The Concise Encyclopedia

of

Ethics in Politics

and

the Media

The Concise Encyclopedia

of

Ethics in Politics

and

the Media

Edited by

Ruth Chadwick

ACADEMIC PRESS

A Harcourt Science and Technology Company

San Diego   San Francisco   New York   Boston   London   Sydney   Tokyo

Academic Press
A Harcourt Science and Technology Company
525 B Street, Suite 1900, San Diego, California 92101-4495, USA
http://www.academicpress.com

Academic Press
Harcourt Place, 32 Jamestown Road, London NW1 7BY, UK
http://www.academicpress.com

Library of Congress Catalog Card Number: 00-109759

International Standard Book Number: 0-12-166255-1

PRINTED IN THE UNITED STATES OF AMERICA
00 01 02 03 04 05 MM 9 8 7 6 5 4 3 2 1

Contents

Civilian Populations in War, Targeting of
GABRIEL PALMER-FERNÁNDEZ

Collective Guilt
GREGORY MELLEMA

Computer and Information Ethics
SIMON ROGERSON

Confidentiality of Sources
MICHEL PETHERAM

Courtroom Proceedings, Reporting of
RUPERT READ AND MAX TRAVERS

Discrimination, Concept of
DAVID WASSERMAN

Indigenous Rights
JORGE M. VALADEZ

Internet Protocol
DUNCAN LANGFORD

Media Depiction of Ethnic Minorities
CHARLES CRITCHER

Media Ownership

EDWARD JOHNSON

National Security Issues

JOHN D. BECKER

Objectivity in Reporting

JUDITH LICHTENBERG

Political Obligation

TERRY HOPTON

Pornography

SUSAN EASTON

Truth Telling as Constitutive of Journalism

JOHN O'NEILL

Violence in Films and Television

MARIAN I. TULLOCH AND JOHN C. TULLOCH

Warfare, Strategies and Tactics

JOHN D. BECKER

Contributors

TIMO AIRAKSINEN
PROFESSIONAL ETHICS
University of Helsinki
Helsinki, Finland

ANITA L. ALLEN
PRIVACY VERSUS THE PUBLIC'S RIGHT TO KNOW
University of Pennsylvania School of Law
Philadelphia, Pennsylvania

SUE ASHFORD
TERRORISM
Murdoch University
Medina, Western Australia

JOHN D. BECKER
NATIONAL SECURITY ISSUES
WARFARE, STRATEGIES AND TACTICS
United States Air Force Academy
Colorado Springs, Colorado

HUGO ADAM BEDEAU
CIVIL DISOBEDIENCE
Tufts University
Medford, Massachusetts

ANDREW BELSEY
ETHICS AND MEDIA QUALITY
Cardiff University
Cardiff, Wales, UK

RUTH CHADWICK
ETHICS AND MEDIA QUALITY
Lancaster University
Lancaster, England, UK

MARGARET COFFEY
BROADCAST JOURNALISM
Australian Broadcasting Corporation
Malvern, Australia

PRESTON K. COVEY
GUN CONTROL
Center for the Advancement of Applied Ethics
Carnegie Mellon University
Pittsburgh, Pennsylvania

CHARLES CRITCHER
MEDIA DEPICTION OF ETHNIC MINORITIES
Sheffield Hallam University
Sheffield, England, UK

SUSAN EASTON
PORNOGRAPHY
Brunel University
Uxbridge, England, UK

SIRKKU HELLSTEN
DISTRIBUTIVE JUSTICE, THEORIES OF
University of Helsinki
Helsinki, Finland

TERRY HOPTON
POLITICAL OBLIGATION
University of Central Lancashire
Preston, England, UK

MARIANNE M. JENNINGS
ELECTION STRATEGIES
Arizona State University
Tempe, Arizona

EDWARD JOHNSON
MEDIA OWNERSHIP
University of New Orleans
New Orleans, Louisiana

STEPHEN KLAIDMAN
FREEDOM OF THE PRESS IN THE USA
Georgetown University
Washington, DC

DUNCAN LANGFORD
INTERNET PROTOCOL
University of Kent
Canterbury, England, UK

JUDITH LICHTENBERG
OBJECTIVITY IN REPORTING
University of Maryland
College Park, Maryland

GARY T. MARX
ELECTRONIC SURVEILLANCE
University of Colorado
Boulder, Colorado

GREGORY MELLEMA
COLLECTIVE GUILT
 Clavin College
 Grand Rapids, Michigan

SEUMAS MILLER
TABLOID JOURNALISM
 Charles Sturt University
 Bathurst, New South Wales, Australia

JOHN O'NEILL
TRUTH TELLING AS CONSTITUTIVE OF JOURNALISM
 Lancaster University
 Lancaster, England, UK

GABRIEL PALMER-FERNÁNDEZ
CIVILIAN POPULATIONS IN WAR, TARGETING OF
 Youngstown State University
 Youngstown, Ohio

MICHEL PETHERAM
CONFIDENTIALITY OF SOURCES
 The Open University
 Milton Keynes, England, UK

RUPERT READ
COURTROOM PROCEEDINGS, REPORTING OF
 University of Manchester
 Manchester, England, UK

SIMON ROGERSON
COMPUTER AND INFORMATION ETHICS
 De Montfort University
 Leicester, England, UK

PHILIP SEIB
CAMPAIGN JOURNALISM
 Marquette University
 Milwaukee, Wisconsin

MAX TRAVERS
COURTROOM PROCEEDINGS, REPORTING OF
 Buckinghamshire College

JOHN C. TULLOCH
VIOLENCE IN FILMS AND TELEVISION
 Charles Sturt University
 Bathurst, New South Wales, Australia

MARIAN I. TULLOCH
VIOLENCE IN FILMS AND TELEVISION
 Charles Sturt University
 Bathurst, New South Wales, Australia

GREGORY UNGAR
ELECTRONIC SURVEILLANCE
 University of Colorado
 Boulder, Colorado

JORGE M. VALADEZ
INDIGENOUS RIGHTS
 Marquette University
 Milwaukee, Wisconsin

DAVID WASSERMAN
DISCRIMINATION, CONCEPT OF
 Institute for Philosophy and Public Policy
 University of Maryland
 College Park, Maryland

JOHN WECKERT
SEXUAL CONTENT IN FILMS AND TELEVISION
 Charles Sturt University
 Bathurst, New South Wales, Australia

BERNARD WILLIAMS
CENSORSHIP
 Corpus Christi College
 University of Oxford
 Oxford, England, UK

EARL R. WINKLER
APPLIED ETHICS, OVERVIEW
 University of British Columbia
 Vancouver, British Columbia

Guide to the Encyclopedia

In order that you, the reader, will derive maximum benefit from your use of *The Concise Encyclopedia of Ethics in Politics and the Media*, we have provided this Guide. It explains how the Encyclopedia is organized and how the information within it can be located.

ARTICLE FORMAT

The articles in this encyclopedia are arranged in a single alphabetical list by title. Each new article begins at the top of a right-hand page, so that it may be quickly located. The author's name and affiliation are displayed at the beginning of the article. The article is organized according to a standard format, as follows:

- Title and Author
- Outline
- Glossary
- Defining Statement
- Main Body of the Article
- Bibliography

OUTLINE

Each article in the Encyclopedia begins with an Outline section that indicates the general content of the article. This outline serves two functions. First, it provides a brief preview of the article, so that the reader can get a sense of what is contained there without having to leaf through the pages. Second, it serves to highlight important subtopics that are discussed within the article.

The Outline section is intended as an overview and thus it lists only the major headings of the article. In addition, second-level and third-level headings will be found within the article.

GLOSSARY

The Glossary section contains terms that are important to an understanding of the article and that may be unfamiliar to the reader. Each term is defined in the context of the particular article in which it is used. Thus the same term may appear as a glossary entry in two or more articles, with the details of the definition varying slightly from one article to another.

The following example are glossary entries that appear with the article "Campaign Journalism."

horse race coverage Reporting that treats a political campaign as a sport-like contest, with principal emphasis on who leads in the opinion polls at any given moment.

media events Campaign events carefully staged by politicians, primarily to serve as the visual content of television news stories. Some journalists resist covering these because they so often offer nothing substantive, just pretty pictures.

DEFINING STATEMENT

The text of each article in the Encyclopedia begins with a single introductory paragraph that defines the topic under discussion and summarizes the content of the article. For example, the article "Censorship" begins with the following statement:

CENSORSHIP includes any kind of suppression or regulation, by government or other authority, of a writing or other means of expression, based on its content. The authority need not apply to a whole judicature, and the effects of its censorship may be local. The term is sometimes used polemically by critics of a practice which would not be described as "censorship" by those who approve of it: in the USA the term has often been applied in this way to the activities of school or library boards in preventing the use or purchase of books which contain sexual scenes or teach Darwinism. It does seem that an activity has at least to be publicly recognized in order to count as censorship; interference with mail by the secret police or covert intimidation of editors would be examples of something else. Accordingly, any censorship implies a public claim of legitimacy for the type of control in question.

BIBLIOGRAPHY

The Bibliography appears as the last element in an article. It lists recent secondary sources to aid the reader in locating more detailed or technical information. Review articles and research papers that are important to an understanding of the topic are also listed.

The bibliographies in this Encyclopedia are for the benefit of the reader, to provide references for further reading or research on the given topic. Thus they are not intended to represent a complete listing of all the materials consulted by the author in preparing the article, as would be the case, for example, with a journal article.

For example, the article "Ethics and Media Quality" lists as references (among others) the works *The Media and Morality*, *Media Ethics*, and *The Virtuous Journalist*.

COMPANION WORKS

This encyclopedia is part of a continuing program of scholarly reference works published by Academic Press. This program encompasses many different areas of science, ranging from life science (e.g., *Encyclopedia of Biodiversity*, *Encyclopedia of Microbiology*) to biomedical topics (*Encyclopedia of Reproduction*, *Encyclopedia of Stress*), to physical science (*Encyclopedia of the Solar System*, *Encyclopedia of Volcanoes*), with special emphasis on social and political issues (*Encyclopedia of Applied Ethics*, *Encyclopedia of Creativity*, *Encyclopedia of Nationalism*, *Encyclopedia of Violence, Peace, and Conflict*, *Encyclopedia of Mental Health*).

For more information on Academic Press reference publishing, please see the Website at:

www.academicpress.com/reference/

Preface

While in the recent history of Applied Ethics it is perhaps fair to say that ethical issues in medicine and the life sciences have been predominant, the debates surrounding ethical issues in politics and the media have achieved increasing prominence in the last few years, partly because of a number of highly publicized events surrounding certain celebrities and political figures, partly because of trends on the world scale such as globalization, and partly because of debates sparked off by events in particular contexts, including developments in the gun control debate in the United States arising out of shootings in locations such as schools. In a number of volumes media ethics has been discussed separately from ethical issues in politics. The decision to treat them together in this volume arises from the view that in a number of respects they are either closely related, or interestingly analogous in some way. The collection of articles is designed to present a snapshot of some of the issues that have been and continue to be most pressing. Although the coverage is inevitably selective, it nevertheless reflects the view that there is benefit in addressing the issues in politics and in the media together insofar as they fall into a number of categories, such as professional ethics, democratic participation, minority issues, privacy, and freedom and responsibility.

Professional ethics. Politics and the media represent two professional groups which raise central questions for professional ethics. As candidates for inclusion in the category of "professions," they are both problematic. While the definition of what counts as a profession is by no means settled, there is a strong tradition that professions are characterized by an ideal of service and by commitment to making some contribution to the social good, partly in exchange for autonomy in practice. In the case of politics or the media, however, does the pattern with which we are familiar in, say, medicine or the law, appear to fit? The model of the autonomous professional serving the interests of a client sits rather

uneasily with the politician's activities in attracting votes and allegiance to party interests, as well as with the journalist's efforts to find and use a good story to sell to readers or attract viewers or listeners.

A debate at the forefront of discussions of professional ethics in recent years has been the question of whether the subject should be addressed through values internal or external to the profession. This raises questions at different levels. First, there is a question as to methodology in Applied Ethics—whether the correct theoretical approach is literally via the notion of "application" of an ethical theory (external to the profession in question) in the sense of deducing conclusions from principles, or whether a virtue ethics approach is more appropriate, where the virtues are "internal" to the profession or practice. From the point of view of an internalist perspective, the question arises as to what the goods are that are necessarily intricately associated with that profession. These have been in dispute with regard to both politics and the media. Interestingly, while there is a view that health care professionals, for example, may aspire to standards and values over and above those to which other non-health care professionals aspire, politics and journalism have both been, however unfairly, to some extent tarred with the same brush in that the question that has arisen here is whether they can be reasonably *expected* to aspire to the same standards associated with common standards of morality, e.g., with regard to honesty and probity. What counts as the "good" journalist? Is it the one who gets the story, at whatever cost? Is the good politician the one who gets his or her party elected or the one who sticks to ideals? The question of the ethics of election strategies is relevant here.

Democratic participation. The ethical issues surrounding the media have also a close relationship with politics in another sense, not only for the obvious reason that journalists report political events, but because, as discussed in the article by Belsey and Chadwick, of the crucial role the media play in supporting the very possibility of democracy. The phenomenon of "spin," however, and the manipulation that is involved therein, raises questions about the validity and strength of that connection. To the extent that politicians use "spin doctors" to manipulate information available to members of the public, there is room for doubt about the implications for the good of the democratic process. There is concern, moreover, at least in some societies, of which the United Kingdom is an example at the time of writing, about the apathy that is apparent in some societies. This is apparent in a number of respects. One manifestation of this is the signs of disaffection in some quarters, leading to opting out of the political process, possibly in a resort to civil disobedience or sometimes violence. Even in the absence of these manifestations, however, the small proportion of the electorate that actually participates in elections raises several issues: the arguments for compulsory voting, the extent to which governments have a genuine mandate, and the role of the media in promoting participation as opposed to providing entertainment.

Minority issues. The concern about apathy takes on a particular aspect in connection with the exclusion of certain groups. The rival claims of group versus individual interests constitute one of the main areas of contention in ethics at the present time. Throughout the development of Applied Ethics as a field of study, one area that has received considerable attention has been that of justice and discrimination—not only through an examination of different theories of justice but also via an application of these in particular areas: sex and race discrimination, and preferential hiring and affirmative action are good examples. There are new phenomena to be addressed however: we see the emergence of both new disadvantaged groups and new ways of disadvantaging groups that have long been identified as such. There is of course room for disagreement about the classifications of characteristics which lead to the identification of groups. Some might be considered to be "essential" to identify, such as race and sex, although even these categories are in dispute; others may be more clearly attributable to environmental factors such as social and technological change. For example, the problem of homelessness is not an "essential" characteristic, but leads to the disenfranchisement of large groups of people. Concerns about new forms of exclusion and divisiveness in society also emerge from developments in information technology—what proportion of the population has access to the benefits of this? When we look at the issue on a global scale, the issue of distribution appears starkly.

Issues related to the rights of indigenous peoples, discussed in this volume, are of course nothing new, but they have the capacity to take on a new twist in the light of technological development. At the same time as the explosion in information technology, the rapid advance in the Human Genome Project has led to concerns among some indigenous peoples about the potential for exploitation of their genetic heritage. The two developments mentioned here, information technology and genetics, have been greeted with both optimism and pessimism. If access to information provides empowerment, and if the Human Genome Project offers the promise of cures for genetic diseases, then they have the potential to relieve disadvantage in a number of respects. If, on the other hand, they lead to greater opportunities for some at the expense of others, then arguably they have the potential to increase social divisions. In the context of developments in genetics and biotechnology, in particular, much has been said about the desirability of raising public awareness, leading to calls for public consultation and of public input into the debate. While the arguments in support of these calls are not always clear and the underlying assumptions regarding deficits in lay knowledge have been challenged, it remains the case that there is an opportunity if not a responsibility here for the media to play a role in enhancing the democratic process surrounding these developments.

In fact it is perhaps with regard to science and technology and their potential social and political implications that the media have their greatest opportunity and power. Developments in science and technology have the potential to change the way we think—for example, work on the human genome and on human diversity may radically reform the categories we use to divide up the world, possibly in ways that we find uncomfortable and challenging. It might be argued, however, that the media are not interested in scientific theories per se, except where they can be used to reinforce some story or stereotype that is already of considerable popular interest for other reasons, such as the differences in brain function between men and women. This may be why, also, medical reporting in the press and other media is at risk of being conducted in one of two ways, both at the extremes—the miracle breakthrough or the Frankenstein scare story. Both make good copy.

The media thus both reflect and have the capacity to influence images of identifiable or disadvantaged groups and reinforce or undermine stereotypes. In this volume articles relevant to this theme include discussions of the media depiction of ethnic minorities; sexual content in films and television; and pornography. Attention to these issues has perhaps been particularly prominent in considerations of tabloid journalism, which has received separate attention. Where the media are concerned, the bottom line is that they are businesses which have to sell newspapers or attract audience figures. These facts may have contributed to a developing lack of trust, but although this may be particularly the case in relation to the media and in light of well-publicized scandals where politicians are concerned, it is important to note that there has been a wider phenomenon of decline in public trust and authority of the professions generally.

Privacy. The preoccupation with the lifestyles of sports personalities, film and rock stars, and supermodels fuels debates not only about the proper role of the media, but also about the rights to privacy of celebrities, as opposed to the public's right to know. There is an oft-rehearsed argument that to some extent celebrities depend on media exposure for their success and thus there may be some justification for intrusion into their private lives. This debate takes on a particular slant, however, where the personalities in question have a public office, as has been demonstrated by the intense scrutiny of the personal life of political figures, including the President of the United States, and the debate about the extent to which a person's private behavior affects his or her suitability for public office. This is one aspect of another wider debate in professional ethics about the extent to which a professional should be expected to observe standards of behavior compatible with being a professional even when "off duty," or whether such a concept even has application for those fulfilling certain roles.

Freedom and responsibility. Another theme that is inevitably raised by the topics addressed in this volume is that of the opposition, or perhaps tension, between freedom and responsibility. In the political arena this has a number of applications. The discussion of gun control, already mentioned, raises the issues starkly—the freedom to bear arms versus the responsibility to contribute toward the safety of others, or at least to reduce the risk of harm. Also, where there is a tradition of freedom of the press, the question is raised as to what service to the community the press should be expected to provide in return for that freedom. In the context of professional ethics, the ideal of service attached to particular professions is mutually supportive of the ideal of professional autonomy, which may be cashed out in terms of both self-regulation and the exercise of individual professional judgment.

The theme of freedom versus responsibility, however, should not be considered to have relevance only to the politicians and media professionals. Individual citizens also have to confront the issue of freedom versus responsibility. The question of whether to participate in elections is one example that has been mentioned. That of political obligation, especially when one finds oneself in disagreement with the government of the day, is another. To what extent is violence justifiable to achieve political ends? Hence articles on political obligation and terrorism are included in the volume. These in turn have the potential to give rise to new ethical issues for the media with regard to reporting. Professionals working in the media may face real conflicts concerning what story is the right one to tell in the light of the competing tensions of national security and reporting what they believe to be the facts. Media ethics thus represents an area of life where access to and dissemination of information is closely related to power, participation, freedom, and responsibility—all key concepts in ethics and politics.

Ruth Chadwick

Applied Ethics, Overview

EARL R. WINKLER

University of British Columbia

GLOSSARY

contextualism A complex theory about moral reasoning and justification that deemphasizes the role of universal principles in determining right actions. In this view, moral judgments are provisionally justified by defending themselves against objections and rivals. The process of justification is essentially continuous with a case-driven, inductive process of seeking the most reasonable solution to a problem. Such justification is carried out within a framework of central cultural values and guiding norms which are seen as having presumptive validity unless they themselves are called into question by rational doubts.

conventionalism The idea that conformity with accepted or conventional moral standards and rules of a community makes actions right. This is an extremely conservative idea, as it leaves little or no room for moral progress or improvement. Hence it is usually considered a fatal weakness in a normative theory if it reduces to, or implies, conventionalism.

metaethics Contrasts with normative ethical theory. Whereas normative ethics is concerned with deciding which actions are right and wrong, metaethics is concerned with the meanings of central moral concepts such as "good" and "right," and with an account of the logic or structure of moral reasoning and justification.

moral expertise The idea that there may be forms of moral knowledge and experience that qualify someone as a kind of expert in moral matters, if not in general then in relation to one or another area of practice, such as medicine.

normative ethical theory A systematically developed theory about the nature and the determination of moral right and wrong.

principalism A traditional view of moral justification in which a particular action is ultimately justified by showing that it conforms to a universal ethical principle which is grounded in the most abstract levels of normative theory. Most contemporary expositions of normative theory involving principalism, however, allow for the operations of reflective equilibrium theory in constructing and testing for principles.

reflective equilibrium theory A theory holding that there is a dialectical relationship between our considered moral judgments about concrete cases and our commitments to principle. Reflection on principles sometimes overrides considered judgment, and considered judgment sometimes forces revisions in our principles. What we are seeking, then, in all systematic moral reflection, is a coherent integration, or equilibrium, between our general principles and our particular judgments.

utilitarianism A form of general normative theory which holds that the rightness or wrongness of actions is wholly determined by the goodness or badness of their consequences. Classical utilitarianism defines the value of consequences in terms of their total contribution to the happiness or well-being of all those affected by an action, counting each persons' happiness as equally important with that of any other. Contemporary forms of utilitarianism may focus instead on aggregate satisfaction of individual interests or preferences.

virtue ethics A general type of normative ethical theory that displaces traditional concentration on the rightness or wrongness of action with a primary concentration on certain defined dispositions of character identified as virtues. In such a theory, virtues are seen as those dispositions that are most important in realizing some ideal, like self-realization, or that are most important to the performance of some morally justified social function, as in the practice of business or medicine.

APPLIED ETHICS is a general field of study that includes all systematic efforts to understand and to resolve moral problems that arise in some domain of practical life, as with medicine, journalism, or business, or in connection with some general issue of social concern, such as employment equity or capital punishment. There are today three major subdivisions of applied ethics: biomedical ethics, concerned with ethical issues in medicine and biomedical research; business and professional ethics, concerned with issues arising in the context of business, including that of multinational corporations; and environmental ethics, concerned with our relations and obligations to future generations, to nonhuman animals and species, and to ecosystems and the biosphere as a whole.

I. RISE OF APPLIED ETHICS

Interest in increasing our understanding of ethical issues concerning health care, business, the professions, and the environment has grown markedly over the last quarter century. When considering the main forces giving rise to this increased interest in applied ethics, one naturally thinks first of biomedical ethics, the most mature and well defined of the divisions of applied ethics. Although abetted by the "liberation" movements of the 1960s and 1970s, biomedical ethics emerged principally in response to various issues and choices that were created by new medical technologies. The traditional values and ethical principles of the medical profession came to be regarded as inadequate in these new situations, because they often seemed to require decisions which appeared to be clearly wrong. For example, the principle of the sanctity of human life permeated the ethos and

ethics of Western medicine for centuries and found formal expression in medical case law. As is now well accepted, however, a central requirement of the sanctity principle—that the physician must make every possible effort to preserve life—simply became too burdensome in the contemporary medical context to continue to support a consensus as to what is right concerning life and death decisions.

There are obvious and important differences, at a general level, between the main divisions of applied ethics. Biomedical ethics is focused within a particular institutional setting and concerns the practices of a closely associated set of professions. Business ethics is broader in scope because the field of business is so much more diverse than the medical field. Environmental ethics obviously has an even broader purview, including the attitudes and behavior of all of us, particularly our basic social patterns of resource use and consumption, and our fundamental moral attitudes toward other animals and the natural world.

In spite of these and other differences, however, business ethics and environmental ethics still have the same basic provenance as biomedical ethics. Within the context of traditional assumptions and values, modern industrial and technological processes, formerly seen as the very engines of progress, have led to global crisis. The *raison d'être* of environmental ethics is to criticize and improve the values and principles in terms of which we understand our responsibilities to future generations, our relationship to nonhuman animals and other living things, and our place in nature generally. Traditional values and principles of Western business practice have also come to seem inadequate for the complex realities of the modern world. This is particularly true regarding the social responsibilities of business, especially those concerning public health and safety and environmental risks. Scandals on Wall Street and the like may prompt endowments for ethics education in business schools, but they are not philosophically significant enough to explain the high level of interest business ethics currently attracts. A more likely explanation will concentrate on such things as the realization that the traditional corporate obligation to maximize profits for shareholders, within the limits of applicable law, can lead much too easily to exploitation, environmental degradation, and other harms.

Viewing the rise of applied ethics generally in this light, it is not surprising that as moral quandaries grew, first in bioethics and then in the other major areas, hope for progress shifted from tinkering with traditional values to moral philosophy and foundational ethical theory. At the same time, the general field of applied ethics has given rise to various subdivisions of a more concentrated kind, such as management ethics, nursing ethics, and journalistic ethics (including all news media). Likewise, the field has developed so as to incude much focused attention on ethical issues connected with a wide range of social concerns, such as discrimination and affirmative action, feminism, world hunger and poverty, war and violence, capital punishment, the rights of gays and lesbians, and so forth.

II. GENERAL ETHICAL THEORY AND PRINCIPALISM

As applied ethics has grown into an established field of study and practice, a number of important questions have arisen about the nature of the field and the problems within it. Paradoxically, perhaps, one of the most fundamental of these concerns the usefulness of ethical theory. Traditional moral philosophy has virtually identified the possibility of genuine moral knowledge with the possibility of universally valid ethical theory, and has supposed that all acceptable moral standards, of every time and place, can be rationally ordered and explained by reference to some set of fundamental principles. *Perfect* theoretical unity and systematization may be impossible to obtain, because there may be a plurality of basic principles that resist ordering. But it is generally assumed that such principles will be few in number, such that substantial and pervasive order may be discovered. A corollary to this conception of moral knowledge is the view that moral reasoning and justification are essentially a matter of deductively applying basic principles to cases.

However, contrary to the expectations created by these methodological assumptions, many philosophers who ventured into clinics and boardrooms were chagrined to discover how little usefulness this deductive approach had in the confrontation with genuine moral problems. Efforts to resolve real moral problems in medicine with some version of Kantian or utilitarian theory, for example, immediately confront the problem of the abstractness and remoteness of general ethical principles. Of course one wants best to serve the important interests of all concerned (utilitarianism) and to respect the rights and personhood of the affected parties (Kantianism); but for real problems of practice the most important and difficult question often is how best to understand the current situation in just these terms. What, for example, does it mean to respect properly the personhood of a potential anencephalic organ donor?

In the field of bioethics, experience of this sort gave rise to a midlevel theory composed of three main principles, those of autonomy, beneficence (including nonmaleficence), and justice. This theory was systematically developed by Tom Beauchamp and James Childress in their modern classic, *Principles of Biomedical Ethics.* This theory claims that its principles are grounded in our most central traditions of normative ethical theory while also offering enough content to guide practical moral judgment in medicine. It thus purports to overcome the problem of theoretical abstractness and also to keep faith with the basic philosophical idea that applied ethics is continuous with general ethical theory. Biomedical ethics, as a primary division of applied ethics, is not a special kind of ethics; it does not include any special principles or methods that are specific to the field of medicine and not derivable from more general sources. Rather, the field of medicine is governed ultimately by the same general normative principles as hold good in all other spheres of human life. As this approach has come to dominate bioethics, it has inspired similar forms of theoretical construction in other areas of applied ethics, notably in business and professional ethics.

Gradually, however, many philosophers and others who have worked extensively in applied ethics have moved toward a rejection of the traditional idea of developing and applying general normative theory. Their experience in the field has convinced them that the appearance of universality achieved by general normative theory is necessarily purchased at the price of too rigidly separating thought about morality from the historical and sociological realities, traditions, and practices of particular cultures. A result of this separation, as already mentioned, is a level of abstraction that makes traditional ethical theory virtually useless in guiding moral decision making about real problems in specific social settings. Moreover, these critics see essentially the same problems of ahistoricism and abstraction reappearing with the standard midlevel normative theories, in bioethics and elsewhere. In addition to this, it appears to many philosophers working in applied ethics that most of the real work of resolving moral problems occurs at the level of interpretation and comparison of cases. Recourse to general normative principles, even midlevel ones, seems never to override case-driven considered judgment. On the contrary, conflict between a putative principle and the extensive consideration of cases seems always to result in refining the interpretation of whatever general principle is involved. This tendency is important in connection with contemporary efforts to refine the deductive model of moral justification by incorporation of wide reflective equilibrium theory. For it is crucial to reflective equilibrium theory and the defense of principalism that general principles override considered judgments, at least much of the time.

Concerns about ahistoricism and abstractness, and the problems of application that they create, have produced a powerful skepticism about the very possibility of constructing a perfectly general normative theory. By now this ancient philosophical quest appears to many to be inconsistent with the most immediate, natural, and defensible conception of morality. Viewed from the perspective of modern history, sociology, and anthropology, moralities are seen as social artifacts that arise as part of the basic elements of a culture—its religion, its social forms of marriage and family, its economy, and so forth. Morality is thus an evolving social instrument that serves a variety of very general ends which are associated with different domains of social life and are pursued within the context of changing historical circumstance and significant epistemic limitations. As such, a morality may be criticized in terms of how well or ill it serves identifiable and worthy social ends. But, by the same token, what is good or right in some realm of life, within a given cultural setting, must be a function of a highly complex set of conditions, including psychological factors and patterns of expectations that are themselves created by social custom and convention.

In light of the very different historical origins of diverse social forms, across so many different cultures, there seems to be no good reason to assume that all defensible moral standards will be explicable in terms of a deductive relationship to some more or less unitary set of basic principles with more or less determinate normative content. Although such a theoretical reduction or reconstruction may be possible, in spite of cultural diversity and in spite of the overwhelming failure of all previous efforts to gain general acceptance of any set of fundamental moral principles, many now regard this enterprise as exceedingly doubtful, even philosophically naive.

III. CONTEXTUALISM AND RELATED DEVELOPMENTS

Skepticism about the possibility of normative theory on a grand scale and growing doubts about the feasibility of solving moral problems by deductively applying general principles have given rise to a plurality of approaches and ways of conceptualizing problems within the field of applied ethics. One general approach to practical moral decision making that is currently gaining favor is *contextualism.* As variously developed in the current philosophical literature, contextualism has tended primarily to be critical of established beliefs about ethical theory, rather than constructive of better models of moral reasoning, but the emphasis is now shifting to include the latter. From the contextualists' point of view, it is unnecessary to strive for a universally

valid ethical theory since there are more realistic ways of accounting for moral rationality and justification. In place of the traditional, essentially top-down model of moral reasoning and justification, contextualism adopts the general idea that moral problems must be resolved within the interpretive complexities of concrete circumstances, by appeal to relevant historical and cultural traditions, with reference to critical institutional and professional norms and virtues, and by relying primarily upon the method of comparative case analysis. According to this method we navigate our way to a practical resolution by discursive triangulation from clear and settled cases to problematic ones.

Moral judgments are thus provisionally justified by defending themselves against objections and rivals. So conceived, justification is essentially continuous with a case-driven, inductive process of seeking the *most reasonable* solution to a problem within a framework of shared values which are seen as having presumptive validity unless rational considerations call them into question.

Closely associated with questions concerning the usefulness of general normative theory is the question of how we should conceive of the enterprise of living and acting morally. While Kantians and utilitarians focus on following appropriate rules and principles, an increasing number of philosophers in the field of applied ethics argue that we should focus on acquiring virtues appropriate to fulfilling our roles in particular cultural and institutional settings. This conception is consistent with a general contextualist orientation in rejecting the deductive model of moral deliberation. In so far as proponents of virtue ethics are concerned with ethical theory at all, it is a much more empirically oriented theory than moral philosophers have traditionally sought. Such theory seeks to understand the instrumental effects of various ways of conceptualizing and judging action and character within the context of the social and institutional roles persons play. Unlike contextualism, however, rather than focusing directly on the structure of moral reasoning about right action, virtue ethics tends to see right action as indirectly determined by considering what actions would flow from the operation of relevant virtues.

As already emphasized, the general question which divides practitioners of applied ethics is where we should look in our quest for standards of justification for moral judgments. For some, the turn away from the deductive model of problem solving in applied ethics has spurred renewed interest in procedural aspects of group moral deliberation and decision. They have begun to consider much more seriously the question of what features a decision procedure must have if its conclusions are to be regarded as morally justified. There seems to be considerable support for the view that a justified moral judgment must represent, in some sense, a free and informed consensus of all interested parties. The central problem is to gain a fuller understanding of the nature of the biases and distortions that affect decision procedures in particular social and cultural contexts, and thus to clarify the conditions under which we can be confident that we have at least approximated such a consensus.

Clearly, rejecting the deductive model of moral problem solving does not entail rejection of all moral theory. Significant moral reform in social life depends upon securing some kind of theoretical purchase on established practice and institutional arrangements. Ethical theory in a form that is sufficient to this purpose is therefore necessary. It is necessary in many other ways as well. For example, theory of some sort is necessary even to approach the problem of moral status—what gives something moral standing such that it is an object of moral consideration in its own right? And only ethical theory can illuminate or resolve such questions as whether the distinction between killing and "letting die" is morally relevant in itself, or whether actual or hypothetical consent under certain ideal conditions is more important in justifying certain kinds of social institutions and policies. These questions, and countless others like them, simply are theoretical questions that arise naturally and unavoidably when attempting to make moral headway in a complex and changing world. Theories dealing with such questions as these, however, do not provide decision procedures for solving moral problems. Rather, they help us to extend and deepen our understanding of the complex set of moral concepts in terms of which we interpret our problems and dilemmas, and so point the way to improving our values and social practices.

The most relevant and useful theoretical constructions in applied ethics are likely to be those that are impelled by an informed understanding of the real conflicts and difficulties of practical life. The recent history of moral philosophy's contributions in the world of practice bears this out. Responses to particular theoretical issues arising in connection with problems like abortion and euthanasia, or concentrated efforts in areas like environmentalism and animal rights, have produced moral philosophy's most significant contributions to the important moral issues of the day. Moreover, the best work of this kind in applied ethics is currently exerting considerable influence on some of the most interesting work concerning ethical theory.

One of the consequences of the turn toward contextualism and virtue ethics has been a renewal of efforts to better understand the nature of practical moral reasoning and the norms governing it. This kind of exploration is presently fostering a kind of redirected metaethics. Rather than concentrating on the analysis of basic ethical concepts and the meaning of moral propositions, the focus is on the structure of actual moral reasoning, including comparisons with law and science; on the conditions for properly evaluating moral precepts and rules; and on the limits of rational decidability in morals. Metaethical theory of this kind, which might strive ultimately to systematically illuminate what abstract conditions social moralities, or their parts, must meet in order to be reasonable or defensible, may be philosophically very valuable. This kind of theory can at least serve, if not finally fulfill, a powerful intellectual desire for ordered, systematic understanding. And it could be helpful indirectly in practical terms as well.

IV. QUESTIONS OF CONVENTIONALISM, MORAL EXPERTISE, AND MORAL PSYCHOLOGY

The intensely practical and consensus-driven nature of applied ethics would alone serve to raise a question of its critical and reformative potential, but given the current trend toward metalevel contextualist accounts of moral reasoning and justification, this issue becomes acute. From such a perspective, how can applied ethics avoid being inherently conventional and conservative? How, in other words, can applied ethics secure a sufficiently critical perspective on conventional moral and evaluative practices to be capable of genuine and, if necessary, radical reform? Environmental ethics perhaps deserves special attention in this regard because so much of its thrust is directed at deep, even revolutionary, reform in moral attitudes toward other animals and the natural world.

Certain fields of applied ethics have developed to include professional consultation and the representation of so-called "ethicists" within institutional settings, on government commissions and committees, and in the media and the courts. This has resulted in much recent discussion of the whole issue of moral expertise. Can there be any such thing as a moral expert, or experts on the important ethical dimensions of certain domains of practice? Of course, if moral reasoning and decision making were primarily a matter of defending some general principle and applying it to cases in a predominantly analytical way, then, presumably, the skills associated with this process would constitute a sort of moral expertise which could be linked to certain sorts of training and preparation. In particular, training in the history of normative theory and analytic philosophy would appear especially relevant, even indispensable. On the other hand, a more contextualist approach to the process of moral reasoning will recognize a central role in moral discourse for a variety of skills and intellectual, imaginitive, and emotional resources beyond those that are typical of the moral philosopher. Psychological understanding and sensitivity will be seen as crucial, as will sociological knowledge, knowledge of religions and of legal and political realities, and so forth. This point of view, therefore, sees applied ethics as inherently multidisciplinary because it is impossible to locate all the skills and attributes necessary to progress in social morality in the training and skills that are typical of any single profession.

Interest in the issue of moral knowledge and expertise is not unrelated to a more general renewal of interest in "moral psychology," as philosophy has, in certain periods, concerned itself with this field. What, for example, are the principal sources of moral hypocrisy in our times? Or how much does the credibility of one's moral views depend on their being based on certain kinds of relevant experience? Or what general conditions support a culture in which ethics and moral values are taken seriously?

Acknowledgment

Much of the substance of this article is derived from the Introduction to *Applied Ethics: A Reader* (E. Winkler and G. Coombs (eds.), 1993.) Basil Blackwell, Oxford.

Bibliography

Beauchamp, T. L., and Childress, J. F. (1979) [1983]. "Principles of Biomedical Ethics." Oxford Univ. Press, New York.

Daniels, N. (1979). Wide reflective equilibrium and theory acceptance in ethics. *J. Philos.* **76,** 256–82.

Jonson, A., and Toulmin, S. (1988). "The Abuse of Casuistry." Univ. of California Press, Berkeley.

Noble, C. (1982). Ethics and experts. *Hastings Centre Rep.* **12**(3), 7–9.

Philips, M. (1995). "Between Universalism and Scepticism." Oxford Univ. Press, New York.

Solomon, R. (1992). "Ethics and Excellence: Cooperation and Integrity." Oxford Univ. Press, New York.

Winkler, E. (1993). From Kantianism to Contextualism: The rise and fall of the paradigm theory in bioethics. In "Applied Ethics: A Reader" (E. Winkler, and G. Coombs, Eds.). Basil Blackwell, Oxford.

Winkler, E. (1996). Moral philosophy and bioethics: Contextualism vs. the paradigm theory. In "Philosophical Perspectives on Bioethics" (W. Sumner, and I. Boyle, Eds.). Univ. of Toronto Press, Toronto.

Broadcast Journalism

MARGARET COFFEY

Australian Broadcasting Corporation

GLOSSARY

broadcast journalism News and information gathering and dissemination on radio and television.

cable television Television programming received in the household via optic fiber cable usually on a user-pays basis.

code of ethics A statement of the values ascribed to by members of a profession.

internet A global network of computers linked through telephone lines and host computers.

organizational code of ethics A statement of values developed for and by members (employers and employees) of an organization such as a corporation or government department.

pay TV Television programming received usually by cable on a user-pays basis.

public broadcasting Radio and television broadcasting funded by subscription and/or government contribution and based on a principle of public access.

public service broadcasting Radio and television broadcasting funded by government out of taxation revenue or licence fees with a charter to provide specified broadcasting services to all citizens.

satellite transmission The sending of radio and television signals via satellite rather than landline or electromagnetic link.

BROADCAST JOURNALISM, like any other kind of journalism, aims to disseminate information to public audiences. Technological innovation means that this information, whether in the form of news, analysis, or opinion, may reach us via radio or television, cable or satellite, or by the (pen)ultimate broadcast medium, the Internet. On the Internet, print journalism is broadcast journalism and vice versa. This fortuitous fusion brings home the fact that ethical considerations with respect to print and broadcast journalism are fundamentally the same. We ask of both that they be truthful, objective, well-informed and accurate, respectful of privacy, and uncompromised by control or influence. Outside of the technical differences and the opportunities these allow, what is distinctive about broadcast journalism is the historical context in which it has developed and out of which claims are made on its behalf.

It is widely understood that the ethical conduct of journalism is of critical importance to us. Journalism is for most people the principle source of information about the world at large. Broadcast journalism's potency is derived from its immediacy and its availability to mass audiences. In the case of television, there is the additional impact of visual images. Studies show, for example, that since 1963 Americans have quoted television rather than newspapers as their primary source of "most" of their news. Paradoxically, journalism is a source of information about our private and domestic worlds as we define these vis-a-vis the information we hear on radio or television or read in the newspaper.

In democratic societies we depend upon journalism not just for information but as a point of engagement with politicians, policies, and issues. Our capacity to act decisively and effectively as citizens or as voters is influenced by how well it serves us. Indeed, nothing less than our individual self-realization as participating members of democratic societies is associated with our access to the knowledge and information journalism conveys.

Moreover, we are faced with many challenges, local and global. Whether they are to do with the survival of the environment and therefore our species, or the just distribution of economic goods (including information), the sustaining and development of democratic institutions, or the maintaining of stable, respectful relations between different peoples and cultures, our ability to face into these challenges turns upon our access to information, its quality, and our capacity to exchange it.

I. HISTORY

Broadcast journalism followed the invention of radio, its experimental popularity in the immediate aftermath of the First World War, and its established use for public broadcasting from around 1920. The earliest developments in the United States, Britain, the USSR, mainland Europe, India, and Japan sketched in an institutional organization of broadcasting which has been seriously challenged only relatively recently.

Print journalism has long enjoyed the idea of the liberty of the press insofar as it has meant freedom from licensing. However, from its early days broadcasting became subject to regulation over and above the restrictions of relevant civil laws such as those relating to defamation, contempt of court, blasphemous or obscene publications, and trespass. In the beginning, regulation was deemed necessary because of both the shortage of available spectrum and the perceived power of the radio broadcasting medium. Governments regulated to ensure a public service dimension to broadcasters' activities and varying kinds of accountability. Two major kinds of regulatory frameworks and institutional organization developed, exemplified by the broadcasting history of the United States and Britain.

A. Commercial Model

On the one hand, in the United States, commercial development went on apace when advertisers realized radio's promise as an advertising medium. Commercial radio stations burgeoned in the early 1920s. The potential for network arrangements was recognized at a very

early point with the establishment in 1926 of the first (New York-based) commercial radio network. And the potential for commercial radio mayhem was countered with federal legislation. As early as 1927 the U.S. Congress passed a Radio Act which set out to inhibit monopoly—with respect to the production of radio equipment and the ownership of radio stations—and to control the allocation of radio wavelengths. The outcome of this approach was the development of four major commercial networks dependent upon advertising revenue and the securing of wavelength for educational radio broadcasting.

Television broadcasting in the United States began similarly as a commercial entertainment and information-oriented venture in 1939. War curtailed its commercial development and it was not until 1952 that the Federal Communications Commission authorized 242 channels for educational purposes. In 1962 the Education Television Facilities Act provided government funds to build new stations. By the mid-1960s a 100-station-strong noncommercial, subscriber-based, national network had taken shape under the impetus of finance from the Ford Foundation. The Public Broadcasting act of 1967 provided a mechanism for government funding of broadcasting via the establishment of a private corporation which would distribute government funds (Corporation for Public Broadcasting). Its rationale was that there were areas of broadcasting delivery which were not supported by advertising and were unlikely to be. In 1970 the already integrated network began operation as the Public Broadcasting Service and PBS now parallels National Public Radio.

Almost from the outset in the United States, the notion of noncommercially funded broadcast journalism has created controversy. (An early PBS cause celebre was the proposed Ford Foundation financed news center in 1971.) Broadcast journalism, the argument goes, requires the democratic restraints of the free market. If taxpayers' money is to be provided for public broadcasting then there must be legislative enforcement of objectivity, balance, and accountability. Strict fairness regulations must be met. The 1992 Public Telecommunications Act was an outcome of this argument: it requires the Corporation for Public Broadcasting to enforce the balance provisions of the Public Broadcasting Act. Subsequent controversies (in 1996 over federal funding, for example) have revealed continuing suspicion of government-funded broadcasting balanced by support from those their opponents describe as leftists, liberals, or Democrats.

On the subject of regulation broadly, there is not such a neat divide between proponents and opponents. While, for example, critics of the Public Broadcasting Service demanded content regulation to counter perceived political partisanship and ambitions for PBS-led social change, some liberals support structural regulation to build rules and constraints into the structure and organization of the media taken as a whole. Their argument is that commercial media represent power and that private power may threaten liberty even as state power does. It may lead to the disproportionate representation of certain views at the expense of diversity, to inappropriate influence on public policy, or to the manipulation of the media to achieve the ends of private owners or corporations.

B. Public Service Model

In Britain, broadcast journalism has followed a different evolutionary path. While early radio initiatives were of a commercial nature, the perceived problems of "commercialization" and the need for order and control exemplified by the clamorous airwaves of the United States soon led to the view that broadcasting was best administered as a public service utility with centralized control. (Already the administration of other resources such as forestry, water, and electricity had been similarly structured.) In 1925 the British Broadcasting Corporation (BBC) was established as a monopoly, ultimately accountable to Parliament but presided over by a Board of Governors enjoined as trustees of the public interest. Broadcast journalism began on the BBC in 1926 in the print news vacuum created by the General Strike. Since broadcasting bans were applied to the leader of the opposition and representatives of organized labor, the BBC was obliged immediately to canvas issues such as its relationship to government, its notion of public service, and its means of estimating public interest. It resolved these issues by accepting the bans and reporting statements by both strikers and strike breakers. It developed a modus vivendi by which it censored itself along government suggested lines in order to forestall the imposition of government regulation. During World War II, when there was an inevitable identification of the common interest with the interests of government, there was even greater complexity in the relationship between the BBC and the British Government. Nevertheless, by the end of the war the BBC's authority as a source of news (and as a cultural institution) was firmly established. For one thing, during the war the BBC had never lied. (That does not mean it was not free of bias.) It was a public service monopoly, committed to the common interest and accountable to Parliament. As James Curran and Jean Seaton have pointed out, that meant that if government were concerned with limiting the amount and kind of information broadcast, the main pressure within the Corporation was to tell people as much as possible.

Until the 1980s broadcast journalism developed in Britain within a framework of reiterated public service notions. These included the idea that broadcasting services should be accountable and made available to everyone, and that programs should be of high quality and wide variety. Even the introduction of commercial television in 1954 occurred under the aegis of these principles, and the new Independent Television Authority was established to regulate commercial stations (ITV, independent television) virtually in the image of the BBC.

More recently there has been a reworking of the public service ideal which would detach it from the notion of a publicly funded utility. In this neoliberal view, corporate media organizations are well placed to serve the public. As Ken Cowley, Rupert Murdoch's sometime chief executive in Australia, remarked, "We take the view, as simple as it is and as corny as it sounds, that what is good for your country is good for your business and what is good for your business is good for the paper, its readers and our employers."

Another kind of reworking of the public service ideal would privatize elements of public service broadcasting organizations under some kind of regulatory oversight such as a Public Broadcasting Council. There are proposals also from the left based on a critique of existing public service broadcasting as expressive of a narrow range of perspectives. These proposals call, for example, for more representative membership of broadcasting authorities and for structures and guidelines which make broadcasters more independent of government and encourage greater ideological range and cultural diversity in program content.

Nevertheless, the paradigmatic ideas governing the broadcasting debate remain those derived from its development history. On the one hand there is the notion that broadcasting is a public good and that to be a broadcaster is to take on a public service while conscious of one's particular responsibilities toward innovation, pluralism, and quality. On the other hand, there is the idea that broadcasting belongs to the commercial arena where market forces (and minimal regulation) will ensure that the requirements of audiences, and advertisers, are met, and where it will flourish under the creative stimulus of the market. Here the broadcast journalist is understood to be a professional, with skills and marketable qualities appropriate to the profession. It is fair to say that this idea (or variations upon it) has been in the ascendant since the 1980s and has already influenced the reshaping of major broadcasting organizations (such as the BBC, the Canadian Broadcasting Corporation, the Australian Broadcasting Corporation, the New Zealand Broadcasting Corporation) and the development of communications policy in response to new technology. It has also influenced the recreation of broadcasting organizations in the former Soviet bloc.

II. RECENT TECHNOLOGICAL DEVELOPMENTS

A. Satellite Transmission

The rise of free market ideology is an important element in the rethinking of communications policy as it affects broadcasting, but the crucial factor has been the scope and speed of technological innovation. It has made redundant, for example, the pragmatic argument for regulation in the first instance, that there would be cacophony on the airwaves given the limited spectrum available. Now that satellite transmission has replaced electromagnetic signals, not only is there no comparable problem with competition, it may seem there are no boundaries either. Western-based media organizations such as Rupert Murdoch's Star TV can broadcast to Pakistan, India, or Iran. By 1994 Star TV was reaching in its target area an estimated 54 million households with receiving dishes. Such broadcasts circumvent any easily applicable state controls since they go direct to their audiences in their homes. (Either governments ban receiving dishes as in Iran or they exert political and economic pressure as with China's acceded-to demand that Star TV stop beaming BBC news bulletins into Chinese households.)

Satellite transmission has also raised questions about diversity. While it proffers a huge increase in viewer choice, its dominance by transnational corporations may be a guarantee only of (Western) cultural hegemony.

Boundaries of another sort have been abolished by the evolution of news coverage as a result of satellite transmission working in conjunction with cable networks in agency arrangements. Journalists with the American Cable News Network (CNN) can be anywhere, anytime, to bring to viewers anywhere in the world via local cable deliverers or major national commercial or public service networks the latest air strike, food crisis, or insurrection. Viewers everywhere hear the news stories told by Americans.

Moreover, CNN's coverage of the 1991 UN-sponsored Desert Storm war against Iraq provided instantaneous images of war which cast viewers in their homes as witnesses to missile attacks and their aftermath. In these circumstances viewers may believe there is yet another kind of boundary crossing going on: that between news and information production/consumption and journalistic /viewer complicity and voyeurism. On the other hand, viewers able to observe the death of 400 civilians in the Al-Ameriya bunker in Baghdad may have experienced the contours of citizenship expanding:

it was, after all, in their names that the war was prosecuted. Why should they not see the bombing, and own to it?

B. Cable Television

The development of cable television invites comment on the hopes held for technological innovation as a means for democratizing broadcast journalism. It has been a form of television slower to develop outside the United States at least in part because of the infrastructure investment required to establish the optic fiber cables to individual households. In Australia, for example, only existing very large media companies have been able to enter the cable market, so that rather than introducing diversity the advent of cable has only confirmed Australia's existing media oligopoly. In the United States public access cable television (in a proportion of one in five cable networks) provides an enormous amount of original community programming of varying quality. Some of it may reflect less diversity than appeal to the First Amendment (which guarantees freedom of speech) as the justification for broadcasts which would elsewhere be banned (for racial vilification, for example).

Moreover the development of cable has meant that abandonment of free-to-air broadcasting as the only model. Cable television has been for the most part a commercial venture and access depends on one's capacity to pay. Hence, "pay TV."

However, there remains hopefulness about technology's democratizing potential. John Keane envisions new digital technologies as contributing to a plurality of communications media in a more democratic order where neither the state nor commercial markets exercise control, but rather publicly-funded, non-profit and legally guaranteed media institutions of civil society (1991. *The Media and Democracy.* Polity London). Certainly, one can point to the use of radio and television among people of indigenous cultures (communities of interest) to demonstrate that the new technologies may indeed offer emancipatory possibilities. Among some indigenous Australian and Canadian communities local radio and television broadcasting is a means of strengthening community cultures and of challenging the powerful incursions of satellite transmission and other Western broadcasts. Here the means of communication belong, in Keane's terms, to the indigenous public at large.

C. Narrowcasting

The next round of technological innovation is focusing on "narrowcasting" and "audience targeting" where information will be offered in response to the individual's choice. Here again the question of diversity arises. It is clear that the quantity of information available to any individual will be enormous and there will be a proliferation of access routes to information. But with existing commercial media organizations positioning themselves to take advantage of these innovations, there are questions to be asked about what diversity will mean in the age of narrowcasting and self-selected news and information.

D. The Internet

The Internet is a communications medium based on a global network of computers linked through telephone lines and host computers. It is capable of transmitting text, images, and sound. Millions of people are linked by the Internet, but unlike conventional media the Internet offers two-way communication, an absence of regulation, and freedom from commercial ownership. However, access to the Internet is dependent on the user's capacity to pay (for equipment, server provider, power, etc.).

The Internet is considered here because of its links to broadcasting: not only do forms of broadcasting—along with other activities—occur on the Net, but major broadcasting organizations have created Internet versions of themselves and make their program material available there. Broadcast journalists use the Internet as an information resource. It is possible, for example, to download texts of Australian Broadcasting Corporation programs within hours of their broadcast, and Radio Telefis Eireann invites the downloading of voice and text news stories as a type of broadcast agency service.

In many ways the Internet is emblematic of broadcasting and the changes being induced by political and technological change. It carries a phenomenal amount of information without any organizing hierarchy of knowledge other than "user selects." It is the subject of arguments about regulation with the balance on the side of open access and freedom from censorship. (However, governments, for example, through the OECD, are investigating forms of regulation primarily to limit access.) Its utility depends on the sharpness of the user's purpose and her competence with the search engines. Its character reflects the overwhelming contribution from the United States. And it too is under pressure from large corporations attempting to take control.

III. CONVERGENCE AND CONCENTRATION

With the dominance by large corporations of the world's supply and delivery of information (and enter-

tainment), many concerns about broadcast journalism have come to be expressed in the terms *convergence* and *concentration.*

The idea of convergence is best illustrated in the way the Internet collapses the boundaries between the distinctive identities of newspaper, radio, and television. A graphic example of convergence in the make is provided by the *Sankei* newspaper in Japan. Its new delivery system, a small box the size of an electronic organizer, may be plugged into a television at night so that each morning it downloads perhaps a thousand news articles and pictures. It is possible to scroll through these stories en route to work and have access to far more information than that provided by a newspaper. A new version will conceivably have audio and video and the user will be able to select and edit what he wishes to hear.

Convergence obviously informs the increasing concentration of media ownership and the spread of media owner activities. Media corporations are involved in telecommunications, information and entertainment (sport and film), computing, and education in addition to radio, television, and newspaper production. Needless to say, the key question here has to do with diversity: what is it and how may it be achieved?

IV. THE BROADCAST JOURNALIST

It is against this background that we must consider the professional role and obligations of the broadcast journalist.

To begin with, such persons will be most likely employed by a profit-seeking corporation and their information-gathering activities will have economic worth. They will have available impressive technological resources, thanks to which they may access information previously unavailable. He or she may be at considerable cultural and social distance from the audience: think of the CNN Gulf War reporter being heard not merely at home—in Wisconsin?—but also in Geelong, Australia, or Colombo, Sri Lanka.

A broadcast journalist will also occupy an ambivalent position in society. Public estimation of journalists is low but rhetoric from both the left and the right casts the journalist in a role central to the maintenance of democratic societies.

A. The Broadcast Journalist as Professional Employee

Journalism has come to be regarded as a profession, if different in status from professions such as law or medicine. What gives journalism its professional status, along with law, medicine, teaching, and nursing, is its relationship to a code of ethics. Its aims and its achievements are judged according to ethical ideas such as truthfulness, accuracy, and objectivity. More and more these ideas are being articulated in formal codes of ethics, the better of which address the peculiar technological context of broadcast journalism.

Implicit in the traditional idea of a professional is a notion of autonomy: this person, whose ethical commitments are held in common with the rest of the profession, nevertheless acts independently to fulfil these commitments. However, most broadcast journalists are employees whose autonomy is limited by the requirements and interests of their employer. Very often this is a large corporation whose interests will not always be best expressed in the journalist's code of ethics: corporations are explicitly about making money rather than about "telling the truth."

The fact that broadcast journalists are employees of a contracting number of employers, or alternatively that they are employees under threat when they work for "downsizing" public service broadcasting organizations, may be assumed to have some effect on journalistic culture. Lack of alternative employment opportunities and competition may foster self-censorship and a less than vigorous journalistic enterprise.

Of course the tension between a journalist's professional values and an employer's interests may be equally strained when the employer is a public service broadcasting organization. Journalists with both the BBC and the RTE are compromised by their respective institutions' adherence to government prohibition on the broadcast of interviews with members of the Irish Republican Army, a ban which is retrospective since it applies to archival material as well. Journalists with the ABC (Australian Broadcasting Corporation) found editorial decision making compromised by their employer's ratings-driven essay into "infotainment" television programming. (The issue became a public scandal in 1994–1995 and led to an inquiry and the establishment of whistle-blowing procedures within the organization.)

An increasing number of organizations are developing organizational codes of practice so that some journalists will find themselves referring to both professional and organizational codes. In Australia, for example, broadcasting organizations are required to notify the Australian Broadcasting Authority of their codes of practice as a first step in a series of measures underwriting accountability.

There is considerable discussion about the merits of professional codes of ethics versus organizational codes. As media organizations grow in size, the trend toward deregulation accelerates, and public service broadcasting is attenuated, professional journalists' organizations will be less well placed to inculcate and enforce values appropriate to broadcast journalism. It may be that, in this age of concentration of media ownership, media self-regulation through organizational codes will have a more productive impact on the quality of broadcast journalism. Such codes can at least broach at the level of the organization issues such as checkbook journalism or the improper influence of advertising or commercial consideration since they embrace those who profit from and control media activities. They may also contribute to media self-regulation across national boundaries since the nature of media organizations is increasingly global rather than local.

However, a professional code of ethics contributes toward a journalist's sense of independence no matter how comparatively weak her position. It is a reminder to all of us that there are interests and aspirations outside those of the market and corporate organizations.

B. The Broadcast Journalist and Technology

Broadcast journalists, like many other professionals, find ethical challenges in the capacities technology allows them. CNN's role in the Gulf War raised a series of such ethical questions as already mentioned. One of them had to do with what might be the proper distance from the action for a viewer.

On a more day-to-day level, broadcast journalists are able to manipulate pictures and sound for effect; they can record sound and pictures without the knowledge of their subjects, and they are able to access with technology people and areas previously inaccessible. The last two raise the issues of consent and privacy—where should the shifting boundary between what should be public and what should be private lie?

Obviously this technology may be used for good purpose, to reveal discrimination, for example. Equally obviously it is often used in breach of commonly accepted ideas about privacy and for reasons which have more to do with entertaining and stimulating audiences than with providing information. Various jurisdictions have felt the need to strengthen laws relating to consent and privacy at least partly in response to perceived problems with the media.

It is nevertheless true that television has created a culture that is less certain about the distinction between public and private and the import of what were once private differences. Alain Ehrenberg writes that tabloid television reassures as it shows that everyone is different and there are no longer any fixed norms that we are to conform to. It is a television of tolerance and what is central is that people accept the need to be true to themselves and be committed to talking about this to the television audience. Hence the kind of infotainment television where people reveal their intimate lives and the prevailing view among certain broadcast journalists that privacy is a middle-class conceit.

C. The Broadcast Journalist and Her Audience

Journalism may figure low on the scale of reputable professions but implicit in this estimation is a view of the journalist as powerful. This ambivalence is expressed in media criticism. One such critique has broadcast journalism giving us information that affects our perceptions; if it is distorted, and it often is, we will find as citizens that our capacity for choice has been corrupted. Broadcast journalism's power to corrupt the culture is a common theme in media criticism.

It is possible that media critics, audiences, and broadcast journalists themselves overestimate the latter's power. It is not clear, for example, that television pictures of the Vietnam War were responsible for opposition to the war's pursuit. Broadcast journalists are not forces in themselves. They are players in complex social and political and economic relationships. It is worth reflecting that so much of the criticism of broadcast journalism in terms of its conduct and ethics is in fact a criticism of modernity itself.

Bibliography

Belsey, A., and Chadwich, R. (Eds.) (1991). "Ethical Issues in Journalism and the Media." Routledge, London.

Coady, M., and Bloch, S. (Ed.) (1996). "Codes of Ethics and the Professions." Melbourne Univ. Press, Melbourne.

Curran, J., and Seaton, J. (1991). "Power Without Responsibility," 4th ed. Routledge, London.

Horowitz, D., and Jarvik, L. (1995). "Public Broadcasting and the Public Trust," Center for the Study of Popular Culture, Los Angeles.

Lichtenberg, J. (Ed.) (1990). "Democracy and the Mass Media." Cambridge Univ. Press, Cambridge.

Marshall, I., and Kingsbury, D. (1996). "Media Realities: The News Media and Power in Australian Society." Longman, Harlow/New York.

Schultz, J. (Ed.). (1994). "Not Just Another Business: Journalists, Citizens and the Media." Pluto, Sydney.

Campaign Journalism

PHILIP SEIB

Marquette University

GLOSSARY

character issue The personal background and beliefs of a candidate. This is important to voters, who are interested in the person as well as issues, public record, party affiliation, and other purely political matters when they decide how to vote. In recent years, however, "character" has come to mean sex life, and coverage has often been more salacious than substantive.

horse race coverage Reporting that treats a political campaign as a sport-like contest, with principal emphasis on who leads in the opinion polls at any given moment.

media events Campaign events carefully staged by politicians, primarily to serve as the visual content of television news stories. Some journalists resist covering these because they so often offer nothing substantive, just pretty pictures.

pack journalism Consensus news coverage that emerges from the often huge press corps that covers campaigns. Once the conventional wisdom is defined, many news stories may conform to it, giving news consumers a constricted view of events.

screening The informal process by which news media decide which candidacies are most viable and therefore will receive substantial coverage, and which will receive less (or none). Through this process, voters have "front-runners" selected for them and receive the most information about these chosen few.

spin Efforts by politicians to influence news coverage by offering their own interpretation of events to journalists. Spin is a form of propaganda. It generally concerns which candidates are doing well or poorly, or which issues are purportedly most important.

truth-testing Coverage by news organizations—often of campaign advertising—that analyzes the accuracy of what the candidates or their surrogates are telling voters.

POLITICAL JOURNALISM includes diverse matters, ranging from the mechanics of running for office to the grand issues of governing. On a daily basis, political journalists who cover federal, state, or local governments concern themselves with executive, legislative, and judicial functions, and the issues (substantive and otherwise) that are part of the governmental process. Campaign journalism is narrower, focusing on the electoral process: The men and women who want to govern, the issues that arise in campaigns, the strategies and tactics used to win votes, and the other factors—mechanical and intellectual—that are part of getting elected. The information that journalists provide the public about all this is an integral part of the democratic process. Voters depend, to some extent, on the news media. Therefore, this part of the news business should be governed by carefully considered ethical standards.

I. WHY ETHICS MATTERS IN POLITICAL JOURNALISM

When people cast their ballots on election day, what factors shape their voting decisions? Each voter makes his or her choices in a unique way, but certain influences affect almost everyone to some degree. Party affiliation; the opinions of family members, friends, co-workers, and others; the politicians' positions on issues the voter considers important; and instinctive reaction to the perceived "character" of the candidates—these are just some elements of voters' decision making. Another factor helps shape almost every voting decision— information provided by the news media. Even those people who say they despise the press rarely avoid its messages altogether. Increasingly ubiquitous—on the printed page, on the airwaves, and on line—the news media provide exhaustive reporting about campaigns for those who care to partake of it. The news mix contains everything from verbatim transcripts of candidates' speeches to intensely partisan editorials. The coverage (or, for some candidates, lack of coverage) does much to shape public perceptions of campaigns. As messengers and arbiters, journalists might not tell people what to think, but they certainly tell them what to think about. That is a tremendously significant role. If it is performed honorably, it enhances the democratic process. If, however, journalists act irresponsibly, they can severely damage that process. That is why ethical political journalism is so important.

Ethics in political journalism is a critical issue in any country that has a free press, although it may be particularly significant in the United States, where the relative absence of press law enhances the importance of ethical behavior. In many other countries, laws governing fairness, defining libel, and imposing limits as to what may and may not be covered act as forceful restraints on journalistic behavior.

There are, nevertheless, certain common problems, such as sensational approaches to "the character issue." During the 1997 British parliamentary campaigns, for instance, the press delighted in lurid allegations about members of Parliament having teenage mistresses, accepting illicit payoffs, and committing myriad other sins. A noted former journalist, Martin Bell, running as an independent "antisleaze" candidate, ousted a Conservative party incumbent whom one newspaper had called (in headlines) "a liar and a cheat." Of course, there were far more important (and far less salacious) matters that shaped the outcome of Britain's 1997 elections. But sensation gets attention. Around the world, scandal— especially when related to the financial affairs or sex lives of politicians—is common journalistic fare, delivered to audiences with a sensational spin that American tabloids must envy.

In nations with established free press traditions and in those tasting press freedom for the first time, ethics in political journalism is an evolving science. In the former Soviet Union and countries that were part of the Soviet bloc, new freedoms have been accompanied, in many cases, by exuberant journalism. This is also the case in other, developing countries where a free press is still talking root after many years during which something such as "truth-testing" would probably land the reporter in jail (or worse). Creating ethical standards is in many respects a trial-and-error process that journalists in these countries are just beginning.

There is no country in which journalists have found ethical perfection in their political reporting, but there are many nations in which news professionals with good intentions are trying to cover politics ethically as well as effectively. These are the laboratories for the further development of journalism ethics.

Some journalists resist overuse of "ethics" when discussing how they do their jobs, preferring the less formal "responsibility." In part, this is because discussions about ethics tend to include suggestions about formal codes or specific guidelines that may prove to be cumbersome and unnecessary. However the semantic issues are resolved, even the less formal approach involves individual journalists recognizing the importance of ethical conduct while doing day-to-day journalism.

II. RESPONSIBILITIES OF POLITICAL JOURNALISTS

A. Fairness and Objectivity

A basic goal, at least in theory, of political journalism is to help the voter cast an informed ballot. Providing that assistance requires more than good intentions. It demands sophisticated knowledge of the workings of politics, and evenhanded presentation of the fruits of that knowledge. This fairness is particularly important given the public's skepticism about the motivations and values of the news media, which flared anew during the intensive coverage of the Clinton–Lewinsky scandal of 1998–1999.

Fairness is an elusive commodity, much praised as an ideal but most often cited for its absence. It is difficult to define, partly because fairness in any particular case may depend on the eye of the beholder. Political partisans might see any coverage of their favored cause or candidate as "unfair" if it does not conform to their views, especially if the coverage seems to depict an opposing viewpoint or politician in what is perceived as an unduly favorable way.

There is little evidence to support allegations that modern political journalists working for mainstream news organizations are deliberately unfair, or that their coverage reflects purposeful partisan bias. If there is unfairness, it tends to come in through the back door, often as a function of sloppy reporting. This was the case in late 1999, when some news organizations reported the allegation that presidential candidate George W. Bush had been arrested on drug charges in the early 1970s. These news stories were not based on independent reporting, but rather relied on a newly published biography of the Texas governor. The story was wrong. The allegation was wholly unsupported, the book's author turned out to be a convicted felon, and the publisher recalled the book from stores. The damage to Bush proved inconsequential, but it simply was not fair to publish those stories. Some news organizations, to their credit, checked out the allegation on their own, found nothing, and did not report it. The lesson for journalists from this episode should be, "Do your own work." Relying on an unfamiliar and uncorroborated source is being lazy to the point of being unethical.

Countless fairness issues arise throughout campaigns, but journalistic malice is rarely a factor. Decisions about what to cover and how much coverage to provide are often based on commercial considerations (what the audience is thought to want) and format constraints (especially on television). The basic ethical mandate for the news media is simple: act in good faith, and when mistakes are made—as in the Bush case—remedy them through corrections and better journalism.

The ideal of fairness can best be achieved by adhering to standards of objectivity. This means dispassionate evenhandedness, with personal biases subjected to self-policing that will protect against their infecting news content. At the heart of this is non-judgmental reporting, which is largely a function of intellectual discipline. Objectivity in the news business is not a philosophical abstraction. It cannot, realistically, be defined as opinion-free news gathering. Any journalist who is interested in and knowledgeable about politics is certain to form opinions about the candidates and issues he or she covers. That is a function of human nature, and it is disingenuous for journalists to pretend that they do not make such judgments. As an ethical principle in this area, what matters is not what journalists think, but what they report. Surveys of members of the national political press corps consistently show that most consider themselves liberal and most vote for Democrats. That should not matter as long as their work product does not reflect it. Granted, partisanship may creep into coverage, even if unconsciously, so reporters should

make every effort to remain as dispassionate as possible. The editing process helps limit this.

Strict definitions of objectivity may collide with "public journalism" (also known as "civic journalism"), a form of coverage that has recently become popular among some journalists. It emphasizes problem solving and public participation in deciding what issues are newsworthy. Public journalism's critics say this is too advocacy-oriented, and that journalists should go no further than telling news consumers what is happening and then let them decide what they want to do about it. To do more, say the critics, is to become part of the story rather than just covering it.

In political coverage, public journalism may involve using polls, focus groups, and other solicitations of opinion to determine what issues voters want to see covered. Journalists, acting as the public's surrogates, then ask the candidates to address those issues.

To the surprise of few, the public in these projects has shown very little interest in campaign tactics, scandal, or any of the other topics that so fascinate political insiders. They want news stories about the economy, education, health care, and other matters that directly affect them.

No one will quarrel with the notion that fairness and objectivity are appropriate standards in political journalism. The ethical challenge is to integrate those standards into the often frantic process of covering politics.

B. News versus Truth

Fairness and objectivity do not, however, mean softness. The healthiest press–politician relationship features dynamic tension, with aggressive journalists always demanding more and better information from the candidates. Most journalists believe that their role is much more than being a conveyor belt that delivers whatever the politicians provide to the voters, because sometimes the politicians' messages are incomplete or even misleading.

At the heart of this is the distinction between "news" and "truth." Some of the darkest days of American politics provide an example of this. When Senator Joseph McCarthy, in a 1950 speech, said that he had a list of 205 communists working in the U.S. State Department, that was news. But was it the truth? By most accounts, the answer is no. So what should journalists do? They cannot very well ignore the allegation, particularly because they do not know, for certain, that the charge is false. One newspaper ran the story under the headline, "State Department Has 205 Commies, Senator Says." Does the "Senator Says" mean that the newspaper is not vouching for the accuracy of the charge?

Will readers interpret that wording as a cautionary note? Perhaps, but perhaps not.

For the next several years, "McCarthyism" wreaked havoc in the United States, and journalists were very slow to challenge the accuracy of McCarthy's allegations and demand proof. This happened a half-century ago, but the news media's sluggish response to McCarthy remains a cloud over the profession.

Although the frightening viciousness of the McCarthy era is long past, some politicians still stray from the truth. Suppose, for example, a candidate says, "My opponent, while governor, presided over a terrible decline in her state's employment rate." The statement is news, but now assume that reliable, nonpartisan sources provide data that prove the charge is false. In such an instance, some journalists might feel that allegiance to truth should supersede mere reporting of the news, and the contrary information should be added to the story.

In many cases, the distinction between news and truth is not so clear. If the candidate says, "My tax cut plan will sustain economic growth," there is no way to prove or disprove the claim. News stories, therefore, should report the candidate's statement and also include comments from experts who agree and those who disagree with the candidate.

News is easy to find. Truth is often much harder to nail down. As a matter of journalistic ethics, the rule often cited is something like this: Never settle for just the news; always include the best obtainable version of the truth.

C. Understanding Issues, Understanding Politics

Voters consistently say that they want the news media to provide more coverage of issues and place less emphasis on candidates' personal lives and political tactics. Many news organizations have tried to respond by providing more thorough issues coverage to give the public a reasonable idea of how the candidates would govern if elected. This means new responsibilities for reporters. Participating in the speculation, gossip, and political rituals that are the underpinning of daily campaign coverage is supplanted by analyzing position papers and researching complex topics. This can be a daunting task, considering the range of issues that are addressed in the course of any campaign. A local contest might feature debate about bond funding, tax rates, and the availability of public services. Issues in a federal race might include proposals to sustain Social Security and develop new superweapons. Reporters must find appropriate background, analysis, and commentary about such matters. As journalist Richard Reeves observed, "Covering politics is fun; covering government is work."

Despite the effort to provide more substantive issues coverage, members of the political press corps must still be experts in campaign mechanics—how candidacies are organized and funded, and how the vote-getting process works. Besides being concerned about issues, the public *is* interested in who is ahead and who is behind at a given point in a campaign, and why these candidates are doing well or poorly. A knowledgeable political reporter should be familiar with the often arcane rules of campaign finance and the nominating process, and should be able to evaluate the proficiency of a candidate's field organization. The journalist also should have a good grounding in political history, knowing what has succeeded and what has failed in past campaigns. Any reporter who is covering a televised presidential debate, for example, should know something about the history of such debates, going back to the 1960 face-offs between John Kennedy and Richard Nixon.

Failure to master such topics will make the journalist susceptible to self-serving pronouncements from the candidates and their handlers. That is likely to result in news stories being laced with politicians' propaganda, which is a disservice to the public. Good reporters should be able to tell news consumers not only what is happening during a campaign, but also *why* it is happening.

Journalistic competence can be considered an ethical issue because an incompetent reporter will almost certainly deliver an inferior news product. This is not merely a matter of a few details being left out of a story. Among journalists' most important responsibilities are decisions about *what* to cover and *how much* coverage should be provided. Setting these priorities requires a sophisticated understanding of the campaign's issues and strategies.

III. CHALLENGES OF CAMPAIGN COVERAGE

A. Pack Journalism

The journalists covering a high-profile candidate often number in the hundreds. The collective body has enough customs and quirks to delight a sociologist. There is stratification, with superstars (television network correspondents and elite newspaper reporters and columnists) at the top and local broadcast and print journalists as the underclass. There is territorial imperative, such as reserving the sacred space with the best view of the candidate for the television cameras (and woe to anyone, especially a print reporter, who tries to usurp that space). There is ritual, in the courtship of journalistic celebrities by campaign staff members trying to influence coverage, which often takes place in the hotel bars that serve as the watering holes along the campaign trail.

Beyond the fact that the dynamics of the political press corps are intriguing and sometimes entertaining are issues of professional responsibility. The nature of the journalistic pack can affect the news product and the public's perceptions of the campaign. The sheer size of the pack is a factor, particularly in national campaigns. With so many reporters and photographers jostling each other, few actually get close enough to the candidates to see or hear them during most of the campaign day. Often a "pool system" is used in which a small number of journalists are allowed close proximity to the candidate with the understanding that they will share their tapes and notes with the rest of the pack. Beyond this, journalists traveling with a campaign spend much of their time talking to each other, picking up pieces of information and gossip. This interaction, coupled with deference to the journalistic superstars' views, tends to produce a conventional wisdom about how the various candidates are doing and what issues are most important. The reporters, unintentionally but inevitably, develop a consensus journalism.

There may be no great harm done by this, but the tendency of many reporters is to gravitate to the safe middle of the pack and not risk original thinking. The public therefore receives a similar product from many news organizations. If the pack's collective judgments are correct, the news product will be accurate, if bland. The danger comes when the conventional wisdom is wrong, such as when the candidate dismissed as having no chance suddenly wins. The ghost of Harry Truman, whom the press wrongly pronounced doomed to defeat in 1948, should haunt journalists even today. As a matter of professional responsibility, many journalists try to resist the inertia that is a function of pack journalism. Rather than relying too heavily on collective judgments of the pack, they want to retain independence in deciding what the public needs to know.

B. The "Character Issue"

The character of politicians has always been an important criterion in voters' decision making. People vote for people, not just for policy positions or party labels. Voters want to know how a particular candidate is different from others, and how personal ideals and background influence that politician's views and actions. In American presidential politics, character has been an important factor since the days of George Washington, but recent press coverage of character has become increasingly lurid, with a heavy emphasis on candidates' sex lives.

Press standards regarding character coverage move through cycles. No president, including the likes of Washington and Abraham Lincoln, has been exempt from being the target of sensational allegations. Bill Clinton's treatment during the Monica Lewinsky scandal was mild compared to what Thomas Jefferson and Andrew Jackson endured. Even mainstream news media (a category that excludes the sensational tabloid newspapers, television shows, and Web sites) have long been purveyors of gossip as well as fact. They have, however, exercised considerable discretion about what they report. When journalists did not write stories about the extramarital adventures of Franklin Roosevelt and John Kennedy, were they being appropriately reticent or negligent? Full disclosure about politicians sounds like a nice journalistic premise, but if it is employed thoughtlessly it can override relevance and good taste.

In the aftermath of the Clinton–Lewinsky scandal, many in the public and some in the press believed that the coverage had gone too far in reporting so many sensational particulars. Nevertheless, journalists seemed little inclined to back off. In the early stages of the 2000 presidential campaign, reporters asked candidates, with no supporting evidence, "Have you ever committed adultery?" and they searched the candidates' personal histories for indiscretions that might produce a headline. Within news organizations, this practice has been debated. Is this solid investigative journalism or unethical snooping?

Among standards that might guide character coverage are these:

- Germaneness. Reporters might concentrate on those aspects of a candidate's background that are most likely to affect his or her performance of official duties.
- Zone of privacy. Even presidential candidates may be entitled to keep some aspects of their lives—such as their marriages and their children—out of public view.
- Timeliness. Journalists could observe a de facto statute of limitations, with its length depending on the nature of the transgression. Recent drug use by a candidate is one thing; occasional college-age marijuana smoking is something else. At some point, old news is no longer news.

In such matters, news organizations face a distinction between what the public has a *right* to know, which is virtually everything, and what the public has a *need* to know before voting, which is more limited. The right to know is implicitly protected by the First Amendment, but as a practical matter news organizations decide daily how far that right extends. Some news is not reported because it does not meet standards of taste or relevance.

In the campaign context, some journalists believe that guidelines are unrealistic because they are too general to be useful to news organizations that must deal with fast-breaking campaign events. Journalists also are wary of guidelines that might limit their right to dig for information. There is a school of thought that self-censorship is never in the public's interest, and so voters should be told everything that reporters can uncover and then decide for themselves what they want to take seriously and what they want to ignore. Some reporters, however, recognize the need for occasional self-restraint. Veteran correspondent Jack Germond wrote that "perhaps the most egregious weakness of those of us who cover politics is our lack of any sense of proportion."

Character, of course, involves much more than sex. Candidates' upbringing and non-political personal history may shed light on how they would perform in office. Recent presidential contenders Bob Dole, Bob Kerry, and John McCain, for example, endured harrowing combat experiences while in the military. Voters deserved to be told about these events because of their possible effect on presidential decisions about sending troops into combat. Similarly, politicians' family members move within the legitimate scope of coverage if they are tied to a public policy matter, as happened when President George Bush's son Neil was involved in the 1988 collapse of a Denver savings and loan.

Politicians' character will continue to be a principal topic for journalistic scrutiny. The ethical challenge for news professionals will be to strike a balance between a commitment to full disclosure and the need for restraint based on respect for some level of privacy.

Character coverage, especially in its sloppy manifestations, has come to be seen as a symptom of weakened journalistic principles. In his autobiography, former British prime minister John Major wrote, "There is more pressure to come up with sensational stories, less hesitancy to print speculative ones. In all this, there has grown up an unscrupulousness, a willingness to give credence to rumor, a refusal to correct or apologize...."

C. Screening the Candidates

Lots of people run for office. Some are well known, with many supporters and a solid campaign organization, and have at least a reasonable chance of being elected. Others are unknown quantities, with little visible support or organization and apparently little chance of winning the election. All these candidates may be equal, however, in the sense that all their names appear on the ballot. Does that mean they should receive equal coverage from the news media?

This is the kind of question that can cause unease among journalists. As a matter of democratic process,

voters should be given a chance to judge all candidates, and the news media should not obstruct that. But as a practical matter, covering *everyone* who announces a candidacy is neither feasible nor desirable. Even the fattest magazine or newspaper does not have unlimited space for news stories, and the public does not have an unlimited attention span. Television newscasts in particular feel squeezed for time. If only two minutes is available on a given night for a story about a campaign, news producers often are faced with this choice: give the two top candidates a minute each, or divide the time among all the candidates, however many there may be. If the latter course is chosen, viewers are likely to get a melange of information nuggets that are so small as to be worthless in terms of providing any real insight into the contenders. This practice, if continued throughout the campaign, can leave voters knowing too little about the candidate who is eventually elected. Therefore, news organizations generally weight their coverage heavily in favor of those candidates who journalists believe have the best chance of receiving serious consideration from most voters.

Those who fall outside this field challenge the fairness of this process. How can they ever hope to make their case to the electorate if they are denied exposure through news coverage? This question is raised at every level of politics, from presidential races to city council contests. Rare is the election year in which at least some offices fail to attract a large number of contenders. (In one U.S. Senate election in Texas, the ballot listed 71 candidates.) Limits on coverage also discourage formation of new parties as alternatives to the Democrats and Republicans. Non-traditional-party candidates must have lots of money (as with billionaire Ross Perot) or lots of celebrity (as with former professional wrestler Jesse Ventura) to be able to get the public's and the news media's attention.

At the heart of the ethical debate about screening is the intrinsically patronizing nature of the process. By covering only a select few candidates, journalists are implicitly telling the public, "We're making choices for you. These are the only candidates you need to consider seriously." Many news consumers, and certainly the candidates who do not make the cut, may view this as journalistic arrogance and a usurpation of the voters' prerogative.

Screening does not take place in secret meetings of the news media elite. The process is haphazard, an evolving reflection of the press pack's conventional wisdom about candidates' viability. These judgments are not made frivolously. Experienced political journalists can make informed—and usually accurate—appraisals of candidates' prospects based on the quality of organizations they have assembled in key states, the amounts of money they have raised, the early public response to their messages, and other such factors. As editors and producers accept these judgments, the shape of coverage begins to conform to them. Certain candidates are in, and others are out.

The absence of invidious intent is unlikely to satisfy candidates in the latter category. All they can do to avoid being screened out is adjust their campaign strategies, such as by starting early and running campaigns that will capture the attention of press and public.

For the journalists, this issue is a classic mix of news business reality and professional responsibility. The reality is the need to cover candidates in a way that is most helpful to prospective voters. The responsibility is to avoid short-circuiting the electoral process. Balancing the two is difficult but extremely important.

The journalists' dilemma is alleviated somewhat by the Internet. A news Web site has what the newspaper or newscast lacks—virtually infinite space. Coverage that does not fit on paper or on the air can find a home on the Web. Some time will pass before the Web audience approaches the size of the major network newscasts' viewership, but when that happens, and if the public takes advantage of the newly available information, the problems of screening will be less severe. Not only will news organizations provide more information on their sites, but candidates will use the Web to attract money and votes (as was seen in the 2000 presidential race). Nonpartisan sources of political information will also use the Internet as a cost-efficient, far-reaching tool to disseminate their messages.

D. Horse Race Coverage

Among the most common synonyms for "campaign" are "race" and "contest." It is no surprise, therefore, that political reporting has certain similarities to coverage of a sporting event. As with sports, the public is interested in who is "winning" at any given moment. The journalistic response often is a frequently updated story line based on polls and other appraisals of the candidates' relative status. This reporting *is* a lot like the call of a horse race: "As they come into the home stretch in New Hampshire, Bush is in the lead, but McCain is closing fast, and Forbes refuses to quit … while Keyes and Bauer trail the field."

For journalists, this is easy work. Gather some polling data, talk to a few political sages, and rank the candidates. The story just about writes itself, and the public's curiosity is satisfied. Assuming that the information in the story comes from reliable sources (respected polls and credible experts), there seems to be a little ethical problem. But this horse race journalism can have an insidious effect on coverage. News organizations may become so infatuated with this facet of the campaign—particularly if there is suspense about the eventual outcome—that they neglect more substantive matters, such as issues analysis. Also, these stories can have a self-perpetuating effect. Reporters might find themselves more race track touts than journalists, developing a proprietary interest in seeing their projections prove correct and subtly shading their coverage in favor of *their* horse. From the candidates' perspective, heavy emphasis on who is ahead and who is not might dissuade voters from giving serious consideration to a candidate who is trailing at the moment, drying up the flow of contributions and volunteers.

Defenders of this kind of coverage make two important points. First, concerning the presidential nominating system, the political parties have created a process that *is* a horse race and must be covered, at least in part, as such. With caucuses and primaries that begin in Iowa and New Hampshire and extend through dozens of other states, a certain amount of quantitative reporting is necessary as delegates are accumulated in the quest for the party's nomination. Also, the essence of the horse race is proving who is the most effective candidate—who can best organize, persuade, and lead. Those characteristics are essential not only in mounting a winning campaign but also in governing effectively, so voters deserve to know about them.

As with most elements of political reporting, no ethical difficulties—in terms of the overall quality of the news product—will arise if balance is maintained. Horse race coverage is fine as long as issues coverage is not slighted. Political journalism is by its nature multifaceted, and as long as news organizations understand and respect that, even intensive reporting about the state of the horse race does no disservice to the public.

E. Resisting Manipulation

In politicians' eyes, "good journalism" means favorable coverage. Much effort is expended by candidates and their managers to foster such "good journalism." As the public's surrogates, journalists have the obligation to resist these self-serving attempts to distort the news.

Campaigns are filled with "media events"—occasions designed to appeal to voters when delivered to them by news organizations. The most common type of media event is the "photo opportunity" in which the candidate carefully poses in a way that will appear appropriately heroic to the camera's eye. Delivering a proposal about environmental issues, for example, is often done with a fitting backdrop; a snow-capped mountain is nice. Or, if the proposal incorporates criticism of an opponent, a negative setting—a sludge-filled harbor, for instance—might work well. These events are designed with a particular emphasis on television coverage, because politicians recognize the power of visual messages. For their part, journalists must not allow themselves to be so carried away by the look of the event that they forget about its substance. In the environmental example, no matter how nice the setting, what really matters is what the candidate says. That should be the principal focus of coverage.

Media events have become the visual cliches of politics. To tout commitment to education, the candidate has an event at a school. If law enforcement is the issue of the day, the politician poses with a crowd of police officers. If older voters are being courted, a retirement home is a heartwarming setting. These events have taken on a generic quality that leads some news organizations to cover them unthinkingly. That is a trap to be avoided. If there is no real substance—just pretty pictures—journalists must decide if the event is worth covering at all. Especially on television, where air time is so scarce, the valuable minutes might be better spent on a story that is less photogenic but has more intellectual content.

Other attempts at manipulation are also common. With increasing sophistication, politicians try to shape news coverage through "spin." This is usually the work not of the candidates themselves, but their staff members who offer their interpretation of events to reporters. After a debate between candidates, for example, supporters of each candidate might literally stand in line to be interviewed about the strengths and weaknesses of the respective presentations. Part of the appeal of spin is that it makes journalists' jobs easier. Editors and producers always like quotes and talking heads in news stories, and the spinners are happy to provide them. Journalists, however, must recognize that the top priority for spinners is to benefit their candidate, with accuracy a distant second. Spin is thinly disguised propaganda, and journalists should treat it as such.

Related to spin is a courtship of reporters that is based on giving journalists easy access to the candidate. In 2000, John McCain used his bus, the "Straight Talk Express," as the setting for endless interviews and conversations. Many journalists were charmed, and much of the coverage of McCain was notably friendly.

A common spin effort is setting expectations. Before a crucial primary in which the candidate expects to get just over 50% of the vote, the preprimary task for spinners may be to convince reporters that the candidate will be happy just to get 40%. That way, if the 50+ level is reached, it will look like a great triumph. On the other hand, if expectations are set too high and they turn out not to be met, news coverage is likely to emphasize the candidate's failure. The politician's classic answer to the question, "How well do you hope to do in tomorrow's vote?" is, "Better than expected." In such vagueness is safety.

The expectations game is part of horse race coverage. It is particularly important in the nominating process because meeting or failing to meet expectations presumably may affect much-desired momentum and the outcome of the next primary on the road toward the nomination. (In the general election, by contrast, there is no tomorrow, so failing to meet expectations becomes just a matter for historians.) A candidate's front-runner or also-ran status will be affected by how performance matches up to expectations. Exceeding expectations can rejuvenate a campaign, while failing to meet them can scare off contributors and volunteers. With the stakes so high, politicians' spin efforts related to expectations receive high priority, so journalists should be on their guard, making their own judgments and resisting the spinners' entreaties.

Yet another area of possible manipulation is campaign advertising. Here the target of manipulation is generally the voter, not the journalist, but this provides an example of the watchdog role the news media must play. Traditionally, campaign advertising attracted little scrutiny from journalists. The ads were part of the candidates' message delivery systems—along with media events, direct mail, and other voter contacts—and the public was left to fend for itself in evaluating the ads. Beginning in the late 1980s, that changed. News organizations began to analyze campaign advertising, especially television spots. This change occurred partly because some ads were so outrageously phony— particularly the attack ads directed at opponents—and partly because as a matter of common sense, there was no reason for journalists to cover other aspects of a campaign while ignoring advertising. If candidates' speeches were critiqued for their accuracy, advertising—which often reaches more people than speeches do—deserved similar attention.

The result is a new minigenre of political reporting: ad truth-testing. Newspapers may print the complete script of a political TV spot and analyze any claims or charges made in the ad. If there are errors of fact, they are pointed out. If claims are based solely on opinion, that too is noted. Television reporters cover ads by showing excerpts, often using a screen-within-the-screen format to avoid simply giving the spot a full-blown replay. As the ad appears, the text or reporter's analysis scrolls beside it. Some TV critiques even go so far as to show an untrue passage from the ad text with "FALSE" in red letters superimposed on it.

The goal of such reporting is twofold: to keep voters from being misled by false advertising, and to discourage politicians from using such ads by making it clear that false or questionable content will be challenged. Although misleading ads have not vanished, the truth tests presumably have heightened the awareness of some voters, and many candidates now offer documentation to support the claims made in their spots.

Resisting political chicanery is an important professional responsibility for journalists acting as the public's surrogate in gathering, evaluating, and disseminating information. In all these cases, the journalists' watchdog role is essential because if the news media are manipulated, the public is being manipulated.

Truth-testing also might be put to use in evaluating politicians' Web sites. More and more candidates use the Internet to reach voters directly—offering news about the campaign, recruiting volunteers, soliciting contributions, and sometimes attacking the opposition. As a source of political information, this is unmediated media. It is much like advertising in its effect, but it looks more like news than ads. As increasing numbers of voters use the Internet to get information about campaigns, news organizations presumably will more closely monitor the accuracy of political Web sites' content.

F. Demands of Real-Time Reporting

Real-time journalism—live reporting—has become increasingly common with the rise of all-news television networks such as CNN, MSNBC, Fox News, and others. Online news providers are making real-time coverage even more commonplace. High-speed technologies coupled with intense competitive pressures create significant ethical challenges for the news business.

In the world of cybernews, traditional news cycles and deadlines are obsolete. Stories are published on line as soon as they are ready. The definition of "ready" can pose problems; the rush to beat the competition can lead to reduced emphasis on corroboration and editing, increasing the chances for errors. Racing against competitors is nothing new. Wire services pull out all stops to beat their rivals to a story, sometimes making mistakes along the way. But their work product goes to other news organizations, which can do their own checking before publishing. When news goes directly on line, however, it can be read by the world.

In political coverage, when charges and countercharges, and claims and counterclaims fly back and forth, careful verification is particularly important, regardless of what medium is used to deliver the news. But as coverage of the Clinton–Lewinsky scandal showed, sometimes getting the story first takes precedence over getting it right. One example of this occurred in February 1998 when a *Wall Street Journal* reporter called the White House for comment about the newspaper's information that a White House steward had told a federal grand jury that he had seen President Clinton

and Monica Lewinsky alone together in the President's study. The White House spokesman told the reporter he would have to check, but moments later the reporter told him that the story had just been posted on the *Journal's* Web site. The report, which cited unnamed sources, also was quickly put on the *Journal's* wire service, and the paper's Washington bureau chief discussed it on cable news channel CNBC. Within 90 minutes, the steward's lawyer issued a statement calling the *Journal's* story "absolutely false and irresponsible." The paper, while standing by the basic information in the story, later changed its report to say that the steward had reported his observation to "Secret Service personnel," not the grand jury (a significant difference). *Washington Post* media critic Howard Kurtz wrote that this case illustrated "the increasing velocity of the news cycle," and noted that one of the *Journal* reporters had explained the rush by saying, "We heard footsteps from at least one other news organization and just didn't think it was going to hold in this crazy cycle we're in."

This illustrates how the high-speed news cycle can entice journalists away from fundamental duties such as thorough fact-checking. Feeling pressure from competitors who may also have had the story, the *Journal* did not give the White House time to comment. As a matter of fairness, the White House response should have been included in the story to provide balance. Readers could then decide whom to believe.

The Internet is a marvelous resource, allowing vast amounts of information to be made available to the public. But it also has vast potential for abuse. Speed can be the enemy of truth. That should be kept in mind as the ethics of political journalism continue to evolve.

IV. RESPONSIBILITIES TO THE POLITICAL PROCESS

A. Influencing Outcomes

The political journalist's job is to report about what is happening in campaigns, not shape election results. That sounds like a good, ethical principle. It is not, however, altogether realistic. If news coverage is interesting and informative, it will inevitably affect how voters perceive candidates and issues, and so will have some impact on voting decisions. All but the most disingenuous journalists accept that. The ethical responsibility, therefore, can be stated as a modified version of the grander principle: journalists should recognize that, regardless of intent, they do exert some influence on election outcomes and therefore should exercise appropriate caution.

A forthright way to try to influence voting is through editorial endorsements. Many news organizations (especially newspapers) do this and observe a basic rule: news coverage is in no way to be affected by the endorsement, and reporters and editors in the newsroom are to do their jobs as if the endorsement by the editorial board did not exist. In practice, this separation between editorial and news functions is not hard to maintain in a good news organization. The problem, however, is one of perception. Readers of a paper that has endorsed a particular candidate might assume that news coverage will tilt in favor of that candidate. Largely because of such perceptions, a case can be made that news organizations should not make endorsements. Presenting institutional opinion may damage the public's faith in the objectivity of the news product.

In addition to the cumulative influence of coverage throughout a campaign, some elements of political journalism can have disproportionate effects on the contest. Reliance on opinion polls, which is a feature of horse race reporting, can cause voters to make what may be premature judgments about the viability of candidacies. The issue for news organizations is not whether to use polls, but rather *how* to use them. If polls are allowed to dominate coverage (in headlines and the way news stories are structured), some voters may decide to embrace or abandon a candidate based solely on his or her perceived chances of winning. Journalist David Broder observed that "much of political journalism is an artful effort to disguise prediction as reporting," which means that issues and qualifications might get less attention than they deserve. One useful guideline is that poll results should be used as supplements to, not substitutes for, reporting about the true substance of a campaign.

News organizations sometimes conduct their own polling, but in cases when they use polls designed and administered by someone else they should examine the polling procedures—sample size and selection, phrasing of questions, and other such matters—before they use the poll results in stories. In addition to well-designed polls, the political season always sees pseudo-polls, such as surveys in which people are invited to call a telephone number to register their for-or-against opinion. These ventures have no control over their sample, and some candidates' supporters may organize a call-in project just to tilt results in their favor. Because of their susceptibility to such abuse, these "polls" usually should be ignored by news organizations.

The electronic media often find themselves involved in controversy about election day projections. Using exit polls (asking selected samples of voters how they voted as they leave their polling places), news organizations' polling experts can project eventual results well before polls close and votes are counted. If they release this information while people are still voting, turnout could be affected. No one is certain how much effect these projections might have, but this practice raises an intriguing ethical question: Should news organizations deliver information to the public as soon as it is available (assuming it is believed to be accurate), or should they withhold it if it might affect voter turnout? If they follow the latter course, news organizations (especially the television networks) might be praised for their restraint, but they also might be criticized for, in journalist Michael Kinsley's words, generating "false tension while suppressing the very information that would dissipate it." Online news gatherers face the same test. The policy observed by many news organizations is to delay projecting outcomes in a given race until the voting in that race has ended, or, in presidential elections, not project how a state's votes will go until that state's polls have closed. This might not be a perfect solution, but given the competition among news organizations to be first with election results, it is probably the best policy that journalists will accept.

B. Covering Political Institutions

Political coverage has become so focused on personalities and any given day's media events that the structural context of politics tends to be overlooked. Candidacies are transient phenomena, while institutions, such as the political parties, are long-lasting. Coverage could better reflect that. For one thing, this would simply be better reporting. Some candidates have surprised journalists because they either mastered or ran afoul of institutional aspects of politics, such as delegate selection procedures or campaign spending rules. Further, no politician—not even a president elected by a landslide margin—can accomplish much without working with other parts of the government. The ability to lead the complex array of democratic institutions should be a criterion by which would-be chief executives are judged, but this is often ignored by the press and so by the voters. The same concept applies to elected officials at all levels—state and local, as well as national.

The structures and histories of the political parties merit attention because even in a television-dominated political world these institutions remain important. Bill Clinton won the 1992 presidential election in part because he pulled the Democratic party toward the ideological middle. George W. Bush became a national figure because he was able to expand the traditional Republican base and win sizable numbers of Hispanic and African-American votes in his 1998 campaign for governor in Texas. These were important stories, but they could not be conveyed to the public unless journalists understood their historical and institutional foundation. Events on the surface do not always tell the tale of what lies below. If *completeness* in reporting is considered a professional responsibility, journalists must look below the surface and describe what they find there.

V. CONCLUSION

Political journalism remains a fertile field for the development of professional ethics because campaigning and reporting are such dynamic businesses. Nothing is sacrosanct; change is constant. Much the same can be said for ethics in journalism and politics: change—if not always progress—is constant. There are positive steps, such as increased truth-testing of campaign advertising, but there are also slips, such as sloppy reporting about "character"-related allegations. Perfection remains in the far distance.

Political journalists are outsiders in the sense that they do not (or at least should not) have a stake in who wins or loses an election. But they are very much insiders because the workings of the electoral process are so dependent on the flow of news to the public. In addition to the independence of journalists and the accuracy of their news product, the tone of coverage is an important factor in influencing how people look at politics and whether they will participate in elections. Unduly sensa-tional and cynical reporting is bad not only for journalism but also for the democratic process. It does not take much to get people to turn away from politics. With that in mind, news organizations should not feel compelled to sanitize political news, but they should understand that by presenting fair and substantive coverage they might spur greater participation.

Ethical performance by the press is important, but in the end, responsibility for the functioning of the political process rests not with the news media but with the people. In *Public Opinion*, Walter Lippmann wrote of the "machinery of knowledge" that the public needs to create in order to have "a reliable picture of the world." Journalists can supply the crucial parts for that machinery.

Bibliography

Ansolabehere, S., & Iyengar, S. (1995). *Going negative: How political advertisements shrink and polarize the electorate.* New York: The Free Press.

Germond, J. (1999). *Fat man in a middle seat.* New York: Random House.

Kovach, B., & Rosenstiel, T. (1999). *Warp speed.* New York: The Century Foundation Press.

Kurtz, H. (1998). *Spin cycle.* New York: The Free Press.

Lichter, S. R., & Noyes, R. E. (1995). *Good intentions make bad news.* Lanham, MD: Rowman and Littlefield.

Sabato, L. J. (1991). *Feeding frenzy.* New York: The Free Press.

Seib, P. (1994). *Campaigns and conscience: The ethics of political journalism.* Westport, CT: Praeger.

Censorship

BERNARD WILLIAMS

University of California, Berkeley

GLOSSARY

censorship Suppression or regulation of publications by a legally constituted authority on grounds of content.

first amendment Provision of the U.S. Bill of Rights governing freedom of speech.

obscenity In English law, technically "a tendency to deprave and corrupt."

pornography Publication in any form with explicit sexual content, intended to produce sexual arousal.

prior restraint A method of control that prevents material from being published.

zoning A system of controlling pornography (or another activity by permitting its sale only in certain designated areas.

CENSORSHIP includes any kind of suppression or regulation, by government or other authority, of a writing or other means of expression, based on its content. The authority need not apply to a whole judicature, and the effects of its censorship may be local. The term is sometimes used polemically by critics of a practice which would not be described as "censorship" by those who approve of it: in the USA the term has often been applied in this way to the activities of school or library boards in preventing the use or purchase of books which contain sexual scenes or teach Darwinism. It does seem that an activity has at least to be publicly recognized in order to count as censorship; interference with mail by the secret police or covert intimidation of editors would be examples of something else. Accordingly, any censorship implies a public claim of legitimacy for the type of control in question.

I. METHODS

The most drastic methods of control involve *prior restraint*: a work is inspected before it is published, and publication may be forbidden, or permitted only after changes have been made. Traditional absolutist regimes sought to control book publication by these means, and the Inquisition similarly regulated publication by Catholic writers. Legal procedures to the same effect still exist in many states for the control of material affecting national security, and in illiberal states for the control of political content and social criticism. Until 1968, theatrical performances in England were controlled in this way by a Court official, the Lord Chamberlain, whose staff monitored the script before production, demanded changes on a variety of grounds (including disrespect to the monarchy), and visited performances to see that their instructions were being carried out. In many jurisdictions, cinema films are inspected by some official agency before release, and its powers may include that of suppressing some or all of a film. However, the emphasis of these inspections has increasingly moved from suppression to labeling, the agency not so much censoring films as classifying them by their suitability for young people (in Britain the relevant body changed its name to express this).

Prior restraint is essential when censorship is motivated by official secrecy: once the information is out, the point of the censorship is lost (the British government attracted ridicule in the 1980s by trying to ban a book on security grounds which had already been published elsewhere). There are other aims of censorship, however, that do not necessarily demand prior restraint. If a work is thought objectionable on grounds of indecency, evil moral character, or its possible social effects, the suppression of it after publication may still be thought to have a point, in limiting people's exposure to it. The word "censorship" is sometimes used to apply only to methods of prior restraint, but legal provisions aimed at suppression after publication can reasonably be seen as having similar purposes and effects, and the term will be taken here to cover these procedures as well. Except in relation to media such as broadcasting, questions of principle are now normally discussed in terms of censorship after publication. It is important that censorship even in this wider sense still aims at suppression. Schemes of restriction or zoning applied to pornographic materials which require them to be sold only in certain shops and only to adults are analogous to film classification, and should be distinguished from censorship.

II. LIMITS

In 1774 Lord Mansfield said, "Whatever is *contra bonos mores et decorum* the principles of our laws prohibit, and the King's Court as the general censor and guardian of the public morals is bound to restrain and punish"[Jones v. Randall (1774)]. Although this dictum was approvingly mentioned by another English Law Lord as recently as 1962, few now would offer quite such a broad justification for censorship. In part, this is because of doubts about what "the public morals" are and by whom they are to be interpreted: pluralism, skepticism, sexual toleration, and doubts about the social and psychological insight of judges have played their part in weakening confidence in the notion. A more basic point is that even where there is a high degree of moral consensus on a given matter, it remains a question of what that may mean for the law, and what, if anything, can count as a good reason for using the law in an attempt to suppress deviant opinions or offensive utterances.

Liberal theories claim that freedom of expression is both an individual right and a political good which can be curtailed only to prevent serious and identifiable harms. They can agree on this even though they may disagree to some extent about the main basis of these values, some emphasizing the danger of political and other power which is not transparent, some the importance of artistic and other expression, and some the ideal, influentially urged by John Stuart Mill, that it is only through an open "market place of ideas" that truth can be discovered. Liberals will agree, obviously, that the presumption against censorship is always very strong. They will differ to some extent, depending on their other views, about the kinds and the severity of harm that may in certain cases justify it. All will want to defend serious political speech; those who emphasize self-expression may be particularly concerned with protecting potentially offensive artistic activity. Those who stress the idea that free speech is a *right* (as Mill usually did not) insist that the reasons for suppression must take the particular form of a threatened violation of someone's rights.

A very strong version of such principles is embodied in U.S. law, which has interpreted the First Amendment to the Constitution ("Congress shall make no law … abridging the freedom of speech or of the press") in such a way as to make censorship on any grounds very difficult. Mr. Justice Holmes in 1919 produced an influential formula: "The question in every case is whether the words used are used in such circumstances and are of such a nature as to create a clear and present danger that they will bring about the substantive evils that Congress has a right to prevent." Restrictions in such terms have been taken to protect even overtly racist demonstrations, let alone publications. The "clear and present danger" test is not used with regard to pornography, but the effect of Supreme Court decisions in that area has been that, at most, hard-core pornography can be suppressed. In many parts of the USA, all that the law enforces is zoning restrictions.

English law allows greater powers of suppresion than that of the USA: publications designed to arouse racial hatred, for instance, may be illegal, and the same is true in other jurisdictions. (In Germany and elsewhere, it is illegal to deny the Holocaust.)

III. PORNOGRAPHY

In the case of pornography, the main concept used in English law is *obscenity*; in a formula inherited from a judgment of Chief Justice Cockburn in 1868, the principal statute defines a publication as obscene if it has a "tendency to deprave or corrupt" those exposed to it. This professedly causal concept of obscenity implies that the rationale of the law is to be found in the harmful consequences of permitting a particular publication. However, as the House of Lords has itself observed, the courts could not apply this formula in a literal sense, and do not really try to do so. No expert evidence is allowed on the matter of causation, and in practice the question is whether a jury or a magistrate finds the material sufficiently offensive. As critics have pointed out, this not only makes the application of the law arbitrary, but reopens the question of its justification. In contrast to the principle that rights to free speech may be curtailed only by appealing to harms or the violation of rights in the particular case—the principle which Holmes' "clear and present danger" test expresses in a very strict form—only those who think that it is the business of the law to express any correct, or at least shared, moral attitude are likely to justify a work's suppression simply on the ground that it is found deeply offensive.

There has been a great deal of controversy about the effects of pornographic and violent publications, and a variety of anecdotal, statistical, and experimental evidence has been deployed in attempts to find out whether there is a causal link between such publications and some identifiable class of social harms, such as sexual crime. It is perhaps not surprising that such studies are inconclusive, and more recent advocates of censorship, such as some radical feminists, have moved away from thinking of censorship in this area on the model of a public health measure, and concentrate on the idea that certain publications unacceptably express a culture of sexual oppression. This approach tends to treat legal provisions against pornography like those against publications that encourage racial discrimination. In some systems, of course, this would still not make such censorship constitutional, even if the problem can be solved of making the provisions determinate enough for them not to be void for uncertainty.

A legal provision drafted by Catharine Mackinnon (which has not been accepted in any U.S. state, though it has influenced Canadian law) would offer a ground of civil action against publishers or manufacturers of pornography by someone who can show that she or he has been damaged by it. This procedure might be said not to be an example of censorship as it is normally understood, but it is relevant to see it in terms of censorship, to the extent that the legal action is based on the content of the material. If a woman is assaulted or raped in the course of making a pornographic film, there is already a ground of legal action; the proposals against pornography will differ from this in being essentially connected with the existence and content of the pornographic material itself.

A radical feminist outlook reinterprets the relation of pornography to other phenomena and, with that,

the rationale of trying to control it. Traditional views, whether liberal or conservative, are disposed to regard pornography as a particular and restricted phenomenon, ministering to fantasy, and extreme sadistic pornography as even more so. The radical feminist thesis is that not just the fantasy but the reality of male domination is central to pornography, and that sadistic pornography involving women is only the most overt and unmediated expression of male social power. The objectifying male gaze to which pornography offers itself is thought to be implicit not only throughout the commercial media, but in much high art. It follows from this that there is a contrast of principle between pornography involving women and other pornography or sadistic material. At the same time, there is a less important contrast, not based on principle, between pornography and other material involving women. Sadistic material involving women will be seen as merely a less reticent version of what is more respectably expressed elsewhere, and if it is specially picked out for censorship, this will be for reasons of policy, somewhat as gross racial insults may attract legal attention rather than trivial ones. In practice, the claim is often made by feminists (in uneasy alliance with conservative forces) that sadistic pornography has worse social effects than other material; this returns the argument to the traditional "public health" approach and its diagnostic problems.

IV. PUBLIC GOOD DEFENSES

It is above all censorship directed against pornography that raises legal issues about artistic merit. With other kinds of censorship, in support of Church or State, it is obvious that works to be censored may have artistic merit, and even more obvious that this will be of no particular concern to the censors, who may well see a good work as more dangerous than a bad one. In the case of pornography, there has been a question, first, whether there can be a pornographic work of art at all. It is not disputed that most pornography is of no aesthetic or artistic interest, but there is disagreement whether this is so merely because it is not worth anyone's while to make it more interesting, or because it is inherent in the content and intention of pornography. It has been argued in favor of the second view that the defining aim of pornography, to arouse its audience sexually, necessarily excludes the more complex intentions and expressive features necessary to aesthetic interest. Against this, there are in fact some visual and literary works which it is hard to deny are pornographic in terms of their content and (it is reasonable to suppose) their intention, but which have been widely thought to have merit.

There is strong pressure to use "pornographic" in an unequivocally negative way—to imply condemnation on moral, social, or aesthetic grounds. If the term is used in this way, there is a danger that different issues may be run together, and some important questions begged: it may be harder to separate, intellectually and politically, the question of whether some objectionable work has merit from the question of whether it should be censored whatever its merit.

The English law is not alone in allowing a "public good defense," which permits acquittal of a work that possesses serious aesthetic, scientific, or other such merits. It is significant that in English law a jury which acquits in a case where this defense has been made is not required to say whether it found the work not obscene or found it meritorious although obscene. The public good defense has secured the publication of serious works that were previously banned, such as *Lady Chatterley's Lover*, but there are difficulties of principle, which are clearly illustrated in the practice of allowing expert testimony on the merits of the works under prosecution. Besides the inherent obscurity of weighing artistic merit against obscenity, and the fact that evidence bearing on this has to be offered under the conditions of legal examination, the process makes the deeply scholastic assumption that the merit of a given work must be recognizable to experts at the time of its publication.

Moreover, the works that can be defended under such a provision must presumably be meritorious, which implies that they are to some considerable degree successful; but if a law is to protect creative activity from censorship, it needs to protect the right to make experiments, some of which will be unsuccessful.

The idea of making *exceptions* to a censorship law for works with artistic merit seems, in fact, essentially confused. Granted that there is a particular value attaching to significant works of art, or, again, that people have an important right to try to express themselves artistically (whether successfully or not), these concerns will not be best met by a system that provides a special exemption just for artistic merit which at a given time can be proved by experts in a court of law. If one believes that censorship on certain grounds is legitimate, then if a work of artistic merit does fall under the terms of the law, it is open to censorship: this point is acknowledged in the practice of traditional political and religious censors. If one believes in freedom for artistic merit, then one believes in freedom, and accepts censorship only on the narrowest of grounds.

Bibliography

Coetzee, J. M. (1996). "Giving Offense: Essays on Censorship." Chicago. Univ. Press, Chicago.

Green, J. (Ed.) (1990). "The Encyclopedia of Censorship." Facts on File, New York.

"Index on Censorship" (1972–). Various issues. Writers and Scholars International, London.

Itzin, C. (Ed.) (1993). "Pornography: Women, Violence, and Civil Liberties." Oxford Univ. Press, Oxford.

Williams, B. (Ed.) (1981). "Obscenity and Film Censorship." Cambridge Univ. Press, Cambridge. [An abridgment of the report of a government committee which reported in 1979.]

Civil Disobedience

HUGO ADAM BEDAU

Tufts University

GLOSSARY

boycott Refusal to buy goods or services in order to protest the policies or practices of the manufacturer or seller.

civil Concerning the body politic or political aspects of a community's life; also decent, courteous conduct.

conscientious objection Refusal to obey the law or commands of higher authority because they violate one's moral convictions.

direct civil disobedience The law being violated in an act of civil disobedience (e.g., refusing to register for the draft) is the law or policy under protest (i.e., an unfair system of selective service).

indirect civil disobedience The law being violated (e.g., refusal to register for the draft) is not the law or policy under protest (i.e., the war for which the draft is instituted).

nonviolence Conduct that does not cause harm to persons or their property.

passive resistance Disobedience of the law followed by passive (unresisting) acceptance of the penalties imposed for such disobedience.

rule of law The principle that disputes are to be settled by appeal to law as determined by an independent judiciary using appropriate rules of evidence and procedure.

satyagraha Nonviolent conflict resolution involving self-purification and respect for one's opponent; originated by M. K. Gandhi. Includes passive resistance.

sit-in A tactic of nonviolent protest in which the ordinary conduct of business is disrupted (e.g., a racially mixed group occupies seats at racially segregated lunch counter in defiance of the store's policy).

tax resistance Refusal to pay one's lawfully required taxes because doing so would support government policies financed by the taxes that are deemed morally wrong by the objector.

CIVIL DISOBEDIENCE is any act in violation of the law done with the intention of frustrating or changing the law, conducted in such a manner as not to involve intentional violence against persons or property, and done in the belief that such disobedience is an appropriate tactic to achieve social justice or some other fundamental moral goal. Borderline cases arise from challenging one or more of the conditions mentioned above on the grounds that it is (or they are) not necessary.

However civil disobedience is defined, it must be done without prejudging the separate question of whether such conduct is justifiable. Not all civil disobedience is justifiable, and civil disobedience is not the only law breaking that can be justified under appropriate conditions. Several features of standard attempts to define civil disobedience have the effect of making such acts either harder or easier to justify. Passive resistance is defended by some as definitionally required in any act properly classified as civil disobedience. The same is true of informing the authorities prior to committing the act of civil disobedience in order to reduce the likelihood of violence and to make the purpose of the protest clear. But some would regard passive resistance or prior notice as only among the many considerations relevant to the justification of such acts.

I. VARIETIES OF CIVIL DISOBEDIENCE

The term "civil disobedience" is sufficiently broad and vague to apply to a wide variety of actual and possible cases, some of which have relatively little in common with others.

A. Individual versus Mass Conduct

Civil disobedience may be undertaken either by an individual acting alone or by a group acting in concert. The political effectiveness of civil disobedience, however, usually depends on large numbers of participants, as in the campaigns for national self-determination in India led by Mohandas Gandhi in the 1930s and for civil rights in the South led by Martin Luther King, Jr., in the 1960s.

Persons acting alone or in small numbers are more likely to be seen as conscientious objectors, testifying by their conduct to what they believe to be an unjust law or policy but not acting with the attempt to change or invalidate the law they protest. Probably the most widely discussed case of civil disobedience in American history illustrates this problem of classification.

In 1846, Henry David Thoreau was arrested for refusing to pay the Massachusetts poll tax (he spent but one night in the local jail, his fine having been promptly paid by a neighbor). In his classic essay, "Civil Disobedience" (first given as a lecture in Concord in 1848), it is evident that Thoreau was not primarily interested in trying to change the laws and practices that he was protesting—the Mexican War, chattel slavery in the South, the Fugitive Slave Law as applied throughout the nation, and to a lesser extent mistreatment of the Indians.

Instead, he seems to have had rather different goals: to use his tax refusal as a tactic that symbolically disconnected him from the wrongs he believed the government was using the tax money to perpetrate, and to encourage others by his example to do the same, regardless of whether that would result in influencing the government to change its practices. In Thoreau's case and cases of conscientious objection, like refusing to report for military duty when drafted, such refusals typically lack the political purpose of changing the law, characteristic of the intention of civil disobedience.

B. Illegal versus Legal Conduct

Whether acts, e.g., a mass rally held in a town's civic center, are classified as civil disobedience depends on whether the law forbids such acts and on what the intentions of the actors are. It is generally agreed that an act cannot be classified as civil disobedience unless some law is violated by the act: Civil disobedience is always *illegal* conduct (even if it is not properly described as *criminal*). Thus, in American society today, with "free speech" interpreted broadly by the Supreme Court and protected by the first amendment to the Constitution, much conduct that in other societies would be illegal is quite within the law here. Accordingly, nonviolent sit-down strikes and boycotts, unless they involve illegal acts, such as a violation of trespass laws, are not tactics of civil disobedience as that term is usually understood.

But whether an act is legal or illegal can itself be controversial, as is illustrated by *Walker v. Birmingham* (1967), one of the important constitutional cases arising out of the Civil Rights movement of the 1960s and decided by the Supreme Court.

Martin Luther King, Jr., and other civil rights leaders planned a mass public protest in downtown Birmingham, Alabama, scheduled for Easter weekend in 1963. But their efforts to obtain a parade permit were frustrated; the undisputed evidence shows they were denied a permit because they were planning to protest local laws and ordinances that mandated racial segregation. Birmingham officials went further and obtained an ex parte court order prohibiting the protest parade. The leaders of the demonstration decided to hold their parade without a permit and to defy the injunction; they were promptly arrested. (While in jail, King penned his famous essay, "Letter from Birmingham Jail," in defense of civil disobedience.)

In court the civil rights leaders argued that their arrest was invalid because they were unfairly denied a parade permit, the injunction was a sham intended solely to turn conduct fully within the protester's rights into illegal conduct, and in any case the segregation laws to be protested were invalid under the federal constitution. In a five to four decision, the Supreme Court ruled on technical grounds to uphold the injunction on its face and thus validate the arrests; the Court sidestepped the two fundamental issues concerning whether the denial of the parade permit was lawful and whether the segregation laws being protested were constitutional.

As seen from the standpoint of lawyers and others sympathetic to the Civil Rights movement but reluctant to endorse violation of the law (even unjust laws), the aim of the disobedience campaigns in the South (such as the one in Birmingham in 1963) was to get the local authorities to recognize the priority of federal constitutional law, especially of the "equal protection of the laws" (14th amendment). Taking that language seriously would require repeal or nullification of local Jim Crow laws, ordinances, and their selective enforcement inconsistent with such equality. On this view, there was no true "disobedience" of the law, because the "laws" being violated were themselves unlawful under the federal Constitution, the moral adequacy of which in principle was taken for granted. Local authorities, such as those in Birmingham, of course saw the matter differently; they viewed the disobedience as criminal conduct and not civil.

C. Violent versus Nonviolent Conduct

Civil disobedience is usually thought of as nonviolent political protest; some of its most influential proponents (such as Leo Tolstoy and Mohandas Gandhi) were pacifists who preached against violence in human affairs generally and explicitly rejected it as a permissible tactic even in a good cause. But controversy surrounds the extent to which civil disobedience must be nonviolent. Some hold that an act of protest can count as civil disobedience even if it involves some violence, provided that the violence (a) was not intended by the protesters, (b) was not carried out by the protesters (rather, it was done by onlookers, opponents of the protest, or by the police), (c) was solely against property, or (d) was not very harmful.

Consider, for example, the Boston Tea Party (1773), in which local patriots disguised as Indians boarded ships in Boston harbor under cover of darkness and dumped bales of tea overboard to protest what they regarded as unfair import duties. If any intentional violence against property by definition keeps an act from being civil disobedience (because violent acts are not "civil," in the secondary sense of that term), then the Boston Tea Party is not a case of civil disobedience. However, if intentional violence is permitted so long as it is not directed against persons, then the Tea Party can be regarded as civil disobedience. (The Tea Party case raises other questions, however; if civil disobedience must be undertaken as a *public* act of political protest, then it is hard to see how those who conceal their true identity can be said to be engaged in an act of civil disobedience.)

A more troublesome case is presented by the self-immolation in the 1960s of Buddhist monks in Saigon, South Vietnam, to protest the Vietnam War (an American Quaker, Norman Morrison, died in a similar fashion outside the Pentagon in November 1965). Leaving aside whether such suicidal acts are illegal, self-immolation would not count as civil disobedience if civil disobedience must by definition be a nonviolent act.

The controversy over violence and nonviolence also shows the extent to which defining an act of civil disobedience may tacitly involve factors relevant to its justification. As a rule, violent acts are harder to justify than nonviolent acts, and so excluding violence by definition from civil disobedience tends to make it easier to justify any act of civil disobedience.

D. Direct versus Indirect Protest

Another controversial issue is whether the law being violated in civil disobedience must itself be the law under protest. This controversy is another example of how the definition of civil disobedience relates to its justification. Some hold that only direct disobedience can be justified. On this view, the purpose of tax refusal must be to protest the principle of public taxation as such; but only a libertarian, anarchist, or nihilist could practice tax resistance in this way. In actual practice, tax resistance is typically aimed at protesting certain uses of tax revenues, e.g., to finance government weapons procurement, without any express or implied moral objections to the principle of taxation as such.

The obvious problem with most tax refusal, unless it is practiced on a wide scale and targeted at a specific public expenditure, is that its primary effect is simply to reduce overall tax revenues available to the government, thus marginally underfinancing government enterprises that most tax resisters approve of (e.g., highway construction, sewer and water supply, and police and fire protection).

Where the law broken is not the law or policy under protest, there are two dangers. First, the general public may regard such indirect disobedience as irrational, implausible, or unjustified, because the gap between the law broken and the law or policy being protested is too large. Thus, it would be virtually unintelligible to protest Congressional refusal to increase the minimum wage by refusing to file one's income tax return (contrast that with organizing a sit-in in the halls of Congress).

Second, indirect disobedience may exert little or no leverage against the laws or policies under protest. Thus, widespread burning of draft cards in the late 1960s at mass rallies to protest the war in Vietnam did not really hamper the government in carrying out the draft or the war; it was at most symbolic of disapproval and disaffiliation. It was also an ambiguous symbol: Were the cards being burnt to protest the very idea of coercive military service, or only to protest the way the draft was administered as an unfair system of selection? Or was the purpose to protest the war in which the draftees would serve? Or were there several such purposes?

On the other hand, if civil disobedience is confined to the breaking of laws that are themselves believed by the protesters to be unjust, then a vast array of law and government policies will be immune from protest by civil disobedience. For example, opponents of the death penalty can chain themselves to prison gates or trespass on prison grounds to protest an execution, but there is no law they can directly violate that will cause a halt to the execution event itself; executions are deliberately carried out within the prison in a manner that makes them inaccessible to direct protest.

E. Criminal versus Civil Disobedience

Law breaking for selfish or purely personal reasons is criminal conduct, not civil disobedience. Disobedience of the law that is kept secret, even if done conscientiously, is not civil disobedience, because the secrecy of such acts prevents them from playing any part in the civic or public life of the community. Disobedient acts without a civic purpose, or without any principled basis, are not civil disobedience.

II. JUSTIFYING CIVIL DISOBEDIENCE

Not all acts of civil disobedience—any more than all law breaking, all lawful political protest, or all conscientious acts—are justified. As a political tactic, a given act or program of civil disobedience must satisfy several conditions before it is justified. What those conditions are, however, is controversial.

Philosophers differ over how civil disobedience is to be justified, in part because they disagree over the strength of the claim on our conduct made by the law and over the grounds of political obligation and responsibility. Traditionally and for the most part, philosophers have assumed that we have an obligation or duty to obey the law, whatever it is, with the result that the burden of justification is on the law breaker. This is a burden not easily discharged. A few other philosophers, especially in recent years, have argued that there is no such obligation or duty—not even in a constitutional democracy. On their view, our only duty is to conform our conduct to correct moral principles, and any law that fails to pass the test of such principles deserves no respect or compliance (except, perhaps, on prudential grounds like avoiding arrest and other inconveniences or worse). On this view, the burden of justification falls on those who insist that there is a presumption in favor of obeying the law whatever its content may be.

As pointed out earlier, it has been argued that respect for the law (in the sense of respect for the principles defining the rule of law) is consistent with violating the law, provided one's illegal conduct is nonviolent, the authorities are fully informed in advance, and one is willing to accept whatever penalties the law imposes.

Others reply that there is no good reason why breaking an unjust law, or attempting to get an unjust law repealed by breaking some other law, requires the disobedient to accept any punishment or to cooperate with the authorities at all.

In a constitutional democracy, where nonviolent political protest and participation are guaranteed by law, breaking the law is more difficult to justify than under tyrannic, despotic, or totalitarian rule. Yet nonviolent political protest is far more likely to be effective in a constitutional democracy than it is under any other form of government. It is difficult to imagine the successful efforts of the suffragettes in Great Britain and the United States in the early 1900s or of the Civil Rights movement of the 1960s except in a society that professes basic principles of political and moral equality of all persons and recognizes civil liberties and rights— precisely what nondemocratic societies reject in theory or in practice, or both.

A. The Problem of Justified Law Breaking in Ancient Athens

Civil disobedience as we know it had no place in ancient society; the idea of mass illegal protest aimed at abolishing some unjust law does not figure in classical thought. Other forms of justified law breaking, however, do. Perhaps Sophocles's *Antigone* (ca. 440 B.C.) is the earliest presentation of the problem: Ought Antigone give her dead brother Polyneices a decent burial as required by divine and customary law, despite the tyrant Creon's express prohibition of such obsequies (because Polyneices had sought to contest Creon's rulership), or ought she to comply with Creon's edict and let her brother's corpse feed the vultures? She decides to defy Creon, to her ultimate doom. (Whether Sophocles intended to side with her or with Creon or only to present a dramatic case of conflicting duties, we need not try to decide; her tragedy in any case does not constitute a philosophical argument.)

Unquestionably the first important discussion of the general problem of justified law breaking is to be found in Plato's dialogue *Crito* (ca. 380 B.C.). Socrates, imprisoned and sentenced to die as the result of conviction after trial on fraudulent charges, entertains arguments from his friend Crito, who urges him to escape from prison before his unjust death sentence is carried out. Socrates demurs; he does not dispute that his sentence is undeserved and unjust, but he argues it would still be wrong for him to try to escape. To do so, he suggests, would be to flout the authority of the laws of Athens, in conformance with which he has lived his whole life to date, and to break the implicit contract between him as a citizen and the state that requires individual obedience in exchange for social protection and nurture.

Socrates's arguments (whether or not Plato wants us to think they are conclusive) stand not only for the proposition that no selfish advantage—such as saving one's own life—is ever a good enough reason for breaking the laws of one's country, they also teach that disobeying the law even in a just cause is unjustified.

B. Christian Doctrine

1. Early Christian Thinking

In *Crito,* Socrates's argument anticipated the even stronger and much more influential doctrine in Paul's Epistle to the Romans (ca. 58 A.D.) that Christians must obey their rulers, because "the powers that be are ordained by God" (13:1). Running counter to this theme is the famous epigram of St. Augustine's, "an unjust law is no law."

As in so many other matters, the epitome of classical Christian philosophy appears in St. Thomas Aquinas. In his *Treatise on Law* (ca. 1265), Aquinas does not discuss civil disobedience as such, any more than his predecessors did, but he does examine how a Christian should react to unjust laws (the central issue of conscientious objection). His is a distinctly conservative view. He builds both on the Pauline doctrine requiring subservience of Christians to whatever rulers God has placed over them and on the Augustinian doctrine that connects law to justice. Aquinas enjoins Christians to obey the law, however unjust it may be, unless the law requires conduct in violation of essential Christian religious tenets, e.g., worshiping false gods. And, of course, history records any number of Christians (and Jews) who went to their deaths rather than place a pinch of incense on Caesar's altar. As for lesser injustices, according to Aquinas, they are to be borne in patience, "lest a scandal [that is, disruption of social order] be caused."

The modern theory of civil disobedience has its origins in religious protests arising out of the Protestant Reformation in the 16th century. The role of conscience as the inner Word of God and thus of sincere personal convictions as the final authority over what one ought to do is a characteristically Protestant doctrine. But the attractions of Pauline doctrine remained strong, especially for Martin Luther; it was the dissenting churches—Quakers, Anabaptists, and Mennonites—rather than the main-line Protestant denominations that cultivated the doctrine of conscience and conscientious objection and passive resistance, and thus laid the basis for later secular theories of civil disobedience.

2. Martin Luther King, Jr.

In his "Letter from Birmingham Jail" (1963), Martin Luther King, Jr., offered a complex theory of justified civil disobedience. First, he defended civil disobedience as the final element in a fourfold strategy, preceded by "collection of the facts to determine whether injustices are alive," "negotiation" between the victims and the oppressors to remove the injustices, "self-purification" of the protesters to ensure that their motives were not purely self-serving, and then "direct action." (The echoes of Gandhian *satyagraha* here are no accident.) King and his associates were convinced that the fourth step (civil disobedience) was justified if the first and third had been achieved and the second had proved of no avail.

Crucial to King's argument on behalf of direct action was his belief that the laws imposing racial segregation and second-class citizenship on African Americans were unjust in several ways. First, the segregation laws did not "square with the moral law or the law of God." These laws failed that test because they "degrade human personality"; legally enforced segregation "distorts the soul and damages the personality." Second, these laws were unjust because they were "a code that a majority inflicts on a minority that is not binding on itself." Third, these laws were unjust because "the minority had no part in enacting or creating" them. King explicitly disavowed "evading or defying the law" as such (by which he meant resisting arrest or lying to the authorities about one's disobedient intentions), for that would lead to "anarchy." He concluded by saying, "I submit that an individual who breaks a law that conscience tells him is unjust, and willingly accepts the penalty by staying in jail to arouse the conscience of the community over its injustice, is in reality expressing the very highest respect for law."

Whether or not one agrees with King's four-step procedure to justify civil disobedience, or with his criteria of unjust laws, it is plain that his theory brings to the surface considerations relevant to justifying civil disobedience superior to those that can be teased out of such earlier writers as Aquinas or Thoreau. And while it is evident that King formulates his theory of justification within the framework of Christian thinking, no great difficulty attends revising and restating his theory in purely secular terms (Bedau, 1969, pp. 78–79).

C. Secular Theories of Justification

Several different kinds of moral theories and moral principles can be invoked to justify acts of civil disobedience. Three at least deserve brief mention.

1. Utility, Natural Law, and Conscience

It is always open in theory for a utilitarian to argue in a given case (whatever may be true in general) that more good than bad would accrue (or more harm would be avoided) by disobeying this or that law as a tactic for getting it repealed in favor of a new law or policy that better serves the general welfare. For anti- or non-utilitarians, of course, such an argument is unpersuasive, since it suffers (in their view) all the familiar difficulties of utilitarianism generally, chief among which is making in advance reliable calculations of future consequences. And it is worth noting that the classic utilitarians, notably Jeremy Bentham and J. S. Mill, never used their utilitarianism to justify breaking unjust laws.

Other theorists, working in effect in the Aristotelian tradition, would appeal to natural law—cross-cultural, universal moral principles—and argue the justifiability of breaking the law nonviolently when a society's positive law is inconsistent with the natural law. Since the advent of utilitarianism two centuries ago, natural law theories have waxed and waned in popularity among legal theorists; in recent years Ronald Dworkin's views beginning with his 1977 book, *Taking Rights Seriously* (Harvard Univ. Press, Cambridge, MA) perhaps best represent this tradition.

Finally, some thinkers would accord to individual conscience a final authority, though the incipient anarchic consequences of such a view will make more cautious thinkers look elsewhere. If each person's conscience is the final authority on right and wrong conduct, then it appears we may have to embrace the paradoxical consequence that certain acts of law breaking are both right and wrong, because the dictates of personal conscience vary radically in many cases.

2. John Rawls

Many writers since the Civil Rights movement and the Vietnam War have offered versions of a purely secular theory of justified civil disobedience. Unquestionably the most influential of these is to be found in the writings of John Rawls, especially his 1971 book, *A Theory of Justice* (Harvard Univ. Press, Cambridge, MA). On Rawls's theory, an act of civil disobedience in a constitutional democracy is "a last resort," and if such acts are to be justified, four conditions must be met: (1) the aim must be to secure society's compliance with a fundamental principle of social justice; (2) the protesters must have tried lawful methods of reform (assembly, petition, election) to no avail; (3) the protesters do not make claims for their tactics and goals inconsistent with allowing others with similar grievances to use similar tactics to secure their goals; and (4) there is some reasonable prospect that the protest will be successful.

Condition (1) rules out using illegal tactics in pursuit of relatively unimportant goals, or goals that cannot be defended on grounds of their justice. Condition (2) rules out impulsive or premature use of illegal tactics to secure

a just goal that reasonable patience using lawful means could have obtained. Condition (3) rules out any presumption of special privilege to break the law in a just cause. And condition (4) rules out causing social turmoil when there is no prospect of accomplishing the goals being sought. As Rawls observes, "we may be acting within our rights [in breaking the law to protest injustice in society] but nevertheless unwisely if our conduct only serves to provoke the harsh retaliation of the majority" (1971, pp. 376). In other words, here as elsewhere, what we have a *right* to do may not be what we *ought* to do.

Of course, there is room for disagreement over the interpretation of these conditions, their scope, and their meaning. (In particular, much turns on how Rawls defines and justifies the principles of social justice that are built into his first condition, a topic to which he devotes the bulk of his book.) And it is possible for reasonable people to disagree over the facts relevant to one or more of Rawls's four principles, though it is easy to see that each of these conditions (or something very like them) is necessary to justify law breaking in a constitutional democracy. Dropping any of these conditions immediately raises questions about how the civil disobedience could possibly be justified given the social costs it usually involves. It is equally difficult to see what further conditions might be needed in the belief they are necessary to make the set of conditions sufficient for justification. What changes would be required to adapt Rawls's criteria to justify civil disobedience undertaken in something less than a nearly just society or in a society not governed by a democratic constitution is another matter. When the whole society is governed unjustly, some form of revolution may be called for in which individual or mass illegal protest would play a very different role (if any) from the one it can play in a constitutional democracy.

III. THE POLITICAL EFFECTIVENESS OF CIVIL DISOBEDIENCE

Has civil disobedience played a constructive role in any nation's political affairs? There is little doubt that using Rawlsian criteria and facts generally available, various tactics of civil disobedience were amply justified as part of the long campaign to invalidate locally enforced racial segregation and in trying to get the national government to withdraw its armed forces from Southeast Asia.

The question of the political effectiveness of civil disobedience is more complex. When it merges into conscientious objection, it will not often have much political effect. To take a hypothetical case, a warden who refuses to administer a lawful execution in his prison, because he believes the death penalty is a violation of human rights, will be relieved of his duties and replaced by an official with no such qualms. While one can imagine all prison wardens and staff refusing to participate in lawful executions, there is no record of any such conduct and little likelihood of such concerted action in the near future in any American death penalty jurisdiction. Without widespread organized refusal, individual acts of protest and disobedience of this sort are unlikely to have political effect—which is not to deny their significance for the dissenters or their influence on sympathetic bystanders.

Civil disobedience can be a powerful tool of public education in a constitutional democracy; this fact tempts activists into taking extreme measures even when they anticipate that their efforts may ultimately be ineffective. The more extreme the act of disobedience, the greater likelihood of publicity in the media; the greater the publicity, the greater the likelihood of public reflection and debate on the rationale of the disobedience—or so the argument goes in theory. Under a Nazi or Stalinist tyranny, however, civil disobedience is likely to be of no avail. The authorities will have no respect for the protesters just because their conduct is public, remains nonviolent, and appeals to principles of justice; the protest will go unnoticed by the government-controlled media and the protesters will be summarily arrested and given harsh punishment. In 1989, the Chinese government literally crushed nonviolent illegal student protest in Beijing. Even in South Africa, India, and the United States earlier in this century, civil disobedience produced reforms only in conjunction with a larger strategy of education and pressure carried out within the law. Civil disobedience by itself in Great Britain and the United States during the Cold War, however, had some effect in curbing atmospheric nuclear bomb tests, but it had little effect on nuclear disarmament. On a wide range of lesser issues, many of them local and not widely publicized, selective, nonviolent law breaking has achieved some notable successes—but, again, usually only in conjunction with lawful efforts publicizing the goals and the strategies of protest.

Perhaps the two most recent efforts at fairly large-scale civil disobedience in the United States have been organized by Operation Rescue, the militant antiabortion group, and by ACT-UP, the AIDS action group known for its disruptive tactics. They are instructive examples when political effectiveness of civil disobedience is under scrutiny.

Beginning in 1987 in Binghamton, New York, Operation Rescue has organized blockades of several hundred abortion clinics around the nation under the banner of "rescuing" the unborn from an undeserved death. Between 1988 and 1990 more than 25,000 protesters were arrested in actions claimed to be "nonviolent in word and deed." Operation Rescue does not, however, describe its blockades as "civil disobedience," arguing that civil disobedience is always "political," whereas rescuing fetal life is not. Be that as it may, there is no evidence that Operation Rescue has so far managed to reach the conscience of the majority and reduce popular support for the availability of abortion services over and above what lawful antiabortion protest has achieved. To be sure, abortion clinics and their staffs have been much threatened and inconvenienced by rescue blockades, but it is quite unclear how many abortions Operation Rescue has actually prevented, as distinct from diverting them to unblockaded clinics.

ACT-UP, also organized in 1987, focused its agenda on forcing pharmaceutical companies to scale down the price of its expensive medications so that more HIV-positive and AIDS-infected patients could purchase them, and on forcing the government to test and approve such drugs more rapidly. Its tactics (including breaking up news conferences and board meetings) have apparently worked. They certainly helped publicize the plight of those with AIDS and helped make progress toward its two main goals. Whether ACT-UP's tactics also won the hearts and minds of the government and industry officials who attempted to carry on business as usual, or only frightened them into partial compliance with ACT-UP's goals, is less clear.

As these two cases suggest, judging the political effectiveness of acts or campaigns of civil disobedience in a constitutional democracy is not easy. Such disobedience is usually carried out in conjunction with other activity wholly within the law (news conferences, demonstrations, or leafleting), so isolating the effects arising solely or mainly from civil disobedience is well nigh impossible. In the Civil Rights and anti-Vietnam War movements, individual and mass disobedience were essential aspects of citizen protest; in the former case, the movement could not have succeeded without direct illegal action. Much the same must be said about the impact of Gandhian *satyagraha* in obtaining self-rule for the Indian subcontinent earlier in this century. Historians and social scientists need to look at other cases where the evidence is less clear, in the hope that such scrutiny will teach us more about the circumstances in which civil disobedience can be politically effective.

Bibliography

Bedau, H. A. (Ed.) (1991). "Civil Disobedience in Focus." Routledge, London.

Bedau, H. A. (Ed.) (1969). "Civil Disobedience: Theory and Practice." Pegasus, New York.

Carter, G. M. (1992). "ACT UP: The AIDS War and Activism." Open Magazine, Westford, NJ.

Greenawalt, K. (1987). "Conflicts of Law and Morality." Oxford Univ. Press, New York.

Haksar, V. (1986). "Civil Disobedience, Threats and Offers: Gandhi and Rawls." Oxford Univ. Press, Delhi.

Harris, P. (Ed.) (1989). "Civil Disobedience." Univ. Press of America, Lanham, MD.

Kraut, R. (1984). "Socrates and the State." Princeton Univ. Press, Princeton, NJ.

Rawls, J. (1971). "A Theory of Justice." Harvard Univ. Press, Cambridge, MA.

Yoder, J. H., *et al.* (1991). Symposium on civil disobedience. Notre Dame J. Law Ethics Public Policy **5,** 889–1119.

Van den Haag, E. (1972). "Political Violence and Civil Disobedience." Harper and Row, New York.

Zinn, H. (1972). "Disobedience and Democracy: Nine Fallacies on Law and Order." Vintage Books, New York.

Civilian Populations in War, Targeting of

GABRIEL PALMER-FERNÁNDEZ
Youngstown State University

GLOSSARY

absolutism To determine the moral value of an act, absolutist moral theories consider whether that act is commanded by God, required by a promise made, is in accordance with widely accepted rules or the rights of persons, or can be consistently willed as a universal law. Absolutist moral theories typically deny what consequentialism asserts—that an action is right as a function of what it will produce.

combatant A legal and moral category requiring that a person, to be considered a combatant, be commanded by another responsible for subordinates, have a fixed distinctive insignia recognizable at a distance, carry arms openly, and conduct operations in accordance with the laws and customs of war.

consequentialism Consequentialist moral theories hold that the ultimate criterion of what is morally right is the value of what is brought into being. An act is right if it happens to bring about a better state of affairs than acting otherwise—if it will produce, or is intended to produce, at least a greater balance of good over evil as any alternative action. Such moral theories depend on a comparative evaluation of alternative courses of action.

just-war tradition The dominant moral tradition in the West that governs the rights of states to go to war and the conduct of soldiers in war. It is divided into two parts, the *jus ad bellum,* which considers the conditions under which war is compatible with morality, and the *jus in bello,* which regulates the actual waging of hostilities.

noncombatant immunity A *jus in bello* principle that distinguishes between combatants and civilians with the consequence that the latter, also called noncombatants or innocents, are immune from deliberate military attack. It is sometimes also called principle of discrimination and is generally regarded as an absolutist principle.

obliteration bombing Air-bombing raids, strategies, or policies that fail to distinguish between combatants and noncombatants. It is sometimes also called area, carpet, terror, or mass bombing. Many jurists and moralists consider this kind of attack a prohibited form of warfare.

principle of double effect A principle that distinguishes between the direct and the indirect effects of an action. It asserts (i) that a person is morally responsible only for the direct (or intended) effects and (ii) that indirect (or unintended) evil effects (e.g., the death of civilians), when they are neither the means to or themselves the end, are allowable.

principle of proportionality A principle of the just-war tradition that appears in two forms. First, as a norm of the *jus ad bellum* the principle of proportionality states that the harms which accompany the use of force must not be so great as to outweigh the values defended by force. As a *jus in bello* norm this principle requires that one weigh the harms caused by a particular tactic or strategy against whatever advantage is gained by such means. It is generally regarded as a consequentialist principle.

CIVILIAN POPULATIONS have undergone misery and death in the millions due to 20th century wars of extraordinary scope. Blitzkriegs, obliteration bombing, the threat of nuclear annihilation, guerrilla wars, terrorism, and the recent rise of ethnopolitical conflicts can easily create the impression that the immunity of civilian populations from deliberate military attack belongs to some distant past. That would be a mistaken impression, however. Despite the truth of the assertion that a distinguishing feature of modern war is the slaughter of the unprotected, the principle of noncombatant immunity originated in the 16th and 17th centuries, particularly in the writings of Francisco Victoria and Hugo Grotius, and gradually developed in the body of international law, the tradition of the just war, and in the Hague and Geneva Conventions. But the future relevance of this principle is far from clear. If it is the case that future wars will take the form of widespread indiscriminate destruction by the use of nuclear weapons, terrorist attacks, or ethnic warfare, then the important distinction between combatants and civilians is bound to break down, and the principle of noncombatant immunity may indeed belong to the past.

Thus the clear definition and justification of the principle of noncombatant immunity are major concerns of legal and moral theorists. However, those theorists face a significant problem. The principle is useful only if we can establish a distinction between combatants and civilians, that is, between who may and may not be deliberately killed in war. Civilians, this principle asserts, may not be deliberately killed in war because they are innocent. But the meaning of innocence in war is controversial. Absent a clear definition of who is innocent and why, it will be very difficult to say who may and may not be deliberately killed in war.

I. THE PRACTICE OF TARGETING CIVILIAN POPULATIONS IN WAR

The manner and method of waging war are partly a function of the technology available to a nation. In the days of dynastic wars a battlefield was often safely removed from civilian populations, and the number of deaths was greater among soldiers than civilians. Civilized war, legal and moral texts tell us, is confined to hostilities between armed forces.

> It is with good reason that this practice has grown into a custom with the nations of Europe, at least with those that keep up regular standing armies or bodies of militia. The troops alone carry on war, while the rest of the nation remain at peace. (E. de Vattel, 1740. *The Law of Nations; or Principles of the Law of Nature (in French), iii, p. 226. J. Newbery, London*)

But today death in war has a far wider range. The emergence of modern means of waging war—the airplane, the missile, and chemical, biological, and nuclear weapons—have not only increased the lethality of war, but also expanded combat over large areas and gradually included greater sectors of the civilian population.

It must be recognized, however, that civilians have always faced some risk in war, even when their material contribution to war has been slight.[1] In ancient as well as in modern times, civilians have been attacked along with soldiers. Sometimes they come under direct attack in order to kill soldiers taking refuge among them; at other times, they are directly attacked because of a critical importance identified with them–namely, the morale of a nation, the collapse of which, it is said, leads to surrender. Such is plainly the case in sieges, where war extends beyond the combatant population and the death of civilians, usually by starvation and dehydration, is a means to hasten the enemy's surrender. The long history of siege warfare suggests that attacking civilian populations is a time-honored method of war, for example, the siege of Jerusalem in 72 C.E. or Leningrad by German forces between 1941 and 1943, where more than 1 million civilians died of starvation or disease.

One distinguishing and very troubling feature of 20th century warfare is the extent to which civilians are deliberately put in harm's way. The cities of Hiroshima and Nagasaki were destroyed by a single atomic bomb. This weapon was new and revolutionary. But the havoc, misery, and death that that single weapon caused was only a more effective means of implementing a strategy that had vigorously been pursued against Germany in World War II (WWII) by more conventional weapons, and perhaps had its origins when the Austrians, in the mid-19th century, launched unmanned bomb-carrying air ballons at the city of Venice. The air balloon was a poor weapon—it drifted with the wind. But it had the potential to cause significant panic in civilian populations—as it did, for example, in May 1915, when Germany bombed London by using a propeller-driven dirigible. Guilio Douhet, an Italian officer, predicted some years later in his 1921 book, *The Command of the Air*, that "now it is actually populations and nations," and

---

[1] The risk is only getting larger. Civilian deaths in war have increased dramatically in this century. In World War I, 5% of deaths were civilians; in World War II, 48%; in Korea, 84%; and in Vietnam, 90%.

not their armies, "which come to blows and seize each other's throats (1942. Translated by D. Ferrari, p. 195. New York). For Douhet and his disciples, which included Hugh Trenchard and Charles de Gaulle in Europe and Billy Mitchell in the United States, the first and most vital target in an air war naturally was the enemy's own strategic bombers. But they were quick to point out the bomber's potential for defeating an enemy with a decisive "knockout blow" and for creating havoc, misery, and terror in the civilian population. The capacity to strike from the air—either with airplanes or with missiles—is the single most important element in 20th century warfare. It delivers the war directly to the enemy's civilian population.

A. Strategic Air War and Civilian Populations in Europe

The experience of strategic bombing during WWII shows clearly how the horror of war moved from soldiers to civilians. When the war broke out, the major belligerents restrained themselves from air bombing of the enemy's heartland. The restraint was reflected in an August 1939 communiqué of British and French officers expressing their lack of intent to bomb civilian population as such. But the restraint was short-lived. Precision bombing required daylight low-level attacks, where flak proved deadly. British Bomber Command soon learned that to be effective it had no option but to fight in the dark. By the fall of 1940, British bombing of German territory was an indiscriminate and nocturnal event. For similar reasons, after September of 1940, Germany was also using its Luftwaffe's bombers only at night. But nighttime bombing was extremely inaccurate. When conducted over a city these raids were more likely to miss than to hit any military or industrial site. Indeed British assessment of bombing campaigns over Germany estimated that only one-fifth of its bombers placed their payloads within 5 miles of the specified target. Deficiencies of bomb-aiming technology coupled with the circumstances in which missions were conducted brought a dramatic change in the nature of modern war: *targeting cities themselves.*

By early 1941, the British Air Ministry issued new orders to Bomber Command. Indiscriminate bombing which had been condemned at the beginning of the war became operational policy. Primary targets would no longer be conventional military objectives, but the morale of the civilian population and especially the residential areas of the industrial workers. Bomber Command was instructed to employ its power on those targets without restrictions: lay down a carpet of bombs over urban and industrial areas in which conventional military targets would be hit, but only incidentally and as a bonus to the mass, indiscriminate killing of civilians.

As a matter of policy, death and destruction were brought to civilians in order to destroy their morale. That was certainly the case, for example, in the second bombing of Hamburg where incendiaries started thousands of fires throughout the city, creating terrific winds as the fires sucked for more oxygen and sending charred bodies and debris flying through an atmosphere of nearly 800° centigrade.

As the British had before them, Americans also discovered that daylight precision bombing was a misnomer. Even when the target was discrete—for example, railroad yards and industrial plants—heavy damage to the surrounding residential areas was unavoidable. American commanders at first resisted British policy of bombing civilian populations. Yet the results of American raids were hardly distinguishable from British nighttime indiscriminate bombing. The U.S. Strategic Bombing Survey estimated that 80% of U.S. daylight bombing missions missed by a fifth of a mile or more. As the war progressed, U.S. targeting policy took the form of British obliteration bombing in an attempt to destroy German civilian morale. The climax of targeting civilians in Europe came at Dresden, near war's end. On February 13 and 14, 1945, British and then American forces bombed this German city teeming with homeless refuges from devastated rural towns and advancing Soviet armies. Some 50,000 civilians were killed in those raids.

War in the 20th century became indiscriminate war when the British Bomber Command and then the U.S. Army Air Force adopted the policy of deliberately targeting civilian populations, i.e., the urban and industrial base of a society. As *Target Germany,* a 1943 U.S. Air Force book, put it,

> The physical attrition of warfare is no longer limited to the fighting forces. Heretofore the home front has remained relatively secure; armies fought, civil populations worked and waited.... [But now] we have terror and devastation carried to the core of a warring nation. (p. 19. Simon and Schuster, New York).

Germans, too, tested the morale of British civilians through shock and terror, first by the use of bombers and then by the V-1 and V-2 flying bombs. Though totally ineffective for attacking military targets, these precursors to the intercontinental ballistic missile were, as Goebbels said, awe-inspiring weapons of murder.

B. Strategic Air War and Civilian Populations in Japan

American targeting of civilian populations culminated in a campaign of terror and fire-bombing of Japanese cities. As in Europe, American air strategy at first gave priority to the Japanese air industry and advocated precision bombing of conventional military targets. But attempts to strike these targets from high altitudes proved to be no more successful than in Europe. When Curtis LeMay assumed command of the 20th Air Force in Japan, he was instructed to give targeting priority to cities rather than industrial targets. Bomb loads would consist of incendiaries—i.e., fire bombs—rather than high explosives, with the purpose of striking at the will of the Japanese people to continue the war. With the success of limited fire-bombing raids in January and February of 1945, the American Air Force undertook a campaign of fire-bombing the city of Tokyo in early March 1945 that destroyed nearly two-thirds of the city's commercial district and killed an estimated 100,000 civilians. This and other nighttime incendiary raids on Japanese cities killed more civilians than the atomic bombings of Hiroshima and Nagasaki, both of which were a late emphasis upon the supposed effect of targeting civilian populations by indiscriminate attack.

The post-world War II debate on the effects of strategic bombing gives a mixed assessment to the assertion that air power will deliver victory in modern war. Britain's own bombing survey after the war suggests that targeting civilian populations was successful only in disrupting German transport and communications systems. It did not induce the effect on civilian morale that it hoped for. American's own postwar bombing survey expressed similar doubts about the effectiveness of obliteration bombing in Europe. Matters are somewhat different with the atomic bombing of Hiroshima and Nagasaki. The same American postwar survey claims that the Japanese would have surrendered even if the atomic bomb had not been used. The air war against Japan had already been won, and its defenses were fragile. Yet others maintain that the speed with which surrender followed the bombings of Hiroshima and Nagasaki supports Douhet's thesis that air power would prove decisive in modern war.

C. The Threat of Nuclear Annihilation

Notwithstanding the partially negative assessment by postwar bombing surveys, targeting civilian populations with weapons of massive and indiscriminate destruction was enshrined in American nuclear strategy. As it emerged in the postwar years, American policy of nuclear deterrence aimed at enemy cities. At first, during the Eisenhower years, this policy called for the immediate launch of the entire U.S. nuclear arsenal in response to enemy aggression. The single target list included cities in the former Soviet Union, China, and satellite states, and made no distinction among military, industrial, and civilian targets. As President Eisenhower himself put it, we "cannot afford to preclude [ourselves] from using nuclear weapons even in a local situation, if such use

will best advance [our] security interests" (J. L. Gaddis, 1982. *Strategies of Containment*, p. 190, Oxford Univ. Press, Oxford). Expected fatalities of a massive nuclear retaliatory strike were estimated between 360 and 425 million civilians.

Other nations, of course, pursued their own nuclear programs—Great Britain, France, and the former Soviet Union, for example. But it became increasingly clear that targeting civilian populations, i.e., massive nuclear retaliation against cities themselves, would result in mutual suicide, absent adequate defenses against enemy missiles. Exploration of a flexible nuclear response and advocacy of a "no-cities" strategy were therefore sought in the late 1950s and early 1960s. Robert McNamara, Kennedy's Secretary of Defense, announced in February 1961 that basic military strategy in general nuclear war would target conventional military objectives and seek the destruction of the enemy's military and nuclear forces, and not the civilian population. Targeting only the enemy's forces rather than the enemy's cities (sometimes referred to as counterforce/no-cities) was short-lived, however. By the fall of 1962, McNamara began to favor an entirely different strategic posture, and by the end of his tenure as Secretary of Defense, had come about-face, advocating the very ideas which, upon coming into office, he had criticized and dismissing the counterforce/no-cities doctrine as having only a very limited role in deterring a nuclear-armed adversary.

Subsequent development of U.S. nuclear weapons policy has emphasized either a selective and flexible response to enemy aggression or some form of massive retaliation in which cities themselves are targeted. Whichever of these strategies one adopts, its activation will surely lead to the indiscriminate killing of civilians. Withholding direct nuclear attack from civilian populations has played an important role in the development of nuclear strategy. Yet doctrines of selective and flexible response are fraught with dangerous destabilizing first-strike possibilities and retain the threat of widespread civilian slaughter by the possession of a large nuclear reserve force. McNamara may well have been correct when he said that nuclear forces are totally useless, except to deter one's enemy from using them by the threat of massive retaliation. If ever deterrence fails and nuclear war breaks out, then nuclear weapons will have failed in their purpose and at least one nation will be in ruin.

D. Ethnopolitical Conflict and Civilian Populations

To appreciate fully the extent and manner in which civilian populations are targeted in modern war, it is necessary to consider, finally, the recent rise of ethno-political conflicts. Since the end of WWII, such conflicts have become increasingly prominent in various parts of the world—in Bosnia, Liberia, Sierra Leone, the Caucasus, and Sri Lanka, for example. Armed hostilities between ethnic groups, some observers contend, indicate that the kinds of war we will see in the future will not be wars between nation-states with armed forces as their agents fighting along geopolitical lines. Instead, armed conflicts in the early 21st century will likely occur between groups that define themselves along ethnic (sometimes also religious) lines and make claims on behalf of collective interests against nation-states and other political actors.

The facts seem to support those contentions. First, the number of groups involved in serious ethnopolitical conflicts has increased dramatically in the post-World War II period: from 26 groups between 1945 and 1949 to 70 in the 1990s, with the greatest increase in the 1960s and 1970s (36 and 55 groups, respectively). The main issue in most of these conflicts is the contention of power among ethnic groups in Third World nations. Second, the 50 ethnopolitical conflicts in the 1993–1994 period alone caused some 4 million deaths, the vast majority of which were civilian, and displaced nearly 27 million people. And third, this type of conflict is very likely to increase in the near future as there is greater communal contention for power among ethnic groups in several of the world's regions, particularly in poor and weak states like those of Africa, most notably, Burundi, Rwanda, Zaire, Angola, and Sudan. One can anticipate that forced resettlement of groups, mass repression, genocidal massacres, guerilla warfare, and other forms of political violence will directly effect large numbers of civilian populations.

II. THE PROTECTION OF CIVILIAN POPULATIONS IN WAR

Recent developments in military technology and strategy make possible destruction of a kind and magnitude previously unimaginable. Incendiaries; gas, chemical, and nuclear weapons; and the capacity to strike from the air, coupled with a strategy to destroy industrial centers and weaken the enemy's resolve to fight, create a mode of warfare that brings certain death to combatant and civilian alike. These facts have led contemporary jurists and moralists to stress a principle that stretches back to the early modern period. It appears first among a group of Spanish theologians of the 16th century, was developed by several Dutch jurists of the 17th century, and was then incorporated into the body of international law. Since the 1970s, as moralists, both secular and reli-

gious, have reflected on the massive and indiscriminate power of modern means of warfare, the principle of noncombatant immunity has taken special importance. It is this moral principle which determines that civilian populations are not legitimate targets of war.

A. The Just-War Tradition, International Law, and the Principle of Noncombatant Immunity

The dominant intellectual tradition concerning the morality of war consists of a set of principles that together are referred to as the just-war tradition. The origins of this tradition may be traced to ancient philosophers and jurists, for example, Plato and Cicero. But it was the 5th century Christian theologian St. Augustine who gave us the first systematic formulation of the conditions under which war is compatible with morality. Augustine's formulation of the just war was refined over the centuries, and by the high middle ages had become official teaching of the Roman Catholic church. Today that tradition is embodied in secular international law and informs much of the public debate on the morality of war.

The just-war tradition distinguishes between questions concerning when a state has a right to wage war (referred to usually in the Latin as the *jus ad bellum*) and those on how war is to be waged (the *jus in bello*). For a war to count as just, the following conditions must be satisfied: (i) there must be a just cause; (ii) the war must be waged with the right intention; (iii) the decision must be made by a legitimate authority; (iv) there must be a formal declaration of war; (v) there must be reasonable hope for success; (vi) war should be the last resort; and (vii) it must satisfy the requirement of proportionality. Even when the *jus ad bellum* conditions are met, there remains the further question of how war is to be waged, that is, the *jus in bello*. The just-war tradition requires that the manner of waging hostilities satisfies the principles of noncombatant immunity—civilians must not be deliberately attacked or killed, and fighting is to be directed solely against the armed forces of the enemy—and of proportionality—the means employed in fighting must not be so destructive as to outweigh the good to be achieved.

In its modern secular version, just-war thinking has increasingly stressed one justification for going to war. The injustice which war should seek to correct is the crime of aggression of one state against another; hence the only justification for war is self-defense. This view is found also in modern international law and in Article 51 of the United Nations Charter, which permits the use of force for individual or collective self-defense. Early formulations of the just war, however, allowed the use of force for reasons other than self-defense, for example, to protect the innocent from attack, to restore rights unjustly denied, to reestablish an order necessary for peaceful and decent human existence, and to punish an evildoer.

Since the 16th century, the principle of noncombatant immunity has defined the most important limit on the manner of waging armed hostilities. This principle depends on the distinction between combatants and civilians, and is interpreted as a prohibition against the deliberate killing of civilians, who are usually referred to as innocent, in contrast to combatants, who are referred to as guilty or culpable and are therefore legitimate targets of deliberate attack. But the earlier formulation of the just war had nothing resembling this prohibition. Indeed, some argue that Augustine thought there was little, if anything, wrong in the deliberate killing of civilians, if the necessities of a just war demand it. For Augustine, so it is argued, the requirement to vindicate justice obviates all other considerations, even when the innocent may suffer. Just as Lot's family in the Book of Genesis is an exceptional innocent minority in the wicked city of Sodom, Augustine believed that in an injust state there will be only a minority of truly innocent people. Furthermore, because innocence is an interior disposition that cannot necessarily be ascribed to any individual with certainty, one cannot know who are the truly innocent. So, Augustine counsels the soldier and public functionary to do what is required for justice, and to let God on the last days separate the wicked and the guiltless. Some improvement on the protection of civilian populations in war is found in the work of the 13th century theologian Thomas Aquinas. Though he relied heavily and explicitly on Augustine, Aquinas unequivocally states that it is unlawful deliberately to kill the innocent. But Aquinas' clear condemnation of killing civilians must be weighed against his doctrine of double effect, which allows for the incidental or unintended deaths of civilians in war—what is usually referred to as collateral damage.

It was the Spanish theologian Francisco Victoria who presented to date the most powerful prohibition against the deliberate killing of the innocent and, at the same time, a justification for overriding that prohibition:

> The basis of war is a wrong done. But a wrong is not done by an innocent person. Therefore war may not be employed against him.... [Furthermore] it is not lawful within a State to punish the innocent for the wrongdoing of the guilty. Therefore this is not lawful among enemies. (1917. De indis et de iure belli reflectiones. In *The Classics of International Law* (J. B. Scott, Ed.), p. 178. Carnegie Institute of Washington, Washington, DC)

Victoria defined the class of innocents as all persons who do not directly take part in the waging of hostilities and included in it all children, women, farmers, foreign travelers, clerics, and "the rest of the peaceable population." He understood, however, that this prohibition is hardly attainable in all circumstance and that in war sometimes innocents are killed. To determine whether the killing of innocents is ever permissible, Victoria relies on Aquinas' principle of double effect, but with greater restriction that Aquinas himself employed. Victoria says,

> Sometimes it is right, in virtue of collateral circumstances, to slay the innocent, even knowingly, as when a fortress of a city is stormed in a just war, although it is known that there are a number of innocent people in it and although cannons and other engines of war cannot be discharged ... without destroying innocent together with the guilty. The proof is that war could not otherwise be waged against even the guilty and the justice of belligerents would be balked.... In sum, it is never right to slay the guiltless, even as an indirect and unintended result, *except when there is no other means of carrying on the operations of a just war.* (Italics added. Victoria, 1917, p. 179)

Victoria's restriction on killing civilians is stricter than Aquinas' in at least two ways. First, he requires that there be no other way of "carrying on the operations" of a war, and second, the killing of civilians is to be limited to the prosecution of a war known to be "just." When there is doubt regarding the justice of a war, then war is to be fought with greater retraint and the immunity of civilians should not yield to the necessities of war. The principle of noncombatant immunity might then function as a moral absolute.

While Augustine, Aquinas, and Victoria were the formative figures in the medieval and early modern formulation of the just-war tradition, it is the work of the Dutch jurist and theologian Hugo Grotius, often referred to as the founder of international law, that exercised the most profound influence on the modern secular development of that tradition. Much like Victoria, he lays great emphasis on the immunity of civilians from direct attack: "One must take care, so far as possible, to prevent the death of innocent persons, even by accident (H. Grotius, 1962. *The Law of War and Peace,* translated by F. W. Kelsey, bk. III, chap. 11, XVI, 2, p. 741. Bobbs-Merrill, New York). In this class of innocents, Grotius includes children, women, the aged, farmers, clerics, and prisoners of war. We have here a clear rule prohibiting direct attack on civilians. But this rule is not absolute. Grotius says, "We may bombard a ship full of pirates, or a house full of brigands, even if there are within the same ship or house a few infants, women, or other innocent persons who are thereby endangered." He cautions, however, that one

> must also be aware of what happens, and what we foresee may happen, beyond our purpose, unless the good which our action has in view is much greater than the evil which is feared, unless

the good and the evil balance, the hope of the good is much greater than the fear of the evil. (Grotius, 1962, bk. III, chap. 1, IV, p. 601)

In all this, Grotius depends on the principles developed by his medieval predecessors, namely, noncombatant immunity, the *jus in bello* requirement of proportionality, and double effect.

Grotius, however, departs from the medieval tradition in two ways that are of great importance for the modern understanding of the just war. First, for him, the *jus ad bellum* is met by a formal declaration of war by the sovereign of a nation-state that includes the reasons or causes leading to war without reference to any substantive understanding of justice, thereby making, far more possible than Victoria had, the possibility that both sides to an armed conflict can be just. In the absence of a shared understanding of justice, as the Roman Catholic church had provided for the middle ages, the modern world of separate and sovereign nation-states has no criterion for appeal to determine the justice of a war other than a system of laws that prescribe proper conduct in international relations. The other departure is this. Augustine and Aquinas had given primary attention to the *jus ad bellum*. But Grotius seems far more interested in restricting the methods and conduct permissible in the prosecution of war—that is, the *jus in bello*. This emphasis on the means permissible in war is particularly well suited to the modern secular world of nation-states and their competing political interests, a world profoundly different from the societal conditions of religious strifes that led to the Thirty Years' War and dominated the period of Grotius' own life. Force is justified, as Grotius put it, "to protect rights and maintain order (1962, bk. I, chap. 2, I, p. 73). He thus limits the legitimate causes for war. But far more important has been the prohibition against deliberately killing civilians and the stringent conditions under which that prohibition may be overridden. These contributions still apply to recent discussions of the *jus in bello* and are embodied in existing international law.

A topic of contemporary debate is whether a clear and morally relevant distinction can be made between combatants and civilians, that is, between who may and who may not be deliberately killed in war. Plainly there will be persons who fall into grey areas such that their immunity from deliberate attack might not be clearly established, for example, musicians in an army band, cooks, electricians, and others whose roles may not have a distinctively military character, or civilians working in munitions or airplane factories, as well as research engineers and physicists improving weapons delivery systems whose labors contribute much to the war effort. It is difficult to determine, moreover, whether the political leadership of a nation that commands the armed

forces to war should be considered combatants or civilians. In spite of these areas of indeterminacy, it is assumed that this distinction can and ought to be made, and therefore may be regarded as a morally relevant distinction.

This important distinction between combatants and civilians is recognized by modern international law, the Hague Conventions of 1907, and is quite explicitly incorporated into the 1977 provision attached to Article 51 of the Geneva Convention of 1949. That provision states:

> The civilian population as such, as well as individual citizens, shall not be the object of attack. Attacks or threats of violence the primary purpose of which are to spread terror among the civilian population are prohibited. Indiscriminate attacks are prohibited. Indiscriminate attacks are (a) those which are not directed at a specific military objective; (b) those which employ a method or means of combat which cannot be directed at a specific military objective; or (c) those which employ means or methods of combat the effects of which cannot be limited as required by this Protocol: and consequently, in each such case, are of a nature to strike military objectives and civilians or civilian objects without discrimination. Among others, the following type of attack [is] to be considered as indiscriminate: an attack which may be expected to cause incidental loss of civilian life, injury to civilians, damage to civilian objects, or a combination thereof, which would be excessive in relation to the concrete and direct military advantage anticipated.[2]

Obviously the bombings of Hamburg, Dresden, Tokyo, London, Coventry, and other instances of obliteration (carpet, terror, or area) bombing, including the atomic bombing of Hiroshima and Nagasaki, are prohibited by the above. International law, as articulated by Hague and Geneva Conventions, embodies very strong humanitarian principles, and the protection of civilians is one of its most important tasks. But from the moral point of view, simply drawing a distinction between combatants and civilians is not sufficient to establish that crucial moral difference wherein the former may and the latter may not be deliberately killed. What needs to be determined is why it is morally wrong to deliberately kill civilians, and why it is permissible—indeed, some will say a positive duty—to kill combatants. The standard answer is that civilians may not be deliberately killed because they are innocent. Now, what does innocence in war mean?

B. Who Is Innocent in War?

The international law and the just-war tradition consider civilians to be innocent and therefore illegitimate

---

[2] 1993. Protocol additional to the Geneva Convention of 12 August 1949 and relating to the protection of victims of international armed conflicts. Protocol I, part IV, chap. II, Article 51, in *International Conventions on Protection of Humanity and Environment* (G. Hoog and A. Steinmetz, Eds.) p. 289. Walter de Gruyteer, New York.

targets of deliberate attack. What does it mean to say that civilians are innocent? What is the sense of the word "innocence" when applied to civilian populations in war? When one says that civilians are innocent, does one imply that combatants, i.e., noninnocents, fighting in a just war are guilty of a wrongdoing and for that reason may deliberately be killed? Clearly innocence does not have the same sense as when used to describe, say, children or those we might consider exemplars of the moral life. If it were the former, then we know innocence is short-lived, for children soon become adults; if the latter, then it is applicable only to extraordinary individuals. Either way, innocence would describe only a small segment of a civilian population. When applied to civilians in war, innocence must have a meaning different from its ordinary one and refer to some distinguishing fact about civilians in respect to war. What might that fact be and how is it related to some morally relevant sense of the word "innocence"?

Two approaches to the problem of innocence in war are evident among contemporary moral theorists. I refer to them as the *moral* and the *role-functional* views. The one determines innocence and guilt by reference to the justice or injustice of a war, while the other looks to a person's participation in war. Most theorists assume that the distinction between permissible and impermissible targets of deliberate attack coincides with the distinction between the guilty and the innocent. But if the moral and role-functional views define these terms in different ways, then we have less than a clear distinction between those that may and those that may not be deliberately killed in war.

1. The Moral View

The moral view determines innocence and guilt on the basis of the justice or injustice of a war. The important question of who is and who is not a legitimate target of deliberate attack is therefore a function of the (in)justice of a war. Elizabeth Anscombe says,

> What is required for the people attacked to be non-innocent in the relevant sense, is that they should themselves be engaged in an *objectively unjust proceeding* which the attacker has the right to make his concern; or—the commonest sense—should be *unjustly attacking* him. (Italics added. 1981. In *Ethics, Religion, and Politics*, p. 53. Univ. of Minnesota Press, Minneapolis)

A plausible interpretation of this view maintains that in a conflict one side is necessarily engaged in an "objectively unjust" procedure. Hence, soldiers on that (unjust) side lack the necessary condition of a just cause and are guilty of fighting an unjust war, even when they fight in accordance with the rules of war. It seems, moreover, that combatants fighting on the unjust side—call these "unjust combatants"—act just as badly in killing enemy soldiers—call these "innocent combatants"—as if they were killing children, the aged, and the infirm. Whatever they do in such a war, they do it inescapably without justice. Those who fight for a just cause, on the other hand, are morally innocent, and when they fight in accordance with the rules of war they fight with—or, better yet, on behalf of—justice.

This view is subject to at least two objections. First, it is far from clear how we are to attribute justice to one side in an armed conflict. There will certainly be cases where the injustice of a belligerent is clear and we can, with medieval and some modern writers, for example, Aquinas and Vanderpol, maintain the criterion of fault as the essence of the just-war tradition. The *jus ad bellum* concern with a just cause for war should then be easily and clearly established. Yet the criterion of fault might not be discernable in every war, and we might have to entertain the possibility of doubt and ignorance regarding a just cause. Victoria, for example, long ago stressed the difficulties in establishing objectively the antecedent causes to a war and, moreover, allowed soldiers who in "good faith follow their prince" to fight in an unjust war when the injustice is known only to the ruler. In this way, he says, soldiers "on both sides may be doing what is lawful when they fight (Victoria, 1917, 177). But in Anscombe's view, it appears that when the criterion of fault or justice in a war cannot be clearly established, then it would be impossible to determine who the innocent and the guilty are and, by extension, who may and may not be deliberately killed. Such a war, then, could not morally be fought.

The second objection is this. There is the assumption, at least in modern democracies, that citizens have a positive duty in justice toward the state—for example, to obey its laws. If citizens fight in a war in accordance with this duty, then they cannot be acting against justice, and all soldiers who fight from duty are innocent and thereby immune from deliberate attack. We may suppose, however, that there is a duty prior to obedience to the state to discern the justice of a war. Citizens, before becoming soldiers, must to the best of their ability determine this important matter. Those who do not and simply obey the state might be guilty of an injustice, whether or not their cause is just, and are thereby legitimate targets of deliberate attack. On the other hand, those who do come to the conclusion that their cause is just, whether or not it is objectively so, are innocent soldiers and may not be deliberately killed. And of these there may be very many in any war. As Jenny Teichman observes, in this account of innocence and guilt

> there will always be in any war quite a large number of innocent soldiers. . . . The only way of avoiding the conclusion that killing the soldiers who are on the right side is the same sort of thing as killing unarmed civilians is either to redefine innocence and

non-innocence more radically than Anscombe has done, or drop the notions and construct a distinction in some other way. (1986. *Pacifism and the Just War*, p. 66. Basil Blackwell, Oxford)

It is further supposed by proponents of the moral view that killing in war is justified on the model of punishment. That is the model given us first by Augustine and then by other Christian writers, and it is frequently appealed to by politicians and citizens. The contrast between *moral* innocence and guilt also suggests it. Those who have no legitimate cause in fighting are unjust combatants and may not morally kill opposing (innocent) soldiers. When these unjust combatants kill innocent soldiers they commit an act on par with murder. Just as some people say society has a right to punish those guilty of murder by killing them, so too soldiers fighting for a just cause may similarly punish unjust combatants for their crime. But this model of killing in war seems far from adequate. Because most soldiers fight from duty to the state, they do not seem to be the proper objects of punishment. Rather the political leadership that orders, and the citizens who encourage, the troops to fight are likely to have a greater share of responsibility for the war, and hence to be guilty of initiating and supporting injustice. If this is even remotely correct, then many legitimate targets of deliberate attack in war will lie in the civilian and not the combatant population. Waging such a war would then be very practically impossible.

2. The Role-Functional View

An alternative view determines innocence on the basis of a person's engagement in the business of war. To say that some persons are innocent is just another way of saying that they are harmless and not involved in violent action. The root of the word "innocence" has this sense to it: *nocentes,* a Latin word that means harmful, coupled with the prefix *in,* yields the meaning "harmless" or "one who does not injure." So, while it is always wrong to deliberately kill the innocent, some people, because of what they do, are guilty and lost their immunity from deliberate attack. Some moral theorists have therefore assumed that the terms "innocent" and "guilty" are equivalent to a person's role as civilian or combatant, respectively. That assumption is evident, for example, in the work of Paul Ramsey, who says,

> The distinction between the "guilty" who are legitimate targets of violent repression and the "innocent" who are not ... is reducible to degrees of actual participation in hostile force.... [The principle of noncombatant immunity] takes into account a person's specific function, or lack of function, in the war itself in order to save as many as possible from being absorbed into the thrust of war. (1968. *The Just War,* pp. 153, 164. Scribner, New York)

Thomas Nagel, too, has argued that in discussions of war innocence "does not mean morally innocent but currently harmless.... So we must distinguish combatants from noncombatants on the basis of their immediate threat or harmfulness (1974. In *War and Moral Responsibility* (M. Cohen, T. Nagel, and T. Scanlon, Eds., pp. 19–20. Princeton Univ. Press, Princeton, NJ).

According to the role-functional view, innocent persons are not engaged in an activity that is immediately violent or threatening, and do not contribute directly to, nor are they within a chain of command that may engage them in, war-related violence. The guilty, on the other hand, are those who put in mortal jeopardy others' lives or contribute in a relevant way to those who do. There are then two major categories of people in wartime: combatants who are guilty of posing an immediate mortal threat, and civilians who are innocent of posing any such threat. In the former category we might include certain types of civilians who are not combatants strictly speaking—for example, munition workers, engineers and physicists who work in the war industry, and perhaps political leaders who initiate wars and order soldiers to fight in them. In the latter category we might include military chaplains, cooks, and medical personnel who do not contribute directly to the war effort but assist the soldier as a person.

The international law of war as specified in Geneva Conventions and Hague Regulations is roughly compatible with the role-functional view. A combatant is any person satisfying four requirements: is commanded by a person responsible for subordinates, has fixed insignia, carries arms openly, and conducts operations according to the laws and customs of war. Such persons have the right to kill other combatants and are themselves legitimate targets of attack. Note the lack of reference to the justice or injustice of a war in this definition of combatant status. Unlike the moral view, the role-functional view and the law of war hold *jus ad bellum* and *jus in bello* judgments to be, as Michael Walzer puts it, "logically independent," allowing "for a just war to be fought unjustly and for an unjust war to be fought in strict accordance with the rules (1977. *Just and Unjust Wars*, p. 21. Basic Books, New York). But the international law of war, unlike the role-functional view, makes a modest though important appeal to the *jus ad bellum* when it requires for combatant status that war be formally declared. Without this appeal to a formal declaration of war, we could not draw a further and important distinction between a soldier and a combatant, and absent that distinction it would be hard to say why the killing of soldiers who are not in war (call these "noncombatant soldiers")—for example, the killing of U.S. soldiers in Lebanon and, more recently, in Saudi Arabia—is wrong.

Even when the distinction between soldiers and combatants is established, one must explain why a combatant fighting in a just war is guilty of some injustice such that she may be killed by soldiers of the opposing side. How does it come to be that all combatants are guilty and may be killed while all civilians are innocent and may not? How can we establish a morally relevant distinction between the innocent and the guilty? In its ordinary sense innocence is said to be a condition of moral purity, of being uncorrupted by evil, or of not being culpable for some injustice. But obviously this is not the sense Ramsey and Nagel have in mind. Theirs is an innocence emptied of moral content. For them, what is crucial in determining innocence and guilt is a person's *role* regarding the waging of hostilities. Therefore innocence and guilt coincide with the role of civilian and combatant, i.e., with being illegitimate or legitimate targets of deliberate attack.

Proponents of the role-functional view will admit that the terms "innocent" and "guilty" are, as Ramsey says, "misleading," and then they might go on to make a further and finer distinction: while a soldier fighting in a just war might be *formally* innocent (i.e., morally innocent of injustice), he is nonetheless *materially* or causally culpable of a direct and immediate mortal threat. This distinction allows the use of the terms "innocent" and "guilty" without the usual connotations of moral innocence and guilt, and should be understood, as Michael Walzer says, as "term[s] of art" ascribing moral innocence and guilt to no one. Yet if one cannot ascribe moral innocence or guilt, how can killing be justified?

Merely occupying a role is not sufficient to justify killing. Killing, after all, is a most serious act and it should have a very clear justification. Unlike the moral view, the role-functional view justifies killing in war not on the model of punishment, but on that of self-defense against a mortal threat. Nagel says, "The attack is aimed specifically against the threat presented by a dangerous adversary.... The prosecution of conflict must be directed to the cause of danger" (Nagel, 1974, 18, 20). The implication here is that killing is justified only to repel an immediate mortal threat to one's life and that it is otherwise unjustified. But if self-defense provides the model on which killing in war is justified, we should have to admit that soldiers seldom, if ever, go to war to defend themselves and that therefore there are relatively very few cases when killing in war is justified—the threat justifying self-defensive action must be immediate and lethal. Should one try to extend the cases in which killing is justified, one is likely to raise the question of who is responsible for a war. Perhaps then the political leadership, that seems more morally responsible than most combatants, would become legitimate

targets of deliberate attack. At any rate, to kill deliberately a person who is not an agent of danger—i.e., a civilian—is beyond the scope of justifiable killing, while to kill an agent of danger—i.e., a combatant—is justified as self-defnese. It is important to note that self-defense justifies only the killing of "the cause of danger." But it does not justify the killing of combatants as such.[3]

This account of innocence and guilt does not draw upon ordinary meanings of those terms, nor does it appeal to the *jus ad bellum* concern with the justice of a war. Any ordinary meaning of the word "innocence" applied to war will likely include so many combatants and exclude so many civilians that it would make the just prosecution of a war impossible. Moreover, any definition of guilt drawn from the *jus ad bellum* concern with the justice of a war will, like the moral view, allow innocent soldiers on the right side to kill guilty soldiers on the wrong side, but will render the killing of the former by the latter as morally equivalent to the killing of children, the aged, and the infirm. Unless this view draws the line between innocence and guilt on the distinction between civilian and combatant—i.e., refers to one's role as agent of a mortal threat—it could not distinguish between who may and may not be deliberately killed in war.

One wonders at this point whether the concept of innocence is at all useful and whether a suitable moral concept is available. Barrie Paskins' and Michael Dockrill's modified Kantian concept of respect for persons is suggestive of a solution. Might it do the important work the language of innocence and guilt wants to do? For them, treating people as ends rather than as objects, as mere means to an end, leads to a "very important distinction between two kinds of death in war":

> Some people, in virtue of what they are doing, can regard death in battle as, however terrible, neither more nor less than suffering the consequences of their own actions. Some other people who might be killed in war do not have this thought open to them. The distinction coincides pretty closely with that between combatant and noncombatant. For the combatant must recognize that death in war would be a fate internally connected with the activity in virtue of which he is a combatant. But, except in very special circumstances, this does not apply

---

[3] Ramsey, unlike Nagel, holds not only a self-defense justification of war, but also a second and much broader justification that allows the use of force to "maintain a just endurable order in which [women and men] may live" and to protect the victims of injustice—or as he puts it, "to deliver as many of God's children from tyranny.... [L]ove for neighbors threatened by violence, by aggression, or tyranny, provided the grounds for admitting the legitimacy of the use of military force." It is doubtful that this second justification for the use of force challenges my classification of Ramsey within the role-functional view. Even when force is used to defend others, or a political system, the justification for killing another extends only to, as Ramsey says, "the bearer of hostile force"; that is, the agent of danger. (Ramsey, 1968, 143–144)

to the noncombatant.... Because of the internal connection between combatancy and being killed, a combatant has the option and opportunity to regard the prospect of death in war as meaningful: written into what he is doing is a connection with being killed that gives his own death a meaning.... But the death in war of a noncombatant does not have any such guaranteed meaning. (B. Paskins and M. Dockrill, 1979. *The Ethics of War*, pp. 224–225. Univ. of Minnesota Press, Minneapolis)

To assume that death can have any "guaranteed meaning" is highly problematical. That aside, Paskins and Dockrill make an important point: soldiers in war know they take on a high risk of, and might even expect, death. It is in the nature of their activity. Killing them does not fail to respect them as persons engaged in purposeful activities. As Nagel puts it, "A coherent view of this type will hold that extremely hostile behavior towards another is compatible with treating him as a person—even perhaps as an end in himself (Nagel, 1974, 14). But civilians do not take a similar risk nor have the same expectation. So for them, death in war is not related to any activity or goal they might pursue, and deliberately killing them fails to respect this fact about their lives. A view of this type, however, seems hardly distinguishable from the role-functional view—note the emphasis on the role of combatants in the above quotation—and may face similar difficulties.

C. May Innocents Ever Be Directly Killed?

No explicitly moral justification for the British policy of strategic bombardment of cities was given during World War II.[4] Yet there are now some people who think that it was justified. What moral justification might that policy have? If the killing of innocent people is morally wrong—is murder—how can a policy that aims deliberately to kill innocent civilians be justified? It is a simple matter of logical consistency, one might object, that because murder is by definition the unjustified killing of innocent people, the bombing of German civilians is incapable of justification. Yet perhaps, others say, there are rare moments of grave crisis when the inno-

[4] An exception is William Temple, Archbishop of Canterbury from 1942 to 1944, who defended the bombing of German and Italian cities on the simple thesis that, as Stephen L. Lammers puts it, "citizens of all modern states are implicated with the actions of their state" (S. L. Lammers, 1991. William Temple and the bombing of Germany: An exploration in the just war tradition. *J. Religious Ethics* **19**(1), 71–92). We should note also that very few criticisms of city bombing were advanced in the moral literature of the day. Public opinion in England strongly supported city bombing: 76% of those polled in areas that had not suffered city bombing—e.g., Cumberland, Westmoreland, and North Riding—approved of the RAF adopting a policy of bombing the civilian population of Germany, while only 45% of Londoners approved and 47% disapproved. The remaining 8% were undecided.

cence of persons does not render them immune from deliberate attack.

The deliberate killing of innocent civilians, unlike the destruction of the enemy's combatants, is not a legitimate goal in war. But large-scale killing of civilian populations is in some circumstances justifiable, according to some interpreters of the just-war tradition. In those circumstances the principle of proportionality, rather than noncombatant immunity (or discrimination), is usually appealed to. That principle is said to require that the harm done by military force be proportionate to some military goal. It prohibits gratuitous harm—i.e., harm that does not serve a military aim—but allows a great deal of harm so long as a legitimate war aim is served. So stated, proportionality is a consequentialist principle that weighs, say, the loss of civilian lives against victory. In Germany, the bombing of cities killed over 300,000 civilians. From the point of view of the *jus in bello* absolutist principle of discrimination, British bombing of German cities was nothing short of murder. Whatever end or goal is supposed to have been achieved by that policy does not justify the deliberate killing of civilians. But the just-war tradition as well as the international law of war contains this second and more permissive *jus in bello* principle that looks not at the distinction between precision and obliteration strategic policy. When applied to the bombing of German cities during WWII, this principle asks whether the military goal sought by strategic bombing justifies the civilian casualties it produced.

1. Supreme Emergency

In *Just and Unjust Wars* Michael Walzer offers the most respectable defense available for the deliberate killing of innocents in war. In several sections of that book and elsewhere, Walzer examines Britain's predicament shortly after the outbreak of WWII. He contends that unless Bomber Command was used systematically against German cities, Britain would very likely suffer defeat and an immense evil power would be let loose on the world. The bombers coupled with a policy of terror bombing against German civilians offered the only hope to avoid defeat by an enemy who posed, as Walzer says, "an ultimate threat to everything decent in our lives (1977, 253). What should one do? Kill tens of thousands of innocent civilians—children, the aged, and infirm—in order to stop a Nazi triumph, or respect the lives of innocent persons knowing that an age of barbaric violence will come to every nation in Europe?

Walzer gives a controversial response to this dilemma. In the life of nations there are rare moments of supreme emergency when the rights of innocent persons must be violated if a nation is to avoid defeat. In those rare moments military success might be so critically important that justice is more properly measured by the evil one prevents than by evil done. Walzer's proposed solution to such desperate times is that political leaders may take whatever measures are necessary to meet the task. He says,

> [C]ommunities in emergencies seem to have different and larger prerogatives [from individuals]. I am not sure that I can account for the difference, without ascribing to communal life a kind of transcendence which I do not believe it to have. Perhaps it is only a kind of arithmetic: individuals cannot kill one another to save themselves, but to save a nation we can violate the rights of a determinant but smaller number of people. (1977, 254)

Before one can justify the deliberate killing of innocent civilians, however, a nation has to face an evil of an ultimate nature. Simple military necessity will not do. The threat has to be such that defeat of the defending nation will result not merely in the establishment of a new balance of power, but in the triumph of evil, of a power so terribly awful that everything decent is radically jeopardized. Nothing less than an evil of this kind can justify the claim of emergency and the deliberate killing of innocent civilians. Accordingly, the threat must be, first, imminent, and second, not simply the loss of honor, but of a most serious nature.

With the criteria of imminence and seriousness of danger, Walzer distinguishes between the legitimacy of British bombing of German cities between 1940 and 1942, and the continuation of this practice during 1944–1945, when Britain was no longer in a condition of emergency, making the attacks on the cities at the end of the war immoral. It is important to note that Walzer's defense of British bombing does not diminish the injustice done to innocent German civilians. The decision to bomb the cities was made at a time when Germany posed a rare danger to the survival of Britain and defeat was ever present. It was a response to a condition of supreme emergency. But while a condition of supreme emergency justifies extreme action, an important wrong was nonetheless committed against German civilians. He says,

> Supreme emergency describes those rare moments when the negative value that we assign—that we can't help assigning—to the disaster that looms before us devalues morality itself and leaves us free to do whatever is militarily necessary to avoid disaster.... [Its essential feature is this:] that we recognize the evil we oppose and the evil we do and set ourselves, so far as possible against both. (Walzer, M., n.d. Emergency ethics)

Walzer's doctrine of supreme emergency and his defense of British bombing policy are subject to various lines of criticism. Here are two in outline form. First, in *Just and Unjust Wars* Walzer asserts that the rules of war are derived from individual rights. These rights, he argues, are more basic than considerations of utility. Yet when the stakes are high, utility has a certain priority over individual rights. Here, if anywhere, the ends to be achieved justify the means. But if utility overrides individual rights when a nation faces great disaster, why not follow utilitarian calculation all the way and consider the interest not only of one but of all communities, or, as Grotius says, "of the whole human race"?[5] It seems that if Walzer considers only the interests of one nation, say, Britain, he has to show why it is morally preferable that innocent civilians in this, rather than in another nation, say, Germany, survive. Second, whether absolutists and consequentialists moral principles, e.g., discrimination and proportionality, can be reconciled is a matter of great theoretical importance. Each contains quite different ideas about the content of morality. The first clearly is concerned with what we do to others, while the other attends to what happens to certain values and interests when we adopt one course of action over its alternative. When and on what grounds do we choose one understanding of morality over another?

Walzer describes supreme emergency as a very rare moment. It was the unique circumstance facing Britain that justified the deliberate killing of innocent civilians. Given the great evil Britain had set to defeat one could only choose the more permissive morality, knowing all the while the evil one does: become "murderers," he says, "for a good cause" (Walzer, 1977, 323). But the fact is that Walzer thinks supreme emergency is not that rare at all. Supreme emergency has become in the nuclear age, Walzer says, "a permanent condition" (1977, 274). One might then assume that a nation may do, or threaten to do, in this permanent condition of emergency just what Britain was justified in doing in the period 1940–1942. If this assumption is correct, then Walzer's argument is self-defeating, justifying on a permanent basis what initially was justified only for a rare and unique event—namely, the killing of civilians.

2. The Principle of Discrimination, Terrorism, and Ethnopolitical Violence

As noted in the first section of this article, there are forms of political violence other than war between states that aim deliberately to kill civilians. Terrorism is usually understood to be one of those forms. Although there are some vexing questions regarding the definition of

---

[5] The entire sentence reads, "Kings who measure up to the rule of wisdom take account not only of the nation that has been committed to them, but of the whole human race." The implication here seems to be that the political leadership of a nation must consider war's consequences not only for its own citizens, but also for the entire international community. (Grotius, 1962, Prolegomena, 24, p. 18)

terrorism (e.g., is it different from freedom fighting, guerilla warfare, and other forms of political violence carried out by nonstate agents?), the application of just-war principles to acts of terrorism yields an unequivocal condemnation. To the extent that terrorism is designed to create fear and despair among civilians by sabotage, assassination, subversion, and other violent acts with indifferences to the legal and moral rules governing the use of force, terrorism is condemned on *jus ad bellum* and *jus in bello* grounds, for example, formal declaration of war and discrimination. The international law of war concurs with this judgment, and Protocol I of 1977 to the Geneva Conventions extends no legal protection to terrorists. Violence is sanctioned when carried out between groups of combatants who wage hostilities in accordance with the rules of war and distinguish themselves from civilian populations. Terrorists, however, do not fight in accordance with those rules, nor do they distinguish themselves. But, as some commentators contend, there may be a bias in the just-war tradition and the law of war in favor of the system of states such that violence by nonstate groups is immediately rendered an impermissible use of violence. Such bias, some say, is fairly obvious in standard definitions of war that allow only states to engage in armed hostilities by armies of combatants as their agents recognized as such by international conventions.

From the point of view of the just-war tradition what distinguishes terrorism from acceptable forms of violence is that its victims are persons who in no way, either morally or causally, are responsible for the harm inflicted on them. Rather the targets are often innocent members of the civilian population, as in the bomb attack at Harrods in London in 1984 and the Achilles Lauro incident in 1985. Terrorism is a form of political violence, so it is different from other uses of violence, say, for private gain. But terrorism is an objectionable use of violence because it is by its nature indiscriminate. For the sake of some political objective it aims deliberately to maim and kill civilians and other persons by virtue of their religion, ethnic heritage, or nationality. Even when the distinction between the innocent and the guilty cannot be clearly drawn, the killing of civilians by terrorist attacks treats them as mere things, as instruments in a political struggle, and fails to respect them as agents and persons.

The same conclusion can be shown to follow from the principle of discrimination applied to ethnopolitical violence. As noted in the first part of this article, since the end of WWII violence between ethnic groups has been steadily increasing, and total civilian casualties number in the millions. Gradually we are moving from nation-state conflicts fought along national borders to conflicts where the borders are determined by linguistic,

religious, and ethnic differences, for example, between Hindus and Muslims in India, Turkic Muslims and Slavic Orthodox Russians in Central Asia, and Orthodox Christians and Muslims in the former Yugoslavia. Indeed we face a new and very troubling type of armed conflict without governments and armies as their agents fighting among themselves according to established rules of war. In this new type of conflict we encounter a breakdown of the traditional division of government, armies, and civilians. To the extent that such conflicts do not adhere to this important division and deliberately kill civilians because of their ethnic or religious identity, they are not a form of war. The law of war and the just-war tradition concur that these conflicts are nothing short of murder on a grand scale.

D. May Innocents Be Indirectly Killed?

The word "killing" describes an action the result of which is someone's death. It is not a moral term as such. From the moral point of view, what we wish to know is whether an act of killing is justified or not. An act of killing that is not justified we call murder. So murder is, by definition, the unjustified killing of a human being. As a general rule, deliberately killing innocent persons is unjustified—is, in other words, murder. Yet it is said that sometimes not all killing of innocent persons is murder. In some circumstances the killing of an innocent person, though reasonably foreseen as a result of the course of action one undertakes, is not murder because death was neither the means to some end, nor itself the end, one intended to bring about. There are a number of controversial issues regarding life and death that are frequently discussed in just this way, including therapeutic abortions, e.g., the removal of an ectopic pregnancy or cancerous uterus that results in the death of the fetus, and palliation of a dying patient by use of morphine hastening the patient's death. In cases such as these, the death of those who have done no harm—who are innocent—although tragic, is said to be permissible.

Consequentialist moral theories typically define a right action by reference to the state of affairs that action brings about. Roughly, an action is right if it happens to bring about a better state of affairs than acting otherwise. It does appear that when deliberating on what one ought to do, a person needs to consider (and is likely responsible for) all reasonably foreseen direct and indirect effects of a given action. The former usually refers to what a person intends to bring about, and the latter to what is foreseen but unintended—often referred to as a secondary or side effect to the action. For the consequentialist, the direct–indirect effects distinction is relatively unimportant. Both effects are the result of one's action and are to be assessed in terms of the state of affairs they produce. For the absolutist, however, the distinction is of great significance. A person, the absolutist will say, is responsible for the direct, but not for the indirect (or unintended) though foreseen, effects of her action. If an action, say, obliteration bombing, aims directly to bring about the death of innocent civilians, then that action is wrong—is, in other words, murder. But when the intention is, say, to destroy an enemy shipyard, a munitions factory, or a communications center (all legitimate targets of deliberate attack) and innocent civilians are killed, their death is a secondary or indirect effect of legitimate military conduct. Their death is, so the view goes, coincidental and collateral.

It is the principle of double effect that makes the just-stated distinction between intended (or direct) and unintended (or indirect) consequences. For example, I perform an act A that intends good G and foresees some evil effects E. Assume that I want to bring G about and have no wish for E, nor is E part of my intentions. E just happens. The principle of double effect is ready to say that I am not morally responsible for E, which is merely a side effect even if foreseen. But matters are different when E is my intention or a means for G, or when E is disproportionate to G. When E is my intended end or a means to some end, or when it is needless, this principle condemns my action. So, intending or using evil, or inflicting needless harm even for a good end, makes the act morally wicked. According to Anscombe, this principle is

> absolutely essential to Christian ethics. For Christianity forbids a number of things as being bad in themselves. But if I am unanswerable for the foreseen consequences of an action or refusal, as much as for the action itself, then these prohibitions will break down. If someone innocent will die unless I do a wicked thing, then on this view I am his murderer in refusing: so all that is left to me is to weigh up evils. Here the theologian steps in with the principle of double effect and says: "No, you are no murderer, if the man's death was neither your aim nor your chosen means, and if you had to act in the way that led to it or else do something absolutely forbidden." Without ... this principle ... the Christian teaching that in no circumstances may one commit murder, adultery, apostasy (to give a few examples) goes by the board. These absolute prohibitions of Christianity by no means exhaust its ethic; there is a large area where what is just is determined partly by prudent weighing up of consequences. But the prohibitions are bedrock, and without them the Christian ethic goes to pieces. (Anscombe, 1981, 58)

One does not, however, have to be a Christian or theist of any kind to adopt this principle. Any absolutist system of morality is likely to have some dependence on it: some things are absolutely wrong and may never be done even if the heavens are about to fall. So, one may not perform an act that is absolutely prohibited (say, torture) to save someone else's (an innocent's) life. But the principle of double effect does allow the indirect and proportionate killing of innocent persons. How does a principle which belongs to an absolutist system permit the killing of innocent persons in war?

Consider one application of this principle. Suppose orders are issued to bomb certain important enemy military targets, say, a command, control, and communications center, a munitions depots, and several highways and bridges used for military transport. Bombing these targets will kill combatants, an action permissible in war. But suppose that a number of civilians are also likely to be killed. They either live or work nearby the munitions depots and bridges. It is, of course, wrong to deliberately kill these civilians. But the principle of double effect says that absent the intention to kill them, their death, though an evil, is not a moral evil but a side effect of a legitimate act of war. Acts that produce such evils are said to be justifiable when (i) the action is either morally good or indifferent, (ii) the intention of the agent performing the action is upright, (iii) the evil is causally related to the intended good, and (iv) there is proportionately grave reason for allowing the evil to occur. Supposing that all four conditions are satisfied in the above example, then the death of civilians is incidental to the act and considered collateral damage.

Indeed that was the reasoning evident in official statements by the U.S. chain of command in the 1991 war against Iraq. We were told repeatedly during that war that the U.S. choice of targets was designed not to hit civilians directly. So, the principle of discrimination was adhered to. Moreover, many of the weapons used in that war—so-called "smart weapons"—gave the assurance that hitting targets within cities would not be hitting the cities (i.e., civilians) themselves. There was no intention, nor need, to rely on WWII strategies of obliteration bombing against civilians. Yet reports attested that due to continual strikes, oftentimes of the same target, particularly in Baghdad near civilian areas, a significant number of civilian casualties were produced. Is there a threshold at which indirect and foreseen effects gain at least the appearance if not the reality of intended aims, when it no longer makes sense to say that civilian casualties are collateral or incidental to permissible conduct in war? At which point do collateral civilian deaths become disproportionate to legitimate military conduct?

Combatant casualties in this war were rather high. Intelligence sources estimated that some 150,000 Iraqi soldiers were killed. The vast majority of them were conscripts who cannot be held responsible for the war. The same sources estimated that civilian casualties may have been equal to combatant deaths. Is this number of civilian deaths acceptable on proportionality grounds? Suppose that American bombing did not intend to kill civilians, only to destroy various aspects of Iraqi infrastructure having some military value. How shall we think of a highway or bridge, an electric power plant, or sources of communication that have some military value but are used regularly by civilians? What if the destruction of those targets has a greater impact on a society than on its armed forces? Are these civilian or military targets? Destruction of infrastructure targets in Baghdad has to date affected the health and living standards of civilians more than the military. To say that these are strictly military targets and so the misery their destruction causes is collateral seems, on consequentialists grounds, to be an evasion of responsibility.

These remarks suggest the following criticism of the principle of double effects. It is extremely difficult to determine what are the intended and unintended effects of a course of action. The fact that our actions often have more than their intended effect does not necessarily mean that we have no responsibility for their unintended effects. When we know our actions bring about the death of innocent persons, even when they are indirect, it seems too narrow a sense of responsibility to say that those deaths, though tragic, are permissible. Is it really possible to engage in a course of action knowing that civilians will be killed and say that their death is only incidental and that one therefore is not responsible for them? To be sure, responsibility may admit of degrees. In some circumstances a person may be less responsible for what is allowed to happen than for what she does. That is an important distinction. But when what is allowed to happen is some 150,000 innocent deaths, as was the case in the war against Iraq, the magnitude seems disproportional to any legitimate military goal, and those deaths begin to take the form of a deliberate action.

This line of criticism is particularly well suited to debates on nuclear deterrence. Some argue that a policy of nuclear deterrence is an effective way to prevent nuclear war. By threatening unacceptable loss to a potential adversary, whatever gains might obtain from aggression are offset and a sort of peace is retained. It has been the readiness to use nuclear weapons that has produced peace in Europe since the end of WWII. But this claim is highly controversial. That to date there has not been a nuclear war is no real evidence that deterrence has this preventive function. Europe has enjoyed other periods of peace without nuclear weapons, even when European governments were more militaristic than now—for example, the 40 years of peace after the Franco-Prussian War of 1871. It is a common and simple fallacy to mistake what is not the cause (deter-

rence) of a given effect (absence of nuclear war and peace) for the real cause. From the moral point of view what is important to determine is the morality of nuclear deterrence. If nuclear weapons are immoral means of warfare because they cannot satisfy the principle of discrimination and will produce effects disproportionate to any goal, and if it is immoral to intend what one may not do, it seems then that nuclear deterrence is itself immoral. Nations ought, therefore, to disarm themselves immediately and unilaterally of these weapons of mass destruction. Proponents of deterrence argue, however, that so long as a nation does not deliberately aim nuclear weapons at civilian populations but rather at military targets—so-called "counterforce deterrence"—however many civilians deaths result from the use of these weapons are only collateral and incidental to legitimate military conduct. It is the principle of double effect that, for the absolutist, opens this line of reasoning. For the consequentialist, however, even when deterrence aims only at strictly military targets, the side (i.e., unintended) effects of a nuclear attack are hardly different from the intended end. Indeed, if an adversary's fear of collateral damage is one of the things that deters, it is then one of the means by which deterrence is achieved. And means to an end are always intended actions. So, the killing of civilians is intended even in counterforce deterrence.

Acknowledgments

I am grateful to my colleagues Drs. Cynthia Brincat and Thomas Shipka, and to two anonymous reviewers, for their detailed and helpful comments on an earlier draft of this paper.

Bibliography

Clark. I. (1990). "Waging War: A Philosophical Introduction." Clarendon, Oxford.

Cohen, S. (1989). "Arms and Judgment: Law, Morality, and the Conduct of War in the Twentieth Century." Westview, Boulder, CO.

Detter De Lupis, I. (1987). "The Law of War." Cambridge Univ. Press, Cambridge.

Holmes, R. L. (1989). "On War and Morality." Princeton Univ. Press, Princeton, NJ.

Johnson, J. T. (1981). "Just War Tradition and the Restraint of War." Princeton Univ. Press, Princeton, NJ.

Lackey, D. P. (1984). "Moral Principles and Nuclear Weapons." Rowman & Allanheld, Totowa, NJ.

Miller, R. B. (1991). "Interpretations of Conflict: Ethics, Pacifism, and Just-War Tradition." Univ. of Chicago Press, Chicago.

Palmer-Fernández, G. (1996). "Deterrence and the Crisis in Moral Theory." Peter Lang, Berlin/New York.

Van Creveld, M. (1991). "The Transformation of War." The Free Press, New York.

Collective Guilt

GREGORY MELLEMA
Calvin College

GLOSSARY

collective guilt The guilt attaching to a collective group for a harm for which the collective is either responsible or for which the collective is tainted due to the wrongdoing of a moral agent or agents outside the collective.

collective responsibility Responsibility for a state of affairs borne by a collective consisting of two or more moral agents.

metaphysical guilt A term coined by Karl Jaspers to describe a collective guilt based upon the idea that a person's identity is shaped by the group, that choices of people affect others in the group, and that guilt is produced as a result of this process.

moral taint That which results from the transferring of the contagion of an agent's moral wrongdoing to others who are connected to this agent.

original sin The sin committed by Adam, the first man, for which the entire human race is allegedly held accountable.

shared responsibility Responsibility for the same state of affairs borne by two or more moral agents.

stain A term employed by Paul Ricoeur for moral taint.

COLLECTIVE GUILT attaches to a group consisting of moral agents as the result of the group bearing moral responsibility for a harm which has occurred. Collective guilt can also attach to a group of those who are tainted by others bearing moral responsibility for a harm. Typically, the collective to which the guilt attaches will subsequently experience guilt for this harm. Suppose several students from the same high school bear collective responsibility for murdering a victim, and they subsequently feel guilt for this state of affairs. Their guilt may be described as a collective guilt. However, those who are tainted by these actions, such as other students from the same high school, may also experience feelings of guilt for this harm. If so, they likewise experience collective guilt.

Two features of this account are noteworthy. First, although guilt is typically experienced when collective guilt attaches to a group, one need not have the experience of guilt in order to be a member of such a collective. And even if the members of such a collective experience guilt, this is not to say that they must be aware of experiencing guilt. The possibility is left open that they experience guilt in a less than fully conscious manner. Furthermore, the guilt experienced by those to whom collective guilt attaches is typically not a sense of personal guilt for a harm. Second, collective guilt is always relative to a harm which has in fact occurred. Those who attempt to bring about a harm and fail do not bear collective guilt for this harm, for it does not occur, though they can bear collective guilt for attempting to produce the harm, for this state of affairs does occur. In addition, at any given time a person might belong to various collectives which are collectively guilty for various states of affairs.

Collective guilt cannot attach to those who neither belong to a collective responsible for a harm nor are tainted by the actions of those who do belong to such a collective. Such people are sufficiently remote from the harm that guilt fails to attach to the collective to which they belong. Accordingly, feelings of guilt are not reasonable or appropriate in this type of context. Of course, people can have feelings of guilt which are unreasonable. But some connection must exist between these people and those responsible for the harm for them to share in the collective guilt and for their feelings of guilt to have a legitimate basis.

There is a great deal of controversy over what this connection consists in. Some have maintained that collective guilt for the sin of Adam, the first man, extends to the entire human race. The Doctrine of Original Sin, as it is sometimes called, teaches that all human beings have in some manner sinned through Adam and have come to bear guilt for the sin which caused evil to enter the world. The collective which is guilty for the fall from Paradise, then, is judged to be all human persons, past, present, and future. All of humanity is said to bear collective guilt for what Adam did in the Garden of Eden.

Two questions are raised by the assertion that all of us bear collective guilt for Adam's sin. First, to what degree do people experience guilt for this sin? Although the experience of guilt is not a necessary condition for membership in a collective which bears guilt, it is plausible to suppose that at least some people will experience guilt for Adam's sin if the doctrine of Original Sin is a true doctrine. No doubt some people will attest that the guilt they experience for this sin is real, but there will certainly be others who deny the experience of guilt for this sin. Regarding this latter group, one who supports the notion of collective guilt for Adam's sins may wish to argue that the experience of guilt in certain people is less than fully conscious.

A second question is this: What connection exists between the sin of Adam and others of the human race? For collective guilt to occur, members of the human race must at least be tainted by the sin of Adam. How, then, does this take place? Theologians who have attempted to answer this question have produced accounts of this connection which are not always easy to comprehend, and it is safe to say that the Doctrine of Original Sin is a notion which remains controversial.

Other Biblical accounts also seem to embody cases of collective guilt which rely on the tainting of many people as the result of one person's sin. In the book of Joshua a man named Achan returns from a battle with possessions of those who have been conquered, in spite of having been forbidden to take them. Achan returns to his tent and buries these possessions in a hole. When he is discovered to have done this, Achan is put to death. But members of his extended family are likewise put to death. Here many will be inclined to raise questions about the severity of the punishment. But for present purposes, the point of this account is that it is an example of being tainted by the wrongdoing of those to whom we are related by birth.

I. COLLECTIVE GUILT AND MORAL RESPONSIBILITY

One of the ways guilt attaches to a collective is when a collective bears responsibility for a harm which has occurred. In the literature there are two primary ways in which collective responsibility is characterized. First, collective responsibility is sometimes characterized as the sharing of responsibility for the same state of affairs by two or more individuals. Second, collective responsibility is sometimes characterized as the view that a nonhuman entity, a collective which is composed of human beings, bears responsibility for a state of affairs. The primary difference between these two notions is that an individual who does not bear responsibility for a state of affairs cannot be a member of a collective bearing responsibility for this state of affairs in the first sense, but it is possible for this individual to be a member of a collective bearing responsibility for it in the second sense.

The first conception of collective responsibility can be illustrated by a case in which several people deface a public building by spraying graffiti on it. Each person bears moral responsibility for a common state of affairs, the defacing of the building, and hence they share responsibility for this state of affairs. Individuals who share responsibility for a harm do not always bear the same degree of responsibility for the harm. But when this type of collective responsibility occurs, each member of the collective bears at least some degree of responsibility. Consequently, the members of the collective bear collective guilt as the result of their participation.

The second conception of collective responsibility can be illustrated by a variation of the same example. Here the members of an established gang deface a public building by spraying graffiti on it. But in this example not all of the members participate in the activity. Some members spray the building, others offer words of encouragement to those spraying the building, and others simply stand and watch. Of those who stand and watch, some secretly wish that the others would stop spraying graffiti and find something else to do of a less destructive nature. However, they do not express this wish, for they do not want to risk being expelled from the gang.

In this example it is plausible to judge that the members of the gang form a collective which bears moral responsibility for the defacing of the building. But the responsibility of the collective does not automatically distribute to all of its members, as in the case of shared responsibility. Here those members of the gang who wish that the others would stop defacing the building arguably do not bear responsibility as individuals for the defacing, for they wish that the building not be defaced. If so, then the gang could be divided into those who bear individual responsibility for the defacing of the building and those who do not. But all the members of the gang still belong to a collective which bears moral responsibility for the defacing of the building (since those who wish that the others not deface the building are members of this collective as long as they do not in any manner express dissent to the actions of fellow gang members).

The collective which bears moral responsibility is not itself a human being, but it is composed of human beings. Of the human beings who compose it, some bear responsibility for the defacing of the building and some do not. Unlike shared responsibility, the responsibility of a collective does not invariably distribute to all of its component members. But the members can nevertheless constitute a group which bears collective guilt.

Some philosophers have held that a collective can bear moral responsibility for a state of affairs even if no member of the collective bears responsibility for the same state of affairs. D. E. Cooper proposes the example of a club which closes due to lack of *esprit de corps* among its members. He argues that the members are collectively responsible for the closing, but no individual member need bear responsibility for the closing. If cases such as this are possible, and there is considerable dispute as to whether or not they are, then collective guilt is likewise possible in situations where no member of the collective is responsible for the harm producing the guilt. Then several people could bear collective guilt for a harm for which none of them bears individual moral responsibility.

Those who support the notion of collective responsibility are far more inclined to countenance cases in which at least one member of the collective bears responsibility for the outcome for which the collective itself bears responsibility. Consider the collective of German citizens during the second world war. It has often been claimed that the German people were collectively responsible for the occurrence of the Holocaust. The vase majority of German citizens played no role in the events which led to the deaths of countless Jews, and hence they do not bear responsibility as individuals for the Holocaust. But various Nazi officials bear responsibility as individuals for the Holocaust as the result

of their individual contributions to the events of the Holocaust. Accordingly, the collective of German citizens consists of some who bear responsibility and others who do not. The same is presumably true of those German citizens who experience collective guilt for the Holocaust: some but not all bear individual responsibility for it.

II. COLLECTIVE GUILT AND MORAL TAINT

The other way that a collective comes to experience collective guilt is through being morally tainted by those who bear moral responsibility for a harm. Moral taint results when harm is produced by a certain person or group of persons, and the contagion of their wrongdoing is transferred to others who have had no involvement in bringing about the harm. Those German citizens who played no role in the events of the Holocaust were tainted by the wrongful actions of the Nazi officials who were involved in these events. These German citizens bear no moral responsibility for the events of the Holocaust, but, because they are tainted by the actions of the Nazi officers, they are in a position to experience and bear collective guilt.

Anthony Appiah has led the way in philosophical circles in explicating this concept (his account is similar to an account of moral stain offered by Paul Ricoeur, but it is considerably clearer). According to his account, a person who is tainted by the wrongdoing of another moral agent experiences a loss of moral integrity. When a person who happens to have some connection to us produces harm, then our own moral integrity can be affected. Appiah applies moral taint to an understanding of the issue of divesting shares of stock in companies doing business in South Africa in the 1980s. A shareholder in such companies was not in any manner responsible for the harmful effects of apartheid, but he or she was nevertheless tainted by those practicing apartheid. Consequently, shareholders in these companies experienced a loss of moral integrity.

Appiah believes that a feeling of shame is appropriate when one is tainted by the wrongful acts of others. Feeling a personal sense of guilt is not appropriate to the situation, for one has no personal involvement. But the appropriateness of a feeling of shame makes possible collective guilt. Because I and several others feel shame over the wrongful actions of one to whom we are connected, the possibility exists that collective guilt attaches to us. Of course, it is not a foregone conclusion that collective guilt attaches to people whenever they are tainted by the wrongful actions of another. Frequently people feel neither shame when they are tainted nor a sense of collective guilt. But the presence of taint is a condition which makes collective guilt possible.

From this it follows that experiencing a sense of collective guilt is not the same as experiencing a personal sense of guilt. Those holding shares of stock in firms doing business in South Africa need not feel a personal sense of guilt for the harmful effects of apartheid, but they can experience collective guilt. If they experience guilt at all with respect to apartheid, the guilt appropriate for them to experience is collective in nature. And the type of guilt appropriate for those German citizens who experience guilt as the result of being tainted by the harmful actions of Nazi officials is collective guilt.

III. COLLECTIVE GUILT IN EXISTENTIALIST THOUGHT

In his book, *Sharing Responsibility,* Larry May argues that 20th century existentialist thought can shed much light on questions connected with moral responsibility and moral taint. The understanding of the concept of responsibility in 20th century existentialist thought is shaped largely by the writings of philosophers such as Jean-Paul Sartre, Karl Jaspers, and Hannah Arendt. Writing in the years immediately following the second world war, they tried to come to terms with the widespread failure of their fellow citizens to prevent the horrible actions of the Nazis. May notes that they turned to existentialist thought in an effort to explain this profound failure, and they likewise appealed to the resources of existentialist thought to design an adequate theory of responsibility. To their way of thinking, an adequate theory of responsibility is marked by its ability to take seriously society and the problems which afflict it.

Inspired by this tradition, May develops an existentialist approach to questions of group or collective responsibility. His approach is built upon the notion that groups have a very powerful influence over their members, and specifically over their attitudes and behavior. As the result of belonging to the group, one's personal values undergo a transformation; people belonging to groups discover that the members influence and transform the values of one another. And along with this sharing of attitudes and values comes a sharing of responsibility for group actions. May argues that belonging to groups also tends to make people insensitive to certain harms in such a way that they come to share responsibility for these harms.

Sometimes groups are responsible for inaction. May refers to situations in which the members make a decision not to act as a collective omission. There are also cases in which people with the ability to form a group to prevent a harm from occurring fail to act, and he refers to this phenomenon as collective inaction. These putative groups can frequently be judged collectively responsible for their inaction, or even for the harms they fail to prevent. The members of these putative groups are not necessarily guilty for their inaction or for these harms; it is more appropriate for them to feel shame for their inaction or collective guilt for these harms. May emphasizes that there is the potential for great social good when people seek solutions of a collective nature, since groups are far more likely than individuals to be able to prevent significant harms from occurring.

May's discussion is intended to push to the limit how we ought to think of agency and responsibility. People who are the products of Western culture tend to think of agency in individualist terms and to think of responsibility as set at a very modest level, and May is attempting to challenge these ways of thinking. He quotes Hannah Arendt as stating, "This taking upon ourselves the consequences for things we are entirely innocent of, is the price we pay for the fact that we live our lives not by ourselves but ... [within] a human community." This statement provides a basis for understanding why the German people feel shame and a sense of collective guilt for the actions of Nazi officials. Because we live in a human community, Arendt believes that there is a sense in which we take upon ourselves the consequences of the harmful acts of others. Although the German people were entirely innocent of the actions of the Nazi officials, existentialists such as Arendt can help us to understand why they experience collective guilt.

Another existentialist writer who has much to say about guilt in the context of groups or collectives is Karl Jaspers. Jaspers's discussion is framed in terms of a particular type of guilt known as metaphysical guilt, and, although he does not offer a precise definition of this notion, it is quite evident on the basis of what he says that this notion is related to the notion of taint.

Consider these words from his book, *The Question of German Guilt:*

> There exists a solidarity among men as human beings that makes each co-responsible for every wrong and every injustice in the world, especially for crimes committed in his presence or with his knowledge. If I fail to do whatever I can to prevent them, I too am guilty.... That I live after such a thing has happened weighs upon me as an indelible guilt. (1961. Translated by A. B. Ashton. p. 36. Capricorn Books, New York)

Jaspers speaks here about a type of guilt which is neither legal, political, nor moral. He describes it as a guilt which attaches to people for failing to prevent wrongs and injustices in the world. And the expectations for them to prevent these wrongs and injustices is high. Even if they must risk their lives to prevent injustices, the failure to do so weighs upon them in the form of guilt which is indelible.

In this passage Jaspers also makes a startling statement that human beings are "co-responsible" for every wrong and injustice in the world. People are first and foremost coresponsible for wrongs and injustices that are known to them. However, to a certain extent they are coresponsible for *all* wrongs and injustices in the world. Commenting upon this passage, May states that Jaspers comes dangerously close to stating that each member of the human race shares responsibility for all of the world's harms.

Two important ideas underlie the notion of metaphysical guilt in Jaspers. The first is that a person bears metaphysical guilt only through being a member of a group or groups. An important element of Jaspers's thought is that people's identities are shaped partly through their group memberships. Who they are is shaped in part through the various groups to which they belong. For this reason it makes sense from an existentialist point of view to judge that some people in a group are implicated by the actions of others in the group.

But there is more to metaphysical guilt than membership in groups. The second important element of metaphysical guilt is that individuals make choices regarding the behavior of others in their groups. If others in one's group are causing harms, then one must make a choice whether to act to prevent the harms, at least to indicate disapproval of the harmful behavior, or to do nothing. If one does nothing, then one has failed to distance onself from these harms, and metaphysical guilt will attach to one who fails to distance oneself from these harms.

Choosing whether or not to distance oneself from the harms which others in one's group are causing is also closely connected to one's identity as a person. In a real sense one is choosing who to be when one makes this choice. Metaphysical guilt in this manner is not only based upon one's actions, but it is based upon the concept of choosing to be a person of a certain type. If a person chooses silence when others are perpetuating harms, then the person's choice of silence is the choice to be a certain kind of person. This type of choice is a crucial part of what enters into how Jaspers conceives of metaphysical guilt.

It is different with moral guilt. There are situations in which one incurs both moral and metaphysical guilt by choosing silence when others are perpetuating harms. But it is possible for one to incur metaphysical guilt without incurring moral guilt. Sometimes the only way to prevent or speak out against certain harms is to risk

one's life; these cases are of special interest to Jaspers. One who chooses silence in these cases incurs metaphysical guilt, as has already been seen. But Jaspers seems to believe that it would be a mistake to judge that one incurs moral guilt as well in situations of this type. Although metaphysical guilt and moral guilt are frequently incurred jointly, they are not always.

It is a consequence of these ideas that Jaspers views moral guilt quite differently from moral responsibility. Moral guilt is not necessarily borne by people who choose silence in the face of harms, but responsibility (or, more precisely, coresponsibility) for every wrong or injustice in the world is shared by everyone who fails to speak out against them. Thus, there are presumably many instances in which one's silence renders one responsible for harms brought about by others, even though one does not bear moral guilt for these harms. In the end, it is not clear to what extent responsibility is comparable to metaphysical guilt in Jaspers's thought, but responsibility is definitely broader than moral guilt.

In May's opinion, shame or taint are the moral concepts which come closest to metaphysical guilt. When someone bears metaphysical guilt because of wrongs committed by others, it seems that one can likewise describe the situation as one in which the moral agent is tainted by this wrongdoing. Of course, Appiah denies that taint involves guilt, but it is moral guilt that Appiah has in mind in making this denial. Metaphysical guilt, by contrast, seems to attach to people in the scheme of Jaspers in the very sorts of cases where Appiah would postulate the appearance of taint.

Jaspers's notion of metaphysical guilt is not, however, exactly the same as what Appiah describes as taint. As pointed out already, metaphysical guilt is also bound up with the matter of choosing one's identity. One's choice of whether to distance oneself from the harmful acts of others is partly a choice of who one is. Whether one comes to bear metaphysical guilt in Jaspers's scheme is partly a matter of one's relationship with other moral agents and partly a matter of what one has done in terms of choosing an identity. Taint is characterized by Appiah in terms of one's relationship with other moral agents, and, regarding the choosing of one's identity, his account has nothing to say. This is not to say that the choice of one's identity is completely irrelevant on Appiah's account; by choosing to be a certain kind of person one will take actions which may preclude one's being tainted. But whatever relevance we can find here is only incidental; by contrast, it appears to be essential to Jaspers's understanding of metaphysical guilt.

May's preference is to think of taint along the lines of what Jaspers suggests. He agrees that Appiah is correct to think that taint is the right concept to employ in cases where people react with silence to the harmful acts of others with whom they are associated. But it is preferable to take into account the question of who one is. The optimal way of understanding taint is that it is determined not only by what one does but also by who one chooses to be.

Appiah describes a case in which one of the co-owners of a store is carrying a box of knives up the stairs from the storeroom while the other co-owner is about to sell a knife to a youth who, they both know, plans to use the newly purchased knife for murder. The co-owner coming up the stairs knows that if he hurries, his partner will sell the youth a knife from the new box; otherwise, his partner will select one from the top shelf. Appiah believes that the partner is tainted by the stabbing if and only if the knife used in the stabbing comes from this box. Hence, on Appiah's view, if he delays in coming up the stairs he escapes taint.

But there is more to the story from the perspective of Jaspers. Suppose the partner decides to bring the box up at once, but he does not do so because the telephone begins to ring. Although the partner's choice to bring the box up at once does not result in his actually doing so, he does make a choice. This may appear to be a trivial choice, but those in the existentialist tradition have repeatedly urged that choices such as this are choices of who one is. The partner is choosing to be a certain kind of person, the kind of person willing to be connected with a stabbing. For this reason a follower of Jaspers will argue that the choice itself is enough to taint the partner. Regardless of whether he follows through on his choice, he is nevertheless tainted.

The view one takes about examples of this type has large implications for collective guilt. For, once again, collective guilt presupposes collective responsibility or moral taint. If one neither belongs to a collective responsible for a harm nor is tainted by the harmful acts of another, then no reason exists for ascribing collective guilt. If the youth murders a person with his newly purchased knife, then if the knife was not from the new box, the co-owner is not tainted by the murder (in Appiah's view), and there is no reason for the co-owner to experience collective guilt.

IV. COLLECTIVE GUILT AND CONTEMPORARY SOCIETY

People frequently express the judgment that groups or collectives are guilty for what has taken place or for what has failed to take place. In debates on abortion, for example, those holding a prolife position sometimes judge that society bears collective guilt for the occur-

rence of legal abortions. It is sometimes maintained that all human beings bear collective guilt for the atrocities of war which occurred in places such as Bosnia. And the dramatic rise in violent crimes committed by teenagers and preteenagers is another area in which society might be said to bear collective guilt.

On the basis of the foregoing discussion, it is dubious that society as a whole bears collective guilt for abortion, civil warfare in other nations, or a rise in crime, for it is unlikely that all members of society are connected to these states of affairs either by taint or by collective responsibility. Moreover, it is sometimes a matter of controversy whether the alleged harms (such as legal abortions) are in fact harms.

Nevertheless, ascriptions of collective guilt for problems in contemporary society are important to take seriously. For although they are sometime exaggerated, they frequently contain a core element of truth. Many people in our society are closely enough connected to the problem of teenage violent crime to warrant membership in the collective which experiences guilt. Thus, although society as a whole does not warrant membership in this collective, a sizable segment of society arguably does. And an additional segment of society no doubt is connected to the crimes committed by teenagers through taint.

As May indicates, many of society's problems can be adequately addressed only when the collective nature of responsibility for these problems is acknowledged. Accordingly, the collective guilt experienced by those collectively responsible for or tainted by these harms serves as a motivator to undertake solutions for these problems.

This line of thinking suggests that collective guilt has the potential for playing a very positive role in contemporary society. While the term "collective guilt" often suggests something negative or even sinister in human life, there is clearly a positive dimension to the role it plays in the life of a community. As a community we can band together to find solutions to the problems that we and others experience. On an individual level, the experience of guilt can motivate a person to actions of a positive nature. But the effectiveness of an individual's solutions to the problems of society is limited. Collective guilt, by contrast, has the potential for motivating an entire group to undertake the solutions of societal problems on a large scale.

There are problems of a practical nature which arise when a group undertakes to solve the problems of society. Perhaps the greatest challenge lies in the initial organization of a group of individuals into a unit which can undertake to solve these problems. But the presence of collective guilt is a factor which makes this organization more manageable than otherwise, for it motivates individuals to desire to participate in groups which can find solutions to these problems.

Collective guilt also has the potential for leading a group of individuals to a greater self-understanding. The experience of guilt can function to shake a group out of its complacency, force it to concentrate upon a harm which has occurred, and take a new look at itself and its relationship with the harm. The collective guilt experienced by the German citizens for the events of the Holocaust led these citizens to ask questions about themselves and their relationship with these events which they would not have been motivated to ask in the absence of collective guilt. In the end they achieved a greater understanding about themselves and about human nature in general.

In some cases collective guilt has the potential for playing a type of purifying role in the consciousness of a group. When the group confronts the feelings of collective guilt and examines its relationship to the harm which has given rise to the experience of collective guilt, there is an opportunity to give expression to feelings of regret or remorse for the events associated with the harm. Depending upon the precise circumstances, this process could reasonably be regarded as a type of purifying process. Collective guilt resulting from the phenomenon of moral taint is perhaps not the type of collective guilt for which this designation would be appropriate. But when collective guilt results from a situation in which a group bears collective moral responsibility for harm, there is reason for the members of the group to express feelings of regret or remorse, and this can result in the consciousness of the group undergoing a process of purification.

Bibliography

Appiah, A. (1987). Racism and moral pollution. *The Philosophical Forum* **18,** pp. 185–202.

Arendt, H. (1987). Collective responsibility. In "Amor Mundi (J. W. Bernauer, Ed.), p. 50. Martinus Nijhoff, Dordrecht.

Cooper, D. E. (1968). Collective responsibility. *Philosophy* **43,** pp. 258–268.

French, P. (1992). "Responsiblity Matters." Univ. Press of Kansas, Lawrence, KS.

Jaspers, K. (1961). "The Question of German Guilt, translated by A. B. Ashton. Capricorn Books, New York.

May, L. (1992). "Sharing Responsibility." Univ. of Chicago Press, Chicago.

May, L. (1987). "The Morality of Groups." Univ. of Notre Dame Press, Notre Dame, IN.

Morris, H. (1976). "On Guilt and Innocence." Univ. of California Press, Berkeley.

Ricoeur, P. (1967). "The Symbolism of Evil," pp. 8–9, 35–37. Harper & Row, New York.

Computer and Information Ethics

SIMON ROGERSON
De Montfort University

GLOSSARY

information systems A multidisciplinary subject that addresses the range of strategic, managerial, and operational activities involved in the gathering, processing, storing, distributing, and use of information, and its associated technologies, in society and organizations.

intellectual property rights Rights that encompass confidential information, patents, trademarks, and copyright.

software A general term encompassing all programs that are used on computers; it can be divided into **systems software,** which controls the performance of the computer, and **application software,** which provides the means for computer users to produce information.

teleworking Working in flexible locations and at flexible times using computers while ensuring that the needs of the organization and of the individual are catered for.

COMPUTER AND INFORMATION ETHICS came into being as computer technology advanced and people started to become aware of the associated pitfalls that threatened to undermine the potential benefits of this powerful resource. Computer fraud and computer-generated human disasters were indicative of a new set of problems arising from this advancing technology. Perhaps the earliest recognition of this new set of problems was Donn Parker's "Rules of Ethics for Information Processing" (1968. *Communications of the ACM,* **11,** 198–201). By the mid-1970s such issues had been grouped together under the term "computer ethics" (coined by Walter Maner) that represented a new field of applied professional ethics dealing with problems aggravated, transformed, or created by computer technology. Deborah Johnson (D. G. Johnson, 1985. *Computer Ethics.* (1st. ed.). Englewood Cliffs, NJ: Prentice-Hall) defined computer ethics as being the study of the way in which computers present new versions of standard moral problems and dilemmas, causing existing standard moral norms to be used in new and novel ways in attempt to resolve these issues.

This is a narrow scope of computer ethics that focuses on the application of ethical theories and decision procedures used by philosophers in the field of applied ethics. Gradually this scope has been extended, as illustrated by James Moor's definition of computer ethics as the analysis of the nature and social impact of computer technology and the corresponding formulation and justification of policies for the ethical use of such technology (1985. In T. W. Bynum (Ed.), *Computers and Ethics.* Oxford: Blackwell).

The current broad perspective of computer ethics embraces concepts, theories, and procedures from philosophy, sociology, law, psychology, computer science and information systems. The overall goal is to integrate computing technology and human values in such a way that the technology advances and protects human values, rather than doing damage to them (T. W. Bynum, 1997. *Information ethics: An introduction.* Oxford, Blackwell). The term "information ethics" is becoming widely accepted as a better term for this area of applied ethics. This is because, firstly, the computer has evolved into a range of forms including the stand-alone machine, embedded computer chips in appliances, and networked components of a larger, more powerful macro-machine, and so the word "computer" is now misleading. Secondly, there has been an increasing convergence of once-separate industries to form an information industry that includes computers, telecommunications, cable and satellite television, recorded video and music, and so on.

I. THE UNIQUENESS OF COMPUTERS

The case of a company operating a nationwide network of service engineers illustrates what can go wrong if the implications of using computer systems are not carefully and fully investigated. The company had been suffering from several thefts of its service vehicles when parked at night. The attraction was not the expensive, though specialized, service equipment in the vehicles, but the engines of the vehicles themselves, which apparently had a high resale value. The company decided to attach electronic tags to the vehicles, enabling vehicle movement to be monitored from a central office. At night it was possible to place an electronic fence around the vehicles, and should an attempt to move the vehicle beyond the fence occur an alarm was triggered at the central office and the police alerted. The system proved highly successful and thefts were reduced dramatically. The management of the company then realized that this system could be used to monitor indirectly the movements of the sales engineers throughout the working day, providing information about abnormal activity instantaneously and without the knowledge of the engineers. The computer manager was briefed to develop this spin-off system, and therein lies the problem—the legitimate use of technology giving rise to the opportunity of questionable unethical action by the company which would affect every service engineer and ultimately anyone who used a company vehicle. The computer manager was placed in a very difficult position because of the conflict in professional responsiblity to the company on one hand and to the employees as members of society on the other.

This situation arose because of the uniqueness of computers. While spying on employees can be done without the use of computers, it is the power of computers that makes such activities viable in this situation. According to Walter Maner (1996. *Science and Engineering Ethics,* **2**(2), 137–154), the characteristics of the computer's uniqueness include storage, complexity, adaptability and versatility, processing speed, relative cheapness, limitless exact reproduction capability, and dependence on multiple layers of codes. This uniqueness has resulted in a failure to find satisfactory non-computer analogies that might help in addressing computer-related ethical dilemmas. Indeed this is an area that raises distinct and special ethical considerations that are characterized by the primary and essential involvement of computers, exploit some unique property of computers, and would not have arisen without the essential involvement of computers.

There is a need to discover new moral values, formulate new moral principles, develop new policies, and find new ways to think about these distinct and special ethical considerations, particularly in the organizational context (Maner). The sections that follow consider the major issues within information ethics with the exception of issues specifically related to the Internet.

II. PRIVACY AND MONITORING

Privacy is a fundamental right because it is an essential condition for the exercise of self-determination. Balancing the rights and interests of different parties in a free society is difficult. Problems of protecting individual privacy while satisfying government and business needs are indicative of a society that is becoming increasingly technologically dependent. Sometimes individuals have to give up some of their personal privacy in order to achieve some overall societal benefit.

Organizations are increasingly computerizing the processing of personal information. This may be without the consent or knowledge of the individuals affected. Advances in computer technology have led to the growth of databases holding personal and other sensitive information in multiple formats, including text, pictures, and sound. The scale and type of data collected and the scale and speed of data exchange have changed with the advent of computers. The potential to breach people's privacy at less cost and to greater advantage continues to increase.

There are two important types of privacy: consumer privacy and employee privacy (R. A. Spinello, 1995. *Ethical aspects of information technology.* New York: Prentice Hall). Consumer privacy covers the information complied by data collectors such as marketing firms, insurance companies, and retailers; the use of credit information collected by credit agencies; and the rights of the consumers to control information about themselves and their commercial transactions. Indeed the extensive sharing of personal data is an erosion of privacy that reduces the capacity of individuals to control their destiny in both small and large matters. Organizations involved in such activities have a responsibility to ensure privacy rights are upheld. Consumer privacy focuses on the commercial relationship. Expanding this concept to client privacy includes consideration of non-commercial relationships where privacy is equally important. For example, medical, penal, and welfare relationships have, without doubt, serious privacy relationships. According to Spinello the issues that need to be addressed regarding movement of consumer data (and client data) can be summarized as:

- Potential for data to be sold to unscrupulous vendors
- Problems with ensuring the trustworthiness and care of data collectors
- Potential for combining data in new and novel ways to create detailed, composite profiles of individuals
- The difficulty of correcting inaccurate information once it has been propagated in many different files

Employee privacy deals primarily with the growing reliance on electronic monitoring and other mechanisms to analyze work habits and measure employee productivity. Spinello explains that employees have privacy rights which include the rights to control or limit access to personal information that he or she provides to an employer; to choose what he or she does outside the workplace; to privacy of thought; and to autonomy and freedom of expression.

In the modern workplace there are increasing opportunities to monitor activity. It is important to ensure that the use of monitoring facilities does not violate employee privacy rights. Some of the potential problem areas are:

- Personal computer network management programs that allow user files and directories to be monitored and to track what is being typed on individual computer screens
- Network management systems that enable interception and scrutiny of communications among different offices and between remote locations
- E-mail systems that generate archives of messages that can be inspected by anyone with authority or the technical ability to do so
- Electronic monitoring programs that track an employee's productivity and work habits
- Close circuit television surveillance systems that are computer controlled and have extensive archiving facilities and digital matching facilities

A modification of the data protection principles within the United Kingdom's Data Protection Act (1984) provides a framework that can be used to address the issue of privacy, develop a reasonable privacy policy, and ensure that the development and operation of information systems (IS) are sensitive to privacy concerns. The modified principles are as follows (E. France, 1996. *Our answers: Data protection and the EU Directive 95/96 EC.* Wilmslow: The Office of the Data Protection Registrar): (i) Personal data shall be processed fairly and lawfully. (ii) Personal data shall be collected for specified, explicit, and legitimate purposes. (iii) Personal data shall not be further processed in a way incompatible with the purposes for which they are collected.

(iv) Personal data shall be adequate, relevant, and not excessive in relation to the purposes for which they are collected or further processed. (v) Personal data shall be accurate and, where necessary, kept up to date. (vi) Personal data shall not be kept longer than is necessary for the purposes for which they are collected and further processed.

(vii) An individual shall be entitled, at reasonable intervals, without excessive delay or expense and under no duress, to be informed by any controller when he or she processes personal data of which that individual is subject and to certain information relating to that processing; to access the personal data of which the individual is subject and to any available information as to their source; and to knowlege of the logic involved in any automatic processing of data concerning him or her involving certain automated decisions; and, where appropriate, to have such personal data rectified, erased, or blocked, and to have details of such rectification, erasure, or blocking available to third parties to whom personal data have been disclosed.

(viii) Appropriate security measures shall be taken against unauthorized access to, or alteration, disclosure, or destruction of, personal data and against accidental or unlawful loss or destruction of personal data.

III. INFORMATION PROVISION

Information has become one of the most valuable assets, for it is through information that people gain knowledge that can then be used in both current and future decision-making activities. Information is concerned with communicating a valuable message to a recipient. Thus information must be clear, concise, timely, relevant, accurate, and complete. A message which has no value to its recipient is simply termed data. The majority of information provision is likely to use computer-based IS. The integrity of information is reliant upon the development and operation of these systems. The responsibility for these activities is a complex issue. For example, it is not clear whether IS provision is a service or the supplying of a product, nor is it possible in the case of a large IS for a single individual to fully understand it, and therefore no single individual can be held responsible for the whole system. It often turns out that an organization together with several individuals within that organization have a shared responsibility.

It is important to understand the nature of responsibility, which, according to D. G. Johnson, comprises four concepts (1994. *Computer ethics* (2nd. ed.). Englewood Cliffs, NJ: Prentice-Hall):

1. Duty—a person has a duty or responsibility by virtue of the role held within the organization
2. Cause—a person might be responsible because of undertaking or failing to undertake something which caused something else to happen
3. Blame—a person did something wrong which led to an event or circumstance
4. Liability—a person is liable if that person must compensate those who are harmed by an event or action

Specific responsibility issues often include several of these concepts. For example, a computer programmer knowingly reduced the testing procedure for a program in order to meet a deadline by not using the supplied test data that were for very infrequent cases. This resulted in a major operation failure several months after implementation. In this situation the programmer was to blame because failure to complete the specified testing had caused the program malfunction, and it was the programmer's duty and responsibility to ensure adequate testing. In this circumstance the programmer may be found legally liable.

One practical way of dealing with responsibility is to assign it to individuals involved in information provision within an organization. Individuals can be grouped into three broad categories: development, implementation, and maintenance of IS; collection and input of data; and output and dissemination of information. Responsibility clauses should be included in each job specification within these three areas of organizational work. Each clause should explain the extent of responsibility. Both management and nonmanagement jobs should be covered. Individuals should be adequately briefed on their responsibilities regarding the authenticity, fidelity, and accuracy of data and information. They should be encouraged to accept such responsibilities as part of their societal responsibilities. Should an undesirable event occur it should be considered on its own merits, and responsibilities can be identified using the responsibility framework already in place.

IV. SOFTWARE AS INTELLECTUAL PROPERTY

Intellectual property rights (IPRs) raise complex issues which organizations have to address. IPRs related to software and data are particularly difficult to assign and protect, and require careful deliberation before executive action occurs. Society has long recognized that taking or using property without permission is wrong. This extends not only to physical property but also to ideas. It is generally accepted that software is a kind of intellectual property and that to copy it or use it without the owner's permission is unethical and often illegal.

Ownership might not be clear. Johnson (1994) argues that a consequentialist framework is best for analyzing software IPRs because it puts the focus on deciding ownership in terms of affecting continued creativity and development of software. Software may be developed by a number of people, each making a contribution. Individuals might have difficulty determining which elements belong to them and to what degree they can claim ownership. Individuals may be employees or contractors. The development of software on behalf of a client raises fundamental IPR issues. It is important that agreement concerning the ownership of IPRs is reached at the onset before any development commences.

If an organization or group of individuals invests time, money, and effort in creating a piece of software they should be entitled to own the result by virtue of this effort and be given the opportunity to reap an economic reward. For the sake of fairness and equity, and to reward initiative and application, one should have the right to retain control over intellectual property and to sell or licence the product. However, the extent of these rights is debatable. Parker, Swope, and Baker explain that there is a responsibility to distribute software that is fit for the purpose for which it was developed, so the owner does not have the right to distribute software that is known to be defective and that has not been thoroughly tested (D. B. Parker, S. Swope, & B. N. Baker, Eds., 1990. *Ethical conflicts in information and computer science*. Wellesley: QED Information Sciences). Software embodies ideas and knowledge that can often benefit society as a whole. To have unrestricted rights may curtail technological evolution and diffusion, which will disadvantage the consumer and society. For example, there may be a piece of software that is deemed to be societally beneficial but which is withheld on commercial grounds. It is questionable whether the owner has the right, simply on grounds of optimizing economic gain, to withhold distribution. Some reasonable limit must be placed on the IPR so an equitable balance is struck. For example, currently copyright legislation in the USA protects the expression of an idea and not the idea itself. This constraint appears to achieve a balance between the right to private property and the furthering of common good.

There is reasonable agreement in countries of the West that individuals or groups of individuals have intellectual property rights regarding software. The law in many countries recognizes that computer software is worthy of protection because it is a result of a creative process involving substantial effort. The principal instrument of protection is copyright. However, the interpretations in other countries and situations are sometimes different. For example, IPR safeguards in countries of the Far East are minimal mainly due to a different philosophy that tends to treat intellectual property as communal or social property. In economically poor developing countries the view often taken is that the right to livelihood takes precedence over other claims on which IPRs are based. It is only when prosperity increases that there is a shift from a social well-being interpretation of IPRs to one with more emphasis on the individual. Such differences will have an impact on organizations involved in international trade and must be considered carefully.

V. ORGANIZATION STRUCTURE AND THE LOCATION OF WORK

With the advent of computers there has been a shift from traditionally stable organizational structures toward more flexible working arrangements. New computer-enabled working practices are creating more dynamic structures that are highly flexible and capable of responding to environmental uncertainty. For example, with the advances in telecommunications and IS, many jobs can be redefined as telework, which involves working remotely via a computer link. Many organizations are now using teleworking, communal office desks and computers, and geographically dispersed virtual teams to reduce organizational operating costs, but there may be serious disadvantages in this. For example, teleworking might result in the breakup of social groups in the workplace and the disenfranchising of those without the resources to participate. This may detrimentally affect organizations and society in the long term.

The impact of computer-enabled work will continue to grow. Work that is capable of being transformed into computer-enabled work must have a low manual labor content, be undertaken by individuals rather than teams, require minimal supervision, be easily measurable, and not depend upon expensive or bulky equipment. This means that there are many activities that might be organized as flexible computer-enabled work, including:

- Professional and management specialists such as accountants, design engineers, graphic designers, general managers, and translators
- Professional support workers such as bookkeepers, proofreaders, and researchers
- Field workers such as auditors, sales representatives, insurance brokers, and service engineers
- Information technology specialists such as software programmers and systems engineers
- Clerical support workers such as data entry staff, telesales staff, and word processor operators

Without doubt there are opportunities for benefit gains through the use of computer-enabled work for both organizations and individuals. However, this change in work practice raises many ethical dilemmas, and as computers evolve the dilemmas will continue to change. The following list illustrates some of the dilemmas and questions that may arise:

- The ability to employ people and sell goods and services globally through technological support may result in localized ghettos comprising people who have redundant or overpriced work skills and people who cannot afford the goods and services produced. Does an employer have a responsibility to the local community to ensure such ghettos do not exist or are minimized?
- Is it right to exploit low labor costs in the economically poor areas of the world, ignoring the injustice of wage differentials and an employer's responsibility to the community in which its employees live?
- Given the access to a global workforce and an increased need for flexibility to respond to the dynamic needs of the marketplace, the permanency of jobs and job content are likely to change. Is this acceptable to individuals, and how might organizations support individuals in coping with this often stressful situation?
- Computer-enabled communication only supports some of the elements of human communication. The loss of non-verbal communication or body language and the creation of electronic personalities could have an impact on the way people interact. Will this have a detrimental effect on individuals and the way they work?
- The workplace provides a place for social interaction at many levels. Individuals cherish this interaction. Commuting provides psychological space that separates work from home, which is important to some people. The move to teleworking radically changes this situation, potentially causing social isolation and disruption in home life. How can organizations safeguard individuals when adopting teleworking?

VI. COMPUTER MISUSE

As computers become more widely used, the risk of misuse and abuse increases, and the impacts of such acts are likely to be greater. For example, in the United Kingdom there was a threefold increase in the number of computer abuse incidents reported in 1993 compared with 1990, with virus infection, fraud, and illicit software accounting for 40% of the total incidents. Computer abuse covers a wide spectrum of activity, as summarized as follows (Audit Commission, 1994. *Opportunity makes a thief.* London: HMSO):

- Fraud through unauthorized data input or alteration of data input; destruction, suppression, or misappropriation of output from a computer process; alteration of computerized data; and alteration or misuse of programs, but excluding virus infections
- Theft of data and software
- Use of illicit software by using unlicensed software and pirated software
- Using computer facilities for unauthorized private personal work
- Invasion of privacy through unauthorized disclosure of personal data and breaches of associated legislation, and disclosure of proprietary information
- "Hacking" through deliberately gaining unauthorized access to a computer systems, usually through the use of telecommunication facilities
- Sabotage or interfering with the computer process by causing deliberate damage to the processing cycle or to the equipment
- Computer virus infections by distributing a program with the intention of corrupting a computer process

Spinello (1995) argues that organizations and individuals are ethically obliged to protect the systems and information entrusted to their care and must strive to prevent or minimize the impact of computer abuse incidents. He suggests that those stakeholders at greatest risk from a computer abuse incident might be party to decisions made concerning security arrangements. He argues that computer abuse offenses should not be treated lightly, even if the detrimental outcome is negligible, because, at the very least, valuable resources will have been squandered and property rights violated. Spinello also points out that a balance has to be struck regarding stringent security measures and respect for civil liberties. There is a dual responsibility regarding computer abuse. Organizations have a duty to minimize the temptation of perpetrating computer abuse, while individuals have a responsibility to resist such temptations.

VII. DEVELOPING INFORMATION SYSTEMS

Developing a computer-based IS is frequently a complicated process requiring many decisions to be made. As well as economic and technological considerations, there are ethical and social issues that need to be taken into account, but these are sometimes overlooked. It is generally accepted that IS development is best undertaken using a project team approach. How the project is conducted will depend heavily upon the perceived goal. The visualization of this goal should address many questions, including:

- What will the goal of the project mean to all the people involved in the project when the project is completed?
- What will the project actually produce? Where will these products go? What will happen to them? Who will use them? Who will be affected by them and how?

These types of questions are important because through answering them an acceptable project ethos should be established and the project's scope of consideration defined, so that consideration of ethical and societal issues is included, as well as that of technological, economic, and legal issues. The problem is that in practice these fundamental questions are often overlooked. It is more likely that a narrower perspective is adopted, with only the obvious issues in close proximity to the project being considered. The holistic view promoted by such questioning requires greater vision, analysis, and reflection. However, the project manager is usually under pressure to deliver on time and within budget, and so the tendency is to reduce the scope and establish a close artificial boundary around the project.

Within computing there are numerous activities and decisions to be made, and most of these will have an ethical dimension. It is impractical to consider each minute issue in great detail and still hope to achieve the overall goal. The focus must be on the ethical hotspots where activities and decision making include a relatively high ethical dimension because they are likely to influence the success of the particular information systems activity and promote ethical sensitivity in a broader context. The scope of consideration is an ethical hotspot and is influenced by the identification and involvement of all stakeholders both within and outside the organization.

The widespread use of and dependence upon IS within organizations and society as a whole means that the well-being of individuals may be at risk. It is therefore important that in establishing the scope of consideration of an IS project the principles of due care, fairness, and social cost are prevalent. In this way the project management process will embrace, at the onset, the views and concerns of all parties affected by the project. Concerns over, for example, deskilling of jobs, redundancy, and the breakup of social groupings can be aired at the earliest opportunity. Fears can be allayed and project goals adjusted if necessary.

An IS project is dynamic and exists in a dynamic environment. Appropriate information dissemination is essential so that the interested parties are aware of occurring change and assignments can be adjusted accordingly. Being over-optimistic, ultra-pessimistic, or simply untruthful about progress can be damaging not only to the project but also to both the client and the supplier. This is true whether the supplier and client are in the same or different organizations. Typically, those involved in this communication would be the project team, the computer department line management, and the client. An honest, objective account of progress which takes into account the requirements and feelings of all concerned is the best way to operate. Thus the second project management ethical hotspot has to do with informing the client. No one likes to get shocking news, so early warning of a problem and an indication of the scale of the problem are important. The key is to provide factual information in non-emotive words so the client and project manager can discuss any necessary changes in a calm and professional manner. Confrontational progress meetings achieve nothing. The adoption of the principles of honesty, non-bias, due care, and fairness help to ensure a good working relationship.

Turning to the overall development process, there are numerous methodological approaches to information systems development. Few deal adequately with the ethical and societal dimensions of the development process, instead tending to stress the formal and technical aspects. Consideration of the human, social, and organizational consequences of system implementation must not be overlooked during the development process. Management should encourage systems developers to adopt the principles of non-bias, due care, fairness, and consideration of social cost and benefit. In particular they should include the social design of computerized systems and work settings in the overall systems development project; build systems that are attractive to those whose work is most affected by them; and undertake information systems development in parallel with any necessary reorganization of work, taking into account changed responsibilities, relationships, and rewards.

VIII. COMPUTER PROFESSIONALISM

In discharging their professional duties, computer professionals are likely to enter into relationships with employers, clients, the profession, and society. There may be one or several of these relationships for a given activity. Quite often there will be tensions existing between all of these relationships, and particularly between the employer and societal relationships. There are three skills that a computer professional should possess so that professional duties might be undertaken in an ethically sensitive manner: (1) the ability to identify correctly the likelihood of ethical dilemmas in given situations; (2) the ability to identify the causes of these dilemmas and to suggest appropriate, sensitive actions for resolving them, together with an indication of the probable outcomes of each alternative action; and (3) the ability to select a feasible action plan from these alternatives.

Codes of conduct can be useful in helping computer professionals discharge their duties ethically, because the code provides a framework within which to work, and indicates to the new professional what are acceptable work practices. An excellent example of a code of conduct is that adopted by the Association for Computer Machinery (ACM) in 1992. The extract in Box 1 shows one of the 24 imperatives and its associated guideline that sets the overall tenor of the code and relates to many issues of computer and information ethics, for example, those raised in this article about the location of work and privacy.

Focusing on obligations makes it possible to consider carefully the implications of advancing computing technologies. There are four types of obligations for computer professionals: those as a supplier, those as a client, those as an end user, and those as a member of the community (W. R. Collins, K. W. Miller, B. J. Spielman, & P. Wherry, 1994. *Communications of the ACM*, **37**, 81–91). These obligations can be summarized as follows:

Obligations as a supplier to the client are to provide a reasonable warranty and be open about testing processes and shortcomings. Those to the end user are to provide clear operating instructions, give reasonable protection from, and informative responses to, use and abuse, and offer reasonable technical support. Obligations to the community are to ensure reasonable protection against physical, emotional, and economic harm from applications, and to be open about development processes and limits of correctness.

Obligations as a client to the supplier are to negotiate in good faith, facilitate adequate communication of requirements, and learn enough about the product to make an informed decision. Those to the end user are to provide quality solutions appropriate to the end user's needs within reasonable budgetary constraints, be prudent in the introduction of computing technology, and

Box 1

Extract from the ACM Code of Ethics and Professional Conduct

Imperative: 1.2 Avoid harm to others.

Guideline: "Harm" means injury or negative consequences, such as undesirable loss of information, loss of property, property damage, or unwanted environmental impacts. This principle prohibits use of computing technology in ways that result in harm to any of the following: users, the general public, employees, employers. Harmful actions include intentional destruction or modification of files and programs leading to serious loss of resources or unnecessary expenditure of human resources such as the time and effort required to purge systems of "computer viruses."

Well-intended actions, including those that accomplish assigned duties, may lead to harm unexpectedly. In such an event the responsible person or persons are obligated to undo or mitigate the negative consequences as much as possible. One way to avoid unintentional harm is to carefully consider potential impacts on all those affected by decisions made during design and implementation.

To minimize the possibility of indirectly harming others, computing professionals must minimize malfunctions by following generally accepted standards for system design and testing. Furthermore, it is often necessary to assess the social consequences of systems to project the likelihood of any serious harm to others. If system features are misrepresented to users, co-workers, or supervisors, the individual computing professional is responsible for any resulting injury.

In the work environment the computing professional has the additional obligation to report any signs of system dangers that might result in serious personal or social damage. If one's superiors do not act to curtail or mitigate such dangers, it may be necessary to "blow the whistle" to help correct the problem or reduce the risk. However, capricious or misguided reporting of violations can, itself, be harmful. Before reporting violations, all relevant aspects of the incident must be thoroughly assessed. In particular, the assessment of risk and responsibility must be credible. It is suggested that advice be sought from other computing professionals.

Reprinted with permission of the ACM, 1515 Broadway, New York, NY 10036-570 Email: acmhelp@acm.org

represent the end user's interest with suppliers. Obligations to the community are to acquire only products having reasonable public safeguard assurances and be open about product capabilities and limitations.

An obligation as an end user to the supplier is to respect ownership of rights. Those to the client are to make reasonable requests for computing power, communicate needs to the client effectively, and undertake to learn and use the products responsibly. Obligations to the community are to make a conscientious effort to reduce any risk to the public and encourage reasonable expectations about computing technology capabilities and limitations.

Obligations as a community member are to become aware of the limitation of computing technology, encourage effective economic and regulatory frameworks, support societally beneficial applications, and oppose societally harmful applications.

Organizations are an essential part of society. Those in charge of organizations have a responsibility to ensure that when computers are applied in pursuit of business objectives it is done so in a balanced manner that accounts for the needs of both individuals and society, as well as those of the organization. Senior executives must strategically manage computer usage to ensure that issues such as privacy, ownership, information integrity, human interaction, and community are properly considered. Computer professionals and their managers must be trained so that they are sensitive to the power of the technology and act in a responsible and accountable manner. The adoption of a broader approach that addresses economic, technological, legal, societal, and ethical concerns will help to realize a democratic and empowering technology rather than an enslaving or debilitating one, both now and in the future.

Bibliography

Berleur, J., & Brunnstein, K. (Eds.) (1996). *Ethics of computing: Codes, spaces for discussion and law. A handbook prepared by the IFIP Ethics Task Group.* London: Chapman & Hall.

Bynum, T. W., & Rogerson, S. (Eds.) (1996). Global information ethics, special edition. *Science and Engineering Ethics,* **2**(2).

Huff, C., & Finholt, T. (Eds.) (1994). *Social issues in computing: Putting computing in its place.* New York: McGraw–Hill.

Johnson, D. G., & Nissenbaum, H. (Eds.) (1995). *Computer Ethics and Social Values.* Englewood Cliffs, NJ: Prentice-Hall.

Langford, D. (1995). *Practical computer ethics.* London: McGraw–Hill.

Rogerson, S., & Bynum, T. W. (Eds.) (1997). *A reader in information ethics.* Oxford: Blackwell.

Confidentiality of Sources

MICHEL PETHERAM
Open University

GLOSSARY

consequentialism The view that the value of an action derives entirely from the value of its consequences. The best-known form of consequentialism is utilitarianism.

House of Lords The final court of appeal in the United Kingdom for both civil and criminal cases.

promise A declaration that one will or will not do something.

WE ARE entrusted with other people's secrets; we entrust others with our own. This entrusting requires that we or they do not pass on the secret information contained in these avowals, and this keeping of confidences is something we all value. Professional people, including journalists, often receive such confidential information. But in the case of journalists the information is to be made public; it is the source of the information that is required to be kept confidential. Much valuable information comes to journalists from individuals who wish to keep their identity secret.

A civil servant passes to a newspaper a document that reveals that the government has lied on a particular issue. If her request for anonymity is not observed, she will lose her job. A journalist investigating drug dealing in a town obtains an interview with one of the drug dealers; the police then demand that he give them the name of the dealer, so that they can prosecute him.

Because, for journalists, obtaining information is their raison d'etre, this practice of confidentiality has long been recognized. Journalists further believe that if they were not able to offer confidentiality, then many of these sources of information would not make themselves available. Some journalists have been prepared to go to prison to defend a promise of confidentiality.

I. THE VALUE OF CONFIDENTIALITY

Journalists themselves often express a strong belief in the need for confidentiality of sources. A recent account of journalism in the United Kingdom by noted journalist Raymond Snoddy remarks: "It is impossible to exaggerate the importance for a journalist of being able to obtain information in confidence from a private source and then being allowed to protect the confidentiality of the source" (Snoddy (1992). *The good, the bad and the unacceptable.* London: Faber). The author also refers to the still secret identity of "Deep Throat" who helped Woodward and Bernstein in the Watergate investigation. Conrad Fink in *Media ethics* describes confidentiality as "an essential tool of the trade" (p. 47) (Fink (1988). *Media ethics.* New York: Mc-Graw-Hill). To turn to more official views, the Society of Professional Journalists, Sigma Delta Chi, from the United States, says in its code of ethics, dating from 1973: "Journalists acknowledge the newsman's ethic of protecting confidential sources of information." Less platitudinous was the 1934 code of ethics of the American Newspaper Guild, which says: "Newspapermen shall refuse to reveal confidences or disclose sources of confidential information in court or before judicial or investigating bodies." In Great Britain the National Union of Journalists, in its code of conduct, says that "a journalist shall protect confidential sources of information."

Surveys of the press in the 1970s indicated that a substantial number of newspaper stories are based on information that could only be obtained through confidential reporter–source relationships (Van Gerpen (1979). *Privileged communications and the press.* Westport, CT Greenwood Press). The *Wall Street Journal* reckoned that 15% of its articles are based on confidential information. Memoirs of journalists and journalistic textbooks all refer to the necessity of preserving the confidential relationship between reporters and their sources.

It should be noted that the issue of confidentiality arises for other professions. Doctors, lawyers, and priests are traditionally recipients of information that the donor, so to speak, does not wish to have passed on. It is hard to see how the relationship between lawyer and client can work at all, without such an understanding. As modern society becomes more complex, with more information being recorded, other professions come to hold confidential information, such as bank managers, accountants, social workers. But, as mentioned above, the relationship between reporters and sources is rather different, in that it is a means to making information available to the public, whereas the other relationships are to keep the information itself confidential.

II. THE PHILOSOPHICAL ARGUMENTS

A. Sissela Bok

The most substantial discussion of confidentiality is to be found in the book *Secrets* by Sissela Bok in the chapter "The Limits of Confidentiality" (Bok, S. (1986)). In this she argues that the justification for confidentiality rests on four premises, of which three support the general practice of confidentiality, and the fourth supports professional secrecy in particular. The first premise is that of individual autonomy over personal information; people can have secrets. The second holds that it is not only natural but often also right to respect the secrets of intimates and associates, secrets that might have been shared with one, and that human relationships could not survive without such respect.

The third premise asserts that a pledge of silence, should one be made, creates an obligation beyond the respect already provided for by the two previous premises, for persons and for existing relationships. Such a promise raises the stakes. But then, as Bok points out, there may be times when these premises have to be overriden, for example, if maintaining confidentiality would lead to violence being done to innocent persons, or to someone becoming an unwitting accomplice in crime. In such circumstances, she says, a promise of silence can be breached. But her fourth premise "enters in to add strength to the particular pledges of silence given by professionals. This premise assigns weight beyond ordinary loyalty to professional confidentiality, because of its utility to persons and to society."

This point about the social utility of the silence of the professional is important, because it is easy for professionals in any field to advance confidentiality as a shield (the medical profession is particularly prone to do this). An absolute insistence on confidentiality can be unreasonable. It can be used as a means for deflecting legitimate public attention. (And indeed it is often this kind of confidentiality that journalists frequently need to breach to discover something of public concern.) Bok concludes her chapter: "The premises supporting confidentiality are strong, but they cannot support practices of secrecy—whether by individual clients, institutions, or professionals themselves—that undermine and contradict the very respect for persons and for human bonds that confidentiality was meant to protect." A system of ethics cannot excuse any group from the rules of moral reasoning predicated simply on the role of that group within society.

So Bok believes that confidentiality is not an absolute value; it is something that can be overridden by other, weightier considerations.

B. Other Arguments

Another way of setting up the argument is in a two step argument as follows. The first step is to say that confidentiality is justified in journalism because it is necessary to do the job, it is a tool of the profession. The second step is the claim that journalism itself is important, that is, to give the justification for the profession.

The first step is a consequentialist one; but does the second step have to be consequentialist? For example, a doctor may argue for the practice of medicine as a whole, not simply that it is concerned with the reduction of pain (consequentialist) but that it shows respect for the individual's physical integrity (nonconsequentialist). When the argument takes a consequentialist turn, we will have to compare the benefits of revealing confidences in problem situations with the benefits of keeping them, and then it is clear how well the two-step argument succeeds.

But if a plausible nonconsequentialist defense of professional activity can be put forward, it may be possible to argue that the two-step argument introduces values that are more important than social utility and therefore should not be weighed crudely against the benefits of disclosure. (Bok's discussion was couched in terms of social utility.) Whether it is possible to put forward a nonconsequentialist justification of journalism is doubtful.

The argument most frequently proposed by journalists to defend their activity is in terms of aiding the functioning of democracy by creating or ensuring well-informed citizens. This is clearly a consequentialist approach. A second line of argument often invoked is that freedom of speech and thereby journalism aid the pursuit of truth. This again is a consequentialist argument, but also rather more double-edged, in that if one is pursuing truth, one is appealing to the virtue of making things known, whereas in this instance the journalist wishes to conceal information.

The harsh truth seems to be that as journalists themselves invoke social utility (usually by appeal to the "public interest"), they have no moral high ground of values that override this utility to fall back on.

Finally, it may be said that what is at stake here is the keeping of a promise, and this can be considered an obligation or a duty, irrespective of the consequences. And it is a duty that is widely acknowledged. So, because breaking promises is wrong, it is wrong to break a promise of confidentiality. But does the keeping of a promise have an absolute force? Although a perhaps simplistic evaluation of the consequence of an action is avoided when we refer to duty, this does not of itself avoid moral conflict. Here, as happens in many other areas of life, the duty of promise-keeping can be in conflict with other duties, or with other's rights, such as the right to a fair trial.

III. THE LEGAL ARGUMENTS

Some of the confidential professional relationships mentioned earlier are considered important enough to receive recognition by the law, for example, those between lawyers and clients, priests and penitents, bank managers and clients. Journalists have this legal protection in Sweden, but not in the United Kingdom or the United States.

Journalists feel that they are often summoned to court without serious alternative attempts by the police or the courts to obtain for themselves the information they want. In these circumstances, the press claims that it is being used as an investigative arm of government.

A watershed decision was made in the United States in 1972 in what is known as the *Branzburg* case, which resulted from the refusal of a journalist to give the names of his sources for an article on drug use. A majority in the Supreme Court ruled to deny constitutional protection for the reporter–source relationship. According to this judgment, reporters had no privilege under the First Amendment to refuse to testify before grand juries.

"The great weight of authority is that newsmen are not exempt from the normal duty of appearing before a grand jury and answering questions relevant to a criminal investigation.... These courts have ... concluded that the First Amendment interest asserted by the newsman was outweighed by a general obligation of a citizen to appear before a grand jury or a trial pursuant to a subpoena, and give what information he possesses.... We are asked ... to grant a testimonial privilege that other citizens do not enjoy. This we decline to do." (Quoted from Hulteng (1985). *The messenger's motives* (2nd Ed.). Englewood Cliffs, NJ: Prentice-Hall). One of the judges, however, dissented from this judgement: "A reporter is no better than his source of information. Unless he has a privilege to withhold the identity of his source, he will be victim of governmental intrigue or aggression. If he can be summoned to testify in secret before a grand jury, his sources will dry up and the attempted exposure, the attempt to enlighten the public, will be ended." (Ibid.)

Following this dissenting opinion, many lower federal courts and state courts in the United States have protected journalists. This judge had proposed a three-part test, which should be met before government could compel grand jury testimony from a journalist. First, there should be probable cause to believe that the journalist has information "clearly relevant to a specific probable violation of the law." Second, that the information sought could not be obtained by alternative means less destructive of First Amendment values. Third, there should be a "compelling and over-riding need" for the information.

However, according to Van Gerpen (1979), p. 177, there is a substantial record of case evidence that a so-called "chilling effect" set in after the 1972 case. There were concrete illustrations of stories that were not published because assurance of confidentiality could not be extended to sources.

In the United Kingdom the issue is covered by the Contempt of Court Act 1981, section 10. This lays down that a court may not require journalists to reveal their sources "unless it is established to the satisfaction of the court that it is necessary in the interests of justice or national security or for the prevention of disorder and crime." Some have argued that this requirement is too wide, especially the phrase "in the interests of justice" (Robertson and Nicol (1992)). There have been few cases in the courts: one occured in 1990 when a journalist was fined £5000 for refusing to disclose a source. The case went all the way to the House of Lords, where one of the judges argued: "no one has a right of conscientious objection which entitles him to set himself above the law if he does not agree with a court's decision. That would undermine the rule of law and is wholly unacceptable in a democratic society. Freedom of speech is itself a right which is dependent on the rule of law for its protection and it is paradoxical that a serious challenge to the rule of law should be mounted by responsible journalists."

In reply, journalists might say that this is to beg the question about where their responsibility lies and that their dispute is not with the system of justice itself, but with the interests (for example, governments or large corporations) that are using the system to protect themselves.

Overall, it is not that journalists wish to put themselves above the law, but a question of where the burden of proof should lie, and what conditions need to be fulfilled to require a journalist to reveal his source. If they are too easy to meet, then it becomes likewise easier to intimidate the press, so that they are less able to carry out their socially useful tasks. Part of the problem in the United Kingdom is that there is no written agreement, comparable to the First Amendment in the United States and Freedom of Information Acts elsewhere, on the role of the press.

IV. PROBLEMS WITH SOURCES

So far, we have been assuming, with journalists, that the reporter's privilege of keeping confidences is a good thing. It may sometimes, perhaps often, be necessary. However, in principle, sources should be made known. For one thing, the reader is often only able to judge the value of the information provided, if he or she is able to evaluate the source from which it comes. Confidentiality can act as a smokescreen. As an editorial from the *Washington Post* put it (1969, December 2. Quoted in Hulteng, 1985. *The messenger's motives* (2nd Ed.). Englewood Cliffs, NJ: Prentice-Hall):

"Walter and Ann source (née Rumor) had four daughters (Highly Placed, Authoritative, Unimpeachable, and Well-Informed). The first married a diplomat named Reliable Informant. (The Informant brothers are widely known and quoted here; among the best known are White House, State Department, and Congressional.) Walter Speculation's brother-in-law, Ian Ru-

mor, married Alexandre Conjecture, from which there were two sons, It Was Understood and It Was Learned."

Thus, confidentiality deprives the audience of the opportunity to decide for itself how much faith to put in the information. In other words, the names of the sources are an important part of the story.

In addition, news sources act from a variety of motives, not all of which are praiseworthy. They may be providing information out of self-interest or for revenge. How is the journalist to know whether this information has been altered, edited, or selected out of context? What interest is he serving? There is a very real danger that journalists and through them the public can be deceived by this use of confidentiality. In the United Kingdom, the government uses a system of informal unattributed briefings to the press, known as the "lobby system." This has allowed governments and individual politicians to manipulate the news to the point of "disinformation" (Cockerell, M., *et al.*, 1984. *Sources close to the Prime Minister: the hidden world of the news manipulators.* London: Macmillan). "When journalists are presented with secret information about issues of great import, they become, in a very real sense, agents for the surreptitious source." (Epstein (1974, April 20). The American press: some truths about truths. *The National Observer*).

It may not be in journalists' long-term interests to connive in such practices. The extensive use of unattributed sources promotes distrust and even cynicism toward reported stories. Journalists should not let their desire to obtain information undermine the long-term credibility of the information they present to their readers. More generally, journalists stand for openness in public discourse; they challenge secrecy. They should, therefore, avoid it in their own practices; reliance on reporter's privilege can lead to accusations of hypocrisy.

V. CONCLUSION

The main consequence of all this is that because a journalist may be in the position of being taken to court to divulge a source, he or she should be very careful about promising to protect a source's anonymity. One textbook of media ethics has put it quite strongly: "Never promise to protect a source's anonymity unless you are prepared to go all the way—to jail, even—to keep your promise. Whatever the source's motives, you must be known far and wide as a completely reliable, ethical reporter who stands by a promise.... No reporter can work effectively without complete trust from sources" (Fink, 1988, *Media ethics,* Mc-Graw-Hill, New York).

The practical consequence of this ethical burden is that in many newsrooms, editors have taken it upon themselves to make the decision as to whether a news source should be granted anonymity, and so reporters must ask permission of their editors. One of the main considerations in making such a decision will be, how important or valuable is the information being offered?

It may be useful to note what journalists think of confidentiality. In a survey carried out in the United States in the mid-1980s, publishers, editors, and journalists were asked about their view of the issue. Twenty-five percent of the total said that a pledge of confidentiality to a source should always be kept no matter what the circumstances, even if it means a long jail term for the reporter and heavy financial cost to the newspaper (although, interestingly, this broke down into 40% of the journalists, 18% and 20%, respectively, for publishers and editors, who worry more about financial consequences). A further 62% thought as a whole that a pledge of confidentiality should always be taken seriously, but it can be violated in unusual circumstances (Meyer, P. (1987). *Ethical journalism.* New York: Longman). Unfortunately, a survey of this kind does not give the answer to the question that immediately arises, in what circumstances? For if a journalist is not going to follow the rigorous course of action suggested above, then this is just what a source seeking a pledge of confidentiality needs to know.

Here it may be useful to return to the three part test suggested after the *Branzburg* case (see Section III). Two of the conditions are relevant. First, the information should be relevant to a specific violation of the law. When a case like this arises, one would expect a newspaper to have worked out a policy as to whether it would resist or comply with a demand to reveal confidentiality, and if to comply, whether it would argue its

case up to the highest appeal court. The second condition was a "compelling and over-riding need." These are difficult to specify. Obviously, if the promise of confidentiality concerned a life or death situation, then life should be preserved. Another consideration follows from the fact that a promise of confidentiality requires trust on both sides. If it should turn out that the information provided under the promise of confidentiality should be false, then the journalist or newspaper may reasonably no longer feel bound to his or to its side of the bargain.

In view of these considerations, and taking into account the fact that individuals can vary considerably in how seriously they take their promises and the weight that they then give to reasons for overriding their promises, the source who seeks confidentiality would be advised to act on the principle of "caveat emptor" and inquire as fully as possible into the journalist's or newspaper's attitude to their promises of confidentiality.

Nevertheless, it is clear that, whether the ethical argument is in terms of consequences or of duty, promises of confidentiality should be kept. The doubts raised in Section IV suggest, not that such promises may be broken more easily, but that they should be given more carefully and less frequently.

Bibliography

Bok, S. (1986). *Secrets.* Oxford: Oxford University Press.

Day, L. (1991). *Essays in media communications: Cases and controversies* (chap. 6). Belmont, CA: Wadsworth Publishing.

Robertson, G., & Nicol, A. (1992). *Media law* (3rd ed.). London: Penguin.

Van Gerpen, M. (1979). *Privileged communication and the press.* Westport, CT: Greenwood Press.

Courtroom Proceedings, Reporting of

RUPERT READ
University of Manchester

MAX TRAVERS
Buckinghamshire College

GLOSSARY

defendant The accused person in a court case.

freedom of speech The right to speak or write whatever one wishes, so long as the speech itself does not constitute a harmful *action*.

journalistic practice What journalists—reporters—actually do.

party In a legal case, the person(s) on one side or another of it.

plaintiff The accusing person in a court case, "the complainant," "the wronged party."

rape-shield laws These are laws designed to protect—"shield"—an alleged rape victim from having to reveal her *prior sexual history* to the court (thereby also restricting the availability of that information to the press). The term is also sometimes used to refer to laws shielding her from having to have her *identity* revealed to the public.

COURTROOM PROCEEDINGS, that is, what happens in courts of whatever type, are generally highly routinized and routine affairs (although of course not without consequence to the parties to them). The reporting of such proceedings is normally a similarly routine matter—if it occurs at all, it will generally be very brief and entirely uncontroversial. It will be a public record of certain ordinary matters of public record.

In major trials, court cases of distinctive public interest, the (more detailed) reporting of the proceedings will take on additional importance. In particular, concerns may arise about the prejudicing (in one direction or another) of the trial by widespread or biased reporting. It is then that the mode of (and any limits imposed upon) the reporting of courtroom proceedings is most likely to become a matter of distinctive ethical interest.

I. INTRODUCTION

The extent to which the press should be allowed to report courtroom proceedings has been an issue for public debate and discussion in America for many years and is increasingly becoming an issue in Britain. This review will examine some possible applications of ethics, as a branch of applied philosophy, in this area of human conduct. It will begin by providing a historical account of the relationship between courts and the press in

America and Britain, providing illustrations of how both reporting, and restrictions on reporting, have been viewed as a problem. It will then consider the ways in which different philosophical perspectives can perhaps assist in clarifying the issues raised in these debates. Finally, it will consider the prospects for incorporating ethical standards into this area of journalistic practice, and it will make a critical point about the purpose of ethical codes in the professions.

II. THE RELATIONSHIP BETWEEN COURTS AND PRESS IN AMERICA AND BRITAIN

American courts have only recently taken measures to prevent journalists gaining access to the courtroom, as a result of growing public concern about the prejudice suffered by defendants in a number of trials during the 1960s. Restrictions on the freedom of the British press to report court proceedings date back to the eighteenth century, and give judges wide powers to hold journalists in contempt of court for publishing material that prejudices the outcome of trials. The objective of courts, and legal authorities, in each country has been to preserve the principle of "the open court" (i.e., public access to whatever is going on in the courtroom—which is regarded as a fundamental safeguard of justice), while at the same time preserving the right of the defendant to a fair trial. It is recognized by all commentators that it will not always be possible to reconcile these two principles, and that there will always be some potential for conflict between the press and the courts.

A. Restrictions on the Press in America

In America, the two opposing principles relating to reporting courtrooms are enshrined in the U.S. Constitution. The First Amendment states that "Congress shall make no law ... abridging the freedom of speech, or of the press." The U.S. Supreme Court has stated that "with respect to judicial proceedings in particular, the function of the press serves to guarantee the fairness of trials and to bring to bear the beneficial effects of public scrutiny on the administration of justice" (*Cox Broadcasting Co. vs. Cohn*, 420 US 469 (1975)), and journalists continue to rely on this Amendment to oppose reporting restrictions imposed by particular courts (see, for example, *Nebraska Press Association vs. Stuart*, 427 US 539 (1976)).

The Sixth Amendment, on the other hand, provides that "in all criminal prosecutions, the accused shall enjoy the right to a speedy and public trial, by impartial jury of the State and district wherein the crime shall be committed." The extent to which freedom to report

under the First Amendment prejudices this right has always been a matter for concern and debate in American public life, especially since the infamous Lindbergh baby kidnapping trial in the 1930s, in which some accused parties were given a severe "trial by the press" before and alongside their actual trial in court.

In its investigation into the 1963 Kennedy assassination, the Warren Comission roundly criticized journalists for their irresponsible reporting of police leaks in the course of the investigation, complaining that—as a result—"it would have been a most difficult task to select an unprejudiced jury, either in Dallas or elsewhere." The case that produced most public discussion of the issue, and resulted in legal change, was that of Dr. Sam Sheppard, an osteopath who was convicted of murdering his wife in 1954. The Supreme Court ordered a retrial 12 years later on the grounds that the media had prejudiced his right to a fair trial. The court noted that:

> Much of the material printed or broadcast during the trial was never heard from the witness stand, such as the charges that Sheppard had purposely impeded the murder investigation [through refusing to take a lie detector test] and must be guilty since he had hired a prominent criminal lawyer; that Sheppard was a perjurer; that he had sexual relations with numerous women; and finally, that a woman convict claimed Sheppard to be the father of her illegitimate child. As the trial progressed, the newspapers summarized and interpreted the evidence, devoting particular attention to the material that incriminated Sheppard, and often drew unwarranted inference from his testimony (Kane, P. (1992). *Murder, Courts, and the Press: Issues in Free Press/Fair Trial*, p. 18. Carbondale: Southern Illinois University Press).

According to another account:

> At one point, a front-page picture of Mrs. Sheppard's bloodstained pillow was published after being re-touched to show the alleged imprint of a surgical instrument—inferentially, her husband's (Gerald, E. (1983). *News of crime: Courts and press in conflict*. Westview, CT: Greenwood Press).

The Supreme Court in the Sheppard case[1] urged that judges should make more use of their existing powers to protect defendants by measures such as changing the venue of trials, sequestering juries, or enabling the defense to make greater use of voir dire (a procedure designed to select jury members uncontaminated by the influence of the media). They were also asked to be more proactive in controlling the release of information by the district attorney's office and the police, and in using court orders to prevent the press publishing prejudicial stories. This was also the central recommendation of the American Bar Association's Reardon Committee in 1966, which drew up professional standards for lawyers and judges in their dealings with the press. These included placing an obligation on the media not to re-

---

[1] New DNA evidence, available only in 1997, suggests more strongly than ever that Sheppard was in fact innocent.

port a defendant's previous convictions before or during a trial.

Since 1966, there have been a whole raft of Supreme Court appeals relating to this issue. Some have been brought by *defendants,* complaining that they have been denied their constitutional right to a fair trial (O. J. Simpson, for example, could and very probably would have tried to appeal on these grounds, if he had been convicted of murdering his wife and her companion in his infamous 1995 criminal trial). Others have been brought by the press, seeking to protect their first amendment rights against "gagging orders" (e.g., *Nebraska Press Association vs. Stuart,* 427 US 539 (1976)). Finally, there have been a few suggestions recently that the increasingly fine-grained nature of the spotlight that the media is able to apply to the evidence and so on in high-profile cases may—if the defense uses the opportunity effectively—work against *plaintiffs,* through making it more difficult to successfully prosecute high-profile defendants (here again, the O. J. Simpson case has been said by some to be a case in point).

In general terms, it would seem that the Supreme Court sees its role as preserving the freedom of the press wherever possible, so that the onus lies on judges to find ways of protecting the rights of defendants without placing blanket restrictions on reporting. However, journalists have tended to argue that the press has the more difficult task of defending freedom of speech against the institutional power of the courts.

B. Restrictions on the Press in Britain

The desirability of open justice is an important principle of long standing in British law. Eighteenth-century jurist Jeremy Bentham argued that it was important for the courts to be open in order to ensure that judges behaved properly and fairly in their public duties:

> Publicity is the very soul of justice. It is the keenest spur to exertion and the surest of all guards against improbity. It keeps the judge himself, while trying, under trial.

According to Robertson and Nicol, society derives a number of other important benefits from having an open system of justice:

> The prospect of publicity deters perjury: witnesses are more likely to tell the truth if they know that any lie they tell might be reported, and provoke others to come forward to discredit them. Press reporting of court cases enhances public knowledge and appreciation of the working of the law, and it assists the deterrent effect of heavy sentences in criminal cases. Above all, fidelity to the open-justice principle keeps Britain free from the reproach that it permits 'secret courts' of the kind that have been instruments of repression in so many other countries (Robertson, G., & Nicol, A. (1992) *Media Law* (3rd ed.), p. 15. Hammondsworth: Penguin.).

This common-law principle is the British equivalent of America's First Amendment, although freedom of the press to report courtroom proceedings is significantly curtailed by a number of statutory and common law exceptions. To give some examples: *in America,* it is left to the discretion of the court whether to make orders preventing the press disclosing information about the identity of the alleged victims in rape trials, or of juvenile defendants, and the court has discretion to allow the media to televise courtroom hearings. *In Britain,* the Criminal Justice Acts of 1987 and 1991 govern the position on reporting juveniles (although one aim of the 1996 Criminal Justice Act, which is gradually coming into force, is to remove this protection from convicted 16- to 18-year-olds, with the aim of adding "public shaming" to the punishment they receive from the courts). The Sexual Offences (Amendment) Act 1976 responded to a decade of campaigning for a change in the law, by making it an offense to identify the complainant in rape cases. Section 41 of the Criminal Justice Act 1925, which makes it an offense to photograph or make sketches in court, effectively prevents televising court proceedings.

However, the most far-reaching restriction operating on journalists in Britain, at least in principle, is the law of contempt, which is now governed by the 1981 Contempt Act. This gives judges or the attorney general the power to impose an unlimited fine or to imprison journalists for up to 2 years for influencing the result of a court or tribunal.

It is worth noting though that when British courts have had to decide whether actions by the media amount to contempt, they have tried, wherever possible, to maintain the open-court principle, by finding that, although stories in the press may be prejudicial, they still need not affect the outcome of trials. The judge in the Jeremy Thorpe murder case dealt with the problem of two prejudicial books by asking prospective jurors to stand down if they had read either of the books.

But perhaps the best example of the reluctance of British appeal court judges to support the widespread use of contempt orders can be found in their views about the susceptibility of jurors to media influence. In the trial of two well-known London gangsters, the Krays, the judge observed that "I have enough confidence in my fellow countrymen to think that they have got the newspapers sized up and they are capable of looking at the matter fairly and without prejudice even though they may have to disregard what they read in a newspaper" (see p. 342 of Robertson and Nicol, 1992). In another case, the Court of Appeal noted that juries tend to forget reporting that took place a long time before the trial. This was because "an inward-looking atmosphere built up during the trial and the jury and judge tended less and less as the trial proceeded to look outwards and more and more to look inwards at the evidence and arguments being addressed to them" (*Gee vs. BBC* (1986), 136 NLJ515, CA).

Robertson and Nicol argue that, notwithstanding this judicial reluctance to restrict the press, journalists and editors in Britain take the threat of being held in contempt seriously, to the extent of being unduly cautious in reporting news relating to the courts, in a way that would astonish journalists in America. There has, however, been a flurry of recent cases that have considerably raised the temperature of debate in Britain.

Perhaps the most-influential of these cases was that of the Taylor sisters in 1994, in which their conviction for murdering Alison Shaughnessy, the wife of Michelle Taylor's former lover, was quashed by the Court of Appeal on the grounds that the outcome of the trial had been affected by reporting in a number of tabloid newspapers. One front-page article in *The Sun* showed a still photograph taken from a video of Alison Shaughnessy's wedding that appeared to show Michelle Taylor kissing the groom full on the mouth (whereas the video viewed as a whole shows that it was an innocent "peck on the cheek"). This was published under the title "Cheats' Kiss." The Taylors spent 11 months in prison, and in 1995 made an (ultimately unsuccessful) attempt in the High Court to force the attorney general to make a contempt order against the offending newspapers.

Since then judges have become more outspoken in criticizing the press. When there was extensive newspaper coverage of the previous convictions of Geoff Knight (the boyfriend of the soap opera actress Gillian Taylforth), the judge abandoned the trial, complaining that "I have absolutely no doubt that the mass of media publicity in the case was unfair, outrageous and oppressive." In a very recent case, the trial of six prisoners charged with breaking out of Whitemoor prison was abandoned in January 1997 as a result of the press publishing details of the involvement of five defendants in the IRA and the previous convictions of the sixth. The judge ordered the newspaper editor concerned to report in person to the court, along with the prison officials who provided the story, in order to explain why they should not be held in contempt. (Ironically, the barrister representing these defendants has suggested that the collapse of the case may represent a cover-up that prevents the public from hearing about an allegation that prison officers colluded in the escape.)

III. REPORTING COURTROOM PROCEEDINGS: AN ETHICAL PERSPECTIVE

As should be evident from the case studies considered above, it is extremely difficult to envisage the creation and enforcement of a general purpose ethical perspective on issues around the reporting of courtroom proceedings, a perspective that would be genuinely *cross-cultural* (for even between Britain and America there are deep differences as to what counts as a matter for ethical concern in this regard), and that would be able to cope with the different and specific issues raised by the *variety* of cases that any such perspective would have to handle.

Any attempt to apply, say, Utilitarian—or even Kantian—considerations to a case in which an issue has arisen as to whether reporting of a trial should be restricted by either self- or other-imposed censorship must take fully into account how the *weighting* is to be undertaken of the public right to know, the check on dishonesty in the court, the rights of the defendant and of the plaintiff to privacy, and to a fair trial, and so on. Such weighting will need to be undertaken in the light of the concrete sociopolitical context of the court and of the question that is being tried in it. It may well be, then, that the complex perspectives of the various institutional forces involved (i.e., the judge, the journalists, the parties to the case, etc.) are more evidently well-founded and grounded in reasonable precedent, than are any theoretical ethical perspectives that can be brought to bear on the issues from outside of them.

However, there may be ethical issues relating to the reporting of courtroom proceedings that are not *recognized* as significant or important by the courts or media in America or Britain, and it is possibly in *this* regard that an applied ethics perspective can be most useful, in at least helping getting these recognized *as* issues, *if* politicians or movements are not already effectively doing so. Two potential examples are:

A. Reporting Rape Trials

There is a law protecting the identity of complainants in Britain, although this is still largely a matter for the discretion of judges and the press in America. However, some—for example feminist critics of the legal system—might want to argue there are wider ethical issues, which are not recognised in debates about courtroom reporting. Soothill and Soothill (1983, Prosecuting the victim: A study of the reporting of barristers' comments in rape cases. *The Howard Journal*, 32, pp. 12–24) suggest that the media tend to portray rapists as "deviants," whereas in fact rape is a "far-reaching social problem" that affects women much more ubiquitously than the special circumstances of a rape trial might suggest. This is a much broader political critique of the role of the media, which is neglected by writers on the fair trial/ free press debate. Thus, a group who might have a reasonable complaint about the media in relation to rape trials (and arguably more generally: see Lorraine Dusky (1997), *Still Unequal: The shameful truth about women and justice in America.* New York: Crown Press), are women plaintiffs. They are often exposed in the courtroom to allegations of sexual impropriety, and so on; and the harm this may cause is argued by feminist legal theorists to be massively magnified by currently operative reporting methods and newspapers' assumptions about women.

However, another group who might have just cause to feel aggrieved are the defendants. Someone accused of a crime may suffer all kinds of damage to livelihood and reputation, even if the trial ends in an acquittal and there is no bias or prejudice in the reporting. It might also be argued that the anonymity given complainants to varying degrees in rape trials, which is intended to make it easier for victims to come forward, may also make it easier to make ill-founded allegations.

B. The Myra Hindley Case

Hindley, one of "the Moors Murderers," was convicted of enticing and murdering young children in Northern England in the 1960s, and was sentenced to life imprisonment. Despite strong evidence of her having undergone a personal transformation, of having been successfully "reformed," successive British Home Secretaries have turned down her appeal for parole, partly on the grounds of public opinion. It could be argued that the media have been partially responsible by reprinting extracts from the trial, including photographs of her and her accomplice Brady taken at the time of the murders. This is perfectly legal, but supporters of Hindley and critics of the judicial system might argue that nevertheless the press are acting unethically.

IV. ETHICAL ARGUMENT AND JOURNALISTIC PRACTICE

Academics in the field of applied ethics tend to present philosophy as a means of attaining a clearer—or more rational—understanding of difficult moral dilemmas than is available to the ordinary citizen, without a philosophical training. Here are two typical statements, from a textbook on philosophy of law, and an introduction to media ethics respectively:

> Legal philosophy provides clarity, intellectual order and structure and standards of rational (often moral) criticism and evaluation. It thus gives insight into the relevant questions to ask when laws are being discussed, or legal reforms are proposed, and it can help to introduce reason into areas where passion often dominates (Murphy, J., & Coleman, J. (1990) *Philosophy of Law: An Introduction to Jurisprudence.* Boulder, CO: Westview Press).

> Too often . . . students and practitioners argue about individual sensational incidents, make case-by-case decisions, and do not stop to examine their method of moral reasoning. Instead, a pattern of ethical deliberation should be explicitly outlined in which the relevant considerations are isolated and given appropriate weight. Those who care about ethics in the media can learn to analyze the stages of decision making, focus on the real levels of conflict, and make defensible ethical decisions (Christian, C., Rotzoll, K., & Fackler, M. (1991). *Media Ethics: Cases and Moral Reasoning* (3rd ed.). New York: Longman).

In media ethics textbooks, students are usually asked to consider real or invented case studies in which there is no clear answer on dilemmas which arise in the course of day-to-day practice, and are not governed by a professional code of conduct or by law. Christian *et al.,* for example, use the example of a fire in a gay cinema, in which two local newspapers took a different view on whether they should print the names of people killed in the fire. Other examples might include the question of when it is ethical for a journalist to lie in order to obtain information that might benefit the public.

The study and discussion of ethics has only recently been taken up by bodies responsible for training journalists, and one can view this sociologically as part of a wider trend toward professionalisation in America and Britain. As Max Weber and others have noted, codes of ethics function as "gatekeepers," and are one means by which occupational groups seek to enhance their status and economic position in society; while, as many studies have shown, practitioners on the ground frequently fail to live up to the ideals envisaged by their professional associations.

In the case of the legal profession, Carlin showed that firms at the bottom end of the profession could not afford to be ethical (and indeed regarded "ethics" as a means used by firms at the top to prevent competition, by enforcing impossibly high standards). Ethical breaches which formed a routine part of practicing law in these firms for business and doing disreputable things for clients. Travers in his study of a firm of criminal lawyers representing legal aid clients, found that rules such as avoiding conflicts of interest were simply not feasible for this type of practice, in which prosecution witnesses were regularly ex-clients, and that breaches were ignored by the local courts.

The gap between professional ideals and actual practice is arguably similar in journalism; the British quality press often criticizes the tabloids for damaging the reputation of journalism as a profession. It seems unlikely that ethical reasoning (in the sense of weighing up the moral pros and cons of alternative actions) plays much part in journalistic practice when the latter is dictated by the need to "scoop" rivals in a vicious circulation war; although the necessary empirical studies of news gathering, and editorial decision-making have not yet been undertaken by British or American sociologists.

What one might predict such studies might well find, if they focused on the way in which the media report courtroom proceedings, is that editors and journalists routinely do not view this as an ethical issue, and certainly rarely if ever as one requiring the services of a philosopher, in that they see no ethical or moral problem in their task of reporting news, and in so doing making money for their proprietor. One would also imagine that they regard the law not as the embodiment of ethics, but as an obstacle they have to work with, in order to avoid being held in contempt by the courts. On this view, which is admittedly cynical about the role of ethics in the professions, teaching journalists skills of moral reasoning, while it might be worthwhile educationally, should not be expected to produce any great transformation in journalistic practice. And it may require sustained political will, including a wide-ranging critique of the organization of the media in contemporary "open"

Western cultures—rather than (or—at least—as well as) intelligent applied ethics discourse—to successfully alter or "ethicalize" any aspects of legal journalism that are considered to be problematic or, more plainly put, wrong.

Bibliography

Bunker, M. (1997). *Justice and the media: reconciling fair trials with a free press.* Mahwah, NJ: Lawrence Erlbaum Associates.

Carlin, J. (1976). *Lawyer's ethics: A survey of the New York bar.* New York: Russell Sage Foundation.

Fish, S. (1994). *There's no such thing as free speech ... and it's a good thing too.* New York: Oxford University Press.

Mill, J. S. (1869/1991). *On Liberty and Other Essays.* Oxford: Oxford University Press.

The Guardian (1997, January 24, p. 7). Editor faces judge as IRA jail break trial collapses.

The Guardian (1995, July 31, p. 6). Judgement day: Unprecedented high court action after two year's imprisonment.

Travers, M. (1991). *The reality of law: An ethnographic study of an inner-city law firm.* Doctoral dissertation, University of Manchester.

Discrimination, Concept of

DAVID WASSERMAN
University of Maryland

I. Introduction
II. Intentional Discrimination as an Individual Moral Offense
III. Discriminatory Institutions and Stigmatized Groups: Racial Discrimination as a Paradigm
IV. Individual Responsibility and Discriminatory Institutions
V. Discrimination and Difference
VI. Conclusion

GLOSSARY

affirmative action The general name for a variety of policies that target people of a particular race, ethnicity, or gender for a range of benefits, from aggressive recruitment to preference in hiring, in order to reduce discrimination toward members of a group or to alleviate the adverse effects of that discrimination.

disparate impact Significant differences in the effect of a given practice or policy on different racial, ethnic, or other groups (for example, on the proportion of applicants from those groups who are hired), differences that are typically to the disadvantage of a group or groups that have been subject to discrimination.

facially neutral practices Practices governing hiring, admission, promotion, or termination that do not make explicit reference to the race, ethnicity, gender, or other group affiliations of those affected by them.

race-conscious remedies As used in this article, a synonym for affirmative action policies.

racial, ethnic, and gender preferences Policies that con-

fer an advantage in hiring, admission, promotion, or similar decisions on the basis of race, ethnicity, or gender, an advantage that may range from treating membership in a particular group as a slight "plus" factor to applying different minimum standards to people of different groups.

DISCRIMINATION was once a neutral term, referring to the capacity to make distinctions; its valence depended on the appropriateness of the distinctions made. A person was praised for his discrimination in judging character, horses, or wines; he was condemned for making distinctions without any moral or aesthetic difference. In recent decades, however, "discrimination" has become identified with a specific way of distinguishing among people, and its negative valence has become dominant. A person is said to discriminate if she disadvantages others on the basis of their race, ethnicity, or other group membership. The older, neutral sense of the term survives in some grammatical forms; a person may still be praised for *being* discriminating, and for discrimination in making a particular kind of judgment. But she is condemned for discriminating, or for discriminatory acts and practices. To claim that someone discriminates is to subject her to reproach or challenge her for justification; to call discrimination "wrongful" is merely to add emphasis to a morally laden term.

Some claim that there has been a further shift in the meaning of "discrimination." At the dawn of the civil rights era, they argue, discrimination was a simple concept; now it has become complex. It used to be that a person discriminated only if he deliberately excluded certain people from his factory or school because of their race or other similarly irrelevant characteristics; now, he is said to discriminate if he fails to encourage people from underrepresented groups to apply, if he employs a standardized aptitude test on which members of those groups get disproportionately low scores, or if he fails to modify his entrances, workspaces, job descriptions, training programs, or curricula so that applicants from those groups may more readily compete for scarce openings.

To some, this shift in the meaning of discrimination is disturbing, if not insidious: a bait-and-switch that smuggles in a controversial agenda of redress and reform under a broadly accepted ban on intentional discrimination. To others, the shift in understanding is necessary, reflecting an awareness of how deeply intentional discrimination by individuals has distorted our social practices and institutions, and how, as a result, the harmful effects of intentional discrimination can be perpetuated by actions that do not themselves express hatred or contempt.

I. INTRODUCTION

This article will trace the conflict over the meaning of discrimination through current debates about disparate impact and affirmative action. It will begin by examining the complexities in the supposedly simple concept of intentional discrimination. That concept encompasses a number of overlapping but distinct features, which differ in moral significance: (1) failing to treat people as individuals; (2) failing to judge them on their own merits; (3) taking account of their group membership in ways that disadvantage them; and (4) treating them as moral inferiors by virtue of their group membership. Over the past generation, moral and legal analyses of discrimination have tended to regard the last—the hatred and devaluation of a group—as the core evil in discrimination, to be understood in the context of social practices and institutions that stigmatize and systematically disadvantage the disfavored group.

This emphasis on the social context of individual discrimination has led to two conclusions that are troubling or unacceptable to many people who regard themselves as strongly opposed to discrimination. First, because social practices and institutions come to function independently of the individual attitudes and conduct that originally shaped them, the harmful consequences of intentional discrimination by individuals may be perpetuated by less objectionable acts and practices, including many that are neutral and reasonable on their face. Second, and relatedly, it will sometimes be necessary to adopt policies with the first three features of intentional discrimination in order to eliminate the fourth—the

hatred and devaluation of a person because of her group membership. As Justice Blackmun declared in the *Bakke* case, "in order to get beyond racism, we must first take account of race."

The legal regulation of acts and policies with inadvertently disparate impact, and the imposition of "group-conscious" remedies for discrimination, have a common premise: that although discrimination may begin in the hearts of individuals, it does not end there, but is embedded in institutions and social practices. Those institutions and social practices reinforce individual prejudice, ensuring that it will proliferate in a variety of covert and subconscious forms even when it has been publicly renounced. More important, perhaps, they maintain the effects of past prejudice through actions and policies that are not themselves motivated by prejudice. The administrative and judicial responses to discrimination that fall under the rubric of "affirmative action" are designed (albeit not always very well) to modify the institutions and practices that perpetuate the exclusion and disadvantage of stigmatized groups.

As important as it is to recognize the social context and institutional embeddedness of individual discrimination, however, it is also important to maintain the moral distinction between conduct that displays contempt for a group of people and conduct that inadvertently maintains the adverse impact of such contempt. This distinction is obscured when the term "discrimination" is used to cover the latter as well as the former. Unfortunately, that is just what the law does when it treats facially neutral practices with adverse impact on Blacks and women as presumptively discriminatory. And yet the judicial extension of the concept of discrimination has certainly helped to counter the effects of generations of deliberate discrimination. The fact that this practical success has been gained at the cost of so much public confusion and resentment suggests the difficulties of separating the parallel discourses of a moralized law, for which "discrimination" is an evolving term of art, and a legalistic morality, for which "discrimination" has, happily, become a term of opprobrium.

The emerging understanding of the role of institutions in mediating individual discrimination and group disadvantage is particularly controversial as applied to women and people with disabilities, groups defined, unlike racial and ethnic groups, partly in terms of physical characteristics thought to have some effect on major life activities. While there is a broad consensus that women and people with disabilities have often been treated as unworthy of equal concern and respect, there is considerable disagreement about whether it is appropriate to treat them as subordinated "minority" groups. There is also considerable disagreement about whether individual prejudice and its institutional manifestations adequately account for the unfair disadvantage they suffer.

Some writers have located the source of that disadvantage in the norms by which the defining attributes of women and people with disabilities are classified as abnormal, and in the physical structures and social practices that limit their participation. They argue that these norms, structures, and practices embody an unjustifiable bias in favor of the dominant group—men or the "able-bodied." But those who regard this pervasive structural bias as the central problem for women and people with disabilities disagree about whether the concept of discrimination can be enlarged to accommodate it.

II. INTENTIONAL DISCRIMINATION AS AN INDIVIDUAL MORAL OFFENSE

The classic bigot, who refuses to hire, serve, or sell to "those people," might be condemned on several grounds: he fails to judge "those people" by their merit or qualification for the good, service, or activity he withholds; he fails to treat them as individuals; he takes their race, ethnicity, or other group membership into account in denying them that good, service, or activity; and he treats them as moral inferiors because of their group membership.

The first two characterizations are of limited use in identifying the core moral offense. Merit and qualification surely play a role in our understanding of discrimination: we generally do not regard it as discrimination to deny a benefit to someone because he is unqualified for it. Yet "merit" and "qualification" are notoriously vague, elastic terms: many qualities are desirable to an employer or a school, and there are many ways of assessing those qualities, so "merit" and "qualification" often fail to provide clear benchmarks against which to measure discrimination.

Similarly, the second characteristic—the failure to treat the disadvantaged person as an individual—is not adequate to explain the moral offense. Discrimination does seem to require some kind of adverse generalization: an employer who refused to hire someone because of a specific aversion to him, rather than a general aversion to "people like him," might act irrationally, but she would not, in common parlance, discriminate. Adverse generalization, however, is hardly a sufficient condition for discrimination. An employer who required a minimum grade level or standardized test score for a given job because of its rough correlation with job performance would ordinarily not be said to discriminate against an applicant who lacked that minimum, even if on closer inspection, the applicant would prove to be highly qualified. Although he has failed to treat her as an individual or, arguably, to judge her by her merit, he would be said to discriminate only, and quite controversially, if grade levels or test scores were also correlated with race, ethnicity, or gender.

The third characteristic associated with discrimination—taking account of a person's race, ethnicity, or other group membership in denying a good or service—appears to specify the kind of generalization involved in discrimination. But it raises the obvious and controversial questions of what groups besides racial and ethnic ones can be discriminated against, and of why adverse generalizations involving those groups are particularly objectionable. Some courts and legal scholars have seized on immutability as the critical feature of the attributes that can be subject to discrimination. However annoying or offensive it is to be disadvantaged because of one's "membership" in an accidental or transient group (for example, to be frisked because one happens to be on a crowded subway car just after a gun is fired), this hardly counts as discrimination. On the other hand, certain mutable attributes such as religious affiliation have often been the basis of invidious discrimination.

If not the immutability of membership, what distinguishes the groups that can be subject to discrimination? Two features seem pertinent. First, however vague their boundaries may be, these groups generally have deep social significance: their members are perceived and treated differently in a variety of important respects by the larger society. Second, and relatedly, membership in the group is generally important to the members' self-identity.

But while these features help identify the groups that can be subject to discrimination, they leave open the question of why it is especially objectionable to take account of membership in such groups in denying a benefit or imposing a burden. When we look only at the effects on individual group members, the harm of taking group membership into account is highly contingent. If members of certain groups have been subject to worse treatment in a wide array of circumstances, it adds to the imbalance to disadvantage them on the basis of group membership. That effect will be amplified if members of those groups have a heightened concern about the treatment of other members, or about the fact that the adverse treatment they suffer is based on their membership. But these considerations appear to make the moral appraisal of discrimination depend too heavily on the existing balance of advantage among groups and the varying sensitivities of group members.

A distinct concern is the social cost of taking account of race, ethnicity, and other socially significant groupings in imposing substantial burdens. Precisely because those groupings have been a source of so much injustice and hostility, disadvantaging people on that basis contributes to destructive and often lethal social discord. But groups can be subject to discrimination even if they lack broad social recognition, and even if their mistreatment does not create or exacerbate social discord.

A final concern about taking account of group membership rests on a belief that the tendency to categorize people into "basic kinds" is a deep, recalcitrant, and damaging one. People tend to impose rigid classification schemes on human variation, and they tend to endow the resulting classes with greatly exaggerated diagnostic and predictive value. The use of such categories reflects a deeply ingrained essentialism, which licenses a vast range of generalizations from group membership to important physical, psychological, intellectual, and moral attributes. While they are rarely distinguished, these three concerns—cumulative harm to individuals, social disharmony, and group essentialism—may all contribute to the moral onus of taking group membership into account in imposing burdens or denying benefits.

The fourth characteristic associated with discrimination—the treatment of a person as a moral inferior by virtue of his group membership—can be seen as an aspect of group essentialism. Just as people tend to judge individuals in terms of their "kind," they tend to see kinds as constituting a hierarchy, in which some are superior to others. Such hierarchies are most explicitly developed in caste systems, but they may be present in virtually all social classification schemes. The classic bigot is not just taking account of group membership in refusing to hire, serve, or sell to "those people"; he is treating those people as members of a morally inferior group. While it may be wrong to treat a person as a moral inferior for reasons other than his group membership, it is not discriminatory. And while it may be discriminatory to take account of a person's group membership without treating him as a moral inferior, such conduct arguably lacks the moral onus of classic bigotry.

Much of the contemporary debate over the meaning of discrimination concerns the comparative importance of the third and fourth features—taking account of group membership in denying a benefit and treating people as moral inferiors by virtue of that membership. The debate centers on the evaluation of actions and policies that display the third but not the fourth feature: that disadvantage people on the basis of their group membership without treating them as moral inferiors. Some writers regard the third feature as the core evil of discrimination, the fourth merely as an aggravating factor; others regard the third without the fourth as injury without insult—a far lesser, more venial form of discrimination.

These conflicts typically surface in two settings: (1) the appraisal of racial preferences and other race-conscious policies that disadvantage some members of the dominant race in order to improve the social prospects of other races seen as oppressed or subordinated, and (2) the appraisal of actions by members of those races that harm or disadvantage members of the dominant race on the basis of race. I will focus on the first setting later in the article. The second setting is important because it suggests the difficulty of judging whether certain actions that disadvantage people on the basis of group membership do in fact treat them as moral inferiors, and because it suggests the importance of social context in making that judgment.

A Black manager who shows a strong preference for Black applicants out of loyalty to "his kind," or from a commitment to reducing the underrepresentation of Blacks in his field, does not thereby treat Whites as moral inferiors, even if he displays an inappropriate or excessive partiality. The character of his policy is less clear-cut if he declines to hire White people on the basis of a group generalization, for example, because he assumes that all or most White people are prejudiced, or because he believes that White employees will enjoy unfair advantages over Black employees once they are in the workforce. While the first generalization is more unfair, and arguably less accurate, than the second, neither displays the kind of contempt and denigration shown by the White manager who refuses to hire Blacks because he believes that most of them are lazy or stupid. To be thought incompetent on the basis of one's race is at least marginally more demeaning than to be stereotyped as prejudiced or overprivileged. Although it is certainly possible for members of a minority group to treat members of the dominant group as moral inferiors, many of the actions by minority group members that are commonly denounced as reverse discrimination may be more aptly characterized as defensive overgeneralization.

Social context affects not only the "message" conveyed by actions that disadvantage people on the basis of their group membership, but also the moral appraisal of actions that clearly do treat the members of a group as moral inferiors. What makes the conduct of the classic bigot particularly reprehensible is that he is actively affirming an oppressive social system. The people that he despises are worse off in significant ways because a range of institutions mirrors his judgment of their inferior worth.

The social context of discrimination is also relevant to the moral appraisal of actions and practices that are *not* discriminatory in either the third or fourth sense above, for example, an employer's good-faith use of a standardized test that is moderately predictive of job performance but has a severely disparate impact on minority applicants. Such actions and practices disadvantage members of subordinated groups without necessarily taking their group membership into account or treating them as moral inferiors. To understand the controversies that have arisen over the moral and legal status of such actions and practices, we need to look more closely at the relationship between individual discrimination and group disadvantage.

III. DISCRIMINATORY INSTITUTIONS AND STIGMATIZED GROUPS: RACIAL DISCRIMINATION AS A PARADIGM

Most contemporary societies have grossly unjust disparities in well-being, however defined, that are highly correlated with membership in ascriptive groups. The worst-off groups are very often those that have been, and continue to be, the most widely despised and the most fully excluded from the political processes by which social benefits are assigned. In the United States, the most despised and excluded group has long been people of African descent. A number of U.S. commentators have seen discrimination in terms of the social and institutional structures that oppress African Americans. They describe a "system of racial oppression" (Wasserstrom); a "caste system" (Fiss); "the social construction of a stigmatized class" (Koppelman). Koppelman, who has developed perhaps the most comprehensive account, identifies three features of group subordination in a discriminatory system: (1) members of the group are systematically excluded from the processes by which political decisions are made and resources allocated; (2) members of the group are devalued and stigmatized; and (3) members of the group are disadvantaged on almost any index of well-being. The first is a matter of familiar constitutional and legal history, from the "social death" of slavery to the poll tax and at-large representation; the second is illustrated by Dr. Kenneth Clark's influential findings, cited in *Brown v. Board of Education*, on the lasting injuries to the self-esteem of Black children caused by segregation; the third is suggested by the extent to which we can predict the future lives of infants in the maternity ward simply by their skin color.

In late twentieth-century America, the claim that an action or policy discriminates against a group of people typically involves an explicit or implicit comparison to race or ethnicity; it suggests that the members of that group are, or may be, treated like a disfavored racial or ethnic minority. Thus, those who oppose genetic testing by insurers argue that the widespread use of such tests will help create a "biological underclass," a group that is likely to be treated, in the shadow of eugenics, much like other groups that have been regarded as genetically or biologically inferior, from African Ameri-

cans and Southern European immigrants to people with intellectual and physical disabilities. Opponents of genetic testing recognize obvious differences in membership criteria and membership between the groups targeted by eugenicists and the "group" that is likely to be disadvantaged by genetic testing, mainly people with hidden disabilities and late-onset diseases (and their relatives). Their point is that the latter may, despite these differences, come to be perceived and treated like the former.

We should not expect to find the same constellation of attitudes and social structures in the case of all stigmatized groups in all societies. Widespread hatred and contempt often coexist with economic advantage or privilege, as they have to some extent for overseas Chinese and Indians, medieval Jews, and contemporary Ibos and Tutsis. But although the "places" to which despised minority groups are consigned by the larger society have widely varying economic, social, and political characteristics, it is always a position the larger society holds in contempt.

There is a complex interdependence between a discriminatory system and discrimination by individuals. Such a system could hardly arise without individual prejudice; a regime that did not express hatred or contempt toward disadvantaged groups might be unfair, but it would arguably not be discriminatory. And while individual prejudice could certainly exist outside a discriminatory system, it would be both idiosyncratic and ephemeral. Individuals do not regard groups as morally inferior on a random basis, or feel undifferentiated hostility toward groups other than their own. Rather, their contempt for and devaluation of the members of a group is informed by a social and institutional structure that consigns the group to a particular "place" and endows its members with particular attributes.

That social and intellectual structure also reinforces conscious prejudice by social validation, and it perpetuates both conscious and unconscious prejudice in a variety of less direct ways:

(1). By maintaining social conditions that appear to support prevailing beliefs about the indolence, criminality, promiscuity, and so on, of the subordinated group. In the contemporary United States, racial stereotypes are fed by the concentration of poor Blacks and Hispanics in highly segregated, physically decaying urban areas with chronically high unemployment.

(2). By encouraging those outside the subordinated group to ease the discomfort they feel about its status and treatment by convincing themselves that its members deserve no better.

(3). By giving negative claims about the subordinated

group an exaggerated or spurious credibility, by encouraging a very low standard of proof for accepting such claims, and by encouraging their overgeneralization.

(4). By developing an "independent" aversion to qualities or traits associated (but not exclusively) with the subordinated group (e.g., I don't dislike him because he's Jewish, but because he's so calculating) where the source of the aversion is really a dislike for the group, which the aversion serves to rationalize.

We can gauge the extent to which prejudice pervades the attitudes and practices of people who would publicly reject it through experiments, such as those done by HUD and the Urban Institute, that track carefully matched Black/White pairs of housing, loan, or job applicants. Despite being equal on every arguably relevant dimension, Black applicants fare significantly worse. While some small fraction of the real estate agents, loan officers, and employers who reject Black applicants do regard their race as a disqualification or negative factor, it is likely that most do not. They see themselves as evaluating all applicants equally, but their deeply ingrained prejudice operates like a hidden thumb on the scales: they give different weight to the same attributes presented by Black and White applicants, give negative weight to irrelevant attributes found more frequently in Black applicants, or give greater credence to the claims made in support of White applicants.

There has been more sophistication in the detection of these sorts of bias than in their moral appraisal. The persistence of bias in reflex actions and judgments has often been seen as aggravating the offense, as if the biased individual compounded his prejudice with subterfuge or deception. The tendency to condemn unconscious bias as harshly as conscious bias may reflect not only rhetorical excess but also a misleading picture of repression as deliberate concealment—the recalcitrant bigot protecting his prejudices by concealing them—or of the biased subconscious as a homunculus in a white hood, a malevolent intelligence waging a covert campaign of racial oppression.

Although unconscious bias is less reprehensible than conscious bias, it may also be more recalcitrant. Unconscious prejudices are unlikely to give themselves up to sustained inquisition or introspection. On an individual level, they are less easily purged than counteracted (for example, by a deliberate effort to review minority applications in the most favorable light). On a collective level, they may be more effectively remedied by long-term changes in social structure than by exhortations to cease discriminating.

Other harmful effects of a discriminatory system are perpetuated by acts and policies that do not themselves express conscious *or* unconscious prejudice. It is characteristic of such a system to make the perpetuation of group disadvantage the path of least resistance. One obvious way it does so is through the need to accommodate the prejudices of other people. Undoubtedly, many Southern restaurant and hotel owners did not want Blacks in their establishments. But many, perhaps more, barred them largely because they feared the loss of business from White customers. In declining to make such "business necessity" a defense, the 1964 Civil Rights Act prohibited a form of conduct that could not be regarded as intentional discrimination in the fourth sense above—that is, discrimination motivated by racial animus. It also helped to eliminate the "necessity" for such conduct, because all public accommodations fell under the same ban.

The 1964 Civil Rights Act was understood to prohibit another form of exclusion that was not always motivated by racial animus: the use of race in most circumstances as a marker or proxy for other characteristics that *were* a legitimate basis for exclusion. If a restaurant owner could not exclude Blacks because his White customers disliked them, he also could not exclude them because they were more likely to steal from him—even if his statistics were correct, even if he would welcome particular Blacks whom he knew posed no such risk, and even though he could exclude members of other groups, like a particular family, on that basis. The unrestricted use of such generalizations would impose far too great a burden on the innocent, law-abiding members of the stigmatized group. The ban on statistical or proxy discrimination has proven to be far more complicated than the ban on actions that merely accommodate the prejudice of others. But it too reflects an early recognition that in order to dismantle a discriminatory system, the law could not limit its proscription to intentional discrimination based on racial animus.

An even more difficult set of issues is presented by allocative actions and policies that are neutral in appearance and design, but that have the effect of perpetuating the harmful effects of deliberate exclusion. The company that now bases promotion on a seniority that only Whites have been able to acquire because of its prior exclusion of Blacks is perpetuating the effects of its own past discrimination, and it may make little moral difference if it does so intentionally or inadvertently. But a company's responsibility for the disparate impact of certain facially neutral practices is less clear if it has never practiced intentional discrimination (for example, if it has only recently gone into business). Many apparently neutral hiring practices, such as the requirement of a recommendation from a senior employee in a once-discriminatory industry, perpetuate the effects of a regime that excluded Blacks from the social networks in which such contacts are usually made. And even the requirement of a minimum score on a standardized test may perpetuate the adverse effects of an educational system, funded by local property taxes, that has long shortchanged Blacks.

There are obvious moral differences between facially neutral policies that perpetuate the effects of a company's own past discrimination and those that merely perpetuate the effects of industry- or society-wide discrimination. Despite these important differences, courts have largely ignored the distinction between these two kinds of cases in applying the 1964 Civil Rights Act. They have treated the use of facially neutral standards in both kinds of cases as prima facie discrimination and have permitted the continued use of such practices only as a business necessity.

The divergence between legal usage and common-sense moral judgment about what counts as discrimination has significant costs. On the one hand, employers with no history of intentional discrimination are indignant at being held liable for "discrimination" when their conscientious efforts to recruit or promote Blacks fall short of current judicial or administrative guidelines. On the other hand, civil-rights administrators and activists, frustrated by massive institutional inertia, tend to be impatient with pleas of innocent intentions. Ironically, it is the moral consensus forged around the passage of the 1964 Civil Rights Act that makes this conflict over the understanding of "discrimination" so highly charged.

IV. INDIVIDUAL RESPONSIBILITY AND DISCRIMINATORY INSTITUTIONS

As we have seen, the concept of discrimination that has evolved in the past generation, which emphasizes the role of social institutions in mediating individual prejudice and group disadvantage, has focused attention on two issues: (1) the extent that African Americans and other minorities continue to suffer from conscious and unconscious prejudice, and from disadvantages that can be attributed directly or indirectly to past prejudice; (2) the extent that individuals, organizations, and institutions can be expected to change to reduce existing prejudice and the effects of past prejudice. The two issues are closely related, because the fairness of antidiscrimination policies may depend on the magnitude and the recalcitrance of the problem they address. Much of the disagreement about affirmative action concerns the need for remedial policies: opponents tend to see discrimination as a thing of the past, or on its way out, while proponents see it as entrenched and pervasive. But even among those who accept the latter view, there is disagreement about which remedial measures are fair.

Thus, some critics of affirmative action acknowledge the pervasive effects of discrimination but insist that, except to compensate for one's own discrimination, it is not appropriate to take race into account in attempting to eliminate those effects: disadvantaging a White on the basis of race may be less maligning or harmful than disadvantaging a Black, but it is still wrong. Most defenders of racial preferences reject this charge of "reverse discrimination," arguing that there is a basic asymmetry between allocative decisions that disadvantage Blacks and those that disadvantage Whites on the basis of race. In a society where Blacks have always, and Whites have never, been a stigmatized group, policies that disadvantage the latter for the sake of the former may be unfair, placing a large burden on a small number of people, but they do not and perhaps could not express the view that Whites are moral inferiors, unworthy of equal concern and respect. The debate about affirmative action reflects conflicting views of the core evil of discrimination. Defenders regard the core evil as the treatment of people as moral inferiors, and thus regard race-conscious remedies that express no disrespect for the people they disadvantage as potentially acceptable; critics regard the core evil as the imposition of burdens on the basis of race, ethnicity, or other group membership, and thus regard race-conscious remedies as fundamentally immoral.

If there is a fierce debate about the morality of policies that take race into account to undo the effects of past discrimination, there is also a fierce debate about the morality of practices that perpetuate those effects without taking race into account. Some people condemn practices that perpetuate the harmful effects of racial oppression by oversight or self-interest, such as an exclusive reliance on old-boy networks for hiring, almost as harshly as intentional discrimination, especially because such oversight and self-interest often reflect latent bias: we give less weight to the interests of people we see as less worthy of concern and respect. Others see such blanket condemnation as excessive and counterproductive, provoking a fierce backlash precisely because most of the people against whom it is directed regard intentional discrimination as a great evil. Clearly, we need a more nuanced conception of individual responsibility for continuing social injustice, which recognizes the role of neutral acts and practices in perpetuating the effects of intentional discrimination without treating those acts and practices as the moral equivalent of intentional discrimination.

V. DISCRIMINATION AND DIFFERENCE

The effectiveness of discrimination claims in mobilizing public indignation and state intervention, and in exposing the harmful impact of facially neutral policies, has encouraged the application of the concept of discrimination beyond racial, ethnic, and religious groups to groups defined by categorically different criteria: elderly people, women, and people with disabilities. The debate over the applicability of the concept of discrimination to these groups has focused on their social recognition and internal cohesiveness, and the extent to which their members are really treated as moral inferiors by virtue of their group membership.

A. Elderly People

Age discrimination is an interesting case, because the group discriminated against is not a minority in quite the same sense that racial and ethnic groups are. While "the elderly" are almost always (sometimes by definition) a minority of the population at any given time, the vast majority of people will be elderly sooner or later. It might seem that extending the concept of discrimination to the elderly involves the "reification" of a life-stage through which almost all of us pass.

Conflict between specific cohorts, like "baby-boomers" and their parents, certainly contributes to the stigmatization of the age groups to which those cohorts currently belong. But contempt for specific age groups does not require such intergenerational conflict. Many societies have restricted full humanity to the middle range of the human life-span, treating both children and elderly people as intellectually, physically, and morally defective. The denigration of youth and old age has not been based solely on a recognition of the general developmental limitations of the young and the general effects of aging on the elderly. Often, a host of other unattractive moral qualities has been attributed to those age groups. This contempt toward, and devaluation of, children and the elderly has hardly been precluded by the fact that people in their middle years were once children and expect to be adults—people are quite capable of despising what they have been and will become.

B. Women and People with Disabilities

The claim that women and people with disabilities should be seen as "minority" groups subject to widespread discrimination in contemporary American society has been challenged from several directions: not only by those who oppose the "proliferation" of rights and victimized groups, but also by those who doubt that an antidiscrimination analysis can capture the entitle-ments and grievances of women and people with disabilities.

Some raise questions about the status of women and people with disabilities as stigmatized groups. Although few would deny that American men, and the institutions they dominate, have often had dismissive, condescending attitudes toward women, some find those attitudes fundamentally less malign and virulent than the attitudes of American Whites toward Blacks. And some question whether American men treat women as a distinct group, given the pervasive interconnectedness of their lives. Parallel questions arise about people with disabilities. Although people with certain types of disability, such as limited mental development, have long been regarded as moral inferiors, there is disagreement about whether similar attitudes prevail across the spectrum of physical and mental conditions classified as impairments, and about whether those attitudes are mitigated or exacerbated by the compassion and solicitude many disabilities elicit. The range of those conditions also raises questions about the extent to which people with disabilities are seen, or see themselves, as members of a single stigmatized group.

But even if women or people with disabilities are seen as stigmatized groups, the physical (and mental) differences that demarcate those groups raise difficulties in applying the concept of discrimination. Those differences are at once stigmata—markers for group membership—and attributes with functional significance, which appear relevant to a variety of allocative decisions. At the same time, much of the disadvantage experienced by women and people with disabilities arises from the way those functional differences are treated in the physical and social organization of society. For this reason, an analysis of the disadvantages suffered by women or people with disabilities would be incomplete if it treated the differences demarcating those groups *only* as stigmata, and if it considered only the direct and indirect effects of hatred and contempt toward those groups.

Thus, women, like Blacks, have often protested the disparate impact of facially neutral policies, such as tests of physical strength used by fire and police departments, which are only loosely tailored to the demands of the job. Although the courts have imposed the same standard of business necessity in evaluating tests with disparate impact on women that they have used in evaluating tests with disparate impact on Blacks, the underlying issue is different in one important respect: there is broad (but not universal) agreement that the adverse impact of standardized aptitude tests on Blacks can be attributed to the effects of past discrimination; there is no such agreement about the disparate impact of standardized strength tests on women. Although the average strength of women might well be greater in a more egalitarian society, few believe it would equal the average strength of men.

But this difference should not, or so it is argued, give aid and comfort to those who would exclude women from police and fire departments; it rather suggests that the norms used to evaluate prospective police and fire-fighters are inherently "gendered," biased in favor of the dominant group. The norm of the qualified fire-fighter is of a fire*man*; it places a gratuitous premium on the brute physical strength associated with men. Women who can satisfy that norm are the conspicuous exception, which is why we are so much more inclined to refer to "female firefighters" than to "male" firefighters—the "male" is understood. On this view, the employer's strength standards do not so much perpetuate the effects of past discrimination as embody a fundamentally sexist norm of what a firefighter should be. While the women assessed by that norm have undoubtedly faced conscious prejudice as well, to focus on the latter is to miss the real locus of injustice.

Writers influenced by this feminist approach to sex-ism have developed a similar analysis of disability. They argue that the physical structures in, and social organiza-tion of, most modern societies are designed to accommo-date only those who fall within an extremely narrow range of physical and mental variation. The formal neu-trality of such practices masks a structural bias against people with disabilities, much as the formal neutrality of seniority and standardized testing have masked the historical oppression of African Americans.

But other writers who share this general understand-ing of the structural disadvantage faced by people with disabilities doubt that the concept of discrimination, even in its extended form, can adequately accommodate it. Structural bias, they argue, is better seen as a matter of injustice—as a failure to give sufficient weight to the interests of people with disabilities in the physical and social organization of society. While animus toward peo-ple with disabilities may help to account for the origins or persistence of grossly unjust arrangements, we cannot ascertain what justice requires merely by eliminating that animus or its effects. What is needed in the case of disabilities is not merely an injunction against discrim-ination, or the recognition of access rights for people with particular impairments, but a broader theory of distributive justice that would specify how society as a whole should be organized to accommodate impair-ments. Others, however, doubt whether any account of distributive justice is up to that formidable task, given the difficulties such theories have had in judging distri-butions of resources among the "able-bodied." Still oth-ers suspect that the very idea of distributive justice for people with disabilities involves compensating them for "natural disadvantages," thereby treating their disad-vantages as personal rather than social and their needs as "special."

VI. CONCLUSION

Several unresolved issues lie behind contemporary debates about the concept of discrimination. The debate over the moral significance of imposing burdens on the basis of group membership suggests that we have a weak grasp of the relevance of group affiliation, ascribed or chosen, for assessing the treatment of individuals. The debate over the morality of practices with inadvertently disparate impact suggests that we need a far more nu-anced account of individual responsibility for main-taining harmful social conditions—not in terms of the actual contribution of specific acts to those conditions, which will often be slight or unknown, but in terms of the agent's degree of complicity with harmful institutions. Finally, the debate over the adequacy of the concept of discrimination for capturing the grievances of women and people with disabilities suggests a broader disagree-ment about the primacy of individual prejudice and par-tiality in understanding and evaluating harmful social conditions. The concept of discrimination is likely to remain a subject of contention as long as these issues are unresolved.

Bibliography

Alexander, L. (1992). What makes wrongful discrimination wrong? Biases, preferences, stereotypes, and proxies. *University of Penn-sylvania Law Review* **141**, 149–219.

Fiss, O. (1976). Groups and the equal protection clause. *Philosophy & Public Affairs* **5**, 107–177.

Fullinwider, R. (1986). Achieving equal opportunity. In R. K. Fullin-wider & C. Mills (Eds.), *The moral foundations of civil rights.* Lanham: Rowman & Littlefield.

Garcia, J. L. A. (1996). The heart of racism. *Journal of Social Philoso-phy* **27**, 5–45.

Koppelman, A. (1996). *Antidiscrimination law and social equality.* New Haven: Yale University Press.

Lawrence, C. R. (1987). The ego, the id, and equal protection: Reck-oning with unconscious racism. *Stanford Law Review* **38**, 317–389.

Lichtenberg, J. (1992). Racism in the head, racism in the world. *Report from the Institute for Philosophy and Public Policy* **12**, 3–5.

MacKinnon, C. A. (1986). Difference and dominance: On sex discrimi-nation. In R. K. Fullinwider & C. Mills (Eds.), *The moral founda-tions of civil rights.* Lanham: Rowman & Littlefield.

Wasserstrom, R. (1986). One way to understand and defend programs of affirmative action. In R. K. Fullinwider & C. Mills (Eds.), *The moral foundations of civil rights.* Landham: Rowman & Little-field.

Wendell, S. (1989). Towards a feminist theory of disability. *Hypatia* **4**, 104–124.

Distributive Justice, Theories of

SIRKKU HELLSTEN

University of Helsinki

GLOSSARY

atomism The view that things are composed of elementary basic parts. In modern moral and political philosophy, the atomist view is seen to mean that social institutions and political communities are just collections of egoistic and isolated individuals promoting their own benefit and advantage.

collectivism The principle that what applies to a group collectively applies to it as a whole only. Also used as another name for political holism. Usually contrasted with individualism.

deontology The ethical theory that takes duty as the basis of morality, that is, as a view that sees that some acts are morally obligatory regardless of their consequences.

empirical Based on experiment or sense-experience. Empirical knowledge is, for instance, knowledge that we get through experience of the world, and it is not innate.

holism The view that social institutions and certain sorts of events and processes are more than merely the sum of their parts, and thus they can be understood only by examining them as a whole. We cannot, for example, understand the concept of justice by examining what is going on the basis of individual people's actions and intentions, because these can gain significance only by virtue of facts about the whole society.

laissez-faire A doctrine that government should have no control at all over economic matters, therefore, it promotes an economic policy of free competition.

metaphysics A study of the ultimate components of reality, the types of things that exist.

methodological individualism Individualism is a form of atomistic social explanation and is often contrasted with holism. It asserts that the social whole has to be reduced to its parts in order to understand it; that is, social institutions and the principles of justice can be explained by studying the individual members of the societies.

primary goods In John Rawls' welfare liberalism, primary goods include such social goods as rights and liberties, powers and opportunities, income and wealth, and self-respect and liberty, and they are defined as people's needs as citizens, that is, as equally rational and autonomous decision-makers.

teleology The study of aims, purposes, or functions of the universe. Teleological ethics, for its part, asserts that the aim of our actions can be derived from the purpose of human nature, that is, from the realization of our moral capacities.

utility As used by philosophers and economists, utility means the quantity of value or desirability people's preferences have whether thought of as actual or

The Concise Encyclopedia of Ethics in Politics and the Media

idealized choices. It is the basic unit of desirability when the values of particular things or actions are compared.

virtue Moral excellence or uprightness; the state of character of a morally worthwhile person; a mean between two extremes. Virtues are often defined as character traits that lead people to a morally good life.

WHAT IS DISTRIBUTIVE JUSTICE? In modern moral, political, and social philosophy the theories of justice are presently divided into three overlapping but still distinguishable spheres. There are (1) theories of political justice or political order, (2) theories of law and punishment, and (3) theories of distributive or social justice. Even if the different spheres of justice are often overlapping, we can say that in this division political justice covers the scope of the other two spheres. Political justice is concerned with the justification of political authority and political order, and it focuses on issues that concern the constitution and legislation of a state. Consequently, the distributional and legal issues are usually included in the conception of political justice. Theories of punishment, for their part, are concerned with the justification of the punishment of those who break the law or disregard generally accepted moral and social norms. Finally, distributive justice focuses on the distributional issues of society's resources; that is, it is concerned with yielding, allotting, assigning, or resigning to the members of society what they need, deserve, or are entitled to. Distributive justice is equated with distributional questions of a society (whether we talk about a particular society or a global community). In this context the terms distributive justice and social justice are, in general, used interchangeably.

This article introduces the main modern Western philosophical theories of distributive justice. Even if certain views may have to be presented through the ideas of particular theorists, the purpose is not to discuss in depth the differences between various theorists, but rather to explain and explore the basic elements, ideas, and terms that are relevant to the contemporary theories of distributive justice. Thus, in order to give the reader an idea of the complexity of the issues involved in the distributional questions, the article gives a general overview of the different features, aspects, and problems that the diverse collection of the theories of distributive justice have.

I. THE PARADOXICAL NATURE OF THE CONCEPTION OF JUSTICE

Questions of justice have always been some of the most fundamental and the most complex questions in our social, political, and moral thinking. On the one hand the questions of justice initiate an abstract philosophical speculation about what is meant by the term justice: what is the just society like? What is the good of a society and what is the good of a human being? What makes governments legitimate, and how can we justify political authority? On the other hand the questions of justice focus our attention on the concrete and practical social problems of our imperfect world. When we define the conception of justice and construct theories of justice, we are not only trying to describe what the perfect world would be like, but we are trying to improve the imperfections of the world we live in. Thus, we also have to ask: how can we justly distribute the social goods and resources? Can it be just that there are poor and starving people living next to those so rich that they have more money and material resources than they can spend in a lifetime? How can we maintain the just balance in rewarding those who work hard and in taking care of those who have no work and who do not contribute to society's public resources? How are we to solve the problems of equality and inequality in distributional issues? (On the conception and definition of justice see also Solomon and Murphy, Eds. (1991). What is justice? *Classic on Contemporary Readings* pp 4–5. Oxford University Press).

Theories of justice are concerned with both the theoretical definition of the word as well as with the normative objectives that guide actual policy-making. On the one hand, they attempt to describe what is meant by the concept of justice and to provide us with an explanation of the concept of justice or, rather, the definition of the word. On the other hand, the theories of justice try to find the means to strive for a more just and harmonious society and are thus concerned with the social and political issues that are related to the maintenance or the return of social harmony. This means that they also try in a prescriptive sense to develop the kind of concept that—substantively and particularly—justice actually requires in practice. They attempt to provide us with normative guidelines as to what a just society should be like.

This dual sense of the conception of justice makes different theories of justice use the same conception, that is the conception of justice, and it makes these theories agree that there is a need to make our societies more just. Yet, simultaneously, they may profoundly disagree with what it is that the realization of a just society would demand from us, because it is extremely difficult to find a definition for justice that is simultaneously sufficiently general to command a broad consensus and sufficiently specific as to permit its useful application. However, even if the theories of justice may disagree as to how we can best reach a just society, in general they seem to agree that the essential element of distributive justice is some variation on the theme of allotting or yielding to each their own.

To make matters more complicated, the conception of justice also points in two different directions. The ideal society and the practical measures to be taken in order to reach this ideal can at a theoretical level be divided into corrective and distributive elements that either stretch backward or forward. The corrective element of distributive justice essentially looks backward. It is an individualistic ideal of securing for all individuals their presumed rewards and entitlements by ordering punishments or redistributing social resources and thus correcting the prevalent injustices. This notion of justice requires empirical preparatory research into the conduct and background of all of the various persons and institutions concerned, and into their several and consequent deserts and entitlements. The *egalitarian collectivist ideal* of imposing equality of outcome, for its part, is forward-looking. Since Aristotle (384–322 B.C.) distributive justice has been distinguished from corrective justice. Corrective (sometimes also called retributive) justice is concerned with who ought to get what social goods, and with punishment for offenses commited. (On the dual nature of the conception of justice see also Anthony Flew (1979), *A dictionary of philosophy.* (Revised 2nd ed.), p. 188, New York: St. Martin's Press.)

This starting point leads modern theories of justice easily into a debate in which the promoters of different theories discuss the problems of justice on very different levels. In such a situation no consistent solution can be found to this dispute. Hence, often the real issue of the dispute is not so much the contents of the conception of justice, but rather fundamental disagreements, usually of a methodological nature. For instance *Robert Nozick's* (b. 1938) procedural redistributive "entitlement theory" is a backward-looking theory of a just society, whereas *John Rawls's* (b. 1921) more egalitarian view on justice as fairness is essentially forward-looking. Because these theories have incommensurable methodological premises, their suggestions about the practical political measures that are to be taken cannot directly be compared with each other either—and one cannot be simply considered to be better than the other.

Theories of justice, and particularly those of distributive justice, always reflect, at least partly, the social, political, and economic environment they were born in. Consequently, the meaning and the substantial structure of the conception of justice changes over time. Particularly during the last couple of centuries, the emphasis on questions of justice has shifted from an analysis of justice *tout court* to that of distributive or social justice. One reason for this is that modern social and economic development has made it evident that individual justice,

that is justice between wrongdoer and victim, is today seen to be a form of justice that is too incomplete and inadequate. The development of the welfare state, which in itself can be considered an application of the notion of distributive and social justice, has shifted the emphasis from the classical Aristotelian view based on individual morality, to a more impersonal view based on right procedure—from acting subject to the object that is acted on. This means that whereas the classical conception of justice focused on the just man, the person who is to act justly, the modern view focuses on more general demands of just treatment and the concept of a citizen to whom just treatment is due. Simultaneously, the method that is used to derive the principles of distributive justice has changed its emphasis from a holistic viewpoint toward the more atomistic viewpoint of methodological individualism, that rejects virtue ethics and instead uses the idea of the social contract as its method of justification of the principles of justice.

II. POLITICOECONOMIC ASPECTS OF MODERN THEORIES OF DISTRIBUTIVE JUSTICE

The concept of distributive justice is usually defined as meaning the fairness of distribution of redistribution of social and material goods, including liberties, rights, and entitlements. There seems to be general agreement that distributive justice is related to the distribution of social goods and material resources, and that these should be distributed according to what one deserves or needs. However, there is wide disagreement on the content and meaning of "desert" or "need." Thus, different theories of justice promote very different views on distributional issues. According to their politicoeconomical views and their normative conclusions, modern theories of distributive justice are traditionally divided into three categories based on the ideological background assumptions. These categories are:

A. The *egalitarian* theories of distributive justice, which can be further divided for instance into "minimum egalitarianism," "welfare egalitarianism," and "socialist egalitarianism."
B. The *utilitarian* theories of distributive justice, which are sometimes called "welfarism" or "welfarist consequentialism."
C. The *liberal* theories of distributive justice, which are further divided into "welfare liberalism" and "libertarianism," and sometimes also described as "neoliberalism."

These categories of theories of distributive justice often overlap, and their politicoeconomic views are closely linked with each other. Many of the theories of distributive justice have been created as criticism of the already-existing theories or of prevailing social practices. Thus, in order to understand the fundamental features of a particular theory, it is often essential to be familiar with the main features of some other theories that have preceded it as well as the social situation it in which it was originated. Thus, when introducing some of the central features of a particular theory it may often be necessary to refer to other theoretical formulations and politico-economic views that have, in one way or another, inspired these approaches. This means that in order to understand socialist egalitarianism or Marxism, we have to first understand the central features of capitalism and the problems of the market economy; in order to grasp the central aspects of contemporary libertarianism, we have to know the main problems of socialist egalitarianism; in order to understand the main focus of welfare liberal reasoning, we have to have an idea of what is meant by the utilitarian and the libertarian views of distributive issues; and in order better to understand the communitarian view of the justification of the distributional issues, we have to be at least somewhat familiar with both Aristotle's conception of justice as well as with Rawls's welfare liberalism.

A. Egalitarianism

The egalitarian concept of distributive justice promotes the view that people are equal and are entitled to equal rights and equal treatment in society. Egalitarianism emphasizes the ideal that all political distribution should be done according to people's equal worth. In principle this means that all citizens of a state should be accorded the same rights, privileges, social services, and material resources. There are, however, conflicting interpretations of what is really meant by *equality* and what the commitment to equality requires in practice. This means that even if the egalitarian conception of distributive justice is in general seen to promote left-wing politics and state socialism, nonsocialist theories may also present certain egalitarian features. For instance, conservative right-wing libertarians see that John Rawls's welfare liberalism, which promotes the equality of opportunity, is an egalitarian form of a liberal conception of distributive justice. The main difference is that the socialist view emphasizes the equal distribution of material resources and liberal egalitarianism emphasizes the equal distribution of political rights and basic social services. Thus, in order to clarify the central features of egalitarianism we should first make a distinction between the three major stands of egalitarianism:

1. Egalitarianism can mean that all *political rights* should be the same for all adult human beings. In terms of access to politics, suffrage, and equality before the law, social class, religion, ethnicity, or other criterion should not be allowed to produce inequality. This is the *minimum definition of egalitariansim,* and this part of it is accepted, at least in theory and often also in practice, in most Western democracies, and also some other types of states. It is also promoted by most of the liberal rights-based theories.

2. Egalitarianism may also be held to involve *equality of opportunity,* which implies that regardless of the socioeconomic situation into which someone is born, one should have the same chance as everybody else to develop one's talents and to acquire the same qualifications that others have. When individuals then, for instance, apply for jobs, their cases will be considered entirely on the basis of such talents and qualifications, and will not depend on their social status or on other random factors that they cannot themselves influence. Realizing this kind of egalitarianism requires, at the very least, an education and a social-welfare system that will train and will provide for the less-advantaged so that they can really compete on equal terms with those from more favorable social backgrounds. Politically, this could be seen as the philosophical justification for a social democracy, which allows some state involvement in distributional affairs. In practice, states try to achieve this situation by the application of a mixed economy, that is, partly capitalist and partly nationalized and planned, with high taxes and extensive welfare services. Philosophically or theoretically, for instance, Rawls's welfare liberalism can be interpreted as giving a justification for this sort of *welfare egalitarianism.* Even if no modern state can be said to actually have achieved the goal of equality of opportunity, most of the modern welfare states have adopted this, at least in principle, as their ideal.

3. The most extreme version of egalitarianism is *socialist egalitarianism,* which would require not only equality of opportunity, but actual equality in material welfare and perhaps, at least in theory, also in political weight. Most Communist states accepted this socialist egalitarianism as the final aim, at least in principle. At its simplest, the core meaning of the socialist conception of distributive justice is its promotion of a politicoeconomic system where the state controls, either through planning or more directly, and may legally own the basic means of production and the distribution and redistribution of material and social resources. By its ownership of these resources the state controls industrial, agricultural, and other plants in order to produce what is needed by society, without regard to what may be most profitable to produce. The goal of the socialist theory of distribu-

tive justice is to produce an egalitarian society, one in which all are cared for by society, with no place for poverty and with no need for relief from poverty by private charity. The principles of socialist distribution are summarized in a famous dictum of Karl Marx (1818–1883): "From each according to his ability, to each according to his need."

Socialism or socialist egalitarianism, as a politicoeconomic theory, has gone though many variations, and dating its exact origin is impossible. Modern socialism stemmed from the industrial revolution. It arose as a reaction to capitalism after the development of extensive industrial private property in a society based on contractual rather than on semifeudal status relations. The general feature of the modern socialist view of distributive justice is that it sees the abolition of private ownership of property as essential, because the control of property is the very definition of a class system. Man takes his essence from labor in pursuit of material ends, and the control of material resources creates upper and lower classes and it gives the upper class control over politics, including the construction of ideologies and a social consciousness. According to socialism there are implacable economic rules that ultimately determine economic development. These economic laws make it inevitable that, ultimately, capitalist society will collapse because of its own inherent contradictions; then Communism will emerge. When summarized, the three tenets of the modern socialist theory of distributive justice are: (1) that economic matters ultimately control political and cultural phenomena; (2) that abolition of private property is necessary to ensure equality and an end to exploitation; (3) that the road to such a Communist society must come about through the proletariat and its leaders, with the development of a revolutionary consciousness. However, the essential ideas of material equality and the demands for common property can be also found in earlier views on distributive justice such as those found in Plato's (c.428–347 B.C.) *Republic*, and in the works of the such earlier social reformers as Fourier (1772–1837) and Saint-Simon (1760–1825).

1. The Problem of Egalitarianism

The problem of egalitarianism, and particularly socialist egalitarianism, is that such total equality in distribution of social and material goods, as suggested by it, is not regarded as possible, either theoretically or in practice. The practical difficulties of a fully equal distribution of material resources within one country or even just one city would be immense; to distribute equally among all the citizens would be logistically very difficult.

Even if the socialist egalitarians were to settle for the idea that the equal distribution of material resources could be accomplished, for instance, by giving equal wages to everybody, there would still be problems. And only short-lived equality would be achieved by an equal distribution of wealth in this way. Different people tend to use their money in many different ways; the clever, the deceitful, and the strong would quickly acquire the wealth of those who are weaker, more gullible, or ignorant. Some people would squander their money, others might save it. Some might gamble their property away as soon as they got it, others might steal or cheat to increase their shares. The only way of maintaining anything like an equal ditribution of wealth and material resources would be by the forceful intervention of coercive authority. This would no doubt involve intrusion into people's private lives and would limit their freedom to do what they want to do. Thus, it is argued that equal distribution of material welfare, social services, and money is not only an unattainable but is also an undesirable goal in political reality. First, because such a sitution of total equality could only be attained by the extensive loss of liberty and, second, because it would be economically inefficient because it would provide no material incentives that reward effort. Empirical proof for this is evidenced from the states in Communist socialism that accepted the socialist egalitarianism as their ideal but failed tragically in realizing it.

B. Utilitarian Conception of Distributive Justice

At is core *utilitarianism* is the moral, social, and political theory that presents a simple equation between the good and happiness or pleasure. It claims that whatever measures, polity, choice, or decision we make, we judge our actions in terms of their consequences, whether these consequences are defined in terms of happiness, absence of pain and suffering, preferences, or "utility." The term utility does not refer merely to the usefulness of a particular thing, but rather means the quantity of value or desirability some things have in the utilitarian calculation. Generally, the aim of the utilitarian calculation is the greatest happiness of the greatest number.

We can distinguish three different features of utilitarianism:

1. Consequentialism: the rightness of actions—and more generally of the choice of all control variables (e.g., acts, rules, motives)—must be judged entirely by the goodness of the consequent state of affairs.

2. Welfarism: the goodness of states of affairs must be judged entirely by the goodness of the set of individual utilities in the respective state of affairs.
3. Sum-ranking: the goodness of any set of individual utilities must be judged entirely by their sum total.

Utilitarianism can then be discussed in two different roles: on the one hand as a theory of personal morality, and on the other hand as a theory of public choice, or of the criteria that are applicable to public policy. In this context utilitarianism is considered almost exclusively from the latter point of view, or as a theory of the correct way to assess or assign value to states of affairs that claims that the correct basis of assessment is welfare, satisfaction, or people getting what they prefer. The utilitarian tradition of Jeremy Bentham (1748–1832), James Mill (1773–1836), and John Stuart Mill (1806–1873), the maximization of social utility of all individuals, was made the basic criterion of morality and of the justification of public policies. What these classical utilitarians saw as social utility would now be the social welfare function of modern welfare economics. There have been many adjustments and refinements to the basic utilitarian theory over the years. Some of the most well-known contributors to the utilitarian theory of distributive justice include Henry Sidgwick (1838–1900), G. E. Moore 1873–1958), R. B. Brant, R. M. Hare (1919–), and John C. Harsanyi.

Modern utilitarian theories of distributive justice often present a particular form of utilitarianism called "welfarism" or "welfarist consequentialism." This requires the simple addition of individual welfares or utilities to assess the consequences, a property that is sometimes called sum-ranking. Sum-ranking, for its part, is a principle commonly used in economics, in which actions are judged entirely in terms of consequences, and consequences in terms of the welfare level of the worst-off person. The utilitarian calculation is seen to offer not merely a descriptive way of answering questions of the form, "How is society really going?" but also a prescriptive criterion of public action. It therefore must assume a public agent, some supreme body that chooses general states of affairs for the society as a whole: an ideal formulation of public rationality. In utilitarian theory this public rationality is usually described as an ideal of the "fully rational observer" who can calculate all the consequences of all our actions. There is also a utilitarian calculation that is based on the expected or foreseeable consequences and thus does not assume that all actual consequences were to be known. (On the utilitarian conception of justice and its criticism see Amartya Sen and Bernard Williams, *Utilitarianism and beyond*.)

The aim of utilitarianism is to escape, as much as possible, from reliance on any source of moral authority,

whether this authority is religion, another metaphysic, or whether it appeals to such abstractions as "natural law." Although is not always explicated, nearly all parties and governments in the Western world tend to operate according to utilitarian reasoning. Most of economic theory, the whole of welfare economics, and many of the theoretical models of justification for democracy appear to be based, at least partly, on utilitarian views. Policy analysis, especially as developed by civil servants and academic specialists in the 1960s, is also based on utility calculus. And until recently the prevailing theories of law and jurisprudence were mainly derived from utilitarianism. Only after the 1970s did non-Marxist political theories begin to develop nonutilitarian general political philosophies and theories of distributive justice. It is also worth noting that even the new liberal approaches that were created as critical alternatives to utilitarian approach to distributive issues, such John Rawls's welfare liberalism and Robert Nozick's libertarianism, are, at least partly, based on a return to the classic liberal social contract tradition, which had clear utilitarian features built into its very structure. Mainly this is the tradition that started from John Locke (1632–1704) and developed to liberal utilitarianism by John Stuart Mill (1806–1073). In a modern secular society that has left behind the intellectual view of "scientific socialism," and that attempts to operate with minimal coercion in a more-or-less democratic manner, it seems to have been very difficult to find a serious alternative to an appeal to rational self interest, which is what also utilitarianism amounts to. (A summary in the utilitarian approach of political and economic decision making is to be found in Robertson, David (1985), *The Penguin dictionary of politics* (pp 328–339), Middlesex: Penguin Books.)

1. The Problems of Utilitarianism

There are three more obvious criticisms presented against utilitarianism. First, there is the practical difficulty of its application. It is extremely difficult to measure utility or happiness and to compare the utility or happiness of different people in different circumstances. How can we accurately assess the amount of utility or happiness that is likely to be yielded by particular actions, general rules, or distributional policies? A person's experience, the information one has, circumstances, and personal capabilities affect what one actually desires or what makes one happy. Should, for instance, those living in luxury with gourmet tastes receive more than those who live in more modest or even in poor circumstances with "cheap" tastes? Second, a utilitarian account of distributive justice is often criticized for its unfairness. The happiness of the majority may best be served by the sacrifice of some innocent party (i.e., for instance by sacrificing an individual in the name of the maintenance of social harmony) or by some manifestly unjust institution, such as slavery. And third, the utilitarian view of justice is seen to be too one-sided when it analyzes morality and justice entirely through actions and their consequences. When utilitarian reasoning is applied to practical politicoeconomic issues, it leaves individuals as mere rational and egoistic maximizers of their own utility, preferences, interests, or happiness. This makes the questions of justice an automatic rational calculation, and it ignores other moral intentions or motives, such as personal integrity and honesty.

C. Liberal Conception of Distributive Justice

A liberal conception of justice is, in general, seen as a rival or alternative view to both the socialist and the utilitarian conceptions of justice. However, despite the fact that liberals themselves are critical of both the socialist and the utilitarian approaches toward distribution in their own theoretical constructions, liberals have adopted, either explicitly or implicitly, some of the same features that appear to present a form of egalitarianism or that have some consequentialist elements in them. On the other hand a liberal conception of justice itself presents a collection of diverse views on distributional and other political issues. By its politicoeconomic agenda liberal theory is divided into two quite different approaches: welfare liberalism and libertarianism. Both of these approaches are liberal at the core because they promote liberal values of freedom and "natural" individual rights, particularly the right to property. Politically and economically, however, they present very divergent and even incommensurable views. When it comes to the practical measures that are needed to realize the liberal values of freedom and equality, they further almost opposite measures.

1. Welfare-Liberal Theory

For welfare liberals such as John Rawls, Will Kymlicka, and Ronald Dworkin, fairness, or a right to basic welfare and a right to equal opportunity, is the ultimate political ideal. Thus, welfare liberalism advocates *positive freedom* with more government intervention, especially when this is thought necessary to achieve what is valued by contemporary welfare liberals: for freeing people from ignorance and misery, or for solving other social problems, such as poverty. Today, welfare liberalism is sometimes used merely to politically designate any left-wing position, and it is said to be close to social

democracy. In its promotion of equality of opportunity the welfare-liberal view clearly has some egalitarian features in it.

A welfare-liberal view on the distributional issues is most fully presented by John Rawls in *A Theory of Justice* (1971) and in *Political Liberalism* (1993). We now examine the main features of the welfare-liberal view of the distribution of social resources. Rawls's welfare-liberal theory was an attack on the prevailing utilitarian theories of social justice. It tried to reestablish some form of Natural Rights arguments that claimed that there are some values we all hold as absolute, such as the right to liberty and a right to equality. Rawls wanted to replace the utilitarian cost-accounting methodology with a more absolute form of argumentation. In order to do this he introduces a modernized form of the traditional social contract that can be used as a simple test to see whether a political or social institution is fair or not. When the contracting parties select the principles of justice in the "original position," they are not in a state of nature, but the parties are presented as rational and reasonable people. However, because "justice as fairness" emphasizes blindness to random differences between individuals, the bargaining advantages that inevitably arise within the background institution of any society (from cumulative social, historical, and natural tendencies) have to be eliminated. Thus, the parties of selection are subject to certain constraints on their motivation and knowledge. Though self-interested, these rational and reasonable agents are also disinterested in the other's interests and they are concerned only with their share of the primary social goods (such as rights and liberties, powers and opportunities, income and wealth, and self-respect and liberty). People in the original position operate behind "a veil of ignorance," which prevents them from knowing their natural characteristic and endowments, their social or economic position in society, their values or personal goals, or the historical period they are born into. The point then is that if you do not know whether you are to be slave or ruler, man or woman, of the twentieth or the twenty-first century, you could not opt for "unfair" rules, lest you end up on the wrong side of the bargain. Given these conditions Rawls believes that two principles will be selected: the first, which guarantees equal liberty, and the second, "the difference principle," which permits inequalities in other goods if they help the least-advantaged. The difference principle also then requires that those with various natural talents must be harnessed to benefit the least-advantaged.

There are several important critiques presented against the welfare-liberal view. First, Rawls's theoretical formulation of a welfare-liberal conception of justice is seen to be too abstract. In reality there are no such rational agents as the fictive social-contract method of justification describes. People are more or less tied to their social environment and to their existing social ties. In its attempt to be impartial and morally neutral, the welfare-liberal view may actually end up promoting inequality in practice by disregarding the actual relations of dependence and interdependence. Consequently, the problem of Rawls's distributive principles of the primary goods is that by assuming that justice as fairness means "difference blindness" it ends up assuming that people are quite similar, or indeed are each other's clones. In reality, however people are diverse in various ways, and they need different amounts of (different) goods to maintain the same level of well-being. Variations related to sex, age, genetic endowment, and many other features give us unequal powers to build freedom in our lives even when we have the same bundle of goods. Hence, equality in holding Rawlsian primary goods can go hand-in-hand with serious inequalities in actual freedom enjoyed by different persons.

Second, welfare-liberal theory also fails to explain what motivates us to adopt these two principles of justice. Why should people who are not in the original position believe it important that those subject to its stringent constraints happen to choose certain principles? Why should their choice "justify" our adopting these two principles of justice?

2. Libertarian Theory

Even as recently as the 1960s libertarianism or neoliberalism was somewhat of a fringe politicoeconomic theory that held extreme versions of liberal capitalist beliefs. Lately there has been a considerable upsurge in interest in libertarian thinking in some quarters, especially in the United States and in the United Kingdom, but also in some other modern Western welfare democracies. This is due to, first, the failure of state socialism, and second, the bankruptcy of most other non-Marxist political theories in the postwar world that have resulted in the political and economic crisis of the modern welfare democracies. The central feature of the libertarian view on distributive justice is that it is totally individualist. It rejects any idea that societies, states, or collectives of any form can be the bearers of rights or can owe duties. Social collectives are legitimate only insofar as they are voluntary aggregations of individuals, and not just because they may, as a matter of fact, make most or all their individual members betters off. Consequently, libertarian political theory is semianarchist in that it regards as legitimate only the very minimal state power that is necessary to uphold the prior existing rights, particularly the property rights, of the individual citizens. The essence of the libertarian approach is laissez-

faire economics and a deep distrust of government intervention that would put social and legal constraints on individual freedom. Libertarianism, then, promotes *negative freedom* and sees that political liberty and the freedom of the markets are the most important things in society. Thus, restrictive laws, taxes, welfare, state economic control, and so on, should be eliminated or minimized. The libertarian theory holds that all individual human beings have a certain sort of natural rights, which are indefeasible. The prime natural right is the right to property. These natural rights cannot be given up, and they may not be taken away in the interest of the collective. Unlike in welfare liberal theory the state may not intervene to balance the rights and to ensure, for example, that someone who is starving is given welfare payments by breaching the property rights of another.

Hence, the libertarian view is politically farthest from socialist egalitarianism in distributional issues. Libertarians are individualists who see that different people deserve different amounts of financial rewards for the jobs that they do, and for the contribution that they make to society. They can argue that industrial and commercial proprietors deserve their wealth and affluence because of their relatively greater contribution to the city or the nation. After all, they make it possible for other people to work and to increase the general economic well-being of the whole geographic area or country in which they operate. On the other hand the higher wages are seen to be needed as an incentive for getting the important jobs done efficiently. No one capable of doing a difficult or a hard job, which may also require long training or an expensive education, would be willing to take one without the incentive of higher pay and a more prestigious social status. Thus, in the libertarian view the utilitarian features (although they are not usually explicated as such) come out when they justify inequality by appealing to the greater overall benefits to society that are seen to outweigh the costs of social inequality. Without big businesses, industrial production, and specialists there might be much less to go around for everyone. Libertarians believe then that gross inequalities in wealth between individuals are acceptable, and that everyone is mainly responsible for his or her own fate. Libertarians see that it is the attempt to distribute money and wealth equally that violates the equal rights of individuals, particularly the right to own property. According to libertarians this violation of the individual's right is always morally wrong because rights always trump any other considerations.

The theoretical formulation of contemporary libertarian political ideas has occurred as a criticism of the welfare-liberal theories of justice, as in Robert Nozick's *Anarchy, State, and Utopia* (1974), which heavily criticized Rawls's welfare-liberal political and economic ideas, for instance the idea that all goods that either exist already or are yet to be produced are the collective property of the social contractors, to be distributed among themselves at their absolute collective discretion. Nozick insists, first, that economic goods are not "manna from heaven," but instead usually are subject to prior claims of possession. Second he insists that we are all individually entitled to possess whatever we either have acquired without injustice, or will so acquire in the future. This also includes the products of our personal talents. This view emphasizes the Lockean classical liberal view of "self-ownership" that sees that individuals are entitled to whatever they produce by their own labor. According to Nozick when an individual has a right to property, this can come about in two ways: one may have legitimately acquired that property in the first place as an original act, or one may have had it transferred to him by a legitimate process from someone else who had a legitimate entitlement. As long as any distribution of property is covered by such rules, then the distribution is just, however inegalitarian it may be. Views such as Rawls's welfare liberalism, which concentrates on the justice of an "end state," that is, a particular distribution of property rights that seems valid in itself, miss the point that actual distribution arises from historical processes that give people entitlement, and justice inheres in the justice of the entitlement chain, not in the consequences of the momentary distribution. Nozick's libertarian enthusiasm for the free-market economy is also present, for instance, in the works of David Gauthier, F.A. van Hayek, and Milton Friedman, who all would like to return to the classical liberalism's historic concern to enhance for individuals the pliability and subtleness of life in regard to the constraints of social institutions, cultural traditions, and norms.

3. The Problems of Libertarianism

Libertarian right-based theory usually views the natural right to property as preceding political life and not being the product of the state. However, it fails to state where these rights come from. Thus, by natural rights libertarians do not mean legal rights, although such rights may coincide with legal rights in a just society: legal rights are those laid down by government or the appropriate authority. Natural rights, for their part, are rights that can be derived from "natural law," and ideally they should guide the formation of legislation and laws. But it is uncertain what the "natural law" is that gives people these property rights.

Second, it is argued that the contractarian conception of justice (thus, up to a certain degree this criticism is valid also with the welfare-liberal view) is based on the idea that sees justice as reciprocity, and thus ignores the social needs and rights of those who cannot fully contribute to the production of the social goods. This would leave the disabled, the old, the ill, and other marginal groups justifiably outside the scope of justice. The politicoeconomic problem of libertarianism is then that it leaves those who are the worst off in the hands of private charity and at the mercy of other people. However, because it is based on the idea that human beings are egoistic and think only of their own benefit, it does not encourage private morality or altruism. In practice libertarian policies then create broad social inequalities that tend to divide society between the rich and the poor. In this society there is a danger that the social harmony cannot be maintained and that the tension between these classes will turn into crime and violence.

III. CATEGORIZING THEORIES OF JUSTICE BY THE STANDARDS OF DISTRIBUTION

The politicoeconomic division does not succeed in covering all the central aspects of the theories of distributive justice. It leaves aside particularly the contemporary methodological discussion on the foundations of justice. Thus, it is justifiable to present another categorization that is achieved by dividing the theories of distributive justice by the standards these theories use as the basis of the distribution of social goods and material resources. (This is a division that was first presented by Thomas A. Spragens, Jr., in his article "The Antinomies of Social Justice," in *The Review of Politics* Vol. 55, Spring 1993, No. 2, but is further developed and discussed here.)

If we divide theories of distributive justice by the standard of distribution we arrive at three different categories. These are:

A. Hegemonic. Defending a single determining standard, such as needs for Marx, rights for Rawls, and entitlements for Nozick.
B. Skeptical. Finding that any standards for distributive justice are radically indeterminate if not meaningless, and thus the only proper way to distribute social goods is to rely on a rational decision-making strategy—the means and the practical outcome of this strategy vary depending on the circumstances. Such a protoutilitarian theorist as Hume, a utilitarian such as Harsanyi, and libertarians like Gauthier and Hayek would fit in this category.
C. Pluralistic. Claiming that we can disqualify all but a handful of standards but that we cannot definitely adjudicate among these, and thus we should

rather focus on determining what it is that we want to realize with the just distribution. For example, human flourishing in Aristotle, autonomy and ideal citizenship in Michael Walzer, and human capabilities in Martha Nussbaum and Amartya Sen.

A. Hegemonic Theories of Distributive Justice

The hegemonic approaches to the questions of distributive justice define a single standard for the distribution of social goods and resources. In this hegemonic category we could then place such otherwise diverse liberal thinkers as Rawls, who uses the concept of individual rights, and Nozick, who uses entitlements as such a standard. These adherents of the hegemonic approach believe that it is in fact possible to ascertain a single substantive standard of social justice that is rationally persuasive. They believe that their conception of distributive justice should be capable of universal acceptance—by, at least, all rational people of good will. If the principles of justice are derived from eternal ideas, or from the demands of pure reason as is in the case with the social contract theory, or from the inevitabilities of a rational cosmos, one might attribute to them a legitimate hegemony over any contrary notions. In very different ways, the Marxist distribution according to need can therefore also be pressed with hegemonic force.

B. Skeptical Theories of Distributive Justice

Diametrically opposed to hegemonic theorists of distributive justice are the skeptics. The skeptical theories of distributive justice see that attempts to find any standards for distributive justice are radically indeterminate, if not meaningless. Thus, the only proper way to distribute social goods is to rely on a rational decision-making strategy—the means and the practical outcome of this strategy vary depending on the circumstances. In this category we could place at least the utilitarian calculus and even some of the most radical libertarian views.

For instance, the utilitarians theory expressly denies, at least in its earlier versions, any ordering, moral or otherwise, of the sources of pleasure as the highest good. Except for the distribution principles, "each man should count as one, and none for more than one," utilitarianism allows no other moral or political criteria of decision but the rational calculation. Utilitarians argue that, at least in principle, it ought to be possible directly to quantify and sum the positive and negative consequences in terms of pleasure or utility. Policy-making for society, as much as private moral decision-making

for an individual, would then become essentially an automatic process. The skeptical approach denies the very possibility of a universal conception of social justice. For skeptics justice is merely a word, an illusory and artificial moral concept, customarily deployed in a hypocritical fashion to give a cover of fraudulent legitimacy to acts that are in fact based on pure self-interest. No matter how this is concealed or disguised in a theory the idea of justice in practice always receives a definition that coincides with the interests of the strongest party in society. Thus, the utilitarian theorists could be seen as skeptics who displace distributive justice with prudential calculation. Different outcomes are produced under this heading, depending upon the interpretation given to "utility." An example of this approach can, for instance, be found in the social philosophy of David Hume. As Hume notes, the abstract meaning of justice is "to each to his due." However, Hume argues, it is social convention that determines what shall be "due" to particular individuals. No transcendent criterion antedates the legal and conventional determination of this standard. What determines the content of social justice, then are the overriding general interests of society, and, in Hume's account, these general interests center upon peace and security. Thus, rules of social justice are conventions of property distribution that civil societies create and enforce in pursuit of their happiness and tranquillity. (See Spragens, 1993, pp. 196–197).

On the other hand some of the libertarian theories, such as those of von Hayek and Gauthier, may be said to deploy a similar skepticism about social justice to different effect: the libertarian insistence that every individual has his or her own goals and his or her own standard of justice. These goals and standards differ. The goals are legitimate expressions of individual preference, and the standards are, presumably, the product of sincere belief. No one is entitled to determine for others what their goals should be, and no one seems to be able to gain universal acquiescence in his or her particular conception of justice. We must choose, then, between tyranny and laissez-faire: either one party gains the power to impose his or her particular standards upon unwilling and unbelieving subjects, or each individual conception should be permitted to retain sovereignty over his or her own resources. Fidelity to market outcomes, it is concluded, provides the most perfect embodiment of the latter, nontyrannical alternative. (See Spragens, 1993, p. 196).

C. Pluralistic Theories of Distributive Justice

The pluralistic theories claim that we can disqualify all but a handful of standards, but that we cannot definitely adjudicate among these and thus we should rather focus on determining what it is that we want to realize with the just distribution. Thus, in order to choose the right procedure or right standards of distribution we have to know first what is the goal that we want to realize by just distribution. The pluralist position begins then by contesting both the hegemonic and skeptical claims. The pluralist approach to distributive justice finds unpersuasive the hegemonic-theories claim that a single substantive account for social justice can be demonstrated to enjoy superiority over all others. The pluralist approach also denies the skeptic's conclusion that a potentially infinite number of conceptions of justice can be generated—corresponding to a potentially infinite multiplicity of human interests—none of which may be deemed better than any other. Instead, in this view, theories of justice may be analytically reduced to a small finite set. Not one of this small finite group of conceptions of social justice can achieve a clear priority over the others. Each of them rests upon persuasive considerations adduced from rationally defensible moral principles. As a group, however, they exhaust the field of persuasive theories: no other theories are extant that can compare in logical or moral force. Hence, it is not appropriate, with the skeptic, to identify conceptions of justice with mere tastes, preferences, or simple interests.

Historically, we could say that the pluralistic tradition starts with Aristotle, with his criticism of Plato's hegemonic totalitarian socialism (not yet named in those terms). Aristotle developed an economic formulation of distributive justice that was close to that of modern social democracy. However, rather than trying to define the fair procedure of distribution, he focused on the goal of the distribution, that is, to the good that is to be realized by this distribution. Aristotle's theory was pluralistic in two senses. Aristotle not only saw that the goods should be distributed in consideration of how they realize human flourishing, but, as already mentioned, he also noted that there were two different spheres of justice to begin with: the distributive, or the forward-looking one, and the corrective, or the backward-looking one.

The modern pluralistic theories present very different views, but all of them tend to have their roots in an Aristotelian approach to distribution and in the instrumental value of social goods and material wealth. The similarity between Aristotelian and contemporary views is that they all base the standards of distribution on the ends that are to be realized. The difference, however, is that the contemporary view starts with redefinition of the concept of equality, whereas Aristotle started with the definition of "the good life." *The communitarian view* to distributive justice has been most fully explicated by Michael Walzer in his *Spheres of Justice* (1983),

where he claims that each social good determines its own criterion of just distribution. Walzer's account is also pluralistic in a second sense, particularly when applied in practice. Walzer claims tht many different kinds of social goods (and evils) whose distribution is a matter of justice have their own particular criterion of distribution. For instance, the criteria used to determine who should get public honors cannot be the same as the criteria used to determine who should get medical care. He, however, does not provide any underlying principles that stand behind all of these distributive criteria, no core idea that might explain why honors are to be distributed in one way and medical care in another. Despite the fact that Walzer deliberately rejects the search for any fundamental principles of justice, he nonetheless wants to make one general claim about societies that respect distributive pluralism of the kind just outlined. The ultimate goal of distribution is to realize individual autonomy and ideal citizenship. This can be done only by creating a "complex equality" among the members of society. Complex equality occurs when different people get ahead in each of the various spheres of distribution, but because they are unable to convert their advantages from one sphere into another, none is able to dominate the rest.

Complex equality in this sense can be understood as an idea of equal citizenship. Complex equality is not a fundamental principle in the way in which equality, need, desert, or inalienable rights have served in the hegemonic theories. Complex equality cannot generate spheres of distribution, but it is better understood as an ethically important byproduct that, according to Walzer, appears in liberal societies when the autonomy of each distributive sphere is maintained. Walzer then follows the Aristotelian idea that the meaning of each social good determines its criterion of just distribution. Once we know what we have to allocate, Walzer argues, we also know how we should allocate—to whom and by what means. In the case of medical care, for instance, the distributive criterion is need; in the case of money and commodities, it is free exchange in the market, in the case of education, it is equality at the basic level and a capacity to benefit at a higher level. If there is disagreement about the distributive criteria, this must reflect disagreement about the nature of the good itself, so once we have settled the latter issue, the distributive question will resolve itself. Once we can establish for instance what medical care really means to us, we shall know by what methods and criteria it ought to be allocated among potential claimants.

The capability approach, for its part, was developed by Martha Nussbaum and Amartya Sen (it should be noted here that despite their emphasis on human capabilities, their separate approaches have different starting points). The capability approach attempts to replace the idea of a quantitative standard of living by quality of life. It defends the moral appropriateness of the concepts of functioning and capability in contrast to such alternative concepts as commodity and utility. The capability approach therefore heavily criticizes utilitarianism, libertarianism, and Rawlsian deontological liberalism. It attempts to build a distributive theory of justice that takes the goal of the distribution into account, that is, it sets the aims prior to the means. Following the Aristotelian view and Marxist criticism of capitalism, the capability approach sees that most of the modern views of justice, particularly the liberal ones, are based on "commodity fetishism," which gives intrinsic value to material goods and prosperity instead of the actual well-being of individuals. This means that material goods and commodities are valued as intrinsically good and thus the mere means are transformed to ends. The capability approach emphasizes that material goods and commodities are not good in themselves but are good only by virtue of their relationship to—and what they do for—human beings. It considers them to be mere means to well-being rather than having intrinsic value. Thus, we should ask, "what can goods do for people" or rather "what people can do with these goods," rather than seeing them as the end in themselves. Nussbaum and Sen also claim that modern views of justice disregard variations among individuals, and they ignore the fact that the same commodity has very different value for diverse people in different circumstances. It is evident that very different types of clothing promote our basic functioning in Africa than at the North Pole, or that a disadvantaged and incapable person gets less from primary goods than many other people. The capability approach suggests, therefore, that instead of focusing on the mechanically equal procedure of distributing individual rights, other primary goods, and commodities, we should look for the final goal of this distribution, that is, human well-being. According to the capability approach, this well-being can be defined in the form of human "capabilities" and "functionings," or "doings" and "beings." If we asked which things are so important that we will not count a life as a human life without them, we would end up agreeing with a list of the capabilities that make life worth living. The object of distributive justice is the enhancement of these valuable and valued capabilities that reflect an individual's actual freedom to choose between alternative lives (i.e., functioning combinations). The capability approach is introduced, for instance, in the works of Nussbaum, (1993), *Human Functioning and Social Justice*; in "Defense of Aristotelian Essentialism" (*Political Theory*, Vol. 20, No. 2, pp. 202–246); and in Sen (1992, *Inequality Reexamined*, Oxford: Clarendon Press).

To summarize, the three fundamental features of the pluralistic theories follow. First, the pluralistic theories create a view that rejects the idea of some universal fundamental principle or example that is believed to be behind all the more concrete beliefs and judgments that we express when we say that this or that action or practice is a fair or just one. This view is developed in conscious opposition to the hegemonic approaches, and it is radically pluralist in nature. There are no universal laws of justice or single standards of justice. Instead, we must see justice as the creation of a particular political community at a particular time, and the account we give must be given from within such a community. Because there is no single standard that can be used to distribute social goods, it is the goal of the just distribution of social goods that ultimately determines their distribution. This teleological nature of the pluralistic account seems to require that there is either a metaphysical or at least a conceptual link between the meaning of the goods and their principle of distribution. Hence, if someone proposed to distribute the goods in another way, this would, in the most literal sense, mean that he or she has failed to understand what the good in question really is. Thus, in the pluralistic theories, the meaning of the good and its criterion of just distribution really are tightly interlocked.

The second feature that the pluralistic theories of distributive justice have in common is their attempt to redefine and clarify the vague conception of equality. Rather than seeing equality as having intrinsic value, it is seen as a means to further ends. According to pluralistic accounts, equality as "blindness to difference" does not take into account the differences between people—the differences in their actual needs. The pluralist view sees that the theories based on ideal rationality present a "view from nowhere," which has no connection to reality and to the real problems and injustices of our world. A pluralistic approach involves the claim that justice needs more than abstract principles, and it needs to pay more attention to interpersonal and cultural differences rather than to merely ignore or disregard them.

It follows, then, that the third feature that these accounts share is their attempt to find a method of justification that does not argue from abstract principles but rather from meaning that is grounded in everyday social experience. This more empirical method is defended as a means that brings the theories of distributive justice closer to everyday politics and to the life of people, and that takes real injustices into account.

The problem of the pluralistic account lies in its vagueness and its ambiguity. For instance, it is difficult to define what is actually meant by valuable capabilities, and how the relevant capabilities can be distinguished from the irrelevant ones. It is also unclear how else, apart from merely following our intuition, we can know what kind of distribution different goods require. And finally, it seems that the emphasis on cultural and other differences between people may easily lead the pluralistic approach toward cultural relativity or conventionality, despite its teleological aspects.

IV. CONCLUSION

The categorical division presented here is not exhaustive and it does not attempt to cover all the central aspects of the theories of distributive justice. However, the purpose is to introduce the different types of theories and to emphasize the complexity of the issues of distributive justice. The modern distributive theories of justice, such as socialist egalitarianism, utilitarianism, or liberalism lately have been criticized for their abstractness and their failure to take into account the personal differences, local circumstances, and social ties that all affect our ability to enjoy our share of social goods. Thus, besides the traditional policoeconomic division of the theories of distributive justice, there is a renewed interest in developing theories of justice that focus on the goals of just distribution rather than on procedures that are merely right. These pluralistic theories attempt to replace abstract philosophical analysis and speculation with more empirical methodological views of the problems of distributive justice. In general, comparisons between different theories of distributive justice are very difficult. The theories themselves are often methodologically incommensurable, but they still overlap politically. The difficulty of a direct comparison between different theories is then due to their methodological incompatibility rather than to the economic or political views they present.

Bibliography

Barry, B. (1989). *Theories of justice.* Berkeley and Los Angeles: University of California Press.

Crocker, D. (1992). Functioning and capability. The foundations of Sen's and Nussbaum's development ethic. *Political Theory,* **20**(4), 584–612.

Flew, A. (1985). The Concept, and Conceptions, of Justice. *Journal of Applied Philosophy,* **2**(2), 191–196.

Kymlicka, W. (1990). *Contemporary political philosophy.* Oxford and New York: Clarendon Press.

Miller, D., & Walzer, M. (Eds.). (1995). *Pluralism, justice and equality.* Oxford: Oxford University Press.

Sen, A., & Williams, B. (Eds.). (1982). *Utilitarianism and beyond.* Cambridge: Cambridge University Press.

Solomon, R., & Murphy, M. (Eds.). (1990). *What is justice? Classic on contemporary readings.* New York and Oxford: Oxford University Press.

Election Strategies

MARIANNE M. JENNINGS

Arizona State University

GLOSSARY

commercial speech Ads and any other forms of communication regarding products, services, or business.

Federal Election Campaign Act (FECA) A federal law governing maximum levels of campaign contributions with requirements of public reporting of campaign donations and expenditures.

Federal Election Commission (FEC) A federal agency charged with enforcing FECA and location for filing of required campaign financial information.

First Amendment A provision in the U.S. Constitution that guarantees an individual the right to speak without censorship of content (with only limited exceptions).

political action committee (PAC) A formally created group of citizens, trade associations, businesses, or employees organized for the purpose of raising funds or making campaign expenditures to or on behalf of candidates or ballot propositions.

political speech Ads and any other forms of communication regarding candidates or ballot initiatives.

Senate Election Ethics Act A set of voluntary guidelines passed by the U.S. Senate on campaign spending limits, PACs, independent expenditures and soft money.

ELECTION STRATEGIES are the methods and techniques used by candidates to gain the support of the electorate. These strategies can involve either an effort to influence voters to favor a candidate or to influence them against an opposing candidate. Election strategies raise important ethical questions concerning issues such as campaign funding, political advertising, and the limits of negative campaigning.

I. INTRODUCTION

When George Washington ran for a seat in the Virginia House of Burgesses in 1767, he gave away approximately 160 gallons of liquor in order to win the support of the 391 voters in his district. Since that time, the strategies used to gain the support of voters have grown in variation and expense. For example, in 1860, both candidates for the office of U.S. President spent $150,000. Ronald Reagan and Jimmy Carter spent $58 million in the 1980 presidential election. Bob Dole and Bill Clinton spent a total of $250 million in 1996. The average cost for an incumbent in the U.S. House to win reelection in 1994 was $389,000. Liquor or money may be parts of effective strategies designed to gain votes. However, there are both legal and ethical issues in the strategies candidates use to seek the votes of the electorate.

Copyright © 1998 by Academic Press.
All rights of reproduction in any form reserved.

TABLE I Election Strategies

Fund-raising and contributions: Limitations, disclosures and uses

Polling: Consultants and nature of polls

Opposition research: Privacy vs. character vs. voter information

Advertisements: Truth vs. negativity

Platforms and promises: Misrepresentation vs. emotion

There are five different election strategies commonly used by candidates in order to win votes. Those strategies are summarized in Table I and include: fund-raising and contributions; polling; opposition research; advertisements and platforms coupled with promises.

II. FUND-RAISING AND CONTRIBUTIONS

A. The Problem of Quid Pro Quo

Since 1867 (see Table II), the United States has struggled legislatively with the conflict of interest issues that exist when funds are raised by or donated to candidates for public office.

The ethical issues that surround fund-raising and contributions arise because of concerns about degrees of influence as well as the appearance of impropriety. The notion that an individual, group, or business can "purchase" power in government operations is one that creates a conflict between the public servant's fiduciary duty and the concept of representative government and being in a possible position of payment in exchange for favorable government action toward the donor. There is an abundance of money available to candidates from corporate, union, and trade organizations. These groups

form political action committees to raise and disburse funds to candidates in order to assist those candidates in their election campaigns. The problem of perception of a quid pro quo relationship or favorable legislation in exchange for donation is one exacerbated by the legislative successes of the richest PACs. Tables III and IV provide the lists (as of 1996) of the richest corporate and noncorporate PACs, respectively, in federal election campaigns.

However, the reality of elections is that dissemination of information about candidates to voters is both necessary and expensive. The value of the free exchange of information has been a cornerstone of democracy in the United States. Justice Holmes of the U.S. Supreme Court wrote in his dissenting opinion in *Abrams v. United States* that it is the dissemination of information to the electorate that is critical for voter autonomy and noted, "truth is the only ground upon which their wishes can be carried out."

B. Government Regulation

It is through regulation of funds that many of the ethical issues surrounding campaign contributions and fund-raising have been resolved. To avoid excessive influence, federal law places maximum limits on contributions one individual can make to any one candidate. To provide full public information about the nature and sources of fund-raising and remove the secretive nature of donations, federal law also requires that candidates file disclosure statements with full disclosure of the names of donors, the amount of their donations, and the nature and amount of expenditures made with those funds. While these federal laws are applicable only to campaigns for federal office, most states and local gov-

TABLE II Federal Regulations on Campaign Fund-Raising and Expenditures

Statute	Date	Purpose
Naval Appropriations Act	1867	Illegal to solicit campaign contributions from government workers in U.S. Navy yards.
Civil Service Reform Act	1883	Federal employees prohibited from soliciting or accepting political contributions from other federal employees.
Tillman Act	1907	Corporations prohibited from making contributions to election campaigns.
Federal Corrupt Practices Act (FCPA)	1925	Mandated campaign contributions and expenditures disclosures.
Hatch Act	1939	Limits on individual campaign donations.
War Labor Disputes Act	1943	Labor organizations prohibited from making contributions in federal elections.
Federal Election Campaign Act	1971	Repealed FCPA 1) Required detailed disclosures on spending; 2) Limits of $1,000 per candidate and $25,000 preelection donations for anyone; 3) PAC maximum limitations of $5,000 per candidate donation.
Presidential/Election Campaign Fund Act	1971	Permitted taxpayers to contribute funds to presidential campaigns.

TABLE III   Top 20 Corporate PACS (1996 Elections)
(Funds raised and available)

1. American Telephone & Telegraph Company Political Action Committee (AT&T PAC)
2. United Parcel Service of America Inc. Political Action Committee (UPSPAC)
3. Black America's Political Action Committee
4. Federal Express Corporation Political Action Committee "FEPAC"
5. Lockheed Martin Employees Political Action Committee
6. Banc One PAC
7. Team Ameritech Political Action Committee
8. Union Pacific Fund for Effective Government
9. Philip Morris Companies Inc. Political Action Committee (AKA PHIL-PAC)
10. BellSouth Telecommunications Inc. Employees Federal Political Action Committee
11. RJR Political Action Committee RJR Nabisco Inc. (RJR PAC)
12. UST Executives Administrators and Managers Political Action Committee (AKA USTEAM PAC)
13. General Electric Company Political Action Committee
14. MBNA Corporation Federal Political Committee
15. Compass Bancshares Inc. Political Action Committee (Compass BANCPAC)
16. Tenneco Inc. Employees Good Government Fund (AKA Tenneco Employees Good Government Fund)
17. Civic Involvement Program/General Motors Corporation
18. Ford Motor Company Civic Action Fund
19. WMX Technologies Inc. Employees' Better Government Fund ("WMX PAC")
20. Employees of Northrop Grumman Corporation Political Action Committee (ENGPAC)

ernments also have similar limitations on contributions and disclosure requirements for state and local elections.

C. Gray Area One: Personal Expenses and Campaign Funds

Within these extensive state and federal election regulatory systems, however, there are certain gray areas. For example, the proper use of funds raised for a candidate's election has been a subject of great debate. In 1967, after having been in public office for 20 years, Senator Thomas Dodd was censured by a U.S. Senate vote of 92–5 for his use of campaign funds to make improvements on his Connecticut home, pay household bills and country club dues, and finance a trip for him and his wife to the Caribbean. Then Senator Dodd stated on the floor of the Senate,

This ... strikes at my heart because it has the connotation of treachery, deceit, dishonesty—the connotation that I fooled people—which I did not do. If you want to mark me as a thief, do it today. Do it before the sun goes down, and let me skulk away, ashamed to face you tomorrow.

Senator Dodd lost his next election and retired from public life. Today, however, the notion of the "proper" use of campaign funds has changed dramatically. Alan Keyes, a candidate for president in the 1996 election, is paid $8,500 per month from his campaign treasury. Most members of Congress have two residences (one in their home districts and one in the Washington, D.C., area) and they maintain one of those residences at campaign treasury expense. Car purchases or leases for candidates are considered routine campaign expenditures.

D. Gray Area Two: Consulting Firms and Spouse Employment

Other candidates use campaign treasury funds in the more creative fashion of paying them to media consulting firms owned by them and operated by their spouses or other members of their families. In many cases, the media consulting firms are operated from their

TABLE IV   Top 20 Noncorporate PACs (1996 Elections)
(Funds raised and available)

1. Emily's List
2. Campaign America
3. National Committee for an Effective Congress
4. Americans for Free International Trade Political Action Committee Inc.
5. National Conservative Club (FKA) National Congressional Club
6. Voters for Choice/Friends of Family Planning
7. Time Future Inc. (FKA Bill Bradley for U.S. Senate)
8. National PAC
9. Majority Leader's Fund
10. Hollywood Women's Political Committee
11. Ernst & Young Political Action Committee
12. New Republican Majority Fund
13. Arthur Andersen PAC (FKA) Arthur Andersen/Andersen Consulting PAC
14. Effective Government Committee
15. GOPAC Incorporated
16. Monday Morning Political Action Committee
17. Deloitte and Touche LLP Federal Political Action Committee
18. Council for a Livable World
19. Coopers & Lybrand PAC
20. American AIDS Political Action Committee

homes. These consulting firm payments are disclosed in public records only as payments for services to consulting firms when the funds are actually being used as a means of paying a spouse and supplementing a candidates' income.

While both the Senate and the House have ethics rules that prohibit personal use of campaign funds, the line for what constitutes personal versus campaign use is difficult to draw and the rules of both bodies are no longer enforced. As these rules are written, they permit uses of campaign funds for "officially connected" purposes. However, some legislators see the use of campaign funds for the personal expenses of public office as a means of saving taxpayers' money. Rather than fund expenses through their offices, they use campaign funds to allow donor funds to pay them. The only legislators to be punished in the last 15 years at the federal level for misuse of campaign funds were those who used funds for escorts for donors, for investments in the commodities markets, or to pay off personal debts.

Some members of the House of Representatives have argued for a strict rule that prohibits the use of campaign funds for anything that personally benefits the candidate rather than offering a sole and exclusive benefit to the campaign. However, other members respond that the need for elected officials to continue an ongoing campaign even while in office justifies the recoupment of living expenses from campaign funds. While the Federal Election Commission (FEC) is responsible for the oversight of expenditures, it has been reluctant to become involved in the review of these expenditures and their debatable benefits to a campaign.

For candidates, the ethical high road is to have disclosure of all uses of campaign funds and to put in place the necessary internal controls so that the funds do not become simply a personal account for the candidate. Those who donate funds to the campaign should be aware of the potential uses of the funds so that there are no misunderstandings between donor and candidate about the purpose of funds solicited or given.

E. Gray Area Three: Soft Money

Yet another gray area in campaign funding is what is referred to as "soft money." Soft money is money available for use on behalf of a candidate, although not directly under the candidate's control. A political party can raise unlimited funds with unlimited amounts given by individual donors. That party, in theory an autonomous entity, is then free to expend or donate funds as it sees fit in order to advance its ideals. However, federal law does not permit the parties candidates themselves to control the flow nor use of the funds. Nor can any candidates be part of the decision-making process for

expenditures of "soft money." Former Senator Robert Packwood wrote in his diaries of a meeting he had in 1992 in his office with Senator Phil Gramm in which Packwood alleged that Gramm promised to use $100,000 in soft money to help Packwood. Packwood wrote, "What was said in that room would be enough to convict us all of something."

F. Gray Area Four: Independent Expenditures

Another aspect of campaign financing that is fraught with ethical issues is the right of independent organizations to expend funds on behalf of any candidates. However, the expenditures of these independent organizations on behalf of individual candidates are often made in consultation with the campaign managers of these candidates. It is the element of independence that is at the heart of the statutory exemptions for independent organizations on spending and fund-raising. In *Buckley vs. Valeo,* the U.S. Supreme Court ruled that the First Amendment mandates that those who are not affiliated with a particular candidate be permitted to speak at any time and expend any amount of money in so doing. The absence of direct candidate involvement is the distinction that permits these expenditures and exempts them from limitation and regulation. Candidate control of fund-raising and spending by independent organizations is a violation of the spirit of the First Amendment. Nonetheless, the relationship between independent organizations and candidates continues to be an area of concern because of the potential for close contact with candidates. At one point, the U.S. Senate proposed ethics rules to prohibit contact between a candidate running for office (and any of the candidate's staff or consultants) and any independent organizations engaged in campaigning for the candidate or issues particularly associated with the candidate. The Senate Ethics Act continues to be a subject of debate as the members of the Senate grapple with the First Amendment protections of independent organizations and the need for their arms length relationships with candidates.

In all areas of campaign finance, the keys to avoiding ethical breaches are disclosure of sources and uses of funds, arm's-length transactions in fund disbursements and in relationships with other independent organizations, and clear guidelines on proper and improper campaign expenditures.

III. POLLING

The purposes of polling may be to discover voters' feelings on particular issues, certain candidates, or reactions to advertisements. A poll may also be conducted in a way to determine how demographics affect voters' reactions to issues, positions, and candidates. Polls are necessary and enormously useful devices in structuring and executing a campaign. It was in the 1996 presidential election that the term "push polling" evolved. The strategy of push polling is to commission a political consultant who will conduct a poll that produces the result desired by the candidate. That result could be obtained honestly, but is guaranteed to be obtained using certain constructs that might not be part of a valid statistical sample. For example, a polling consultant could release the results of a poll of a random selection of residents of a city. Or a polling consultant could release the results of a poll of a random selection of residents who voted in the last election. In other words, the results of a poll can be manipulated according to the "n" group chosen by the consultant as the data base.

Once the favorable results for a candidate are released, the voters may be influenced by the results with the poll then serving the purpose of pushing voters in a certain direction. The results of a poll may also cause those who favor the opposing candidate to resign themselves to a loss and have a resulting effect on the turnout on election day. The poll results from one narrowly defined group can often control the issue focus of a campaign. In the 1996 presidential election, the polls on the highly publicized "soccer moms" revealed that single women with children were more likely to vote for President Clinton because of his campaign proposals on college funding, hospital stays for delivery, and daycare policies and facilities.

The critical ethical issues in any polls commissioned or released by candidates are disclosure of who conducted the poll (for possible bias), the nature of the group polled, the phrasing of the questions, and the margin for error in the poll. While that information is generally always provided by media organizations conducting a poll, similar disclosures are not made in polls commissioned by candidates. Whether candidates have such an obligation presents an ethical dilemma that many would say raises a discovery responsibility on the part of the opposition rather than an affirmative duty of disclosure on the part of the candidate conducting the poll.

IV. OPPOSITION RESEARCH

The novel, *Primary Colors,* by Joe Klein ("Anonymous") highlights a character known as "Libby" who has the responsibility of collecting information on her candidate's opponent in order to have ammunition against that opponent. Her damaging information harms the opponent but is also used to silence detractors. Her skill is searching long and hard for background and history on opponents and detractors. Her background work is simply research put to effective political use. One political consultant has observed that "elections are won in the library."

Opposition research consists of gathering information about a political opponent on everything from a voting record to whether there are tax liens on his or her property. Some candidates have been embarrassed by the revelation that they failed to vote in the last general election. Within the political consultant field, a new group of researchers has emerged. These consultants are the experts in researching public records for revelations that are embarrassing to a candidate's opponents. An estimate for the 1996 federal elections puts the total expenditures on opposition research at between $25 and $30 million.

For some, private-eye sleuthing such as that conducted as opposition research is offensive. For others, these research consultants are simply performing a function that used to be done by the media: providing the voters with information about the background, lifestyle, character, and record of candidates for public office.

The ethical issues that arise in this sophisticated snooping include whether it is appropriate to go beyond public records. For example, a question often asked among opposition researchers is whether it is ethical to search through an opponent's trash looking for potentially damaging information because of the privacy implications associated with such a search. Other experts worry that the level of opposition research turns political campaigns into nothing more than a game of "Trivial Pursuit," in which the candidates try to outdo each other with disclosures that may have little to do with the issues of the campaign or the concerns of the voters. The information may, however, have some impact on those issues. In the 1992 California U.S. Senate race, Republican Bruce Herschensohn accused incumbent senator Barbara Boxer of "lacking" religious values. Opposition research in the form of following Herschensohn revealed that he had been to nude bars. Herschensohn confirmed that revelation as true and lost the election. The ethical issue that remains in many minds was whether the election should turn on such a revelation.

Personal versus public information has emerged as the definitive line for opposition research. Voting records, litigation, liens, and compliance with campaign finance laws are all issues of relevance in terms of a candidate's character. When information such as this is not disclosed, voters make their judgments without evidence that may be relevant. A candidate in a California legislative race uncovered, through opposition research, a significant number of mortgage defaults by his opponent. He declined to use the information against his opponent. He lost the election. The mortgage-defaulting candidate has been ranked as a very poor legislator. Voters were deprived of this relevant information obtained through opposition research.

V. ADVERTISEMENTS

A. The Nature of Political Ads

Political ads (as summarized in Table V) run from those that simply describe the candidate to those that associate a voter hot-button issue with the opposition. Other ads use information on the candidate's record or personal life to provide voters with a negative image. Still other ads tie a societal harm to an opponent or focus on a hot-button issue that reflects negatively on the opposition.

In the 1988 presidential election, George Bush ran an ad that described the conduct of Willie Horton, an African American who raped and murdered a woman while he was on furlough from a Massachusetts prison. Mr. Bush's opponent, Michael Dukakis, was the governor of Massachusetts at the time Mr. Horton was furloughed and committed the crimes. The ad was a classic example of a single issue that hit voters' hot button. Concerns about crime, parole, and recidivism were all social issues of great concern to voters. The Horton ad became a turning point in the election and is often cited by political scientists and consultants as an example of the power of political advertising.

In the 1996 presidential elections, President Clinton's ads on Speaker Newt Gingrich and presidential candidate Bob Dole and their roles in the reduction of Social Security and Medicare had the effect of frightening many senior citizens into voting for Mr. Clinton. Mr. Dole's ads, which included a clip of Mr. Clinton telling an MTV audience that he might inhale if given another chance at smoking marijuana, were used in conjunction with statistics on drug use being up among teenagers. The ad was one used to try to have voters associate

TABLE V   Political Advertisements

| Touting personal record |
| Touting personal characteristics |
| Revealing/describing opponent's record |
| Revealing/describing opponent's character |
| Societal harm—cause and effect |
| Single issue hot-buttons |

Mr. Clinton's personal views as the cause of the drug use increase.

B. Regulation of Political Ads

These ads represent the most dramatic forms of political advertising. Whether the ads are true or false or fair or deceptive is not the issue. The Supreme Court has carved out a clear niche for political advertisements. While commercial speech, or ads for products are subject to government regulation for accuracy and fairness, political speech, or speech on behalf of issues or candidates, enjoys an immunity from such regulation. As noted earlier, the desire to have a fully informed electorate fuels the protection candidates enjoy in making their cases through television, radio, and print ads. Any form of content regulation of election ads would fall under a constitutionally mandated and highly suspect category of regulation. To date, states have not enjoyed much success in passing constitutional content regulation on political advertisements. Some states have passed statutes requiring all candidates to participate in public forums in order to give voters more information than that offered in carefully constructed political ads. Other states have required that pamphlets with position statements from candidates be distributed to voters to supplement the slanted candidate-constructed political ads. With respect to ballot initiatives and propositions, many states have disclosure requirements on the sources of financing for such ads. For example, an organization opposing a smoking ban initiative would be required to disclose that one of its sources of funding was a tobacco company.

The fairness of political advertising, the issues of mudslinging and the rough-and-tumble nature of politics have been with us since the days when Alexander Hamilton engaged in a duel to protect his political reputation. In 1850, Mississippi Senator Henry Foote pulled a pistol on Missouri Senator Thomas H. Benton during a debate on slavery. However, recent campaigns have caused political scientists, such as Kathleen Hall Jamieson to remark, "never before in a presidential campaign have televised ads sponsored by a major party candidate lied so blatantly as in the campaign of 1988." Alexander Kroll, the chairman of Young & Rubicam noted, "Political advertising is so wretched that most of it wouldn't be approved by our own self-governing boards."

C. Self-Regulation of Political Ads

Based on the concerns about the truth and political ads, proposals have been advanced for forms of self-regulation of these forms of political speech. For example, during her 1994 campaign for governor of California, Kathleen Brown asked all candidates for office to sign a notarized document that read, "We pledge to be honest." Thomas Jefferson's response to pledges and claims of honesty was, "The more he spoke of his honesty, the faster we counted our spoons." Paul Alvarez, chairman of Ketchum Communications, proposed that political ads be held to the same standards as are other ads: no lies and no disparagement. Mr. Alvarez has proposed a committee to work on a code of ethics for political advertisements that would offer to consultants and candidates the opportunity to establish standards for political ads that would not violate the U.S. Constitution because of their voluntary nature.

Others maintain that the function of political ads is to place information for the public to evaluate and consider. Just as not all products are purchased by all people because they are skeptical about the claims, not all candidates win voter approval simply because an ad offers certain claims about him or her or the opposition. H. L. Mencken once wrote that the role of every philosopher is to establish that every other philosopher is an ass. Mencken also noted that they all accomplished their goal. There are those who maintain that political ads are reviewed by voters with the idea that there is an agenda at work, and that voters are capable of scrutiny and discernment.

Difficulties also arise in controlling forms of ads. While candidates may pledge to conduct an "issues" campaign, many do view the character and personal life of a candidate as an issue. Negative information about one's opponent record is negative, but it is also relevant information for voters. One distinction that has emerged in the debate over the control of political ads is that the line on content should be drawn on truth and falsehood. In other words, it is not the negative aspect of the ad that creates the ethical issue, it is whether the information that gives rise to the negative perception is true or false. If an incumbent has been absent on 50% of all votes taken in the last legislative session, that information is negative, but it is not unethical to advance that information in the form of an ad if in fact the 50% figure is accurate.

VI. PLATFORMS AND PROMISES

In recent years, no campaign platform promise has been more recalled or had greater significance than George Bush's 1988 campaign promise of "Read my lips. No new taxes." During his administration, Mr. Bush did raise taxes and those words were used by Mr. Clinton in the 1992 campaign to demonstrate a contrast between his character and that of Mr. Bush in the sense of keeping promises. It was a campaign promise not kept, and Mr. Bush's credibility suffered in his reelection campaign.

With election platforms and promises, there is perhaps a prevailing Albert Carr philosophy of "so long as we all understand we're lying to each other, it's okay." There is a certain acceptance in election strategy that the rhetoric of a candidate is different and does not carry accountability. Therefore, many promises are made during campaigns that simply cannot be fulfilled. In the 1992 presidential primaries, Democratic candidate Bruce Babbitt became a household name when he stood in a debate and said that he was standing up for new taxes because they were inevitable. His honesty was the demise of his candidacy. Some have compared campaign promises to romance—the words must later be discounted. However, the Bush experience taught campaign strategists that clear and unequivocal promises carry expectations with voters.

Bibliography

Alexander, H. (1984). *Financing Politics: Money, Elections, and Political Reform* (3rd. ed.). Washington, DC: CQ Press.

Carr, A. (1968). Is Business Bluffing Ethical? *Harvard Business Review.*

Colford, Steven W. (1994, December 8). Coming clean on political ads. *Advertising Age.*

Corn, D. (1995, October 9). Money Talks. *The Nation*, p. 373.

Faber, R. J. *et al.* (1993). Negative political advertising and voting intent: The role of involvement and alternative information sources. *Journal of Advertising, 22*(4): 67–76.

Hazlett, T. W. (1994, June). And that's the truth. *Reason*, p. 66.

Impoco, J. (1996, October 21). The fine art of digging dirt. *U.S. News & World Report*, 44–45.

Moran, T. J. (1992). Political Debate without Suppressing Free Speech. *Indiana Law Journal, 67*, p. 663.

Note, Constitutional Law. (1986). Campaign finance reform and the first amendment—All the free speech money can buy. *Oklahoma Law Review, 39*, p. 729.

O'Neil, R. M. (1992). Regulating speech to cleanse political campaigns. *Capital U. L. Rev., 21*, p. 575.

Overby, P. (1992, September). Charge it to my campaign. *Common Cause*, p. 23.

Shipper, F., & Jennings, M. M. (1989). *Business Strategy for Political Arena.* Westport, CT: Quorum Books: Greenwood Press.

Sittig, R. F. (1995, January). Campaign reform: Interest groups, parties and candidates. *Annals*, p. 537.

Teinowitz, I. (1996, July 8). The politics of vice. *Advertising Age*, p. 1.

Electronic Surveillance

GARY T. MARX and GREGORY UNGAR
University of Colorado at Boulder

GLOSSARY

minimization A principle of personal data collection in which only the amount of information essential to the goal is gathered

new surveillance A term for a family of technologies for extracting personal information, such as computers, video cameras, and electronic location monitoring devices, in which data can often be gathered, combined, and analyzed inexpensively without a person's consent or knowledge

personal borders The boundaries (whether physical, spacial, relational, or symbolic) that separate the individual from others

privacy An expectation that an individual can control his or her personal information

SURVEILLANCE of individuals has changed markedly with recent developments in electronic, biochemical, and data base forms of personal information collection and analysis. Computer data bases, video cameras, drug testing, and work monitoring are routine. They are or will be joined by new means that may become equally prevalent: DNA screening and monitoring for insurance and employment; electronic location and other forms of monitoring via computer chips that are worn or even implanted under the skin; Internet monitoring that keeps a record of what one has viewed on a computer and for how long; "intelligent" highway systems that record where a vehicle is and its speed; "smart cards" that contain extensive personal information (e.g., passport, banking, credit, medical, and arrest records, driver's license); satellite photography; the linking of video and facial recognition technology that permits scanning faces to find subjects of interest; and "smart homes" in which data flows (whether electricity, communications, or energy) into, or out of, the home are part of the same monitored system.

I. THE NEW SURVEILLANCE

These technologies constitute the "new surveillance". The new surveillance has a number of characteristics that separate it from traditional forms. It can

1. transcend boundaries of time, distance, darkness, and physical boundaries such as walls and skin that traditionally protected privacy;
2. permit the inexpensive and immediate sharing, merging, and it can
3. permit combining discrete types of information such as voice, computer data, facsimile, electronic mail, and video;
4. permit simulating realities and altering data;
5. involve remote access;
6. often be done invisibly;
7. often be done without the subject's knowledge or consent;
8. permit more intensive information collection, probing more deeply;

9. permit more extensive information collection, covering broader areas.

The boundaries that have defined and given integrity to social systems, groups, and the self are increasingly permeable. The power of governmental and private organizations to compel disclosure (whether based on law, circumstance, or technology) and to aggregate, analyze, and distribute personal information is growing rapidly.

We are becoming a transparent society of record such that documentation of our past history, current identity, location, and physiological and psychological states and behavior is increasingly possible. With predictive profiles there are even claims to be able to know individual futures. Information collection often occurs invisibly, automatically, and remotely—being built into routine activities. Awareness and genuine consent on the part of the subject may be lacking.

The amount of personal information collected is increasing. New technologies have the potential to reveal the unseen, unknown, forgotten, or withheld. Like the discovery of the atom or the unconscious, they bring to the surface bits of reality that were previously hidden, or did not contain informational clues. In a sense people are turned inside out.

To be alive and a social being is to automatically give off signals of constant information—whether in the form of heat, pressure, motion, brain waves, perspiration, cells, sound, olifacteurs, waste matter, or garbage, as well as more familiar forms such as communication and visible behavior. These remnants are given by contemporary surveillance technologies. Through a value-added, mosaic process, machines (often with only a little help from their friends) may find significance in surfacing and combining heretofore meaningless data.

The ratio of what individuals know about themselves (or are capable of knowing) versus what outsiders and experts can know about them has shifted away from the individual. Data in diverse forms from widely separated geographical areas, organizations, and time periods can be easily merged and analyzed. In relatively unrestrained fashion new (and old) organizations are capturing, combining, and selling this information, or putting it to novel internal uses.

To a degree these technologies are controlled by laws, organizational policies, etiquette, and countertechnologies that seek to protect personal information. Such efforts imply ethical assumptions that are often unstated. In this article we suggest an ethical framework for thinking about personal surveillance.

II. ETHICS

It might appear that an ethics for surveillance is an oxymoron. Is surveillance with its connotation of spying and suspicion incompatible with ethics? This article suggests that an ethics of, or for, surveillance is not only possible, but necessary. Yet given the gravity and complexity of the issues and the risks, we suggest this gingerly and tentatively. There are extremes of surveillance and good and bad uses. Reasoned discussion can enhance the former and minimize the latter.

Surveillance, broadly defined as attentiveness to one's external environment, is a fundamental part of complex living organisms. Societal attitudes in democracies are profoundly ambivalent about it because it can offer protection via the eye of a benevolent God, leader, or parent or domination by a Leviathan. We cannot live without it, but neither should we live with its excesses. It can be linked (although not necessarily always reduced) to issues of power and authority.

This chapter suggests an ethics for those who carry out the surveillance or data collection. It assumes that under appropriate conditions they may have a *right* to do this, but they also have a *duty* to do it responsibly. Reciprocally, those subject to legitimate surveillance may have duties as well (e.g., not to distort the findings), even as they also have rights not to be subjected to some forms of surveillance. Given the tilted (if not outrightly downhill) nature of the playing field, in which powerful interests and organizations are practically unopposed in emphasizing their rights to gather personal information rather than their duties, and offensively take the behavioral initiative, our emphasis is on creating an ethics that applies to them rather than to their subjects. Yet it is also well to note that given the multiple roles we play, we all rotate between being ''surveillors'' and the surveilled, if hardly equally.

Our discussion is based on conventional domestic settings in a democratic society for those with full adult citizenship rights. In situations of extreme crisis, such as war, when dealing with very different countries or cultures, children, the ill, the incompetent, or those juridically denied certain rights such as prisoners, a different discussion is needed and the lines in some ways will be drawn differently. That, however, does not negate the value of the principles to be discussed here as ideals that should apply more broadly, other factors being equal.

One form of ethical theory or principle is sweeping, categorical, and absolutist. It declares certain behaviors as either prohibited or required. Biblical commandments are an example. The Bible, for example, does not say ''in considering whether to kill the following factors should be considered.''

In contrast, the form of ethics treated here considers right and wrong in relative, context-specific terms. In doing so it recognizes the contingent nature of many ethical assessments—that principles may conflict and be subject to different understandings and weighing, that the facts on which an assessment is to be made may be unclear, in dispute, or subject to different interpretations, and that complex situations likely involve multiple dimensions, each subject to ethical analysis.

The relational perspective would say "a situation becomes more or less morally acceptable to the extent that the following conditions are present," or "situations in which these elements are present are morally preferable to situations where they are lacking." Such a perspective requires one to compare a given means to alternatives and to the consequences of taking no action.

In evaluating any behavior we might begin with the law and with whether or not a behavior does what it claims to. While there is much to debate regarding what the law ought to be or how it is to be interpreted and whether or not a tactic works, one does not need to be an ethical theorist to know that the application of a technology should be legal and it should make sense. We take that for granted. But just because an extractive technology is legal and valid does not necessarily make it morally acceptable. Ethical criteria also need to be considered. Of course these can be related—laws can be grounded in morality or be immoral and to use an invalid technique can be unfair and wasteful, but they are empirically and, for some purposes, analytically distinct.

Many positive uses are not in dispute—video cameras and sensors for monitoring the flow of anonymous traffic or a data base containing the names of doctors and lawyers with suspended licenses. Other cases represent obvious abuses—surreptitious video or audio taping among friends or selling of confidential information by medical or criminal justice personnel. Of much greater interest theoretically and for public policy are the cases in which there is disagreement—listening in to a cell or cordless telephone communication that is equivalent to a radio broadcast; drug testing in noncritical contexts such as the employees of retail stores, the selling of consumer lists, or going through a person's trash.

Here we operate inductively. Rather than starting with an ethical framework and applying it to behavior, we start with behavior and examine the beliefs and feelings it engenders. What arguments underlie beliefs about whether personal surveillance is justified or not? Of course, ideas from the major deductive ethical systems such as Kant's emphasis on consistency and dignity or utilitarianism are reflected in commonly held attitudes, although not in an integrated and consistent manner.

Let us begin the analysis by making a distinction between (1) *the means* (instrument) of data collection, 2) *the context and conditions* under which the data are gathered, and 3) *the uses/goals* to which the data are put. There is a temporal sequence here as we start with the means and then move to collection and use.

A given means such as video can be used for a variety of goals and a given goal such as drug testing can be done in a variety of ways. Means and goals apart, the conditions under which these appear also show enormous variation. The ethical status can vary from cases in which the means, the context, and the use are all abhorrent to those in which they are all acceptable or even desirable, to varying combinations. Ethical analysis needs to consider all three factors. Beyond different value priorities and interpretations, disagreements in evaluation often involve persons emphasizing one rather than another of these elements.

A. The Means

Are there some means of personal information collection that are simply immoral? Torture is the obvious case. For many observers the polygraph with its tight-fitting bodily attachments, manipulation, and questionable validity; a drug test requiring a person to urinate in front of another; and harming or threatening friends or relatives of a suspect in order to obtain information, are also generally unethical. Similarly, most persons recoil at the thought of certain coercive bodily intrusions such as pumping the stomach of a suspect believed to have swallowed evidence or removing a bullet from the body for ballistics matching (practices that the courts have generally also prohibited).

For many moral theorists and much of society, lying, deception, and manipulation are a cluster of means that in and of themselves are ethically questionable. These come together in the case of undercover tactics. Such means (unlike many other surveillance means) always present a moral dilemma. This is not to suggest that under certain conditions and for certain ends they may not on balance be appropriate. But no matter how compelling the latter, this does not alter the fact that in our culture neither lying and trickery nor physical force and coercion are morally preferred techniques.

We have identified a folk or common sense morality that underlies judgments made about the collection of personal information. A popular expression claims "if it doesn't look right, that's ethics." And when the means do not look right, the act of collecting personal data is likely to involve saying "yes" to one or more of the following questions:

1. Does the act of collecting the data (apart from its use) involve unwarranted physical or psychological harm?
2. Does the technique cross a personal boundary without permission (whether involving coercion or deception, or a body, relational, or spatial border)?
3. Does the technique violate trust and assumptions that are made about how personal information will be treated such as no secret recordings?

4. Does the technique produce invalid results?

To the extent that one or more of these concerns are present the means as such raise ethical concerns.

Of course, the generality of these concepts offers ample room to ask when they apply. With cleverness or sophistry one can make them problematic. Is harm to be measured by objective or subjective accounts? What about culture or individual differences in definitions of harm, trust, and the drawing of personal boundaries? However, our argument in the first instance is empirical and even intuitive, like Supreme Court Justice Stevens's definition of pornography ("I can't define it, but I know it when I see it"). Within American culture certain data collection means simply feel wrong. Whether this sense extends empirically (or ought to extend morally) to other Western or industrial societies, or more broadly to all societies (if one accepts the idea that there are universal human rights that all persons should be entitled to) is an important question, but beyond our concern here.

In spite of the fact that some data collection or surveillance means are inherently undesirable, most contemporary disputes do not involve the means as such; rather, they involve the context and the end. Ethical disagreements and problems are more likely to be found in the conditions around the data collection and/or in the use of the data.

B. The Data Collection Context

With respect to the context, we ask how the technique is applied and we ask about its social setting. Even if we have a means that is morally acceptable, that is not sufficient justification. We also need to attend to the context of its application and then to its use.

A distinction here can be made between (1) the actual collection of the information, and (2) the broader conditions surrounding this. In the first case we are again concerned with the presence of harm, unwarranted border crossings, trust, and validity. At the most general level these represent respect for the dignity of the person. In this case we assume that it is possible to collect the information in an ethically acceptable fashion. We draw attention to the discretion surveillors have to behave *within* or *beyond* ethical bounds in their use of a means that *is* capable of being ethically applied.

1. Data Collection

With respect to harm during the process of information collection, tactics such as interviews, psychological tests, drug tests, and searches can be done to minimize or maximize discomfort.

Validity here refers to whether the tactic is applied correctly and measures what it claims to measure. Situations in which invalid readings result (whether out of malevolence, incompetence, good faith errors, faulty machines, or unaccounted-for confounding factors) are obviously unfair and wasteful (not to mention the liability issues involved in wrongful application and use). There must be a means to verify results, and those in charge must have enough confidence in the system that they would willingly submit to it themselves when appropriate. It must not be assumed that fallible humans can design and operate infallible machines (or given the complexity, that machines are infallible).

Lack of validity may apply to an individual case, as with the switching of a positive for a negative drug test or factors that can confound a drug test, such as that the subject ate poppy seeds prior to giving a urine sample. Or problems of validity can apply to a broad group as when a large number of false readings result because of faulty lab procedures. A pattern of systematic errors is particularly troubling given what amounts to the institutionalization of unfairness.

Borders have legitimate and illegitimate crossing points and interstitial and gray areas. Being invited in the front door is very different from breaking it down or sneaking in the back door. Information collected in a public setting such as a street or park is different from that taken in a private setting. Regardless of the setting, information available to the unaided senses has a different moral status than that which can only be assessed with sense-enhancing technologies.

Personal border crossings and trust are related to (and even defined by) whether (1) individuals are *aware* that personal information is being collected and, if so (2) whether they agree to the collection and subsequent uses of the data. These are difficult concepts because no one can be fully aware of all the possible consequences of the act of data collection, nor of subsequent uses. In the same way, "consent" is always conditioned by the range of choices and their relative costs and benefits.

While to consent means to be aware, the reverse is not necesarily true. Whether or not consent is sought is perhaps the most important ethical question with respect to the collection of personal data. Of course, there are social roles granted the right to transcend personal boundaries without consent, such as police and emergency medical personnel. However, in conventional settings the failure to inform, or a coercive lack of choice, is of a different order.

Taking information without consent may also be seen to violate a proprietary right the individual has to control his or her personal information. At one extreme this is reflected in the Fifth Amendment's protection against self-incrimination.

A component of justice is fair warning—providing people with information about the rules, procedures, rewards, and punishments they are subject to. Beyond showing respect for the person, full disclosure can be a means of shaping behavior, as individuals know they will be assessed and they may behave accordingly (e.g., paying bills on time to avoid being data base-labeled as a bad credit risk). Openness about data collection can also help bring accountability to the data collectors because it comes with an address.

We can also ask if consent has the quality of "opting in" or "opting out." In the latter case individuals are told that if they give their permission their individual data will be collected. In the former, individuals are told that their data will automatically be collected *unless* they request that it not be. Those with an interest in gathering the data strongly prefer the latter system of opting out—that is, requiring persons to ask that they *not* be included. To be sure that is better than offering no choice at all. But because many persons will be ignorant of the possibility of opting out or will not want to take the time, not remember, or be unaware of the potential negative consequences, "opting in" is preferable.

There are also degrees—such as full awareness that a tactic may be used, versus knowing that it will be used but not in precise detail where and when (e.g., where a hidden camera is, or whether or not there is a monitor/recorder behind a known camera). A nice example of being informed and consenting are some Internet websites that inform users that "cookies," a program that charts what the individual views, may be activated or blocked as the user chooses.

Even if the data gatherer does not offer a formal choice, it may be possible to, in effect, have this by using a countertechnology to block the collection of personal information. If devices to prevent the unwarranted collection of personal information are widely available but nevertheless are not used, then there is a sense in which persons do choose to release their information. Yet that is not the case if such means are very expensive or are difficult to use.

An element of choice may also be present when privacy becomes commodified such that persons can choose by payment or compensation the level of privacy they desire. Yet it is still important that privacy thresholds be available below which no one falls.

The concept of consent, of course, can be very problematic, given the role of culture in shaping perceptions and the fact that choices always occur within situations that are not fully free, or within the making of the person choosing. For example, the meaning of choice with respect to agreeing to take a drug test is very different in a one-industry town than in a setting where one can find equvialent work settings in which not all employers require such a test.

In flying on a domestic Canadian airline a friend saw the following sign:

> Notice: Security measures are being taken to observe and inspect persons. No passengers are obliged to submit to a search of persons or goods if they choose not to board our aircraft.

Rather than spend days in the car or on the train, the friend had chosen to fly and "agreed" to be searched. Most persons would do the same. But to claim the choise is somehow voluntary as the sign suggests is disingenuous in the extreme. Choice to be meaningful should imply some genuine alternatives and refusal costs that are not wildly exorbitant.

We also need to ask, "consent to what?" Thus, a mass marketing executive reports "the data isn't out there because we stole it from them. Someone gave it away, and it's out there for us to use." In a legal sense that is true. But the element of "giving it away" was not a willful choice in the obvious sense. Rather, the data became available indirectly as a result of taking some other action. At the time, were the individuals to be asked if they agree to have their information used for marketing purposes, it might not be "out there" waiting for specious disclaimers about its nontheft.

We can also ask "who consents?" Thus, when children follow the advice of a television clown and hold their telephone receivers in front of their set and a remote signal sent through the television set activates the phone and sends its number over a toll-free line, they have acted voluntarily. But they did not know that this was to be used for direct mail marketing purposes for candy and even if they did, the "consent" of small children obtained by a clown seems specious.

Given the complexities and competing values, the absence of informed consent is not automatically a sign of unethical behavior, but situations where it is present are clearly morally preferable to those where it is not.

One aspect of harm and crossing into possibly perilous personal borders involves going farther than is required or than has been publicly announced (and perhaps agreed to by the subject). Here we ask, does a principle of *minimization* apply to the collection of personal data?

One should go no farther than is necessary for the task at hand, in spite of temptations and incentives to go beyond. Granted that many of these tactics by their very nature cross personal boundaries and may subject the person to feelings of embarrassment, shame, and powerlessness, we can still ask was this done in a professional manner and only to the extent necessary to obtain the informational end, or does it go beyond that? For example, is wiretapping applied in a categorical way such that all communications are listened to or only those pertaining to the focused goal? If federal minimization rules are followed regarding wiretapping it will be only the latter. A related example is the very precise time and place limits of well-drawn search warrants.

In contrast, many private-sector data gatherers face no such limits. As an "insurance" policy, data collectors often favor gathering more rather than less information, because they can never be sure that sometime in the future they might not need it, or that a new way of using it might not be discovered. Consider large retail chains that may routinely ask (even cash purchasers) for names and telephone numbers, or the extraneous data collection about life-style and demographic characteristics that accompany warranty forms. Much of that information ends up in a massive data base in Denver. Medical samples taken for employment purposes may be analyzed for conditions for which informed consent has not been given.

The potential to go too far is also found with the system operators for many networked computers. For example, some interactive computer games or other services that involve using software at a company's Web page also give the company the opportunity (although certainly not the right), to explore everything in a user's computer. There may be valid reasons for doing this (e.g., to see if a player has stolen or misused files), but there is no justification for looking at other unrelated files. In the same way, providers of telephone and e-mail services may need to monitor communication to be sure their systems are working, but to listen to conversations or read e-mail beyond what is technically required for service reasons is wrong. Yet the temptation can be great.

2. The Social Setting

The second aspect of the conditions of data collection involves the broader social context, rather than the direct application of the tactic as such. We identify 10 procedural conditions. In the absence of these, problems are more likely to occur. The presence of these policies and procedures does not make a tactic ethical, but it does increase the likelihood of ethically acceptable outcomes.

Some procedural conditions:

1. *Public decision-making:* Was the decision to use a tactic arrived at through some public discussion and decision-making process? For example, are the conditions of computer and telephone work monitoring of reservation clerks jointly developed through a management-union or worker's council committee?

2. *Human review:* Is there human review of machine-generated results? Given the acontextual nature of much of the data the technology generates and the possibility of hardware and software failure, this is vital. Generally, individuals as interpreters of human situations are far more sensitive to nuance than are computers, even if they are much more expensive.

3. *Right of inspection:* Are people aware of the findings and how they were created? Being entitled to know the evidence and, as the next condition suggests, to challenge it are fundamental aspects of procedural justice.

4. *Right to challenge and express a grievance:* Are there procedures for challenging the results, or for entering alternative data or interpretations into the record?

5. *Redress and sanctions:* If the individual has been treated unfairly and procedures have been violated, are there appropriate means of redress? Are there means for discovering violations and penalties to encourage responsible surveillant behavior? In Europe and Canada there are official data commissioners who may actively seek out compliance. But in the United States it is up to individuals to bring forward complaints. But in order for that to happen they must first be aware that there is a problem and that there are standards.

6. *Adequate data stewardship and protection:* Can the security of the data be adequately protected? There must be standards for who has access to the data and audit trails, for whether and when data is to be updated, for how long it is to be kept, and the conditions under which it is to be destroyed.

Finally, three more general questions deal not with a given individual, but with broader social consequences:

7. *Equality-inequality regarding availability and application:* This involves three questions:

    a. Is the means widely available or is it restricted to only the most wealthy, powerful, or technologically sophisticated?

    b. Within a setting, is the tactic broadly applied to all people or only to those less powerful or unable to resist?

    c. If there are means of resisting the provision of personal information (whether technically, economically, or legally) are these equally available, or restricted to the most privileged?

The first question applies particularly to conflict and hierarchical settings and relates to Kant's principle of universalism or consistency, which asks "would it be acceptable if all persons or groups used the tactic?" The democratization of surveillance through low cost and ease of use can introduce a healthy pluralism and balance (as well as reiprocal inhibitions in use for fear of retaliation). On the other hand this may also help create a more defensive and suspicious society with an overall increase in surveillance.

We can also apply a principle of consistency that asks if the tactic is applied to everyone (which is different from asking what if everyone applied it?) Here we ask about equality within a setting—is the tactic (particularly if it is controversial) applied to all, or only to some (usually those lower in status)? For example, are executives drug tested and are their phone and e-mail communications subject to monitoring as with other employees? If there is inequality, is the rationale for differential application clear and justifiable?

Finally, we need to consider (in the absence of being able to just say no) whether there are means available that make it possible for people to maintain greater control over their personal information and, if so, how widely available these are. Some, such as providing a false name and address when the request is irrelevant (as with paying cash for consumer electronics) or free, anonymous e-mail forwarding services, are available to anyone. In other cases privacy may come with a price tag, as with the purchase of a device for shredding records, having an unlisted phone number, or possessing the technical skill to encrypt one's e-mail or telephone communications.

8. *The symbolic meaning of a method:* What does the use of a method communicate more generally? Some practices simply look bad in being deeply violative of a broad principle such as respect for the dignity of the person. Something much broader than the harm to a particular individual seems present here. There is a sense in which a social value is undermined and the community as a whole may be harmed.

9. *The creation of unwanted precedents:* Is it likely to create precedents that will lead to its application in undesirable ways? Even if a new tactic seems otherwise acceptable, it is important to apply a longer range perspective and consider where might it lead. The social security number, which has become a de facto national identification card that Congress clearly did not intend when it was created, is an example.

10. *Negative effects on surveillors and third parties:* Are there negative effects on those beyond the subject? For example, what is the impact on the personality of being a professional watcher or infiltrator? In another example, there is some evidence that police who use radar guns in traffic enforcement have higher rates of testicular cancer. Audio and video tapping may record the behavior of suspects, as well as that of their family and friends. Tactics rarely stand alone, and their possible implications for persons beyond the subject need to be considered.

III. USES OF SURVEILLANCE DATA

Let us move from the tactic itself and the social context in which information is collected to its actual use. The first two may be ethically acceptable even as the uses to which the data are put is ethically unacceptable.

It is easy to identify relatively noncontroversial positive goals such as productivity, health, and crime prevention. It is more difficult to identify questionable goals because by their very nature they are less likely to be publicized (e.g., DNA insurance exclusion examples based on future predictions). These may involve using inappropriate means for strategic gain or profit, an effort to enforce an employer's morality, politics, or opposition to unions onto employees, or illogic or ignorance. The gray area here is large, even if cases at the extremes are clear. For example, is use of a pulmonary lung test to measure whether employees are not smoking (in conformity with a company's nonsmoking policy), a necessary health and cost-saving measure good for both the company and the employee, or is it a wrongful crossing of the boundary between work and nonwork settings?

In considering goals we need to be alert to the possibility that the publicly stated goals may mask other less-desirable goals. Even when that is not the case, moral worth must be sought in the consequences of the use, beyond the good intentions of those applying the technology.

To help in assessing the "use" issue the following questions need to be asked. Other factors being equal, the first response suggests an ethical use and the second an unethical use.

1. *Appropriate vs. inappropriate goals:* Are the goals of the data collection legitimate? Are they publically announced? Consider the following contrasting cases:
    —drug testing bus drivers vs. junior high school students who wish to play in the school band;
    —a doctor asking a female patient about her birth control and abortion history in a clinical setting vs. asking this of *all* female employees (as one large airline did) without indicating why the information was needed.

2. *The goodness of fit between the means and the goal:* Is there a clear link between the information collected and the goal sought? How well a test measures what it claims to—drug and alcohol use, miles driven, or location—can be differentiated from second-order inferences made about goals only indirectly related to the actual results of the measurement. As we move from the direct results of a measure that is immediately meaningful given the goal (e.g., a drug test to determine if a person has abided by the conditions of their parole), to more distant inferences about goals, questions may

arise. For example, some research suggests that drug tests may not be associated with the employment performance behaviors they are presumed to predict. In that regard a test for transportation workers that directly measures reflexes is preferable to a more inferential drug test.

3. *Information used for original vs. other unrelated purposes:* Is the personal information used for the reasons offered for its collection and for which consent may have been given? Does the data stay with the original collector, or does it migrate elsewhere? For example, are the results of medical tests undertaken for diagnostic and treatment purposes sold or otherwise obtained by potential insurers, employers, or pharmaceutical com-

panies? Using data for unrelated purposes may violate shared understandings and can also involve deception, if collectors know from the start how it will be used and do not reveal that.

4. *Failure to share secondary gains from the information:* Is the personal data collected used for profit without permission from, or benefit to, the person who provided it (or at least participated in its generation)? This implies a private property defense of personal information and contrasts with a definition based on universal human or democratic citizenship rights. To sell another person's information without asking them and without letting them share in the gain might even be seen as a kind of theft. The issue of ownership of personal infor-

---

TABLE I   Questions to Help Determine the Ethics of Surveillance

A. The Means

1. *Harm:* Does the act of collecting the data (apart from its use) involve unwarranted physical or psychological harm?

2. *Boundaries:* Does the technique cross a personal boundary without permission?

3. *Trust:* Does the technique violate trust and assumptions that are made about how personal information will be treated, such as no secret recordings?

4. *Validity:* Does the technique produce invalid results?

B. The Data Collection Context

5. *Awareness:* Are individuals aware that personal information is being collected?

6. *Consent:* Do individuals consent to the data collection?

7. *Minimization:* Does a principle of minimization apply?

8. *Public decision-making:* Was the decision to use a tactic arrived at through some public discussion and decision-making process?

9. *Human review:* Is there human review of machine-generated results?

10. *Right of inspection:* Are people aware of the findings and how they were created?

11. *Right to challenge and express a grievance:* Are there procedures for challenging the results, or for entering alternative data or interpretations into the record?

12. *Redress and sanctions:* If the individual has been treated unfairly and procedures have been violated, are there appropriate means of redress? Are there means for discovering violations and penalties to encourage responsible surveillant behavior?

13. *Adequate data stewardship and protection:* Can the security of the data be adequately protected?

14. *Equality-inequality regarding availability and application:*
    a. Is the means widely available or restricted to only the most wealthy, powerful, or technologically sophisticated?
    b. Within a setting, is the tactic broadly applied to all people or only to those less powerful or unable to resist?
    c. If there are means of resisting the provision of personal information are these equally available, or restricted to the most privileged?

15. *The symbolic meaning of a method:* What does the use of a method communicate more generally?

16. *The creation of unwanted precedents:* Is it likely to create precedents that will lead to its application in undesirable ways?

17. *Negative effects on surveillors and third parties:* Are there negative effects on those beyond the subject?

C. Uses

18. *Appropriate vs. inappropriate goals:* Are the goals of the data collection legitimate? Are they publically announced?

19. *The goodness of fit between the means and the goal:* Is there a clear link between the information collected and the goal sought?

20. *Information used for original vs. other unrelated purposes:* Is the personal information used for the reasons offered for its collection and for which consent may have been given, and does the data stay with the original collector, or does it migrate elsewhere?

21. *Failure to share secondary gains from the information:* Is the personal data collected used for profit without permission from, or benefit to, the person who provided it?

22. *Unfair disadvantage:* Is the information used in such a way as to cause unwarranted harm or disadvantage to its subject?

mation raises novel copyright issues, whether they involve sale of information about a person's purchases or a clone of their cell structure.

5. *Unfair disadvantage:* Is the information used in such a way as to cause unwarranted harm or disadvantage to its subject? There is, of course, much room for debate over whether these occur and are warranted or unwarranted. Yet some major types can be identified and at the extreme examples are easy to find:

a. An unfair strategic disadvantage or with respect to a situation in which there is a conflict of interest (for example, a bugged car sales waiting room that permits the seller to learn a customer's concerns and maximum payment).

b. Unfairly restricting social participation, for example, denying someone an apartment, insurance, or employment based on information that is invalid, irrelevant, discriminatory acontextual, or according to policy, not to be a factor in the decision made (e.g., not hiring someone because their DNA suggests they have a better-than-average chance of developing a serious illness in the future).

c. The unwarranted publication or release of personal information that causes embarrassment, shame, or otherwise puts a person in a negative light. The emphasis here is on the subjective harm the individual experiences as a result of the release of confidential information, apart from its validity. State laws that protect against the "tort" of privacy invasion apply here. Direct tangible, material harm can more easily be determined than subjective harm involving embarrassment, shame, stigma, humiliation, and the uncomfortable feeling of being invaded by the prying eyes of others, whether known or unknown.

d. A feeling of betrayal of confidence. The failure to use information only as promised or to maintain confidentiality and security as promised applies here. This can involve friends telling something they should not, violations of professional confidentiality, or a phone company revealing unlisted numbers through a new service such as caller-ID.

e. Intrusions into solitude. An important element of privacy is the right to be left alone in a busy world. The indiscriminate traffic in personal information may result in unwanted mass market-ing intrusions via telephone, mail, e-mail, or face-to-face solicitations.

Given the variety of tactics for extracting personal information and the conditions under which they are applied, an ethics of surveillance must be very general, and categorical imperatives mandating prohibition, or use, are difficult to defend. It is unrealistic to expect a general principle to apply equally in all contexts and across all technologies. But we can talk in relative terms and contrast tactics, situations, and uses as being more or less ethically acceptable depending on the play of the factors discussed.

The questions asked about the means, data collection context, and use offer a guide for assessing surveillance ethics. The more the principles implied in these questions are honored, the more ethical the situation is likely to be, or, conversely, the fewer of these present, the less ethical. We intend this additive approach as a sensitizing perspective and do not suggest that equal moral weight necessarily be given to these factors. But, hopefully, they do touch the major ethical elements. There are no simple equation, or cookbook, answers to the varied and complex situations in which personal data are collected and used. Suggesting an ethics for a particular tactic such as computer data bases or drug testing can be worthwhile in offering focused guidelines, but it is important not to ignore the commonalities and to see the broader social picture. In spite of the above limitations, awareness of the complexity and asking the questions in Table I (which summarize our argument) will likely yield better results than ignoring them.

Bibliography

Foucault, M. (1977). *Discipline and punish: The Birth of the prison.* New York: Vintage.

Gandy, O. (1993). *The panoptic sort.* Boulder, CO: Westview Press.

Johnson, D. (1994). *Computer ethics.* Englewood Cliffs, NJ: Prentice-Hall.

Lyon, D. (1994). *The electronic eye: The Rise of Surveillance Society.* Cambridge: Polity Press.

Marx, G. T. (1994). New telecommunication technologies require new manners. *Telecommunications Policy,* Vol. 18, no. 7.

Marx, G. T. (1986). The iron fist in the velvet glove: Totalitarian potentials within democratic structures. In J. Short (Ed.), *The social fabric.* Beverly Hills: Sage:

Regan, P. (1995). *Legislating privacy technology, social values and public policy.* Chapel Hill: University of North Carolina Press.

Rule, J. (1973). *Private lives, public surveillance.* London: Allen-Lane.

Ethics and Media Quality

ANDREW BELSEY
Cardiff University

RUTH CHADWICK
Lancaster University

GLOSSARY

code of practice A set of principles and standards expressing the collective commitment of a professional group to certain ways of behaving in their professional role.

quality Excellence in relation to its kind.

self-regulation The monitoring and policing of professional standards by mechanisms internal to the profession, such as a code of practice, as opposed to by an external mechanism such as legislation.

virtue A disposition to act virtuously. As expressed in virtue ethics, an approach to ethics which prioritizes character rather than, say, consequences or rights.

virtues Traits of character which are regarded as morally valuable, because they enable human beings to live well, flourish, or fulfill certain kinds of human purposes or practices.

MEDIA QUALITY is important, given the connection between the media and democracy. A recurring theme in this discussion is the distinction between positive and negative aspects of media quality: what is required and what is prohibited. The legal route to media quality is necessary, but not sufficient, requiring supplementation by the ethical route, which is understood as a competence to deploy ethical consideration in professional practice. Ethical standards can be promoted by a code of practice, such as that of the (British) Press Complaints Commission. Analysis of this Code suggests that such formulations have their limitations, but that overall the ethical route is indispensable, although in need of further exploration.

I. QUALITY AND THE MEDIA

How ought journalists to behave in their professional lives? What are the freedoms and responsibilities involved? Two recent events have raised public awareness of the ethics of journalism to unprecedented levels: the case of Princess Diana, in which the media were accused of hounding the princess (and her companion) to death, and the Clinton–Lewinsky case, in which new depths of public prurience were plumbed. But however extreme these cases appeared, the underlying issues were not new, and so fundamentally these examples join a long list of similar cases which exercise the minds and consciences of journalists and commentators whenever they turn to questions of quality. The questions are not new, and neither will they go away, for deeper issues are involved—issues that transcend merely sensational cases because they go to the heart of society and the principles of social organization.

The social psychologist Urie Bronfenbrenner once

wrote that "the only safe way to avoid violating principles of professional ethics is to refrain from doing social science research altogether" (in Barnes 1979, 5). Such an option is not open to the journalist. Although the nature of the media is changing, particularly with the enhancement of the role of electronic media at the expense of traditional print, it is a reasonable assumption that the media are here to stay. Given the importance of the media to society as a whole, how then can the quality of the media be protected and promoted? Is quality assurance in the media a matter of professional ethics?

The media are important to society because of their close connection with democracy. It is generally agreed that free media are a necessary condition of a democratic society. A democracy is an association of citizens who participate in a wide range of social processes, including especially the political. Democratic political participation requires an informed citizenry, and one of the roles of the media is to enhance the level of participation by providing the information, opinion, comment, and debate on a wide range of social and political issues. (Clearly, the media are not alone in having a democratic role, but are building on the work of, for example, the education system.) However, although in fulfilling their democratic role the media require freedom, this is not sufficient. There is also the issue of the quality of the information and opinion that the media make available to the public. "Diversity" is often put forward as the watchword here, especially as far as the circulation of opinion is concerned.

Although this sounds like a common assumption of much modern democratic theory, it is not without its problems. In particular, it could be argued that there is a conflict between the theory of the role of the media in a democratic society and the market ideology which dominates political and economic practice in the world today, including those parts of the world, especially Western Europe, North America, and Australasia, normally assumed to be the paradigms of a democratic approach to social and political organization. According to this dominant ideology, the media and their content are commodities, subject to the laws of supply and demand just like any other product, and as such should be outside the sphere of state regulation.

Where deregulation and market forces predominate, there are two possible approaches to the question of media quality. The first would rule out the question altogether, as representing an unwarrantable intrusion of non-market forces into the free market. The second approach is slightly more sophisticated. This would reinterpret questions of quality in terms of the satisfaction of consumer preferences, as measured by sales and audience figures. Thus the best newspaper would be the one with the largest circulation, the best television channel the one with the largest number of viewers, etc. In other words, "quality" would be decided by the market.

Whether either of these approaches is a satisfactory response to the question of media quality is debatable. The first refuses to recognize the question at all, while the second avoids the question by a quantitative redefinition of "quality." Both approaches, by adopting an overnarrow idea of regulation, assume wrongly that regulation is necessarily hostile to the media, and thus fail to notice that the idea of regulation, as a constitutional or legal framework within which the media operate, is neutral in itself. The consequences of regulation in practice depend on the particular content of the framework in some particular state and jurisdiction. Some content can be highly positive, as can be argued in the case of the First Amendment to the American Constitution, where the legal guarantee of a free press permits journalists to focus on questions of quality in the ethical sense. Other content can be highly negative, as can be argued in the case of British libel law, where both uncertainty and the possibility of a draconian outcome have a severely inhibiting effect on investigative journalism and editorial comment.

Furthermore, at a more fundamental level the whole market approach can be criticized not just for ignoring questions of quality but for failing to deliver democratic media at all. John O'Neill, for example, has criticized the supposed connection between a free market and a free press, arguing that "the market inhibits the dissemination of information and diverse opinion required of a democratic society" (1992, 15). A narrow range of ownership and control in the media results in an unduly narrow output—one that reflects the interests of those with ownership and control.

The market approach does not face up to the problem that a democracy cannot be indifferent to questions of media quality. Not just any set of media institutions, even if free by market standards, is likely to assist in achieving democratic expectations unless the question of quality is faced squarely. It is clear that inaccurate news, biased discussions, and manipulative opinion pieces will not serve the ends of democracy.

The question of media quality remains, then. But before directly addressing this question it is worthwhile to briefly draw attention to a distinction that has already been mentioned and will recur in various guises in this article—the distinction between positive and negative aspects of quality assurance. This distinction accords fairly well with common sense. In general terms it is the distinction between what the media should and should not do—between what should and should not appear in the media. The positive aspect of media quality is concerned with the media's contribution to democracy through the dissemination of information and opinion in terms of range, depth, diversity, etc. The negative aspect of media quality is concerned with what should be avoided: manipulation, exploitation, obscenity, and pornography, for example.

It appears that there could be two approaches to the question of media quality in the terms outlined: the legal and the ethical. Which, then, is the best route to follow for quality assurance, the legal route or the ethical route? Or do they both lead to the same goal?

II. THE LEGAL ROUTE TO MEDIA QUALITY

The legal route to media quality has both positive and negative aspects. The positive aspect, however, rather than addressing the question of quality directly, can instead be thought of as providing an enabling framework, within which good journalism can be practiced. The obvious example, already mentioned above, is the First Amendment to the American Constitution, which lays down that "Congress shall make no law ... abridging the freedom of speech, or of the press." Another important example is freedom of information legislation, which not only makes information available but, ideally, by so doing encourages an atmosphere of openness and debate about political and social issues. A legal framework which guarantees press freedom and promotes the free flow of information is serving not just the ends of good journalism but also the ends of democracy.

The negative aspect of the legal route to media quality concerns the prohibition or restriction of what may be published, and introduces a concomitant panoply of police action, criminal or civil proceedings, interdicts, injunctions, writs, sanctions, penalties, and other legal processes. Although this tends to conjure up images of a police state, even democratic countries have laws which restrict or regulate the media in some ways, though they differ in extent and often reflect accidents of history and tradition. It seems that there will be an inverse proportional relationship between the negative aspect and the positive aspect of media law: a country with a legal guarantee of press freedom and freedom of information legislation will have few laws restricting the media. Conversely, a country with no statutory press freedom and no freedom of information will have fewer inhibitions about restricting the media, and here the United Kingdom provides an example, with its considerable battery of legislation on official secrecy, confidence, contempt of court, race hatred, blasphemy, obscenity, defamation, and many other matters. In such a system media freedom exists in the interstices of the legal

framework, though of course the interstices are much larger than in totalitarian states.

Is the legal route a necessary part of quality assurance in the media? Clearly, yes, both the positive and negative aspects assist in promoting media quality. Admittedly some of the possible negative legal restrictions are highly controversial—blasphemy, for example, or the severely restrictive British law on official secrecy. But some legal restriction on the publication of libel, pornography, or racist material is compatible with media quality and with democracy—the problem is where to draw the line and how to frame legislation that rules out the genuinely objectionable without stifling justifiable circulation of information or expression of opinion. But the issue is perhaps clearer if the negative restrictions are balanced by a commitment, enshrined in legislation, to a positive framework which has the task of promoting rather than hindering the contribution of the media to a democratic polity.

But however necessary and however desirable, the legal route to media quality will not be sufficient. Neither legal rights for journalists, nor legal restrictions on the media, will in themselves produce good journalism. Quality in the media requires an additional route, the ethical.

III. THE ETHICAL ROUTE TO MEDIA QUALITY

No legal framework guarantees ethical behavior in any area of life, though the law does provide an arena in which some forms of behavior are encouraged or discouraged. There will be (dis)incentives in the form of sanctions and penalties, but ultimately a society depends on the sense of morality and responsibility of its members. And this is how it ought to be in a democracy. Similarly, neither the negative nor the positive aspects of the legal route will guarantee media quality. Unless media professionals too have a sense of morality and responsibility the quality will be lacking.

But in relation to the media (as indeed elsewhere in society) there is an important interplay between law and ethics. To put the point simply, too many legal prohibitions and restrictions force journalists to concentrate on what they can get away with in legal terms, and thus distract their attention away from matters of ethics. This has a distorting and a trivializing effect on the output of the media, to the detriment of quality. Conversely, giving legal rights and freedoms to journalists places them under an obligation to pay attention to the ethical issues of their profession. Even the American First Amendment, for example, does not guarantee standards in journalism—far from it. But awareness of this point has given rise to vigorous debate in the United

States about the role of the media, often contrasting individualistic notions of free expression with more communitarian emphases on media responsibility. Klaidman and Beauchamp summarize the point at issue in their influential discussion of media ethics when they point out that "freedom from legal constraints is a special privilege that demands increased awareness of moral obligation" (1987, 12).

This is because a legal right to publish does not mean that it is morally right to publish. Even when the law is satisfied there are still ethical questions in areas such as obscenity, character assassination, privacy, confidentiality, deception, sexism, and homophobia. Journalists need to select from the mass of possible information what should be included and what should not, and judgments about what is important, significant, trivial, or tasteless are, basically, ethical judgments. Similarly, judgments about presentation are also ethical, inasmuch as they raise issues of, on the one hand, sensitivity and taste, and on the other sensationalism and vulgarity. All these ethical issues can be summed up in the concept of professional competence, as this requires not just a command of technical skills but also the ability to deploy moral qualities. Thus, for example, a commitment to truth-telling, often put forward as constitutive of journalism (and therefore basic to journalistic competence), requires honesty, integrity, tenaciousness, and no doubt other ethical qualities on the part of the journalist.

One interesting and important way of spelling out further what is involved in this ethical notion of competence in the media is by referring to Klaidman and Beauchamp's prescription for journalism in terms of virtue and the virtues: every journalist the "virtuous journalist." The virtuous journalist will display a commitment to many virtues, including fairness, accuracy, honesty, integrity, objectivity, benevolence, sensitivity, trustworthiness, accountability, and humor. More important, though, than a list of specific virtues is virtue: the virtuous journalist is one who has a virtuous character—one who therefore has a disposition to act virtuously not only in familiar but also in novel situations. It is in this sense that the competent journalist is the virtuous journalist, and is also the journalist with a commitment to quality.

But are there universal virtues, or more specifically universal virtues for journalism? Journalists operate in different times and societies, and face different regimes (democratic or authoritarian) and circumstances (war or peace, for example), so to what extent are virtues dependent on time and place? Although there is a long tradition of muckraking journalism, the mainstream has tended to be deferential toward those with power and authority. But this has changed, and with it the understanding of what is good journalism. Consider as an example the changing relationship between the media and the private life of the president of the United States, from F. D. Roosevelt to Kennedy and Clinton. Or in the different context of the United Kingdom, consider the changing attitude of the media to the monarchy, which in the view of many contributed to the fate of Princess Diana.

These examples show some of the questions that remain. When does sympathetic respect deteriorate into obsequious deference? When does decent reticence become a corrupt cover-up? And, more generally, there is the point that the pursuit of virtues can lead to situations of ethical conflict, as, for example, when the desire to respect someone's privacy can be at odds with the requirement of truth-telling. In spite of the difficulties, however, emphasis on virtue and the virtues can produce an ethics which is a vehicle for media quality. As before, it is a vehicle which can travel the ethical route in two ways, a positive aspect emphasizing the ethical requirements for maintaining quality in the media (the virtues, like truth-telling), and a negative aspect emphasizing the prohibitions (the corresponding vices, such as lying).

IV. THE ETHICAL ROUTE VIA A CODE OF PRACTICE?

The ethical route to media quality requires a commitment by individual journalists and other media practitioners to certain ethical principles and standards—a commitment which may be conveniently expressed by the notion of the "virtuous journalist." But should this commitment be further demonstrated by adherence to an ethical "code of practice," incorporating the various principles and standards?

While not essential, such an approach has advantages. It joins journalism with other occupations that have promulgated codes of practice, and is one of the moves which demonstrate an aspiration to move beyond mere occupation to professional status. Adherence to a code brings journalists together as professionals recognizing common aims and interests and accepting responsibilities to the public. Adherence to a code thus shows a collective public commitment to acknowledged ethical principles and standards, rather than a purely solitary conscientiousness about ethical matters. Putting ethical principles and standards into a published code is not just a convenience but a declaration, announcing to both professionals and the public that there is a commitment to quality and to the standards of behavior and practice necessary to achieve quality.

An ethical code of practice will have both positive and negative aspects, detailing what is required and what is prohibited. Both aspects clearly have a contribution to make to media quality. A code of practice for the media, for example, could require journalists to be honest and accurate in all matters, to be impartial and objective in reporting news, to publish corrections, to offer a right of reply, and to protect the identity of confidential sources. It could also, presumably, prohibit deception, harassment, invasions of privacy, doorstepping the victims of traumatic events, exploiting children, and buying the stories of criminals. It is noticeable that these prohibitions tend to be much more specific than the positive requirements.

However, a code of practice could be seen as having functions other than just listing requirements and prohibitions. First, a code could have a disciplinary function, linking breaches of requirements and prohibitions with sanctions. A code could also have an educative function, in that it would teach what was expected of a journalist and would both state and encourage the standards of competence and the underlying thinking that constitute journalism as professional practice. Related to this, a code could also have a "utopian" function, which would be a statement of the ideals and aspirations of the profession, going beyond a list of requirements and prohibitions. In the case of a code for the media, such ideals could go back to First Amendment aspirations, linking press freedom with the requirements of democracy.

V. AN EXAMPLE: THE PRESS COMPLAINTS COMMISSION'S CODE OF PRACTICE

In the United Kingdom, press self-regulation dates from 1953. In spite of the amount of time that a system has been in place, there is usually little agreement about the foundations, both political and ethical, on which self-regulation should be based. In 1991 there was a major reorganization in the UK press self-regulation, and one result was the birth of the Press Complaints Commission (PCC). The Commission, a nonstatutory body with both media and lay members under an independent chairman, has the task of monitoring and enforcing press standards in the United Kingdom through a Code of Practice.

Examination of this Code of Practice can throw considerable light on the advantages and disadvantages of attempting to encapsulate avowedly ethical conduct in a code. But the very existence of the Code and of the PCC itself is illuminating in regards to the issue of the relationship between legal and ethical regulation of the media. The Commission and the Code exist not because of a dedicated commitment by the British press to ethical conduct, nor even to the principle of self-regulation, but precisely to avoid further restrictive legislation. The

British press has in recent years shown what the government regarded as an unhealthy disregard for its authority, in that the press took a considerable interest in the *Spycatcher* case and many other matters involving the security and intelligence services—matters that the government regarded as its secrets. When the press went on to take an even more unhealthy interest in the sex lives of prominent figures—many of them senior establishment politicians or even ministers—the government took this as an opportunity to try to reign in what it regarded as the excesses of the media through such mechanisms as a statutory regulatory body for the press and privacy legislation.

The problem was that such mechanisms would threaten to reach beyond the main immediate offenders, the tabloid newspapers, to inhibit serious and responsible investigative journalism, and so far the solution has eluded the drafters of possible legislation. But the press responded—with no great enthusiasm, it must be admitted—to the threat of further restrictive legislation with an attempt to "put its own house in order" (the politicians' favourite cliché in the circumstances) by creating the Press Complaints Commission and the self-imposed Code of Practice.

The PCC Code is fairly brief, occupying the equivalent of only two sides of a piece of paper. The current version (December 1999) consists of a preamble followed by 16 substantial clauses and a statement on "the public interest." The headings of the clauses are:

1. Accuracy
2. Opportunity to reply
3. Privacy
4. Harassment
5. Intrusion into grief or shock
6. Children
7. Children in sex cases
8. Listening devices
9. Hospitals
10. Reporting of crime
11. Misrepresentation
12. Victims of sexual assault
13. Discrimination
14. Financial journalism
15. Confidential sources
16. Payment for articles

Several of these clauses (3, 4, 6–11, 16) are subject to possible exceptions on grounds of the public interest.

The text of the Code has been through several revisions in the almost 10 years of its existence, and the current text is undoubtedly a considerable improvement on previous versions. Nevertheless, similar problems have persisted, because in the absence of a clear foundation, amendments have been made ad hoc in response to difficult cases, such as that of Princess Diana. The current text still immediately suggests one problem which is inherent in any attempt at producing a code of conduct, in that little thought appears to have gone into making the Code well ordered, with a coherent theoretical base. There is not much attempt to state what its basis or purpose is, or to demonstrate that the clauses are individually necessary and jointly sufficient to achieve whatever the aims of the Code are. The Code does not explicitly mention such obvious virtues as truth-telling and objectivity, for example. Nor does it clearly differentiate between the way in which material is gathered and the manner in which it is presented to the public, so although both these aspects of journalism are considered to some extent, their ethical bases remain unexplored.

The preamble does offer a few hints at an underlying purpose when it says, "All members of the press have a duty to maintain the highest professional and ethical standards. This Code sets the benchmarks for those standards. It both protects the rights of the individual and upholds the public's right to know." Here the reference to the public's right to know does indicate the connection between the media and democracy, but the point is left vague and unexplained, as is the link between the right to know and the reference to professional and ethical standards.

The Code is no clearer or better at explanation in its claim that "it is essential to the workings of an agreed code that it be honoured not only to the letter but in the full spirit. The Code should not be interpreted so narrowly as to compromise its commitment to respect the rights of the individual, nor so broadly that it prevents publication in the public interest." The obvious difficulty here is that there is no guidance on how to adjudicate conflicts between the two rights—those of the individual and those of the public. As a result, the Code is left floundering, with no substantial basis to fall back on. A clearer statement of basis and principle would be more helpful, especially if it also enabled the user or reader of the Code to see how each particular clause was developed in a coherent way from the foundation.

The clauses themselves, a mixture of positive requirements and negative prohibitions, are not presented in any obvious sequence but are just a series of unconnected do's and don'ts, which can be summarized as do be accurate; do publish corrections and apologize for mistakes; do offer a right of reply; do distinguish between fact and comment; do respect people suffering from grief or shock, and people who are merely relatives or friends of those involved in criminal cases; and do protect the identity of confidential sources; but don't invade privacy or harass people, especially if hospital patients, innocent victims, or children are involved, or if the case concerns sexual crime; don't eavesdrop; don't misrepresent; don't pay witnesses in court cases or criminals; don't be sexist or racist; and don't profit from inside knowledge if you are a financial journalist.

There are two further problems with the clauses as they appear in the Code. The first is vagueness and generality, and as a result many of the prescriptions would need further interpretation or elaboration before they could actually be put into effect. Journalists must "take care" not to publish inaccuracies; an apology is required "whenever appropriate"; a "fair" opportunity for reply should be given; approaches to victims of traumatic events should be made "with sympathy and discretion"—and so on. This problem is particularly prominent in the note added to the privacy clause, which reads, "Private places are public or private property where there is a reasonable expectation of privacy." But it would not be fair to blame the Code for resorting to circularity, given the failure of philosophers to produce a workable criterion for distinguishing between the public and the private.

The second further problem is that exceptions to some of the substantial clauses are built into the statement on the public interest. Thus privacy is not totally protected, nor is eavesdropping, misrepresentation, harassment, and payments to witnesses and criminals totally banned, provided there is a public-interest defense for breaches of the provisions of the relevant clauses. Even the protections offered to children can be overridden, provided that an "exceptional" public interest can be demonstrated. The public interest is defined in terms of detecting or exposing crime and serious misdemeanor, protecting public health and safety, and preventing the public from being misled by individuals or organizations. These are useful provisions, but once again there is much scope for further interpretation and elaboration. One problem is that although the phrase "the public interest" has a reasonably well-understood technical meaning in political philosophy, both journalists (sometimes deliberately) and members of the public (usually inadvertently) confuse it with "what the public is interested in." Perhaps the Code would be helped if it stated that exceptions of the substantial clauses would have to be justified by demonstrating that the exceptions contributed to the public *benefit*.

But just because criticisms can be made of the Code, it does not follow that it is without value. Such a code also has many advantages. First, it does offer journalists some guidance in areas that are going to be problematic in their practice, and the individual requirements and prohibitions are, in themselves, relevant and sound.

Even though some of the clauses cannot be acted on without further interpretation, the Code does at least draw the attention of journalists to the type of situation in which some care and reflection would be desirable. It thus might even stimulate journalists to become interested in ethical problems and to seek further interpretation though reflection and mutual discussion—and by such a process to further improve the Code itself.

The Code also has the advantage of making a public declaration of attachment to maintaining high ethical standards in professional practice and to serving the public interest. This is particularly important when the Code is considered in its historical and political context. Of course, given this context many members of the public will greet the Code with a degree of cynicism, believing that it was introduced merely to avoid further restrictive legislation and that the press is unlikely to make any great efforts to live up to its provisions.

The third advantage of the Code is that it does include a disciplinary function which might have some success in combating the cynicism of the public. The sanctions that a self-regulatory system can bring to bear are not great, but the preamble of the Code does speak of the Press Complaints Commission "enforcing" the Code of Practice. The main sanction is that any publication found by the PCC to have breached the Code is required to print the critical adjudication in full with due prominence. This, and the related sanction of bad publicity for the offender, shows that the PCC's system of self-regulation amounts to operating a "shame" culture within which the media feel obliged to act with higher ethical standards.

The fourth advantage is that the Code as part of a system of self-regulation, even if backed by only weak sanctions, is surely better than statutory regulation. Self-regulation is preferable in a democracy—or perhaps this should be put more strongly: self-regulation is a necessary part of a society which hopes to call itself democratic.

VI. ETHICS AND MEDIA QUALITY

Examination of the PCC Code shows some of the problems in taking the ethical route to media quality via a code of practice. A code which consists of a series of positive and negative rules cannot cover every case nor every type of case. Life in general throws up novel situations which are ethically problematic, and it is these which create the most serious problems for everyone, and professionals are no exception. Journalists already know (it is to be hoped) that they should not use deception in gathering ordinary material, but what should

they do if they think they have come across a serious case of corruption? A code might help, but what is more important are the principles and standards on which a code ought to be based.

A well-thought-out, well-constructed, and ethically sound code—one that is clearly based on a coherent set of moral principles—is likely to be more successful in doing what a code ought to do: to produce in journalists internalized competence, including competence in the ethical sense, or in other words (since the language of virtue is helpful here), a virtuous character—one that has a disposition to act virtuously in the journalistic sense which includes a commitment to quality. It will also be a bonus that such a journalist will have a greater likelihood of coping with problems that are ethically novel.

It is the virtuous disposition which is necessary, not the code. A good, properly based code can be useful, but the code itself is merely a convenient way of conveying the principles and standards with which it should be informed. It is principles and standards that form the ethical route to quality in the media, and it is explicit and reflective acknowledgment of the ethical route that offers the best chance for quality assurance, if this is regarded as an issue separable from quality itself.

There are still many areas that require further exploration and explanation in media ethics. There is first the requirement for principles soundly based in ethical theory, and second the application of these principles to actual issues and cases in the practice of journalism. Then there is the third issue of how the application of ethical principles is to promote media quality, and, finally, the question of the role of an explicit code of practice in achieving the desired level of ethical competence and quality in journalism. The ethical route to media quality is, therefore, still something of a rocky path, but through further ethical reflection and discussion there is hope that it can become easier to travel.

Bibliography

Article 19 (1991). *Freedom of expression and information in the United Kingdom.* London: Article 19, The International Centre against Censorship.

Baird, R. M., Loges, W. E., & Rosenbaum, S. E., Eds. (1999). *The media and morality.* Amherst, NY: Prometheus Books.

Barnes, J. A. (1979). *Who should know what: Social science, privacy and ethics.* Harmondsworth: Penguin.

Ewing, K. D., & Gearty, C. A. (1990). *Freedom under Thatcher: Civil liberties in modern Britain.* Oxford: Oxford University Press.

Hooper, D. (1987). *Official secrets: The use and abuse of the act.* London: Secker & Warburg.

Keiran, M., Ed. (1998). *Media ethics.* London/New York: Routledge.

Klaidman, S., & Beauchamp, T. L. (1987). *The virtuous journalist.* New York: Oxford University Press.

O'Malley, T. (2000). A degree of uncertainty: Aspects of the debate over the regulation of the press in the UK since 1945. In D. Berry (Ed.), *Ethics and media culture: Practices and representations* (pp. 297–310). Oxford/Boston: Focal Press.

O'Neill, J. (1992). Journalism in the market place. In A. Belsey and R. Chadwick (Eds.), *Ethical issues in journalism and the media* (pp. 15–32). London: Routledge.

Press Complaints Commission (1999). *Code of practice.* London: Press Complaints Commission.

Stephenson, H. (1994). *Media freedom and media regulation: An alternative white paper.* Birmingham: Association of British Editors, Guild of Editors and International Press Institute.

Freedom of the Press in the USA

STEPHEN KLAIDMAN

Kennedy Institute of Ethics, Georgetown University

GLOSSARY

communitarian Someone who believes that the rights of the community should generally be given preference over the rights of individuals.

deontology The doctrine that some acts are morally required, irrespective of their consequences.

libertarian Someone who believes that the rights of individuals should generally be given preference over the rights of the state.

utilitarianism The doctrine that morality is most effectively calculated from consequences.

NO CONTEMPORARY EVALUATION of the roles and responsibilities of the American news media is possible without revisiting core historical issues: the social, philosophical, and legal content of freedom of speech and of the press. This is so because many of the most important unresolved questions having to do with press freedom in the age of megamedia corporations and satellite feeds are left over from the age of printer-publishers and political pamphleteers. We are still groping, for example, to discover the moral and legal limits of inquiry in reporting on public persons. We have no settled idea of what values, if any, ought

ever to prevail in a conflict with the right to free speech or freedom of the press. We have no clear conception of whether the press has specific moral obligations to provide public benefits or to avoid harms to the general public or to particular individuals. And it remains unresolved precisely what is meant by the language in the First Amendment to the Constitution that says "Congress shall make no law abridging ... the freedom of the press."

The debate about what the media ought and ought not do is sometimes framed as a conflict between libertarian and communitarian perspectives on the problem of freedom of the press. For libertarians, press freedom is as much a vehicle for individual self-expression as it is an instrument for informing the public. The fact that it provides an opportunity for individuals to realize their human potential by the relatively uninhibited expression of opinions and ideas is seen as central to its value. It is viewed as an extension of a fundamental right to self-expression recognized in the free-speech clause of the First Amendment. Communitarians value press freedom principally because it encourages an open exchange of ideas, opinions, insights, and information, and such an exchange is essential to the functioning of a representative democracy in which the people regularly choose their own leaders and have additional means of influencing public policy. Because libertarians place an extremely high value on individual expression and the rights of the individual generally, they are more likely to be absolutists about press freedom. Communitarians, who are more concerned with the general welfare than with individual liberty, are more often inclined to balance the social worth of press freedom against competing social values such as national security, privacy, and fair trial.

It is central to this discussion that the First Amendment treats freedom of the press as distinct from freedom of speech. The amendment's specific recognition of the press, and much of the surrounding debate, reflects the framers' opinion that the press is something other than just a vehicle for self-expression. If that were not so, the press clause would be redundant. It is true that in the 18th century the American press was a highly politicized vehicle for often scathing self-expression that could be exercised by anyone who owned or had access to a small print shop. James Madison and his colleagues shared the views of Milton, Bentham, and Hume on freedom of expression for individuals, and they respected the rights of all citizens to publish broadsheets and pamphlets venting their personal views. But it is clear from the debate surrounding press freedom in colonial America that the extraordinary protection the press was granted under the law derived mainly if not exclusively from its value to society as a disseminator of news and opinion.

Madison, the principal drafter of the First Amendment, viewed the press as a social institution whose free and independent existence was a condition of democracy. Nevertheless, it is not self-evident from the 18th-century debates that Madison, Thomas Jefferson, or any of their contemporaries believed that press freedom had to prevail every time it clashed with the imperatives of other valued social institutions. Jefferson characterized the importance of the press as it was understood by 18th-century American democrats in its most memorable form:

> The basis of our government being the opinion of the people, the very first object should be to keep that right; and were it left to me to decide whether we should have a government without newspapers, or newspapers without a government, I should not hesitate a moment to prefer the latter.

> (letter to Col. Edward Carrington, 16 Jan. 1787)

The role Jefferson envisaged for the press was to provide the people with the information they needed to reach informed conclusions about the nation's business. However, Jefferson, like the First Amendment, was silent on the question of the responsibility of the press. And neither he nor Madison had much specific to say about balancing press freedom against other values, in either moral or legal contexts. It has been left to the philosophers and lawyers of succeeding generations to sort out these questions. Law professor Paul A. Freund, put it this way:

> Whatever the philosophic bases for freedom of expression—whether as an indispensable means to the discovery and spread of truth or as a fulfillment of the human vocation to seek to persuade, to inform, to entertain, and to astonish one another—

the freedom is, as I have said, defeasible in smaller or larger measure. To regard it as never requiring accommodation with the interests of integrity, security, personal reputation, and human dignity would be to take part of the values of life—however grand a part—in place of the whole, in the realm of public policy to commit the offense of political synecdoche.

> (Autumn 1975. *Am. Scholar,* 546)

Much of the rest of this chapter is devoted to specifying and defining some of the responsibilities of the American press, specifically in its role of reporting news in contrast to providing a forum for opinion. But first let us briefly outline some principles involved in dealing with conflicts between press freedom and other values. To do that, it is essential to distinguish between conflicts that arise in law and those that, because they raise no legal questions, arise in a strictly moral framework.

I. DEALING WITH CONFLICTS BETWEEN PRESS FREEDOM AND OTHER VALUES

Because democratic societies, if they are to function, must vigorously protect individual liberty to speak and promote a free flow of information and opinion, the law must provide a high degree of protection to all forms of speech, including, of course, the form exercised by the press. This protection of expression is especially important because what seems true today may seem false or even invidious to the well-being of society tomorrow, and what seems true and fair to one thoughtful, intelligent person may seem false, scurrilous, or both to another. One way to grasp the point is to consider the history of split decisions on the Supreme Court and to recognize the great dissenting opinions among them that subsequently became law (A. Barth, 1974. *Prophets with Honor.* Knopf, New York).

Although most Americans are not so naive as to believe that in the marketplace of ideas truth always drives out falsehood, at least not in a timely fashion, they have found no better way to test ideas and opinions than to let them circulate freely. It is a matter of societal consensus in the United States, therefore, that no matter how unpopular the ideas or opinions being expressed, they are entitled to the full protection of the law. This broad consensus, however, is a mid-20th-century phenomenon, and it is not without exceptions that remain unsettled in law, such as expressions of obscenity in some circumstances. This legal presumption in favor of free speech and press freedom does not mean that journalists have a moral right to speak, broadcast, or publish without consideration for competing values or the consequences of their actions. No utilitarian calculus would support such a view, and the best-known of all deontological theories, Kant's, is of little use when moral imperatives collide. The British philosopher Isaiah Berlin offered this context for considering what happens when values clash:

> What is clear is that values can clash—that is why civilizations are incompatible. [Values] can be incompatible between cultures, or groups in the same culture, or between you and me. You believe in always telling the truth, no matter what; I do not, because I believe that it can sometimes be too painful and too destructive. We can discuss each other's point of view, we can try to reach common ground, but in the end what you pursue may not be reconcilable with the ends to which I find that I have dedicated my life. Values may easily clash within the breast of a single individual; and it does not follow that, if they do, some must be true and others false. Justice, rigorous justice, is for some people an absolute value, but it is not compatible with what may be no less ultimate values for them— mercy, compassion, as arises in concrete cases.... Some among the Great Goods cannot live together. That is a conceptual truth. We are doomed to choose and every choice may entail an irreparable loss.

(March 17, 1988. *N.Y. Rev. Books,* 15)

Sir Isaiah has simply stated the human condition: life is about hard choices. Press freedom is a cardinal social value, but there are times when it must compete with other cardinal values, and times when it should yield. As Sir Isaiah's argument suggests, value disputes cannot be resolved by rules of thumb. Because values are fundamental beliefs, it is no simple matter to weigh one against another. Yet that is what must be done. For example, intuitively, it sounds right to say that press freedom should give way when innocent lives are at stake. But suppose the life at stake is that of a clandestine agent on a mission in a foreign country that violates U.S. law, and the risk of the agent's being killed if a story is broadcast or published can be calculated at about 10%. Similarly, when it appears that someone's right to a fair trial would be prejudiced by disclosure of certain information, should not the press withhold that information? Maybe, but what if the information is verifiably true and the result of not publishing it is likely to be that a murderer who has threatened to kill 10 other people will go free?

Morally it makes no sense to hold out press freedom as an absolute value, because it will inevitably clash with other values that have equally good or, rather, equally poor claims to being treated as absolutes. The question of how much freedom the press should be given under the law, however, is somewhat more complicated. Because it is often difficult or even impossible to calculate the relative benefits and harms of publishing or broadcasting specific pieces of information, because the suppression of free expression is such an obvious and important harm, because the circulation of information is such an obvious and important good, and because the temptation on the part of the powerful to suppress information that is contrary to their interests is so strong, a potent argument can be made against imposing any legal restrictions on the press. Yet many who are otherwise avid First Amendment absolutists do not argue against a ban on publishing information about the movement of troop ships in wartime, to cite a classic example. And many who are virtual First Amendment absolutists would ban the publication of child pornography.

A more difficult case, recently decided by a federal appeals court, involved the delivery of classified photographs to a British military publisher by a U.S. Navy analyst (*U.S. v. Morison,* U.S. Court of Appeals for the Fourth Circuit, Richmond, VA). In 1984 Samuel Loring Morison turned over to Jane's Publishing Company, for whom he did freelance work, three secret spy satellite photographs of the Soviet Union's first nuclear aircraft carrier, which was under construction at a Black Sea shipyard. In 1985 Morison was convicted by a federal court in Baltimore of theft of government property and espionage (*U.S. v. Morison,* U.S. District Court, Baltimore, MD). A three-judge appeals panel unanimously upheld the verdict in April. Morison was not convicted as a journalist, which he was in his freelance role for Jane's, but as a government employee; as a result the appeals court's main opinion by Judge Donald Stuart Russell declared the First Amendment essentially irrelevant to his defense. It is true, nonetheless, as Judge J. Harvie Wilkinson III pointed out in a concurring opinion, that the First Amendment interests in the case were not "insignificant" because "criminal restraints on the disclosure of information threaten the ability of the press to scrutinize and report on governmental activity."

The *Washington Post* wrote in an editorial, "Surely the government has a right—even an obligation—to protect the kind of national security information that could, if secretly slipped into the hands of a foreign power, harm the nation.... But never before has anyone been convicted of espionage for giving secret information to the press." The *Post*'s conclusion was, "The ruling ... should be overturned by the full court of appeals or the Supreme Court" (6 April 1988. *Washington Post,* A-24). The Morison case represents a clear-cut clash between two values: the government's right to protect secrets essential to the national security and the press's need for a broad mantle of protection under which it can report freely on issues that might be improperly classified and about which the public might have a need to know. (The Soviet Union already had had the manual for the KH-11 spy satellite in question "secretly slipped into [its] hands," so it seems unlikely that Morison's breach of security had grave implications. The precedent set by the court, however, could significantly influence future rulings in cases involving all classified information.)

The *Post* argued that, because the Morison decision has the potential for chilling reporting on classified matters, it should be reversed. But the *Post*'s argument does not come to grips with the central issue. The photographs Morison provided to the British publisher were printed in *Jane's Defence Weekly,* a publication readily available to anyone who cares to buy it, and subsequently some of them were published in several general circulation newspapers. It is possible, therefore, even if in this specific instance it might not be likely, that Soviet analysts, by studying the photographs in the journal, might have learned something detrimental to U.S. security interests. It is logical to wonder, therefore, how great the difference would be if the information were "secretly slipped into the hands of" the Soviet Union? In either case the potential might have existed to compromise national security.

At the same time, it seems equally clear that an all-encompassing legal ban on government employees' disclosing classified information would have an undue chilling effect on the free flow of information. One solution could be narrowly drawn legislation that specifically bans what Morison did, that is, make available for publication (or broadcast) photographs (or information) that compromise U.S. intelligence sources. But it will not do to imply that whenever there is a possible chilling effect, the real conflict of values involved need not be addressed at all.

Therefore, although there is a strong historical and philosophical case for giving freedom of speech and freedom of the press extraordinary protections because of their intrinsic value, and their value as a precondition to many other freedoms, the case for protecting them absolutely is unsustainable. Even as staunch a defender of free speech and free press as the philosopher Alexander Meiklejohn wrote,

> No one can doubt that, in any well-governed society, the legislature has both the right and the duty to prohibit certain forms of speech. Libellous assertions may be, and must be, forbidden and punished. So too must slander. Words which incite men to crime are themselves criminal and must be dealt with as such. Sedition or treason may be expressed by speech or writing. And, in those cases, decisive repressive action by the government is imperative for the sake of the general welfare. All these necessities that speech be limited are recognized and provided for under the constitution.

> (1948. *Free Speech,* p. 18. Harper & Brothers, New York)

Although debate continues about whether the First Amendment was meant to be as absolute as its language suggests, there is fairly widespread agreement that anything that does not constitute a "clear and present danger" to the national security, with the emphasis on "clear and present," may be published. Punishment, if any, is to be meted out after the fact. The judicial history supporting this view runs through a series of Supreme Court cases known to First Amendment scholars as *Schenk, Abrams, Near,* and the *Pentagon Papers* cases, to name perhaps the best-known among them. There are those who argue as well that even penalties after the fact are an unwarranted encroachment on press freedom, but that remains a minority position. Here again it is important to note that the legal right to publish provides no moral sanction for publishing.

To make the transition from legal rights to moral duties is, in effect, to introduce the subject of responsibility. If the press has the *right* to publish just about anything in just about any fashion, *responsibility* entails making choices about what to publish and in what fashion. It seems a truism to say that the press ought to be responsbile. Yet Alan Barth, one of the most thoughtful journalists and civil libertarians of our time, calls it into question. Barth wrote,

> Now, a press which enjoys such independence of the government [as the American press does] is, almost by definition, in some degree irresponsible. And no one ought to be surprised if it behaves at times altogether irresponsibly. A measure of irresponsibility was the price which had to be paid—and which the Founders were quite prepared to pay—for the independence without which the press could not discharge its vital function.
>
> A great deal has been said in a great many lectures by a great many eloquent lecturers concerning the irresponsibility of American newspapers. I do not propose to add to that indictment.... On the contrary, I mean to raise a rather different question for your consideration. I want to ask—and not altogether rhetorically by any means—whether the press in the United States today has not become excessively *responsible,* whether it has not, in fact, to an alarming degree, become a mouthpiece and partner of the government, rather than a censor.

> (1984. In *The Rights of Free Men* (J. E. Clayton, Ed.), pp. 292–293. Knopf, New York)

Barth's concern is not idle, but his language might be misunderstood outside the culture of journalism. If I understand correctly, what he means by "excessively responsible" is too careful, or too easily co-opted by official sources. In other words, if the press is too docile, it is unlikely to fulfill its responsibility as a watchdog of government. Nowhere, however, does Barth argue that the press *ought* to be irresponsible. He saw some degree of "irresponsible" conduct as an unwelcome but unavoidable side effect of doing what the press does in the circumstances in which the press does it. He had a clear personal sense of what it meant to be a responsible journalist and practiced his craft accordingly. What follows is an attempt to define responsibility in American journalism in a way that would satisfy the exacting criteria of a journalist of the probity and intelligence of Barth. The following criteria are ideals in the sense that they do not reflect commercial pressures exerted on newsrooms in the highly competitive media market-place. They are, however, attainable, at least in print journalism. Many reporters and editors meet them regularly.

II. RESPONSIBILITY OF THE PRESS

Responsibilities in journalism, or in any profession for that matter, fall into two categories: role responsibilities, that is, those that go specifically with the calling, and general moral responsibilities such as fairness and telling the truth. Role responsibilities, of course, vary by definition. As for general moral responsibilities, some are more relevant to certain professions than to others. For example, the duty of beneficence, to do good, specifically and concretely, seems more applicable to medicine than to journalism. What follows are a brief description of the role responsibilities of journalists and an effort to give content to the most relevant general moral responsibilities.

The press, as has already been indicated, is both an outlet for expression and a means of circulating news, ideas, opinions, and other kinds of information. But it is as a disseminator of information, not as a vehicle for anyone's self-expression, that the press has been given explicit constitutional protection, and therefore it is from this role that responsibility most directly flows. When the two values clashed, the issue was decided by the Supreme Court. A political candidate's suit to force a newspaper to publish a reply to editorials criticizing his record was denied. The court ruled that the newspaper was not obliged to give him access to its columns (*Miami Herald Publishing Co. v. Tornillo*, 1974). Chief Justice Warren Burger wrote the following opinion for the Court:

> A newspaper is more than a passive receptacle or conduit for news, comment, and advertising. The choice of material to go into a newspaper, and the decisions made as to limitations on the size and content of the paper, and treatment of public issues and public officials—whether fair or unfair—constitute the exercise of editorial control and judgment. It has yet to be demonstrated how governmental regulation of this crucial process can be exercised consistent with First Amendment guarantees of a free press as they have evolved to this time.
>
> (*Tornillo*, 1974)

The ruling denies access to someone seeking to be heard with the underlying purpose of protecting the press's ability to inform people without inhibition about all the matters that are material to their concerns as citizens. From such powerful protection of the prerogatives of the press flows a profound responsibility to report on these matters in a way that meets the public's needs. What are these needs? In asking whether "the news as we experience it [is] promoting democratic liberty?" William Henry III suggests an answer (Spring 1987. *Gannett Center J.,* 114). But the formulation is vague. It can be made concrete by specifying the informational requirements of an idealized reader or viewer who represents the public. The section that follows attempts to do that and thereby to give content to the fundamental responsibility of the American press. Although it is not a verbatim account, it is based substantially on my earlier research with Tom L. Beauchamp published in a volume titled *The Virtuous Journalist* (1987. Chap. 2. Oxford Univ. Press, New York).

III. THE REASONABLE READER

As a rough standard, what the press collectively has a duty to report is correlated with what the public has a need to know. In reflecting on how the press can meet that standard, it is useful to draw on a legal model known as "the reasonable person," which for purposes of greater specificity can be transformed into a model called the reasonable reader or viewer. This model is designed to incorporate the common body of assumptions that members of a society make about their fellow citizens in order to cooperate efficiently. The reasonable person is never to be understood as either a specific person or an average person. In the words of William Prosser, "he is a prudent and careful man who is always up to standard.... He is a personification of the community ideal of reasonable behavior (1971. *The Law of Torts,* 4th ed., p. 151. West, St. Paul, MN). Under a standard such as this, a journalist can be found negligent even if the information provided is well within the bounds of accepted professional practice.

As this suggests, the reasonable reader standard is to be understood from the point of view of a reader's needs for information rather than from the perspective of routine media practices. The reasonable reader is the community ideal of an informed person with informational needs that the so-called "quality," general news media are designed, or at least ought to be designed, to serve. This general model provides a guide for establishing standards of completeness, accuracy, understanding, and objectivity that are intended to yield, within attainable limits, useful, fair, and impartial journalism.

To make the concept more concrete, consider this question. In a first story about the 1979 nuclear accident at Three Mile Island in Pennsylvania, what would the reasonable reader living in California need to know and have a right to expect from a local California newspaper? Initially, there is a need to know what happened and what is known about the safety, health, and economic implications of the event. The reasonable reader would not be interested in the press's comparisons of the event to a contemporaneous film (*The China Syndrome*) that treats the subject of a nuclear accident in fictional form. But the reader would need to know how much risk was associated with the accident and whether there were similar nuclear plants located in the reader's area. As the story develops, more information will be needed about how the utility and the government were handling the aftermath of the accident, what had been learned about how the accident happened, how it could be expected to affect the physical and mental health of persons living in the area, and what implications the accident had for the nuclear power industry. As is always the case with an unfolding event or series of events, it would take more than one story to meet the reasonable reader's needs. Follow-up stories should continue to appear as long as those needs remained unmet.

A. Completeness

Given the constraints of print and even more so of electronic journalism, any standard of completeness must be reasonably flexible. If the concept of completeness is viewed as a continuum with "no truth" at one end and "the whole truth" at the other end, the threshold standard that journalists should satisfy is the point along the continuum marked "substantial completeness." This would be the point at which a reasonable reader's need for information would be satisfied. A decision about where to situate substantial completeness on the continuum depends on practical, institutional, moral, political, and policy considerations. Providing substantially complete coverage means that within the constraints of these competing values, as well as the availability of staff, space, and other resources, and the accessibility of sources and documents (a professional level of resourcefulness in uncovering information is assumed), a news organization would, over the course of its coverage, publish enough information to satisfy the needs of an intelligent nonspecialist who wanted to evaluate the situation.

B. Understandability

Completeness is not enough, however. News reports must meet several other tests to fulfill their responsibility. Among other things, they must be understandable to the reasonable reader. As with the whole truth, complete understanding, in some senses, is an unattainable ideal. A person could be said to understand a situation or event fully only if that person were to grasp all relevant propositions or statements that accurately describe events that are reported, as well as their possible outcomes or consequences. What journalism can legiti-

mately be expected to produce is, of course, far short of this ideal. Moreover, even if news organizations could provide all the information that was relevant and material to all of the stories published and broadcast, that amount of information would overwhelm rather than inform readers and viewers. The goal should be substantial understanding. In addition to providing the vital facts clearly, a story that strives to promote substantial understanding should leave out the irrelevant and trivial; should make clear what relevant facts are not known; should set new facts in an appropriate context; and, especially in complex technical stories, should begin at a point that is sufficiently elementary for the intended audience and frame information in a way that is neutral rather than encouraging, unintentionally or otherwise, a particular reader response.

C. Objectivity

Stories written for the reasonable reader must also strive to be objective. According to the *American Heritage Dictionary of the English Language,* objectivity entails being "uninfluenced by emotion or personal prejudice." It is, of course, unrealistic to expect even the most objective persons to be totally uninfluenced by these sources. Nevertheless, although a reporter might be motivated to pursue a story from a tangle of emotion and reason, it is possible in the writing and reporting to distinguish personal attitudes, religious or political dogma, and so forth from facts and justified beliefs. This statement does not mean that such facts and beliefs are not subject to legitimate dispute, but rather that, in reporting news, journalists should strive to identify disputed areas even when they personally favor one side over another. In other words, in the American context, reporting on the news ought not be politicized, ideological, or in any way polemical. News stories should be written and organized so as not to suggest or express a preference for one set of values over another.

Objectivity does not, however, require the mindless balancing of viewpoints when the preponderance of evidence is heavily weighted in one direction. Similarly, objectivity is a journalistic responsibility in the selection of stories to be published in the main news section of a newspaper or aired during the main portion of a network news program. Generally speaking, priorities should be assigned according to criteria having to do with the public's need to know in areas bearing on important matters such as political choice and public health.

D. Accuracy

Finally, the reasonable reader demands accuracy from journalism. To be accurate means to present as facts only that information for which there is good and sufficient evidence. If, after checking the evidence, a reporter or editor remains even minimally doubtful about the accuracy of the information, that doubt should be incorporated into the story if the information is used. Accuracy also requires precision in such things as quotation, paraphrasing, and description. And proper attribution is a hallmark of accurate reporting. Reporters usually should describe without attribution only what they have witnessed and what is common knowledge; one possible exception is the reporting of an event that was witnessed by a trusted colleague.

Attribution, of course, does not authenticate information. It only lets the reader or viewer know its source and therefore what bias if any it might reflect. The duty to be accurate and the constraints of the fast-moving world of journalism are often incompatible. As a result, it would be foolish to think that mistakes will never be made. But a high standard of accuracy is consistent with the importance of the role assigned to journalism in America. The best journalists take this test daily and pass it with remarkable regularity.

By serving the reasonable reader as indicated, and by providing space or air time for the circulation of diverse opinions, print and broadcast media fulfill their role responsibly. And, as a result of aspiring to this level of journalism, they are likely to provide coverage that is maximally fair and minimally biased. In so doing, however, they do not necessarily meet all their responsibilities. The media may have a duty to perform public services that go beyond the mere provision of information that is deemed newsworthy. For example, newspapers may have a responsibility to publish the telephone numbers of hot lines for information on AIDS or drugs. And some television news organizations, such as WJLA-TV in Washington, intervene on behalf of citizens frustrated by government bureaucracy.

Is there a duty to weigh harm to the public, sources, and subjects of stories against the benefits of publishing or broadcasting? Suppose, for example, that a newspaper learns that a public figure had a single homosexual encounter five years before he was elected to office and seven years before his marriage. Publishing the story could wreck both his marriage and his career. Should the paper publish it? And finally, what about accountability? Because the American media are so protected and privileged, are they, as a result, essentially unaccountable? The industry argues that the media are ultimately accountable to readers and viewers who can buy another paper or flick the TV dial to another channel. But given the patterns of media ownership in America, with most cities limited to a single newspaper that very likely is chain-owned, it is fair to ask just how much *accountability* is likely to be imposed at the newsstand.

Similarly, it is obvious to people who follow network news coverage that the evening TV news programs are so much alike that little real accountability can be enforced in the living room either.

I think that the media have a duty to perform public services, to avoid harms that are greater than the correlative public benefits, and to be accountable. Space does not permit a full explication of these views, but the main points are briefly summarized in the section that follows.

E. Public Service

The record in support of a public service role for the press goes back at least to the 18th century. In making its case for independence, the Continental Congress offered the following rationale for an independent press:

> The importance of this [press freedom] consists, besides the advancement of truth, science, morality and arts in general, in its diffusion of liberal sentiments on the administration of government, its ready communication of thoughts between subjects, and its consequential promotion of union among them.
>
> (quoted in L. W. Levy, 1985. *Emergence of A Free Press*, p. 174. Oxford Univ. Press, New York)

In modern times, the American Society of Newspaper Editors (ASNE) says in its statement of principles that "the primary purpose of gathering and distributing news and opinion is to serve the general welfare by informing the people and by enabling them to make judgments on the issues of the time" (as printed in J. L. Hulteng, 1981. *Playing It Straight*, p. 85. American Society of Newspaper Editors, Chester, CT).

Both these quotations relate to promoting the public good, or the general welfare, as the ASNE statement puts it. And they both tend to support the thesis that the implicit contract between the press and society, on which the privileges of the press are based, extends to providing adequate information to the public in spheres other than politics. The measure of the adequacy of the information published and broadcast is the degree to which it promotes autonomous deliberation and choice. That standard would indicate a duty to publish hot-line numbers when they would facilitate choice, but no duty to intervene directly in disputes between citizens and government.

F. Doing Harm

The question of doing harm in journalism is more complex than the question of what public services the press has a responsibility to perform, because some public benefits of reporting news entail harms. Moreover, the benefit might be marginal or ambiguous and the harm significant and concrete. For example, exposing the fact that a Supreme Court nominee has smoked marijuana during his tenure as a law professor or that a candidate for president has jeopardized his campaign by spending time in compromising circumstances with a woman who was not his wife harms the nominee and the candidate, but some observers find the benefits questionable. From their perspective, reporting of this kind might even hurt the public by denying qualified persons the opportunity to serve in public office. It might also be that some harms are deserved, resulting more from the act itself than from the fact that the act was reported in a newspaper or on television.

A principle is needed to help determine in what circumstances, if any, press freedom should be overridden to avoid harm. That principle is provided in John Stuart Mill's monograph, *On Liberty* (1955. Henry Regnery, Chicago). Mill's harm principle says, in effect, that a liberty may be restricted if the harm caused outweighs the value of that liberty. There are many ways to define harm, but the philosopher Joel Feinberg has devised one that works well for journalism. Feinberg proposes that a harm is something that thwarts, defeats, or sets back an interest such as that which one might have in property, privacy, confidentiality, friendship, reputation, health, or career (1984. *Harm to Others*, pp. 34–35. Oxford Univ. Press, New York). Taken together, the ideas of Mill and Feinberg provide a conceptual framework for weighing harms against the benefits provided by a free press, but they are no help in determining whether a specific harm outweighs a specific benefit.

In an ideal world, there would be a formula that a journalist working on deadline could use to decide whether to include in a story a paragraph with some news value that might harm someone. There is no formula, but there are ways to think about whether potential benefits outweigh potential harms. For example, invading the privacy of a public official to report on matters relevant to the carrying out of his or her public responsibilities would be a more justified harm than invading the privacy of a mother to report on the death of her child in an accident. This is so partly because, by accepting public office, the official has given up part of his or her claim to privacy and partly because the public has a legitimate need to know about matters relevant to the carrying out of official duties. The mother, in contrast, has a full claim to privacy, and there is no compelling need for the public to know how she feels in her time of grief.

Not every case is so clear-cut, however. Suppose a reporter invades the privacy of a reclusive actress to report on her affair with the husband of her best friend. Does her right to privacy outweigh the interest of her fans in reading about the affair? The trade-offs in matters of this kind are not peculiar to journalism, so I will not belabor them here. The main point is that there is a benefit–harm equation and responsible journalism entails taking it into account.

G. Accountability

Finally, there is the conflicted question of accountability in journalism. To be both free and accountable is the democratic ideal, but like most ideals it remains distant from reality. Journalism in the United States is not absolutely free, but it comes a lot closer to being absolutely free than it comes to being absolutely accountable. Journalists are sometimes co-opted through cleverness or flattery by their governmental adversaries, but they are rarely if ever deterred from publishing or broadcasting for fear that they will have to give an account of their actions afterward. Because Congress is permitted to "make no law abridging the freedom … of the press," the government has little power to make the press accountable, which, given the potential for abuse of that power, is as it should be. The press is even less accountable than the liberal professions, which, although self-policing in many areas, also are subject to licensing restrictions. The print press in America is not licensed, nor should it be, especially because the government could use the licensing process as an instrument to enforce accountability. (The knotty problem of broadcast licensing in the cable and satellite age is beyond the scope of this article.)

In the end, the press remains accountable to the public because it is privileged and protected so that it can serve the public. Because the press is the public's surrogate for keeping tabs on the government, it stands to reason that it would be inappropriate for the government to enforce press accountability. Who, then, is to do it? The answer is some combination of the press itself, monitoring bodies not dissimilar to the defunct National News Council composed of media and public members with power to publicize their findings but not to punish offenders, and the public, by exercising its right to switch channels or newspapers.

A more fundamental question is, What does it mean for the press to be accountable? To be accountable is to be answerable to someone or some group to whom accountability is legitimately owed. Press accountability therefore cannot be satisfied by providing space for letters to the editor or by running an ombudsman column that criticizes the paper's coverage. It requires explanations and justifications of why controversial stories were reported as they were, why an unidentified source was allowed to malign a public figure, and so on. Traditionally the American media have feared any formal structure of accountability as the first step on a slippery slope toward media regulation. In fact, however, the opposite might be true. A media-supported mechanism of accountability would more likely serve to defuse media bashers and enhance media credibility than to promote a trend toward control of the press by outsiders, governmental or otherwise.

IV. CONCLUSION

This article does not attempt to present a comprehensive account of the role and responsibility of the press in the United States. To do that would require a substantial book. It is only an effort to suggest some essential elements of that role and responsibility. Nonetheless, it stands to reason that if journalists seek to serve the reasonable reader in some of the ways described here and to reflect on questions of harm and public benefit, and if they consider themselves accountable to the public, much else will take care of itself.

Bibliography

Dickerson, D. L. (1990). "The Course of Tolerance: Freedom of the Press in 19th Century America." Greenwood, New York.

Garry, P. M. (1990). "The American Vision of a Free Press: An Historical and Constitutional Revisionist View of the Press as a Marketplace of Ideas." Garland, New York.

Leahy, J. E. (1991). "The First Amendment, 1791–1991: Two Hundred Years of Freedom." McFarland, Jefferson, NC.

Lichtenberg, J. (ed.) (1990). "Democracy in the Mass Media: A Collection of Essays." Cambridge Univ. Press, New York.

Miller, W. L. (ed.) (1995). "Alternatives to Freedom: Arguments and Opinions." Longman, New York.

Murphy, P. L. (1992). "The Shaping of the First Amendment, 1791 to the Present." Oxford Univ. Press, New York.

Powe, L. A., Jr. (1991). "The Fourth Estate and the Constitution: Freedom of the Press in America." Univ. of California Press, Berkeley.

Wilkinson, F. (1992). "Essential Liberty: First Amendment Battles for a Free Press." Columbia Univ. Graduate School of Journalism, New York.

Gun Control

PRESTON K. COVEY

Carnegie Mellon University

GLOSSARY

assault rifle A technical military term derived from a World War II German innovation, the Sturmgewehr ("storming rifle," "assault rifle"). Three features are essential to the assault rifle: (1) selective fire, as between semiautomatic and fully automatic modes; (2) chambering for a cartridge intermediate in case length (and consequent power) between larger battle rifle rounds and submachine gun (pistol) rounds; and (3) relative compactness and light weight.

assault weapon A nontechnical term applied to a variety of repeating pistols, shotguns, and rifles, with the general sense that the firearms in question are useful only for what is termed military or criminal "assault," that is, mass or wanton violence, devoid of any legitimate sporting or defensive function.

automatic firearm A firearm that can automatically reload its chamber after initial manual discharge and continue to fire as long as the trigger is depressed. Such firearms are often called "fully automatic" to emphasize the contrast with semiautomatic firearms. In popular, but not technical, use, the term "automatic" often refers to both fully automatic and semiautomatic firearms.

BATF Bureau of Alcohol, Tobacco and Firearms, an arm of the U.S. Department of the Treasury empowered to supervise the production and distribution of firearms; often shortened to ATF.

discretionary licensing A firearm licensing system that imposes criteria such as "good reason" or "special need," allowing for relatively subjective judgment and discretionary latitude as to who qualifies for a license.

gun ban A law or policy that prohibits the manufacture or import, sale or transfer, acquisition, or possession of given firearms for the general population within a certain jurisdiction. Laws that disqualify some identifiable portion of the general population, such as minors or those with felony records, from possessing firearms are not usually referred to as bans because they do not affect the general population.

semiautomatic firearm A firearm that operates automatically to the extent that it can reload its chamber by an automatic process, but which requires that the trigger be released and pressed again for each successive shot.

shall-issue licensing Firearm licensing schemes that, in contrast to typical discretionary licensing regimes, allow far less judgmental discretion on the part of licensing authorities. Typical criteria for shall-issue licensing include being of a certain age, having no record of criminal conviction or involuntary commitment for mental disability, and (for a license to carry a concealed firearm) passing a certified course on relevant law, safety standards, or marksmanship.

The Concise Encyclopedia of Ethics in Politics and the Media

GUN CONTROL assumes myriad guises among over 20,000 current laws, the endless array of proposed legislation at all levels of government, evolving case law, administrative policies, consumer-product safety regulations, and novel liability and litigation stratagems. The topic embraces a wide variety of arguable means and social ends and therefore involves a maze of issues. Any instant case of gun control policy serves, in effect, as a rabbit hole leading to an underlying warren of issues: questions of fact, questions of value, and questions of how to try the facts and weigh the values at stake. Consequently, gun control is a matter which few can count themselves for or against simpliciter, notwithstanding the hard and fast battle lines drawn by partisans on either side of the nominal issue. Indeed, the controversy over gun control has been called a "culture war," because it evokes impassioned conflict amongst people's deepest sensibilities and convictions about how best to secure human life and limb, individual liberty, social order, or an appropriate balance of these values. So construed, the controversy over gun control in the United States has few rivals as a potential threat to that very social order or as a challenge to our collective ability to give both the factual disputes and the competing values at stake a fair hearing and trial.

I. THE VARIETIES OF GUN CONTROL

A. Defining Gun Control

Gun control opponents prefer to define "gun control" as proper grip, presentation, stance, sight picture, and trigger control. This quip calls the question of how to parse the ambiguity of "gun control" as it refers to a complex of social policy. "Gun control" as social policy typically refers to law that regulates such specifically firearm-related activities as the manufacture, import, sale, ownership, transport, or carrying of firearms. However, there is more dimension to gun control policy and controversy than statutory law, including constitutional law, case law, and administrative regulations as well as discretionary administrative, judicial and enforcement policies, civil litigation stratagems, and private-sector policies enabled under law. Because generic definitions do not reveal the variegated landscape of either gun control or its attendant controversies, a rough taxonomy is helpful. Different types of gun control, as well as their different strategies, give rise to different sorts of controversy.

B. Categories of Gun Control

The following (adapted from Kleck, 1991, see Bibliography) are dimensions along which gun controls can be categorized and which occasion controversy: the type, level, or jurisdictional scope of the agency effecting

regulation; the targets of regulation (the gun-related activity, the category of persons or the type of firearm targeted); and the dimensions and degree of restrictiveness of the regulation (from extremely permissive to extremely restrictive or prohibitory).

1. The Agency Effecting Regulation

The type of agency or institution enacting or effecting regulation is typically some level (federal, state, or local) or branch (executive, legislative, or judicial) of government, although private-sector entities (such as businesses, other private institutions, or their agents) can lawfully restrict otherwise lawful gun-related activities (a source of controversy endemic to conflicts among enabling laws).

a. Private-Sector Agency

Private-sector gun control, or lack thereof, as allowed within the law is a salient social concern. For example, when within a year and a half there occurred seven suicides and one murder-suicide with rented handguns at shooting ranges in California, there was an outcry for ranges to stop renting guns. In the absence of a law prohibiting the rental of firearms at shooting ranges, the controversy concerned what the private-sector policy should be. Airlines have policies regarding how firearms are to be declared for transport on passenger airliners, over and above what is required by the Federal Aviation Administration.

More salient examples of private-sector agencies of gun control policy are enterprises (such as pizza chains or delivery services) that prohibit licensed employees from carrying concealed firearms when delivering goods or services, businesses that prohibit concealed carry by licensed customers and employees on their premises, or churches and private schools that have similar policies. Social controversy in such cases arises over whether the law should favor proprietors' rights over those of employees or clientele, whether such discrimination against legally armed citizens is justified, or, conversely, whether citizens should be restrained from being armed on certain premises even when the law generally allows it.

According to the National Institute of Occupational Safety and Health (NIOSH), empirical evidence shows that three of four murdered workers are killed by armed robbers, and that permitting concealed carry by armed license holders not only occasions virtually no wrongful violence, but in fact has occasioned many successful defenses against criminal offenders and probably deters even more such offenses. Nevertheless, many proprietors and clientele of businesses, churches, and private schools object to the very idea of guns kept or carried even for self-defense. Thus cultural attitudes toward guns and gun control run deeper than beliefs amenable to empirical evidence.

b. Government Agency: Level, Branch, Jurisdiction

While the category of gun control that enjoys the widest controversy is highly visible federal gun law, the vast majority of firearms laws are at the state and local level, where more restrictive controls and more intense controversy tend to be found. The multilevel distribution of controls can make for an inconsistent patchwork of laws, which run to such extreme variations as the ban on handguns in Morton Grove, Illinois, and the mandate that every household possess a firearm in Kennesaw, Georgia. The inconsistency of gun laws across jurisdictions is itself a matter of controversy. Control critics argue that it is unfair to treat citizens with similar qualifications differently on account of their location or residency, while advocates complain that controls legitimately established in one area are undermined by "leakage" from more lax jurisdictions. A collateral and more fundamental issue is the proper apportionment of jurisdictional powers among federal, state, and local government.

The Brady Law, requiring a national 5-day waiting period to enable point-of-sale background checks by local law enforcement, has raised issues of states' and local rights against compliance with unfunded federal mandates. Brady is contested on 10th Amendment grounds (that all powers not specifically granted the federal government by the Constitution remain with the states) and, along with the federal ban on so-called assault weapons, has intensified the antifederal sentiments of state- and local-rights partisans (including members of the populist militia movement). Similarly, state preemption laws, which reserve authority for all or certain gun controls to the state legislature, address the pragmatic problem posed by an inconsistent patchwork of laws across localities but run afoul of partisans of local autonomy (as when, for example, the Pennsylvania General Assembly forced Philadelphia to change from discretionary to "shall issue" licensing for concealed carry).

Inconsistencies among the patchwork of state and local laws thus raise controversies both pragmatic and philosophical. Just as gun control advocates argue that firearms should be uniformly subject to registration as are motor vehicles, for pragmatic reasons (such as to aid criminal investigations), gun rights advocates argue that concealed carry licenses issued by one jurisdiction should be honored uniformly in others, as are drivers' licenses, collateral with the right of self-defense, which presumably knows no borders. The latter right itself is, in turn, contested by certain pacifists and other opponents of the private use of deadly force even in self-defense. For example, some American gun control advocates prefer the policy of England, Canada, and Australia, according to which self-defense is not regarded by the law as a valid reason for owning a firearm.

Here also, state or local jurisdictions with more stringent controls complain that the efficacy of their laws is unfairly undermined by more permissive regimes elsewhere (as when the District of Columbia, which prohibits the sale and acquisition of firearms, suffers "leakage" from nearby Virginia, where sale and purchase are permitted). While the leakage problem affects only certain forms of gun control, such as restrictions on acquisition and possession, it is cited in support of the preemption of state and local authority by uniform federal law. Likewise, rights afforded by federal law can be compromised by state or local policy. For example, federal law allows lawful owners to transport their firearms in their vehicles for purposes of interstate travel to destinations where possession of the firearms is legal.

The patchwork problem is, therefore, compounded by different layers of authority within branches of the federal, state, or local government. For example, the federal judiciary encompasses district and appellate courts (which have made conflicting rulings on the constitutionality of the Brady Law and on challenges to the federal "assault weapon" ban) as well as the Supreme Court, which may, within its discretion, ignore certain constitutional controversies, as it has done regarding the Second Amendment since the 1930s. Enforcement of firearms laws, a crucial dimension of gun control, is conditioned by discretionary policies on the part of U.S. Attorneys, States' Attorneys General, and local District Attorneys as well as by the policies of lower layers of authority within law enforcement agencies and the judiciary.

A case in point is the discretionary executive, enforcement, and judicial policy that determined how lower-echelon BATF officials pursued suspected illegal firearms at the Branch Davidian compound in Waco, Texas, and led a Texas magistrate to issue the ATF agents a warrant on the basis of an arguably dubious affidavit as probable cause. Another example is the policy that led federal agents to entice Randy Weaver into illegally sawing off and selling two shotguns in order to enlist him as an informant and later to mount a siege on his Ruby Ridge home, precipitating a chain of events that cost the lives of Weaver's wife and son and a U.S. marshal, as well as several million tax dollars. The costs of gun-law enforcement initiatives in both the Waco and Ruby Ridge incidents have been characterized as well out of proportion to the initial violations at issue (as one report on Waco noted, "90 People Dead Over Gun Parts"), thus illustrating how lower-echelon enforcement and judicial policies can become a salient dimension of gun control controversies at the national level.

2. The Targets of Regulation

Gun controls can be categorized according to the firearm-related activity, the category of persons, or the type of firearm (or ammunition) being targeted for regulation.

a. Types of Activities

Types of firearm-related activity regulated include use, manufacture and importation (also exportation), transfer (including sale and purchase), transport, and possession (which includes both the "keeping and bearing" of firearms).

i. Use Actual deployment, including the intentional presentation of a gun as well as the firing of a gun for some purpose, is distinguished from the possession or carrying of a firearm. General criminal or civil law covers crimes, torts, or justifications for the use of force (such as self-defense) that happen to involve the use of guns but whose actionable nature is not instrument specific. (For example, general laws defining murder or self-defense are indifferent to whether a gun or some other instrument is used.) "Place and manner" laws specifically regarding where or how firearms may be used provide sentence enhancement for crimes committed with a gun and forbid uses such as the reckless display of a gun or discharging a gun within certain areas.

The most salient type of law governing the use of firearms imposes sentence-enhancement for the commission of certain crimes with a firearm. For example, the Gun Control Act of 1968 made the overt use (or even covert possession) of a firearm in the commission of a federal crime a discrete offense in its own right subject to an additional minimum penalty beyond the sentence prescribed for the primary offense. The Firearms Owners Protection Act of 1986 added serious drug offenses to the crimes that entailed an added penalty in case a gun was used. It also doubled the prescribed penalty for any crime if it was committed with a machine gun or a firearm equipped with a sound suppressor. State and local laws likewise often make the use of a firearm in the commission of certain serious crimes a separate offense entailing an enhanced penalty.

ii. Manufacture and Importation The manufacture of firearms is regulated in a number of respects. A federal license is required for virtually all firearms manufacture and, by federal law, all firearms must be made with unique serial numbers and with a minimum metal content identifying them as firearms. The latter requirement, known as the "plastic gun bun," was motivated by the possibility that firearms technology might someday permit the manufacture of nonmetallic firearms that could not be recognized as such by metal-detection equipment.

Local zoning ordinances can prohibit the manufacture of firearms, as well as commercial sale. Certain states (Hawaii, Illinois, Maryland, Minnesota) and localities (in California) prohibit the manufacture and sale of certain types of firearms, such as so-called Saturday Night Specials.

Unlike manufacture, the importation of firearms is regulated exclusively by the federal government and, like manufacture, requires a federal license. The Gun Control Act of 1968 introduced the "sporting purpose" requirement for purposes of an import ban on "nonsporting" firearms, in particular military-surplus rifles (such as the Carcano carbine involved in the assassination of President John F. Kennedy) and handguns that failed the test of being "particularly suitable for or readily adaptable to sporting purposes" (typically, small, inexpensive handguns).

The motivation for the exemption of privileged "sporting" arms in even draconian prohibitionist schemes has historically been political and economic expediency: it allows governments to outlaw certain firearms while appeasing large political constituencies and economic sectors, namely hunters and "sport" shooters and the economic enterprises dependent on them. In the present day, while the European Economic Community has debated total bans on cross-border transport and civilian-owned firearms, certain "sporting" arms have so far been spared in the interest of commerce.

The concept of "sporting purpose" has also been established as a standard for domestic bans in the U.S. This test was invoked in 1989 to ban, by Executive Order, the importation of certain "assault weapons," consonant with the movement to ban them domestically. In 1994, lack of "sporting purpose" was used for the first time to ban firearms of domestic manufacture under the authority of the Secretary of the Treasury (in this case, the BATF).

iii. Transfer, Sale, and Purchase The transfer of firearms typically involves either a sale-purchase transaction or the commercial sale of a firearm by a licensed dealer; private transfers between individuals qualified to possess the firearm in question (by sale, barter, gift, or bequest) are generally lawful (with the exception of machine guns, which may be transferred only through a licensed dealer). This is a bone of contention for those who believe that all firearms transfers should be subject to the same regulations. For example, the Gun Control Act of 1968 prohibited only licensed dealers from knowingly transferring a firearm to an underage person or a member of a disqualified category; however, the Firearms Owners Protection Act of 1986 made it unlawful for anyone to do so, thereby including private transfers.

Washington, DC, Chicago, and some other cities ban the sale of handguns, and some states and localities ban the sale of certain small, inexpensive handguns. Where the sale and purchase of firearms is allowed, some regulations affect licensed dealers, while others target purchasers. Firearms dealers are required to have a federal firearms license and some states and localities require state and local licenses as well. The Gun Control Act of 1968 prohibited the sale or delivery of any firearm to anyone from or in another state, except for long guns which could be sold to residents of bordering states. The Firearms Owners Protection Act of 1986 allows long guns to be sold and delivered by licensed dealers directly to qualified individuals in other states in which sale and possession of the firearms are lawful. However, interstate sale and delivery of handguns must be mediated by a licensed dealer in the purchaser's state.

Some states and localities have adopted "gun rationing" laws that prohibit multiple sales and limit how many firearms may be purchased in a given period of time, such as one handgun a month. Advocates argue that this measure obviates multiple purchases by proxy buyers for illegal resale on the black market; opponents argue that notification of multiple purchases is a better law enforcement mechanism, because it allows investigation and apprehension of strawman buyers.

Federal restrictions on firearms purchasers include a minimum age requirement (18 for long guns, 21 for handguns), a waiting period (where an instant check system is not available), and background clearance on a number of criteria of legal disability for acquiring or possessing a firearm. To the federal criteria for legal disability, some states add criteria such as alcohol addiction.

While the Brady Law established a national application-to-purchase system, state and local law may impose further restrictions on purchasers. There are two such mechanisms: purchase permits and licenses to possess a firearm. Permits to purchase require a background check and may be valid for some period of years and for multiple purchases, after which they can be renewed and at which time a background check may again be required. Alternatively, a separate purchase permit (and background check) may be required for each purchase. Purchase permits are usually required for acquisitions from private individuals as well as for transfers from licensed dealers, and they may apply only to handguns or to all firearms.

Licenses are required for the possession of firearms as well as for making new acquisitions. They also require a background check and commonly take the form of a Firearms Owner Identification Card. Some propose that a national card should be required to possess or purchase any firearm.

iv. Transport   Transport of a firearm simply for purposes of getting it from one location to another can be distinguished from carrying a firearm on or about one's person for purposes of protection. Transport regulations are a form of "place and manner" restriction insofar as they dictate where and in what condition a firearm may be kept for purposes of transporting it off one's own private premises. Transport regulations are of two types: those regulating how a person may privately transport a firearm and those regulating how commercial carriers must transport firearms.

v. Possession ("Keeping and Bearing")   Possession includes legal ownership as well as having a firearm (which one might not own) on one's premises or on or about one's person. Laws or policies regarding possession, in effect, regulate the keeping and bearing of firearms: who may or may not keep or bear them, the places and manners in which they may or may not be kept or carried, and the form of permission required to keep or carry them.

Possession, in the sense of ownership, beyond purchase or acquisition, might be regulated in four ways: (1) a license might be required to own any firearm (or a handgun) in some states or locales; (2) some state or local jurisdictions might require registration of any firearms (or handguns) one owns; and (3) many states require that all firearms be kept secured from unauthorized hands, in particular from children, in certain specified ways (a "manner" restriction) and/or impose criminal liability for firearms that are not properly secured and consequently misused.

Most states have special exemptions, or special carry permits, allowing hunting firearms to be carried openly in vehicles or about one's person in designated areas during hunting season. In general, possession in the sense of carrying a firearm on or about one's person, openly or concealed, is lawful on one's home or business premises, but carrying an uncased firearm, loaded or unloaded, on or about one's person beyond one's private premises is prohibited unless one has a license to do so. Vermont is the one state that allows concealed carry in public without a license, provided that the firearm is lawfully possessed and the bearer has none but lawful intent. Open carry in public is in theory or by default legal in many states, but, in the modern cultural climate and urban or suburban settings, this may cause alarm and be construed as disturbing the peace. On the other hand, in certain rural areas, carrying a long gun or handgun openly may be both lawful and unremarkable.

Besides restricting the manner in which a firearm is carried under a license, federal, state, and local law may restrict the places in which firearms can be carried even by licensed carriers. Possession of a firearm is prohibited in all federal buildings and in airport terminals. Commercial railroad or bus lines can prohibit carry by passengers, and carry by operators is generally prohibited by company policy. Many states prohibit even licensed carriers from carrying in bars (or eating establishments that serve liquor), and in sports stadiums or at sporting events.

Private establishments such as stores, restaurants, shopping malls, and amusement parks may prohibit firearms possession by legal carriers on their premises. In Texas, when the new mandatory carry licensing law took effect in January, 1996, many establishments and commercial chains posted signs prohibiting concealed carry. However, many of these rescinded the prohibition because of (a) threatened boycotts, or (b) because the postings might serve as an invitation to armed robbers, or (c) out of concern for liability in the event of an incident like the Killeen massacre (where Luby's Cafeteria patrons had firearms in their vehicles with which they might have defended against the perpetrator had they been allowed to carry them inside).

Most states prohibit possession on school grounds. Congress passed the Gun Free School Zone Act in 1990 to make this prohibition uniform nationally, but the Supreme Court found the law unconstitutional. An amendment to the Omnibus Consolidated Appropriations Act of 1997 reinstituted a national prohibition on the possession of firearms on school grounds and included findings to show the relevance to interstate commerce and thus to federal jurisdiction.

Federal, state, and local regulations may prohibit the possession of firearms in federal, state, or local parks. Such an ordinance in Tucson, Arizona, was ruled in violation of Arizona state law, which preempts local authorities from regulating the possession or carrying of firearms within the state.

The idea of "gun free zones" (especially when they are hallowed places such as schools for children, churches, or recreational areas for families) may seem unassailable until one examines the logic of such restrictions. However, firearm possession by criminals or minors and firearm use for criminal intent is already outlawed and penalized everywhere. Moreover, according to numerous studies in Texas, Florida, and elsewhere, firearm possession by licensed law-abiding citizens, even

in hallowed places, is (a) not a significant problem and (b) useful for deterring criminal violence.

Criminals who possess and carry guns illegally in society, the whole of which is in effect a "free zone" for them, are not likely to be any more respectful of special "gun free zone" laws. However, the effect of such policies is likely to disarm the law abiding, depriving them of the means of self-defense and depriving society of the utility of responsible armed citizens.

Thus, the rationale for many special "gun free zones" appears to be merely symbolic. One might as well call for "bullet free zones," because it is not the presence of guns but rather their misuse that is the greater concern. On reflection, the symbolism of special "gun free zones" is also perverse: it implies that human life is more sacred in some places than in others, as well as that the right to defend innocent life varies with place and, worse, that this right shall be restricted in those very places that society considers most hallowed.

This line of objection to many "place" restrictions on possession of firearms by licensed carriers does concede that there may be places where even lawful, defensive response by armed citizens can be too hazardous to risk. Airliners are a likely candidate, where a stray bullet can compromise the air-worthiness of the aircraft, thereby threatening all aboard; training and marksmanship standards for air marshals, who routinely carry aloft, are consequently higher than for law enforcement generally.

Courthouses and airport terminals are exceptional because they are so closely policed that the law-abiding who are disarmed are less likely to encounter armed criminals who successfully ignore the law. However, schools, workplaces, commercial establishments, and parks are places where some of the worst incidents of mass violence have occurred, violence that might have been averted by armed citizens. The Killeen, Texas, massacre at Luby's Cafeteria is a case in point, and it galvanized the movement to reform the Texas carry law. Dr. Suzanna Gratia watched as her parents were fatally shot at close range before her eyes, knowing that she could have shot the perpetrator with the pistol she had duly left in her vehicle, in order to abide by Texas law at the time. At the least, the controversy over "place" restrictions on possession and carry, whether imposed by government or by private enterprise, calls for close scrutiny of both their empirical and their philosophical rationales.

b. Types of Persons

That certain qualifications should be required for acquiring and possessing firearms, as well as for being licensed to carry or deal in them, is, on its face, among the least controversial of all gun control propositions. Presumably, the general criterion for prohibiting certain types or categories of persons from acquiring or possessing firearms, or certain types of firearm (such as handguns), is being at "high risk" for misusing them criminally or for failing to use them responsibly and safely.

However, the specific criteria employed for determining legal disability are not necessarily relevant to such risk. For example, convicted felons are not permitted firearms regardless of whether the conviction was for a violent crime or for a nonviolent "white collar" crime; minors are not permitted handguns, regardless of the fact that some minors are more responsible than many of their seniors; persons dishonorably discharged from the armed services are not permitted firearms, although a dishonorable discharge does not necessarily equate to being at "high risk" for violence or firearm misadventure. On the other hand, some factors, such as alcohol or drug addiction, mental impairment, or a history of chronic violence, are statistically relevant to being at higher risk for criminal misuse of firearms. Thus, depending on the category in question, it may or may not make sense to consider people who are in that category as "high risk." This raises the question of what the rationale for a category of legal disability actually is.

The federal Gun Control Act of 1968 as amended by the Firearms Owner Protection Act of 1986, provides the following criteria for legal disability from acquiring, possessing, selling, transporting, or importing firearms: (1) being under indictment or having been convicted of a crime punishable by imprisonment for a term exceeding 1 year; (2) being a fugitive from justice; (3) being an unlawful user of, or addicted to, a controlled substance (as defined in the Controlled Substances Act, 21 U.S.C. 802, Section 102); (4) having been adjudicated as a mental defective or committed to a mental institution; (5) being an illegal alien (firearms possession is not proscribed for legal adult aliens); (6) having been dishonorably discharged from the armed services; and (7) having been a citizen of the United States and having renounced that citizenship. In addition, one must be 18 years of age to acquire a rifle or shotgun and 21 years of age to acquire a handgun.

Some states add addiction to alcohol as a disability, which raises the question of which standards should be used to determine whether a person fits a given criterion. Some criteria carry a cut-and-dried standard: one is either a certain age or not. Similarly for the seven criteria listed above; all are objective measures. But, for example, what is the standard for being addicted to, or an abuser of, alcohol? Some states use the standard of having been convicted of driving while intoxicated a certain number of times. Being a DWI offender may be a good reason for legal disability, but not all DWIs are alcoholics and not all alcoholics are convicted as

DWIs. Extending the standard to include other evidence runs afoul of privacy and confidentiality issues regarding therapeutic records and relationships, fairness issues regarding discriminating against alcoholics who seek help, or evidentiary issues regarding the reliability of "expert" opinion or other diagnostic indicators (which are especially fallible predictors of violence predicated on mental or emotional difficulties). Similar problems have been encountered by proposals to extend the standard for mental or emotional impairment beyond adjudication or commitment for same, which are verifiable matters of public record. Current controversy revolves around just such efforts to extend the criteria and standards for "high risk" categories.

c. Types of Firearms and Ammunition

A federal license is required to acquire a fully automatic firearm, but in most states no license is required to acquire other firearms, be they handguns or long guns. However, where licenses are required to purchase or own more ordinary firearms, handguns rather than long guns are typically the targets of the requirement. While federal law prohibits possession of all firearms by convicted felons, some states prohibit only their possession of handguns. Presumably, it is the utility and popularity of handguns for criminal purposes or their alleged susceptibility to misuse in general that motivates their differential treatment. Other gun types selected for special treatment include machine guns (associated in the public mind with indiscriminate or mass violence and with use by gangsters in the 1920s and 1930s) and short-barreled rifles and shotguns (singled out for their concealability and popularity for criminal purposes). In 1986, the Gun Control Act of 1968 was amended by the Firearms Owner Protection Act to double the prescribed penalty for any federal crime, in particular drug offenses, if a machine gun or a firearm equipped with a sound suppressor was used in the commission of the crime. Similar sentence enhancements are prescribed by some state and local laws for the use of an assault weapon in the commission of a crime.

When it comes to the most restrictive form of gun control, outright gun bans, selected targets include handguns generally and specifically the "Saturday Night Special" subcategory of handgun, machine guns (in several states), and "assault weapons."

Certain firearm accessories are also targets of control. For example, detachable magazines holding more than 10 rounds and manufactured after September, 1994, were banned for civilian use by the federal "assault weapon" ban, part of the Violent Crime Control Act of 1994. This act also banned firearms that had any two of the following "military style" accoutrements: a pistol-grip shoulder stock, flash suppressor, or bayonet lug.

Specific types of ammunition are also targeted for special regulation or prohibition from civilian use; for example, expanding, hollow-point handgun ammunition and so-called armor-piercing or "cop-killer" bullets.

II. EVALUATING GUN CONTROL POLICY

A. Perspectives on Gun Control

The following are three particularly salient perspectives on gun control that emphasize different sorts of consideration or different priorities vying for public attention and allegiance. Although these perspectives are not mutually exclusive, partisan strategies often assume the authoritative mantle of one or another of them, so it is useful to examine critically how they are employed.

1. Criminology and Criminal Justice

Criminology studies, among other things, the behavior of criminals and influences thereon, including the feasibility and efficacy of policies aimed at reducing criminal violence. Criminal justice, among other things, is concerned with the law and other norms governing agencies and policies tasked with reducing criminal violence. Criminal violence is a natural focus from this perspective, as is gun control policy whose strategic priority is reducing criminal violence, which by some lights was the exclusive focus of gun control research and policy into the 1980s.

The other side of the criminology/criminal justice coin is concern with noncriminals as victims and resistors and noncriminal activities (such as legal firearms commerce and ownership) as enabling or deterrent influences on criminal violence. While criminology and criminal justice heed the distinction between justifiable and criminal homicide, their perspectives may be essentially agnostic regarding how noncriminal violence, such as gun accidents and suicides, should be addressed. However, researchers who are ostensibly criminologists are, fundamentally, sociologists who are not limited by artificial disciplinary boundaries; in fact, they assume a broader social-scientific purview on gun violence and policy that embraces noncriminal violence such as suicide and accidents, and they are duly concerned with the reduction of all forms of gun crime and violence.

2. Public Health

Insofar as an exclusive preoccupation with reducing criminal gun violence is a limited strategic perspective for gun control (fully half of all gun deaths are suicides), the public health perspective that evolved in the 1980s is an important complement. Public health policy today is concerned with addressing many contributing factors to human death and injury, not just disease; hence, the establishment of a division within the National Institutes of Health (NIH) and its Centers for Disease Control (CDC), the National Center for Injury Prevention and Control (NCIPC).

The general perspective of public health as such is properly agnostic on matters of essential concern to the criminology/criminal justice perspective: the distinction between justifiable death or injury and criminal violence and such a positive role as legally held firearms can play in reducing or defending against criminal violence. From a public health perspective, injury is injury and something to be prevented, not just treated: the ramifications of preventative medicine can quite naturally include efforts to reduce access to and use of lethal instruments such as firearms. Hence, several health maintenance organizations encourage doctors to advise their patients against keeping household firearms as a health risk, the American Medical Association has officially supported all manner of gun control proposals at the federal level, and the CDC/NCIPC has supported an intensive research program expressly devised to demonstrate that firearms pose a public health risk far greater than any social benefit attributable to their legal ownership or use.

However, what has come to be known, by advocates and critics alike, as "the public health approach" (PHA) to gun control policy has evolved from a research perspective on noncriminal and unintentional gun injury into a strategic political agenda that has proven to be controversial. It is useful, then, to distinguish between the general public health perspective, which is complementary to the study of human injury (including gun suicide and accidental death), and the PHA as a strategic policy perspective with a specific political agenda.

A general public health strategy aims to reduce all death and injury by gun, specifically avoidable death by suicide and accidental injury. Under the same mantle of medical-scientific authority, the PHA political strategy is to advance this laudable goal by reducing private gun ownership and use. The problem, then, with PHA as a research strategy is its predisposition to find against noncriminal firearm possession and use.

The PHA focus on death and injury and the view that firearms themselves are the "vectors" of death and injury are effectively, if not intentionally, biased in important regards. The analogy of firearms to what epidemiologists call "vectors" of disease, such as bacteria and viruses, is problematic as a premise for research design in two ways: guns are not animate, as are viruses and bacteria; and gun-related injury is also a function of the behavior of animate agents (people) possessing intentionality, unlike viruses and bacteria. The PHA research program, modeled on an epidemiological disease metaphor, quite naturally focuses on firearms-related pathology, death, or injury, but can be regarded as myopic in framing its results.

A telling example of this focus is a highly publicized statistic in the current gun control debate, the finding of a 1986 *New England Journal of Medicine* article that a gun in the home is 43 times more likely to be used to kill a family member or acquaintance than to kill an intruder. This suggests frightfully bad odds for people who keep a gun in the home (86% of the gun fatalities were suicides and 12% accidents, making the ratio of justifiable to criminal homicides 1 to 5, which still looks like a bad bargain). The imputation is that the presence of guns in homes, like deadly viruses, are much more apt to bring death to a user or her loved ones than anything good. The statistic itself is unassailable, the straightforward result of simple arithmetic on the gun fatalities that occurred over 5 years in homes in King County, Washington. It is the focus on fatalities as the measure of the risks/benefits of household firearms that is misleading: less than 1% of defensive uses of firearms are fatal, so intruders killed, as compared to householders or acquaintances killed, is an incomplete measure, just as the number of felons killed by police officers is not the whole, or the most significant, measure of the protective value of the police force in a society.

In addition, the focus on the gun as the "vector" of the pathology (death), to the exclusion of the characteristics of the killers and their victims, ignores critical dispositional, demographic, or environmental factors: the vast majority of householders and their acquaintances who perpetrate or suffer homicide or fatal accident by gun have certifiable histories of violence, recklessness, substance abuse, or drug dealing and are no more representative of risks endemic to the general population of gun owners than the deaths of people who drink and drive are representative of all drivers' risks. Cruder numbers provide some global perspective: in a given year, the ratio of all gun fatalities (at 40,000) to gun owners (at 60 million) is 0.066%. The horrific-looking *NEJM* odds for people who keep a gun in their home is an artifact of the PHA study's perspective: an exclusive focus on pathology (fatalities), the use of the single criterion of intruders killed rather than a complete view of defensive gun use, and the emphasis on one "disease vector," the gun, to the neglect of well-known criminological factors.

3. Constitutional Law

Constitutional issues regarding gun control can be raised both on the state and federal level. On the federal level, issues regarding the constitutional feasibility and justifiability of gun control policies, or the status of the right of citizens to keep and bear arms, have been raised especially on Second Amendment grounds.

a. State Constitutional Provisions on the Right to Arms

State constitutions tend to be very explicit about the right to arms being both a right of individuals and being for the purpose of self-defense as well as the common defense. For example, this excerpt from the state constitution of Delaware: "A person has the right to keep and bear arms for the defense of self, family, home and State, and for hunting and recreational use." (Article I, Section 20)

In fact, a majority of state constitutional provisions are explicit about issues that are contested by different schools of thought about the Second Amendment to the U.S. Constitution, namely: (1) that the right to arms is an individual right, not merely a collective right of the state to equip and muster a militia; (2) that one function of this right to arms is to ensure effective means for self-defense (some states specify it more broadly to include defense of others and property as well); but (3) that the exercise of this right is properly subject to certain forms of regulation, in particular that the state may regulate the manner in which arms may be carried.

Selective gun bans represent one issue that remains ambiguous or arguable even on state constitutional provisions that are more explicit than the Second Amendment. For example, "assault weapon" bans in California, New Jersey, and Connecticut have survived constitutional challenges. This leads to an interesting line of constitutional argument in favor of selective gun bans, which was used by the Connecticut Supreme Court. The issue is whether the government's power to impose certain regulations even as against an individual right to arms includes the power to prohibit the lawabiding from possessing some types of firearm. The argument on behalf of the Connecticut ban was that it left a sufficient remainder of legal firearms unmolested so as to comport with the state constitution's provision that "every citizen has a right to bear arms in defense of himself and the state."

The generally used term "arms" is ambiguous regarding just what kinds of firearms merit protection. For self-defense purposes, could the state not prescribe a narrow assortment of handguns or long guns as sufficient? Would the right to bear arms in self-defense be violated by being limited to a few kinds of state-approved guns? Of course, there are important intervening empirical issues about what the criminal potential and defensive utility of assault weapons actually are, but the issue of principle concerns the power of the state to define what constitutes a sufficient selection of arms for defensive purposes. What reasons does the state need to constrain the otherwise unfettered choice of arms by citizens? This leads to another related issue: whether another function of the right to arms is to help secure the citizenry against tyranny, an issue central to debate about the Second Amendment.

b. The Second Amendment

A well regulated militia being necessary to the security of a free state, the right of the people to keep and bear arms, shall not be infringed.

The complex of issues about the meaning and scope of the Second Amendment, and the vast scholarship to which they have given rise, are beyond the capacity of this article. An outline of the general lay of the land must therefore suffice.

There are basically two schools of thought: what may be termed the individual right view (IRV), that the Second Amendment refers to a right of individuals; and the states' right view (SRV), that it refers to a collective or state right (as in a right of the several states) to maintain a militia as one check against the federal government, whereby the states retain the discretion to determine how citizens shall be armed and regulated for this purpose. The "militia clause" is taken by the SRV proponents as evidence of this intent, whereas the IRV position observes that the term "the people" is distributively, not collectively, used in other amendments in the Bill of Rights and that "rights" therefore pertain to individual citizens while "powers" pertain to government entities.

Supervening this controversy is the presumption that the "original intent" of the Framers is crucial to the current meaning of the Second Amendment. Some opponents of the idea of an individual right to arms break with this presumption in one of two ways. Some aver that the Framers did indeed hold the IRV but argue that in deciding constitutionality, original intent needs to be balanced against modern exigencies and may be discounted; others accept both the IRV and original intent, but conclude that the amendment should be repealed rather than finessed. The former believe the Framers had no idea what havoc modern firearms technology would produce, so that if they were alive today they would allow that the IRV may be constrained in whatever ways necessary. The second view holds that regardless of what reaction we might presume the Framers would have to the current world, that is not good enough reason to override the protections of the First, Fourth, or Fifth Amendments. The only proper way to correct the constitution, in this view, is by formal repeal or by a counteramendment.

IRV opponents point out that the U.S. Supreme Court has never proscribed gun control on Second Amendment grounds. Since the Supreme Court has addressed Second Amendment issues only once in this century, in a very circumspect decision (U.S. v. Miller, 1939), the only thing that can be fairly said about Supreme Court Second Amendment jurisprudence is that there is a dearth of it to argue about. As to the IRV/SRV controversy, it is argued that *Miller* supports the IRV, but this is true only in dicta, incidental to the decision, which skirts this fundamental issue. The basic fact of the matter about Supreme Court jurisprudence on the Second Amendment is judiciously put by Nowak, Rotunda, and Young in the Third Edition of *Constitutional Law* (1986): "The Supreme Court has not determined, at least not with any clarity, whether the amendment protects only a right of state governments against federal interference with state militia and police forces … or a right of individuals against the federal and states government(s)." That this observation is relegated in the text to a footnote is symbolic of the marginal status of the Second Amendment in the purview of the Supreme Court.

SRV advocates gain more ground in their appeal to the authority of lower court decisions, many of which construct an SRV from their interpretations of *Miller*. While SRV advocates arm themselves with the authority of court rulings, IRV supporters appeal to constitutional scholarship, where the weight of authority breaks down as follows. Of the approximately 60 law review/journal articles that have been published on the Second Amendment, they run over 6 to 1 in favor of the IRV position. Among the minority SRV authorities, it is pointed out, most are not law professors but are employees of gun control advocacy organizations; and their articles appear in inferior reviews or invitational symposia that are not peer-reviewed. Among the majority IRV authorities, whose articles appear in the most prestigious peer-reviewed journals, are many of the most distinguished constitutional law professors who happen not to be gun owners and who are personally hostile to firearms and the private use of force. Of course, none of this says anything about the merits of the scholarship or its arguments. But it indicates a remarkable growth in Second Amendment research in general, as well as among scholars who are not by disposition or personal philosophy gun-rights advocates.

III. TRYING THE FACTS

The great enemy of the truth is very often not the lie—deliberate, contrived, and dishonest—but the myth—persistent, persuasive, and unrealistic.

(JOHN F. KENNEDY)

It isn't what folks don't know that's the problem. It's what they know that ain't so.

(WILL ROGERS)

Former President Kennedy's and Will Roger's caveats apply to much of what is taken as conventional wisdom about firearms and violence. Pace Will Rogers, in addition, what people don't know or care to know is also a problem for public policy dispute. Of course, the controversy over guns engages many of the strongest and least attractive of human passions: the fears evoked by the apparent ubiquity or randomness of human violence (fears exacerbated for some, assuaged for others, by the availability of guns); contempt for others with alien, seemingly threatening values (be they "gun nuts" who are seen as "Wild West" vigilantes or do-gooder "gun grabbers" who would throw the citizenry, disarmed, to the wolves); and cultural beliefs akin to apocalyptic religious faith (visions of bloody anarchy or cold-blooded totalitarianism, either of which might bring an end to the world as we wish to know it). Phobia, paranoia, and bigotry reign at both extremes. Extreme control advocates see the gun culture as paranoid and bloodthirsty, but are viewed in turn as paranoid enemies of liberty by their opposite numbers.

Perhaps more than the abortion controversy, which tends to turn on metaphysical and moral issues more than upon empirical matters, the gun control controversy is rife with factual disputes. On the factual front, there is bad news and good news. The good news is that there are many well-researched findings of fact available, as well as informed and reasoned analysis on irreducibly speculative matters. The bad news is that a lot of the comforting faith and conventional wisdom about guns and gun control does not hold up under factual scrutiny. But this bad news should not make a virtue of ignorance: we still need to know what there is to know and to identify what of what we think we know that "ain't so." The following description of factual issues provides only a summary of a sample of the pertinent research.

A. Effects Attributable to Firearms

Presumably, we are interested in factual matters of the following kind for purposes of informing some cost/benefit assessment of private firearm ownership and use (as well as controls thereon), whatever role cost/benefit analyses may play within our respective ethical orientations. For purposes of illustrating the empirical contours of the task of policy evaluation, the following discussion will focus on well-defined indicators of social cost and benefit: the chief categories of firearm fatality, violent crime, and the defensive and deterrent effects of firearms.

1. Criminal Gun Violence

From the indisputable facts that America has a high level of violent crime, a high level of gun ownership, and a high level of crime committed with guns, and the fact that America's levels of both gun ownership and violent crime are higher than other nations, the inference is often drawn that the level of gun ownership "causes" or occasions the higher violent crime rate in America. There are two, decidedly less popular, alternative hypotheses: the substitution hypothesis, that the violent crime rate is accountable to other factors and would occur by other means without the guns, and the reverse causation hypothesis, that the crime rate motivates gun ownership.

There are two possible connections between gun possession and violent crime that need to be distinguished: (a) the effect of illegal gun posession by criminal aggressors on the patterns and lethality of violent crime and (b) the effects of legal gun ownership in the general population on violent crime rates.

a. Effects of Illegal Gun Possession on Criminal Aggression

On the level of individual incidents of violent crime, one question of interest is how the type of weapon possessed by a criminal aggressor influences the disposition to commit aggression via threat, whether threats escalate to attacks, whether in the event of attack injury results, and whether in the event of injurious attack death results. These are questions about what are called instrumentality effects. What are the instrumentality effects of firearms when used by criminal aggressors? Does the use of guns in violent crime tend to increase the likelihood of attack or serious injury and death from attack?

i. Effect on Criminal Threat It has been found that guns are used in homocides more often in the following types of cases (as compared with the reverse situations): where the victim is male, where the attacker is female, where the attacker is under 16 or older than 39, where the victim is 16 to 39 and the attacker is outside this "prime" age span, where there is a single attacker, and where a single aggressor attacks multiple victims. Such homicide data suggest that guns, compared with other weapons, can facilitate criminal aggression where attack is contemplated or where victim resistance is a contemplated risk. But these data do not prove that guns induce aggression or attack where they would not otherwise have been attempted for lack of a gun. It is possible that criminal aggressors would be sufficiently motivated to threaten or even attack victims, absent a gun. However, the advantage of a gun as a threat and remote-control weapon might well embolden criminals to be aggressive where they would not do so without a gun. This might be true particularly where the aggressors perceive themselves to be at risk or at a disadvantage as compared with anticipated victims; for example, by virtue of some disparity of bodily force in stature or strength or because of age or gender. A gun can certainly facilitate aggression by equalizing disparities in force, real or perceived.

ii. Effect on Criminal Threat Escalating to Attack
Similarly, it seems reasonable to hypothesize that a gun would facilitate weaker or smaller criminals' escalating their aggression from mere threat to attack, even where attack was not originally contemplated, but particularly where victim resistance is seen as a risk. Guns may also enable physically strong and able criminals to commit attacks where they would be loathe to do so with weapons requiring physical contact. This facilitation hypothesis holds that guns enable some criminals to attack in situations where they would not do so with bare hands or contact weapons because guns equalize disparities of force for aggressors (just as they do for victims) or because guns allow attack without requiring contact with the victim.

In addition, a triggering hypothesis holds that guns can increase the likelihood of criminal aggression or attack because their very presence or possession can incite aggression. This has also been called "the weapons effect," because it could apply to other weapons. Experimental studies on this effect are about evenly divided between those that support a triggering effect and those that do not. No study provides evidence that mere possession of a gun by itself stimulates aggression or, as the triggering hypothesis is aptly summarized to hold, that "the trigger pulls the finger." Indeed, some "weapons effect" experiments showed that the mere sight of a weapon could inhibit "aggression," but various expressions of aggression are one thing, while lethal attack is quite another (and certainly not an option for experimental subjects).

A further inhibition hypothesis holds that, probably because a gun creates such a disparity of force and is effective at a distance (the very features delineated by the facilitation hypothesis), when a gun is presented by the aggressor, both the aggressor and the victim tend to refrain from attack or resistance, respectively. The victim is, predictably, more apt to comply with the aggressor's mere threat and, because this is likely, the aggressor is inhibited from gratuitously raising the ante by escalating from threat to attack. Evidence for the inhibition hypothesis comes from victim survey data. Complementary evidence for the inhibition hypothesis is found in the fact that victims who resist aggressors with a gun fare better, for all categories of criminal threat, than victims who do not resist or those who resist by other means.

iii. Effect on the Injuriousness of Completed Attacks
Once an attack ensues, for whatever reason, what effect does the use of a gun by an aggressor have on the likelihood of the attack being completed and resulting in injury? Conversely, how likely is it that an attack involving the firing of a gun (as opposed to using the gun as an impact weapon) will miss and not injure the intended victim, as compared with an edged or impact weapon attack? According to National Crime Survey data for 1990–1987, only 19% of gun attacks resulted in hits on victims. By contrast, NCS data on knife attacks show that they connect 55% of the time. However counter-intuitive it might be for those unfamiliar with the impact of stress in lethal encounters and the difficulty of shooting accurately even at close range, the net effect of the use of firearms in criminal attacks is to reduce the frequency of completed attacks and resultant injury. More generally, it is found that the more lethal the weapon involved in an attack, the less likely it will be used to inflict injury.

iv. Effect on the Fatality of Injurious Attack
It is natural to expect that the surprising infrequency with which gun attacks are completed and prove injurious would be counter-balanced by the greater lethality of the gun-shot wounds that do occur. This intuition turns out to be correct: given an injury, the injury is more likely to prove fatal if it is a gunshot wound than some other kind. Actuarially, there is a hierarchy of fatality running from, at the top, gunshot wounds to knife wounds to blunt-instrument injuries to damage produced by the use of the hands and feet.

How does the greater frequency of fatality from injury interact with the lower frequency of injury from firearms as compared with other modes of attack? The matter is too complex for summary analysis here, but the use of a gun by an aggressor, all things considered, increases the probability of a victim's death by 1.4%. Thus, the countervailing "good news/bad news" effects of firearm use at different stages of aggression almost cancel one another out.

b. Effects of Legal Gun Ownership on Criminal Violence

The vast majority of violent crime is not committed by law-abiding gun owners who turn rogue, but by small, high-risk or recidivist subsets of the population disposed to criminal violence. Nevertheless, the institution of private gun ownership is suspected of increasing violent crime by increasing general gun availability (for example, for theft), thereby enabling illegal possession and use, and by enabling, or even inducing, legal gun owners to commit violent acts.

The question about gun "availability" as affected by legal gun ownership is whether, or to what extent, the level of lawful ownership of firearms is positively correlated with either criminal gun violence or criminal violence in general. For example, do areas with higher rates of legal gun ownership have more crime? Do crime rates increase over time when gun ownership rates increase? These questions are ambiguous, insofar as a positive correlation between levels of gun ownership and levels of crime could have at least four explanations:

1. Gun ownership enables illegal possession and crime; thus higher levels of gun ownership promote higher levels of crime.
2. Reverse causation: higher levels of crime motivate higher gun ownership.
3. Reciprocal causation: each has a positive effect on the other.
4. Confounding factors: many other variables, demographic and cultural, are determinants of crime rates.

Although space cannot be afforded here to summarize the amount and variety of the research on this matter, the bottom line is instructive: the net impact on violent crime of the various combined effects of gun possession by criminals and by prospective victims (the general public) is a virtual nullity. "Consequently, the assumption that general gun availability positively affects the frequency or average seriousness of violent crimes is not supported. The policy implication is that there appears to be nothing to be gained from reducing the general gun ownership level. Nevertheless, one still cannot reject the possibility that gun ownership among high-risk subsets of the population may increase violent crime rates" (Kleck, 1991). Thus, as a policy matter, while trying to reduce levels of legal gun ownership is not helpful and might even be counter-indicated for reducing the rate and severity of violent crime; it might nonetheless be effective to target illegal gun possession and to screen against high-risk persons' acquiring firearms.

c. International Comparisons

A popular tactic in the U.S. gun control debate, employed by both sides, is to make comparisons between the United States and other countries. Japan and Great Britain, it is observed, have far lower rates of homicide but far stricter gun controls; therefore, America's being awash in uncontrolled guns must be the reason that it is awash in violence. Switzerland, comes the rejoinder, is not only awash in guns but also requires its citizens to keep fully automatic assault rifles in their homes, yet Switzerland has one of the lowest violent crime rates in the world, lower even than Great Britain's. Hence, the availability of guns throughout a given population is not uniformly associated with violent crime.

The obvious difficulty with international comparisons regarding gun ownership/control and violence derives from important cultural differences, such as the relative presence (or absence) of such factors as: social solidarity, ethnic homogeneity, racial conflict, hierarchical rigidity, obedience to authority, and a subjective sense of unjust deprivation. (For example, Switzerland not only keeps and bears its private firearms with noteworthy civil discipline, but is also noteworthy for citizens who pay public transit fees on the honor system.) In many cases, reliable and uniform data are not available either on these and other cultural variables or on gun ownership levels. Consequently, systematic study of a large comparison set is impaired.

However, despite the obstacles in the way of accurate comparisons, certain approaches have proven instructive. For example, to partially control for cultural differences between the U.S. and Japan, Kleck examined homicide rates among Japanese-Americans in the U.S., where gun availability is widespread, with homicide rates in virtually firearm-free Japan, finding rates of 1.04 per 100,000 for the former and 2.45 for the latter. Of course, there could be many cultural differences between Japanese-Americans and Japanese citizens that might defeat this comparison, but that is just the point: international comparisons are readily vitiated. The lesson that Kleck draws from his exercise is that even a simple attempt at controlling for cultural variables can obviate an apparently enormous difference in violence rates.

An example of an obviously fallacious but popular comparison is that between the U.S. and Great Britain: not only is the U.S. overall homicide rate higher, but its gun homicide rate is also higher, which is then taken to imply that the greater rate of gun ownership in the U.S. must account for its higher rate of homicide. But Britain also has lower rates of homicide from the use of the hands and feet, yet no one would suppose that this fact is accountable to Britons' having fewer hands and feet.

Another illustrative study surveyed gun ownership levels in 14 countries and noted, for pair-wise comparisons, that higher gun ownership levels generally correlated with higher total homicide rates and with higher gun homicide rates. What the study did not notice or mention was that greater gun availability correlated equally strongly with higher nongun homicides, which suggests an alternative to the hypothesis that more guns cause more homicide; namely, the reverse causation hypothesis that higher homicide rates motivate higher levels of gun ownership. *A priori*, there seems more reason to expect nongun homicide to motivate gun ownership than to expect gun ownership to motivate nongun homicide. Another alternative explanation is that both the higher levels of gun ownership and the higher homicide levels are correlated with other cultural variables, such as attitudes on the use of lethal weapons against others. In any case, international studies are not yet conclusive on the nature of the relationship between gun ownership levels and violence rates, and they therefore provide no definitive comparisons for the U.S.

d. Demographics

The tendency to isolate firearms as a major factor accounting for American violence is understandable: America has distinctively high levels of gun ownership and also of violent crime and gun crime. However, solutions to the problem of American violence are not apt to become apparent if the problem itself is oversimplified and other factors in the patterns of American violence are ignored.

For example, it is axiomatic that violence correlates to demographics. Perhaps the most distressing recent manifestation of the effect of demographic factors in the U.S. is the sharp rise in violent crime, and gun crime in particular, among juveniles and young adults. It is not surprising, from the criminological perspective, that as the youth cohort of the general population increases the overall crime rate can increase, because the highest rate of crime in any population in every age and country occurs in the subset of those aged roughly 15 to 24. In turn, the highest crime rate in the youth cohort is in the subset of males and the highest crime rate in the male youth cohort is in the subset of the socioeconomically deprived. Despite the steep increase in gun crime among the youth cohort and the increase in the relative size of that cohort in the 1980s in the United States, the overall violent crime rate did not so markedly increase, indicating that in other age groups violent crime actually decreased. Aside from the increase of drug trafficking and associated incentives for American youths to resort to firearms in the 1980s, the general factors of youth, gender, and socioeconomics play an influential role in the national crime rate.

For example, data from the 1992 FBI Uniform Crime Reports and the *Economist,* reported by Jarod Taylor in the May, 1994, *National Review,* show that European murder rates in 1990 per 100,000 people were: Great Britain, 7.4; France, 4.6; Germany, 4.2; and Italy, 6.0; with an average of 5.5, compared to the 1992 U.S. rate of 9.3. If the socioeconomically deprived cohort is removed from the U.S. tally, the U.S. murder rate falls below Great Britain's and compares to the European average.

Removing the youth cohort aged 15–24 has a similar, dramatically deflationary effect. This in no way diminishes the more severe violent crime problem in the United States, because the same manipulation would also deflate the murder rates in the European countries. It simply illustrates the magnitude of the association of violence with general demographic factors. The point is not that the problem of violent crime is not significant, but that the problem is not uniform across U.S. society.

Beyond the role of general demographic, socioeconomic, or geographic factors, more specific influences on the patterns of violence in American society can be discerned. Analogous to the question "Why is America more violent than its neighbor to the north, Canada?" is the question "Why was the American western frontier more violent than Canada's?" (Significantly, the American West was no more uniformly violent than American society is today.)

David T. Courtwright explores this question in his article "Violence in America" in the September, 1996, *American Heritage*. He identifies many regional peculiarities and differences in American violence through history that cannot be explained simply by the demographics of age and gender, whereby young men, as in all societies and times, are at highest risk for violent crime and misadventure. More specifically, it is young men who lack parental supervision or marital partners, family, or other communitarian identities, who are at greatest risk. For a variety of reasons and for most of its history, "America has had a higher proportion of itinerant, single men in its population than the nations from which its immigrants, voluntarily or otherwise, came." American immigration patterns were such that there was a surplus of men every year until 1946, producing what Courtwright calls "the abnormal structure of the population" that accounts in significant part for America's abnormal history of violence "played out with a bad hand of cards dealt from a stacked demographic deck." The surplus of men, many of whom would necessarily remain single, combined with "the ubiquity of bachelor vices" (such as liquor, gambling, and prostitution purveyed in places of commercialized vice) created ample opportunity for violent conflict, which in turn created ample reason for this volatile population to resort to arms. Unlike the Canadian frontier, which attracted families and women in greater numbers and was characterized by a more balanced and rooted population, single men disproportionately populated the notoriously violent zones of the American frontier.

Courtwright's case in point is California during the Gold Rush. The population was 95% men in 1849, 20% of whom were dead within 6 months of their arrival from disease, suicide, or violence brought on by competition for scarce prostitutes or gambling quarrels, all of which were exacerbated by alcohol abuse. For a complex of reasons, the excesses and ravages of life in communities dominated by single men abated with the influx of women and, in established communities with more balanced populations, violent conflict was localized to the establishments and mining camps where men exclusively caroused.

Mining communities were several times more violent than urban crime centers today. For example, where the latter post homicide rates of 20 to 30 per 100,000, the former produced rates of 60 to over 110. However, an exception was the Gold Hill area of North Carolina, which was settled by immigrant Cornish miners who brought and created families and suffered nothing like the premature death and homicide rates of the female-scarce and, hence, family-scarce California environs.

By Courtwright's analysis, the key factor differentiating the more violent from the more pacific communities across "frontier" regions as well as across time (as havens of violence became increasingly domesticated and peaceful or vice versa) was the difference in gender balance: the more balanced the population, the greater the social order. The complexion of this relationship, of course, reflects far more than the mere head count of male and female co-inhabitants, but the dynamics of the relationship and the salient role played historically by undomesticated men in America's violent "hot spots" illustrate a level of demographic detail worthy of attention today.

2. Suicide by Gun

There are two different kinds of issues regarding guns and suicide. The empirical questions concern the effect of firearm possession on the frequency of attempted suicide and the effect of the use of a firearm on the success of suicide attempts. While there may be little philosophical question about the propriety of the law being used to try to reduce criminal violence, there is a philosophical question, albeit a delicate one, about the law being used to prevent suicide. If objection can be raised against medical paternalism, it can also be raised against paternalism (limitation on, or interference with, a person's liberty for the presumed good of that person but regardless of, or against, that person's express or apparent wishes) exercised by coercive state authority.

Suicide prevention, at least gun-suicide prevention, is part of the rationale for imposing special criminal liability for negligence in securing firearms from unauthorized hands. And suicide reduction is one rationale for gun bans or gun-scarcity programs, on the assumption that eliminating or reducing gun suicides will reduce total suicides. Prohibiting minors and the mentally/emotionally impaired from possessing guns, imposing liability for the insecure keeping of guns, and banning guns are three different types of gun control aimed at suicide reduction.

A brief summary of the facts and findings about guns and suicide is helpful for determining how suicide-targeted gun controls might be argued. Gun suicides regularly outnumber gun homicides and account for roughly half of all gun deaths. If in a given year gun fatalities were 40,000, 20,000 would typically be suicides, 1,500 accidents, and 18,500 homicides (10 to 15% of which could be in justifiable self-defense).

Guns were used in 57% of U.S. suicides in 1985, compared with hanging, the second most popular method, at 14%. The frequency of both gun suicides and the preference for firearms for suicide in general suggest to some that the immediate availability of a gun can induce suicide (analogous to the "triggering" hypothesis regarding guns and criminal aggression, that "the trigger pulls the finger") or that the general availability of guns is conducive to suicide. Alternative notions are that the suicide who chooses a gun is a determined, not an ambivalent or impulsive, suicide attempter; that the gun is preferred because the suicide attempter wants to ensure success (fatality); that ambivalent or call-for-help suicide attempters, for this reason, do not prefer guns. Proponents of this line of hypothesizing have generated a mass of research, as have its opponents, but it culminates in the substitution hypothesis, which holds that virtually all gun suicides would have been committed by some other means had a gun not been available. The substitution hypothesis is one empirical challenge to proposals to reduce firearm ownership in order to reduce suicide overall.

Overall, by Kleck's analysis (1991) and as is the case in other areas, the research fails to make a case for the effectiveness of gun controls for reducing the overall suicide rate (as opposed to the gun suicide rate). As is the case in other contested areas of research on the efficacy of gun controls, the research is about evenly divided regarding whether any given gun control measure appeared to reduce overall suicide rates or failed to do so.

There are two studies paradigmatic of what can be said for the partisans and opponents of the substitution hypothesis, respectively. A 1990 study of average suicide rates in Toronto 5 years before and after Canada imposed stricter gun controls found a decrease in the gun suicide rate but no significant drop in the overall suicide rate, consonant with the substitution hypothesis. However, a study of the effects of the Washington, DC Firearms Control Act of 1975 (which went into effect in February, 1977) from 1976 to 1977 found that the gun suicide rate decreased by 38% while the total suicide rate decreased by 22%, even as the national suicide rate was increasing. The DC law prohibited handgun sales as well as handgun possession by previous handgun owners who failed to register their handguns prior to passage of the law; it is the latter provision that could have had an impact in the study's short time frame. Factors that detract from the impressive drop in overall suicides include the facts that (a) the study did not control for any other variables besides the handgun ban and (b) that the results represent only a 1-year period. Factors that enhance the impressiveness of the D.C. study's results include the facts that (c) the substitution of more lethal long guns for handguns, if it occurred, left a marked decrease nonetheless, contrary to one version of the substitution hypothesis, and (d) any "leakage" effect from other jurisdictions that helped make Washington the "murder capitol of the world" despite its gun ban evidently did not erase the effect of the handgun ban on the suicide rate in the first year; "leakage" might have more of an effect over time, but suicide attempters are more law-abiding and less apt to seek illegal guns than criminals.

By contrast with the dramatic suicide rate drop and contrary to the study's authors' claim, the DC handgun ban, according to Kleck's analysis, did not result in decreases in overall violent crime. This is consistent with two general facts: few crimes, but most suicides, are committed by people without certifiable criminal identities; broadly targeted gun controls, such as gun bans, reduce gun possession only among the law-abiding if they reduce gun possession at all. While the reliability or generalizability of the DC study's result, limited to 1 year of the past two decades, might be questioned, the study poses an instructive question. The Canadian toughening of gun controls that effected no reduction in total suicides, according to the aforementioned 10-year Toronto study, was not tantamount to a handgun ban. The discrepancy might be taken to suggest that only sufficiently draconian controls, such as outright bans, are rewarded with the intended effect, a net reduction in some category of violence. The challenge, then, is to decide how to weigh the benefits against countervailing costs. Washington, DC is a case in point: on the assumption that overall suicide reduction has remained a result of the 1975 handgun ban, the question is whether the suicides saved counter-balance innocent lives lost to criminal violence for lack of a defensive firearm. Two questions remain: whether the prospect of suicide reduction can itself justify gun bans and, if not, what other forms of gun control might hope to reduce suicide.

There are two important firearm-specific instrumentality effects to consider, whatever one's position on suicide-preventative gun control. (1) Firearms are among the most lethal suicide instruments. Also, delayed-success methods like drug overdoses provide more opportunity to interdict suicide, should that be justifiable. The lethality of guns as suicide instruments suggest that even if gun suicide attempters would have seriously attempted suicide absent the availability of a gun, more attempters might survive (and survive with less damage) absent a gun. (2) A secondary effect of a handgun ban, were it to be effective in reducing handgun possession, could be to induce firearms users to substitute long guns (rifles and shotguns) for handguns; in the case of gun suicide attempters, this substitution would prove yet more lethal. While the Washington, DC handgun ban, at least in the first year, resulted in a significant net decrease in suicides whether or not long guns were substituted as an instrumentality, handgun bans or handgun ammunition bans can still have the perverse effect of inducing some suicide attempters to resort to more lethal firearms.

3. Accidental Death by Gun

As in the case of suicide, there is more philosophical argument about how the law should be used to prevent accidents (which can involve harm to self as well as harm to others) than about how the law should be used to prevent crime (harm to others). As with suicide, accident-prevention measures that target minors or children are less contestable than those that constrain adults for their own safety. With respect to coercive accident-prevention measures aimed at adults for their own safety, some might be welcomed by their supposed beneficiaries, while others can objectionably interfere with the liberty or other interests of their would-be beneficiaries.

Unlike the case of gun suicides, which typically outnumber gun homicides, fatal gun accidents are relatively small in proportion to all gun deaths (typically, less than 5%) and in number (1400 to 1500 per year in the 1990s), and their rate has been steadily decreasing since early in the century. For example, accidental firearm fatalities among children and juveniles age 14 and younger dropped 63% between 1979 and 1993; and the National Center for Health Statistics puts accidental firearm death at the bottom of their list, below drownings, falls, and choking. While 1500 deaths are hardly a negligible issue, the magnitude of the problem they represent is hardly on the order of the "thousands of deaths a year, most of them children" advertised by some gun control proponents. For example, the January 10, 1997, issue of the *Weekly Reader,* self-described as the "largest newspaper for kids in the world," reported that almost 2000 "kids" died in gun accidents in 1992, whereas the total number of fatal gun accidents for all age groups in 1992 was actually 1400.

Despite the low number of fatal gun accidents (FGAs) at, say, 1500 a year, some control advocates argue that FGAs outnumber justifiable gun homicides in the home and that, therefore, the risks of a gun kept in the home for defense outweigh its defensive value. Allowing that not all but most FGAs occur in the home, the problem with this extremely popular argument is that justifiable homicides represent less than 1% of defensive firearms use and are in no way an adequate measure of their defensive value. As advice that people should disarm themselves, it is a bad argument; as a paternalistic argument for disarming defensive gun owners, it is worse.

One reason to expect that the rate of fatal gun accidents would be below drownings, falls, and choking, among other modalities, is that people's exposure rates are also lower: even most gun owners have cause to handle loaded guns far less frequently than they encounter heights and food. We could expect, then, that an increase in the exposure rate would increase the fatal accident rate. Lott and Mustard did a recent study of all counties in the United States on the effects of right-to-carry laws. Where more people are newly licensed to carry concealed handguns, we might expect that more will carry and that fatal gun accidents would increase with this increased exposure (handling a loaded firearm on a daily basis). Lott and Mustard estimated that the increase in right-to-carry laws might increase fatal gun accidents by 9, which would be an increase of 0.6%, if accidental gun deaths were 1500 per year. This increment as a cost would, then, need to be balanced against the benefits of concealed carry found by Lott and Mustard.

Fatal gun accidents fall into two categories: FGAs that involve a person accidentally shooting himself with a gun he is holding and FGA's that involve another person getting shot by the person holding the gun. About half of FGAs are self-inflicted. It is estimated that 5.5–14% of self-inflicted deaths classified as FGAs are actually suicides. This substantially reduces the already relatively small magnitude of the problem of self-inflicted FGAs. For example, if there are 1500 apparent FGAs in a given year, 750 of which are self-inflicted, and if 100 (13%) of these are actually suicides, then there are actually 650 self-inflicted FGAs. What type and magnitude of legal apparatus is appropriate for reducing this number? What proportion of the self-inflicted FGAs involve children shooting themselves with someone else's gun as opposed to qualified adult gun owners shooting themselves with their own gun? It might be that cases of purely paternalistic controls are too difficult to distinguish from harm-to-others controls

to raise concern, but it is an issue to watch for as new consumer-product safety measures are proposed.

Of course, the relatively small number of fatalities does not capture the whole problem of concern, accidental gun injury (fatal or not). The Consumer Product Safety Commission (CPSC) estimated from a national sample of emergency room data (which included intentional injuries among youths 15 and younger) that guns accounted for 60,000 injuries. Guns thus ranked 36th among 183 products or groups of products. The CPSC had previously weighted injuries by seriousness. On the CPSC injury index that took into account both frequency and seriousness, guns ranked 46th among 159 products, just behind prescription drugs and three ranks ahead of pens and pencils. Bicycles ranked first, with a rating 15 times as high as firearms. For the prudent, these figures counsel due care. For some policymakers, the implication is that there is always room for more concerted governmental controls. The potential for reducing accidental gun death or injury by government action will be a function of how gun accidents come about.

Using the common "reasonable and prudent person" standard of negligence, the vast majority of gun "accidents" are morally if not actionably negligent. The implication is that gun accidents are occasioned by some manner and discernible degree of carelessness. Even purely mechanical discharges that result from dropping a gun can be foreseeable and avoidable. The keeping of an unsecured and loaded firearm in one's bedroom, where a child or other unauthorized person may find it while one is away, is needless and careless, irresponsible or foreseeably risky. This general characterization of the problem of gun "accidents" comports with specific findings about those who cause or occasion them. In 1987, children under age 10 accounted for 122 of the 1400 victims of FGAs, or 13%. It is estimated that 64% of child FGAs might be caused by other children under 10. Even if all these FGAs were either self-inflicted or involved other children as shooters, children, of course, cannot be accounted "negligent" or responsible. The responsibility, or negligence, lies with the adults who allowed them access to the firearms.

Adults who allow children access to guns match the high-risk/reckless profile of adults and juveniles who are typically the shooters (and also victims) in gun accidents, who in turn match the profile of high-risk/aggressive offenders who perpetrate violent crime. The most accident-prone as well as the most violence-prone categories are these: male, single, 15 to 24 years of age, minorities, socioeconomically deprived, abusive of drugs or alcohol with histories of accidents or violence (such as vehicular accidents and offenses, prior arrests for assault).

By contrast, middle-class professionals are at virtually no risk for gun accidents; indeed, the vast majority of the general population, as well as the population of lawful gun owners, are likewise at negligible risk for gun misadventure of any description. This fact raises a general philosophical question regarding not just gun accidents but also criminal gun violence and gun suicides: How should the vast majority of any population, or their liberty, be restricted in the hopes of restricting the untoward or heinous behavior of a fractional and marginal element (notwithstanding that the effects of this element's behavior are significantly harmful, but granting that would-be controls to date have been largely ineffective)? At bottom, and in the main, the problem of gun accidents is a behavioral problem, not a mechanical safety problem, and this perspective needs to govern the deliberation of gun controls contemplated or crafted to reduce gun accidents.

4. The Defensive Utility of Firearms

The defensive utility of firearms against personal criminal threat (of murder, assault or rape, robbery, or the burglary of inhabited premises) is a quantifiable or actuarial component of their personal protective value as well as their social value and a function of two factors: the frequency and the efficacy of defensive use. The efficacy of defensive use, in turn, has two dimensions: the effect of defense with a firearm on the completion of an attempted crime and on the injuriousness of an attempted crime (including attempted homicide).

Doubt about the defensive utility of firearms is often based on one or more of the following common beliefs: people who own guns hardly ever use them defensively, because the guns are not likely to be available when needed; even whey they are, people who try to defend against crime with guns will not prevail and usually have their guns taken away and used against them; gun-armed defenders just escalate conflict and the likelihood of attack and injury from attack, whereas the best advice is to comply with criminals' terms or run away; civilians lack the ability to use guns effectively and probably shoot more innocent people than criminals; people can and should rely on the police for protection rather than "taking the law into their own hands."

a. The Frequency of Defensive Firearm Use

Kleck and Gertz have conducted a comprehensive critical analysis of all past research on the frequency of the defensive use of firearms as well as the most recent and systematic survey research. The major finding is that guns are used by civilians in defense against criminal threat from 2 million to 2.5 million times a year. Assuming approximate round numbers for gun deaths at 40,000 a year, with 18,500 homicides, 1,500 accidents, and 20,000 suicides (variations in actual numbers in any year

will make a negligible difference to the comparisons below), we can derive the following comparative frequency figures based on the Kleck and Gertz finding.

- Guns are probably used defensively to save lives nearly 20 times more often than they are used criminally to take life. Reportedly, 314,000 lives are "almost certainly" saved by the defensive use of firearms; this divided by 16,250 criminal homicides yields 19.28.
- Guns are used 50 times more often to defend against criminal threat than to kill anybody— defensively, criminally, suicidally or by accident. Kleck and Gertz estimate justifiable gun homicides at fewer than 3,000 (or less than 1% of the lives reportedly saved by defensive gun use).
- Guns are used 100 times more often to defend against criminal threat than to kill another person intentionally or to commit suicide. Two million gun defenses divided by 20,000 gun suicides is 100.
- Guns are used 480 times more often by law-abiding citizens to defend against criminal threat than to commit criminal homicide. Assume the finding of Chicago Police Department studies of 20,264 homicides from the period 1965–91 that approximately 75% of criminal homicides are committed by criminals with prior records. Assume 18,500 annual gun homicides and a low rate of justifiable gun homicide at 10% or 1,850, leaving 16,650 criminal homicides. 25% of 16,650 criminal homicides yields 4,163 criminal firearm homicides by people with no prior criminal record.

The last comparative frequency estimate addresses the question of how often previously law-abiding gun owners turn rogue and commit criminal homicide as compared to how often they use guns defensively. It provides perspective for those who presume the worst of gun owners (as one gun ban advocate put it, "the homicide fantasy is the engine that drives America's fascination with guns") and it gainsays widely believed and authoritatively propagated allegations such as "The overwhelming majority of people who shoot to kill are not convicted felons; in fact, most would be considered law-abiding citizens prior to their pulling the trigger."

b. The Efficacy of Defensive Firearm Use

By the forgoing findings, the defensive use of firearms is far more frequent than misuse resulting in criminal homicide, suicide, or accidental death. But just how effective is it? There are at least five significant indicators of the efficacy of gun defense or lack thereof: (i) How effective is defensive gun use in foiling crime? (ii) How many lives are saved? (iii) How well do the gun defenders fare compared to those who do not resist or who use nongun resistance? (iv) Are guns taken away from these defenders and used against them? (v) How often do would-be defenders mistakenly shoot innocent people?

i. Efficacy in Preventing the Completion of Crimes
Victims who resisted robbery with a gun or other weapon were less likely to lose property than those who resisted in any other way or those who did not resist. Kleck's analysis of National Crime Survey (NCS) data for 1979 to 1985 found the following completion rates for attempted robberies: guns, 30.9%; knives, 35.2%, other weapon, 28.9%; physical force, 50.1%; threatening or reasoning with robber, 53.7%; no self-protection, 88.5%.

NCS data on rape attempts provided too small a sample to analyze, since fewer than 1% of rape victims report resisting with a gun. Kleck and Sayles grouped resistance with guns, knives, and other weapons together and found that armed resistors to rape were less likely to have the rape completed against them than victims using other methods of resistance (such as reasoning with their assailant) and armed resistors did not suffer greater injury beyond the rape itself. From the finer breakdown of data on completion and injury rates for robbery and assaults, it seems reasonable to infer that the same results would hold for rape: in general, the more lethal the weapon used to resist, the less likely is the chance of completion of the crime.

ii. Estimation of Lives Saved
Defensive gun use is not limited to self-defense but often involves or includes the defense of some person(s) other than or in addition to the gun wielder. The Kleck and Gertz study asked the following question: "If you had not used a gun for protection in this incident, how likely do you think it is that you or someone else would have been killed?" Reportedly, 15.7% of respondents "almost certainly would have been killed," 14.2% "probably would have," and 16.2% "might have," which, given the lower estimate of 2 million defensive gun uses, would translate to 314,000; 598,000; and 922,000 lives saved. At the lower end, the lives reportedly saved by defensive gun use are a good seven times the total gun deaths in any year. If only 15% of the most confident respondent reports were correct, lives saved with guns would still outweigh all gun deaths.

iii. Efficacy in Preventing Attack and Injury
People who defend against criminal insult or threat with a gun are the best off of all the categories of victim-responder regarding the likelihood of suffering injury: better off than those who do not resist, who try to reason with the criminal, who try to flee, or who resist with bare physical force or with any other type of weapon.

Thus, as a matter of actuarial fact, gun defenders are significantly better off than those who employ any of the alternative methods of responding to robbery or assault. This fact contradicts the myths created and propagated by many (not all) police chiefs and other authoritative paternalists to the effect that people are better off not resisting or carrying and using a police whistle or Mace or pepper spray or a "stun gun." Regarding speculation that attempted gun defense is apt to precipitate or escalate a criminal attack, Kleck found to the contrary that the defensive use of firearms appeared to inhibit attack on defenders in threatening confrontations with criminals as well as, in the event of an attack, to reduce the probability of injury.

iv. Defenders Shot with Their Own Gun
One form of ineptitude attributed to gun defenders by skeptics of the defensive efficacy of private firearms is their liability to having their guns taken away by an assailant and used against them. Because of the prevalence of this allegation, it merits special attention. In fact, this sort of misadventure is extremely rare. By Kleck's analysis, 1% of defensive gun use is the outside estimate for such untoward reversals. These incidents even include situations such as where a burglar did not actually take the gun from the defender's hands but rather confronted an armed defender with another of the defender's guns obtained in the course of the buglary.

v. Defenders' Rate of Mistaken Shootings
Another prevalent myth is that gun defenders are trigger happy, because they are naturally bloodthirsty, skittish, eager to shoot their way into the "Armed Citizen" column of the *American Rifleman,* and so on. Again by Kleck's analysis, fewer than 2% of fatal gun accidents involve a would-be defender shooting an innocent person who is mistaken for an intruder or assailant. Assuming 1500 unintentional gun fatalities a year, this means 30 fatal mistaken shootings annually. Fatally mistaken shootings then represent 0.0015% of gun defenses.

c. Defensive Firearm Use versus Vigilantism

Vigilantism is historically associated with times and places where no official law enforcement or judicial authority was available to apprehend and punish offenders. Whatever its arguable quasilegal rationale in such times and circumstances, vigilantism in the modern American setting is defined here as the use of force by anyone (whether a civilian, police officer, or government official) to impose punishment without due process of law. As such, it is decidedly a criminal offense. By contrast, the use of deadly force is perfectly lawful in defense of innocent human life against the imminent threat of death or grave bodily harm (and, in some jurisdictions, in defense of property or against trespass, where the law grants the householder the presumption that an unannounced intruder poses actionable risk). The threat of the use of deadly force, especially upon one's own premises, is arguably lawful when the defender has reasonable suspicion of the hostile intent of the offender (akin to the standard for investigative detention by a police officer). Such an action, whose intent is defensive and not punitive, is, by definition, not vigilantism.

The defensive use of force is often dubiously described as "taking the law into one's own hands." It is, indeed, precisely that, notwithstanding the ambiguity of the metaphor: when the law is "broken" by an offender who poses a threat allowing defensive force (or the threat of defensive force), the defender is allowed to take the broken law into his own hands, as it were, and forcibly make it right. This is not vigilantism, the unlawful taking of the law into one's own hands for purposes of meting out punishment in the absence of due process of law, but a lawful mending of broken law.

5. The Deterrent Value of Firearms

Crime prevention by interdicting or interrupting an attempted crime is different from deterring a person from even attempting a crime in the first place. Crime deterrence means the prevention of the very attempt to commit a crime by people who are or might be otherwise disposed to break the law, presumably by engendering fear of negative consequences. A deterrent effect attributable to private firearms possession would be another component of their protective value and their social value in addition to their defensive utility. While, unlike the defensive utility of firearms, their deterrent value is difficult to determine, let alone quantify, there exist reasonable grounds as well as direct evidence for positing a deterrent effect. There are at least two questions of interest: whether there is reason to assume a deterrent effect and, if so, how to assess its magnitude or significance.

a. A Plausibility Argument for a Deterrent Effect

Apart from direct empirical evidence, there is a plausibility argument to the effect that there probably is a deterrent effect and, whatever its exact magnitude might be, that it is probably greater than, or at least similar to, any deterrent effect attributable to the criminal justice system, whose presumed deterrent effect is itself notoriously hard to prove. Thus, the plausibility argument is conditional: if the justice system has a deterrent effect, the deterrent effect of private firearms and the private use of force is probably greater.

Deterrence theory holds that deterrence, in part, is a function of three factors: (1) the certainty of penalty, (2) the severity of penalty, and (3) the promptness of penalty. Kleck observes that the risk a criminal faces from armed civilians is at least more prompt (the armed victim is, by definition, at the crime scene) and potentially more severe (death or grave injury) than the risk of penalty from the criminal justice system (where the likely legal penalty for robbery, burglary, rape, assault, or even murder is a few to several years in prison). While less than 1% of defensive gun uses by civilians are fatal, civilians fatally shoot thousands of criminals a year, more than do the police and more than are executed for capital crimes. The frequency of defensive gun uses that involve actual confrontations (at 2,000,000 per year) is twice the 1980 arrest rate for violent crime and burglary (at 988,000), so the risk of confronting an armed citizen is at least as likely as arrest but far more likely than conviction.

Of the estimated 600,000 police officers in the U.S., less than 25%, or 150,000, are on duty at any given time; whereas there are tens of millions of civilians with access to firearms and high motivation to use them for protection of themselves or their families. For example, if 1% of the adult population carries a concealed firearm (in states that have licensed concealed carry, 3–5% of the population are license holders, which need not mean that all of them carry all or most of the time), then there could be more armed civilians abroad than armed police on most shifts. In sum, if there is reason to attribute any deterrent effect to the criminal justice system, there seems to be reason to attribute a deterrent effect of at least similar magnitude to armed civilians.

b. Evidence of a Deterrent Effect

Until recently, the direct evidence for a deterrent effect has been of two kinds: self-reports obtained from surveys of incarcerated criminals, which are extremely persuasive but not conclusive, and quasiexperimental or observational studies of the before-and-after effects of well-publicized firearms training programs. In addition, there is recent evidence, for example, one study by Lott and Mustard of all counties in the United States, on the effects of right-to-carry laws. Insofar as concealed carry by civilians has a deterrent effect, it could affect violent crime abroad or in general, not just violent crime or burglary in the home or business establishments in which guns are apt to be kept.

Kleck reports as follows on the classic Wright and Rossi study (1986) that interviewed 1874 imprisoned felons in 10 states about their encounters with, and their perception of the risks of confrontations with, civilians armed with guns. Interviews of those who admitted having committed a violent crime or burglary in their criminal histories indicated the following: 42% encountered armed victims; 38% were scared off, shot at, wounded, captured, or a combination; 43% on some occasion refrained from a crime because they believed the victim was carrying a gun; 56% agreed with the statement that "most criminals are more worried about meeting an armed victim than they are about running into the police"; 58% agreed that "a store owner who is known to keep a gun on the premises is not going to get robbed very often"; 52% agreed that "a criminal is not going to mess around with a victim he knows is armed with a gun"; 45% of those who had encountered an armed victim thought frequently about the risk of getting shot by a victim, while only 28% of those who had not had such an encounter said the same; and only 27% saw committing a crime against an armed victim as an exciting challenge.

Kleck allows that prisoners are a biased sample because their very imprisonment shows that at least in one instance they were not deterred. It has also been argued that felons who elude arrest might be different in attitude and disposition from those who are captured. However, the latter point suggests only that not all criminals are risk-averse in either attitude or behavior regarding encountering armed victims, which the survey already allows. Moreover, Kleck argues that the bias of the sample renders the survey results more impressive. The prisoners' admissions recounted above are not complimentary; if anything, prisoners' incentive is not to admit such vulnerabilities and concerns, such that the results are likely to underreport the extent of aversion to the risks of encountering armed victims. Because the prisoner sample excludes the criminally disposed who are in fact deterred, the survey results underrepresent the deterrent impact of armed civilians.

B. The Feasibility and Efficacy of Gun Control

Nothing is so firmly believed as that which we least know.
(MONTAIGNE)

Montaigne's remark can be applied to general faith that gun controls actually work as intended or hoped. But what actually is known about the workability and intended impacts of gun controls? And, absent a showing of impact, what remains to be said for them? The following are some examples of gun control policies that have a serious claim to feasibility, efficacy, and justifiability, along with some caveats about their potential controversy.

1. Background screening at points-of-sale by means of a national "instant" records check. The need for uniform screening and centralized, reliable data argues for a federally mandated, and subsidized, policy. Background screening to obviate the possibility of purchase by disqualified applicants, a corollary of the need to disqualify certain categories of people, is presumably as agreeable as gun controls come. Another law enforcement advantage of an instant check system is the capability it provides to apprehend disqualified applicants who may be dangerous or wanted. However, a computerized and nationally networked instant check system arouses opposition from those who fear, and have reason to fear, the creation of a national (or state or city) registry of legal gun owners: its expediency for the confiscation of firearms. Government's lack of response to this fear is causing gratuitous controversy over a gun control measure that should not be problematic.

2. Required background screening for private transfers. The lack of uniformity enables "leakage" of legally disqualified buyers to private sellers, who lack the means to perform a proper background check. The proposal is for a national policy (some states already have such laws) that require private transfers to be processed through a licensed dealer. This policy may be arguable in its impact on the illicit firearms market, but it is also arguably obligatory to do what we can to prevent illegal firearm acquisitions, regardless of net impact, when the burden to law-abiding gun owners of "doing the right thing" is modest. Private automobile transfers are handled by a similar process, requiring a modest notary fee.

3. Legal disability policy. Laws that prohibit certain categories of people from possessing or using firearms may be the least problematic form of gun control. However, two controversial issues are (a) exactly what categories of people (beyond the "usual suspects" such as minors and those with felony records or certifiable mental disabilities) ought to be disqualified from firearm acquisition, possession, or licensing for concealed carry and (b) the standards for granting relief from legal disability, such as for recovered mental patients or convicted felons after some period of time has passed since they served their sentence. There is no question that certain categories of "high risk" people should be prohibited from possessing firearms, but the expansion of the traditional criteria of disability has proven controversial.

4. Improved, concerted, proactive enforcement of carry and possession laws. Illegal carry of firearms occurs in public and is an easily established offense in that setting; laws prohibiting unlicensed carry are more susceptible of enforcement than laws against general possession, whose enforcement requires access to the criminal's residence. Law enforcement programs that have intensified, for whatever purposes, street searches have been found effective for interdicting casual weapon carrying. Sentence enhancement for certain firearms-related offenses can prove an effective tool of enhanced enforcement, although discretionary policies are found

more effective than the popular mandatory enhancement laws. This is an interesting case where many gun control opponents, on the one hand, argue against gun control nostrums on grounds of their lack of proven efficacy and, on the other hand, persist in pushing "tough on criminal" laws such as mandatory enhanced sentencing for gun crimes only to be hoist upon their own petard: evidence that discretionary systems work better than mandatory ones.

One strategy for reducing overall violence is indirect, trying to do so by reducing overall gun ownership; another is to target and try to reduce gun violence directly and thereby reduce the overall violence rate. In general, gun controls do not reduce general gun ownership, either legal ownership among the general public or illegal keeping of guns among "high-risk" groups. While this suggests that the indirect strategy or its proximate goal of reducing gun ownership is not a promising approach to reducing the overall violence rate, it also suggests that in general gun controls (gun bans excepted) do not impair legal ownership.

However, certain forms of the direct strategy, which targets gun violence specifically rather than gun ownership generally, have demonstrable benefits. Kleck reports on the results of 121 tests of the effects of various types of gun control on crime and violence; in 92% of the cases there was no effect on violence rates. However, 6 tests provided ambiguous evidence of efficacy, while 4 provided unequivocal support. For example, mandatory penalties for illegally carrying a firearm and discretionary (rather than mandatory) additional penalties for felonies committed with a gun evidently reduce robbery rates. One possible explanation is that such laws, by whatever mechanism, reduce casual carrying and thereby reduce casual or opportunistic robbery.

Of course, the fact that the preponderance of gun controls have no demonstrable efficacy in reducing violence does not show that gun control in general can have no such effect, because it might be the case, as advocates insist, that different controls, more controls, or stricter controls would prove effective. The point, rather, is to illustrate that common assumptions about the efficacy of gun control are, more often than not, too facile.

IV. WEIGHING THE VALUES

Regarding the balance of harms against benefits associated with private firearms, a question often asked is: At what point does the good of the many outweigh the freedom of the individual? The way such qeustions are framed often presumes that there exists a net balance of harm or risk to the detriment of the many, putting individuals' entitlement to firearms on trial under a presumption of guilt. Such questions also imply a utilitarian presumption about what is required for proof of innocence, that a showing of net benefit would vindicate the putative right to private arms.

A. The Value of Firearms to Individuals

The potential value of firearms to individuals is twofold: their recreational value and their protective value. Individuals may also take an abiding interest in the residual social and political values of private firearms.

1. Recreational Value and "Sporting Purpose"

An unusual facet of the gun control controversy is what might be called the "sporting purpose hypothesis." The concept of "sporting purpose" is one of the tools for discriminating between "good" and "bad" guns. The mantle of "sporting purpose" protects "good" guns from bans, while its denial helps stigmatize "bad" guns. This argument holds that if a firearm (such as firearms particularly suitable for combat purposes) serves no legitimate sporting purpose, then it may justifiably be banned.

The obvious question is why sporting purpose should come into the question of which guns to ban or not ban. If private firearms are to be banned either because they are fundamentally morally objectionable or because they produce greater social harm than benefit, then their recreational value and "sporting purpose" is certainly not going to be sufficient to prevent such a ban.

The category of "sporting purpose" firearms is a puzzlement because many hunting firearms are far more deadly than the firearms targeted as "assault weapons." For example, the Colt Sporter targeted by the federal assault weapon ban fires a relatively small .223 caliber cartridge, while the Remington 7400 rifle fires the vaunted .30-06 round, a U.S. military cartridge from before WWI to Korea, a favorite of big-game hunters and a far more devastating round than the .223. Why is the lightweight .223 an "assault weapon" and the heavy-duty .30-06 a "sporting" firearm? The answer, gun control opponents argue, is that the "sporting purpose" standard is a temporary expedient for allaying opposition to gun bans and that it provides only temporary immunity for the guns of sport shooters and hunters on the perverse pretext that the recreational value of deadly weapons carries special weight in the balancing of the overall harms and benefits of firearms.

Whatever weight it carries in the social balance scales, the value of the recreational use of firearms is twofold: the residual value of the enjoyment of firearms by recreational shooters, hunters, or collectors regardless of their expectable utility, a value to individuals, and the social utility of their use in lawful hunting, insofar as this recreation serves and raises significant moneys for wildlife conservationist policy and local economies. (For example, the Vermont Fish and Wildlife Department estimated that the 1996 fall hunting season brought $68 million into the state's economy.) In addition, social utility is imputed to reactional training and competitions with combat firearms.

2. Protective Value

The protective value of firearms to individuals also has two dimensions: (a) defensive utility, one measure of which is the actuarial rate at which armed civilians successfully defend against criminal threats (as discussed earlier) and (b) the residual value of the right to firearms as an option in self-defense, irrespective of their defensive utility.

a. Defensive Utility

As has been documented earlier, a firearm happens to be one's best option in the gravest extreme when, by the universal standard of justifiable deadly force, an innocent person is in imminent and otherwise unavoidable danger of death or grave bodily harm. The conventional wisdom notwithstanding, gun owners and carriers know this and wish to preserve this option.

b. Residual Value

The second dimension of the protective value of firearms is the fact of having this option in self-defense regardless of the actuarial utility of using a gun defensively or the likelihood or ever having to use it (which, while nonnegligible, may be very low for many people). A person may value this option in self-defense, and many do, regardless of what the statistics say about the defensive efficacy of firearms or the probability of ever having to ward off predatory criminals.

3. The Question of Police Protection

The protective value of firearms to individuals may take on a different complexion and priority depending on one's view of the efficacy or likelihood of police protection, whose functions are essentially general deterrence and reactive apprehension after the fact. As a matter of law, the police are not responsible for protecting individuals, nor liable for failing to do so, in all but a few special cases where they assume this obligation. The legal fact that police have no general duty to protect is well established by statutory law and case law going back into the 19th century.

In light of the fact that police have neither the duty nor the ability to afford individuals protection and given the nonnegligible actuarial risks of victimization (the National Crime Survey estimates indicate that 83% of Americans, sometime in their lifetime, will be a victim of violent crime), the residual value of private firearms possession for protection is predicated on citizens' ultimate responsibility for their own protection in the gravest extreme. People who value the option of armed defense argue that, if they must bear responsibility for their own protection, the options afforded them should be commensurate.

B. The Social Value of Firearms

1. Security, Tranquility, Civility

On the one hand, the prevalence of private firearms may seem to threaten the social values of security, domestic tranquility, and civility. For example, people who advocate domestic disarmament, a state monopoly on force, and oppose self-help against crime for the sake of domestic tranquility and civility, also uphold the value of the security of life and limb for the sake of enjoying the rest. However, they do not hold with private firearms as a means of securing any of these values.

On the other hand, proponents of self-help in the provision of individual and collective security, and of the right to arms for this purpose, who oppose a state monopoly on all means of force, also uphold the social values of domestic tranquility and civility; but they cleave to very different ideas about the means for securing these values and the apportionment of responsibility. As Jeffrey Snyder argues in *The Public Interest* (Fall, 1993), "How can you rightfully ask another human being to risk his life to protect yours, when you will assume no responsibility yourself?"

2. The Social Utility and Residual Value of Private Firearms

By the Snyder ethic, the social value of private firearms is not limited to their utility in defensive deployment or to their role in the reduction of criminal violence or social disorder by either deterrence or defensive interdiction. Rather, their social value, like their protective value to individuals, is twofold: one part social utility and one part residual value (their value regardless of their expectable utility) held by those who take an abiding interest in lawful citizen participation in the maintenance of civil order. There are the empirical, actuarial questions of utility: Does an armed citizenry collectively deter or reduce crime against the person and thereby provide, on balance, an effective measure of aggregate security from harm? Or, rather, does the keeping or bearing of arms by law-abiding citizens undermine private and public safety?

Besides these empirical questions of social utility, there are also residual moral questions: Are citizens morally obligated to contribute to the public safety, as well as to their own defense, not by vigilantism, but by vigilance and, in the gravest extreme, by responsible armed response? Can citizens be fairly expected to fulfill this civic right and duty without being afforded effective means? Or, rather, should the state be afforded a monopoly of armed force and sole responsibility for maintaining public safety and civil order?

C. The Political Value of Firearms

An important controversy beyond that of the social value of private firearms concerns the value of an armed citizenry. This is a fundamental issue for moral-political philosophy, the question of the monopoly of force as a political matter: whether the distribution of checks and balances of power in the society should not properly allot to the people, the ultimate sovereigns, a fair share in the distribution of force. There is a collateral issue: Who should enjoy the greater presumption of trust, the people or their government, irrespective of actual trustworthiness? This question is analogous to the question of which presumption should rule the institution of criminal law: the presumption of innocence, or the presumption of guilt. Should the government presumptively mistrust the people in the apportionment of liberty? Or should the people presumptively mistrust their government in the apportionment of power?

1. Political Utility and Residual Value

The political value of an armed citizenry is perhaps the most controversial, insofar as its empirical dimension is so largely speculative. This putative value presumably consists in the role of an armed citizenry as a defense or deterrent against government violation of the social contract as well as their utility for the common defense. But this political value is one part expected utility (the deterrent or defensive efficacy of an armed citizenry against government transgressions and the likelihood of the need therefore, or success) and one part the residual value of citizens' being entrusted with a share of armed force (as against a paternalistic or arrogated monopoly of force by the state).

Again, there are two kinds of question of value. There are the obvious empirical, albeit speculative, utility questions: Whether an armed citizenry is any longer necessary or likely useful for the protection of the state against disorder from within or invasion from without;

or, whether an armed citizenry is either a necessary or even viable impediment to governmental abuse of power. Be that as it may, there remain fundamental philosophical questions: the propriety in principle of entrusting the state with a paternalistic monopoly of armed force as versus the value of methodical mistrust of government, the value of sharing all manner of power (including the right to arms) with the people as part and parcel of the system of checks and balances, the value of investing a measure of coercive (not just procedural) power in the people themselves, individually as well as collectively. The residual moral value of so entrusting and empowering the people is not a function of expected utility (whether it is likely that it would ever be necessary or feasible in fact for the people to pose a threat of armed resistance against their government); it is rather a matter of the principles upon which the governance of a free people should arguably be founded, a question of residual moral value rather than expected utility alone.

2. Speculative Issues

The question of the need for an armed citizenry as a check on the abuse of governmental power is simply dismissed by many as both anachronistic and anathema in our modern and high-mindedly optimistic times. But the question is relative, as the need or capacity or efficacy of armed resistance pertains to any level of government: federal, state, or local. In fact, armed American citizens have mustered in order to resist corrupt governmental authority on the local level. That an armed citizenry is a factor to be reckoned with even by a government superior in arms is, by some lights, shown by many insurgency actions around the world, not the least by our own forebears' historic war of independence.

But today the very idea of a people having to take up arms against their own government invites images of anarchy as well as futility and is, in any case, a discomfiting thought. While granting this, Sanford Levinson, in his judicious treatment of the Second Amendment controversy ("The embarrassing Second Amendment," in Cottrol, 1994), provides a temporizing perspective on this sensitive and irreducibly speculative issue: "One would, of course, like to believe that the state, whether at the local or national level, presents no threat to important political values, including liberty.... But it seems foolhardy to assume that the armed state will necessarily be benevolent. The American political tradition is, for good or ill, based in large measure on a healthy mistrust of the state.... In any event, it is hard for me to see how one can argue that circumstances have so changed as to make mass disarmament constitutionally unproblematic."

In the end, the empirical fact of the matter, the likelihood of whether the people could, or would need to, resist their government in the gravest breach of power, is not dispositive on the moral and political-philosophic question, whether a free people should nonetheless be so empowered. In addition, political-philosophic commitment to such empowerment is part of the residual value of firearms for many individuals, who value it regardless of its speculative utility. The individual, social, and political value of privately owned firearms are all arguable, on both empirical and philosophic grounds. But that is to say that they must be fairly accounted and weighed in the balance scales on their merits, not summarily ignored as counter-conventional wisdom.

V. PARADIGMS OF RESTRICTIVE AND PERMISSIVE POLICY

Gun bans and permits to carry firearms concealed in public are probably the two most controversial types of gun control measure among political proponents and opponents of gun control, by virtue of the fact that they are viewed, respectively, as extremely (too) restrictive and extremely (too) permissive policies. Both restrictive control advocates and a large part of the public (as reflected in polls) have favored selective bans on certain types of firearm. In the case of "assault weapons," 70% of Americans apparently favored a ban (whatever they may have construed such firearms to be). Prohibitionist control advocates tend to oppose concealed carry permits, at least the more premissive "shall issue" variety. While a 1996 poll found 60% of Americans in favor of permissive licensing for concealed carry, the outcry against such measures has been as intense as the opposition to equally popular "assault weapon" bans. These cases of gun control are useful to examine not only because of their high profile but because corrigible speculation plays a large role in the associated controversy.

A. Gun Bans

While the ultimate social goal of many ban proponents is complete civilian disarmament, selective bans are taken to be politically necessary incremental steps. The ultimate goal of other ban proponents is reduction of criminal violence, and thus they may be more selective in the guns they see fit to ban. In either case, the gun ban proposals on the public agenda at any time are apt to be selective bans, where total and selective prohibitionists can make common cause. Selective gun bans typically target firearms that can be easily stigmatized in some fashion or seem particularly conducive to criminal violence, such as "Saturday Night Specials"

and "assault weapons" or even handguns in general. Arguments against banning such highly stigmatized guns will presumably tell against more comprehensive bans, the defense theory being that if the most evil-seeming of "bad" guns may not justifiably be banned, no firearms may justifiably be banned. So, we will focus on the forms of argument about selective bans, in particular bans on so-called assault weapons, but we will first examine the salient tactical role that selective bans play in more comprehensive ban strategies.

1. Comprehensive Bans and Civilian Disarmament

The political feasibility of a total ban or even a general handgun ban is arguably nil, because of the size of the political constituency that value guns of some sort, like sporting arms and handguns. On the occasions when popular referendums on categorical handgun bans have been held, in states where public support had appeared significant before the ban campaign, the proposed bans were defeated by large margins. In view of the fact that 60% of Americans now support permissive right-to-carry laws and handguns are the very guns suitable for concealed carry, even a general handgun ban is not feasible politically.

In addition, the moral right of self-defense, while denied by some on moral grounds, is upheld by the law as well as an overwhelming majority of Americans, as is the moral right to firearms as the most effective means of self-defense (a moral position quite separable from any debate over the meaning of the Second Amendment). The number of people cleaving to both of these putative rights as essentially connected probably pose insuperable political opposition to very comprehensive gun bans. The right of self-defense (tantamount to the right to use deadly force) and the right to possess guns for that purpose are, by some lights, segregatable (for example, English and Australian law uphold the quite universal right of self-defense but deny self-defense as a legitimate reason for possessing firearms). However, convincing most Americans of this, that the former right (self-defense) does not entail the latter (a right to arms), is not likely.

Comprehensive ban proponents know this and consequently adopt an incremental strategy against the general store of private firearms, attacking select types of firearms with smaller constituencies. The long list of protected "sporting purpose" firearms in the federal "assault weapon" ban in the Violent Crime Control Act of 1994 was intended to assure hunters and sport shooters that their favorite firearms were not at risk and thereby allay potential opposition from that large population. The "assult weapon" ban portion of the larger 1994 crime bill was called the Public Safety &

Recreational Firearms Use Protection Act to signal its intention to protect "recreational firearms." An important collateral tactic is to assure the large population interested in self-defense guns that "assault weapons" are not legitimate instruments of self-defense.

Similarly, "Saturday Night Special" ban proposals attempt to allay the opposition of both sports shooters and gun-defense advocates alike by arguing that such cheap guns are no good for either purpose, by virtue of being both unsafe and unreliable. "Saturday Night Special" and other stigmatic terms, such as "junk gun," "assault weapon," or "cop-killer gun," are designed to allay public opposition: Who, after all, would want to stand up for "cop-killer guns" or depend for defense on "junk guns"? Ban opponents, in turn, refer to such targeted weapons as "affordable handguns" that are "particularly suitable for defensive purposes."

2. Selective Gun Bans

As a prohibitionist policy, gun banning harks to at least two different strategies, which for convenience of reference may be called the utilitarian ban strategy (UBS) and the fundamental moral objection strategy (FMOS). While there are, in fact, significant numbers of influential gun ban proponents who adhere to or vacillate between each sort of strategy, the UBS and FMOS here serve simply to illustrate radically different approaches to gun bans.

a. The Fundamental Moral Objection Strategy (FMOS)

For the UBS, as will be seen, the ultimate goal is reducing criminal violence; the efficacy of a ban for this purpose is essential to its justifiability. For the FMOS, by contrast, the reduction of the store of private firearms is the ultimate goal as a matter of fundamental moral objection to private force and firearms, so the efficacy of a ban may be expedient to claim and argue, but it is not taken as critical to the justifiability of the ban. The FMOS affords preeminence to certain moral values, such that trying the facts or weighing the balance of social harms and benefits of private firearms is not dispositive. The individual, social, and political values of private firearms are the very sort found objectionable; so, in principle, they are either dismissed or demoted to inconsequential status (even if in practice they are entertained). Any putative rights to firearms for defense against criminal threat, let alone against the state, will carry no weight with the FMOS.

The FMOS has a counterpart among gun-rights positions that resort to empirical and utilitarian argument about the utility of firearms as a tactic but hold that, in principle, the numbers cannot gainsay what they take

to be a fundamental right to arms derived from the paramount right of self-defense. Second Amendment fundamentalists, who believe that the constitutional right in question is not only an individual right but an absolute one, would be one counterpart to FMOS partisans. Such partisanship, based on fundamental and nonnegotiable moral entrenchments inhospitable to empirical considerations, is one reason the gun control controversy is aptly called a "culture war."

b. The Utilitarian Ban Strategy (UBS)

A more prevalent, and more tractable, sort of gun ban strategy is the utilitarian crime-control agenda whose goal is to reduce criminal violence (or, at least, its more indiscriminate, wanton forms, such as mass mayhem and massacres) by reducing criminal access to certain types of firearm with features that are "particularly suitable" to indiscriminate violence or that otherwise make them "criminals' weapons of choice."

Noncriminal misuse of firearms (such as in suicide or gun accidents) is not typically used to promote selective bans, because it is hard to make the case that certain types of firearm are more conducive to gun suicide or accident than any other type. Thus, the UBS seeks to ban certain firearms that are claimed to figure significantly in crime in order to reduce criminal access to these weapons and, thereby, reduce criminal violence. If banning certain weapons did not reduce criminal violence overall, there would be no reason to reduce access to these rather than to other guns according to a utilitarian strategy. Regarding any selective gun ban, then, it is sensible to ask: Why ban these and not other guns, or all guns? From the UBS view, the answer must be that banning certain weapons promises a reduction in criminal violence overall, because there is something special about them that is especially conducive to promoting greater fatality or a greater prevalence of violence.

For example, one feature of handguns that makes them specially suitable to criminal violence and attractive to criminals is the fact that they are convenient to carry and conceal. Handguns are most criminals' weapons of choice and thus are frequently targeted for selective gun bans. But with regard to so-called assault weapons, which include a confusing melange of rifles, shotguns, and pistols, convenience and concealability for carry and stealth cannot be the common features of concern. Thus, the UBS approach can select different guns for banning on the basis of different features, and the specific features are material to the rationale for the ban in question. In fact, it is the specific features that the variety of assault weapons all supposedly have in common that make sense of that very variety. The UBS argument for the efficacy and consequent justifiability of assault weapons bans rests on the following empirical hypotheses and principle of justifiability:

Criminals' Weapons of Choice: Assault weapons are very attractive to violent criminals, making them the criminals' "weapons of choice," which increases the frequency with which they are used in violent crime.

Greater Destructive Potential: Assault weapons are designed to kill or maim many people quickly, even while being fired unaimed from the hip, as in military assaults. They possess certain features that render them capable of perpetrating massive and indiscriminate violence, of shooting more victims, including innocent bystanders, in shorter periods of time than other firearms, because they can fire more rounds more rapidly before being reloaded.

Greater Overall Violence: Given the above factors, criminal use of assault weapons results in higher rates and greater severity of injury overall than would result if no criminals used them.

Reduced Criminal Access: Banning assault weapons will eliminate criminal access or at least reduce criminal access to a negligible level.

Overall Violence Reduction: Banning assault weapons will reduce criminal violence overall, if not its frequency, then the rate and severity of injury resulting from criminal violence.

No Legitimate Sporting Purpose: Assault weapons have no "legitimate sporting purpose," so banning them harms no legitimate recreational or avocational interests.

No Defensive Value: Assault weapons are designed or useful only for military or criminal assault, in neither of which law-abiding citizens have any legitimate interest; at least, assault weapons are unnecessary for self-defense; so, in any case, banning them does no harm to anyone's interest in self-protection.

Since the use or possession of any firearm by criminals or for criminal purpose is already prohibited, extant criminal laws and penalties covering such use and possession have presumably exercised whatever deterrent effect of which they are capable. The UBS proposes to supplement general criminal law with an assault weapon ban in hopes of reducing criminal violence. This is a laudable ambition, but there are problems with each facet of the UBS argument, as follows:

i. Criminals' Weapons of Choice Although it is menacing-looking long guns (such as the AK-47 with its 30-round magazine or the "Streetsweeper" shotgun with its rotund cylinder) that, for rhetorical purposes, are made emblematic of assault weapons, as in ads for assault weapon bans, in fact "normal-looking" semiautomatic pistols are more popular as criminals' weapons of choice. It stands to reason that long guns would not be most criminals' choice because they are less wieldy and less concealable than handguns, the very reason handgun ban advocates give for handguns being criminals' weapons of choice. So-called "assault rifles" figure in perhaps 1% of gun crimes overall (their use varies from 0 to 3% by jurisdiction). For example, in New York City from 1987 through 1992, the highest annual rates of homicide committed with rifles and shotguns were 0.7% and 2%, respectively, according to New York's Division of Criminal Justice Services.

Estimates of assault weapon use in violent crime are inflated by using arbitrary definitions of the term "assault weapon." An example is the Pennsylvania State Police count of the use of such weapons in violent crime in 1994. They used crime data but included in the category of assault weapons not only "military-style rifles and shotguns" (1.33% of the guns used in violent crime) and "high-capacity pistols" (defined as semiautomatic pistols with magazine capacities in excess of 20 cartridges, 1.33%), but also "low-capacity pistols" (9.33%). The federal assault weapon ban defines "high capacity" as over 10 rounds, so the Pennsylvania State Police undercounted, by this standard, while including a category, "low-capacity pistols" (small, concealable semiautomatic pistols), that had not before been regarded as assault weapons.

ii. Greater Destructive Potential Though this hypothesis holds that the use of assault weapons results in more death and injury than the use of other firearms, the "power" and caliber of assault weapon cartridges are actually not greater on average than those of other weapons: cartridges for revolvers and low-capacity semiautomatic pistols cover a comparable range of "power" and caliber, from .22 to .45 caliber, regardless of whether they are categorized as assault weapons; cartridges for what are nominated as "assault rifles" are semiautomatic versions of military rifles, such as the AK-47 in 7.62 × 33 mm or the M16 in .223 (5.56 × 45 mm) and, thus are, on average, less powerful than the wide array of hunting rifle rounds in similar calibers; 12- or 20-gauge shotgun cartridges are as devastating whether fired from a 5-round "sporting" shotgun or an 8-round (or the rare 12-round) combat shotgun. The greater destructive power attributed to assault weapons is rather a function of what is called, ambiguously, their "firepower," which takes into account such factors as ammunition capacity, rate of fire, volume of continuous fire per load, reloading time, and volume of sustained fire per reload.

The hypothesis that assault weapons are potentially

more destructive than nonassault weapons will be true in any specific case insofar as the assault weapon in question is capable of higher volumes of fire. However, this factor (and, hence, the validity of the greater destructive potential hypothesis) is arguably inconsequential to the aggregate of death and injury resulting from criminal violence, as will be seen in the discussion of the Greater Overall Violence hypothesis.

iii. Greater Overall Violence This hypothesis postulates that, given the greater destructive potential of assault weapons, the rate and severity of injury (including death) resulting from their criminal use is greater than would result if no criminals used such weapons. However, criminals are, in the main, notoriously inaccurate with whatever firearms they use, even at close range, at least when they are facing armed defenders. This fact is substantiated by New York Police Department (NYPD) reports of all shooting incidents involving police officers, which shows criminals' hit probability to be on average less than 10%.

Moreover, the same reports show that the number of shots fired by criminals in battles with the police to be fewer than five on average, a number that is attainable by shooting an ordinary revolver. While a high-capacity assault weapon affords the shooter more potentially stray rounds, extrapolation from actual shooting incidents both with police and civilian defenders (where the prepetrator is being shot at) does not support the hypothesis that criminals would fire more errant shots when shooting at unarmed victims (where they have the time and incentive to place their shots more carefully).

Criminological facts, as gleaned from the NYPD reports and similar incident samples for civilians, indicate that gunfights rarely involve more than a few shots on either side, well within the capability of revolvers or low-capacity long guns. In the rare instance of an extended firefight, armed defenders or police can indeed suffer a disadvantage in "firepower," such as being subjected to the high volume of suppressive fire of which assault weapons are capable. But the relevant question is whether these rare incidents result in injury or fatality as compared to other such extended firefights in which assault weapons are not used.

iv. Overall Violence Reduction At best, then, assault weapons might account for some marginal increment in the overall rate and severity of injury (including death). The marginality of the risk or potential increment is a function of the extreme rarity of the situations in which assault weapons could actually cause more human carnage than nonassault weapons. The other side of the greater overall violence postulated to result from the use of assault weapons by criminals is the overall

violence reduction hypothesized as a benefit of assault weapon bans. But if the former increment is marginal, so is the latter.

v. Reduced Criminal Access This hypothesis, that banning guns will translate to getting them "off the street" or out of "the wrong hands," is so firmly and widely believed as to be taken as common knowledge. The "uncommon knowledge" view holds that reduction of access to criminals who seek assault weapons is impossible to achieve, because for criminal demand there will always be a supply, even of contraband. In fact, the most seriously violence prone among the criminally disposed are precisely the ones who would be attracted to instruments supposedly capable of wanton and indiscriminate destruction. Such criminals as are willing to commit capital offenses are the least likely to fear the relatively minor penalties imposed by assault weapon bans.

If there is a way to reduce criminal use of assault weapons, it is not by a supply-side prohibition that targets criminal access while also burdening the law-abiding population, many of whom would comply but many others of whom, unjustly disenfranchised by their government in their view, would prepare, as some have already prepared, to resist. The question to assault weapon ban advocates is whether marginal and likely inconsequential criminal compliance is worth the cost of significant, and possibly violent, civil disobedience; whether deterring some people with prior criminal identities is worth generating a large new class of criminals from the stock of disaffected citizens. This question shifts our focus from the presumed but dubious efficacy or social benefits of an assault weapon ban to its social costs and objections against it.

vi. No Sporting Purpose Firearms that are generally recognized as particularly suitable for sporting purposes are presumptively excluded on that basis from proposed gun bans. By contrast, firearms that are particularly suitable for combat (such as assault weapons), but which are assumed to serve no legitimate sporting purpose, are prime targets of proposed gun bans. The objections brought against this hypothesis are three:

1. The "sporting purpose" hypothesis presupposes that government has the authority or competence to judge what counts as "legitimate" leisure, sport, or avocation and the right to curtail socially harmless and even socially useful leisure activities that some majority deems illegitimate.
2. The discriminatory notion of "sporting purpose" is also problematic because it presupposes without argument that "sporting purpose" should carry spe-

cial privileged weight in the balancing of harms and benefits. On the contrary, the weightiest interest in the balance scales of benefits is not the recreational value of firearms, but rather their protective value to individuals, along with their associated social value and political value.

3. Finally, there is a sport and avocation with ample claim to legitimacy through recreational competition and training with firearms particularly suitable for combat, such as those stigmatized as "assault weapons." The practitioners of combat weaponcraft as a sport or avocation hold that law-abiding civilians have a legitimate interest in combat for their own self-defense. This legitimate interest in combat firearms training for defensive purposes naturally gives rise to both legitimate and socially useful "sporting purposes" for which combat weapons (or assault weapons) are particularly suitable in the sport and avocation known as combat weaponcraft.

vii. No Defensive Value This hypothesis denies that assault weapon gun bans harm the interests of people for whom assault weapons have protective value. This denial is based on one or both of two different arguments.

One argument is that assault weapons are designed solely for military assault (in which civilians as such have no legitimate interest) and are otherwise useful only for criminal assault (in which people obviously have no legitimate interest). That so-called "assault weapons" are inherently "bad" because they are designed only for killing or, worse, only for killing many people quickly, is on the same order of moral obtuseness as the view that assault weapons are "bad" because they are "particularly suitable" for combat rather than for hunting or target shooting. Combat is inherently defensive as well as offensive; its moral or legal justifiability, in either case, must be assessed on the merits of the combat itself and has nothing to do with the instrument used. By the same commonsense reckoning, the martial arts are neither regarded nor outlawed as "assault arts." The good or evil done with a weapon is not a function of the instrument but rather of the intent and consequences of its use. Law-abiding citizens, as well as the police, have use for, and therefore a legitimate interest in, assault weapons for threat management and defensive combat. The fact that assault weapons are not useful solely for indiscriminate murder and mayhem is evident in the interest the police have in these as well as other firearms and the fact that no ban proposes to prohibit their use by the police.

The second argument does not try to obscure the distinction between criminal assault and defense with disingenuous semantic games and does not deny that assault weapons can be used defensively. Rather, it denies that assault weapon bans do any harm to anyone's interest in firearms for protection by alleging that assault weapons are not necessary for defense, that other firearms can serve the defense interest just as well. There is often the added imputation that people who think they "need" an assault weapon lack both good sense and good character. However, recent cases in which semiautomatic shotguns and high-capacity semiautomatic rifles have been dramatically advantageous in deterring packs of rampaging offenders include the Los Angeles riots after the first Rodney King case verdict, the St. Petersburg riots in the fall of 1996, and civil disorders following natural disasters such as Hurricane Andrew.

While extended firefights with multiple assailants are rare, they do indeed occur and represent a nonnegligible risk in the world of random violence. The fact that criminals resort to assault weapons only enhances the argument that assault weapons are reasonably "necessary" defensive options for lawful defense by civilians as well as the police. To ask "What does a decent citizen need with an assault weapon? Why won't more 'refined' firearms do?" is like asking why people "need," or choose to carry, flood insurance in areas where floods rarely occur. The simple answer is: just in case.

B. Right-to-Carry Laws

Basic issues regarding the carrying of firearms in public by law-abiding civilians are: (1) Should this be allowed at all? (2) If so, should it be licensed? (3) If so, by what sort of licensing system?

1. "Shall Issue" versus Discretionary Licensing

Discrimination arises under discretionary licensing systems for concealed carry for two related reasons: that discretion in vetting applications for a license is allowed; and that the typical standards of "special need" or "good reason" exacerbate the inconsistency endemic to discretionary licensing.

Given the judgmental latitude allowed by the subjective nature of such criteria, a licensing official may, at one extreme, effectively institute a ban on concealed carry or, at the other extreme, effectively waive the requirement to show need by approving otherwise qualified applicants who simply cite the general reason of self-defense. In states imposing such subjective criteria, the policies of local officials are notoriously variable between both extremes. Unfairness arises if equally qualified, or equally disqualified, applicants are differentially issued or denied a license on the morally irrelevant basis of where they happen to reside. This is not merely a theoretical possibility but a prevalent reality in states with discretionary licensing (such as New York, Massachusetts, and California). It poses not only problems of fairness, but also criminological problems: (1) where politics or favoritism allows, otherwise unqualified applicants may obtain licenses and (2) where very restrictive discretionary practices are known to be the rule, violent crime may increase as a function of criminals' expectations that victims will be unarmed and there will be a consequent displacement of crime from jurisdictions where more citizens are apt to be armed.

Endemic unfairness notwithstanding, if concealed carry is to be permitted, its opponents may prefer a discretionary system precisely because it is apt to be more restrictive overall in practice. However, the criminological factors, the effects of legal concealed carry on crime and violence in the balance of social harms and benefits have to be reckoned.

2. The Effects of Permissive Carry Laws

Negative reaction against allowing concealed carry where it has been proposed is easy to conjure, along with the dramatic visions of mayhem that sustain it: blood in the streets, shootouts over minor insults and fender benders. More sober speculation holds, not that an armed society would fail to be a polite society, but that any defensive or deterrent utility of allowing concealed carry would be outweighed by criminals becoming preemptively more violent. Contrary to the hypothesis that criminals' uncertainty about whether prospective victims were armed would result in fewer victimizations, opponents of concealed carry hypothesize that criminals would go armed more often themselves and shoot first, to obviate the risk of injury from encountering an armed victim. However, this "preemptive strike" hypothesis does not stand up to the years of victimization survey data analyzed by Kleck: although, by definition, in gun rapes and robberies, criminal assailants pull guns first, they do not tend to shoot first and then rape and rob later. The idea that it would make sense for criminals disposed to commit rape, robbery, or assault to raise the ante to murder or attempted murder as a preemptive strike may seem plausible to some, but it is a phenomenon that has not appeared in the many states where concealed carry has already been permitted for years, nor was there a sudden rise in gun assaults, robbery, or rape in the highly scrutinized states where concealed carry was recently legalized. So, there is no reason to expect that criminals will suddenly become so imprudent in states that pass new concealed carry laws.

Unlike the deliberate violence escalation described above, speculation that the number of gun accidents are likely to increase along with concealed carry stands to reason on reflection. It is reasonable to suppose that the chances for a gun accident will increase as the occasions for people to handle loaded guns increase, which they do when more people start carrying concealed firearms that have to be holstered and unholstered daily. But, instead of speculating about defender and offender misadventure, we need to look at the available evidence.

While, of course, not all law violators are caught, if licensed concealed gun carriers are really gun-flashing or trigger-happy misadventurers, we would expect to find some significant record of revoked licenses, in particular licenses revoked for violent gun crimes. So, the phenomenon is easy to check, especially when new state carry laws mandate close scrutiny of the behavior of license holders. Texas, whose "shall issue" law is among the newest, and Florida, whose law initiated what became a wave of such measures, are two cases in point.

The Texas "shall issue" concealed carry law took effect on January 1, 1996. In the following year 1202 applicants were denied, 111,408 licenses were issued, and there were 57 incidents in which licensees committed offenses on the order of carrying a gun while intoxicated or failing to keep the weapon concealed. The overall offense rate by licensees at that point was 0.05% and the violent offense rate was 0.0009%.

Florida passed a "shall issue" concealed carry law in 1987. The Florida Department of State compiles data on carry licenses denied and revoked and the reasons therefore. According to Secretary of State Sandra Mortham, in a January 11, 1996, letter responding to published criticism of the Florida law, her Department had so far denied 723 applications and had issued 207,978 licenses, of which 324 were revoked for some manner of offense, of which 54 involved a firearm and 5 were violent crimes (none of which resulted in fatalities): thus 0.16% were revoked for some offense, 0.026% for an offense involving a gun and 0.0024% for a violent crime.

One hypothesis to explain the extremely low incidence of (apprehended) misadventure by licensed gun carriers is the training that is required to obtain a carry permit. For example, the Texas law requires a training course that includes not only basic marksmanship, firearm safety, and the law on the use of defensive deadly force, but also techniques of conflict resolution. But while training requirements are typical of the new wave of carry laws, they are by no means universal among the older laws. For example, concealed carry has been permitted without training in Pennsylvania for decades and the record of licensed gun carriers is basically as clean as elsewhere. The violent crime rate in Pennsylvania outside the city of Philadelphia is as low as Europe's. New Hampshire, the "Live Free or Die!" state, likewise has no training requirement and enjoys one of the lowest crime rates in the country. Vermont, which enjoys the lowest of violent crime rates, has neither a training requirement nor even a license requirement: concealed carry with lawful intent is a right of every adult citizen without a criminal record.

3. The Overall Impact of Concealed Carry Laws

The following three studies of the effects of concealed carry laws differ in illustrative ways: one is an intrastate study comparing violent crime across counties whose policies varied widely in permissiveness and restrictiveness under a discretionary licensing system; the second is a before-and-after study of the homicide levels associated with the introduction of "share issue" laws in a collection of five urban areas; and the third is a national study of crime rates across all U.S. countries with all manner of carry laws.

a. The California Study

Cramer and Kopel did a study accounting for demographic factors, comparing violent crime rates by county in California, which has a discretionary carry law resulting in extreme variation in policy from prohibitory to very permissive. They claimed to find that counties with high numbers of licensed concealed gun carriers and permissive policies had lower violent crime rates than counties with restrictive policies, which in turn had lower rates than counties with prohibitive policies.

b. The Violence Research Group Study

McDowall, Loftin, and Wiersema of the Violence Research Group at the University of Maryland did a study that compared gun homicide versus other homicides in five select urban areas in three states before and after new "shall issue" laws went into effect: Tampa, Jacksonville, and Miami, Florida; Jackson, Mississippi; and Portland, Oregon. The study found that after the new laws the number of people killed by guns in four of the cities increased (74% in Jacksonville, 43% in Jackson, 22% in Tampa, 3% in Miami) while the average number of homicides by other means stayed the same. The suggestion is that the relaxation of restrictions in the carry laws is the cause of the homicide increases. (In Portland the homicide rate fell about 12% after the new law, which the researchers suggest could be explained by the fact that Oregon instituted background checks for firearm purchases coincident with the new carry law).

Regarding the relevant homicides committed outside the home, where one would properly look for effects of concealed carry, the authors suggest that while licensed gun carriers may not be committing homicide, the new laws might increase incentive for unlawful car-

rying by the criminally inclined (which is tantamount to the "preemptive strike" hypothesis discussed above). The study does not distinguish criminal from justifiable homicides, leaving open the alternative to the preemptive strike hypothesis that justifiable homicides might account for the overall increase in homicides, especially in the violent environs studied where licensed gun carriers are apt to be assaulted.

The study's analysis also does not control for confounding factors such as demographic shifts or trends in drug trafficking. Worse, the study results are attributable to the artifact of selecting different stating points for establishing the before-reform homicide baselines, thereby ignoring higher-homicide years that would have shown a post-law decline. Finally, the researchers do not provide a rationale for their particular selection of so few urban areas as opposed to looking at the data for the whole states themselves. Florida's statewide homicide rate fell 21% from 1987 through 1992, after enactment of "shall issue," and has held consistently below the national rate after having been 36% higher before "shall issue." The authors do not explain why their "preemptive strike" hypothesis does not apply to the state as a whole or how the homicide rate in the rest of the state could decrease so far as to greatly offset the increases in Tampa, Jacksonville, and Miami.

Advocates of concealed carry are certainly not willing to grant, as an ethical matter, that an increase in criminal homicide would undermine the defensive efficacy of the practice; quite the contrary, the defensive rationale for concealed carrying and for the right to do so would only increase. To defeat the heavy interest so many have in the arguable right to effective means of self-defense, even on purely utilitarian grounds that grant no presumptive weight to this right, the evidence showing concealed carry laws to be the culprit in any observed increase in criminal violence must be very strong. The Violence Research Group study has been widely touted as proof in the media and by carry critics who see it as the thumb in the dike against the rising tide of "shall issue" laws. But it is not a compelling case for the proposition that laws permitting law-abiding citizens to carry guns for protection are the probable cause of increased criminal homicide.

c. The Lott and Mustard Study

Lott and Mustard (1997) set out to address what they take to be "the crucial question underlying all gun-control laws: What is their net effect? Are more lives lost or saved? Do they deter crime or encourage it?" These questions of efficacy are not the only or last issues for the justifiability of gun controls; there are strong rights-based objections to restrictive gun control on the one hand and, on the other hand, fundamental nonutilitarian moral objections to firearms and their use and, supervening both, the metaissue of how to weigh such residual moral values in the balancing of social goods and ills. But a rigorous address to the efficacy of firearms and their regulation is certainly the foremost if not the final word on justifiability.

Like the Kleck and Gertz study of defensive gun use, the Lott and Mustard study is meticulously designed to anticipate criticism. It analyzed the FBI's crime statistics for all 3054 counties in the United States from 1977 to 1992. Lott and Mustard's (most conservative) estimates and major observations follow:

- "Shall issue" laws reduced murders by 8.5%, rapes by 5%, aggravated assaults by 7%, and robbery by 3%.
- If states that did not permit concealed carry in 1992 had allowed it at that time, the citizenry would have been spared 1570 murders, 4177 rapes, 60,000 aggravated assaults and 12,000 robberies.
- Enjoyment of the deterrent effects quantified above are generally distributed, not limited to those who carry guns and use them defensively. This phenomenon is a major advantage of concealed carry: the uncertainty of who is carrying and the possibility that any potential victim, or potential defender nearby, may be armed renders everyone an unattractive target for many criminals. Unarmed people are thus in effect "free riders" on their armed fellow citizens.
- There is some displacement of criminal activity from violent crimes to property offenses like larceny (such as automobile theft). This is likely an acceptable trade-off in aggregate cost saved, let alone lives.
- In large cities, where typically both crime rates and gun control advocacy are highest, right-to-carry laws produced the largest drops in violent crimes. For areas with concentrated populations of over 200,000, the decrease in murder rate averaged 13%.
- Carry laws seem to benefit women more than men. Murder rates decline regardless of the gender of the gun carrier, but the impact is more pronounced when women are considered separately. An additional female licensed gun carrier reduces the murder rate for women three to four times more than an added male carrier reduces the rate for men. (Victims of violence are typically weaker than their assailants; thus armed women defending themselves enjoy a greater relative increase in their advantage than do armed men.)
- Contrary to the alleged beneficial impact of the Brady Law on crime rates (predicated by defenders simply on the number of applications for purchase denied, without acknowledging the high rate of false positives later corrected or the extremely low yield, 7, of felon-applicants brought to trial), the law's introduction is associated with higher rates of assaults and rapes.
- While the number of fatal handgun accidents is only 200 a year, if states without "shall issue" laws adopted them, there would be at most nine additional accidental handgun deaths, an increase of 4.5%.

The nearly 50,000 observations in the data set allowed for more rigorous controls for more variables than in any previous gun control study, including regression controls for arrest and conviction rates, prison sentences, changes in handgun laws such as waiting periods and background checks, enhanced-sentencing policies for using a gun in a crime, income, poverty, unemployment, and demographic changes.

Lott has modestly commented that the rigor and results of the study should "give pause" to opponents of permissive "shall issue" concealed carry laws: "The opportunity to reduce the murder rate by simply relaxing a regulation ought to be difficult to ignore."

The initial reaction to the study by many of those opponents was illustrative of how passion can rule the gun control controversy. A public press conference was called by prominent political gun control advocates at which Lott's scholarly integrity was attacked; in particular, it was alleged that he was in the service of the firearms industry. This inference was based on the fact that Lott is the John M. Olin Fellow at the University of Chicago Law School, together with the presumption that the Olin Fellow would be dedicated to the interests of Olin/Winchester, the noted ammunition and firearms manufacturer and a subsidiary of the Olin Corporation.

In fact, the Olin chair is funded by the Olin Foundation, which was created by money from John Olin's personal fortune upon his death, not by the Olin Corporation, which neither chose Lott as a Fellow nor approved his topic. Researchers have since embarked upon the appropriate response to the challenge of the Lott and Mustard study, critical analysis, the first wave of which Lott has rebutted but the most promising of which is yet forthcoming from a new center for violence research at Carnegie Mellon University.

Bibliography

Cottrol, Robert J. (Ed.). (1994). Gun Control and the Constitution: Sources and Explorations of the Second Amendment. Garland Publishing, New York.

Covey, Preston K. (1995). Legitimacy, recreation, sport and leisure: 'Sporting purpose' in the gun-control controversy. Gerald S. Fain (Ed.), Leisure and Ethics, Vol. II. American Association for Leisure and Recreation, Reston VA.

Covey, Preston K., and Stell, Lance. (forthcoming 1998). Gun Control: For and Against. Rowman and Littlefield, Boston.

Kates, Don B., Jr., and Kleck, Gary (Eds.). (1997). The Great American Gun Debate. Pacific Institute for Public Policy Research, San Francisco.

Kleck, Gary. (1991). Point Blank: Guns and Violence in America. Aldine de Gruyter, New York.

Kopel, David B. (1992). The Samurai, the Mountie, and the Cowboy: Should America Adopt the Gun Controls of Other Democracies? Prometheus Books, Buffalo.

Walker, Samuel (1994). Sense and Nonsense about Crime and Drugs, Third Ed. Wadsworth Publishing Co., Belmont, CA.

Wright, James D., and Rossi, Peter H. (1986). Armed and Considered Dangerous: A Survey of Felons and Their Firearms. Aldine de Gruyter, New York.

Indigenous Rights

JORGE M. VALADEZ

Marquette University

GLOSSARY

cultural integrity The quality that a cultural tradition exhibits when its principal values, customs, and sociopolitical and economic institutions remain relatively cohesive and whole over time.

ethnic group Group of individuals who share a common cultural tradition. In contrast to indigenous groups, when they form part of a multicultural society it is more likely that they are, or wish to be, integrated into the larger society.

globalization The economic, cultural, political, and technological processes through which countries and peoples throughout the world become increasingly interconnected.

indigenous group Group of individuals with a culturally distinctive character who are the living descendents of preinvasion inhabitants. They are part of larger settler societies and they generally have profound connections to their land and a continuity of identity with their ancestral past. Often, the terms "native" and "aboriginal" are used synonymously with the term "indigenous" to describe this category.

neoliberalism An economic doctrine that emphasizes international free trade, production for export, privatization of national services, minimal government intervention in economic activity, and domestic markets open to foreign investment and ownership.

self-determination The right of a group to control its own destiny by choosing and sustaining its economic and sociopolitical institutions and preserving its cultural heritage.

territorial autonomy The right of a group to control the access and use of a particular territory and its natural resources without interference from the larger society or external societies.

INDIGENOUS RIGHTS are rights designed to protect the vital interests of certain culturally distinctive groups with ancestral connections to precolonial peoples who inhabited areas now occupied by settler societies. What makes indigenous rights different from universally applicable human rights is that they answer to the particular social, political, and economic needs of nondominant indigenous groups who live in societies formed as the result of colonization. Historically, many indigenous groups have been socially and politically marginalized through racial discrimination and have been deprived of ownership and control of their ancestral homelands. According to political philosophers, indigenous leaders, and human rights activists, the special circumstances faced by indigenous groups make it necessary that they be protected by rights that take into account their special group needs and interests. Prominent examples of indigenous rights are the rights of territorial autonomy, self-governance, preservation of cultural integrity, and nondiscrimination.

I. HISTORICAL BACKGROUND

A. Early Treatment of Indigenous Rights

Up until the middle of the 20th century, indigenous rights were generally unrecognized because indigenous groups, occupying an intermediate position between individuals and states, were not regarded as legitimate bearers of rights. According to the 17th and 18th century philosophical model of rights adopted, among others, by Emmerich de Vatell and Thomas Hobbes, rights could be exhaustively divided into the rights of individuals and the rights of states. Since indigenous groups were obviously not individuals, they could be granted collective rights only if they could satisfy the criteria for statehood provided by this state-centered model. But while indigenous groups were collectivities like states, often they did not exhibit the hierarchical, centralized structures of governance and authority characteristic of states. To be sure, some indigenous groups, such as the Aztecs in Mexico and the Incas in Peru, had highly centralized and hierarchical governance structures at the time of the arrival of the European colonizers, while other indigenous groups had complex nonhierarchical sociopolitical systems whose sophistication was denied or ignored by the colonizers. But typically, indigenous groups had horizontal, decentralized political structures, and, unlike states which had clearly delineated territorial boundaries, they often inhabited territories that overlapped with those of other indigenous groups.

Thus indigenous groups did not satisfy the criteria for statehood provided by the state-centered model. Since some of the most important rights of indigenous groups, such as the right to self-determination, are collective in nature, the failure to grant indigenous groups due recognition as rights bearers was an important loss for them. The state-centered model served, whether accidentally or by design, to further colonial interests and empire building. Further, since indigenous people were often regarded as "uncivilized" and "primitive," they were seen as less than fully human and were thus denied even their most basic individual rights. Many indigenous groups suffered brutal injustices at the hands of the colonizers, such as enslavement, mass killings, and forcible displacement from their homelands.

B. Recent Developments Concerning Indigenous Rights

In recent years there has been increased interest in issues related to indigenous rights and a resulting move-

ment toward their legitimation. This has been due to several interconnected factors, the most prominent of which are the greater demand for natural resources found in native homelands, increased awareness and political activity of indigenous groups, and changes in the global political climate.

As nations throughout the world become more integrated into the global economy, and as their populations increase, they are being compelled to make maximal use of their natural resources. Economic integration often means acceptance of the neoliberal paradigm of economic development which emphasizes open access of a country's economy to foreign ownership and investment. Thus indigenous groups find themselves besieged by the territorial intrusions of transnational and domestic companies in the logging, mining, fishing, oil, and agricultural industries as these companies try to identify and exploit new resources.

For example, the Tarahumaras of northern Mexico are battling logging companies and encroachment from settlers; the indigenous peoples of Irian Jaya (West Papua) are engaged in an intense, bloody struggle for control of their lands with the Indonesian government; and the Yupik of Alaska are competing with commercial fishing interests and fighting attempts by the U.S. government to control their hunting and fishing practices. The struggles of indigenous peoples to protect their lands and resources from outside interests and to retain their traditional forms of economic subsistence are a major cause of conflict in the world.

While the "resource wars" many indigenous peoples are engaged in sometimes take the form of violent struggle, oftentimes they proceed through legal battles in domestic and international courts and political participation in national and international forums. Aided by indigenous and nonindigenous human rights activists and organizers, indigenous groups in South America, Asia, North America, Africa, and Australia are taking a more active role in determining their destinies by demanding government compliance of early treaties and legitimation of their collective rights. The realization that their way of life and even their survival as a cultural group are at stake has contributed to a resurgence of political awareness and activity among indigenous groups throughout the world.

Of pivotal importance in the development of this process of heightened indigenous political participation was the International Nongovernmental Organization Conference on Discrimination against Indigenous Populations in the Americas that was held in Geneva in 1977. Representatives from indigenous groups in North and South America initiated a process of political dialogue and engagement that eventually came to include not only peoples in the western hemisphere, but indigenous groups throughout the world. The struggle of indigenous peoples for their collective rights has extended beyond control of land and natural resources to include cultural rights such as the right to an education in their native language and government support of programs that promote the retention of their cultural heritage. The decline of military dictatorships and the process of democratization, particularly in Latin America, has also encouraged the political participation of indigenous groups fighting for their self-determination.

Another factor in the latter part of the 20th century that has facilitated the legitimation of indigenous rights is the changed global political climate. During this period there has been a shift from a state-centered normative framework in which issues such as the ethical treatment of indigenous groups were seen as matters of domestic law to a universalistic framework which focuses on essentialist normative conceptions. According to this universalistic framework the rights of indigenous peoples transcend the particular sociopolitical norms of the settler societies where they reside. The UN now officially disavows both external (overseas) and internal forms of colonialism.

Furthermore, the end of the cold war and the corresponding decrease of ideological polarization has created a more propitious environment in international supragovernmental institutions like the UN for discussing questions of human rights from a universalistic perspective. While the state-centered model still remains the dominant model, the voices and perspectives of nonwestern cultural groups have attained greater prominence in the international community. Having noted the advances made by indigenous groups, it must also be pointed out that formal recognition of the rights of indigenous groups is quite different from the implementation of these rights by the countries where these groups reside. Widescale abuses of indigenous people still take place in many countries.

Three central issues have arisen in discussions of indigenous rights: (i) the nature and scope of these rights, (ii) their philosophical justification, and (iii) the criteria for determining which groups are entitled to these rights. Each of these issues will be discussed in turn.

II. THE NATURE OF INDIGENOUS RIGHTS

A. Some Philosophical Questions Concerning Indigenous Rights

What kinds of rights are indigenous rights? What areas of life do they affect, i.e., what is their scope? Concerning the first question, a great deal has been written about whether indigenous rights (and more generally, rights granted on the basis of cultural membership) are collective rights that are irreducible to individual rights. For some philosophers a central issue is whether indigenous groups *qua* collectivities are the bearers of rights, that is, whether it is the group that properly speaking is entitled to indigenous rights and not its individual members. Individualists deny the rights-bearing priority of collectivities and maintain that despite the fact that the language of group rights gives the impression that the group is the bearer of rights, ultimately it is the individual members of the group who exercise and are entitled to the rights.

Collectivists, on the other hand, argue that the interests of groups or communities are not identical with, and not exhausted by, the interests of individuals, and that since rights are designed to protect interests, we cannot equate group and individual rights. Thus, concerning a particular indigenous right such as the right to self-governance, the collectivist would emphasize that it is a right that a indigenous community requires to preserve its own existence and that by definition it is a right that only a collectivity can exercise. Individualists, however, would contend that even though self-governance is a right that individuals must exercise within a group context, ultimately it is out of respect for the right of individuals to govern themselves as they see fit that we grant the right in the first place.

It is possible to mediate between the individualist and the collectivist positions by noting that there are different aspects of indigenous rights on which we can focus, and that these rights can be understood as collective or individual rights depending on which of these aspects we emphasize. There are at least four aspects of indigenous rights that we can distinguish: (i) the basis on which indigenous rights are granted, i.e., whether one is entitled to them because of group membership or merely because one is a human being; (ii) the fact that since there are certain characteristics that only groups can exemplify—such as ownership of communal property—only groups can be entitled to rights ensuring the preservation of such characteristics; (iii) the claim that indigenous rights inhere not in collectivities themselves but in the individuals composing those collectivities; and (iv) whether the legal declaration and exercise of indigenous rights is best understood in terms of groups or individuals. It seems reasonable to maintain that indigenous rights are collective rights in senses (i) and (ii), that they are individual rights in sense (iii), and that in sense (iv) they can be seen, depending on the particularities of the case at hand, as either collective or individual rights.

Before proceeding, an additional observation must be made concerning the individualist–collectivist debate. This debate is considered philosophically significant because it has a crucial bearing on the question of whether the community or the individual has moral priority. Adopting a collectivist position would mean that when there are conflicts between the interests of the community and the interests of some of its members we would grant moral priority to the community, while adopting an individualist position would mean favoring the interests of the individual vis-a-vis the community. Despite its prominence in the literature, however, it is not clear whether the individualist–collectivist debate clarifies more than it obfuscates the important issues surrounding indigenous rights. As Will Kymlicka points out, the individualist–collectivist debate, by conceptualizing the issue of indigenous rights in terms of the relative moral primacy of the individual or the community, diverts attention from central questions concerning their function and legitimacy (W. Kymlicka, 1995. *Multicultural Citizenship: A Liberal Theory of Minority Rights.* Clarendon Press, Oxford).

When we take the debate about indigenous rights as essentially a controversy about whether individuals or communities have moral priority, we construe indigenous rights only in terms of the internal restrictions that indigenous communities can place on their members. In other words, we conceive of indigenous rights as rights that an indigenous group can appeal to in order to prohibit or require certain actions of their members. But it is equally important, if not more so, to understand indigenous rights as external protections that indigenous groups can rely on to defend themselves from the detrimental decisions of the larger society. Understanding indigenous rights as external protections is particularly crucial in societies where the rights of minority groups have been systematically violated by majority groups.

To be sure, there are important questions concerning the restrictions that liberal democracies should place on the authority that indigenous groups can exercise over their own members, but clearly the issues concerning indigenous rights are not exhausted by such questions. In addition, taking the individualist–collectivist debate as pivotal to understanding indigenous rights is bound to bias the case against them in societies which prize individual autonomy over collective needs and interests. If we construe support for indigenous rights as support for the primacy of collective over individual interests, it is unlikely that indigenous rights will receive the reasoned and fair consideration that they deserve.

B. The Content and Function of Indigenous Rights

In order to understand more fully the character and function of indigenous rights, it would be instructive to examine some generally recognized indigenous rights and their interconnections. Among the most prominent are the rights of self-determination, territorial autonomy, and preservation of cultural integrity.

Self-determination can be considered as an overarching indigenous right because it incorporates a number of other indigenous rights. At the core of self-determination is the conviction that people should be free to determine their own destinies by choosing and sustaining their own economic and sociopolitical institutions, patterns of governance, and ways of life. Self-governance for indigenous communities means not only political governance that accords with the will of indigenous peoples, but also governance that is consistent with their historical modes of sociopolitical organization. Thus it would not be appropriate to merely incorporate indigenous communities into the existing western political-legal systems, because such systems may be at odds with indigenous patterns of self-governance.

Most indigenous groups have traditionally functioned with consensual systems of decision making and procedures of conflict resolution that differ markedly from those of liberal democratic societies. In contrast to legal systems based on an adversarial orientation, for example, Navajo courts of conflict resolution focus on identifying the reasons why the conflict occurred and strive to restore broken community solidarity. Similarly, consensual decision making is preferred by indigenous communities because systems of democratic majority rule are seen as potentially divisive and unfair since the interests and preferences of those who are outvoted are diminished or neglected. In short, we cannot assume that political inclusion and assimilation to the mainstream society can ensure adequate self-governance for indigenous groups.

In the case of indigenous peoples, self-determination is closely connected with such rights as territorial autonomy and the preservation of cultural integrity. Control of land and natural resources by indigenous people is important for their self-determination because of their profound spiritual and material connections to the land. For many groups their means of subsistence—which typically consist of fishing, hunting, and farming practices—have intrinsic cultural significance. For Maya communities in Guatemala, for example, some of the practices related to the cultivation of corn are replete with religious meaning. The ancestral homelands of indigenous peoples also contain sacred sites and ancient burial grounds that connect the community to earlier generations. Most indigenous groups see themselves as connected to their ancestral past through continued stewardship of the land, and they consider caring for the land that future generations will inhabit as a great moral and cultural responsibility. The land and its creatures are seen as parts of a great biotic web of which the members of the indigenous group are also an integral component. Breaking this connection to the land would mean severing a pervasive bond that they have with the natural world.

The preservation of cultural integrity—which includes maintaining one's language, religion, and economic and sociopolitical institutions—is also important for the exercise of self-determination. Since the preservation of a cultural tradition cannot be carried out by isolated individuals, the right to preserve cultural integrity must take place within a communal context. It is also the case that maintaining cultural integrity is meaningless without the existence of a vibrant indigenous community. In practical terms, this means that positive efforts must be made, and material resources provided, for the development and maintenance of indigenous communities. This is particularly important given the fact that indigenous groups have suffered pervasive racial discrimination, religious bigotry, and attempts at cultural destruction at the hands of the majority society.

In the United States, for example, the General Allotment Act of 1887 negated traditional communal land patterns in Indian reservations and replaced them with a system of individual private property ownership. The destruction of traditional communal ownership was made with the expressed purpose of disrupting the cultural cohesion and communal solidarity of Native American peoples. Other attempts by the U.S. government to undermine the cultural integrity of Native Americans include the subverting of indigenous tribal governments by the assassinations of their leaders, the withholding of official recognition of certain tribes through the Extermination Act of 1953, and the forced schooling of Native American children in English in an effort to eradicate their cultural identity. Indigenous groups in other parts of the world have also faced forced assimilation or attempts at cultural and physical annihilation. This legacy of oppression has typically left indigenous groups socially and politically marginalized, impoverished, and communally fractured. The oppression suffered by indigenous groups strongly supports a remedial component in the right to preserve cultural integrity.

Our observations on self-determination, territorial autonomy, and cultural integrity reveal the special interrelatedness of indigenous rights. In many cases, an indigenous community cannot maintain cultural practices that are central to its cultural integrity without a secure land base. Likewise, granting indigenous groups the right to self-determination involves respecting their reliance on traditional forms of self-governance and dispute resolution, which are essential components of their cultural traditions. We can also readily discern that other generally recognized indigenous rights, like nondiscrimination and the promotion of social welfare, comple-

ment and reinforce self-determination. In short, indigenous rights form a cohesive and interconnected set of principles that lay the groundwork for the survival and flourishing of indigenous communities.

III. THE PHILOSOPHICAL JUSTIFICATION OF INDIGENOUS RIGHTS

The justification of certain indigenous rights raises some interesting philosophical issues. Defending certain rights, like the right to nondiscrimination, poses no particular problems because everyone (at least in a liberal democratic society) is recognized as having the right to be protected against invidious and arbitrary discrimination on the basis of race, color, creed, and similar characteristics. Other indigenous rights, however, like the right to territorial autonomy, appear to be problematic. What justifies granting special rights, like the right to fish and hunt in areas that are off limits to others, to the members of certain groups only? In societies that are based on principles of equality and justice, how can we justify rights based on group membership?

Some indigenous rights based on group membership can be justified by reference to the idea of the "inequality of equals." This idea gives due recognition to the fact that in certain situations special protections will be necessary to ensure equal treatment of all members of society. Consider the fundamental right in a democratic multicultural society to pursue one's conception of the good life. For many people this endeavor may involve maintaining their cultural identity, including keeping their language and cultural traditions. Preserving cultural identity may be taken for granted by the members of the majority cultural group because their own language is used in official government transactions and in the schools, the society provides public funds for museums and art organizations that preserve their culture's artistic heritage, the justice system conforms to the conceptions of justice of their cultural tradition, etc.

However, the situation is very different for indigenous groups who are in a position of social and political inequality vis-a-vis the larger society. For them it will be extremely difficult to exercise the right to pursue their vision of the good life because of the lack of support given to their cultural traditions by the majority society. Without rights specifically designed to preserve their cultural heritage, such as rights guaranteeing education in their own language, these indigenous groups will be unable to pursue and realistically achieve their vision of a good and satisfying life. Thus, indigenous rights protecting language and cultural heritage are not designed to provide indigenous groups with special privileges that other members of the society do not have; on the contrary, they are meant to ensure that indigenous groups have the same freedoms and opportunities that everyone else in the society enjoys.

Sometimes the argument is made that group rights protecting cultural integrity would not be necessary if indigenous groups assimilated into the majority society. This view is supported by the claim that it is reasonable for a society to expect that its members assimilate into the national culture. After all, many other ethnic groups who were once discriminated and marginalized have integrated successfully and now enjoy the social benefits that full acceptance and participation in the society bring. By demanding special group rights, indigenous groups willfully separate themselves from the rest of society and thwart the process of assimilation that ethnic minority groups in a pluralistic society must undergo in order to function successfully.

This view fails to make the crucial distinction between ethnic minorities and indigenous groups. Ethnic minorities are groups with a common cultural background who have voluntarily immigrated and who typically favor integration into their adopted country. They have not strenuously resisted assimilation into the mainstream society; in fact, many immigrant parents teach their children only the mainstream language and willingly adopt the prevaling cultural norms of the new country. Even though sometimes the self-identity of first generation immigrants is closely connected with the cultural traditions of their native countries, that is generally not the case with succeeding generations.

Indigenous groups, on the other hand, did not immigrate from a foreign country but were forcefully annexed or conquered by the dominant society. Before the arrival of the settler society, they were self-governing autonomous communities or nations with their own distinctive economic, social, political, and cultural institutions. Most indigenous groups have for many generations vigorously resisted assimilation, and have fought not so much for civil rights that would guarantee them full membership in the society, as for rights of political liberty and self-determination. Keeping in mind the distinction between ethnic minorities and indigenous groups is important for understanding why it may be reasonable to expect the former to integrate into the society but not the latter. Distinguishing clearly the two groups is also helpful for alleviating fears of the larger society that ethnic minorities will use the same reasoning as native groups to demand the same collective rights.

Other indigenous rights have a different justificatory basis. The important right of territorial autonomy, for example, can be defended by reference to the historical injustices committed when disputed indigenous territories were expropriated through conquest or unilaterally annexed by the larger society. The justification here is a kind of compensatory justice where a significant wrong inflicted on a particular group needs to be redressed. Additional support for the moral obligation for rectification comes from the fact that the denial of territorial autonomy for indigenous groups is the cause of continuing social and political oppression. If an indigenous group has maintained a strong continuity of identity with its ancestral past and with its homeland, then the rationale for granting them at least some form of territorial autonomy is compelling.

In justifying the indigenous right of self-determination, several considerations have to be taken into account. Self-determination is a right that is recognized by the international community as belonging to all people, but in the case of indigenous groups it acquires a special meaning. We have already seen how for indigenous people self-determination is closely connected to the rights of territorial autonomy and the preservation of cultural integrity. But the right of self-determination as it applies to indigenous groups must be further qualified by the recognition of the diversity of historical circumstances, present sociopolitical conditions, and collective decisions of particular indigenous groups. For some indigenous groups self-determination may mean having control of their natural resources and of the immigration policies for residency in their homeland, for others it may entail retaining traditional forms of self-governance and dispute resolution, and for yet others it may mean secession from the larger nation-state in order to achieve complete sovereignty.

The right of self-determination has often been equated with the right to secession and independent statehood. Indeed, resistance to claims of self-determination has often been based on this erroneous assumption. Many indigenous groups, however, are not seeking complete sovereignty but some form of political and territorial autonomy within the boundaries of the nation-state where their lands are located. Various types of federalism, where significant control of political, economic, and cultural affairs is devolved to local and regional subunits, could accommodate the demands of some indigenous groups for self-determination.

Thus, different indigenous groups may seek various forms of self-determination. A number of considerations must be kept in mind when attempting to justify particular forms of self-determination. Among the factors to be considered are the needs and interests of the indigenous group in question, the historical facts surrounding the group's colonization or incorporation by the larger society, the cultural cohesiveness of the indigenous group and its continuity of identity with its ancestral communities, the likelihood that the proposed form of self-determination will bring about the survival and flourishing of the indigenous group, and the consequences of the proposed form of self-determination for the larger society. The philosophical justification of the principle of self-determination is a complex matter involving a number of empirical and conceptual considerations.

IV. CRITERIA FOR THE GROUPS ENTITLED TO INDIGENOUS RIGHTS

Different criteria for defining indigenous groups have been proposed in various contexts, and it is difficult to arrive at a universally accepted definition. Governments have sometimes employed excessively narrow criteria of who is indigenous in order to avoid or lessen financial and legal responsibilities. Different indigenous groups have used different criteria for group membership, for tribal voting rights, and for holding office in tribal government. American Indians, for example, have used group membership criteria that range from requiring one-half tribal blood to one-sixteenth. Specifying criteria for indigenous group membership sometimes takes political overtones within the groups themselves, as opinions differ about how to best employ them to maintain community solidarity or achieve political goals. It is important to note that many indigenous groups traditionally took a liberal approach to the question of who is a group member. Nonindigenous persons could be adopted as members of the group if they accepted its perspectives and way of life.

A key issue in defining indigenous groups is whether they are to be characterized primarily in ethnological (racial) or cultural terms. Ethnological criteria are based on percentages of native blood while cultural criteria involve adoption of cultural beliefs and practices and affinity with other group members. There are advantages and disadvantages in using ethnological or cultural criteria for group membership. Ethnological classification can contravene charges of arbitrariness concerning indigenous group membership and can make more compelling the demands for restitution from the colonizing society for past injustices. It would be highly implausible, for example, for a group to demand the return of lands illegitimately expropriated from their ancestors if the group's hereditary connections to those ancestors were nonexistent or indeterminate.

On the other hand, culturally based criteria do not exclude individuals who are deeply committed and knowledgeable of the needs and concerns of the indigenous group but who do not have the required degree of ancestry. In addition, cultural criteria conform more closely with the traits and practices which indigenous groups are concerned with preserving. If the core demand of indigenous groups is to attain self-determina-

tion and live according to their chosen way of life, it makes sense to adopt criteria for group membership based on how committed an individual is to defending and embodying that way of life. Cultural criteria based on a set of sociopolitical convictions and commitments are also more likely to enhance the credibility of indigenous group demands in liberal democratic societies that are deeply suspicious of race-based rights and privileges.

Reasonable standards for indigenous group membership should take into account the strengths and liabilities of ethnological and cultural criteria. While ethnological criteria do not appear to be necessary for every case for group membership, a "critical mass" of group members with ancestral connections seems to be an essential component of group identity. Otherwise, as we have seen, the moral legitimacy of certain indigenous rights would be undermined. Indeed, relations of descendance are part of the very meaning of the terms "native" and "indigenous." It is perhaps impossible to determine in precise terms what this critical mass should be, but it is reasonable to suppose that past a certain point of hereditary attenuation, there will be a decline in the moral exigency of some, although not all, indigenous group claims. Besides ethnological considerations there are other criteria that are straightforwardly relevant. The most important of these are that the members be cognizant of the cultural traditions of the group and that they exhibit a discernible commitment to those traditions, that they have a continuity of identity with the group's ancestral past, and that they value the continued existence and intergenerational transmission of the group's cultural heritage.

Ultimately, however, it should be up to indigenous groups themselves to determine the criteria for group membership. There are advantages gained and responsibilities incurred in adopting particular criteria for group membership, and awareness of these should restrain excessively broad or overly restrictive standards for group membership.

V. CONCLUSION: PROSPECTS FOR INDIGENOUS RIGHTS

There are some encouraging developments that support the understanding, development, and recognition of indigenous rights. After centuries of neglect, this subject is currently being researched by philosophers, legal scholars, and political scientists. Interest in indigenous rights has been bolstered by the increasing interest in the cultural pluralism that now characterizes societies throughout the world. Scholars in different disciplines are recognizing that a proper understanding of democracy and human rights must take into account the diversity of perspectives, needs, and interests of the different cultural groups that make up the global human community. Developments in information technologies and telecommunications have also facilitated research and scholarly exchanges between researchers interested in indigenous groups.

There has also been an increased interest in the legal status of the rights of indigenous peoples by the international community. Of special importance in this connection are the drafts that United Nations committees have written on the rights of indigenous groups, particularly the "Draft United Nations Declaration on the Rights of Indigenous Peoples." This document represents a milestone in the international recognition of indigenous rights.

However, prospects for the implementation of indigenous rights and the preservation of the cultural integrity of indigenous groups are uncertain. Governments routinely give rhetorical recognition to such rights but do little to carry out social welfare projects or enforce formally granted rights. Sometimes this is due to lack of resources and sometimes to neglect or persisting racist attitudes toward indigenous groups. But perhaps the greatest danger to the cultural survival of indigenous groups is the current global western cultural homogenization driven by commercial interests and put into effect by ubiquitous media technologies. Should this process succeed, the world will have lost the cultural richness of indigenous groups which is our common human heritage.

Bibliography

Anaya, S. J. (1996). "Indigenous Peoples in International Law." Oxford Univ. Press, Oxford.

Buchanan, A. (1993). The role of collective rights in the theory of indigenous peoples' rights. *Transnational Law Contemporary Problem* **3**(1), 89–108.

Clinton, R. (1990). The rights of indigenous peoples as collective group rights. *Arizona Law Rev.* **32**(4), 739–747.

Jaimes, M. A. (Ed.) (1992). "The State of Native America: Genocide, Colonization, and Resistance." Sound End, Boston.

Kymlicka, W. (1995). "Multicultural Citizenship: A Liberal Theory of Minority Rights." Clarendon Press, Oxford.

Kymlicka, W. (Ed.) (1995). "The Rights of Minority Cultures." Oxford Univ. Press, Oxford.

Pacari, N. (1996). Taking on the neoliberal agenda. *North American Congress on Latin America: Report on the Americas* **29**(5), 23–32.

Pevar, S. L. (1992). "The Rights of Indians and Tribes," 2nd ed. Southern Illinois Univ. Press, Carbondale/Edwardsville.

Internet Protocol

DUNCAN LANGFORD

University of Kent at Canterbury

GLOSSARY

electronic address A unique address detailing the name, organization, type of organization and usually also the country of a company or individual.

electronically published Describing or relating to information that has been created, distributed, or made available over networked computers.

electronic communication Interaction between two or more individuals carried out by means of networked computers.

E-mail Short for electronic mail; messages sent between individuals over networked computers.

Internet A high-speed worldwide network of computers.

mailing list A means of distributing e-mail to a group of individuals.

modem A device to connect a computer to a telephone line.

network A group of computers connected in such a way that their users may share information.

newsgroup The name given to the equivalent of a global electronic notice board, classified under a subject heading. Electronic messages posted to it by individuals may be accessed and replied to by any interested person.

newsreader A computer application used to access newsgroups.

on-line/Internet community Those individuals who have access to the wider Internet.

(on-line) service provider An organization that exists to provide a connection to the wider Internet.

site The name given to a specific location on the Internet.

World Wide Web (WWW) or the Web An approach to Internet use, potentially incorporating text, graphics, video, and sound. An individual establishes contact with a specific site containing desired information and accesses it directly. WWW documents, or pages, may be readily connected together.

INTERNET PROTOCOL describes the expectations on the part of existing users of the Internet of the manner in which users should behave. For many years after establishment in the 1960s of the original precursor to the Internet (ARPAnet), the users of globally networked computers tended to be predominantly academic, and to have a strong belief in the virtues of free speech and individual responsibility, together with stress on shared information, rather than proprietary or secret knowledge. This collective view led to the establishment of written and unwritten rules which, through the impossibility of local or national enforcement, were adhered to by members of the Internet itself. This shared acceptance of a protocol allowed the Internet to function efficiently and productively.

However, in recent years newcomers to the Internet, increasingly unaware of this underlying philosophy, have wittingly and unwittingly acted to undermine the protocols. What was originally viewed as a cognate national environment has become a diverse, global one. For the Internet to continue functioning, there is an urgent need to re-establish acceptance by its users of the existing Internet protocol, or establishment of a workable replacement.

I. NETWORKS AND THE INTERNET

A. What Is the Internet?

1. Background

The creation of globally interconnected networks of computers has given individuals the ability to directly communicate with each other, linking across national and international boundaries as easily as across the street. Global publication is trivially easy; this means, for example, that views which may be abhorrent to large numbers of individuals can be propagated and automatically distributed. Material such as pornography, instructions on breaking into computer systems, or even details on building bombs is potentially freely available. However, despite the wishes of politicians and others, it is technically quite impossible to realistically censor or otherwise limit electronically published material. Although national policing may be attempted, operation of the global computer networks known generically as the Internet is, quite literally, out of political control.

2. Networking in Practice

Wide-scale networking means, in effect, that any person or organization possessing a suitable computer, together with a telephone line and modem, has the ability to establish links with other computers. Such links are normally made through a paid-for commercial link to a service provider, the Internet equivalent of a telephone company, offering a connection to the wider Internet community. (For many office workers, connection to a service provider is frequently provided automatically by an employer.) Once joined to any Internet-connected network, a user has the ability to post messages to any connected electronic address, situated anywhere in the world.

Begun as a vehicle for experimental network research, the Internet was originally designed to survive nuclear war. In consequence, there is no central control whatever—any part of it may be removed without damage to the whole.

In attempting to understand how such a devolved system can work, it is essential to appreciate the very strong ethos of the Internet. Its users are very much in favor of internal control and against outside influence. In effect, the Internet is a fully functioning anarchy. Until comparatively recently, most actual users of the Internet were technically aware individuals who understood the technical background to this form of networking and who (because of their experience and background) were perhaps biased in favor of academic freedom and individual autonomy.

What is ethically appropriate must reflect what is technically possible. In order to appropriately consider protocols in electronic communication, there is consequently a need for some understanding of the technical setting. A brief description of the background to computer networking and the Internet therefore precedes consideration of some potential ethical problems involved in networked communications.

Use of the Internet is typically through three main channels—electronic mail, newsgroups, and the World Wide Web.

3. Personal Mail—"E-mail"

Once a service provider has allowed connection, electronic messages may be generated from any computer connected to the Internet. Messages can be "mailed" or "posted" to any user with a similarly connected computer. Given the electronic address of a target, electronic mail can be dispatched in seconds to someone working at the next desk, or on the next continent.

4. Newsgroups

Connection to the Internet also allows access to an enormous number of newsgroups, which cover the whole range of human activity. Although those newsgroups concerned with sexual matters may have gained a high profile, there are, literally, tens of thousands of others. Reading the contents of an Internet newsgroup is very straightforward; simple newsreaders are available for virtually every Internet-linked computer.

"Posting" an article simply involves sending mail to the electronic address of a newsgroup, rather than directing mail to an individual. Although some newsgroups are moderated, which means a human acts as a filter for postings to them, the huge majority have no such control. Whatever is posted to the newsgroup is then automatically distributed to every Internet site subscribing to it. Posting to an Internet newsgroup is consequently the nearest thing on earth to absolute free speech—unmediated, uncensored, and far reaching.

B. How Newsgroups Work

As will be further discussed, there have been demands that the Internet and its newsgroups be censored.

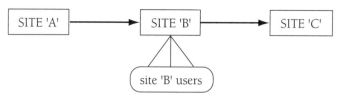

FIGURE 1 Transmission of typical newsgroup message.

Once the workings of the Internet are understood, though, it will be seen that, even if justified, such censorship is technically impossible.

Electronic messages are constantly being sent along links between service providers, or "sites." When a site receives a message, it checks that the newsgroup to which the message belongs is accepted by that site. The message is then made available to a site's individual members by storing a copy "on site." The site will also send a cloned copy of each message to the next site in the wider network. Millions of messages are continually passing around the Internet in this way.

In the typical example illustrated in Figure 1, a message originates at site A and is passed to site B, which distributes it not only to its own subscribers, but also onward, to site C. Copies of the message will then move on to subsequent sites in the network.

What would happen if, instead of passing on the message, site B decided it was subversive of morals or authority, and refused to circulate either the message or the newsgroup to which it belonged? Clearly, those users who depended directly upon the site (site B users) would be unable to access the newsgroup. However, site C and its users, downstream in Figure 1, would be only temporarily inconvenienced. The Internet is not called "net" casually. The pattern of its links forms a spider's web; so, if one connection is damaged, information can be obtained from any other. The Internet interprets censorship as damage, and, of course, it was designed from the first to survive massive damage. Site C can consequently obtain a "censored" newsgroup from any other of its connections—or it may readily establish a new connection to an unrestricted news "feed."

This pattern holds at whatever scale the Internet is viewed. A single user banned from accessing or contributing to a newsgroup can just telephone a different service provider, while, even if a whole country decided to ban a particular newsgroup, at worst this would only effect the country itself. The global Internet community would continue.

It is very important to keep this state of affairs in mind, not only when considering requests for punitive action against publications on the Internet, but when debating appropriate user conduct.

C. How the World Wide Web Works

The World Wide Web (WWW), graphically based and consequently very visual in nature, is inherently easy to use. In structure, it can be considered as a static approach to service provision. Here, instead of the contents of a newsgroup being constantly transmitted around the world, an individual uses freely available software to establish direct contact with a site containing desired information and specifically accesses it. A great advantage of this approach is that Web sites are easily connected to each other. A user may, by clicking buttons on their personal computer's screen, move between the display of Web pages in different states—or different continents—without realizing they are doing more than accessing the next page of data. Communication may be two-way: companies and individuals may establish their own Web sites; any connected computer may then read presented information. Access to Web sites is very easy indeed—they form the simplest way of accessing electronic information, and have played a large part in the recent enormous growth of the Internet (see Fig. 2).

Although their purposes—access to desired information—may seem similar, Internet Web sites and Internet newsgroups are very different. A newsgroup has no "real" location and cannot therefore be said to exist in any one place, while a Web site must, by definition, have a unique home address.

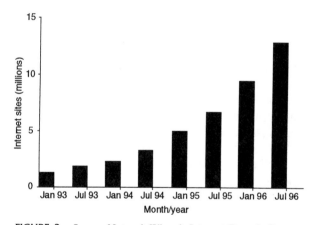

FIGURE 2 *Source:* Network Wizards Internet Domain Survey.

D. Summary

Anyone with a full Internet connection may post electronic messages to any Internet address anywhere in the world. In addition, anyone may read from and contribute to Internet newsgroups, which cover the whole range of human activity. Such groups cannot effectively be banned. Graphically based, World Wide Web sites also contain information, but such sites, unlike newsgroups, have specific locations. Both rely on the Internet, a paradoxically unorganized and ad hoc arrangement of connected computers which has evolved to its present position of global dominance from an origin as a nuclear attack-proof research network.

The underlying ethos shared by long-standing users of the Internet has always been very strongly in favor of freedom from external controls and internal self-regulation.

II. PROBLEMS IN ELECTRONIC COMMUNICATION

In considering appropriate protocols, two areas of computer networking and communications may be viewed as particularly relevant. The first relates to *individual* communications, and the second is concerned with *publication*—that is, reading or publishing information through access to newsgroups and World Wide Web sites.

A. Ethical Issues in Individual Communications

When moving into new circumstances, it is natural to assume previous experience may be relevant. Consider an apparently simple task, such as writing a letter. It may seem logical to bring to composing and sending an electronic letter an established cognitive model which has worked well in generating similar paper mail. However, unthinking transference to the Internet of experience gained in other settings may lead to serious problems.

One such problem lies in classifying an electronic message. Is it, for instance, best treated as a traditional paper memo? There can be similarities, but there are also important differences. A typed memo involves several stages, at each of which an author may modify the text, or even decide to scrap the whole idea. This extended process does not fit the generation of an electronic message, which, in contrast, is very quick and easy to produce. Many people create and send e-mail spontaneously, often without pausing to consider use of tone and language, or even if the message is really appropriate or necessary. Of course, an electronic message can easily be printed as well, so a casual electronic jotting may instantly and unexpectedly achieve the formal authority of a typed memo.

Unlike paper communications, electronic mail appears transitory. A message can flash across a screen before seeming to vanish into electronic limbo. However, it is a serious mistake to think of e-mail as temporary. Although messages can certainly be impermanent, the opposite is also true. Once sent, a copy of an unguarded personal message may easily be stored by a recipient, perhaps for years, before, in the memorable phrase of one businessman, "It comes back to haunt you."

This is an instance of an individual problem which is likely to follow misunderstanding of the electronic medium, possibly leading to the inappropriate establishment of protocols—protocols which may have been quite appropriate in a different setting. For example, sending a paper letter is predicated upon the assumption that its contents will remain personal to the addressee. It is therefore both logical and appropriate to use a paper letter to convey confidential information, and to consider that a third party who then reads it is, normally, acting unethically.

However, in addition to the potential problems already described, there are also manifold possibilities for inadvertent distribution of electronic mail. Accidentally posting to a mailing list (which copies mail to everyone on the list) or unthinkingly sending multiple copies is deceptively easy. Given such a very different distribution model, transference of paper mail protocols to electronic mail is not appropriate.

This e-mail example illustrates the importance of applying an appropriate cognitive model to the consideration of electronic communication. In this case, the protocol which has evolved with the Internet itself suggests it is unethical to distribute electronic mail inappropriately, or to publish personal messages.

B. Ethical Issues in Networked Communications

In addition to the issues concerning personal communication, networked computers allow spreading of information in a way which is directly analogous to traditional broadcasting, or publishing on paper. Once distributed electronically, such "published" information is potentially seen by very large numbers of individuals indeed. Discussed next are two illustrative examples of inappropriate Internet broadcasting.

1. Personal—"Spamming"

Sending multiple copies of messages to many different newsgroups, although very easy, is always considered inappropriate. Doing so is called, in Netspeak, "spamming," after an old Monty Python sketch.

Distributing many hundreds of thousands of copies of your message and presenting it to the readers of every newsgroup might, perhaps, be useful to you, but the disadvantages to everyone else are very clear. Who does this, and why?

The most infamous example to date was probably the 1994 Green Card Lottery Spam, perpetrated by the U.S. law firm of Canter & Siegel. The firm considered the Internet to be an ideal, low-cost, and perfectly legitimate way to target their advertising at people likely to be potential clients. Although spreading their "spam" message cost others thousands of dollars, and much inconvenience, they had done nothing illegal or, in their consideration, improper. Among Internet users this was certainly a minority view—the reaction of the Internet population was overwhelmingly hostile.

Users felt that, firstly, Internet newsgroups were the wrong place to conduct commercial business. Its origins, and long-standing academic bias, had created a long tradition of non-commercialism. Secondly, although it may not be obvious to users, global use of the Internet is not free—the costs of infrastructure, transmission, and storage must be borne by someone. Canter & Siegel were alleged to have posted to over 6000 groups, which must surely have involved expenditure of quite a lot of other people's money.

Finally, in order to be established, newsgroups have individual "charters," setting out their aims. Many of the charters of the Internet newsgroups and connected sites specifically prohibit offers to do business. (A few do accept them, but restrict buyers and sellers to individuals, not companies.) Of course, being the Internet, such charters have only moral force. Understandably, though, people reading a particular newsgroup can become very annoyed by irrelevant postings concerning subjects outside the group's charter. This is analogous to, say, a neighborhood group meeting together to discuss the needs of their local school and being constantly interrupted in their debate by someone trying to sell telephone chat lines.

Noncommercial spamming may be used by antisocial individuals as a deliberate irritation; to this a typical response would be "flaming," which is the sending of personally abusive e-mail or the posting of similarly abusive news items.

Respecting the rights of groups and individuals is part of the Internet ethic. Someone who, for their own purposes, casually overrides the interests of other users by generating spams is consequently acting unethically.

2. Technical—Broadcasting of "Inappropriate" Material

Once a computer is connected to the Internet, running appropriate software allows easy creation of a World Wide Web site. Tens of thousands of such sites exist, and numbers are increasing exponentially. Most such sites are well designed and well conducted—but there are some WWW sites, for example, which exist to distribute pornography, both hard and soft, as well as those devoted to propagating extremist political views. All that is needed to view them is the correct electronic address.

As was mentioned earlier, Internet newsgroups are only controllable by refusing to allow news packages to enter a service provider's site. Newsgroup access may also be made more difficult by a "censoring" site refusing to pass information along the networked chain of computers.

In contrast, a Web site cannot be controlled at all, beyond refusing it permission to exist at a particular location. Sites created by individuals but felt to be unsuitable by their service providers have been closed down, but there is no way whatever of forbidding them to exist. A closed site may just spring up somewhere else—potentially, even in a different country, perhaps in the Third World. Such use is directly analogous to telephone sex lines in the United Kingdom. Although protests resulted in them being banned by United Kingdom operators, the lines continued—using numbers located outside the United Kingdom.

The ethical issues involved here are inherently enormously complex, and this complexity is exacerbated in the electronic world. It would be foolish to pretend there are easy or obvious solutions. The mix of Internet users is increasingly being diluted from its specialist origins by a vast influx of additional users from a range of different backgrounds. The well-established Internet philosophy of open access and free communication is consequently in direct conflict with the social and moral mores of many of its new users. If the trend continues, the philosophy itself must, at best, be in a state of flux. What is certain, however, is the inescapable fact that censorship is not possible. Whatever decisions are eventually reached must inevitably reflect this reality.

III. THE ISSUES

So far we have discussed a selection of examples intended to illustrate some problems in using the Internet. These range from minor difficulties—unexpected responses to personal mail—to the more serious, and potentially involve abuse or limitation of free speech.

Difficulties faced by new users in attempts to communicate effectively by electronic mail are probably typical of the teething problems to be anticipated in the use of most new facilities. Advice to tread warily, together with effective education, should go a long way to answering their problems.

In contrast, the impossibility of exerting effective censorship is hard for many individuals to understand. Politicians, especially, are understandably reluctant to consider anything other than legislation as the ultimate sanction on behavior. Within the Internet, though, local or even national legislation simply will not work.

There are two main reasons why this is so. Policing the Internet is technically impossible, and, in any event, much of the Internet lies beyond the reach of any national police force. This means that any Internet site may make available whatever it likes, provided only that the country *within which it is located* does not object. Although access to such sites from the United States may be officially forbidden, it would be as difficult to prevent as a ruling forbidding faxes. Anyone with a computer and telephone could access any site. In reality, enforcement is quite impractical.

Given the impossibility of exercising political or technical control over the Internet, the need for appropriate education is growing increasingly urgent. In the past, the Internet worked well; it has done so since it was first established. The principal reason we are experiencing problems now lies in a dramatic shift which has taken place in the Internet population. No longer are the majority of users experienced in the use of computers, familiar with an academic approach to free speech, and aware of established expectations of user behavior. Letting loose new users on the Internet without training or education is perhaps analogous to letting loose new drivers without instruction—except that even the worst new driver does not have the ability to inconvenience several million people, a task well within the powers of even a neophyte Internet user.

Quite apart from a massive increase in personal use, we are also seeing an explosion in commercial use of the Internet, principally through the World Wide Web. What was formerly a largely academic network is now a promotional goldrush. Hundreds, if not thousands, of companies from the very large to the very small are racing to seize the enormous potential market represented by those with Internet connections. This commercial rush shows no signs of decreasing—indeed, all the indications are that it will continue to accelerate. What decisions should be taken on defining what is appropriate commercial use of the Internet, and who should be responsible for framing such definitions? How long can the established ethic, which is essentially a shared understanding on the part of users, be sustained under a stunningly rapid dilution of user experience? There appears a real need for establishment of an updated 'Internet ethic', if only an acceptable defining body can be found or established.

IV. CONCLUSIONS

This entry has outlined some of the practical and ethical problems concerned with appropriate behavior in electronic communication. It has emphasized the impossibility of effective network policing, and the associated need for a greatly increased level of education.

Before the advent of the Internet, few individuals could expect to have their views and opinions considered by more than a handful of friends and acquaintances. In contrast, a simple posting to a popular Internet newsgroup may potentially be read by hundreds of thousands of people.

It seems clear that automatic carrying over of "small-scale" behavior into a large-scale forum will lead to inevitable difficulties. Such difficulties are likely to be compounded by the greatly increased opportunities the Internet offers for antisocial behavior. Users with even limited knowledge may, for example, employ electronic mail to "spam" newsgroups, while the more technically advanced may use the World Wide Web to distribute extreme political propaganda.

Until now, the Internet has worked through acceptance on the part of its users of a belief, which might perhaps be viewed as an evolved general ethic of behavior. While reflecting what may be a purely pragmatic approach to Internet use, this evolved approach has proved both effective and functional. Six protocols have been particularly emphasized:

- The Internet is very strongly against external control and in favor of internal self-regulation
- Rights of groups and individuals should always be respected
- Individual actions should always reflect awareness of the wider Internet community
- Person-to-person communications should be private
- No message should be broadcast without proper cause
- The ability to post globally is so powerful it must always be voluntarily limited

Underlying these points is the well-established Internet philosophy of open access and free communication.

As the number and variety of new Internet users are constantly increasing, the situation is dynamic, and prediction risky. However, there is a strong case for some form of coordinated encouragement of appropriate ethical standards, ideally founded upon those established during development of the Internet. If such standards are agreed upon, they might then be included in appropriate education of new users of the Internet. New users surely need to demonstrate awareness of the responsibilities, as well as the advantages, of Internet use. Further research into the ethos of the Internet is clearly essential.

The Internet undoubtedly provides a tremendous global opportunity, analogous to the invention of the printing press in its power to educate and inform. Should it develop without an ethical foundation known to all users, we should all surely be the poorer.

Bibliography

Bynum, T. W. (1997). *Information ethics: An introduction*. Oxford: Blackwell.

Gotternbarn, D. (1996). Establishing standards of professional practice. In Myers, Hall, Pitt (Eds.), *The responsible software engineer*. London: Springer.

Johnson, D. G. (1994). *Computer ethics*, 2nd ed. Englewood Cliffs, NJ: Prentice-Hall.

Langford, D. (1995). *Practical computer ethics*. London: McGraw-Hill.

Langford, D. (1997). Ethical issues in network system design. *Australian Journal of Information Systems* May, **4**(2).

Rogerson, S., and Bynum, T. W. (Eds.) (1997). *A reader in information ethics*. Oxford: Blackwell.

Media Depiction of Ethnic Minorities

CHARLES CRITCHER

Sheffield Hallam University

GLOSSARY

assimilation The view or assumption that ethnic minorities should adopt the culture of the ethnic majority.

ethnocentricity A view of the world in which other groups are judged according to the cultural values and ideals of one's own ethnic group.

genre A particular type or format of media output, e.g., soap opera, situation comedy, or news.

multiculturalism The view or assumption that ethnic minority and majority cultures should coexist on equal terms.

news values A working set of criteria that govern how the newsworthiness of a story is assessed by journalists.

stereotype The attribution of a set of fixed characteristics to all members of a particular social group, usually of a negative kind.

THE MEDIA DEPICTION OF ETHNIC MINORITIES is an ethical issue for media practitioners, media regulators, and media publics. The ethics of professionalism and the ethics of media policy are intimately related to the ethics of public life. Ultimately at stake is the cultural right of any group to an accurate media representation of its way of life, part of a general claim to equal citizenship. Our discussion of the issue begins with a clarification of key concepts.

The conventional definition of *mass media* is that they are communicative forms involving the simultaneous transmission of noninteractive messages to large, heterogeneous audiences. They are also normally operated for commercial profit and subject to some form of government regulation. Such a definition encompasses what we commonly think of as the major mass media: television and radio, and newspapers and magazines. Film is a mass medium in definitional terms, though traditionally film scholars have studied it separately. It will be included here. More ambiguously placed are what are more often termed products of mass culture such as popular literature and music. As a consequence, they will occupy a tangential place in this discussion.

The term "mass" has become more problematic since it is an inheritance from a time when media outlets, especially in broadcasting, were restricted by the availability of wavelengths. When only a few television or radio stations are available, they will divide the large audience up between them. However, the use of FM bands on radio and the multiplicity of channels made

---

available by cable and satellite (likely to expand further via digital technology) have rapidly increased the number of outlets. The result has been to begin to fragment the audience and reduce the extent to which it follows the same programs.

There is no simple way of objectively defining the existence of an *ethnic minority*. In any society there will exist groups who in some way are regarded or regard themselves as different from the rest of the population, but there is no simple threshold beyond which they qualify as an "ethnic group." Ethnic minorities are distinguished from the rest of the population by a range of attributes, the most important of which include religion, language, kinship, dress, diet, music, cultural heritage, and even body language. A group exhibiting just one of these characteristics, such as religion or language, will not necessarily be an ethnic group, though their combination is likely to provide a foundation for ethnic identity.

"Race" is a further complication. Though few now claim biological differences between "races," skin color remains a powerful signifier of difference. It may serve to define an ethnic minority even in the absence of many of the other characteristics so far considered. Over generations the constituent elements of ethnicity may change, as children lead a bilingual and bicultural experience. Ethnic intermarriage may blur the boundaries of the group.

Any attempt to arrive at a consistent definition of ethnic minorities must also recognize the enormous variety of experience among such groups which may belie any attempt to cateogrize them together. What all ethnicities share is a dependence for their existence on members' sense of belonging. People belong to ethnic groups when they subjectively identify with them. Ethnic membership is a result of choice; people can opt to move out of or, more rarely, into an ethnic group, whereas they can never leave or join a racial grouping. Overall, ethnic groups may be seen to exist to the extent that groups see themselves as ethnically distinct.

The term "minority" implies that ethnic groups do not constitute the numerical majority. There is, however, a linguistic sleight of hand here. It appears that minorities possess ethnicity while majorities do not. One rarely hears the term "ethnic majority," but that is the logical corollary of "ethnic minority" and is the term that will be used here. Sometimes implicit in the political use of the term "minority" is emphasis on ethnic minorities' subordination to the majority group. This may vary across political, economic, and cultural dimensions but is rarely totally absent. This structured inequality built into majority–minority relations will be a consistent aspect of our discussion.

The messages of the media are complex. Some, such as radio, are exclusively oral. Newspapers rely heavily on language but their use of typography and photographs means they also depend upon the impact of visual messages. Television uses speech, written language, and still and moving pictures. The manipulation of such techniques in film is more self-conscious and resource-intensive than in any other medium. This is also the only mass medium to be almost entirely fictional, all the others containing both factual and fictional material. In looking at media representations of ethnic minorities, we are concerned with what is said, what is written, what is shown in still photographs and in film, and sometimes with all these simultaneously. What the media say cannot easily be divorced from how they say it.

I. THE CONTEMPORARY CONTEXT

A. The Ubiquity of Ethnic Minorities

The presence of ethnic minority groups is now the rule rather than the exception in most nations of the world. Many societies comprise several ethnic groups, with considerable variation in the extent to which any one group is dominant.

While the terms ethnic minority and ethnic majority may be universally applicable, there are very great differences between the groups who may be similarly categorized. Important are differences in size, geography, and history. Ethnic minorities may severally or together be a small or a large proportion of a given country's population. They may be geographically concentrated in one area or type of area, such as urban conurbations, or they may be dispersed in small clusters throughout the country. History provides some of the greatest differences because it is there we find the reasons why such minorities have come to be where they are.

There are at least six historical categories to which any ethnic minority can belong:

1. Indigenous peoples where the majority are settlers (e.g., American Indians or Australian aborigines)
2. Indigenous peoples who have been incorporated into a new society by the formation of a nation-state, often as a result of colonial conquest (e.g., Africa, Asia)
3. Peoples forcibly transported as labor through systems of slavery or indentured labor (e.g., peoples from Africa, the Indian subcontinent, and China)
4. Peoples who are economic migrant settlers (e.g., from Europe in previous times to Europe today)
5. Peoples who are temporary economic migrants or "guest workers" (e.g., Turks in Western Europe)
6. Peoples who are political refugees from persecution (e.g., Jews who fled fascism)

Ethnic minorities may have resided in their current location from time immemorial, for the past 150 years, for the last 30 years, or only for the last decade. This is bound to affect minorities' perceptions of their old and new homelands and the majority's acceptance of the legitimacy of their presence.

B. The Economic and Political Disadvantages of Ethnic Minorities

Whether newcomers or old-timers, ethnic minorities appear to experience difficulty in achieving significant access to the commanding heights of political and economic power. They may find a niche in the middle ranges of powerful institutions, in the polity as government administrators, and in the economy as small-scale entrepreneurs. However, in any society where ethnicity is a significant way of differentiating between groups, the majority group is likely to resist any minority attempt to compete for political and economic power. This invariably extends to a cultural struggle over the right to be heard, in which the media are crucial.

C. Media Representations as Status Indicators

Since the media tend to be produced and consumed by the majority ethnic group, representations of ethnic minorities are an important indicator of how majorities view minorities. At one extreme, ethnic minorities might be accepted as an integral part of the society (part of us) and its self-image; at the other extreme, they may be represented as permanent outsiders who are unable to fulfil the conditions necessary for full membership of society (the category of them). One way of conceptualizing this insider or outsider status is in terms of citizenship.

D. Ethnic Minorities, the Media, and Citizenship

Ethnic minorities are frequently denied, and thus attempt to claim, civil rights, either at basic levels of rights to permanent settlement and to vote or at more advanced levels of rights to equal opportunities in education and employment. In this apparently inevitable conflict, the media occupy a strategic role as reporters and commentators. A frequent point of evaluation of their performance is the extent to which they give a fair hearing to the minority's claim to rights. They may act as referees to the conflict or they may favor one side. The media themselves may operate to exclude minorities from their production staff or output. The media

thus perform this dual role: they are the forum where the arguments should be heard and are themselves implicated in the power structures which the minorities may wish to reform.

E. Variations in Media Systems

Across the world, media systems vary in their state of development, the extent of government control, and the degree of commercialization. In democracies, the press acts as a commercial enterprise free from direct government control, so that ethical standards cannot easily be enforced. Television and radio systems normally operate under licence, to which there may be attached some obligations to serve the whole community. This is a usual requirement of public service broadcasting systems. Advertisements in the press and broadcasting are subject to general laws, but otherwise tend to be self-regulated by the industry itself. There is a global tendency to deregulate media systems which causes problems for the enforcement of basic ethical standards. How sensitive the media are to serving ethnic minorities and to granting them equal representation may depend in part on the extent and kind of the ethical standards required by regulatory systems.

II. KEY QUESTIONS

A. Inclusion versus Exclusion

An initial question about media representation might be, to what extent is the presence of ethnic minorities acknowledged or ignored? In an ideal situation, the media would acknowledge ethnic diversity within a framework of common citizenship. Then we might expect ethnic minority members to appear in the media in the same proportional frequency and on essentially the same terms as members of the ethnic majority. This would apply to appearances as members of the public, reporters, artistic performers, and spokespersons, across the full range of the media: in newspapers and magazines, on radio and television, and in film and popular culture. Alternatively ethnic minorities might appear in the media more unevenly, for example, in sport and entertainment rather than in news and current affairs. And when they do appear in the latter, it may be mainly when they represent a "problem" to the dominant group. In the most extreme case, the media may simply act as if ethnic minorities do not exist.

B. Accuracy versus Distortion

The second question is, how far are media accounts of ethnic minorities accurate or distorted? There is clearly some difficulty defining what an "accurate" portrayal of an ethnic minority might be. Nevertheless there are some areas of "fact" where such accuracy can be defined and, if necessary, measured. These include: (i) historical facts about minorities—how they came to be part of the society, and how they were treated in the past by dominant groups; (ii) demographic facts about minorities—their size, age distribution, birth and marriage rates, etc.; (iii) cultural facts about minorities—languages spoken, religious practices, kinship networks, dietary and dress customs, and the like; and (iv) social facts about minorities–their proportional membership of the workforce or the unemployed, educational attainment, involvement in the welfare system, and role as perpetrators and victims of crime.

Extensive data of this kind about ethnic minorities are known, at least in advanced democratic societies, because they are routinely collected by government and related agencies. These can then be compared with media portrayals to assess their degree of accuracy and the nature of any systematic distortions. It is also possible to check the accuracy of specific news stories, especially where subsequently there are official investigations, the results of which can be compared with the way the media represented the event.

C. Sensitive Understanding versus Rigid Stereotyping

This question is, to what extent do media representations contribute to sensitive understanding or to rigid stereotyping of ethnic minorities? This discussion frequently hinges around accusations that the media tend to indulge in stereotypes of ethnic minorities. Perceived characteristics of an ethnic minority—how they look, speak, or behave—are exaggerated and rigidified so that all members of the group are assumed to conform to the stereotype. This may prevent ethnic minorities being presented as both sharing cultural affiliations and being individually unique—much like the dominant majority.

D. Multiculturalism versus Assimilation

This last question is, do the media support multiculturalist or assimilationist ideals of ethnic relations? Multiculturalism accepts that society will be enriched by the equal coexistence of many cultures whose varying customs and institutions can be accommodated within a society based upon principles of common humanity. Assimilation assumes that the ultimate goal is for all members of society to share one culture and become similar to one another. That culture is, unsurprisingly, the culture of the ethnic majority, with some minimal adjustments to incorporate its new recruits. Evidence

for the kinds of view adopted by the media are most often to be found when the media are in a editorializing or a didactic mode—when they directly address the "problem" of ethnic minorities.

III. EVIDENCE ABOUT MEDIA REPRESENTATIONS

A. News Coverage

Analysis of the ways ethnic minorities are depicted in the news media has proceeded by identifying the themes and issues with which ethnic minorities tend to be associated and those which are ignored (see Tables I and II). It thus deals with sins of commission and sins of omission. Despite the differences in media systems and ethnic minority populations, there is a remarkable degree of unanimity among researchers in the USA, Western Euorpe, and Australia about which issues and themes emerge most consistently in news coverage of ethnic minorities.

1. Immigration

Most ethnic minority groups are immigrants of one kind or another. The question of immigration policy, how many should be allowed in and from where and under what conditions, looms large in news coverage.

TABLE I   Frequencies of General Subjects in the Dutch Press, August 1985–January 1986

Subject	% All subjects
Immigration	20.8
Discrimination	16.7
Crime	9.1
Social affairs	5.7
Research	5.7
Work, unemployment	5.1
Politics	4.6
Race relations	4.2
Housing	3.9
Education	3.7
Culture	3.5
Religion	2.5
Health	2.3
Other	10.7
Total	100

Source: Van Dijk, T. A. (1991). *Racism and the Press*, table 4.4, p. 111. Routledge, London/New York. Reproduced by permission.

TABLE II Frequencies of General Subjects in Stories about Black Americans during Three Local Television Newscasts in Chicago on December 1–7, 1989

Category	% All categories
Violent crime	41
Intraparty political conflict	19
Candidacy of black judge for county board	15
Nonviolent crime	1
Other	24
Total	100

Source: Entman, R. (1990). Modern racism and images of blacks in local television news. *Crit. Studies Mass Commun.* **7**(4), 332–345. Reproduced by permission.

It is generally triggered by a news event, such as the actual or imminent arrival of refugees, or by a news issue, such as recurrent concerns with the problem of illegal immigrants. Immigration is generally perceived as a threat. Its desirability is calculated in terms of the costs to the ethnic majority of accepting people who are economically destitute and culturally different. Where the causes of refugee status are political, there is a constant preoccupation with the possibility that asylum seekers are bogus, since their motivations are actually economic. It appears difficult to find in the news media any view of immigration as natural or desirable, rather than an unwelcome imposition. These trends have been found in relation to migrant Mexican workers in the USA, African-Asians and Hong Kong Chinese in the United Kingdom, Sri Lankan Tamils in the Netherlands, and Boat People in Australia.

2. Law and Order

Ethnic minorities frequently appear in the media as perpetrators of crime, either individually in relation to specific incidents or generally as part of crime waves or trends. In both the USA and the United Kingdom, controversies have arisen over the media's tendency to reproduce uncritically police statistics which claim a disproportionate involvement of ethnic minorities in street crime. Hence the term "mugging," which has no legal standing, has become synonymous with gratuitously violent crime committed by young black men on the streets. In fact, ethnic minority crime is rarely disproportionately high and most violent crime is intraethnic, but this does not dissuade the news media from contributing to the belief that young men from ethnic minorities constitute a physical threat to members of ethnic majorities, to whom they are represented as a symbol of fear.

Next to street crime in importance is drug taking, especially associated with African-Americans in the USA and Afro-Caribbeans in the United Kingdom. The emphasis is on any violent event which can be related to drug gangs. Individual drug takers are less likely to be seen as victims of their habit than as resorting to crime in order to support it. That members of ethnic majorities may take and deal in drugs as frequently as ethnic majorities is largely ignored in favor of depicting drugs as an ethnic minority issue.

Violent crime and the drug problem are only two manifestations of the general problem of law and order associated with ethnic minorities. Coverage of political demonstrations by ethnic minorities is generally commensurate with the level of conflict and violence, especially with the police. Such demonstrations are ignored when they are peaceful and reported solely in terms of violence when they are not. Often there is an implication that political activity is only a cover for the real objectives, to attack people, property, and the police.

Coverage of urban unrest in the USA and the United Kingdom demonstrates most of these characteristics. The immediate trigger for such disturbances or their long-term economic and social causes are generally marginalized in order to emphasize damage to property, injuries to police, and the helplessness of innocent victims, all of which are more newsworthy and photogenic than long-standing grievances over equal opportunities or relations with the police, as the following attests to:

> The media report and write from the standpoint of a white man's world. The ills of the ghetto, the difficulties of life there, the Negro's burning sense of grievance, are seldom conveyed. Slights and indignities are part of the Negro's daily life, and many of them come from what he now calls "the white man's press"—a press that repeatedly, if unconsciously, reflects the biases, the paternalism, the indifference of white America. (National Advisory Commission on Civil Disorders, 1968. *Report of the National Advisory Commission on Civil Disorders,* p. 366. U.S. Government, Washington, DC)

Attributions of motive are simplified into mob mentalities, criminal tendencies, and opportunistic vandalism. Rather than as a desperate form of social protest, urban unrest is seen as primarily a problem of law and order, the solution to which is to restore order on the streets and apprehend as many of the culprits as possible.

More than any other of the major news issues in relation to ethnic minorities, that of law and order seems to be racialized. It is black youth, rather than those from Asian or other ethnic minority groups, who are associated with crime and disorder. The victims of such crime are presented as members of the ethnic majority or other law-abiding ethnic minorities. This has been found to be so of African-Americans in the USA, Afro-

Caribbeans in the United Kingdom, Surinamese in the Netherlands, and aborigines in Australia.

3. Welfare and Social Problems

Ethnic minorities are generally portrayed less in terms of what they put into society than what they are seen to be taking out. Ethnic minorities are seen as troublesome, causing or exacerbating social problems which require public expenditure in such areas as social security, housing, and education. Whether or why their needs might be greater than those of the majority population are rarely considered. The implication, sometimes made explicit in media editorials, is that ethnic minorities are being accorded special privileges not available to the majority population who nevertheless have to pay for them through taxation. These trends appear regardless of the type of welfare system.

4. Politics

All the issues reviewed so far have direct implications for political leaders. The media are therefore likely to reproduce the pronouncements of ethnic majority leaders who, almost inevitably, call for measures to control immigration, crime, and welfare expenditure. Crucial for any kind of balance is the extent to which such views are challenged by other political views, especially those of ethnic minority leaders. Evidence suggests that ethnic minority interests are more likely to be represented by "liberal" members and groups from within the majority community than by their own leaders. Even when represented, such leaders are likely to be the subject of hostile questioning or investigation into their alleged links with "extremist" groups or statements. Thus ethnic minority leaders' experience of the mass media is that they are likely to be marginalized, required to respond to an agenda set by the ethnic majority or liable to be dismissed as extremists. This pattern is reproduced in all democratic societies so far studied.

5. Ethnic Minorities as Victims

It has thus been demonstrated that ethnic minorities appear in the news as and when their existence and presence is seen to create a problem for the ethnic majority. The question then arises as to how the media cover those issues where the ethnic majority constitutes a problem for the ethnic minority. About these the media are reticent. Discrimination receives some minimal coverage but is regarded as caused by a few prejudiced individuals. The possibility that discrimination is a pervasive and persistent ethnic minority experience is rarely addressed by the news agenda. Even its most

extreme manifestation, violence against ethnic minorities by members of the ethnic majority, is habitually underrepresented. Ethnic majority members are much more likely than ethnic minority members to commit acts of racial violence, but only rarely are such events recognized as news. The prevailing image is one of the ethnic majority as the victims of ethnic minorities; the reverse is rarely considered.

The general pattern of social disadvantage experienced by ethnic minorities is not a central news issue. That such groups live in the worst housing, go to the worst schools, and receive the worst treatment by the police and other public services remain peripheral. Even the attempts to remedy this situation, known variously as equal opportunity policies or affirmative action programs, are now regarded by the media with suspicion. A news story is more likely to occur when a member of the ethnic majority is denied access to a resource as a result of such programs than when an ethnic minority member demonstrates their benefit.

6. Summary

Wilson and Guttierez hypothesized five stages in the press representation of ethnic minorities: excluded, threatening, confrontational, stereotyped, and accepted (C. C. Wilson and F. Gutierrez, 1995. *Race, Multiculturalism and the Media.* Sage, London and Thousand Oaks, CA). Evidence supports the pervasive presence of the first four, and a general absence of the fifth, in contemporary news media coverage.

B. Media Entertainment: Television

Television entertainment is more complex to analyze than news. We are dealing here with programs which set out to entertain rather than inform, with no obligation to be balanced or impartial, and which incorporate a whole range of genres: situation comedies, soaps and drama, and game and chat shows. It is less easy to ask straightforward questions about the content or meaning of such entertainment forms.

With the exception of some Australian work, almost all the evidence about the representation of ethnic minorities in media entertainment comes from the USA. The generalizability of its findings cannot therefore be guaranteed, though the export of American programs across the world means they are a universal source of ethnic minority imagery.

1. African-Americans on U.S. Television

Greenberg and Brand have summarized quantitative research findings about ethnic minorities in U.S. prime-time television in the 1980s (B. S. Greenberg and J. E. Brand, 1994. In *Media Effects* (J. Bryant and D. Zillmann, Eds.), pp. 273–314. Erlbaum, Hillsdale, NJ). Of every 100 prime-time characters, African-Americans constituted no more than 8 and other minorities together 4. African-American females were much less prominent than males, and females from other ethnic minorities were virtually absent. Analysis of the roles they played or performed indicated that they were nearly always peripheral or subordinate to ethnic majority performers and in positions of low social status. Inter-ethnic relations were generally formal and work-related rather than informal or sociable. The overall conclusion was that ethnic minority members on television appeared to be apart or separate from ethnic majority members, even when they appeared together.

There is some agreement that African-Americans now appear more frequently in television entertainment but that this quantitative gain does necessarily imply qualitative improvement. Game and talk shows that involve the audience appear to be the only genres where ethnic minorities appear on television as frequently as they do in the population at large. They are rarely central in soap opera and drama serials, except those located in a work setting, such as hospitals and police stations, where ethnic presence seems to be more easily accommodated.

2. African-Americans in Situation Comedies

The genre in which African-Americans appear to have achieved the most prominence is situation comedy, even though some of the most popular and frequently exported situation comedies of the mid-1990s largely exclude an ethnic minority presence. Prominence in situation comedies is double-edged: though it invites identification with black characters, it may also draw on established stereotypes of African-Americans as comic figures. Further complexity arises from the fact that situation comedies stand or fall by their ability to make the (largely ethnic majority) audience laugh. Accurate representation of ethnic identity is secondary to this overriding objective.

The debate about the terms on which African-Americans can succeed in U.S. prime-time television is encapsulated in the arguments about the phenomenal success—not least with minority audiences—of the all-black situation comedy "The Cosby Show." On no other program has the "burden of representation" fallen so heavily.

On the one hand, critics of the show argue that it is a misrepresentation of African-American experience. In their professional jobs and affluent lifestyle, the Huxtables are atypical. Despite its internal conflicts, the Huxtable family is basically harmonious, its teenagers immune to the temptations of sex or drugs. Though there is a positive identification with black culture, the Huxtables never experience personal or institutional racism. This is a black family sanitized for the consumption of a white audience.

On the other hand, the show is viewed as positive in several senses. First, it demonstrates, not least to a white audience, that African-Americans are not necessarily welfare dependents or living in dysfunctional families. Second, it normalizes blackness, since the audience is invited to laugh at recognizable universal human situations. Third, and as a consequence, it demonstrates that African-Americans can appear on prime-time television without inhabiting the stereotypical roles to which they might otherwise be allocated.

These two views are not wholly incompatible. It is possible to argue that the show simultaneously reveals the extent to which African-Americans can penetrate entertainment television and the conditions which have to be met for that incursion to be acceptable. Similar arguments can be applied to the most prominent Afro-Caribbean star on British television, Lenny Henry, who has an unrivaled capacity to raise questions of ethnic difference while ridiculing them through laughter.

3. Ethnic Minorities on Australian and British Television

Evidence from Australia suggests that entertainment forms tend to exclude ethnic minority performers. Successfully exported soap operas deny or marginalize the existence of aborigines. Asians and Pacific peoples appear to occupy the same position as Hispanics in the USA, being largely absent from entertainment television. Other than the occasional situation comedy, European ethnic minorities, such as Greeks or Italians, appear infrequently. Their only contribution to the Australian way of life seems to be culinary.

In the United Kingdom, Afro-Caribbeans have appeared as hosts of game and entertainment programs, though systematic evidence is lacking. Some of the most popular soaps habitually feature ethnic minority characters, issues of racism being neither exaggerated nor ignored. However, the Asian ethnic minority appears much less frequently, and other groups, such as Africans, hardly at all.

4. Summary

Television entertainment features ethnic minorities even less than the news. Only African-Americans in the USA and Afro-Caribbeans in the United Kingdom appear with any frequency. Even then, they are restricted to particular genres, such as occupational soaps or situation comedies. It would appear that ethnic majorities wish to be entertained largely by members of their own group and will tolerate ethnic minorities only under very restrictive conditions.

C. Media Entertainment: Films

Analysis of the representation of ethnic minorities in film has largely concentrated on Hollywood, given its domination of the international market. The recycling of films on television means that past representations are still readily available in the present and cannot simply be consigned to history. Findings are complex to summarize since research tends, in the tradition of film criticism, to involve very detailed textual analysis of films taken to be exemplars of particular traditions or viewpoints.

1. The Native American Indian

The ethnic minority to have been most misrepresented by Hollywood is the Native American Indian. There has been a move away from the stereotypes of Indians as ignoble savages which disfigured the Western genre in the past. Yet, even as Hollywood has apparently moved to a more sympathetic view, there are still evident tendencies toward historical and cultural inaccuracies, a preference for white stars to play Indian heroes, or for the whole issue to be seen from a white point of view. For example, the film *Dances with Wolves* self-consciously sets out to tell the story of the West from the Indian point of view, inviting the audience to invert its usual ethnic sympathies. The Indian way of life is represented as palpably more civilized than that of the white invaders. Yet the whole narrative is structured around the dilemmas of the white hero, Kevin Costner, with whom we are asked to identify. Thus, even where white people rather than Indians are portrayed as destructive, intrusive, and uncivilized, it is a white point of view on which the film hinges.

2. African-Americans

In Hollywood's portrayal of African-Americans, there are still traces of what have been identified as the five main stereotypes of the African-American, all of which ensured African-Americans a manageable and predictable place in the white world of Hollywood.

In *Toms, Coons, Mulattoes, Mammies and Bucks* (1989, New York, Continuum) Donald Bogle surveys representations of Blacks in Hollywood cinema, especially emphasizing the unequal struggle between Black performers and the stereotypical roles offered them by Hollywood. Bogle's very title announces the five major stereotypes:

1. the servile "Tom" (going back to Uncle Tom in *Uncle Tom's Cabin*);
2. the "Coon" (Step'n Fetchit is the archetypal example), a type itself subdivided into the "pickanniny" (the harmless eye-popping clown figure) and the Uncle Remus (naive, congenial folk philosopher);
3. the "Tragic Mulatto," usually a woman, victim of dual racial inheritance, who tries to "pass for White" in films such as *Pinky* and *Imitation of Life;* or else the demonized mulatto man, devious and ambitious, like Silas Lynch in *Birth of a Nation;*
4. the "Mammy," the fat, cantankerous but ultimately sympathetic female servant who provides the glue that keeps households together (the Aunt Jemima "handkerchief head" in one variant) such as Hattie McDaniel in *Gone With the Wind;* and
5. the "Buck," the brutal hypersexualized Black man, a figure of menace, inherited from the stage, whose most famous filmic incarnation is perhaps Gus in *Birth of a Nation.*

(E. Shohat and R. Stam, 1994. *Unthinking Eurocentrism: Multiculturalism and the Mass Media*, p. 195. Routledge, London/New York.

As in television, African-Americans appear to have moved from the periphery to the center of the action, with some commercially successful films featuring black heroes and even predominantly black casts. Some black directors, such as Spike Lee, have even managed to produce successful films which address in popular form the experiences and dilemmas of the black community.

However, it has been argued that more typically black characters achieve filmic prominence in roles which are assigned to blackness. They are subordinate to narratives and situations defined by the majority culture. The association of African-Americans with crime, for example, is given a new twist but not ruptured if an African-American is not the criminal but the cop, especially if he operates in an uneasy alliance with a white partner. Such black characters, it is argued, live on the edge, always on the verge of transgressing the rules they are supposed to uphold. Thus even where the ethnic blackness of the character is emphasized–in language, bodily posture, dress, and cultural affiliation—his presence in the white world is conditional upon acceptance of the white terms in which the film world is cast. Even such minimal gains have not been enjoyed by female black stars and roles. The most prominent female actors are those who have already achieved prominence as comics, singers, or even models, thus ensuring their acceptability to the largely white audience.

3. Appropriating Ethnic Minority Cultures

While black characters remain peripheral, Hollywood has appropriated aspects of ethnic minority cultures and histories in order to reproduce them through white eyes. Musicals invariably pull on African-American and Hispanic traditions but their stars and settings are invariably white. Black historical struggles, such as the 1960s civil rights movement, are seen through the eyes of white liberals struggling with their consciences with mass black activism as a backcloth. The multiethnic tradition of American culture and history is distorted so that the prime movers are portrayed to be white.

4. Other Ethnic Minorities

Other ethnic minorities fare no better. Latino peoples are represented through another series of stereotypes: bandido, greaser, revolutionary, or bullfighter. Almost all appear in films set in the past; the contemporary experience of this group remains unrepresented. Of Koreans, Chinese, and Japanese, there is no sign, except in the displaced form of the enemy in films about the Vietnam war. The one exception appears to be the Jewish minority, where representation by Hollywood has been at once low-key and careful, attributed to the considerable Jewish influence over development of the film industry.

5. Summary

The evidence to support any generalizations about Hollywood's representation of ethnic minorities is necessarily soft and interpretative rather than hard and factual. Yet the weight of evidence suggests that, as in other media, the film industry finds it difficult to represent ethnic minorities in terms other than those derived from the ethnic majority. It would appear that Hollywood has largely failed to acknowledge the multiethnic nature of the society in which it operates or even of the audiences to which it appeals. The experience of ethnicity is refracted through the lens of the white ethnic majority.

D. Other Media Content

1. Advertising

The purpose of television advertising is to market goods and services to a mass consumer market. Where, as is often the case, ethnic minorities lack significant spending power, we might expect commercials to be directed at the ethnic majority and consequently use the images they find most salient. Greenberg and Brand (1994) have summarized relevant research, mainly on U.S. television commercials in the mid-1980s. African-Americans appeared in less than 20% of commercials, and only 2% featured blacks alone. Though recent data

are lacking, the suggestion is that African-Americans appear more as background than foreground and rarely interact with whites. Also remaining to be updated are data from the 1970s suggesting that African-Americans in commercials were more passive than whites, were less likely to initiate activity, and lacked command over space or technology.

The increasing consumer power of African-Americans and their prominence as sports and music stars with marketing potential may have recently increased their visibility and status in U.S. television commercials but we cannot be sure. Other ethnic minorities, especially Hispanics, are largely absent from television commercials, outside their own cable and satellite stations.

Australian television commercials appear to be even less likely than their U.S. counterparts to reflect multiculturalist ideals, with the exception that the art and music of aborigines may be used in a mythologized form to evoke the spiritual inheritance of Australia. Much of prime-time television advertising is more concerned with conveying an idealized image of the white Australian family with a blonde mother as the key figure. Little research has been conducted in the United Kingdom, but a useful hypothesis would be the replication of the U.S. case, with the slow emergence of Afro-Caribbeans in largely minor roles outside sport and music but the almost total absence of any Asian or other ethnic minorities.

Overall, in their general exclusion or marginalization of ethnic minorities, television commercials would appear to offer images of ethnic minorities even less developed than those in the news and entertainment programs in which they are inserted, certainly in the United States and Australia, probably in the United Kingdom and possibly elsewhere.

2. Children's Television

Demographic trends, educational objectives, and ethnic minority children as a commercial market might be thought to encourage greater ethnic diversity on children's television. Evidence suggests that this is generally not the case. Greenberg and Brand's 1994 summary of relevant U.S. research suggests that only African-American males are marginally more evident on children's than adult television. African-American females, Hispanics, Asians, and other ethnic minorities are virtually absent. Black characters are peripheral rather than central and segregated from white characters so that there is little interethnic interaction. The staple diet of U.S. children's television, cartoons, are considered to be less representative than other types of programs and more likely to contain ethnic minority stereotypes. Advertisements showed more evidence of ethnic diversity, especially in homilies from large food corporations, but girls, Hispanics, and Asians remained underrepresented. The most consistently high-profile and positive images of ethnic minorities occurred in public service programs, where as many as a quarter of all characters were from ethnic minorities.

The importation from the United States of children's programs has led to an increase in the portrayal of ethnic minorities on Australian children's television, but its own ethnic minorities. Asians, aborigines, and Pacific children, remain largely invisible. There is little systematic evidence from the United Kingdom, but Asians are again conspicuous by their absence, despite the prominence of Afro-Caribbeans as children's television presenters.

In an extensive analysis of mainly U.S. imported cartoons, Jakubowicz *et al.* traced a greater diversity of ethnic minority characters who nevertheless occupied marginal roles (1994. *Racism, Ethnicity and the Media.* Allen & Unwin, New South Wales, Australia). Heroic figures were mainly white or occasionally African-American; other ethnic minorities were hardly represented at all, and stereotypes of other cultures appeared in portrayals of foreign lands.

The increasingly global dependence on U.S. children's programs, especially on cable and satellite channels, and the weakness of public service broadcasting cancel out demographic trends so that children's television reproduces the same bias toward ethnic majorities to be found in adult television.

3. Sports

For complex reasons, African-Americans in the United States and Afro-Caribbeans in the United Kingdom are significantly overrepresented as top-level performers in major spectator and televised sports: track and field in both countries, football and basketball in the United States, and soccer in the United Kingdom. Any definition of news or entertainment that excludes sports will thus omit an arena where the achievements of at least one ethnic minority would ensure their prominence in media coverage. This would be no guarantee against stereotyping, since natural athleticism is established as a white view of the black "race." Sport constitutes a useful case study of whether evidence of ethnic minority achievement challenges media stereotypes.

Studies in the 1970s and 1980s, mainly of football and basketball television coverage in the USA, suggested that positive images of African-Americans as athletes were heavily qualified by the white structures of authority, promotion, and audiences into which they were inserted. It was also suggested that mainly white commentators tended to be more disparaging of black than white athletes. The more recent introduction of black coaches and commentators may have modified this bias, though evidence to test this assumption appears to be lacking. Nor are there any substantial studies of the way ethnic minorities in sports are represented in the press or specialized sports magazines. Also unanswered are questions about female ethnic minority sports stars, whose representation may well be doubly skewed by both ethnicity and gender.

Often qualified and subject to stereotyping, the continuing achievements of black people in sports, and their consequent marketing potential, seem likely to act as a positive counterbalance to negative stereotyping elsewhere in the media. It may be of marginal economic and political significance, but its symbolic impact, for both majority and minority communities, may be substantial.

4. Popular Music

Popular music is another area where academic categories may exclude an important sphere of ethnic minority achievement. Music channels, background music on television advertisements, and the music press may include potentially positive representations. There may still be tendencies toward exclusion, such as MTV's initial resistance to black performers or hostility toward the ethnic assertiveness of "gangsta" rap. The stereotype that African peoples are naturally rhythmic may also be drawn upon.

Yet popular music provides evidence of ethnic minority success and even of control, since, almost uniquely, pop videos are a media form where black performers are in charge of their own projected images. The ubiquitous presence in popular music of African-Americans in the United States and Afro-Caribbeans in the United Kingdom has not been adequately studied. This is ironic, since along with sports, music may be the source of much imagery of ethnic minorities among both majority and minority populations, especially the young.

IV. KEY ANSWERS

We can now consider the answers provided by the evidence to the questions posed in Section II.

A. Inclusion versus Exclusion

Many ethnic minorities—Hispanics in the USA, Asians in the United Kingdom, aborigines in Australia—are largely excluded from media representation. The main exception is where they appear in the news as troublesome. Othewise—in television entertainment, in films, in adverts, and even on children's television—they appear hardly at all. African-Americans are more likely to appear in media entertainment but only in the restricted roles of comedians or marginal characters. It is unclear how far this is counterbalanced by their prominence in the sports and music programs. Overall we find, dependent on the ethnic minority, the medium, and the country, a range of representations, from outright exclusion to minimal and conditional inclusion. What we do not find is any evidence of inclusion which is quantitatively and qualitatively equal to that of the ethnic majority.

B. Accuracy versus Distortion

In the news, it has been found that basic facts about ethnic minorities, such as immigration or crime figures, are distorted or glossed over. News events are constructed through the views of white authority while there is little attempt to portray the daily experience of ethnic minorities, especially of discrimination. In the entertainment media, their cultural heritage is inaccurately portrayed and history rewritten to favor the ethnic majority. Whether focusing on an individual event, a social trend, or an historical image, the media generally appear unable to represent the presence of ethnic minorities with any degree of accuracy.

C. Sensitive Understanding versus Rigid Stereotyping

As a compressed form of communication, the media are apt to resort to stereotypes. Media news coverage of ethnic minorities is replete with such images: the illegal immigrant, the street criminal, and the welfare scrounger. Slightly different stereotypes appear in the entertainment media, where differences of accent and lifestyle are the sources of comedy or tension. Where desirable images of social life are being conveyed, as in advertising, ethnic minorities are never central. Even children's television, with the exception of public service broadcasting, fails to reflect the realities of multiethnic communities. Those members of ethnic minorities who achieve public prominence as politicians, broadcasters, athletes, or musicians may escape the stereotypes, but they can also be used to perpetuate them. What seems difficult is for the media to accept ethnicity as one of many diversities of identity which can be recognized without resorting to stereotypical images.

D. Multiculturalism versus Assimilation

There seems little doubt that the media do acknowledge the cultural variety produced by the presence of ethnic minorities but do not appear to value it. The ultimate test comes when the media represent "The Nation" and its way of life. Whether such national images appear in feature films, soaps, or advertisements, ethnic minorities are invariably marginalized or excluded. The least-included groups are those whose way of life cannot easily be assimilated by that of the ethnic majority. It is no accident that Asians are frequently the most excluded group. Adherence to their own languages, religions, food, dress, and kinship systems daily present their otherness to the ethnic majority. Where such variety cannot be accommodated in the representation of "The Nation," then we may conclude that multiculturalist ideals are absent and that assimilation is the implicit model of the integration of ethnic minorities into society.

E. Summary

The evidence suggests that there is an overall pattern to media representations of ethnic minorities. It is one which tends toward their outright exclusion or highly conditional inclusion, to distorted rather than accurate depiction of their lives, to interpretations in terms of rigid stereotypes rather than sensitive understanding, and to underlying ideals which are assimilationist rather than multiculturalist. Some news or entertainment programs, some films or advertisements, and some music or sports channels may be partly exempt from such a judgment. (For a review of some examples from European television see C. Frachon and M. Vargaftig, Eds., 1995. *European Television: Immigrants and Ethnic Minorities*. Libbey, London). However, for the vast majority of media output in all the nations where there has been systematic study, these tendencies have been found to be consistent. We now consider why these have come to be the predominant patterns of media representation of ethnic minorities.

V. EXPLAINING MEDIA REPRESENTATIONS

There is substantial agreement about the main explanations for the nature of ethnic minority representation in the media, though scholars differ about which explanations should be given most weight. Here we look at five possible explanations, working from the most concrete to the most abstract kind of explanation.

A. Media Ownership

The media are major economic institutions, the source of much commercial profit and cultural power. It is thus not surprising that they tend to be owned and controlled by members of majority ethnic groups, who directly or indirectly decide the view of the world which the media convey. This is argued to lead to negative views of ethnic minority groups for two reasons. Firstly, the owners share the cultural perspective of the majority group, which is likely to be hostile or indifferent to the presence and needs of ethnic minority groups. Secondly, such owners are likely to have a heavy investment in society as it is, so are unsympathetic to the reforms which ethnic minorities and their allies may be demanding.

Paper pays for racial bias

Martin Wainwright

A newspaper group is to apologise and pay £13,000 to a black woman who was warned in an interview that she would need to accept phrases like "black bastard" as typical office banter if she was given a job.

Claudia Baptiste, aged 28, who was described as an excellent candidate by the Telegraph and Argus in Bradford, failed to get either of two advertising jobs after saying that she found such language offensive and unacceptable.

A three-man industrial tribunal in Leeds ruled unanimously that the evening newspaper, which last year won a Race in the Media award for its coverage of the city's riots, had discriminated racially against Ms Baptiste. The chairman, John Prophet, said that the episode had been "totally unacceptable". Although the interviewer, advertising manager Jane Holt, has subsequently been promoted, Bradford and District newspapers managing director Tim Blott said she had been disciplined.

The Telegraph and Argus, which serves an area with a large ethnic population, also agreed to give all staff a written warning within two weeks that racially offensive comments would result in disciplinary action, including dismissal.

Ms Baptiste said after the ruling: "Anyone who has suffered from racial discrimination should come forward and protest. No one should accept it." (The Guardian, London and Manchester, UK, October 10, 1996.)

B. Media Staffing

Surveys confirm the impression that ethnic minorities are underrepresented in media personnel. They are particularly excluded from higher levels of management. Apart from their functions in sports and entertainment, they are also conspicuous by their absence as media performers. The media appear to reproduce the patterns of exclusion and discrimination which ethnic minorities experience in other areas of employment.

As in other institutions such as the police, staff drawn almost wholly from the ethnic majority are likely to reinforce each others' prejudices and misconceptions about ethnic minorities. They neither encounter nor have to allow for the views of those from other groups. Even where ethnic minority members do join media staff, they often find themselves regarded as accountable for and experts on the activities of ethnic minorities, and are expected to cover or produce any story or pro-

gram with an ethnic minority slant. This restricts the scope of their activity and career advancement. They are effectively treated first and foremost as members or representatives of their ethnic group, rather than as media staff on an equal footing with their ethnic majority counterparts.

By excluding, marginalizing, and occupationally stereotyping their ethnic minority staff, media institutions often reproduce the same patterns of discrimination in employment to be found in society at large. It may not be surprising if they find it difficult to admit to the pervasiveness of discrimination when they themselves practice it.

C. Professional Practices

This explanation looks at how the media operate, regardless of the ethnic composition of its personnel or ownership. The emphasis is on occupational routines and practices regarded as professionally acceptable which nevertheless militate against adequate representations of ethnic minorities. Such professional practices are to be found across the range of media. In television, the expected formula for a situation comedy may imply that any tensions between characters, such as those arising from ethnicity, should be defused rather than left unresolved. In popular cinema, the expectation that the major protagonists should be male, preferably white, and certainly an adherent of dominant cultural values may implicitly marginalize ethnic minority characters.

The most documented example of professional practices having an observable effect on the representation of ethnic minorities is news coverage on any medium. A set of expectations about what the news is or should be like have been identified: the kinds of people and events who make the news. Less formal prescriptions than a working set of assumptions common among media professionals, such news values contain a set of attributes which any event must possess in order for it to become headline news.

A simple example is that a major news value is negativity. The more negative an event is, the more likely it is, all other things being equal, to become news. Studies consistently find that the news conveys a negative portrait of ethnic minorities, emphasizing their involvement in or presentation of problems, especially around urban unrest, crime, and welfare issues. A conspiracy against ethnic minorities need not be posited to explain this tendency. It is simply how all news works. There is always more bad than good news. To that extent, media representations of ethnic minorities in the news may only be following the implicit rules they follow for all news selection and presentation.

Once selected, news events have to be constructed into a story. They have to be assembled in terms which make sense to the audience: a sequence of events, some notion of cause and effect, and commentary from eye-witnesses and responsible authorities. Here the media tend to rely on official sources of evidence or to give more authority to their views, regardless of the kind of event. When the event relates to ethnic minorities, for example any event involving relations between the police and ethnic minorities, then we may find an in-built bias toward the police version of events. This is the normal procedure of news making: the police belong to that category of official institutions who are perceived as the source of knowledgeable and authoritative statements. Any group which is critical of the police will find itself disadvantaged whenever it seeks to challenge the police version of an event or an issue. This is an integral part of news making; it is not specific to ethnic minorities and reflects the general distribution of power in society.

There are many other aspects of the news-making process which operate in this way. They affect such media practices as headlines, photographs, and who gets quoted in what order. They are not designed to disadvantage ethnic minorities in particular, and it may not be necessary to attribute them to ethnic bias. They are simply the outcome of the application of established routines of news making.

D. Audience Maximization

All media are involved in a constant effort to maximize their audience because their major sources of profit are advertising, sponsorship, and consumer subscriptions. The bigger (or sometimes more affluent) the audience, the greater the profits. The equation is simple. Maximization of audiences requires reaching as many consumers as possible. Since the ethnic majority is by definition the largest and generally the most affluent group, the media will initially look to them for its source of custom. Penetration of the ethnic minority audience may be a bonus but is not a necessity.

The media are thus driven to present the kinds of factual and fictional material they believe will appeal to the majority of their potential audience. This requires news coverage of the kinds of events and people the audience recognize and fictions which speak to their experience. Their view of what is expected and unexpected, normal and deviant, and who are "us" and who are "them" becomes part of the routine of making sense of factual and fictional material. Without it, media output would not make sense to its audience. Hence the media are drawn to the view of the majority group because they constitute most of the audience. It may also be assumed that the majority group expects to be addressed in the media, especially on the television screen, by members of their own group, from whom they also expect their fictional heroes to be recruited.

The media's orientation to their audiences, advertisers, and sponsors tends to make them reluctant to try anything or anyone which would breech the audience's expectations. They perceive the audience to want what it already knows and likes. Ethnic minority members may be acceptable in particular niches, such as comedy, sport, music, or even cookery, but otherwise they are not expected to feature prominently in the media. The few exceptions—ethnic minority performers whose success attracts attention—prove the rule.

All these commercial imperatives impel the media to reproduce the ideas and prejudices of the ethnic majority. As long as ethnic minorities remain an insignificant proportion of viewers, listeners, or readers they will not be seen as a viable media market.

E. Ideologies and Belief Systems

The final explanation moves into a different terrain of argument, moving beyond the detail of media institutions. It argues that the media, whether factual or fictional, are engaged in a process of sense making. In order to understand the news story, situation comedy, or Hollywood feature film, the audience must be presented with a framework of reference which it understands.

Any representation of ethnic minorities will therefore be located in the common understandings of producers and audiences about the nature of ethnic relations. This is indivisible from what is regarded as a crucial ideological function of the media, to demarcate the boundaries of society—to specify "us," who belong to the society and identify with its values and respect its institutions, as compared with "them," who do not really belong, since they seek to undermine society's values and institutions. This makes it difficult for ethnic minorities to avoid being defined as "them." If they demand change, or if they want their values, such as religion, to be enshrined in institutions such as the education system, then they may be seen as trying to redraw the boundaries of membership in society.

Moreover, in its sense of who belongs and who does not, the media will draw on a set of sedimented ideas about groups derived from selective views of history and geography. Ethnic minorities in the West, for example, may be seen as belonging to groups or hailing from parts of the world which have yet to reach the "civilized" level of the West. Their strangeness of religion, language, dress, etc., are regarded as markers of their being both different and inferior. They will become accepted only insofar as they abandon the markers of their ethnicity and adopt the ways of ethnic majority. Even then, they may not be fully accepted if they remain visibly different in terms of "race."

The media's treatment of ethnic minorities cannot, in this view, be divorced from their ideological presuppositions about ethnicity and race which invariably cast the ethnic majority as possessing the most advanced culture to which others are by definition inferior. To an extent, such tendencies work independently of, though they may be reinforced by, other forms of explanation. Changes in media ownership, staffing, professional practices, or audience maximization would not necessarily alter the ideological function of the media. From this point of view, the debate over media representations of ethnic minorities is only part of a wider struggle over ideological domination, which is regarded as in its own way as important as political and economic inequalities.

VI. PROSPECTS FOR REFORM

Each of the explanations of the way the media represent ethnic minorities points to possible remedies for the situation.

A. Media Ownership

The need here is for greater diversity in the ownership of the media to include ethnic minority members or at least those sympathetic to their cause. This is very difficult, since there is a global trend toward the domination of media ownership by large corporations. Governments are generally and increasingly resistant to the regulation of media ownership, other than preventing extreme monopolies. There is thus little prospect for change in the ownership of the press or mainstream television stations, though there is some room for maneuvering on the margins. The franchising of local radio stations may involve a commitment to community broadcasting and a persuasive case can be made for the appropriateness of ethnic minority ownership. New television stations can be designed to represent minority interests not catered for by the mainstream media and ethnic minorities are one such interest. The remit of the Special Broadcasting Service in Australia is one example.

> The Special Broadcasting Service's mission is to contribute to a more cohesive, equitable and harmonious Australian society by providing an innovative and quality multilingual radio and television service which depicts the diverse reality of Australia's multicultural society and meets the needs of Australians of all origins and backgrounds. (Jakubowicz, 1994, 144)

A more enduring one, if only because of its profitability, is Channel Four in the United Kingdom, whose commitment to experimental and minority broadcasting has

given airtime to new kinds of perspectives, including those from within the minority communities.

B. Media Staffing

Prospects for reform here are potentially greater, provided an ethical commitment is forthcoming from media owners and management. The clear underrepresentation of ethnic minorities in virtually all parts of the media industry can be remedied by the application of equal opportunity policies and even some positive discrimination. The BBC in the United Kingdom, for example, has a specialist training program for ethnic minority recruits, and some college training courses openly or tacitly seek to attract ethnic minority students. As important is the need to raise awareness of the issues amongst ethnic majority staff. Journalistic and broadcasting training would benefit from consideration of ethical issues of reporting in a multiethnic society. The current backlash against equal opportunity policies does not give rise to optimism, but it is still possible to question the extent and causes of the apparent lack of ethnic representativeness among media employees.

C. Professional Practices

This area is very resistant to change, since the demand seems to be to reform the very nature of media practices governing the production of news reports, advertising messages, television series, or feature films. The most to be hoped for is the institution of codes of practice to govern professional conduct, such as that of the National Union of Journalists in the United Kingdom. In theory it ought to be possible to extend codes which currently govern the representation of violence and sex to that of ethnicity. The signs are not particularly encouraging, since there is much resistance on the grounds of media freedom. Where there has been change, as in Hollywood's representation of native American Indians, the main cause has been a shift in cultural attitudes outside the media. All that can be done is to draw attention to the worst kinds of abuse in media representation and their relationship to professional practices.

D. Audience Maximization

There are some positive trends here, rooted in the changing economics of the media industries. Especially in broadcasting, the multiplicity of channels means that a viable audience is now much smaller, a trend reinforced by some advertisers' preference for niche rather than mass marketing. Combined with any minimal improvement in the consumer power of one or more ethnic minorities, it means that they can emerge as viable audiences, an example being the proliferation of Spanish stations on cable television in the United States. Paradoxically, the competition for audiences can equally produce a lesser willingness to depart from established formats for fear of losing the audience. While media outlets may emerge which address ethnic minorities as consumers and thus avoid ethnic stereotypes, such representations may not reach the ethnic majority who watch or listen to their own stations. Talk radio in the USA and Australia has a tarnished reputation for giving vent to virulent prejudice against ethnic minorities, often endorsed by host broadcasters. What is known as the fragmentation of the media broadcasting audience may simply mean an increase in the ethnic exclusivity of individual outlets.

E. Ideologies and Belief Systems

These are quite clearly the most resistant to change, though this is not to say that they remain static. In the USA, the United Kingdom, and Australia biologically based theories of racial superiority have become less and less tenable and have been displaced by ideas which stress cultural difference rather than biological inferiority as the basis for ethnic incompatibility. The media are quite clearly one of the important articulators of changes in perceptions of ethnic minorities. There is always room to reveal the inconsistencies within the media, where news coverage or entertainment material is at variance with a media organization's avowed commitment to interethnic harmony. Yet in other ways the media may be seen as a symptom rather than a cause of ethnic ideologies and their reform only one aspect of a wider ideological struggle.

F. Social Change

It has been argued that trends outside the media will bring about change in media representations of ethnic minorities. In discussing the situation in the USA, for example, various commentators have stressed the importance of demographic and economic change. It is possible that early in the 21st century, ethnic minorities may constitute a majority of the U.S. population. In such a context, it may no longer be viable to assume that the media should continue to largely address what was the ethnic majority. At the same time, the emergence of a middle class, especially among African-Americans, will provide an economic incentive to address this audience in terms it appreciates. The fragmentation of the media audience into segments induced by the expansion of channels will further enhance the viability of ethnic minority niche markets.

It remains to be seen whether these changes, still at an embryonic stage, will bring in their wake radical changes in the ways the media represent ethnic minorities. Evidence about local media in U.S. cities where ethnic minorities are already numerically significant does not suggest that such changes will necessarily be rapid or far-reaching. It may be significant that some of the most often cited harbingers of change come from outside the media and are expected to induce reforms by the media following their own established commercial logic rather than from any changes in that logic itself.

VII. CONCLUSION: THE ETHICS OF ETHNICITY

Media representation of ethnic minorities is an ethical issue with public, political, and professional dimensions. For the public, it is an issue of what kind of society we believe we are or wish to be members of. Is it a society which seeks to convert its ethnic minorities to the ways of the ethnic majority, to assimilate them? Or is it one which can tolerate and even welcome a diversity of skin colors, languages, religious practices, kinship structures, dress, and diet, the position of multiculturalism? This issue is directly connected to our conception of citizenship: who is regarded as a member of society and what rights, including the right to accurate media representation, such membership entails.

The second dimension is political, especially the formulation of media policy. There appears to be a reluctance to require the mass media to give equality of representation to ethnic minorities or even to provide an effective means of redress where members of ethnic minorities feel they have been misrepresented. The issue is largely left to the consciences and professional codes of media communicators.

In the third dimension, professional ethics, the issue of representing ethnic minorities does not seem a pressing one. With a few honorable exceptions, media owners, managers, and practitioners have not seen the treatment of ethnic minorities as central to their codes of professional ethics. Such strategically placed individuals have somehow suppressed their professional responsibility for the quality of relationships between ethnic groups. While they may as individuals be genuinely appalled at the ethnic hatreds which cause so much violence around the world, they make no connection to their own failure to contribute to interethnic understanding.

The media may be only one influence, but it is an important one, on the state of interethnic relations in any context. Media personnel may only reflect the unthinking attitudes prevalent in their own ethnic group, but their role in society requires them to do more. Media regulators may fear a backlash from the ethnic majority but have responsibilities to the wider multiethnic community. We, as citizens, need to do more to ensure that the media equally represent humankind in all its welcome diversity. The alternative is the perpetuation of the mutual incomprehension of ethnic groups, from which conflict of many different kinds seems bound to follow.

Bibliography

Cottle, S. (1992). Race, racialization and the media. *Sage Race Relations Abstr.* **17**(2), 3–57.

Downing, J., and Husband, C. (1995). Media flows, ethnicity, racism and xenophobia. *Electronic J. Commun.* **5**, 2/3.

Greenberg, B. S., and Brand, J. E. (1994). Minorities and the mass media: 1970s to 1990s. In "Media Effects: Advances in Theory and Research" (J. Bryant and D. Zillman, Eds.), pp. 273–314. Erlbaum, Hillsdale, NJ.

Jakubowicz, A., Goodall, H., Martin, J., Mitchell, T., Randall, L., and Seneviratne, S. (1994). "Racism, Ethnicity, and the Media." Allen & Unwin, New South Wales, Australia.

MacDonald, J. F. (1992). "Blacks and White TV: African Americans in Television Since 1948," 2nd ed. Hall, Chicago.

Shah, E. (1995). Race, nation and news in the United States. *Electronic J. Commun.* **5**, 2/3.

Shohat, E., and Stam, R. (1994). "Unthinking Eurocentrism: Multiculturalism and the Media." Routledge, London/New York.

Van Dijk, T. A. (1991). "Racism and the Press." Routledge, London/New York.

Wilson, C. W., and Gutierrez, F. (1985). "Minorities and Media: Diversity and the End of Mass Communication." Sage, Newbury Park, CA.

Media Ownership

EDWARD JOHNSON

University of New Orleans

GLOSSARY

cyberspace The representational "place" defined by computerized interactions, named by William Gibson in the 1984 science-fiction novel *Neuromancer*.

factoid A piece of unimportant information whose very existence is an artifact of the power to report it (such as some of the excessively arcane statistics sports commentators like to inject into their coverage); a pseudo-fact; meaningless information masquerading as a fact; presumptuous trivia.

media event An event that exists, or has significance, only for the purpose of being represented or reported in the media.

panopticism Life under conditions of absolute subjection to surveillance.

simulacrum A sign that presents itself *as* a sign, while in fact representing nothing (or, sometimes, representing the fact that it represents nothing).

MEDIA OWNERSHIP is shorthand for a number of interconnected problems concerning access to, and control of, communications media. Briefly, critics assert (or deny) the existence of inequality in people's access to mass communi-cations, and discuss how this is (or is not) connected with inequalities of wealth and power.

I. BAGDIKIAN'S RECKONING

About communications media, at the end of the 20th century, three facts are beyond dispute: more media outlets exist, telecommunications is more important, and media ownership is more concentrated than ever before.

These facts are tied to three important changes during the course of the century. The first change has been *technical*. New forms of communication have been developed—telephone, radio, television, photocopy, fax, computer, the Internet, etc.—and have been repeatedly refined. The second change has been *social*. Each new form of communication has defined a new dimension for human interaction and created new possibilities for social relations and novel categories of human interaction. The third change has been *economic*. Because these technical changes involve the transformation of materials, they define new kinds of property. Because these social changes open up avenues of influence, they define new sorts of social control. Who will own this property? How will this control be exercised? When Ben Bagdikian published the first edition of *The Media Monopoly* in 1983, he pointed out that ownership of most of the major media was consolidated in only about 50 corporations. By the time he published the fourth edition in 1992, the number had dropped to 20.

There are more media outlets and fewer media own-

Copyright © 1998 by Academic Press.
All rights of reproduction in any form reserved.

ers, but what impact (if any) does this have on the content or the effects of the media? The Swedish anthropologist Ulf Hannerz, in *Cultural Complexity* (1992), notes that the issue is typically framed along the following lines:

> Will more media power bring us closer to Orwell's 1984 ... if media power keeps cumulatively concentrating in the same hands? Or will a computer literate society make totalitarianism and its knowledge hoarding impossible, as more people can answer back, and as the hackers will always get the secrets in the end?

Howard Rheingold, in *The Virtual Community: Homesteading on the Electronic Frontier* (1993), formulates the issue in terms of similar poles of opposition: the reinvigorated democracy of a kind of "electronic agora" (the ancient Greek marketplace) versus an electronic Panopticon.

The Panopticon, a design by English philosopher Jeremy Bentham (1748–1832) for a building that would permit absolute and unobserved observation of its inmates, was introduced into current discussion by French social theorist Michel Foucault (1926–1984), in *Surveiller et punir* (1975; translated as *Discipline and Punish* in 1977). This book, along with Foucault's other work, has exercised considerable influence on the radical reconceptualization of modern life. According to its subtitle, it is a study of "the birth of the prison," but it is in fact an examination of the formation of the "disciplinary society." A general theme running through Foucault's several studies—of asylum, clinic, prison, language, knowledge, and sexuality—is the ever increasing imposition of socially defined order on the life of the individual. Foucault explored the emergence of discourses which exercised power through their definition of knowledge, and attempted to excavate the suppressed facts about the struggles that had taken place over the imposition of these disciplinary discourses.

The "panopticism" which characterizes modern life establishes a structure of power that is indifferent as to who exercises it. Foucault asked, "Do you think it would be much better to have the prisoners operating the Panoptic apparatus and sitting in the central tower, instead of the guards?" It also makes those who are supervised themselves part of the mechanism, in two senses. They are part of the mechanism, in the first place, because part of the effectiveness of supervision derives from one's awareness of being supervised; one thus becomes the principle of one's own subjection. One is part of the mechanism also in the sense that one can take part in the supervision of others. The Panopticon even "enables everyone to come and observe any of the observers." The Panopticon thus provides a model for the functioning of a society in which "disciplinary mechanisms" have become ubiquitous.

If there is a central political problem about the prison, in Foucault's view, it involves the fact that the "mechanisms of normalization," for which the prison served as incubator, exercise a widespread and increasing influence throughout society. "Is it surprising that prisons resemble factories, schools, barracks, hospitals, which all resemble prisons?" The extension of this framework to electronic media is obvious. Rheingold sees himself as following Foucault in worrying about whether "the machinery of the worldwide communications network constitutes a kind of camouflaged Panopticon (1993)". Similarly, Mark Taylor and Esa Saarinen see the "media philosophy" they propose in *Imagologies* (1994) as an extension of Foucault's "microphysics of power to the world of media."

A less dramatic picture of the issues of media ownership can be drawn in terms of the handy formula—offered by Werner Severin and James Tankard in *Communication Theories* (1991)—that "media ownership determines media control, which, in turn, determines media content, which is probably the major cause of media effects". Each link in this chain raises questions.

II. MEDIA OWNERSHIP AND MEDIA CONTROL

Ownership and control are not the same thing. People's use of their property operates within the parameters of certain social determinations; the use of an automobile or a gun, for example, is plainly subject to sensible restrictions. Furthermore, if what one owns is some kind of public treasure, then the public can specify limits that define the owner's responsibilities. Some possessions, in other words, involve a public trust.

These points, however, presuppose that the law functions to enforce the limitations in question. To the extent that it fails to do so (whether through incompetence, oversight, or corruption), the power of ownership will not be restrained. A standard argument from anticorporate critics is that the economic power of the corporation is such as to allow it to override legal limits through the exercise of political influence.

William Greider, in *Who Will Tell the People: The Betrayal of American Democracy* (1992), provides a detailed argument that social control (government) fails because those who know the system realize that their goals can be achieved through intervention, licit or illicit, at many points in the path from law to enforcement. The interpretations of administrators can function effectively to reverse the intention of a statute. Indeed, politicians often legislate merely symbolic gestures whose actual effect in practice they know will be (in fact, they *count* on its being) quite different. As politico Stuart

Eizenstat instructed Greider, "The law's always up for grabs. That's why you win elections and appoint judges." Greider himself endorses Bagdikian's suggestion that limits be placed on cross ownership of media, noting,

> Media owners usually hide behind the First Amendment when such questions are raised, but the practical effect of media concentration is actually to restrict the "free speech" of everyone else, the voiceless citizenry. Who gets to enter the debate? The choice belongs to reporters and editors and producers and, really, to the companies they work for.

Lawrence Grossman also argues that First Amendment considerations should not be an obstacle to enforcing antitrust laws against media conglomerates. We must distinguish, he says in *The Electronic Republic* (1995), "between the *medium*, on which reasonable limits of ownership can and must be imposed, and the *message*, which must be kept entirely free from government interference, regulation, and restriction."

Those who are not alarmed by Bagdikian's dwindling list of media owners can insist that ownership is not the same as control for another reason. Operating a media enterprise is a large and complex business, in which many individuals leave (albeit to varying degrees) their personal mark on what happens. Does the corporation's ownership "really" determine the choices of its many agents, the reporters, editors, producers, etc.? An example of a negative answer is given by Martin Seiden in *Access to the American Mind: The Impact of the New Mass Media* (1991). He dismisses Bagdikian's worries and sees the real problem with the media as being the power of journalists, rather than the power of their corporate owners:

> The real corporate conspiracy would appear to be the corporations' bond of uncritical silence regarding the operation of their media. Corporate executives appear to be paralyzed by the fear of being devoured by the mindless swarm if they interfere. What sensible executive would jeopardize his company's profit-and-loss statement by triggering a strike because he took issue with one of the journalists' sacred causes?

Analyses of this kind can also point to pollsters, lawyers, or other minions of corporate power—indeed, even to corporate executives *qua* individual decision makers—as those in whose hands media control actually resides. From this perspective, media ownership does not necessarily determine media control, because those who actually exercise the control, who make the relevant decisions, must be understood as having a culture and an agenda of their own, one not necessarily consonant with the interests of the owners.

Many studies of the actual functioning of complex, and especially bureaucratic, organizations suggest that the processes of evasion and circumvention that characterize the government can be expected to compromise any simple account of the exercise of corporate power.

As Len Masterman points out in *Teaching the Media* (1985),

> ... we have to revise any simplistic notion we may have that commercial ownership of the media inevitably involves the cynical manipulation of audiences, that public service broadcasting is untainted by commercial considerations, or that media institutions necessarily exercise tight control over every aspect of their corporate enterprises. We have to recognise, as always, that the media are sites for struggle between conflicting interests, and that ownership/management power is not absolute, monolithic or uncontested.

Of course, the fact that the behavior of individuals is shaped by factors other than the announced (or, even, real) goals of the organizations of which they are members should not lead us to belittle the shaping influence exerted by economic power and vested, to some degree, in ownership. As Greider observes, "the politicians dare not challenge the structure of media ownership, for that would provoke severe retribution from press and television and their corporate owners.... If the people do not raise these questions, they will not be raised at all."

III. MEDIA CONTROL AND MEDIA CONTENT

Whether owner or manager, *somebody* makes decisions, and those decisions determine what is in fact transmitted through media. At least, this seems true for those media that involve broadcast programming. Not every medium does this. The telephone, for example, largely separates issues of ownership and control from questions of content, at least in principle. The content of conversations is not dictated, and within broad limits not much regulated, by the medium itself. (Though, even here, computerized commercial calling and aggressive telephone marketing have tended to introduce an asymmetric intrusiveness into phone use.)

With regard to broadcast media, however, it can be argued that media control determines media content, and that concentration of control leads to both narrowing and degradation of content. Bagdikian puts the case bluntly: "The greater the dominance of a few firms, the more uniformity in what each of them produces." Changes may sometimes involve an ideological concern, or a desire to manipulate public opinion to advantage, but often they reflect simple adherence to narrow economic interests with little regard to larger social effects. Bagdikian argues that

> ... there is no reason to expect that a person skilled at building a corporate empire is a good judge of what the generality of citizens in a community need and want to know. Today, news is increasingly a monopoly medium in its locality, its entrepreneurs are increasingly absent ones who know little about and have no commitment to the social and political knowledge of a community's citizens.

Local media coverage may be simply reduced or re-placed with less expensive syndicated, or already-owned, material. Lawrence Grossman, a former president of NBC news recalls,

> It did not take long, however, before the press of daily deadlines, budget constraints, and the need to cover the same major unfolding stories as everyone else took us back to the practice of reacting to the themes and priorities of others—mostly what the president, the Congress, and top government departments and agencies decided to announce as the news of that day.

Edward Herman and Noam Chomsky, authors (separately and together) of many books critical of the media as government propaganda, remark in *Manufacturing Consent: The Political Economy of the Mass Media* (1988),

> Partly to maintain the image of objectivity, but also to protect themselves from criticisms of bias and the threat of libel suits, they need material that can be portrayed as presumptively accurate. This is also partly a matter of cost: taking information from sources that may be presumed credible, or that will elicit criticism and threats, requires careful checking and costly research.

Ostensibly "technical" decisions may effectively determine both access and content. Thus, Bagdikian argues that a question such as that of the

> "… allocation of the electromagnetic spectrum" tends to be handled in seclusion as an engineering task, but in reality, once in place the technical decision determines who will be given exclusive rights to broadcast to the public…. [For] by the time the systems are committed to certain kinds of equipment and practices, they effectively exclude the public from access to their media.

Such technical issues may not only determine who is able to afford to operate a broadcast medium, but may also affect the character and persuasiveness of the content. Robert Ray, in *A Certain Tendency of the Hollywood Cinema, 1930–1980* (1985), observes that

> … technological improvements in photography, film, and television have always carried concealed political implications. Each improvement, in effect, has redefined what counts as an acceptable (and therefore "realistic" and "unbiased") picture of the world, escalating the standard so as to keep it always just out of reach of all but the most powerful. Those images that fall short of the accepted norm appear not only as amateurish, but more importantly, as less "real". While the images produced by those in power seem to be merely an "objective" record of the way things are, less-than-standard images always appear as the products of special interests.

Evidently, there is a good deal of ground for concern about the ways in which, in both news and entertainment, more power in fewer hands affects media content. Some analysts, however, continue to see content as ultimately answerable to the audience. According to some, the media give people what they want, because otherwise people will pick something else they like better. This analysis puts emphasis on the increasing number and variety of options. Critics concede the increase in quantity, but dispute the claim of quality or real diversity, seeing the competition as largely among small variants of more-of-the-same—in Bruce Springsteen's phrase, "67 channels and nothing on."

A defender of the status quo may reply that the better alternatives the critic calls for are spurious because, when given a choice, people mostly do not select them. The critic insists that the choice has not been real, etc., etc. And so the largely unedifying debate proceeds. One side insists on what people in fact choose and ignores the shaping effects of the status quo. The other side insists on what people would (or, perhaps, should) choose and ignores the implicit appeal to paternalism. It is not that people are not free to purchase, say, *Mother Jones* instead of (or in addition to) *TV Guide*. If the audience prefers looking at "Baywatch" reruns to watching city council meetings, is that evidence of manipulation, or rather an expression of the very autonomy and diversity democracy aspires to celebrate and protect?

To the critic, of course, there is something doubtful about the idea of mass consumerism of any kind as an expression of individuality, but the relevant notions are difficult to get into focus. A century of debate about highbrow, middlebrow, and lowbrow has settled little, and yet it has been, as Robert Ray puts it, "an age that has seen popular culture become, for most people, the *only* culture." The triumph of popular culture, though still lamented by many, is tied to the capitalistic exploitation of mass media in complex ways that defy easy analysis.

Michael Parenti, a left/progressive thinker who has published a number of books critical of the media, laments in *Inventing Reality: The Politics of News Media* (2nd. ed., 1992) the fate of radical newspapers: "Skyrocketing postage rates effect a real hardship on small dissident publications. While defending such increases as economy measures, the government continues to subsidize billions of pieces of junk mail sent out every year by business and advertising firms." One need not dismiss claims about hostility on the part of the government to observe that, for the typical consumer, the catalog from Sears may in fact be of greater interest than, say, the latest issue of *Lies of Our Times*. How much of the "ideological monopoly" lamented by critics like Parenti is in fact a reflection of the actual shared values of the masses?

Like all chicken-or-egg questions, this one is unanswerable without an appeal to some normative theory about human nature, the good life, the just society, etc. How such an appeal is to be negotiated without begging the question remains a puzzlement. We can appeal, like the influential German philosopher Jürgen Habermas, to the idea of "undistorted communication," but such a notion resolves nothing; it merely provides terminology for further debate.

For some, the very fact that we have become consumers of the "spectacle" provided by society is the fundamental problem. But any gesture to reject the spectacle immediately is co-opted and becomes a part of it. As the Situationist International movement—articulated in such works as Guy Debord's *Society of the Spectacle* (1967) and *Comments on the Society of the Spectacle* (1988)—saw it, "There is no gesture so radical that ideology will not try to recover it." And yet, as Sadie Plant says, in *The Most Radical Gesture* (1992), her valuable study of the movement, "the awareness that even the most radical of gestures can be disarmed continues to encourage a search for irrecuperable forms of expression and communication."

For others, the pervasiveness and intrusiveness of the increasingly inescapable symbolic environment must be accepted as the new reality—indeed, *hyper*reality—of human existence. As Rheingold puts it, "Hyper-reality is what you get when a Panopticon evolves to the point where it can convince everyone that it doesn't exist." It is the age of what French philosopher Jean Baudrillard, in *Simulacra and Simulation* (1981, trans. 1994), calls the "simulacrum." It is the age of the "factoid." It is the age of the celebrity, who is "famous for being famous." It is, in sum, a world in which media (collectively out of control in the sense of producing cumulatively unwanted effects) increasingly take each other and themselves as their content.

IV. MEDIA CONTENT AND MEDIA EFFECTS

If even the seemingly short step from control to content is uncertain, it should be no surprise that the relation between content and effects has been much disputed. Communication theorists have disagreed vociferously over the course of the century, some arguing that media have only "limited effects" on people's attitudes and behavior, with others insisting that they are "powerful agents of social change." The fact that, as Christopher Simpson documents in *Science of Coercion* (1994), communication research had its roots in the government's development of psychological warfare techniques—along with the extensive and expensive use of media for purposes of advertising—make it surprising that so many communications theorists have argued for limited effects. (Or, perhaps, not surprising at all.)

Herbert Schiller, the author of many critiques of media imperialism, from *Mass Communications and Amer-* ican *Empire* (1969) to *Culture, Inc.: The Corporate Takeover of Public Expression* (1989), expresses astonishment at the limited-effects theory: "... the power of the Western cultural industries is more concentrated and formidable than ever; their outputs are more voluminous and widely circulated; and the transnational corporate system is totally dependent on information flows." How is it possible to suppose the effects of all this to be limited? The answer for recent critics is that media power is balanced by *audience* power. "First, it is claimed, the new information technologies afford greater choice. The second support factor derives from an appraisal of the audience, which finds it heterogeneous, comprised of a large number of social subgroups, each with its own history, experience, and interests." Schiller disputes each of these arguments.

The first argument, essentially that put forward by Ithiel de Sola Pool in *Technologies of Freedom* (1983), points to the increase in viewing choice made possible by cable TV and VCRs. At its crudest, the argument amounts to seeing media freedom as "channel surfing," the power to put together one's own viewing experience out of fragments of public meaning. Against this argument, Schiller contends that the actual diversity is spurious, because the power remains in the same place. "Has the sponsor disappeared from cable television? Is commercialism and consumerism absent? Where are the sharply drawn social dramas?" Furthermore, the media are still owned, and the infrequent participation of the community through public-access channels reflects the struggle with "cable owners who find it outrageous to be compelled to yield the tiniest fraction of their revenue-producing facilities for community use."

The second argument is analogous to reader-response criticism and other literary theories emphasizing the priority of how a text is received and interpreted by its audience over whatever its author may have intended: "Diversity, ... in this way of looking at television, does not require a variety of programmatic material. It is provided by the viewers in their capability to produce a diversity of readings or meanings in the single program." Schiller devotes extensive discussion to this second argument, but his basic response boils down to the observation that, as a passsage he quotes puts it, "television—along with most other commercial enterprises—exploits the competitive fragmentation among people who belong to what is objectively, the same, subordinate class." Or, to put the point the other way, "The ultimate message in TV ... is that the dominating class has the same basic problems as the dominated and is itself not in control of its destiny." What is wrong with this message? "Theories that ignore the structure and locus of representational and definitional power and emphasize instead the individual's message transformational capability present little threat to the maintenance of the established order."

Put in other words, Schiller's message, like that of many radical media critics, is that to locate freedom in marginal differentials of response to the mass-mediated environment is counterrevolutionary because it leads one to define one's situation not in (objective?) terms of the interests of one's class but rather in (subjective?) terms of one's creation of an individual style or response to reality. In terms popularized by Richard Rorty, it is to be paying attention to private "irony" rather than public "solidarity." Rorty's (liberal) view is that one needs both, and that there is no way to adjudicate their competing claims.

For the radical critic, the fact that individual styles have themselves become commodities—buy Michael Jordan's basketball shoe and "be like Mike"—only emphasizes the primacy of the need to see who is really doing the defining. But from another perspective, even commodified individualities can to some extent be viewed as grist for the mill of self-creation. They are what John Milton said a good book was, "the precious life-blood of a master-spirit." (Collect the whole set.)

Some writers hold out the hope that the new technologies of communication may yet enable us to reconcile self-creation and solidarity. Russell Neuman, in *The Future of the Mass Audience* (1991), suggests that "narrowcasting" (as opposed to broadcasting) may help us rediscover "virtual communities of like-minded individuals ... who will band together and speak out spontaneously in response to a public concern or event," thereby recreating "the essence of the vigorous citizen-based democracy." Against this optimism must be set journalist Georgie Anne Geyer's warning:

> In some ways, the Internet does give demonstrators across the globe the technological means to bypass national boundaries and to appeal vaguely to 'solidarity'. On the other hand, it tends to weaken and destroy the kind of discipline, organized, across-class-lines appeals that always underlie every real revolution.

Still, Taylor and Saarinen are no doubt right to insist: "Where would Socrates hold his dialogues today? In the media and on the net."

Not only private life and civic life may come together in "cyberspace," but work life is being altered as well. Some have seen electronic communication as enhancing the speed and efficiency of networked knowledge, allowing people to work together from various locations and increasing scheduling autonomy, though not without some important dislocations as individual identity metamorphoses into universal product code. Joshua Meyrowitz explored the impact of electronic media on social behavior in *No Sense of Place* (1985). Barbara Garson foresaw computers turning the office of the future into the factory of the past in *The Electronic Sweatshop* (1988). Shoshana Zuboff provided an insightful study of the future of work and power with *In the Age of the Smart Machine* (1988). Stanley Deetz analyzed developments in communication and the politics of everyday life in *Democracy in an Age of Corporate Colonization* (1992).

The business world has also been transformed by economic changes made possible by the new media. In his valuable study of the film industry, *American Film Now* (Rev. ed., 1984), James Monaco notes

> ... a kind of Gresham's law of culture. As the craft becomes able to accomplish more with less, to realize record-setting profits with the flimsiest of raw materials, bad product drives out good.... The definitive irony of film culture in the seventies (as in all contemporary media culture from television to records to books) is that the refinement of the craft results in less freedom rather than more for the "artists"....

The criterion of the media of the 1970s, he observed, was "form follows finances." The age of the blockbuster was born.

By 1980, the destructive effects of "the big-time, big-money, winner-take-all system" had spread from television, movies, and records to the book trade, as Thomas Whiteside documented in *The Blockbuster Complex: Conglomerates, Show Business, and Book Publishing* (1981):

> The kind of emotional remoteness from "the product" which one senses in the conglomerates' central-management people now seems to be communicating itself to the people who are directly in charge of the publishing houses owned by the conglomerates, and more and more it seems that books are being regarded as interchangeable products.

Wall Street merger guru Felix Rohatyn summed it up succinctly: "Everything in this world has turned into show business."

Robert Frank and Philip Cook argue, in *The Winner-Take-All Society* (1995), that a similar process has spread to many areas of society: "In effect, the reward structure common in entertainment and sports—where thousands compete for a handful of big prizes at the top—has now permeated many other sectors of the economy." The growth of winner-take-all markets, they argue, is due to "the rapid erosion of the barriers that once prevented the top performers from serving broader markets." This erosion is due to a number of factors, but especially to changes in the media. "Perhaps the most profound changes in the underlying forces that give rise to winner-take-all effects have stemmed from technological developments in two areas—telecommunications and electronic computing." They argue that the winner-take-all system is costly and unproductive, and conclude that "rising inequality is more likely to curtail than to stimulate economic growth." The good news is that this would mean that there is no necessary opposition between economic growth and the curtailment of extreme inequality. The bad news is that, as they concede, most economists disagree with them.

V. AGAMEMNON'S SCEPTER

In Book II of the *Iliad*, the founding work of the long cultural tradition that stretches from the poet Homer down to Homer Simpson, Agamemnon's golden scepter functions as a symbol for the divine right of the king. When the troops are in turmoil, Odysseus borrows the scepter and goes to rally them, urging that "we cannot all be kings." Odysseus is soon successful and everyone keeps to his place, except for Thersites, whom Homer describes (in Samuel Butler's translation) as "a man of many words, and those unseemly; a monger of sedition, a railer against all who were in authority, who cared not what he said, so that he might set the Achaeans in a laugh." Thersites is ugly— itself an objection in ancient Greek culture, as Nietzsche liked to emphasize—and he has "a shrill squeaky voice." Thersites complains about Agamemnon's greed and proposes that the armies go home. Odysseus tells him to shut up, and threatens him, and finally beats him with the scepter until he is silent. This provides a fitting emblem of the way in which wealth and violence constrain participation in the debate over public policy. To be sure, a right to speak is not the same as a right to a megaphone. But what if some of the others have megaphones?

In his discussion of impairments in thinking and communication in *Inquiry and Change: The Troubled Attempt to Understand and Shape Society* (1990), Charles Lindblom says: "Among the defects of the existing competition of ideas, none seems more impairing or more easily remedied, given the will, than that well-financed communications, whether well-financed by the state, by private organizations, or by wealthy elites, overpower poorly financed ones." His suggestions for possible reforms include constraints on corporate spending on mass communications (and not just in electioneering) and perhaps limits on advertising and sales-promotion communications. He also calls into question "corporate influence on education and research ... indeed, the whole scope of corporate philanthropy."

Lindblom even goes so far as to broach the issue of the harmful effects on inquiry of inequality of wealth. He holds that genuine competition of ideas

> ... has to go further than [merely] to permit people to listen and read as they wish. If impairing influences have narrowed the range of ideas to which people choose to attend, then their freedom, however prized, to listen and read as they wish will not open them to a competition of ideas, but will leave them impaired.

Underlying Lindblom's project is the desire to distinguish inequalities necessary to the efficient operation of socially desirable mechanisms (functional inequalities) from inequalities that have illegitimately "attached" themselves to the functional inequalities. As we all know, "these 'attached' inequalities are often energetically rationalized, justified, defended, and enlarged when possible by the advantaged. Hence, sorting out useful from attached inequalities in control becomes subordinated to the struggle of the advantaged to maintain their advantages." Such illegitimate inequalities can be criticized not only from an egalitarian point of view (which sees equality as valuable in and of itself, other beings being equal), but also because they impair clear thinking, plain speaking, and the efficient operation of social mechanisms. Their criticism thus is part of the project of increasing the "rationality" of society. This project is, as Lindblom recognizes, a legacy of the Enlightenment. Accordingly, it rouses the enthusiasm and the worries common to such attempts to rationalize life.

Whether one is more enthusiastic or more worried will depend on whether one thinks that what afflicts human life is too much irrationality or too narrow a view of rationality. The former (pro-Enlightenment) attitude characterizes thinkers from Plato to Carl Sagan. The latter view, suspicious of the claim of rationality to be comprehensive, stretches a zigzag course from Aristophanes to Euripides to Edmund Burke to Nietzsche to Foucault. Liberal reformers criticize conservatives for wanting to preserve the status quo, with its ignorance and inequities. Conservatives criticize liberals for being naive about human nature, and for being willing to impose their ideas of the human good on others. Radicals insist that the status quo already imposes on people a particular idea of the human good, a strikingly one-sided idea which is maintained by violence (or the threat of violence) and, thanks to the media, by distraction and illusion—bread and circuses at Eleven.

These views disagree about how values such as freedom and equality are to be understood in the actual conditions of social life. Nowhere is this disagreement more perplexing than in the question of control of media in an increasingly media-dependent world. As anthropologist Ulf Hannerz suggests,

> The problem of the asymmetry of input mode in the cultural apparatus, especially as constituted by the media, then, is that it allows little active participation in the production of certain kinds of symbolic form. At the same time, the presence of the cultural apparatus may allow people to cultivate a sensibility to symbolic forms which, without it, would not have been available at the same level of development at all.

The standard defense of corporate cultural "development" is that it makes life better. Though this is not always true, the interesting questions arise in those cases where it arguably is true, for the standard radical criticism of corporate cultural "imperialism" is that, whatever its superficial benefits, it supplants indigenous cultural systems and substitutes structural inequalities of power. What critics worry about is not so much Orwell's *1984*, as Huxley's *Brave New World*—less the jackboot in the face than designer boots in the window.

Whatever our ultimate destination, there is no doubt that the journey is a short one over the "information superhighway" to the "global village." En route, many now suggest, we are likely to see the end of the nation-state as the dominant force in world politics. James Martin, who in 1978 presciently described *The Wired Society*, observed that

> patriotism is declining and may decline more with decades of advanced global communications. Some people will feel more loyalty to their global cultural thread than to their country.... The shape of cultural patterns is often determined more by money than by aesthetic or abstract values. The imperative to maximize profits will increasingly be an imperative to market internationally and hence design products for international markets.

Theodore Zeldin, in *An Intimate History of Humanity* (1994), has described the change in more personal terms:

> ... the earth is in the early stages of being criss-crossed afresh by invisible threads uniting individuals who differ by all conventional criteria, but who are finding that they have aspirations in common. When nations were formed, all the threads were designed to meet at a central point; now there is no centre any more; people are free to meet whomever they wish.

With the end of the nation-state may come as well the end of the kind of literacy that has been part of nationalism. With this literacy may go, as Bill Readings suggested in *The University in Ruins* (1996), both the book and the university as we have known them. What cultural forms might replace their claim on our attention, or their effect in our lives, remains to be seen. Stay tuned.

Bibliography

Ansolabehere, S., et al. (1993). *The media game: American politics in the television age.* New York: Macmillan.

Bagdikian, B. H. (1992). *The media monopoly* (4th ed.). Boston: Beacon.

Branscomb, A. W. (1994). *Who owns information?* New York: Basic Books.

Ewen, S. (1996). *PR! A social history of spin.* New York: Basic Books.

Frank, R. H., & Cook, P. J. (1995). *The winner-take-all society: Why the few at the top get so much more than the rest of us.* New York: Free Press.

Grossman, L. K. (1995). *The electronic republic: Reshaping democracy in the information age.* New York: Viking Penguin.

Herman, E. S. (1995). *Triumph of the market: Essays on economics, politics, and the media.* Boston: South End.

Poster, M. (1990). *The mode of information: Poststructuralism and social context.* Chicago: Univ. of Chicago Press.

National Security Issues

JOHN D. BECKER

United States Air Force Academy

GLOSSARY

actors Those entities, such as states, alliances, international organizations, and transnational organizations, that play roles in the conduct of national security. Other actors may be selected individuals and groups in a particular state or region.

approaches The methods and manners in which states conduct the business of national security. Approaches derive from national security structures and strategies.

commitments Specific actions at specific times and places. Commitments specify a state's interests and objectives in a given situation.

interests Highly generalized abstractions that reflect a state's basic wants and needs. They are sometimes difficult to identify because they are rarely clean-cut and tend to overlap with other interests.

issues Points of debate or controversy that concern the national security of a state.

objectives The goals or aims of what a country endeavors to do; more tangible and easier to change than interests.

operations other than war (OOTW) Operations that involve the employment of military and nonmilitary resources, but without the intention of using violent force as a primary means to achieve a specific end or set of ends. OOTW include such actions as peacekeeping, counterdrug operations, and disaster relief.

peacetime concerns Those important political and economic concerns that nations normally conduct with each other, when not at war or in hostile conflict.

policies Patterns of actions to attain specific objectives.

power The ability to get others to do things, particularly something they would not do of their own volition. Power is dynamic, subjective, relative, and situational. It is expressed in many ways, such as coercion, persuasion, bargaining, and threats, and through various forms, including the military, political, economic, and sociopsychological.

programs A plan to allocate resources in support of objectives, policies, and commitments.

purpose An expression of an enduring value or values in which a state (or nation) is rooted. A national purpose is more or less permanent, tends to be an end rather than a means, and is desired in and of itself, not simply as a means of attaining something else.

strategy A plan of action, using available resources to obtain certain goals over time. There are national strategies, grand strategies, and military strategies.

structures The organizational arrangement established by a state to allow it to conduct the business of national security.

war A state of open armed conflict between states (or coalitions of states), or between parties in a state, carried on by force of arms for various reasons. There are various types of wars, ranging across the spectrum of conflict, including attack or raids, low-intensity conflicts, limited wars, general wars, and nuclear war.

NATIONAL SECURITY ISSUES are those points of debate or controversy that concern the security of a state. The principal term, national security, has traditionally signified the protection of a state's people and territories against physical assault. Yet, since World War II and the rapid transformation of the international political system, the term has taken on a more comprehensive meaning. National security now includes the protection, through a variety of means, of vital economic and political interests, the loss of which could threaten fundamental values and the life of the state.

National security is conducted in the context of a bifurcated environment, divided into global and domestic parts. The global part of the environment includes factors such as perceived threats of and between states, states' geographic locations and physical conditions, international laws, customs, and agreements, trade relations and other international economic concerns, as well as the flow of strategic information and intelligence. The domestic part of the environment is composed of factors such as states' worldviews, their internal public attitudes, economic conditions including national security budgets, competing political ideologies and elections, bureaucratic agendas and contests, their social and cultural conventions, in addition to respective legal and ethical norms.

The national security environment is, in turn, cast with numerous actors who play various roles. These actors include the states themselves—along with their prominent leaders and private individuals—their corresponding political, military, and economic alliances, international and transnational organizations, and the media and mass communication groups. Additionally, legislative and judicial branches of a state's government play roles in the national security framework, as do other groups, such as prominent minorities and opposing political parties in states' populations.

Within this environment, and among these actors using power, the business of national security is determined and carried out. While there are significant differences in various states as to how those processes are carried out, all states end up with at least three things: a national security structure, a national security strategy, and a national security approach.

Additionally, as part of the process of national security, issues of applied ethics are raised and considered. These issues include traditional just war concerns which are often broken into two types—*jus ad bellum* (justice of war) and *jus in bello* (justice in war). They also include questions about nontraditional issues, such as OOTW and future war concerns, as well as issues like human rights, economic rights, and environmental rights.

I. NATIONAL SECURITY STRUCTURES

A national security structure is the organizational arrangement established by a state to allow it to conduct the business of national security. The national security structure will vary depending upon a number of factors, including the type of government organization and the level of political development. Typically, however, it will be vested in the executive branch of a state and it will include representatives from the state department or diplomatic corps, the armed forces, those involved with foreign trade and commerce, and the intelligence services. It may also include a special coordinator for national security affairs, as in the United States or in Russia. Additionally, it may draw upon other representatives from government or actors from the national security environment, who are concerned or involved with a particular issue or set of issues.

An example of a national security structure can be seen in that of the United States. At the center of the structure is the White House Office—this office houses the staff members of the President, including his personal and political assistants. The specific organization of the White House Office is a reflection of the President's personal style. Another key element is the National Security Council, which serves as the formal coordination and policy planning group. It is composed of the President, the Vice President, the Secretary of Defense, and the Secretary of State. It is supported by a combined military and civilian staff, with the Assistant to the President for National Security Affairs serving as its head. Other key elements include the Department of State, the Department of Defense, the Central Intelligence Agency, and the Office of Management and Budget. And, of course, other agencies, such as the Department of Energy, the Department of Treasury, and the Federal Bureau of Investigation, are involved on an ad hoc basis.

Another dimension of the structure includes the unofficial organization, which may range from a "kitchen cabinet"—personal friends and confidants of the President, to previous Presidents ands former senior officials, key members of Congress, the media, and the business community, to the others like the President's relatives, including spouses and siblings.

The interaction and inputs from all of these actors, in both formal and informal organizations, provide the structure that will shape and develop the strategies and approaches that a state takes to national security issues.

II. NATIONAL SECURITY STRATEGIES

From this structure, the key actors will determine a national security strategy. A strategy is simply a plan of action, using available resources, to obtain certain goals over time. Thus, a national security strategy is a state's plan, which fuses all of its available resources, during peace as well as war, to attain national interests and objectives. A national security strategy will normally include two other strategies—a grand strategy and a military strategy. A grand strategy involves employing national power under all circumstances to exert desired degrees and types of control over a state's enemies or opponents. Threats, force, indirect pressure, diplomacy, subterfuge, and other imaginative means are all employed in grand strategy.

For example, before the Persian Gulf War, the United States developed and employed a grand strategy against Iraq. This strategy included President George Bush's use of media in establishing the "line in the sand"; the use of economic sanctions and ultimately, embargo; the establishment of a political and military coalition to fight Iraq; declarations of support by both the U.S. Congress and the United Nations; and the veiled threats of using nuclear weapons in response to any Iraqi use of chemical or biological weapons. In short, these various tactics were woven together into a single, integrated plan—a grand strategy for going to war with Iraq.

Military strategy, on the other hand, is predicated on physical violence or the threat of violence. It seeks to obtain national security interests and objectives through the use of arms. It involves, as General Karl von Clausewitz noted, the use of engagements to attain the object of war. There are a variety of approaches to military strategy including sequential and cumulative, direct and indirect, deterrent and combative, and counterforce and countervalue.

In the earlier example of the Persian Gulf War, the U.S. military strategy was clearly articulated by Chairman of the Joint Chiefs of Staff, General Colin Powell, who said the military was "Going to cut off it's head, and then kill it." What this meant was that the United States planned first to destroy the command and control structure of the Iraqi's armed forces and second to destroy their fighting forces.

The difference between grand strategy and military strategy is simple then: the first is the purview of statesmen while the latter is the territory of generals. More-over, military strategy should be understood as a subset of the larger, grand strategy.

III. NATIONAL SECURITY APPROACHES

The intermediate step between national security structure and national security strategy is the national security process. While the exact processes differ as do states' structures and strategies, all follow a similar path. This path starts at a nation's purpose and progresses through interests, objectives, policies, commitments, and programs.

Every state has a national purpose. This national purpose is an expression of the enduring values in which a state is rooted. In the United States, for example, the Declaration of Independence and the Constitution are such expressions. In the first case, "... We hold these truths to be self-evident, that all men are created equal, that they are endowed by their Creator with certain unalienable Rights, that among these are Life, liberty, and the pursuit of Happiness...." In the second case, the preamble notes, "We the people of the United States, in order to form a more perfect union, establish justice, insure domestic tranquillity, provide for the common defense, promote the general welfare, and secure the blessings of Liberty ourselves and our Prosperity, do ordain and establish this constitution for the United States of America."

Expressions of national purpose differ depending upon cultural, economic, historical, political, and moral precedents, yet often focus on similar themes including domestic order, the welfare of the nation, and national security. It is important to note that a national purpose is marked by certain characteristics: it is more or less permanent, it tends to be an end rather than a means, and it is desired in and of itself, not simply as a means of attaining something else.

Deriving from a state's national purpose are its national interests. Interests are highly generalized abstractions that reflect a nation state's basic wants and needs. They include such things as political integrity and territorial integrity. They are sometimes difficult to identify because they are rarely clean-cut and they tend to overlap or interlock with other interests.

An example of national interests can be found in Operation Just Cause, the U.S. military intervention in Panama. One of the reasons the administration gave for intervening was the repeated abuse of U.S. nationals and military personnel by local officials and police. This need to protect U.S. citizens abroad is considered a common national interest. Another example of a threatened national interest was the requirement to protect the Panama Canal, in which the United States has economic, political, and military needs. Economically, the Canal is important to our trade relations. Politically and militarily, it is important both as a symbol and carries treaty obligations for the U.S. defense establishment.

Emerging from national interests are national security objectives. These objectives spell out what a country is trying to do. These objectives might be understood as goals, aims, or purposes. They are similar to interests but more tangible and easier to change. If one of the United States' national interests is to ensure access to oil supplies in the Middle East, then some of its objectives might be maintaining stability in the region, strengthening its allies such as Israel in the region, and constraining "rogue" states like Iraq and Iran.

Interests and objectives require specifics actions, like policies, commitments, and programs, to be translated from abstractions to actual activities. Policies are patterns of actions designed to attain specific objectives. In the previous example of the United States objective to have access to Middle East oil, a supporting policy might include providing financial aid to developing countries in the region, providing military assistance to pro-U.S. countries, and denying technology to anti-U.S. countries. Correspondingly, commitments are specific actions at specific times and places, and programs are resource allocation plans. So military assistance to a pro-U.S. country, like Saudi Arabia, might include shipments of a dozen advanced fighter aircraft in one year, shipments of 50 tanks in the next year, and training aid teams, with repair parts, during both years.

This, then, is an example of how states approach the handling of national security issues, within the context of their organizations and strategies.

IV. NATIONAL SECURITY ISSUES

Examples of specific national security issues include arms control, energy resources, environmental problems, foreign trade, international terrorism, the uses of outer space, and the war on drugs. These various issues occur along what might be considered a continuum—a continuum of national security. This continuum includes three key concerns: wars, operations other than war, and peacetime concerns. Let us consider each element in turn.

A. War

On one side of the continuum is war, a state of open armed conflict between states, or between parties in a state, carried on by force of arms for various purposes. There are various types of wars, ranging across a spectrum of conflict, including attacks or raids, low-intensity conflicts, limited wars, general wars, and nuclear war. War is a primary national security issue.

An attack or raid is a limited military action, meant to inflict a minimal amount of damage or destruction on an enemy, for a specific reason. The forces employed in an attack or raid vary from air-launched cruise missle strikes to large-scale land assaults by either an army or marine force. For example, in 1986, U.S. warplanes bombed Libya, targeting Mu'ammar Qaddafi's headquarters at Tripoli, leaving 15 civilians dead. This raid was a retaliatory attack for the Libyan bombing of a West Berlin discotheque that killed and injured several hundred people, including American soldiers stationed in Germany.

Low-intensity conflict (LIC) is a limited political-military struggle, meant to achieve political, social, economic, and psychological objectives. It is often protracted and it ranges from various types of pressure (diplomatic, economic, and psychosocial pressures) through terrorism and insurgency. LIC is most often constrained to a geographic area and is characterized by restraint on weaponry, tactics, and level of violence.

Three examples indicate the breadth and diversity of LIC. First, early American involvement in the Vietnam war, with the use of Army Special Forces troops and other military advisors, was an example of a guerrilla war. Using unconventional tactics, these American forces and their South Vietnamese allies fought against communist guerrillas from North Vietnam. This war was indeed a political-military struggle and it was also a protracted conflict.

For a second example, consider the Israeli response to the terrorist seizure of a civilian airliner in June 1976. Palestine Liberation Organization (PLO) terrorists hijacked an Air France jet and diverted it to the Entebbe airport in Urganda. They held 98 Israeli passengers and the plane's crew as hostages, demanding that numerous PLO prisoners held in various countries be released in exchange. The Ugandan government, then lead by the dictator Idi Amin, cooperated with the terrorists. The Israeli government launched a rescue raid, by commandos, which overcame Ugandan and PLO forces, and liberated the hostages.

Finally, a third example of LIC is psychological warfare. Psychological warfare is really fighting with words, using communications technology to advance both propaganda and psychology. In Haiti, recently, U.S. psychological operations troops sent pamphlets and papers throughout the island, encouraging Haitians to cooperate with American forces as they arrived.

Limited wars or conventional wars are armed conflicts between two or more states. They are most often what we mean by "war." The means and ends are still constrained but are greater than those found in LIC. The resources of all states in a limited war may be fully mobilized and their own survival may be at risk, but it is still limited in that it is not a regional or global conflict. Examples of limited war include the U.S. involvement in Korea, Panama, and the Persian Gulf wars.

Next, there is general war. This is armed conflict between major powers. States such as the United States, Russia, or China employ their total resources—political, economic, military—in the conflict and, in fact, the survival of one or more belligerent may be jeopardized. General wars have included World War I and World War II.

Finally, there is nuclear war. Simply put, this horrific, and so far theoretical notion is that states make use of nuclear weapons in the fighting of a general war. In this type of conflict, nuclear weapons, in various forms—submarine-launched missiles, land-based rocket-launched missiles, and aircraft-launched bombs and/or missiles—attack either countervalue (basically, cities or people) targets or counterforce (military or nuclear weapons) targets. Although nuclear weapons have been used in war, by the United States on Japan in World War II, no nuclear war has ever been waged.

B. Operations Other Than War

Moving toward the middle of the national security spectrum, one finds operations other than war (OOTW). These are concerns that may involve the employment of military and nonmilitary resources, but without the intention of using violent force as a primary means to achieve a specific end or set of ends. OOTW include such actions as peacekeeping, counterdrug operations, and disaster relief.

Recent U.S. national security operations have been almost exclusively OOTW. For example, when the United States and others decided to intervene in the affairs of Somalia, they did so under the rubric of humanitarian intervention. Military forces, in conjunction with diplomatic and relief organizations (both domestic and international) established an infrastructure in 1992 and 1993 that allowed the storage and distribution of food, water, and medical care. Additionally, in the American involvement with Haiti, U.S. Special Forces troops, in conjunction with diplomatic negotiators, worked to achieve a peaceful transition between governments.

Domestically, all national security operations except perhaps civil wars are OOTW, ranging from hurricane relief to assisting firefighters in battling large-scale fires to helping with flooding throughout a country. Combined efforts are also seen in counterdrug operations where U.S. military forces work with intelligence ser-vices, satellite support services, and law enforcement agencies, as well as with diplomatic services and other nations, in an effort to stem the flow of drugs into this country.

Although there has been much discussion as to whether operations of this type are ones that our national security resources should be employed on, it is important to recognize that they are not new. For instance, after the American Civil War, national security resources (specifically the Army) were used in suppressing the Pullman riots in Chicago, repressing the various Indian tribes throughout the west, exploring and mapping the Pacific Northwest and Alaska, conducting excursions into Mexico and other Latin American countries, and construction projects, like the Panama Canal.

C. Peacetime Concerns

On the other side of the continuum of national security is peace. Peace is not simply some type of tranquillity, but consists of those important political and economic concerns that nations normally conduct with each other when not at war or in hostile conflict. Common peacetime concerns include diplomacy, trade and economic interactions, and deterrence.

Diplomacy involves the normal, day-to-day, relationships between states and other transnational organizations. There are both formal diplomatic channels, usually represented by a corps of professional diplomats who work in embassies in other states, as well as informal diplomatic channels, represented by other, nonprofessional envoys, who may work directly for a nation's leadership in dealing with other nations. Both representatives deal with a variety of activities including communications between nations, political dealings, economic issues, and military cooperation. They work on issues ranging from nuclear disarmament talks to trade treaties to refugee settlements.

Economic transactions between states include trade, trade balances with corresponding imports and exports levels, economic growth between and in other states, economic assistance programs such as loans and grants, and also tarrifs and other barriers across respective borders.

Deterrence and defense are also peacetime concerns. Deterrence is simply the notion that a state, through the size and power of its military forces, can affect the actions of another state. For example in the Cold War between the United States and the former Soviet Union, both states' military forces with their large and vast nuclear arsenals served to deter nuclear wars.

Defense, too, is a peacetime concern. States constantly struggle, through the development of their understanding of potential and actual threats, their development of strategies to deal with those threats, and the procurement and sustainment of military forces, with the issue of what is an adequate defense. This is, perhaps, the critical issue in national security, because how strong a state is perceived to be affects all of its dealings with other states. It also impacts on the rest of a state's internal governance through the sharing and distribution of fiscal resources for other domestic departments and programs.

In sum, it remains important to note the wide variety of national security issues that states encounter occur across a continuum. This national security continuum includes war, operations other than war (OOTW), and peacetime concerns. It should also be noted that rarely does a state focus on just one part of the continuum. Rather, it faces various issues across the continuum simultaneously with other different states. Accordingly, the management of national security is difficult but critical to a state's life.

V. APPLIED ETHICS ISSUES

As part of the process of national security, issues of applied ethics are raised and considered. These issues include traditional just-war concerns, which are often broken into two types—*jus ad bellum* (justice of war) and *jus in bello* (justice in war). They also include questions about nontraditional issues, such as OOTW and future war concerns, as well as issues such as human rights, economic rights, and environmental rights.

In the first case, war, including LIC, a great deal of discussion is focused on whether a state is justified in its actions of starting and conducting war. In Western history, the issue has been addressed by just-war tradition or just-war theory. Philosophers ranging from Augustine to Aquinas to Grotius have contributed to this discussion. Considerations include just cause, right authority, right intention, proportionality of ends, last resort, reasonable chance of success, and the aim of peace. The satisfaction of these criteria produces a "just war" versus and "unjust" war.

In the second case, the issues are generally about the conduct of the war itself. The focus is on how soldiers and their commanders conduct the war and whether that conduct is ethical or not. Primary considerations include the proportionality of means and ends, as well as noncombatant protection and immunity.

In the third case, the issues also draw upon ethical principle but in relation to OOTW, including humanitarian intervention and peacekeeping missions. Often efforts are made to balance one ethical principle against another principle—for example, saving the lives of a state's starving people versus violating the political autonomy of that state. Considerations include those found in the earlier cases but with distinctive approach on nonlethal force.

In conclusion, the purpose of applied ethics in national security issues includes justifying the use of force by a political community (or a state), warranting protection of fundamental rights and values, and explaining the relation of ends to means in political life. Ethical issues are addressed in the structure, strategies, and approaches of national security.

Bibliography

Becker, J. D., Gibson, W. H., Hittinger, J. P. (1996). *Moral dimensions of the military profession.* Boulder, CO: American Heritage Custom Publishing.

Hardin, T., & Mapel, D. R. (Eds.) (1992). *Traditions of international ethics.* New York: Cambridge University Press.

Lykke, A. F., Jr. (Ed.) (1989). *Military strategy: Theory and application.* Carlisle Barracks, PA: U.S. Army War College.

Rosenthal, J. H. (Ed.) (1995). *Ethics and international affairs: A reader.* Washington, DC: Georgetown University Press.

Wells, D. R. (Ed.) (1995). *An encyclopedia of war and ethics.* Westport, CT: Greenwood Publishing Group.

Objectivity in Reporting

JUDITH LICHTENBERG

University of Maryland at College Park

GLOSSARY

bias The slanting of news reporting according to the personal views or professional interests of the journalist or the political, economic, and technological interests or constraints of the news organization.

objectivity A guiding principle of contemporary journalism according to which news should be reported without bias; held by many critics to be an impossible and undesirable ideal.

social construction A prominent contemporary theory, deriving from the sociology of knowledge, according to which the political, economic, and social circumstances of a society determine what constitutes reality and knowledge in that society.

OBJECTIVITY is a cornerstone of the professional ideology of journalists in liberal democracies. The distinction between news, where objectivity is thought possible and desirable, and opinion, where objectivity is thought impossible, is deeply entrenched in the journalistic culture. Objectivity is inextricably intertwined with truth, fairness, balance, neutrality, the absence of value judgments—in short, with the most fundamental journalistic values.

Yet the objectivity of journalism has come increasingly under fire in recent years. The criticisms come from a variety of quarters and take several forms. Some say that journalism *is not* objective; others that it *cannot* be objective; and still others that it *should not* be objective. Odd as it may seem, sometimes the same critic seems to be making all of these charges at the same time.

One challenge comes from critics—from across the political spectrum—who claim that the media have misrepresented their views or have not reported their activities impartially. Some say that the media have a "liberal bias," that they overemphasize unrest and dissent, or look too hard for muck to rake. Other critics contend that, on the contrary, the press serves the conservative interests of government and big business. Aggrieved individuals and groups of all kinds charge that news coverage of this or that issue is unfair, biased, or sensational.

Those who attack journalism on these grounds seem to share one crucial assumption with those they criticize. The complaint of bias seems to presuppose that *un*bias is possible. But many contemporary critics, not only of journalism but of every other form of inquiry, reject this assumption. Journalism is not objective, they say, nor could it be. As one recent textbook puts it, objectivity "is a false and impossible ideal," and although all media writers claim it in some way, "they are all wrong."

This view has its roots in the sociology of knowledge and today finds its fullest expression in postmodernism; it is shared by many sociologists, humanists, legal scholars, and other social critics. They believe that the idea of objectivity rests on an outmoded and untenable theory of knowledge, according to which objective knowledge consists of correspondence between some idea or statement and a reality "out there" in the world. "Objectivity," in the words of a former journalism school dean, "is an essential correspondence between knowledge of a thing and the thing itself." But according to the critics, reality is not "out there"; it is, as James Carey has put it, "a vast production, a staged creation—something humanly produced and humanly maintained." Reality, on this view, is "socially constructed," and so there are as many realities as there are social perspectives on the world. There is no "true reality" to which objective knowledge can be faithful.

Perhaps paradoxically, those who believe objectivity is impossible sometimes think at the same time that it is an undesirable and even a dangerous aspiration. According to Catherine MacKinnon, objectivity is a strategy of hegemony used by some members of society to dominate others. Gaye Tuchman calls objectivity a "strategic ritual" enabling professionals to "defend themselves from critical onslaught;" while Dan Schiller describes it as, at best, "a cultural form with its own set of conventions."

I. THE COMPOUND ASSAULT ON OBJECTIVITY

On the face of it, there is something odd in this compound assault on objectivity—that journalism is not objective, that it could not be, that it should not be—for the charges do not seem compatible.

1. The complaint that a particular piece of journalism is not objective makes sense only against the background assumption that objectivity is possible.
2. The insistence that journalism cannot be objective makes the view that objectivity is undesirable seem superfluous.
3. The assertion that objectivity is not desirable makes senseless the complaint that journalism is not objective.

But although the combination of these charges may seem confused, the appearance is somewhat misleading. For the different charges leveled against objectivity, we shall see, are really charges leveled against different understandings of objectivity.

Let us begin with a rough reconstruction of the chain of reasoning leading to the conclusion that objectivity in journalism does not, could not, and should not exist:

- Experience continually confronts us with examples of clashes of belief (between individuals, between cultures) that we cannot resolve—we do not know how to decide which belief is true.

- No one can totally escape his or her biases; no one can be completely objective.
- Therefore, the idea that there could be an objective, true account of things is a fiction.
- Anyone who sincerely thinks there could be such an account is deluded by a faulty understanding of the relation between mind and world.
- This faulty understanding has significant practical consequences; belief in objectivity and adherence to practices thought to be implied by it reinforces existing power relations and cultural and political chauvinism.
- Therefore, the aspiration to objectivity, whether innocent or not, serves as a prop in an ideological agenda.
- So, in other words, real objectivity is impossible and its attempted manifestations are either naive or insidious or both.

The enemy that makes such strange bedfellows—uniting critics from left and right and bringing together abstruse academics with practical politicians, advocates, and journalists—is not a single entity. In elevating objectivity to an ideal one may be endorsing any of several different ends or the supposed means of attaining them. Thus the attack on objectivity can represent a variety of different complaints. Because the values captured by the term "objectivity" vary greatly—in the extent to which they are possible, probable, actual, or desirable—the legitimacy of the complaints varies as well. In what follows we explore the most significant of these values and complaints.

II. METAPHYSICAL QUESTIONS

Our most fundamental interest in objectivity is an interest in truth. We want to know how things stand in the world, or what happens, and why. In this sense, to claim that a particular piece of journalism *is not* objective is to claim that it fails to provide the truth or the whole truth. And to deny that objectivity is *possible* is to say that there is no way to get at the truth, because all accounts of things are accounts from a particular social, psychological, cultural, or historical perspective and we have no neutral standpoint from which to adjudicate between conflicting accounts. To deny that objectivity is possible is often also to insist, not only that we can never get at the truth, but that for precisely this reason it makes no sense to think there is any such thing. Even to speak of "truth" or "the facts," these critics strongly suggest, demonstrates a certain naiveté.

To doubt that objectivity is possible, then, is to doubt that we can know how things *really* are or what *really* happens, where "really" means something like "independently of our own perspective." But there is a crucial ambiguity in the phrase "our own perspective." One way to doubt the objectivity of a story or an account of things is to challenge the particular perspective from which it is told. So, for example, one might doubt that American news accounts of the Persian Gulf War told an objective story. When our worries take this form, we may be doubting that a particular account or set of accounts is objective—that is, true or complete—but we need not be denying that it is possible to tell an objective, or at least a more objective, story. Indeed, we typically have specific ideas about how to go about getting one. We seek out foreign press reports of these events, compare them to each other and to American news reports, and evaluate inconsistencies within and between stories in light of a variety of standards. We inquire into a news organization's sources of information, likely obstacles to the reliability of its judgments, whether it has interested motives that might give it reason to distort the story. So, for example, in attempting to understand what happened in the Gulf War, the cautious inquirer will question the American media's reliance on U.S. military reports and press conferences as a source of credible information, and will attempt to find other sources of information with which to compare and assess U.S. reports. These sources will be subjected to the same kind of scrutiny.

Defenders of objectivity can point, then, to a multitude of standards and practices for evaluating the reliability of information. They do not need to claim that we are often or even usually in a position to determine the whole truth and nothing but the truth, particularly in the hurried and chaotic world that journalists cover. But it is rare, they will say, that we have no guidance whatever. We generally know how to distinguish between better and worse, more or less accurate accounts.

Often, however, the challenge to objectivity connects to deeper philosophical worries, to the centuries-old debate between realists and idealists. The metaphysical realist says that there is a world or a way things are "out there," that is, independently of our perspective. Traditionally, "our" perspective meant not yours or mine or our culture's, but the human perspective, or even the perspective of any possible consciousness. The ideal of knowledge presupposed by this view holds that objects or states of affairs in the world are "intrinsically" or "independently" a certain way, and that knowledge consists in somehow "mirroring" the way they are.

The metaphysical idealist denies that we can know what the world is like intrinsically, apart from a perspective. The world is our construction in the sense that we inevitably encounter it through our concepts and our categories; we cannot see the world concept- or category-free. Kant, the father of the contemporary idealist

critique, described universal categories shaping our perception of the world that are necessary for human beings to experience the world at all. The sense for Kant in which we cannot get outside our perspective is unthreatening, because by "our" perspective Kant meant not that of our clan or culture but that of all human consciousness. So understood, idealism poses no threat to objectivity. The idealist can make all the distinctions the realist can make: between the real and the illusory, what is "out there" and what is "in here," the objective and the subjective. Lions are real and unicorns mythical; trees and sky are "out there" and stomachaches and beliefs are "in here." Idealism leaves everything as it is (D. Luban, 1986).

But Kant opened the door to a more threatening relativism. For having admitted that our knowledge of the world is relative to a framework, it was a natural step to the view that the categories molding our experience depend partly on concrete and particular conditions that vary from culture to culture, community to community, even person to person. When twentieth-century thinkers took this step, arguing not simply that reality is constructed but that it is socially constructed—constructed differently, therefore, by different groups and cultures—they repudiated Kant's consolation that we could accept idealism while preserving objective, because universal, knowledge.

III. GLOBAL DOUBTS AND LOCAL DOUBTS

We need a better understanding of what critics of objectivity mean when, in support of the view that our news accounts of events are not objective, they tell us that reality is socially constructed. Perhaps they mean that our culture, our political and other interests do much to structure and determine the way we (whoever "we" may be) look at the world, and that our news reports reflect, reinforce, and even create these biases. There can be little doubt that this is true. Yet some of the sharpest critics of the press make this argument without calling into question the possibility of objectivity; indeed they rely on it. The assertion that reality is socially constructed suggests something more than that we are strongly influenced by our surroundings, for no sensible person would deny this. There is a finality and inevitability about the claim: we believe what we believe because of our gender or class or cultural attachments; others with other attachments believe differently, and there is no adjudicating between our beliefs and theirs, for there is no neutral standpoint.

Perhaps objectivity's critics mean that we can never get outside the particular worldview in which we have been raised, that we can never look at it, criticize it, judge it. But this seems implausible, because they themselves seem to have succeeded in doing so. The judgment of bias rests partly on other sources of information, which taken separately or together have, the critics believe, proved more consistent or coherent.

The defender of objectivity argues, then, that we can criticize a statement or description as biased or unobjective only against the background of some actual or possible contrast, some more accurate statement or better description. We have a variety of means to settle differences between conflicting beliefs or to establish one view as superior to another. We get more evidence, seek out other sides of the story, check our instruments, duplicate our experiments, reexamine our chain of reasoning. These methods do not settle all questions, but they settle many. In showing us how, say, British news stories construct reality, critics of necessity depend on the possibility of seeing and understanding alternative versions of the same events. And if no means existed to compare these alternative "realities," the charges would have no bite. For the critics' point is not that these alternative "realities" are like so many flavors of ice cream about which *de gustibus non disputandum est* but that those who see things in one way are missing something important, or getting only a partial view, or even getting things wrong.

The social constructionist critique seems to vacillate between two different and incompatible claims: the *general,* "global" assertion that objectivity is impossible because different people and cultures employ different categories and there is no way of deciding which framework better fits the world; and the charge that *particular* news stories or mass media organizations serve ideological interests or represent the world in a partial or distorted or otherwise inadequate way. But it can be argued that insofar as objectivity is impossible there can be no sense in the claim—certainly none in the rebuke—that the media are ideological or partial, for these concepts imply the possibility of a contrast. Conversely, the defender of objectivity may say, insofar as we agree that the media serve an ideological function or bias our vision, we implicitly accept the view that other, better, more objective ways are possible.

IV. TRANSCULTURAL COMMUNICATION

Implicit in the critique of objectivity is the assumption that different cultures possess worldviews so different they are impermeable to outside influence. On this view, different cultures cannot engage in genuine conversation with each other, because they speak different conceptual and evaluative languages and employ different standards of judging. And there are no available yardsticks external to the culture by which to judge these internal standards of judgment.

Against this claim the defender of objectivity can bring two objections. First, despite differences in worldview we share a great deal even with those from very different cultures. Second, even where we see things differently from those of other cultures often we can see *that* we see things differently and we can see *how* we see things differently. So our worldviews are not hermetic: others can get in and we can get out. As we shall see, the two points are not wholly separable: the distinction between sharing a perspective and being able to understand another's perspective is not sharp.

It is easy to fall under the sway of the doctrine of cultural relativism. At a certain point in our intellectual development—often in late adolescence—we are struck with the realization that language plays a crucial role in shaping the experience and worldview of individuals and even whole cultures. But it is easy to misunderstand and exaggerate the truth in this insight. For one thing, what impresses us depends partly on the premise that different "worldviews" take the same underlying stuff, the same data of experience, and shape it differently. The "aha experience" of relativism depends, then, on the commonsense recognition of one world out there—something that, paradoxically, the relativist is often at pains to deny.

Furthermore, the differences between worldviews can be overstated. Even those from very different cultures can agree, despite their deeply different conceptions of time, to meet at ten and to come together at what all recognize as the negotiating table. Intractable disputes between cultures arise sometimes because their values diverge; equally often, however, such disputes arise precisely because their values coincide. Both the Israelis and the Palestinians invest Jerusalem with sacred and irreplaceable value. Do their worldviews clash? As Francis I is supposed to have said about Henry VIII: "Henry and I agree about everything: we both want Calais."

Even where our points of view clearly differ, it's not clear what we should make of this fact. As Donald Davidson puts it:

> Whorf, wanting to demonstrate that Hopi incorporates a metaphysics so alien to ours that Hopi and English cannot, as he puts it, "be calibrated," uses English to convey the contents of sample Hopi sentences. Kuhn is brilliant at saying what things were like before the revolution using—what else?—our postrevolutionary idiom (D. Davidson, 1984).

Worldviews, then, are not hermetic. We can and do come to see things as others see them—not just others from our culture but from radically different ones. Thucydides brings the agony of the Athenians' war to life; Ruth Benedict gets us to see "the uses of cannibalism";

Faulkner shows us how things look to an adult with the mind of a child. The possibility of communication between cultures is perhaps inseparable from the first point: from the outset different cultures possess points of commonality and contact, and these enable us to travel back and forth. There could not be a point to history, anthropology, literature, journalism, biography, if this were not so.

V. ON THE SOCIAL CONSTRUCTION OF REALITY

If other "realities" are not hermetic and impermeable, that deflates the significance of the assertion that reality is socially constructed. For the usual connotations of the word "reality" are exhaustive and exclusive: reality is all, and all there is. If instead there are many possible realities, and ways to get from one to the other, then we can see into each other's worlds, and our realities can thereby be altered.

Perhaps critics of objectivity mean that even when we seem to escape the determination of our perception by a particular social construction, even when we seem to see things in a new light, that new perception is also socially constructed. Suppose, for example, that, partly as a result of changes in American news accounts, over the last 25 years Americans have come to understand the Palestinian point of view in the Middle East conflict better than they had before. (A New York Times/CBS News Poll found evidence of such a change in American attitudes.) It might be argued that this evolution results from differences in the American political establishment's view of its own geopolitical interests. On this view, the change is itself socially constructed out of the web of American ideology.

No doubt changing American interests partly explain the changes in perception. But to insist that apparently divergent views *always and only* derive from the push of the dominant culture's interests, from the powers that be, amounts to an unfalsifiable conspiracy theory. And the claim that reality is socially constructed is then in danger of becoming empty. If, on the other hand, it is acknowledged that other sources, apart from the powers that be, can be responsible for changes in our views, then the question is what work the concept of social construction is doing. Is the point simply that ways of looking at the world do not come into being *ex nihilo*, but are rather the product of . . . of *something*—the total social-political-economic-cultural-psychological-biological environment? And is this anything more than the claim that everything has a cause? It is not clear what, beyond these extremely general assertions, the view that reality is socially constructed adds. For if every view is socially constructed but no view could *not* be socially constructed we learn nothing of substance when we learn that reality is socially constructed.

This is not to deny that the media often present events in a distorted, biased, or ideological way. It is rather to say that we can only explain this fact on the assumption that there are better and worse, more and less faithful renderings of events, and that, despite our own biases, preconceptions, "conceptual schemes," we can sometimes escape our own point of view sufficiently to recognize how it imposes a structure or slant on events.

The word "reality" is to blame for some of the confusion. In an influential article on objectivity and the media Gaye Tuchman argued that "the act of making news is the act of constructing reality itself rather than a picture of reality" (G. Tuchman (1978) *Making news: A study in the construction of reality,* p. 12. New York: Free Press). Tuchman's point trades on ambiguities in the term "reality."

News can illuminatingly be said to construct reality rather than a picture of it in two senses. First, some events are genuine media creations. When *Newsweek* in the 1980s proclaimed on its cover that "Nixon Is Back," then in a crucial sense Nixon *was* back. To have arrived on *Newsweek*'s cover is to be back from whatever realm of nonbeing one formerly inhabited. We have here a variation on the Pirandellesque insight that "It's the truth if you think it is": "It's the truth if they (the major media) say it is." But this rule applies to only a very limited fraction of our beliefs and a tiny portion of the total news product.

Second, the act of reporting news is an act of constructing reality in the sense captured by the sociological commonplace that "if a situation is defined as real it is real in its consequences." If people believe that news stories of an event are accurate, they will behave accordingly, and for certain purposes those stories function as "reality." This is sometimes simply a matter of the bandwagon effect: when a news story describes college-bound students' scramble for admission to elite institutions, more students may panic and start scrambling.

But journalists purport to represent an *independent* reality. Defenders of objectivity argue that although journalists often fall short, without the concept of a reality independent of news stories we undermine the very basis on which to criticize the media's constructions, as well as the motivation for journalists to do better.

VI. THE EXISTENCE AND MEANING OF FACTS

Clearly, whether or to what extent objectivity in journalism is possible depends on what we mean by "objectivity." Belief in objectivity need not mean that every question that can be posed or about which people might disagree has a single determinate right answer.

What, then, does belief in objectivity commit one to? At the very least it means that *some* questions have determinate, right answers—and that all questions have wrong answers. So, for example, it is a fact that in 1992 and 1996 Bill Clinton was elected President of the United States, and that in 1995 the New York State legislature reinstated the death penalty.

Presumably objectivity's critics do not deny that Clinton is President or that the death penalty was reinstated in New York. How, then, do they reconcile these facts with their repudiation of objectivity? We find several strategies.

1. One is to insist that nevertheless such facts are socially constructed. The question is what this means. No one would deny that for there to be such a thing as a President of such a thing as the United States, a variety of complex social institutions must be in place. If that is all it means to say this fact is socially constructed, nothing significant turns on admitting it. But typically the point of emphasizing the constructedness of a fact is to undermine its truth or credibility. Yet however constructed "Bill Clinton is President" may be, it is no less true or credible for that.

A variation on the theme that all facts are socially constructed is the claim that they are all "theory-laden." Certainly every factual statement can be understood to imply decisions about the usefulness or appropriateness of categorizing things in one way rather than another. Should even the most commonsensical of such categorizations be dignified with the label "theory"? If so, we must keep in mind that there are theories and theories. "The human fetus is a person" and "The PLO is a terrorist organization" are laden with controversial theories; "The earth revolves around the sun" and "The lion is a mammal" are laden with theories not seriously contestable in modern times. Facts, then, may be theory-laden; but whether they therefore lack objectivity depends on the particular theories they carry as freight. "Bill Clinton is President" may in some sense rest on a theory or conceptual framework, but it is one so widely shared and innocuous that the label "theory-laden," usually brought as an accusation, loses its bite.

It may be said that the facts just mentioned are not interesting facts, and that this weakens the point they are used to illustrate. In what sense are they not interesting? Surely New York's reinstatement of the death penalty is in many respects interesting. The critic must mean that it is uncontroversial that these *are* facts. But because the social constructionists sometimes seem to include all facts, however humdrum, in the realm of the constructed, this might itself be viewed as a concession to objectivity.

2. A different strategy for the relativist is to exempt such facts from the realm of the socially constructed, but to insist that they are trivial and that all nontrivial "facts" of the kind prominent in news stories are socially constructed in an interesting sense. Yet this is a significant concession. First of all, there will be a very large number of these trivial facts. Second, they will serve as a crucial check constraining all the nontrivial, socially constructed "facts" that are supposed to make up the bulk of the news. Finally, having admitted the existence of some non-socially constructed facts, the relativist may find it difficult to draw the line between these and the socially constructed ones, especially given the constraints the former place on the latter.

3. A third strategy is to admit that some facts are independent of socially produced theories but insist that nevertheless these facts will be interpreted differently by members of different groups or cultures, and that these interpretations, themselves social constructions, will invest the same facts with different meanings. This claim can be understood in at least two ways.

(a) In one sense there is no disputing that these facts will be interpreted differently by different people. We all agree that the New York State legislature reinstated the death penalty, but we disagree about the reasons for it and about the agents ultimately responsible, its consequences, its symbolic significance.

Yet our disagreements about these matters of "interpretation" will in turn depend partly on other facts, such as people's beliefs about crime and about the efficacy of capital punishment. The constraint of facts will rule out some interpretations as wrong, even if it typically leaves room for reasonable disagreement about which interpretation is right. The web of expectations on which everyday life depends rests on the possibility of knowing all sorts of things "beyond a reasonable doubt." So although there is generally room for disagreement, interpretations of the facts are not wholly outside the reach of objective assessments. Some interpretations are better than others, and some are simply wrong.

(b) A second sense in which it may be said that different people and groups will invest the same facts with different meanings is best understood through an example. A study of British, American, and Belgian coverage of elections in Ireland found that the BBC story focused on the potential consequences of the vote for British–Irish relations; the CBS story used the election as a peg to talk about Irish unemployment and its potential consequences for immigration to the United States; and the Belgian account focused on the role of the Catholic Church in Irish politics, the relation between church and state being an important issue in Belgium (M. Gurevitch et al., 1991). It makes sense to say that each story began with the same set of data but interpreted them differently, selecting certain facts for emphasis or interpretation.

The point is important, and the significance of this "meaning construction" function of the mass media should not be underestimated; it bears extensive examination. But those who stress this point often seem to misunderstand its relevance (or lack of it) to the question of objectivity. The British, American, and Belgian news reports invest the Irish election with different meanings—they see it as signifying different things—but they all refer to the same set of events. Indeed, the three stories may not disagree about the truth of basic facts; rather they emphasize different facts as being important. It is no surprise to find that the same events have different significance for people of varying histories, cultures, or interests. We might put this point by saying that the issues raised here go *beyond* the question of objectivity, but they do not subvert objectivity.

VII. BEYOND OBJECTIVITY?

Belief in objectivity need not mean that to every question we might ask there must be a single right answer, or that there is one right way for a reporter to tell a story. Imagine a continuum of objectivity along which to locate the variety of subjects and statements news reporters investigate. At one end we find the relatively straightforward and uncontroversial facts of the kind just discussed. In the middle we find statements about which clearly there is a truth, a "right answer," but where to a greater or lesser extent the answer is difficult to discover. How did the dinosaurs become extinct? Who were the high-ranking Communists in British Intelligence? Did O. J. Simpson murder Nicole Simpson and Ronald Goldman? The answers to some of these questions may depend partly on what we mean by certain terms (like "murder"), but even assuming consistent usage we may reasonably disagree about the answers. Still, no one doubts that there are definite answers.

The line is sometimes thin between cases where clearly there is a truth about the matter although we have difficulty finding out what it is, and those where it cannot be said that there is a truth about the matter. For many of the complex goings-on between people, both at the "macro" political level and at the "micro" interpersonal level, the language of truth and objectivity may be thin and inadequate. When, for example, we have heard in detail "both sides of the story" from two quarrelling lovers or friends, we may sort out some clear truths about what happened, but in the end we may still be left with a residue of indestructible ambiguity, where it is plausible to say not simply that we do not know for sure what happened but that at the appropriate level of description there is no single determinate thing that happened.

Examples of this kind of ambiguity and indeterminacy abound for the most interesting and important subjects covered in the news. Did Clarence Thomas sexually harass Anita Hill? Uncertainty may depend partly on insufficient evidence and doubts about the credibility of witnesses. But disagreement may depend on other things as well: on different understandings of how sexual harassment should be defined and on related questions about the meaning of certain gestures, expressions, and interactions. Depending on the framework in which we embed the bits of evidence, the gestures and utterances, we will get different answers. And the question "Which framework is the appropriate one?" may not always have a determinate answer.

On the other hand, these matters are not always up for grabs. Once we know the context of a given utterance or action, the ambiguous often becomes unambiguous. Did he or didn't he? The answer may be yes or no.

So the defender of objectivity can perfectly well agree with Stanley Fish that "no degree of explicitness will ever be sufficient to disambiguate the sentence [for example, what he said to her] if by disambiguate we understand *render it impossible to conceive of a set of circumstances in which its plain meaning would be other than it now appears to be*" (S. Fish, (1980). *Is there a text in this class?* pp. 282–283. Cambridge: Harvard Univ. Press). But as long as we can know what context, framework, or set of conventions actually governed the circumstances—which we sometimes can—we will be entitled to conclude that in *these* circumstances he meant x or did y.

Questions about the application of concepts such as sexual harassment or racism reside in the murky area where fact meets value, description meets evaluation. Some who would describe themselves as objectivists would deny that values are objective; to the extent, then, that sexual harassment and racism are evaluative rather than descriptive concepts, they would part company with other objectivists who say there can be a truth about such matters as whether a remark is racist or a person has sexually harassed another. Facts can be objective, the first group would say, but value judgments cannot be. Yet our commonsense understanding of concepts like racism and sexual harassment supports the view that they can be applied or misapplied: that it can be true or false that a remark is racist or that one person sexually harassed another. Facts and values are not so neatly separable. The inseparability of facts and values is commonly taken to support the anti-objectivist position: facts are not that "hard," because they are infused with values. But the shoe can be placed on the other foot: values are not that "soft," because they are infused with facts.

The larger question lurking here of the objectivity of value judgments goes beyond the scope of this essay. But two points are worth making. First, the realm in which this question is relevant forms a limited part of the object of journalistic investigation. Journalists are typically concerned with issues at the more factual end of the continuum. Second, the journalist (and indeed anyone who hopes to understand the world) must arrive at the conclusion of indestructible ambiguity or indeterminacy very reluctantly, only after the arduous search for the truth has been found not fully realizable.

This suggests that the journalist must proceed on the assumption that there is objective truth, even if sometimes in the end she concludes that within a particular realm the concept of truth does not apply, or that in any case we will never discover it. It is not irrelevant to note that the vehemence with which defenders of both Thomas and Hill (a group that came to include a large number of Americans and other observers) made their respective cases reveals that *they* had no doubt that there was a right answer to the harassment question. Perhaps they were deluded. But it is significant that people behave and think as if there were a truth about these matters.

Some would argue that they cannot do otherwise, that the concepts of objectivity and truth function for us as "regulative principles," in Kant's sense—ideals that we must suppose to apply, even if at the limit they do not, if we are to possess the will and the ways to understand the world.

VIII. THE POLITICS OF OBJECTIVITY

In the foregoing sections we have seen why critics have thought objectivity is impossible, and also why others find the concept indispensable. But we still do not have a complete answer to the question why many critics not only deny that objectivity is possible but believe it is a pernicious idea.

The main reason is that they see the claim of objectivity as the expression of an authoritarian, power-conserving point of view. Michael Schudson describes this attitude as it arose in the 1960s:

> "objective" reporting reproduced a vision of social reality which refused to examine the basic structures of power and privilege. It was not just incomplete, as critics of the thirties had contended, it was distorted. It represented collusion with institutions whose legitimacy was in dispute (M. Schudson, (1978). *Discovering the news. A social history of american newspapers*, p. 160. New York: Basic Books).

There are a variety of accusations implicit here that need to be sorted out.

First, the assertion of objectivity seems to heighten the status of claims to which it attaches. To insist not only that the enemy is winning the war, but that this statement is objective, seems to elevate it to a higher plane of truth or credibility. The assertion of objectivity then appears to involve a certain arrogance, a setting up of oneself as an authority. Now in one sense this concern seems unwarranted. Ordinarily when we say "The sky is blue" we imply "It's an objective fact (for all to see) that the sky is blue." My belief that what I say is true or objective adds nothing to the belief itself. At the same time, to the extent that we are convinced of our own objectivity or that of others, we are less likely to be open to other points of view. Belief in one's own objectivity is a form of smugness, and may lead to a dangerous self-deception. Belief in the objectivity of others—including the news media—enhances their credibility, often unjustifiably.

So acceptance of the ideology of objectivity—the view that institutions like the news media are generally objective and are sincerely committed to objectivity—has significant political consequences. A person's belief that a newspaper always and only publishes true and objective information will serve as an impediment to her political and intellectual enlightenment, whether she is a consumer or a producer of news. But for the ideology of objectivity to have the political consequences critics suggest, we must add a further premise: not only that people believe the press is objective, but also that the news provided favors the powers that be. (We can imagine an alternative: an opposition press with a great deal of authority and credibility.)

Is the press biased in favor of the powers that be? One reason to think so is that mass media organizations are vast corporate entities; they are *among* the powers that be, and so have interests in common with them. We can also raise a different question, however. Does the commitment to objectivity *itself* create biases in favor of the conservation of political power? This is the implicit claim of some of objectivity's critics: that the methods associated with the ideal of objectivity contain an inherent bias toward established power.

One reason for thinking that objectivity is inherently conservative in this way has to do with the reporter's reliance on sources. Among the canons of objective journalism is the idea that the reporter does not make claims based on her own personal observation, but instead attributes them to sources. Yet sources must seem credible to perform the required role, and official, government sources—as well as other important decision makers in the society—come with ready-made credentials for the job. In addition, they often have the skills and the resources to use the news media to their advantage. Yet such sources are not typically disinterested observers motivated only by a love of truth.

Journalists therefore confront a dilemma. If they provide to such sources an unfiltered mouthpiece, they serve the sources' interests. To avoid this outcome, journalists must make choices about which of the sources' statements are sufficiently controversial to call for "balancing" with another point of view, and they must choose those balancing points of view. And if, where the official view is doubtful, they merely balance the official source's view without even hinting at the probable truth, they mislead the audience. Each of these policies raises troubling questions about objectivity.

The first alternative, simply to provide an unfiltered mouthpiece, characterizes the press's response to Joseph McCarthy in the 1950s. This example, widely cited by objectivity's critics, has helped tarnish its reputation. But although we can see why journalists might have worried about challenging McCarthy's accusations, it seems clear that leaving them unanswered does not satisfy any intelligent conception of objectivity. Objectivity is supposed to be a means to truth; giving credibility to baseless charges—whether by commission or omission—should not count as objective.

If this is so, it follows that journalists must always make judgments about the credibility of sources and what they say. But when does a source's statement invite challenge? The obvious answer is: when it seems controversial. Yet what seems controversial depends on the consensus existing in the culture at a given time. And that consensus derives partly from powerful ideological assumptions that, while unchallenged in the culture, are by no means unchallengeable. So it is that I. F. Stone argues that "most of the time objectivity is just the rationale for regurgitating the conventional wisdom of the day." What goes without saying may be dogma rather than truth.

Supposing, however, that the journalist does recognize that an official view is sufficiently controversial to invite challenge, she must choose which opposing sources to cite and how to frame the debate between the opposing points of view. Is the dispute taken to span a fairly narrow range of the political spectrum? If so, the press may be criticized for simply reproducing the conventional wisdom. Is the opposing point of view chosen an "extreme" one? (Obviously what we take to be extreme depends again on the prevailing consensus at the time. For a hilarious parody, see A. Cockburn (1987). The Tedium Twins. In *Corruptions of Empire*. London: Verso.) In that case the press may sensationalize the issue or marginalize the opposition by making them seem eccentric or irrational. Either way, the journalist cannot avoid exercising judgment.

These dilemmas explain another of the standard criticisms of journalism's commitment to objectivity: not that it necessarily favors established power, but that it

leads to a destructive agnosticism and skepticism. Objectivity must be "operationalized," and this is achieved through the idea of balance. In exploring controversial issues, the journalist does not himself commit to a view, but instead gives voice to different sides of the story. The reader is left to judge the truth. But if the journalist truly balances the views, there may be no rational way for the reader to decide between them. And so he concludes that "there's truth on both sides," perhaps that every view is as good as every other. Rather than connecting with truth, objectivity, according to this way of thinking, leads to cynicism and skepticism.

Yet it might be argued that both these criticisms—that objectivity favors established power, and that it leads to skepticism and indecision—suffer from too mechanical a conception of objectivity. It is easy to see how the problems they address arise in the transition from objectivity-as-an-ideal to objectivity-as-a-method. In part, they may proceed from a confusion between objectivity and the appearance of objectivity. Questioning the remarks of an important public figure may look partisan, while leaving them unchallenged does not; but the appearance is misleading and only skin deep. Similarly, leaving two opposing points of view to look equally plausible where one has the preponderance of reason and evidence on its side is a charade of objectivity. It reflects the common mistake of confusing objectivity and neutrality. The objective investigator may *start out* neutral (more likely, she is simply good at keeping her prior beliefs from distorting her inquiry), but she does not necessarily *end up* neutral. She aims, after all, to find out what happened, why, who did it. Between truth and falsehood the objective investigator is not neutral.

The confusion between objectivity and neutrality may arise because of the belief, alluded to earlier, that "values" are not objective, true, part of the "fabric of the universe." According to the positivist outlook of which this is part, the objective investigator will therefore remain "value-neutral" and his inquiry will be "value-free." But the identification of neutrality and objectivity within a given realm depends on the assumption that there is no truth within that realm. Leaving aside the question whether values are objective, if facts are objective the objective investigator will not be neutral with respect to them.

As a journalistic virtue, then, objectivity requires that reporters not let their preconceptions cloud their vision. It does not mean that they have no beliefs, or that their findings may not be significant and controversial. Nevertheless, it is easy to see why many people confuse objectivity and neutrality. Often the outsider cannot easily tell the difference between a reporter who has come to a conclusion based on a reasoned evaluation of the evidence, and one who was biased toward that conclusion from the start. The safest way to seem objective, then, may be to look neutral.

IX. CONCLUSION

There are good reasons to suspect claims to objectivity. People who insist on their own objectivity protest too much; they are likely to be arrogant, overconfident, or self-deceived. In fact, those who acknowledge their own biases and limitations probably have a better chance of overcoming them than those who insist they are objective. Those who have faith in the objectivity of others may be complacent or dangerously naive. They fail to see the many obstacles—inborn and acquired, innocent and insidious, inevitable and avoidable—on the way to truth.

Often, furthermore, the press can rightly be accused of ideological or other bias. Sometimes these biases result from overt economic or political purposes, as when news organizations suppress damaging information about corporations to which they belong; sometimes from structural or technological features of media institutions, such as television's reliance on good pictures. But it is also true that, paradoxically, the aspiration to objectivity can contain biases of its own, by advantaging established sources or by encouraging an artificial arithmetic balance between views and tempting reporters to maintain the appearance of neutrality even in the face of overwhelming "nonneutral" evidence.

Finally, we must mention one further way in which,

perhaps more than any other, the media shape our thinking. As one observer has put it, "The press doesn't tell us what to think, but it tells us what to think *about*." Journalists select from the innumerable events taking place in the world those to report, and, by giving them more or less prominence in a newspaper, magazine, or program, imply a great deal about their significance. As we saw earlier in the example of the Irish elections, even once an event has been chosen for coverage, there are crucial questions about which aspects to emphasize and how to interpret them. Whether these matters of selection fall squarely within the sphere of objectivity may be debatable; clearly they are intimately related.

Despite the variety of barriers to and limitations on objectivity, however, there are reasons for thinking that insofar as we aim to understand the world we cannot get along without assuming both its possibility and value.

Bibliography

Davidson, D. (1984). The very idea of a conceptual scheme. In *Inquiries into truth and interpretation*. New York: Oxford University Press.

Gurevitch, M., Levy, M., & Roeh, L. (1991). The global newsroom. In P. Dahlgren and C. Sparks (Eds.), *Communication and citizenship: Journalism and the public sphere in the new media age*. London: Routledge.

Luban, D. (1986). Fish v. Fish or, some realism about idealism. *Cardozo Law Review* 7.

Schiller, D. (1981). *Objectivity and the news*. Philadelphia: University of Pennsylvania Press.

Schudson, M. (1978). *Discovering the news: A social history of American newspapers*. New York: Basic Books.

Tuchman, G. (1972). Objectivity as strategic ritual. *American Journal of Sociology* 77.

Political Obligation

TERRY HOPTON

University of Central Lancashire

GLOSSARY

anarchism Rejection of political authority in any form as immoral.

consent Self-assumed, voluntary obligation of obedience to political authority.

contract Historical or quasi-historical, formal act of consent to establish political authority, which is held to be binding on subsequent generations.

hypothetical consent An obligation inferred from the belief that we ought to consent to political authority because it is legitimate, or because to consent would, in any case, be rational.

legitimacy Conformity of political authority to an independent criterion of rightness in terms of origin, procedure, or performance.

nonvoluntarist theory A form of theory of the Right that identifies obligations as a duty binding on individuals, irrespective of their own acts of commitment or consent.

philosophical anarchism An anarchist theory based on the failure of theories of political obligation that, nevertheless, accepts that there may be moral reasons for compliance.

political obligation Obligation of the individual to polit-

ical authority, such as the law, government, or state, which is a moral reason for obedience.

pseudoproblem A philosophical "problem" that arises as a result of conceptual confusion and that is, because of this, incapable of solution.

tacit consent Consent given without an explicit or formal act, but that can be conventionally inferred from absence of dissent.

Theory of the Good The theory that certain acts are obligatory or right because they contribute to a state of affairs independently defined as morally good.

Theory of the Right The theory that certain acts are obligatory or right in themselves, irrespective of their consequences.

utilitarianism A form of theory of the Good that uses the pleasure or happiness consequent on acts as the criterion of what counts as morally good, and as a means of identifying what is right or obligatory by means of their contribution to this.

voluntarist theory A theory that identifies obligations as self-assumed by individuals by means of their acts of commitment or consent.

I. THE CONCEPT OF POLITICAL OBLIGATION

A. The Meaning of Political Obligation

The expression *POLITICAL OBLIGATION* has come to stand for a number of related problems concerning the relationship between politics and morality. Its central question is taken, variously, as asking why the individual morally ought to obey the law, government, state, or political authority generally. But it has also come to include other, more detailed, questions, such as those concerning the role of state intervention in specific areas and, at the other extreme, to include the most general pictures of political life and the human situation.

B. Origin of the Concept

The term "political obligation" only came into use in political theory after T. H. Green's *Lectures on the Principles of Political Obligation* of 1895. Green took political obligation as the core problem of political thought, both as constituting the newly reestablished academic discipline of political theory and as identifying a canon of classic texts from earlier periods. Although Green took the problem to be characteristic of individualist theories, which he was concerned to criticize, by extension it came to represent at a highly abstract level *the* theme of the history of political thought, from Plato's *Crito* to the present. (This was despite the enormous variety of political thought and practice that this encompassed). Green also sought to show how a theory of political obligation could be used to provide practical moral guidance on a range of practical political issues. These ranged from state regulation of the sale of alcohol to the justification of the death penalty. Few subsequent thinkers have shown a similar practical concern, being concerned with the problem at a more abstract level. Nor has much interest been shown in Green's solution to the problem, which consisted of a reinvigorated form of citizenship exemplified in practical service to the community.

C. Political Obligation and Ethics

It is important to emphasise that the problem of political obligation is concerned with *justification*, asking why people *ought* to obey the law, government, and so on, and not with the *explanation* of why, in fact, most people *do* obey. This is so even if their belief that they are justified in obeying is an important cause of their obedient behavior. In this sense some empirical theories, and "realist" theories, which might interpret such beliefs as an ideological sham to legitimate coercive power, are *not* about the problem of political obligation.

D. Classification of Theories

There is a considerable variety of potential solutions to the problem of political obligation, and although it is possible to classify these in different ways for different purposes, it is suggested that the following classification at least has the virtues of simplicity and clarity. It also accords with very general distinctions employed in contemporary ethics, which, given the insistence that the problem is a moral one, seem appropriate. Even so, two reservations must be made for reasons that will soon become apparent. First, the classification is not intended to be hard and fast, but as merely providing some signposts in a difficult landscape. Second, although it is possible to identify most theories with the name of a classical political theorist, because it seems that we have the entire history of political thought to draw on, this retrospective recruitment of contributors will inevitably be at the cost of insensitivity to their particular historical context. Moreover, pigeonholing into even the general classification suggested here might suggest that each thinker had only one solution to the problem. In fact, thinkers like Locke employ elements of different types of theory in an ensemble that seeks to achieve a structure of argument in order to influence a defined audience in a particular ideologically charged context.

It is possible to arrange theories of political obligation into three groups corresponding to basic responses to the question of obeying the law, government, and so on. First, those that claim that we *do* have a political obligation, a view which can be cautiously ascribed to most political thinkers of the past. Second, those that claim that we *do not* have a political obligation, a view identified with anarchist thinkers in the last 200 years. Third, those that claim that the problem has no clear answer because it is a result of conceptual confusion, or a *pseudoproblem,* a view explicitly held by some recent philosophers.

II. THEORIES OF POLITICAL OBLIGATION

A. Arguments for Political Obligation

The pattern of argument employed by theories seeking to show that we have a *political* obligation, is to take a familiar *moral* obligation and attempt to show that the former is analogous to, or a special case of, the latter. Our puzzlement about political obligation is thus solved by the use of a moral principle "writ large" as a model taken from the private to the public sphere. Given the diversity of possible moral principles in history that have come to constitute the substance of our modern moral thought, there are plenty of potential models available, not to mention many possible paradigm examples of each one. These may be broadly grouped into two categories corresponding to the contemporary distinction, popularized by Rawls, between Theories of the Right and Theories of the Good.

Roughly translated into terms of political obligation. Theories of the Right would claim that I ought to obey the law, government, and so on, because it is my duty, and that it is right to do so *in itself.* Theories of the Good would claim that I ought to obey because it will bring about a good state of affairs in consequence.

B. Theories of the Right: Voluntarist Theories

1. Consent

The most influential voluntarist theories have been consent theories of various types. These tend to model our political obligation to the government or other institutions on obligations that arise from promises or voluntary agreements, and to see the state as a voluntary association. They emphasize that obligations are self-assumed individual commitments. Hence, although we have a duty to *keep* promises or agreements that we have made, there is no duty to *make* them. We can bind ourselves, or not, if we choose. Whatever the merits of consent theory in general, it is strongly concordant with modern notions like individual autonomy. Hence, if we believe both that we are politically obligated *and* autonomous, something like consent as a free and rational restriction of one's own freedom *must* be assumed. Similarly, if we believe that people are in some sense politically equal, the exercise of authority as a form of political inequality can only be comprehended as a result of consent if it is to be legitimate. While few doubt that political obligation could be created by consent, the problem is in indentifying when, where, and how this occurs. It is possible to distinguish several forms of consent theory according to their different stipulations of which of our acts count as our political consent.

a. Consent: Contract Theories

The first consent theory, and the theoretical paradigm for later versions, is the idea of a historical contract. By means of a contract, or similar agreement, men had passed from a prepolitical state of nature into a civil society, and this agreement was held to be binding on subsequent generations in that society. This type of theory, generally termed *social contract,* became dominant in the 17th century, when it accorded with the pervasive assumption that historical origins settled questions of legitimacy. Some thinkers were cautious about asserting the actuality of such a historical event. This was understandable because contemporary critics pointed to the lack of evidence for a contract, to its absence from scriptural accounts (taken as historically true and divinely sanctioned), and to the uncertainty of the *terms* of the contract (evidenced by the variety and number of contracts used by different thinkers). Critics also ob-

jected to the idea that we could be bound by the consent of our ancestors (or at least that we could without invoking a separate duty of inheritance). In part, it was a tribute to the genius of contract theorists, to its concordance with new ways of thinking like individualism, and to its ideological value, that it was dominant in the face of such serious objections. In part also, theorists, such as Hobbes and Locke, employed other forms of consent theory alongside the contract. And it is these other forms that have become central to contemporary thinking about consent, while the historical contract idea lost its influence during the 19th century. These forms seek to retain the force of a contract and its conditions of validity, like absence of coercion and deception, without its formality and historicity.

b. Consent: Tacit Consent

In the *Second Treatise,* Section 119, Locke famously claimed that people tacitly consent to their government simply by living within its jurisdiction, although he was careful to indicate that this was so only if it was legitimate. Legitimacy here was defined as respecting and maintaining rights. This argument appears to be more plausible now than in Locke's time, because more people today have a degree of choice of living elsewhere, if they object to a government, in a way that was open to few then. The main objection to this account is that it robs consent of its meaning. Any act by any person, even done unwittingly, is taken as their consent. This is not to deny that there *is* such a thing as tacit consent, whereby even the absence of action, such as dissent, can be taken as consent. This is familiar in group meetings where actual votes are absent. But these cases exist because there are well-understood conventions about the moral significance of inaction at a given juncture. Locke, however, merely asserts that there is a binding convention about residence that takes *all* action at *any* time, or simply the absence of emigration, as constituting consent. There are strong grounds for doubting the existence of a convention, especially when those allegedly acting in compliance with it are unaware that they are doing so. (They may be said to follow the convention, but they cannot be acting in accordance with it.) The consequence would be that people, paradoxically, would be surprised to hear of their own "consent" when, elsewhere, consent conventions normally entail a self-conscious choice. In fact, Locke's tacit consent appears both unavoidable and deceptive in a way that would undermine the validity of more explicit formal acts of consent like contract.

c. Consent: Hypothetical Consent

An alternative form of consent theory, advanced by Pitkin, and attributed by her to Locke, is that of hypothetical consent. This directs our attention even more to the legitimacy of government. If government is fulfilling its moral purpose, however defined, then we ought to consent to it. Actual consent is reduced to the role of providing evidence of legitimacy, rather than creating it. An alternative formulation claims that consent to a legitimate state is simply *rational.* While a degree of rationality is normally required for a person to be counted as capable of consenting, to claim that rationality *is* consent is every bit as dubious as claiming that residence is. That people *ought* to consent, or rationally *would* consent, is simply not *actual* consent, but (at best) a background to it. Moreover, the problem of political obligation is, on this account, merely relocated to the problem of legitimacy, without answering the obvious questions of what makes a government legitimate and why I should obey one legitimate government rather than another, (that is, why is one *my* government?).

Looking at the three versions of consent mentioned so far, all meet the absence of actual consent to government by individuals by postulating a dutiful "double," who consents on our behalf, and yet over whom we have no control.

d. Consent: Voting

A more promising possibility, not widely available to earlier theorists, is to identify our *actual* consent with voting. Because voting is the one conspicuous and "official" political act that most contemporary citizens do every few years, this would go a long way toward the universality of obligation that most theories seem to seek. True, there are those who do not, or cannot, vote, and these presumably are not obligated (mere opportunity of voting cannot be consent). The problem here, as with tacit consent, is whether there is a well-established convention that identifies voting with consent to government. Voters think that they are choosing a representative and a party of government, but are they, at the same time, accquiring or confirming an obligation to obey even if "their" party loses? It could be argued that, by taking part, freely and deliberately, in elections their consent is *implied.* Consent to a procedure is consent to its outcome if it could reasonably be foreseen, as is the case with majority decisions. But such a suggestion seems quite idealistic in view of what we know about voting behavior, the electoral process, and democratic systems generally. And if one votes *against* a party, say the Nazis in 1933, does this obligate you to their government if they win?

e. Consent: Reformist Consent

One response to the difficulties of both the absence of actual consent, and of counting other things as its equivalent, is to admit that the political system cannot be interpreted to fit the theory. Instead, the system must be changed in practice so that it relies on actual consent and also provides the encouragement and reasons for people to consent. This reformist theory, suggested by Beran, for example, requires things like the establishment of "dissenter's territories" to ensure that there is a genuine alternative in order to make consent a reality. It would not be overly cynical to suggest that governments are unlikely to carry out such reforms, preferring nonactual consent that can safely be taken for granted.

A more radical theory, like that of Pateman, insists that a yet more fundamental change is required. Here, the suggestion is that consent is not enough, implying as it does, acceptance of something presented *to us,* rather than a participation *by us,* in creating and shaping it. This leads in the direction of direct participatory democracy.

2. Fair Play

Alongside consent theories it is worth considering another theory that can be conveniently classified as a voluntarist Theory of the Right. This is the fair play theory that originated in the work of H. L. A. Hart and Rawls. It likens the state to a voluntary scheme of cooperation where the benefits of the scheme are made possible by the contributions of the members. It suggests that if one is a beneficiary of the contributions made by others, then one has an obligation to reciprocally contribute and, by so doing, to continue the scheme. By analogy, it is argued that if one benefits from the state in the form of, say, security, and this is made possible by contributions by others in taxation and keeping the law, then one has, in turn, an obligation to pay tax and keep the law when the occasion arises. However, as Simmons points out, this only appears plausible if we are voluntarily members of the scheme, or have become so by voluntarily *accepting,* rather than passively *receiving,* benefits. These requirements serve as the equivalent of consent. While this element does appear to be needed for political obligation to arise, it is difficult to make a distinction between acceptance and receipt when the state's benefits, unlike smaller schemes, are unavoidably open to all (for example: defense). This makes it impossible to identify noncontributing beneficiaries or deliberate free-riders who could be excluded, or conversely, to identify those willingly committing themselves. In effect, the benefits are compulsory, because unavoidable, and few would accept that they create an obligation in return. A commercial equivalent would be receiving unsolicited goods followed by coercive demands for payment. A possible exception suggested by Klosko are "presumptive" benefits, for example: security that we can assume people *must* want (and would *accept* if a convention for doing so was available). However, one might ask whether they want them at *this* cost, and from *this* source (that is, political obligation to the state), especially if there are alternative suppliers. And, in any case, this merely reiterates the problem of hypothetical consent where if we "must" means that we "ought" to consent. And this does not create a political obligation. Moreover, it is important that the scheme *is* fair for fair play to arise. This means that there should be an accepted fair allocation of contributions and benefits across the scheme and some relation between the two in the case of each member. It is neither obvious nor uncontroversial that this is the case with the state, given persistent and undeniable inequalities in society.

C. Theories of the Right: Nonvoluntarist Theories

1. Duties of Obedience

In contrast to the voluntarist theories just considered, nonvoluntarist theories argue that we have a duty of obedience irrespective of our choice. Many of these fail to correspond to modern ideas of individuality, and they presuppose a world view that has largely disappeared from Western societies. For example, highly influential theories that argued for unquestioning obedience to the king on the basis of divine right, by scriptural injunction (especially Romans 13), by appeals to natural hierarchies, or by analogy with children's duties to parents (patriarchialism), have all lost their force. (This does not, however, necessarily apply outside Western societies.) A more sceptical suggestion might be that they have been replaced by consent only in a form that, despite its voluntarist credentials, proves to be as unavoidable as duty ever was. Despite this general picture, two types of duty have been suggested as models for political obligation in recent years, although both contain voluntarist elements.

a. Gratitude

It has been argued by A. D. Walker that our political obligation arises as a debt of gratitude, owed to government, for the benefits that it has bestowed upon us. This may also prove to be the basis for the family duties of children to parents employed in earlier theories like patriarchialism. Gratitude is normally *warranted* when a benefactor bestows an unquestioned benefit, at the cost of some sacrifice on his part and without seeking a return of benefit. Gratitude is normally *expressed* in degree and kind according to conventions of appropriateness that, nevertheless, leave much discretion to the beneficiary. Paradigm cases tend to be of highly personal debts of gratitude such as that owed by someone who had been drowning to his rescuer. Some deny that an institution, for example a hospital, rather than an individual within it, can be treated as a benefactor. Even if a government is not ruled out for this reason, it is difficult to see it as making sacrifices to provide benefits, especially when these are paid for by the taxation of the recipients. It would also be naive to see this provision as disinterested, rather than designed to generate feelings of gratitude and, hence, support. This might be compared with commercial sponsorship, or even bribery, rather than pure beneficence. Another reservation about the gratitude model is that government, in contrast to normal benefactors, demands the degree and kind of gratitude that it expects (namely: political obligation). And although this model drops the idea of a scheme as used in the fair play theory, it does rely on the benefactor–beneficiary relation being continuous in a way that is relatively rare in modern society. It also shares with the fair play model the difficulty of distinguishing acceptance and recipience. This is not normally a difficulty in paradigm cases of gratitude, such as life saving, where acceptance is obvious (albeit in dire necessity). But it may well be so in the case of "open" state benefits.

b. Natural Duty of Justice

The second nonvoluntarist duty suggested as a model for political obligation is that of natural duty. In traditional versions this would crucially depend on shared foundational assumptions about the moral significance of "nature" in a wide sense. In the recent version found in Rawls' *A Theory of Justice* there is a natural duty to obey *just institutions,* including states, on entirely different foundations. This is because parties in Rawls' "original position," a hypothetical situation of fairness, would base their rational political obligation on this. (They would, as hypothetically rational individuals, decide to make obedience to a just state their duty.) It is also, supposedly, in accordance with out intuitions about the necessary arrangements of a just socity. The plausibility of this account crucially depends on the plausibility of Rawls' theory as a whole, and here one can only say that the debate continues. However, it seems that even if this account does not actually turn into a hypothetical consent theory, it will suffer from the same problems.

D. Theories of the Good

Having looked at Theories of the Right, both voluntarist and nonvoluntarist, and found them deficient as theories of political obligations, it is necessary to turn to Theories of the Good. Here the obligation is generated by its contribution to a good state of affairs.

1. Utilitarianism

This is by far the most familiar and influential contemporary version of a Theory of the Good, where goodness is defined as utility (itself defined as pleasure, happiness, welfare, and so on). Here the right action depends on the net utility it produces in consequence (after deduction of its disutility). This appears to rule out action done in accordance with obligation as having any independent or special worth. But in one variety of utilitarianism—rule utilitarianism—obligations are reinstated as rules, the following of which have been found to have indisputable utility. Here it is argued that obligations have to be kept, even when specific breaches would produce seemingly greater utility, because otherwise uncertainty and disappointed expectations (both disutilities), would result. Obligations, including political obligation, are thus justified as contributing to "the greatest happiness of the greatest number." In fact, apart from this, utilitarianism has very little more to say on the subject. It takes the utility of government, and the obedience to it, for granted, by assuming that it is indispensable as a means to the utilitarian end.

The utilitarian account of political obligation is entirely dependent on the validity of utilitarian theory in general. While it was used by Bentham and his successors as a public philosophy, and might be suitable on that account for *political* obligation, it does have major disadvantages. This is in spite of its admission of voluntarism, either in the form of individual choice or discovery by individuals of what makes them happy. (The plurality of many different individual pursuits is "cashed" into the common currency of utility.) It is this individualism, and a kind of economic rationality, that seems to accord with widespread modern ideas.

Although it has not lacked for ingenious defenders, utilitarianism is widely thought to have severe limitations. Many are unconvinced that its account of obligation is really satisfactory. Others doubt that one can really *calculate* utility—especially when only the vaguest examples are offered by utilitarians. Others, too, object to the assimilation of moral reflection to a form of calculation as being a distortion. This is particularly so as it suggests that deep convictions, that form our moral identity, are also merely the contingent product of calculation. And if utilitarianism is meant to uncover the logic of our moral beliefs, there seem to be examples where the sacrifice of individuals for the greater happiness is promoted in a way rejected by common morality. For these reasons, utilitarianism is probably an insecure foundation for political obligation.

2. Other Theories of the Good

Of course the Good need not be defined in utilitarian terms. It could be defined in more specific terms, but this would be at the cost of more general acceptance. This difficulty can be evaded by invoking ideas like *the common* or *public good,* but when these are unpacked they tend to lose their plausibility. In terms of political obligation, this move will still rely on the state as a necessary, or uniquely effective, way of promoting whatever counts as the Good. However, it must be conceded, because many ideas of the Good presuppose political order for their attainment, the role of the state is not obviously easily dispensed with. Hobbes, in particular, was anxious to remind men of this.

3. Aristotle's Theory of the Good

A much older theory of the Good is that of Aristotle, although to call this "a theory of political obligation" is stretching the definition a good deal. Here, participation in the life of the state as a citizen is seen as *intrinsic* to the good life for any human being of full rationality. It is not a *means* to something else, such as an individual's privately chosen good. To be political, for Aristotle, is part of what it means to fulfill the function of a human being, as cutting is to fulfill the function of a knife. The idea of obligation seems out of place here for two reasons. First, the morality is one of virtues or excellencies of character, rather than the modern morality of duties and obligations. It is a human excellence to be a citizen. Second, the state is not something *other* than the citizen, to which he needs to be bound by an obligation. Rather the state *is* the citizen body. This represents an ideal where each rules, and is ruled in turn, as equals. In practice, as Aristotle knew, there is a distinction between being a good citizen and being a good man in any state, short of the ideal. It is this distinction that makes the arguments of Plato's *Crito,* concerning the acceptance by Socrates of the death penalty imposed on him by Athens, seem so central to the problem of political obligation.

Although the recovery of the importance of the Political, that some contemporary theorists call for, would contribute to making a revival of Aristotelian citizenship possible, it is not at all clear how this could be done without the most massive changes in modern society. (This would apply to Green's idea of citizenship also, even if he does not seem aware of this.) Not only that, but a new metaphysical foundation would be required to establish the idea of a human "function." This would be something that is quite alien to modern ways of thought.

III. ANARCHIST THEORIES

A. The Form of Anarchist Theories

Having looked at theories that claim that we *do* have a political obligation, it is worth pointing out that none of them claims that this obligation is absolute. The absence of moral reasons for obligation becomes the grounds for refusal or even for a duty of resistance. It is the defining feature of anarchist theories that they claim that we *never* have a political obligation to government. However, because most envisage anarchy as a form of society rather than chaos, other obligations or communal ties are accentuated to *displace* political obligation, or to *become* political obligation in a nonauthoritarian form. The pattern of argument that emerges is one in which one form of obligation, familiar in everyday morality, is taken as the model, *not* for obedience to government, but for the operation of an alternative form of society. In fact, it can be suggested that every obligation that has been used as a model for government, can be used as a model to replace it.

B. Philosophical Anarchism

A recent type of anarchism, which explicitly addresses the problem of political obligation, philosophical anarchism. In Simmons' version it is a *last resort* following the failure of all other theories. After examining most of the theories mentioned above (citizenship being a notable absentee), and finding none adequate, he concludes that there is *no* political obligation. His argument depends on the list of candidate theories being exhaustive and exclusive of each other. It is thus vulnerable to the production of an additional theory, or to the (admittedly faint) possibility that a composite theory might not suffer from the defects of its constituent theories. It is also vulnerable to counterargument in support of the theories that he rejects.

In fact, the consequences, of Simmons' position are insignificant in practice, because he believes that our ordinary, everyday various moral obligations, *not* treated as models of political obligation, are sufficient to tie us to our political society. At the very least, government is left in place as a significant nonmoral fact of life. Much the same is true of Wolff's theory, where philosophical anarchism is a *first resort*. Wolff argues that the quest for a theory of political obligation is doomed from the start. In a devastatingly simple argument, he claims that to be a moral agent is to be autonomous, but that to obey authority is an abdication of autonomy (and by definition immoral). It follows that autonomy and authority are incompatible, and any theory of political obligation "justifying" obedience *must* fail, because it is necessarily immoral. Wolff's critics, of whom there are many, have pointed out that this idea of authority is so strong that it preludes *any* commitment, because it is a loss of autonomy. Authority, in turn, is defined as something that is obeyed *because* it is authority and for no other reason. There is no compelling reason to accept these definitions, which take common

understandings of them to extremes. Wolff's attempts to fill out his argument become quite confused. He does make clear that there is an exception to his claim that a legitimate state is a "logical impossibility," and that exception is a unanimous direct democracy. This is, however, eventually dismissed as utopian. Surprisingly, despite the radical sound of this theory, it will, Wolff believes, have little effect in practice. He believes that philosophical anarchists will autonomously find good reasons of their own to *comply with* rather than *obey* "their" government and state.

C. Classical Anarchism

In the classical anarchist theories and their contemporary descendants, there is a rejection of the state, accompanied by suggested measures for its abolition. They propose an alternative form of society based on the strength of a moral principle, such as nonviolence in Tolstoy, or collective solidarity in Bakunin. Such arguments rely on the possiblity that a moral principle that some people adhere to some of the time, will be adhered to by just about everyone just about all of the time. This would then serve as the basis for a new society. If this possibility was dismissed, anarchist writers would still serve to remind us that even governments and states that are normally thought of as legitimate have many morally dubious features. And this only goes to emphasize the difficulty of the problem of political obligation.

IV. POLITICAL OBLIGATION AS A PSEUDOPROBLEM

The final response to the problem of political obligation is that of what could be called "conceptualism." This argues that the problem is incoherent and that no justification of obligation is either possible or necessary. This argument was developed as a response inspired by 20th-century analytical or linguistic philosophy to the diversity of previous theories, and to the failure of any to gain wide acceptance. The reason for this scandalous state of affairs was held to be due to the imprecision of the problem, and to the craving for a general theory—when there could only be different reasons for obedience, for different people, in different cases. (Asking why I should obey the state was analogous to asking why I should read books.) While there is much force in these objections, a stronger group of arguments was advanced, which purported to show that the problem could not even arise. The state was compared to the rules of a game like chess. Objections made to following laws, or rules, can only show that we have not understood that *that* is precisely what membership of the state, or playing the game, means. But this obviously depends on an untenable analogy between states and games. A second argument, related to the first, pointed out that a legitimate state *ought to be obeyed* because that is what *legitimate* means. One has, simply by defintion, an obligation to a legitimate state. But even were this true, and the meaning of legitimacy is hardly clear-cut, this only displaces the problem to one of deciding what counts as legitimate, as was noted in the case of hypothetical consent earlier. A final argument asserted that seeking a justification of the state went beyond the bounds of meaningful justification. By analogy, while we can doubt our senses *on occasion* it does not, contra Descartes, make sense to doubt them *always*. We may, then, doubt particular obligations, but not that we are still obligated to the state. But the morality of obedience is hardly as indubitable as the veracity of our senses. Certainly, to doubt specific political obligations presupposes that there can be genuine political obligation, but it does not, *of itself,* establish that there is.

Two things make the conceptual argument persuasive. One is the implied limitation to liberal democracies, where legitimacy is taken for granted. The other is the assumption that any justification of political obligation must be metaphysical and thereore unacceptable in the new philosophical climate. The consequence of the argument is, by denying there is a genuine problem, to assume that there *is* political obligation, but that it is something about which we must remain silent and leave as it is.

V. CONCLUSION

Recently there have been some indications of a new direction in thinking about political obligation. Dworkin has suggested that political obligations most resemble those generated in friendships and other groups that can be classed as neither the result of a voluntary decision or as nonvoluntary. These "associative" or "communal" obligations suggest a move from the individualism that most contemporary theories presume. A related suggestion is made by Horton who argues for a richer understanding of what membership of a polity entails than can be captured by analogy with one particular model of obligation.

None of the theories considered are without difficulties. This is true of theories that seek to show that we *do* have a political obligation, or that we *do not,* or that it is *not a genuine problem*. Yet it is clear that people act as if there was an obligation. The practice of obeying political authority seems to persist, while theories come and go. Perhaps even if no theory is successful, each raises considerations that should have a place in any moral reflection by individuals about politics. Rather than *solve* the problem, such considerations make us aware of the difficulties involved. This applies also to actions and relationships in respect of institutions and practices not normally thought of as political, in our more general social and economic lives, for instance, areas normally thought of as private.

Bibliography

Beran, H. (1987). *The consent theory of political obligation.* London: Croom Helm.

Gans, C. (1992). *Philosophical anarchism and political disobedience.* Cambridge: Cambridge University Press.

Harris, P. (Ed.). (1990). *On political obligation.* London: Routledge.

Horton, J. (1992). *Political obligation.* London: Macmillan.

Klosko, G. (1992). *The principle of fairness and political obligation.* Lanham, MD: Rowman and Littlefield.

Marshall, P. (1993). *Demanding the Impossible: A history of anarchism.* London: Fontana Press.

Pateman, C. (1985). *The problem of political obligation* (2nd ed.). Oxford: Polity Press.

Pitkin, H. (1992). Obligation and consent. In P. Laslett, W. G. Runciman, & Q. Skinner (Eds.). *Philosophy, politics and society* (4th series). Oxford: Basil Blackwell.

Simmons, A. J. (1979). *Moral principles and political obligations.* Princeton, NJ: Princeton University Press.

Walker, A. D. (1989). Political obligation and gratitude. *Philosophy and Public Affairs,* **18,** 359–364.

Wolff, R. P. (1976). *In defense of anarchism* (2nd ed.). New York: Harper and Row.

Pornography

SUSAN EASTON

Brunel University

GLOSSARY

erotica Erotica represents the world of the sensual and depicts sexual activity but, unlike pornography, does not present sexual relations in a degrading or dehumanizing way.

harm principle The principle that the only ground on which intervention is justified is to prevent harm to others; the individual's own good is not a sufficient justification.

moral independence The concept that the individual should not be prevented from freely expressing ideas, provided that no tangible harms to others result directly from their expression, even if others think those ideas are foolish, mistaken, or offensive.

obscenity Material that is indecent, offensive to modesty or decency, expressing or suggesting lewd thoughts, and tending to deprave and corrupt. Obscene materials appeal to a prurient interest in sex and portray sexual conduct in a patently offensive way.

pornography The word "pornography" originates from Greek and means writing about prostitutes. It has also been defined as sexually explicit material that subordinates women through pictures or words.

PORNOGRAPHY has been described as hard to define but easy to recognize. Justice Stewart said in *Jacobellis v. Ohio* (1972, 378 U.S. 184) that he was unable to define pornography but he knew it when he saw it. The word "pornography" originates from Greek and means writing about prostitutes. Pornography should be distinguished from obscenity, which means filthy or disgusting. Obscenity rather than pornography is the term normally found in legal instruments. The *Oxford English Dictionary* defines "obscene" as filthy, indecent, offensive to modesty or decency, expressing or suggesting lewd thoughts. It defines "pornography" as the description of the life and manners of prostitutes and their patrons. Legal usage does not conform to everyday language or to dictionary definitions.

I. DEFINING PORNOGRAPHY

Schauer favors a definition of pornography in terms of sexual depiction rather than obscenity, as obscenity could, but need not, be pornographic, and pornography may, but need not, be obscene (1982. *Free Speech: A Philosophical Inquiry*. Cambridge Univ. Press, Cambridge). In England the Obscene Publications Act 1959 has been used to prosecute leaflets extolling drug use but has been deployed primarily to control pornography.

Obscenity is defined in the Obscene Publications Act in terms of its tendency to deprave and corrupt, that is, its impact rather than content. In considering whether the material in question is obscene, the court will consider whether its effect is, taken as a whole, such as to tend to deprave and corrupt persons who are likely, having regard to all relevant circumstances, to read, see, or hear the matter contained or embodied in it. The material may include books, pictures, films, and video-cassettes. However, the future medium for the dissemination of pornography is likely to be computer disks or CD-ROMs, and as Manchester notes, there may be problems in controlling the electronic transmission of material under existing legislation (C. Manchester, 1995. *Crim. LR,* 546). Does a computer disk constitute an article as defined in section 1(2) of the 1959 Act? If information is transmitted electronically does it constitute a "publication" under the Act? The Home Affairs Committee's report (*Computer Pornography* (1994), H.C. 126) recommended amending the legislation so that the electronic transmission of information from one computer to another constitutes publication.

The Obscene Publications Act includes a public good defense if it can be proved that publication of the article in question is justified as being for the public good on the grounds that it is in the interests of science, literature, art, or learning, or of other objects of general concern. The focus in English law is on the state of mind of the consumer, rather than on harms to others. The legislation was criticized by the Williams Committee for its inconsistency. It noted the difficulty of finding a reliable criterion for separating work of no value from valuable work, and of relying on juries to reach decisions on such matters (B. Williams, 1979. *Report of the Committee on Obscenity and Film Censorship.* Cmnd 77. HMSO, London). It has also been criticized by feminist campaigners because it does not take account of the effects of pornography on women.

Child pornography is covered by the Protection of Children Act 1978 which makes it an offense to publish, distribute, or take an indecent photograph of a child. Section 160 of the Criminal Justice Act 1988 makes it an offense to possess an indecent photograph of a child. The Criminal Justice and Public Order Act 1994 tried to strengthen the law relating to adult and child pornography and to restrict children's access to harmful videos. It amends the Protection of Children Act to cover data stored on a computer disk or by other electronic means which is capable of conversion into a photograph or pseudo-photograph. The question of harm is also recognized by sections 89 and 90 of the 1994 Act which amends section 2 of the Video Recordings Act regarding the classification of video recordings, so that an authority in reaching a decision regarding the suitability of a video recording should have special regard to any harm which may be caused to potential viewers, or through their behavior, to society by the manner in which the work deals with criminal behavior, illegal drugs, violent behavior, or incidents, horrific behavior or incidents, or human sexual activities.

In the United States Catherine MacKinnon and An-dre Dworkin, in drafting Minneapolis and Indianapolis ordinances, defined pornography as sexually explicit material which subordinates women through pictures or words. It includes scenes of women enjoying pain, humiliation, rape, and penetration by objects or animals, or shown as bruised or hurt in a context which makes these conditions sexual. It would also include scenes of men and children being treated in sexually dehumanizing ways.

Recurring themes found in pornography include multiple rape, men planning and executing a rape which the victim enjoys despite initial resistance, sadism, and the profaning of the sacred. The latter dimension has received less attention in current debate, but in the past has been used as a strong motif in pornographic works, featuring in the writings of de Sade. The view of pornography as liberating, radical, and challenging has partly developed because of the shock and outrage caused by profanity.

Feinberg distinguishes three definitions of obscenity. Obscenity may be used in a pejorative, judgmental way, to suggest the offended state of mind of the maker of the statement. It is also used by the courts to refer to material aimed at producing an erotic response in the consumer. Thirdly, obscenity may be used in a neutral way to classify material, for example, describing the fact that it contains certain words (J. Feinberg, 1987. *Harm to Others.* Oxford Univ. Press, London). Obscenity is seen by Feinberg as a particular form of offensiveness, suggesting disgust, producing what he calls a "yuk" reaction, and allurement.

He is critical of the identification of pornography with obscenity. Although the two may overlap they are not identical. Because pornography is used descriptively to refer to sexually explicit writing and pictures, he says it is narrower than the obscene. Pornography is confined to sex, while obscenity is more than sex. But it may be difficult to maintain such a sharp distinction since disgusting materials might still be intended to produce a sexual response and have that effect, however bizarre the taste or the audience.

The U.S. Supreme Court's analysis of obscenity has developed in the context of assessing challenges to the constitutionality of laws passed by state legislatures to control obscenity. Prior to 1957 the Court used the Hicklin Test, the tendency to deprave and corrupt, when considering obscene materials. In *Roth v. United States* (1957, 354 U.S. 476) the Supreme Court excluded obscene material from the protection of the free speech principle, but since then the Court has had difficulties in defining what constitutes obscenity. The test of whether material was obscene was whether the dominant theme of the material taken as a whole appeals to a prurient interest. The effect on the average person is taken into account, applying contemporary community standards to the work. Each of these concepts has raised problems of interpretation. In *Stanley v. Georgia* (1969, 394 U.S. 557) the possession of obscene material at home was held to be protected by the right to privacy.

In *Miller v. California* (1973, 413 U.S. 15) the court defined obscenity to mean works which appeal to a prurient interest in sex, which portray sexual conduct in a patently offensive way, and which, taken as a whole, do not have serious literary, artistic, political, or scientific value. The court affirmed that prohibitions on obscenity do have constitutional validity, but subsequent attempts to ground regulation in harm, such as the Indianapolis ordinance, have received little support from the court.

The aim of the ordinance was to hold pornographers accountable for injuries to others; to provide remedies, including damages and injunctions, for proven injury; and to prevent unjust enrichment from that injury. Men, children, and transsexuals injured by pornography would also have been able to obtain remedies under the ordinance. It encompassed a number of issues, including trafficking, assault, coercion, and the forced consumption of pornography. The Indianapolis ordinance was struck down in the Supreme Court as a violation of First Amendment free speech rights.

In considering the ordinance in *American Booksellers v. Hudnut* (1986, 475 U.S. 1001), the Supreme Court acknowledged the harms caused to women by pornography. But the harms were seen as outweighed by the need to protect free speech rights, and the ordinance was seen as a content-based restriction, which discriminated on the basis of viewpoint. It amounted to "thought control" in defining an approved view of women and it was stressed that the feminist view of pornography was one standpoint among others. Perceptions of pornography varied according to standpoint, and the ordinance could therefore not be justified. While a civil rights ordinance was favored by reformers in the United States, in England consideration has been given to other possibilities, including a criminal offense of incitement to sexual hatred.

A distinction is also often drawn between erotica and pornography, the former representing the world of the sensual and depicting sexual activity, but unlike pornography, not presenting sexual relations in a degrading or dehumanizing way. However, while this distinction is well established in Western culture, in other cultures such as China, erotic or even romantic material may be seen as pornographic.

A useful classification was given in *R. v. Butler* (1992, 89 Dom LR 449) where the Canadian Supreme Court distinguished between materials depicting the following: (i) explicit sex with violence; (ii) explicit sex without violence, but which subjects people to treatment that is degrading and dehumanizing; and (iii) explicit sex without violence which is neither degrading nor dehumanizing. Feminist campaigns for regulation and prohibition are directed at the first two categories.

Demands for the regulation of pornography raise philosophical, empirical, and legal questions. The philosophical issues include the question of whether pornography constitutes speech, the boundaries between speech and conduct, the nature and scope of the free speech principle, and the relationship between the state and the individual. The empirical problems center on the measurement of the effects of pornography. Legal problems have arisen over the drafting of appropriate legislation, evidentiary problems regarding the burden and standard of proof, the appropriate remedies for those harmed by pornography, and procedural issues concerning the responsibility for determining the impact of pornography in a particular case (whether this should lie with expert witnesses, the jury, or the judiciary). Problems have faced the courts in determining the scope of free speech protection and framing appropriate legislation in England and the United States.

II. THE REGULATION OF PORNOGRAPHY

The dispute over pornography and censorship has split both liberals and feminists. The role of pornography in legitimating and perpetuating violence against women has been of great concern within feminism. As well as stimulating theoretical debates, the problem of pornography has also generated political activism, culminating in pickets of sex shops, "off the shelf" campaigns directed at high street retailers, and vigorous demands for legal constraints on the free market in pornography.

The emancipatory potential of pornography in liberating sexual inhibitions and providing affirmation to sexual minorities has also been considered. The demands for the regulation of pornography have been seen as raising the issue of censorship of ideas and publications by the state. Once the regulation of pornography is in place, it is feared that there is a risk of censorship of political, religious, and artistic works, including gay and lesbian literature. There are many literary, artistic, and educational texts which have been suppressed in the past but which have later been recognized as valuable. The risk of suppression is that unconventional political views and artistic expression will be crushed, and the effect of state censorship is to stifle radical thinking.

The problem of pornography has been a central issue within liberalism, and arguments both for and against the regulation of pornography may utilize classical liberal ideas. Mill's "On Liberty" offers a useful source of concepts and methods, including the harm principle, which are used by both sides in the pornography and censorship debate. Liberal defenders of pornography have deployed Mill's notion of moral independence, his plea for toleration, and his focus on the importance of a range of opinions for social and individual improvement to allow for the possibility of learning through errors and experience.

Millian arguments have dominated debates on free speech and censorship. The major justifications of free speech found in English and American jurisprudence, including the democracy and truth justifications, are advanced in Mill's writing and have been used by defenders of pornography. The harm principle has underpinned this debate.

III. THE HARM PRINCIPLE: THE LIBERAL DEFENSE OF PORNOGRAPHY

Mill's objective in "On Liberty" was to chart "the nature and limits of the power which can be legitimately exercised over the individual" (1970, 126). What is needed, said Mill, is one very simple principle to govern the relationship between society and the individual. The principle he offers is the harm principle: the only ground on which intervention is justified is to prevent harm to others, and "his own good, either physical or moral is not a sufficient warrant" (1970, 135).

The feminist demand for regulation of pornography, a matter which properly concerns only the passive consumer, would be seen by defenders of pornography as a clear example of the unwarranted intrusion of public opinion and constraints into the self-regarding sphere. Pornography is seen as "harmless" in so far as no compelling evidence has been offered of any tangible harm to others. Of course one might argue that it is in the consumer's interest to refrain from this activity, and therefore to restrict access to pornographic materials because they are demeaning to users and they divert them from more worthy self-enhancing occupations. It is precisely this type of argument for restriction which is ruled out on Mill's principle, for here the focus would be on the consumer, and "in the part which merely concerns himself ... over his own body and mind, the individual is sovereign" (1970, 135). For Mill, no matter how degrading and depraved an activity is, if no one else is affected by it, the fact that others may think that foregoing this activity would make an individual a happier or better person is not sufficient to justify the imposition of sanctions.

Mill exempts from his doctrine immature and mentally impaired individuals, so children and those who are incapacitated are excluded, but adults' preferences clearly fall within the principle of liberty. Within this domain of personal liberty lie the realms of consciousness, thought, and feeling. Where opinions are concerned, whatever the subject matter, absolute freedom is essential.

The appropriate guardian of the individual's mental, spiritual, and physical health is the individual. If the effect on others infringes their rights or substantially affects their interests, then regulation of the harmful activity might be appropriate, but otherwise the appropriate sanction would be mere criticism.

On this argument, legal regulation of the kind embodied in the Indianapolis Ordinance would seem to be an unjustified intervention, as sexuality is the most private area of self-expression and self-realization. Consequently attempts to control pornography, other than by persuasion, have been firmly resisted by liberal theorists. Any increase in state power is seen as an evil in itself and the specter of state officials investigating private activities and thoughts accounts for much of the liberal fear of feminist protest. This fear has also characterized some feminist approaches, and partly accounts for skepticism over the use of the law as a feminist strategy.

In defending the realm of personal sovereignty, Mill stresses that he is not undervaluing the exercise or development of higher faculties, or treating all pleasures as equal. But the "lowest" preferences deserve protection: no one is warranted in preventing other adults from adopting a particular activity—from doing what they like with their own lives—when they are the best judges of their own feelings. The outsider may offer observations on more edifying pursuits and seek to persuade, but ultimately individuals must decide for themselves.

Mill recognizes that there may be hard cases which lie on the boundary between self-regarding and other-regarding action, but this is precisely why a free and wide range of opinions are necessary, in order to find the best policy to adopt consistent with respect for the individual's rights and interests. If activities such as drinking and gambling are acceptable in private, why should we condemn them because they operate as a business, governed by commercial considerations? Similarly one might argue that if sexual relations conducted by consenting and loving adults constitute a social good, then individuals working in the sex industry should not be attacked simply because the cash nexus is involved. However, Mill recognized that commercial motives and financial interests could lead proprietors to encourage excessive use of drink and gambling.

The fear for the liberal defender of pornography is the prospect of disapproval being hardened into legal and physical restraints on actions—into civil or criminal sanctions. Even if *some* pornography is used for improper means, for example, as an aid to rape by an unbalanced individual with a prior disposition to harm others, this does not justify denial of access to pornography to the vast majority of law-abiding consumers who use pornography for private noncriminal activities, for example, as harmless fantasy or sexual aids.

Claims of a causal link between the circulation of pornography and violent crime have met with considerable skepticism from pornographers, commentators, and investigators, including the President's Commission (The Report of the Commission on Obscenity and Pornography, 1970. Washington, U.S. Government Printing Office, Washington, DC), in the United States and the Williams Committee (1979) in the United Kingdom. But some defenders of pornographers further argue that pornography has positive benefits in contributing to individual and social well-being, including liberating individuals from taboos and constraints at the harmless level of fantasy, promoting personal growth and awareness, and providing a catharsis for individual sexual tensions. Pornography may also be used in therapeutic programs to reeducate sex offenders away from negative perceptions of sexuality into more positive attitudes and behaviors.

Restrictions have found more favor than prohibition with liberal commentators. The Williams Committee (1979) advocated restricting the public display of material which others find environmentally unattractive and denying access to sex clubs to minors, while leaving adults a free choice whether or not to buy the goods or to enter those clubs. Restrictions were also imposed by the Indecent Displays (Control) Act 1981.

Millian principles have often been invoked in defense of free speech. Free speech has been seen as essential to the functioning of democracy and representative government, the promotion of autonomy, and the pursuit of the truth. Applying these justifications of free speech to pornographic materials has proved difficult. Pornography does not constitute political speech and does not contribute to the democratic process, so it is hard to justify it by appealing to the democracy justification. The point was made forcefully by Justice Stevens in *Young v. American Mini-Theatres* (1976, 427 U.S. 50) that every schoolchild can understand the duty to defend the right to speak in relation to political or philosophical discussion, but "few of us would march our children off to war to preserve the citizen's right to see Specified Sexual Activities exhibited in the theater of our choice."

The autonomy justification is also difficult to apply since pornography contributes little to the self-fulfillment of the consumer or to the promotion of autonomy, and the truth justification is problematic since pornography makes no obvious contribution to the pursuit of the truth. In fact it may prevent the discovery of the truth about women's abilities. Some might argue that pornography should not be seen as speech because it lacks the dimension of communication, but is simply a sexual aid, but others would argue that what is pernicious in pornography is precisely the message it communicates about women. If it is seen as speech it might be seen as a form of commercial speech which contributes to sex discrimination and therefore justifies a much lower weighting than political speech.

Nonetheless pornography has attracted considerable and vigorous support from defenders of free speech. Freedom of thought is meaningless without the freedom to publish. A slippery slope argument is also invoked in support of the pornographer's right to publish. If sexual material is restricted, then sex education in schools may be exposed to the risk of control and political ideas, and literary and artistic works will also be under threat. Moreover, it is argued that a free market in ideas and opinions is essential to the public good in affording the possibility of acquiring knowledge of satisfying ways of living.

In modern liberal thought the right to consume pornography has been defended by Ronald Dworkin, who bases his defense on the right to moral independence, that is, the right not to suffer disadvantages in the distribution of social goods and opportunities or in liberties just because others think that one's opinion about the best way to lead one's own life is flawed. He says the right to moral independence demands a permissive legal attitude toward the consumption of pornography in private. His argument would permit a restriction scheme similar to that advocated by the Williams Report. The individual's right to moral independence cannot be breached simply on the grounds that the community as a whole will benefit. For Dworkin the right trumps utilitarian demands for prohibition when the majority find the idea of consuming pornography offensive.

Dworkin's critique of the Williams Report and his defense of the right to consume pornography has been subjected to criticism from within feminist theory, but some feminists have used Dworkinian ideas to support an argument for regulation. For example, if one begins from the premise of mass culture, one might accept a Dworkinian rights-based argument and yet reach an opposite conclusion to Dworkin. One might argue that the effect of a free market in pornography is to violate women's right to autonomy, self-fulfillment, and equal concern and respect, and that the free speech of pornographers silences women's speech. A free market gives more weight to the preferences of producers and consumers of pornography than to women's rights to autonomy and equality. If women's right to autonomy is given more weight, the case for regulation does not rely here on the condemnation of the consumer as a bad person and so does not violate the consumer's right to moral independence.

One could also appeal to Dworkin's notion of integrity in adjudication which demands that consistency be achieved so that moral and political principles held by the community apply equally to all members of the community in all areas of the legal system. The principle of integrity demands equal consideration of women's interests and this encompasses the regulation of pornography (see S. Easton, 1995. Taking Women's Rights Seriously: Integrity and the ''Right'' to consume pornography, *Res Publica*, 1(2), 183). On this argument the regulation of pornography could be construed as compatible with existing principles, in terms of the established limits on free speech.

Acknowledgment of the other-regarding nature of speech is reflected in the civil law of defamation and the criminal law of incitement. The harms of words, as Schauer argues, may in certain cases far exceed harms from physical injuries, if one's whole livelihood, for example, is affected by a libelous statement. The effects of speech may be extensive, affecting community relations or gender relations, for example, in the cases of ''hate speech'' directed at ethnic minorities and women, as well as inciting immediate violence or hatred. Mill recognizes that effect of speech on others and formulates the problem of free speech in terms of calculating the negative consequences of speech against the ill effects of speech suppression. As Schauer observes, the protection of free speech in American law and jurisprudence may be given not because it is self-regarding, but despite the fact that it is other-regarding and in some cases harmful or offensive to others. Offensiveness will not always justify restraints on speech, and toleration of offensive speech may be the price to pay for living in a democratic pluralist society. Pornography can be seen as communicating powerful ideas and statements about the nature of women and the legitimacy of their abuse and degradation. If seen as communicative it is more likely to be included within the scope of the First Amendment.

If speech is seen as other-regarding and resulting in harm, this does not resolve the issue of regulation. The type and extent of harm would have to be sufficiently serious to warrant intervention and one would need to take account of the nature and strength of the opposing rights and interests. Consequently, the pornography and censorship debate has focused on the identification of harms; measuring the extent of harms and their proximity and remoteness; and

balancing these harms against the harms arising from suppression of pornography.

However, even if the harmful effects of pornography are accepted, harm may not be the conclusive factor in the determination of regulation as illustrated by the case of *American Booksellers v. Hudnut* (1986, 106 S.C. 1172). Here the Supreme Court, in considering the constitutionality of the Indianapolis Ordinance, affirmed the opinion of the Court of Appeals in *American Booksellers v. Hudnut* (1985, 771 F.2d, 7th Cir.), which had accepted evidence of harms to women and objective causation, but concluded that the harms to women were outweighed by the need to protect First Amendment speech rights. This contrasts with the approach of the Canadian Supreme Court in *R. v. Butler* (1992, 89 Dominion Law Reports 449) where it was held that section 163 of the Criminal Code, dealing with obscenity, did violate the Charter of Rights and Freedom, but was justified as a reasonable limit prescribed by law.

Although it was difficult to establish the precise causal link, it was reasonable to presume that exposure to pornography affected attitudes and beliefs, including women's own self-perceptions: ''Materials portraying women as a class worthy of sexual exploitation and abuse have a negative impact on the individual's sense of self-worth and acceptance.'' The Court said that, ''Among other things, degrading and dehumanizing materials place women (and sometimes men) in positions of subordination, servile submission or humiliation. They run against principles of equality and dignity of all human beings.'' Legislation aimed at preventing harm to women and children and to society as whole was of fundamental importance and could justify infringement of the right to freedom of expression. So in *Butler* the Court accepted that the harms to women, children, and society arising from pornography could justify constraint on the free speech rights of pornographers. Pornography appeals only to the basest aspect of individual fulfillment, physical arousal, and is primarily economically motivated. Obscenity legislation is directed at the avoidance of harm caused directly or indirectly to women or other groups by the distribution of materials. Although education may be a helpful way to deal with negative attitudes to women, it is insufficient and legal measures may also be required.

IV. THE HARM PRINCIPLE: CRITIQUES OF PORNOGRAPHY

To elucidate the question of harm in relation to pornography, one needs to be clear whose interests are being harmed: the consumer's, whose capacity for self-development could be undermined by consumption, and the interests of women and society as a whole. Here we might distinguish among women's interests as participants in pornographic productions, as real and potential victims of sexual assaults, and as citizens of a society in which pornography flourishes as part of a general pattern of gender inequality. When considering the interests of society as a whole, the impact of pornography on community morality and the quality of the environment is relevant.

The types of harm may include physical or psychological effects along the dimensions of minor or serious, direct or indirect, and proven or speculative. Psychological effects were recognized by Mill as grounds for regulation.

These distinctions are important both at the level of philosophical debates and in terms of the specific problems in construing legislation in England and the United States. For example, considering *who* is liable to the depraved and corrupted is important in interpreting and applying the Obscene Publications Act 1959 in England and in determining community standards using the test formulated in *Miller v. California* (1973, 413 U.S. 15). There may also be difficulties in applying legal concepts of harm, based on tort models, when considering the impact of pornography on women as a group—as tort models are essentially atomistic and linear models. If we are dealing with harms to women as a class, the harms may be indirect rather than direct and the concept of a group injury is undeveloped in English law. If the consumer's interest is the only issue, then there is no ground for social intervention, no matter how degrading the effects of the activity. The key question in considering the regulation of pornography is whether a free market affects the interests of others sufficiently to justify constraint. The case for regulation has principally relied on the claim that obscene or pornographic materials may cause antisocial or illegal acts, including sexual offenses. A number of claims and counterclaims have been advanced, and attempts to establish a causal link raise methodological and evidential problems.

The major sources of evidence in the debate have been the results of experimental studies to test the impact of pornography on subjects' attitudes and behavior undertaken by social psychologists, the President's Commission on Obscenity and Pornography (1970), and the Meese Commission, and the testimony of victims at the Minneapolis hearings.

A review of the research on the impact of pornography was commissioned by the Home Office in Britain and undertaken by D. Howitt and G. Cumberbatch (1990. *Pornography: Impacts and Influences.* HMSO, London), who in their report could find no compelling evidence in the materials surveyed of a causal link between pornography and sexual violence: "Inconsisten-

cies emerge between very similar studies and many interpretations of these have reached almost opposite conclusions" (p. 94). They point to major methodological difficulties in the experimental studies raising doubts regarding their internal and external validity. There are also gaps in our knowledge of the relevant variables; for example, not enough is known about the attitudes which may encourage sexual attacks or the role of pornography in psychosexual development. We do not have sufficiently detailed records of sexual offenses to plot changes through time in relation to changing patterns of pornography consumption. Most of the available research is based on Canadian and American experience rather than European studies. Although reluctant to infer a causal link, the authors were nonetheless skeptical regarding claims of the advantages of pornography:

> … it would be overgenerous to the research evidence to argue a case for the benefits of pornography. The idea that pornography might serve as a substitute for the direct expression of sexual violence has not really been subject to the necessary empirical tests.… However, it is probably unrealistic to believe that there is a major contribution made by pornography in this respect since there is no substantial evidence of any reduction in sexual crime where pornography circulation rates have increased. (1990, 95)

The President's Commission on Obscenity and Pornography was set up in 1967 and reported in 1970. It made a number of recommendations which reflects the liberalization of sexual morality at that time. It reviewed the effectiveness of the existing laws on pornography and obscenity, examined methods of distribution and its effect on the public and its relation to crime, and made recommendations accordingly. The Commission could find no empirical research to firmly establish a causal relationship between the consumption of pornography and criminal behavior. It therefore recommended the repeal of existing legislation prohibit the sale, exhibition, and distribution of sexual materials to the consenting public. It could find no grounds for state interference with the reading or viewing materials of adults. The Commission's report was criticized for its selective use of statistics, and a further study undertaken by the Meese Commission came to quite different conclusions.

The question of harm was central to the Meese Commission's inquiry. This federal commission was briefed by Edwin Meese, the attorney-general, in 1985, to find new ways of controlling pornography. It reported in 1986 and recommended stronger enforcement of existing obscenity legislation as well as enactment of new civil remedies. The Report concluded that pornography does cause individual, social, moral, and ethical harm and proposed further restrictive measures. Sexually violent pornography, it concluded, is causally related to antisocial and possibly unlawful acts of sexual violence. The Commission also supported the work of citizen action groups seeking to use nonlegislative measures to reduce the availability of pornography. While the Meese Commission did not undertake its own research, it did examine research undertaken by others, including that of Malamuth and Donnerstein, who testified to the Commission.

The claim that pornography is harmless has been challenged on a number of grounds.

A. Imitative Harms

The assertion of a link between pornography and sexual crime is one of the most controversial claims advanced by critics of pornography. Murder and rape trials in the United States and the United Kingdom have, in some cases, revealed instances of apparent imitation of particular practices found in literature on the accused's person at the time, or identical to those shown in films seen by the offender. The influence of pornography on sexual offenses has been referred to in a number of English and American cases by judges, counsel, expert witnesses, and defendants [see, for example, *R. v. Taylor* (1987, 9 Cr. App. R. (S) 198) and *R. v. Holloway* (1982, 4 Cr. App. R. (S) 128)]. Pornography may be shown to the victims of sexual offenses, as in the case of *Liddle* (1985. 7 Cr. App. R. (S) 59), where the accused had a history of sexual offenses which included showing the victims pornography. In the United States, in *Hoggard v. State* (1982, 27 Ark. 117 640 S.W.2d 102), for example, which concerned the sodomy of a 6-year-old boy, the court recognized that pornography could have an instrumental role: "the pornography was used as the instrument by which the crime itself was solicited—the child was encouraged to look at the pictures and then encouraged to engage in it" (at 106).

B. Harms in the Production Process

Harm may also be involved in the production of pornography if participants suffer bodily harm as part of the filmmaking process or are coerced into taking part. Once individuals have been persuaded to appear, the film itself may be used as proof of their participation to ensure further compliance, or by threats to tell parents where minors are involved. Substantial evidence of coercion, including physical coercion and blackmail to ensure further cooperation in pornographic productions, was admitted at the Minneapolis hearings in 1983. The harms caused to the victims in these cases may be exacerbated by the repeated showings of the film. For this reason the use of injunctions where coercion has been proven was seen as a key component of the Indianapolis Ordinance.

C. The Credibility of Victims of Sexual Offenses

The effect of a free market in pornography on particular groups, namely, child and adult survivors of rape, abuse, and violence, for whom a major problem is gaining credibility, also needs to be considered. The relationship between pornography and the credibility of survivors of sexual violence is complex. Although to defenders of free speech it might seem too remote to warrant intervention, the issue needs to be addressed. It is only relatively recently that the extent of child sexual abuse has been acknowledged. New doubts regarding the credibility of child witnesses have been expressed following the Cleveland and Orkney investigations. Numerous challenges to children's evidence have been mounted, including the contentious "discovery" of false memory syndrome. Complaints of rape by adult women have for long been treated with suspicion by the police, judges, juries, and the general public. Until recently both children and women were subject to corroboration warnings when giving evidence. Proving absence of consent in rape cases has been a major problem for prosecutors, which has resulted in a reluctance to proceed with complaints from certain categories of women who are unlikely to be believed in the witness box.

If women and children are portrayed in pornography as acquiescing and enjoying violence and abuse—if these assaults are portrayed as normal sex—then it becomes harder for the survivors of sexual violence to establish their credibility and to be taken seriously.

The legitimation of nonconsensual violent sex is an important dimension of pornography. Women's subordination is portrayed as natural and normal; their rape is depicted as having a "positive outcome."

A number of small-scale studies have been undertaken to ascertain the effects of exposure to pornography on tolerance of sexual crimes and the process of desensitization (see, for example, D. Zillman and J. Bryant, 1982. *J. Comun.* **32**(4), 10–21; 1989. *Pornography: Research Advances and Policy Considerations.* Erlbaum, Hilsdale, NJ). If sex is defined in pornography as violence, then the tolerance of crimes of sexual violence may increase. This may be more pronounced as pornography becomes more violent. Some experimental studies have found that men exposed to pornography become more tolerant of rape and violence against women than men who have not been exposed to pornographic stimuli. The former are more likely than the latter to accept rape myths, seeing rape victims as having less worth and suffering fewer injuries. Social psychologists also gave evidence at the Minneapolis hearings in 1983. Laboratory experiments on "normal" males have found that exposure to pornography increases acceptance of rape myths and of violence against women (Malamuth and Donnerstein, 1984). While these studies on their own might be seen as inconclusive, the impact of pornography may be further corroborated by the experience of victims on the "receiving end" of pornography, although their experience has been underresearched.

D. The Effects on Community Morality

Constraints on pornography might also be seen as a means of upholding a community's moral standards. The focus on using law to enforce a society's moral standards has its roots in the 18th century but is associated more recently with Lord Devlin, who advanced a view which contrasts sharply with that of Mill.

Lord Devlin challenged the assumption that morality was a matter for private judgment. Society may pass judgment on moral issues and society may use the law to protect and preserve morality to enforce its moral judgments. Without this morality, society could not survive but would disintegrate. A common morality is the price paid for social cohesion. If we accept society's right to make moral judgments and that common morality is necessary to society, then society may use the law to protect morality. In practice the law should accord the maximum freedom to individuals which is compatible with the integrity of society. Privacy should be respected as far as possible but the law may justifiably intervene to protect society.

On this argument, then, if a community decides that it does not wish to live in a culture where pornography freely flourishes, it would be legitimate to use the law to express this view. Here we are taking account of the effects on society as a whole as well as on participants. A similar argument was used by Justice Burger in *Paris Theatres v. Slaton* (1973, 413 U.S. 49) where he referred to the adverse effect of pornography on "the mode,... the style and quality of life, now and in the future."

At the time Lord Devlin's view seemed out of tempo with the mood of sexual liberation. But in recent years the right of society to intervene in the private sphere has gained more support from the courts.

E. Environmental Harms

Environmental harms have also been cited in support of the case for regulation. Various ways of dealing with the environmental effects have been proposed, including limiting the number of shops which sell pornography, dispersing them through the city, or confining them to particular streets or areas through planning controls. One form of regulation used in the United States is zoning, which is usually justified in terms of offensiveness. Because it restricts rather than prohibits access to pornography, it meets with more support from de-

fenders of pornography and free speech. Pornographic bookstores have been subject to zoning laws in the United States.

The Supreme Court in 1976 upheld a Detroit ordinance confining the bookstores to certain areas. Municipal zoning ordinances will be upheld if they permit the bookstores to survive, but not if access to them is significantly restricted. In *Young v. American Mini-Theatres* (1976, 427 U.S. 50) the court held that the Detroit ordinance prohibiting the location of adult cinemas and bookshops in certain locations has a valid means of regulation because of the city's interest in protecting the character of its neighborhoods, and this interest supported its classification of films, although it included some films which might be constitutionally protected. In England a form of zoning has been deployed through planning regulations and controls on sex shops and cinemas. The Williams Report also favored the use of restriction rather than prohibition.

Although the environmental effects of sex clubs, shows, and shops may be contained by zoning, some neighborhoods are protected at the expense of others so that residents in the selected areas suffer loss of their property values as well as a poorer quality of life and a decline in their visual environment.

From a Millian perspective, a liberal feminist could advocate regulation on the harm principle on the ground that it is other-regarding and harmful to the interests of others. But even if the link between pornography and physical harm were refuted, other arguments might be advanced on which to ground a claim for regulation, including the argument from autonomy, which builds on the perfectionist strand in liberalism, associated, for example, with Joseph Raz, which sees the government having an obligation to provide a range of options which enable individuals to lead autonomous lives, to encourage those options which promote autonomy, and to discourage those which negate or undermine autonomy.

From a perfectionist standpoint, pornography may be seen as undermining women's capacity to develop their human faculties by circulating images which emphasize their unreflective nature; instead of generating new ideas pornography reaffirms women's subordination and passivity. The depiction in pornography of women as creatures lacking autonomy contributes to the perpetuation of gender inequality.

Some liberal feminists have focused on pornography as a violation of women's civil rights, including the right to equality. MacKinnon in recent writings has argued that even if pornography is deemed to be protected by First Amendment speech rights, it nonetheless violates the equal protection clause of the 14th Amendment. The Supreme Court, she argues, should acknowledge that pornography raises a conflict between two fundamental principles of liberty and equality. The use of government intervention to promote equality is accepted in other areas, such as sexual harassment, so the prohibition of pornography may be justified by an appeal to equality. The Indianapolis ordinance aimed to protect the civil rights of women and construed pornography as a civil rights violation and a practice of sex discrimination. If the pornography issue is approached from the standpoint of emphasizing the autonomy and self-fulfillment of women as moral agents and their rights to dignity and to equal concern and respect, then the argument for a free market in pornography may be effectively challenged.

Bibliography

Abel, R. (1994). "Speech and Respect." Sweet and Maxwell, London.

Butler, J. (1997). "Excitable Speech." Routledge, London.

Dworkin, R. (1996). "Freedom's Law." Oxford Univ. Press, Oxford.

Dworkin, R. (Mar. 3, 1994). Pornography: An exchange. *N.Y. Rev. Books,* 48–49.

Dworkin, R. (Oct. 21, 1993). Women and Pornography. *N.Y. Rev. Books,* 33–42.

Easton, S. (1994). "The Problem of Pornography, Regulation and the Right to Free Speech." Routledge, London.

MacKinnon, C. (Mar. 3, 1994). Pornography: An exchange. *N.Y. Rev. Books,* 47–48.

MacKinnon, C. (1993). "Only Words." Harvard Univ. Press, Cambridge, MA.

Privacy versus the Public's Right to Know

ANITA L. ALLEN

University of Pennsylvania School of Law

GLOSSARY

first amendment A provision of the Bill of Rights of the U.S. Constitution providing that "Congress shall make no law respecting an establishment of religion, or prohibiting the free exercise thereof; or abridging the freedom of speech, or of the press; or the right of the people peaceably to assemble, and to petition the Government for a redress of grievances."

privacy The inaccessibility of persons, personal information, personal property, and personal decision making to others.

public figure A person of notable, noteworthy, or notorious accomplishment or misconduct in any field of human endeavor who thereby earns the sustained attention of the general public.

public official An elected government officerholder or any responsible government agent or employee.

right to know The claim that society is obligated to adopt laws and promote practices that channel useful and important information to the general public or to an interested member or segment of the general public.

right to privacy The claim that society is obligated to adopt laws and promote practices that shield against unwanted intrusion, disclosures, and publicity, and against interference with matters of personal decision making and conscience.

sunshine law/act Any legislation requiring that government procedures or records be open to the light of inspection by the general public.

A RIGHT TO KNOW is commonly ascribed to the public. The public is also commonly ascribed a "right to privacy." Can it have both? To an extent, the public can have both the information it wants and the privacy it wants. However, conflicts between public access to information and personal privacy are common the world over. This article will describe some recurrent conflicts and efforts to resolve them through ethics, politics, and law.

I. CAN THE RIGHT TO KNOW AND PRIVACY COEXIST?

A. Social Boundaries

For the most part, the right to know and the right to privacy enjoy a peaceful coexistence. Shared cultural norms define certain kinds of information as appropriately public and others as appropriately private. By virtue of these complex and highly contextual norms, those who channel information to the general public accept social boundaries barring unwanted surveillance, disclosures, publication, or interference. Yet the boundaries between public and private are sometimes uncertain and contested. Western society is undergoing rapid cultural change. Along with other ethical, legal, and social norms, norms of public and private are in flux. Social boundaries are often unclear.

Privacy values are evolving and diverse. For example, in the United States egalitarian, informal modes of interpersonal exchange are more pervasive than in the past. More people willingly share personal information with strangers, whether for the sake of personal expression, entertainment, or public health education. In addition, the availability of more opportunities for women outside the home has altered privacy norms by bringing issues of child care, home management, and domestic violence to the public's attention. The cellular telephone, the pager, the personal computer, and other communication technologies are altering privacy expectations. Knowingly and unknowingly, users of the Internet and the World Wide Web routinely pass along personal information to reap the business, professional, and personal benefits of electronic mail, research, and commerce.

B. Contested Boundaries

At peace for the most part, the right to know and the right to privacy are sometimes at war. Conflicts and controversies over the limits of the public's right to know and the right to privacy arise when one person, group, or entity seeks or discloses information that another person, group, or entity wishes to conceal. Precisely how individual privacy rights and the private sphere are defined is culturally relative, but conflicts and controversies between public knowledge and privacy abound, worldwide. A few examples are illustrative.

In 1999, Ayumi Kuroda was forced to leave her job as a popular television talk show host when it was learned that she had divorced her husband without informing the viewing public. A common, though by no means universal, sentiment in Japan is that professional women are accountable to the public for their private lives and, moreover, that the public has a right to know about the family life of a woman who has become a public figure.

In April 2000, Japanese Prime Minister Keizo Obuchi lapsed unexpectedly into a stroke-induced coma. The governing Liberal Democratic party leaders kept news of Obuchi's illness secret for 22 hours, leading some to charge that the public's right to know had been violated.

The government and press cited the need to ensure an orderly succession of leadership and a tradition of medical privacy for public officials as reasons for delaying public notification.

In March 2000 in Israel, the private truth that a popular singer had died of AIDS was finally reported a week after her death. The singer was pop diva Ofra Haza, a Sephardic Jew, originally from Yemen. Out of respect for Ofra's medical privacy, the press initially kept the cause of her death secret. A week after she died, citing the need to replace pervasive, feverish rumor with truth, the daily newspaper *Haaretz* reported that Ofra had died of complications of AIDS.

In the United States, a number of popular television shows are premised on the belief that the public has a right to know about the secret misconduct of government, corporations, and professionals who serve the public. ABC's "Prime Time Live" used deception to infiltrate Food Lion supermarket and expose dubious food handling practices such as bleaching malodorous fish and grinding dated unsold meats into sausage. "Prime Time Live" also used deception to expose doctors who performed 10,000 cataract operations in a single year and told healthy ABC employees disguised as patients that they, too, needed eye surgery. Food Lion and the eye doctors sued, arguing that the deceptive practices "Prime Time Live" used to gain access to their offices and employees in the name of the public's right to know amounted to trespass and violated privacy rights. ABC relied heavily on the First Amendment in its defense. By tradition, the principle of freedom of the press, enshrined in the United States in the First Amendment of the federal Constitution, is closely associated with the idea of the public's right to know. The American media have staked out turf as the constitutionally empowered defenders of this right. The law books are filled with cases of newspapers, magazines, and television networks seeking judicial approval for the acquisition, publication, or investigation of family, medical, sexual, employment, or financial information others deem appropriately private.

II. DEFINING THE RIGHT TO KNOW

The public's right to know is in essence a right to be well informed. The right to know is the claim that society is obligated to adopt laws and promote practices that channel useful and important information to the general public. Notwithstanding the language of "rights," the public right to know is not reducible to one specific legal entitlement satisfied by one specific law, or to one specific moral entitlement satisfied by one specific act. In fact it might be helpful to think of the public right to know as a collection of several distinguishable *rights* to know, each with its own set of correlative obligations. The public's rights to know include:

- The right to know how government conducts itself
- The right to know how government officials and candidates for government office conduct themselves
- The right of access to information contained in government files and records
- The right to important information, both about current events and issues, and about the history and achievements of the past, insofar as they bear on current events and issues
- The right to know the opinions and ideas of fellows citizens
- The right to know how public figures conduct themselves
- The right to know how businesses and other nongovernmental entities receiving government aid or affecting the public welfare conduct themselves

The idea that the public has a right to know in some or all of these seven senses plays an important role in democratic political systems. In the ideal democracy, citizens are free and self-governing. Access to information enables each person to make the sound, independent judgments about matters of personal and collective concern that are required by responsible citizenship. Access to information also enables citizens to evaluate and criticize government and the other institutions that affect public well-being effectively.

A free press, freedom of information statutes, public schools, public libraries, and consumer advocacy groups are some of the many institutions and practices that can fulfil societal obligations implied by the public's right to know. The role of the free press is especially noteworthy. Major media have taken on the professional responsibility of channeling news and information to the public. The American people, like people in countries the world over, are vitally dependent upon their newspapers, radios, televisions, and computers to keep them informed. The media have invested heavily in court battles to vindicate publications and investigative tactics that they believe are warranted by the public's right to know.

A. Access to Government and Government Records

Although we can distinguish between the right to know how government conducts itself and the right of access to government files and records, the two rights to know are closely related. Open files and records is one way a government might give the public an opportunity to discover what it is up to. But it is not the only way.

Governments reveal to the public how they conduct their business by inviting the general public to witness their legislative, judicial, and executive processes; by making official and unofficial statements to the general public or to selected media; and by granting the general public, the media, or researchers access to official files and records. In short, the public's right to know how the government conducts itself is protected by (1) open procedures, (2) public statements and reports, and (3) open files and records.

First, many government proceedings are open to the press and the general public. Laws requiring that government processes be open to the public are sometimes called "sunshine laws." Public officials, including the president of the United States, commonly invite the press and community leaders to accompany them on official state visits and fact-finding missions. Moreover, sessions of Congress, meetings of federal agencies, meetings of state legislatures, city council meetings, judicial hearings, trials, and public school board meetings can be attended by interested citizens. Some branches and departments of government are not open to the public. In the name of national security, many activities of the Pentagon, the Central Intelligence Agency, and the National Security Agency are cloaked in substantial secrecy.

Second, government officials speak on and off the record to private citizens and the media about the conduct of the government's business. On the record, federal, state, and local governments issue press releases and reports detailing activities, plans, and findings. Off the record, government insiders "leak" information to selected members of the press.

Third, the public is able to obtain copies of government records and files. Modern governments are sophisticated bureaucracies that collect and store vast quantities of information. The exercise of the government's power to tax requires the collection of financial and other personal data from individuals and businesses. National defense and public programs are effected through departments and agencies with the need for vast quantities of information. The principle that the public should have access to public records is realized legislatively in the United States in the federal Freedom of Information Act (FOIA) and in similar laws in the 50 states and other countries. Under FOIA, citizens, the media, or business may file written requests for information held in government record systems. Subject to a number of exceptions designed to safeguard personal privacy and national security, FOIA requests must be granted. FOIA prohibits releasing to the general public "personnel and medical files and similar files the disclosure of which would constitute an unwarranted invasion of privacy."

The potential for conflict between the right to know how government conducts itself and privacy is well illustrated by press efforts to obtain "rap sheets." So-called "rap sheets" are the comprehensive records of criminal arrests, indictments, acquittals, convictions, and sentences assembled by Federal Bureau of Investigation (FBI) investigators to aid their law enforcement efforts. In *United States Department of Justice v. Reporters' Committee for Freedom of the Press*, 489 U.S. 749 (1989), CBS News made a request pursuant to the federal Freedom of Information Act for copies of the rap sheets of four suspected Medico crime family members. At the time of the CBS News suit, the FBI maintained rap sheets on over 24 million people, few of whom posed a threat warranting public attention. The Justice Department did not wish to turn the rap sheets over to CBS and argued that rap sheets contain private information, similar to personnel and medical files. CBS brought a lawsuit seeking to compel disclosure. The Supreme Court held that FOIA's privacy protection provisions require a balancing of interests by the courts, and held that when the media seek access to criminal histories prepared by government investigators for potential law enforcement purposes, rather than to official information about government activity as such, the balance characteristically should tip in favor of privacy interests.

B. Access to Government Officials and Candidates

It is widely agreed that government officials are accountable to the general public for their official acts and misconduct while in office. Like officials, candidates for high office may be required to disclose financial and medical information to the public so that their fitness and suitability for office can be judged. The price of accountability for public officials and candidates for office is very high, and can include justifiable, but humiliating, privacy losses. Former U.S. senator Robert Packwood was forced to open his personal diaries to public scrutiny in proceedings to oust him for sexual and financial improprieties. Other members of Congress accused of inappropriate sex with teenagers, sexual harassment, and sexually motivated nepotism have faced humiliating public exposure of what they considered their personal lives.

Controversies about the public's right to know arise when officials and candidates are asked to account for purely moral misconduct, such as marital infidelity, or for recreational illegal drug use that occurred years earlier. One topic for debate is whether and where a boundary line can be drawn between public and private aspects of the lives of officials and would-be officials. One school of thought maintains that, when it comes to high public

officials, virtually every aspect of their lives is a matter of legitimate public concern. The ideal of the transparent public official is defended by appeal to the value of trust. The assumption made is that the public can better trust officials who have no secrets and who are willing to account for all aspects of their personal and professional lives. Another school of thought argues for a reserve of privacy for public officials in high office, on the ground that privacy is a moral and social need of everyone. The difficulty facing the perspective that officials should be opaque rather than transparent is the need to decide what categories of information should be off limits. Matters of health are usually considered private, but these may affect the public assessment of fitness for office. Matters of marriage and child rearing are considered private, but these may affect public assessment of character and judgment—properties valued in public employees and especially in high public officials.

C. Access to Public Figures

"Public figure" is an expression used to describe a person who is not a government official, but who is known to the general public. Entertainers, professional athletes, television journalists, major criminals, and accident victims are public figures. United States courts distinguish between voluntary and involuntary public figures. Famous entertainers are voluntary public figures because they have sought out the limelight of public attention and adoration. Accident victims, like Elian Gonzalez, the Cuban boy who became the focal point of an international custody battle between family members in Cuba and the United States, may become involuntary public figures. The spouse of a public figure can become an involuntary public figure, as the former husband of feminist Betty Friedan discovered when he unsuccessfully sued for unauthorized use of his name and photograph in a magazine article. Courts further classify certain persons as limited purpose public figures. The heads of the American Civil Liberties Union and the Planned Parenthood Federation of America may be public figures for purposes of news relating to their organizations missions, while not being public figures for the purposes of gossip about their intimate relationships.

When it comes to voluntary public figures, it is often said that the public has a right to know how they conduct themselves and their affairs. They are thought by many to have obligations of transparency. It has been argued that the high salaries and invited attention paid voluntary public figures carries with it a loss of privacy and a responsibility to be accountable to the public. Some public figures flatly reject the role modeling responsibilities ascribed to them and thought to justify intrusions into their personal lives. Realistically, a person who wants recognition as a champion ice skater, academy award winning actress, civil rights advocate, or religious leader may have to accept the curiosity the public will naturally develop about aspects of their lives that may be none of its business.

D. Access to News, Information, and Opinion

The sentiment that the public has a right to know can be seen at work in the laws that mandate compulsory free public education. So vital are the information needs of citizens, youth normally are required to submit to formal schooling until they are at least 16. Virtually every American town and city boasts a free lending library in which can be found government documents, reference books, and the histories and literary achievements of human societies. Attempts to exclude materials from public and school libraries invoke the cry of censorship. Opposition to censorship is based on the idea that the public is entitled to information and ideas contained in printed form, however ideological, sexually explicit, irreligious, or otherwise controversial. The formation of independent ideas and judgments vitally depends upon access to controversial and uncontroversial materials.

In pluralistic societies being informed about the perspectives of fellow citizens is also vital to the democratic process. The idea of a right to know has come to include a right to information about others' perspectives. The emphasis on polling in recent years reflects the media's sense that people are interested and should be interested in opinions, sorted demographically. The ethical guidelines of the Gannett Company's news division recognize that diversity breeds information demands. In pursuit of the public interest Gannett promises that public that it will "provide a public forum for diverse people and views," and "reflect and encourage understanding of diverse segments of our community." While many fellow citizens will think as we think, many will not. In order to know what policies and laws are best, one must have an idea of the preferences and values of the others. In order to know who will best represent voters in one's district, one needs to know something about other residents. Consider, for example, the difference in perspectives reportedly held by rich and poor, black and white, men and women, Protestant and Catholic, and immigrant and native born on issues such as taxation, crime, welfare, education, and immigration. Given patterns of residential and school segregation in the United States, a middle class black woman may need to read the newspaper and watch television to find out how the poor white men in her town feel about public issues.

The publication of news and information can directly clash with the desire of persons for privacy. Some people do not want to be subjected to public attention, even when the attention does them honor. Common conceptions of the right to privacy allocate to the individual the power to decide whether information about her affairs or her photograph will appear in a publication. In fact it is a common law offense in most states to invade privacy in either of four senses: by intruding upon seclusion (intrusion tort); by publishing embarrassing private facts (disclosure tort); by publishing a misleading story or image of a person (false light tort); and by appropriating a person's name, likeness, or identity (appropriation tort). But the law recognizes a number of exceptions relevant here. State common law permits newsworthy publications, even if they offend privacy sensibilities. Thus courts have permitted publication of the names and photographs of rape and other crime victims, even naked crime victims. The First Amendment bars states and the federal government from most actions that would inhibit freedom of the press, even in the name of keeping private information out of the news.

Thus any truthful fact or image of a person may be published without consent if it is "newsworthy." Media have wide discretion in determining what is newsworthy. It is not merely affairs of state and the economy that are newsworthy. Business misconduct, sporting events, entertainment spectacles, and highway accidents can be newsworthy. A person caught up in a current event, such as a crime or dramatic rescue, may find that family or medical privacies have become news. A person who is a public official or a public figure will find that aspects of their lives that would not be newsworthy were they an ordinary private citizen become newsworthy by virtue of their governmental responsibilities or notoriety. It appears that false and misleading statements about or images of a person may be published without liability, if the publication is made without "actual malice." While the actual malice standard was developed in the law of defamation, it may apply to limit liability in privacy law as well. Facts about long-forgotten or obscured events and people may be published, but courts may disapprove revisiting the past if doing so requires fresh, highly offensive intrusions into a person's home or interferes with the public interest in criminal rehabilitation.

III. DEFINING THE RIGHT TO PRIVACY

The right to privacy is a right to be let alone. The right to privacy is the claim that society is obligated to adopt laws and promote practices that shield against unwanted intrusion, disclosures, and publicity, and against interference with matters of personal decision making and conscience. "Privacy" has been described as a vexing, indefinable term. Yet, "privacy" has a handful of straightforward common usages reflected in cultural practices and the law.

Under one familiar usage, the term denotes a degree of physical inaccessibility to others' five senses, as where a person is alone at home and cannot be seen or heard. Seclusion, solitude, and isolation are examples of *physical privacy*. Under a second usage, the term denotes limited access to information or data about a person, as where medical records are stored in a locked cabinet. Data protection, secrecy, and confidentiality are examples of *informational privacy*. Under a third usage, the term denotes a degree of control or ownership with respect to one's good name or other attributes of personal identity, as where a person prohibits use of her photograph in a magazine advertising campaign. I call this *proprietary privacy*. Under a fourth and final usage, the term denotes autonomous, independent decision making, as where the choice to abort a fetus is left to the pregnant woman rather than the state. This is *decisional privacy*.

While it is possible to speak about an overarching right to privacy, one might speak as well about:

- The right to physical privacy (solitude, seclusion, and bodily integrity)
- The right to informational privacy (confidentiality, secrecy, data protection, and anonymity)
- The right to proprietary privacy (including publicity and reputational rights)
- The right to decisional privacy (autonomy and choice)

Ethicists and political theorists have assigned a key role to privacy and privacy rights in all of the aforementioned senses in the creation and sustaining of moral persons and responsible individuals.

A. Theories about the Value of Privacy

Individualism is a distinct theme in ethical accounts of privacy, though not the exclusive one. Ethicists and political theorists emphasize the benefits to intimate relationships, families, groups, and society as a whole. Thus, it is argued that privacy is essential for the response and reflection that makes individuals fit for family, social, and civic participation. It is also argued that privacy ensures the flourishing of intimacy and friendship. Privacy is a valuable condition presupposed by democratic institutions, such as the private ballot, and by liberal political norms such as freedom of conscience, freedom of religion, and, even, freedom of speech. According to one account prompted by the challenges of the information age, privacy has special value for the

creation of the societal managers required of market economies in liberal democracy:

> It is for the ultimate good of society as a whole that privacy is preserved, even at the expense of legitimate social control. Without some preserved private spaces, society would lose its most valuable asset: the true *individual*. Without an appropriate environment the system would die. Without privacy, individuals would not mature into responsible managers.... If we understand that privacy creates the "clearing" from which autonomy, trust and accountability can emerge, then privacy will become part of the ... agenda, not merely some annoying "nice to have" liberal value.... The idea that people should be let alone also plays an important role in liberal, democratic political systems. Part of what it means to be free is to have the opportunities for solitary, intimate and private thought, reflection and repose presupposed by the ideal of meaningful participation in civic life. Freedom also means having the opportunity to develop and act independently, even in accordance with unpopular values and beliefs. (Introna, 1997)

Although there is a wealth of literature extolling the value of privacy, privacy has its critics. Feminist theorists, critical theorists, communitarians, civic republicans, and new technologists have argued against conceptions of privacy that harm group interests.

Feminist academics and intellectuals have attacked privacy as a value in league with male domination and as an obstacle to gender equality. For women saddled with care-taking responsibilities, family homes are no private sanctuaries. Catharine MacKinnon and other leading contemporary feminist critics equate traditional ideas of privacy with, first, barriers to escaping domestic confinement, traditional roles, and violence, and, second, ideals of isolation, independence, autonomy, or individualism that conflict with the reality of women's existential experience and obstruct egalitarian social justice. Robin West has argued that childbearing, breast feeding, and heterosexual sex connect women physically and psychologically to others. Ideals of ethical care, compassion, and community responsibility dominate women's lives, not privacy and autonomy. According to West, woman are not and do not see themselves as autonomous in the way men are or see themselves.

Some critical race theorists raise similar concerns about privacy and isolation. Anthony Cook has argued that the quest for privacy is a quest for isolation and unaccountability that contradicts the inescapable social nature of the self, and that is inimical to a community's flourishing. Other critical legal theorists offer a general critique of the public–private distinction within liberal jurisprudence, condemning it as incoherent, contradictory, and oppressive. They argue that "public" and "private" are incoherent and indeterminate concepts because everything that is supposedly private has a public aspect or is vitally dependent upon public order. Family life is "private" but is highly regulated by "public" law. Marriage laws, divorce laws, child abuse and neglect laws, education requirements, and adoption strictures all make the so-called private sphere a matter of public scrutiny and control. Critical legal theorists stress that legal privacy rights cannot function as secure protections against intrusion in personal affairs, because liberals can interpret privacy as a negative liberty and use "privacy" as an excuse for abrogating responsibility to the poor and vulnerable. In *DeShaney v. Winnebago Department of Social Services* (489 U.S. 1989), for example, the Supreme Court held that state government need not take responsibility for the serious consequences of failing to remove a boy severely beaten by his father from the father's private home.

Communitarians attack individualistic conceptions of privacy as a threat to the common good. Amitai Etzioni has advanced what he calls a communitarian critique of American privacy law. According to Etzioni, "immoderate champions of privacy have ... engaged in rhetorical excesses [with] ... significant and detrimental effects" (Etzioni 1999, 7). Those effects including "delaying for years needed public actions by bottling them up in the courts," blocking "the introduction of other needed public policies," and having "a chilling effect on the consideration of other public policies that would advance the public good...." To illustrate his points he argues that privacy advocates blocked HIV testing of newborns, opposed laws to alert communities when convicted child molesters move into the neighborhood, blocked efforts to institute national ID cards or other identifiers, and opposed mandatory government access to encryption keys.

Civic republicans worry that liberal conceptions of privacy lead to policies that neglect the importance of traditional sources of civic virtue and education, such as families and religious groups. Michael Sandel condemns liberal approaches to privacy law in constitutional cases. The liberal strain in constitutional law is apparent in decisions that treat privacy rights as autonomy rights to individual self-determination. An older and more "republican" vision of privacy, Sandel argues, sees privacy rights as rights that allow persons to flourish in families, intimate relationships, and communities that are constitutive of their identities.

New technologists are focused on the upside potential of cyberspace and computing. Some fear an overemphasis on privacy will thwart the development of highly efficient information management systems and novel modes of communication and community. They also fear that the government will enact heavy-handed privacy regulation in advance of market solutions to privacy problems, including the development of privacy-enhancing technologies, encryption, and privacy-sensitive architectures for cyberspace.

The most strenuous critics of liberal conceptions of privacy in fact maintain some belief in the value of opportunities for solitude, selective intimacy, confidentiality, and nongovernmental decision making. And while the quest for privacy can be isolating and constraining, it can also be rejuvenating in ways that make us more fit and ready for our roles in the family and community. The trick is to stress that the lines between public and private are socially constructed, and must be renegotiated and redrawn as necessary to further dignity, safety, and equality.

B. Privacy Rights in the Law

The right to privacy in each of these four senses—physical, informational, proprietary, and decisional—is incorporated into the positive law of developed nations and into international law and covenants. The United States, Canada, Germany, France, and most other western nations have laws either expressly conferring privacy rights or protecting privacy-related interests.

The European Union's 1998 data protection directive limits the ability of firms conducting business in member states to sell or share personal consumer or customer information. Article 8 of the European Convention on Human Rights provides that "everyone has a right to respect for his private and family life, his home and his correspondence," and that "there shall be no interference by a public authority with the exercise of this right except such as is in accordance with the law and is necessary in a democratic society...." In a single provision, physical, information, proprietary, and decisional privacy interests are similarly recognized by the Universal Declaration of Human Rights, adopted by the UN General Assembly in 1948. Article 12 provides that "no one shall be subjected to arbitrary interference with his privacy, family, home or correspondence, nor to attacks upon his honour and reputation. Everyone has the right to the protection of the law against such interference or attacks."

The United States has a uniquely broad array of legal rights of privacy protecting interests in physical, information, propriety, and decisional privacy. These interests are protected through federal and state constitutional law, through a host of federal and state statutes, and through the common law. Significantly, the Supreme Court has interpreted 5 of the 10 original Bill of Rights guarantees and the Fourteenth Amendment as protective of privacy.

1. Constitutional Law

The First Amendment provides that "Congress shall make no law respecting an establishment of religion, or prohibiting the free exercise thereof; or abridging the freedom of speech, or of the press; or the right of the people peaceably to assemble, and to petition the Government for a redress of grievances." The Supreme Court has held that this provision guarantees a right of free association for individuals, and consequently a right of group privacy. Citizens are entitled to form exclusive political, social, or civic organizations whose meeting places and membership lists are beyond the reach of state and federal government. In *NAACP v. Alabama,* 357 U.S. 449 (1958), the Court held that government officials in Alabama were not entitled to copies of the membership lists of the National Association for the Advancement of Colored People (NAACP). The Court explained that the "inviolability of privacy in group association may in many circumstances be indispensable to preservation of freedom of association." In a concurring opinion, Justice William O. Douglas defended the principle of group association, linking both physical and informational privacy to First Amendment values of speech and assembly: "Whether a group is popular or unpopular, the right of privacy implicit in the First Amendment should create an area into which the government may not enter." Douglas further observed that "if the files of the NAACP can be ransacked because some criminal may have joined it, then all walls of privacy are broken down.... State and the Federal government by force of the First Amendment are barred from investigating any person's faith or ideology by summoning officers or members of his society, church or club."

Reflecting the sentiment of James Otis that "a man's house is his castle," the Third Amendment provides that "no Soldier shall, in time of peace be quartered in any house, without the consent of the Owner, nor in time of war, but in a manner to be prescribed by law." Even before America had been settled, the home had come to be seen as a place of shelter and privacy. A sphere of secluded private conduct free from coercive governmental interference is implied by both the Third Amendment and the Fourth Amendment.

The Fourth Amendment limits government's ability to engage in search and seizure. The Fourth Amendment provides that "the right of the people to be secure in their persons, houses, papers, and effects, against unreasonable searches and seizures, shall not be violated, and no Warrants shall issue, but upon probable cause, supported by Oath or affirmation, and particularly describing the place to be searched, and the persons or things to be seized." When the government intrudes in an area where a person has justifiably relied upon a sense of privacy, its intrusion is a "search and seizure" under the Fourth Amendment. In *Katz v. United States,* 389 U.S. 347, 351 (1968), the Supreme Court famously observed that what a person "seeks to preserve as pri-

vate, even in an area accessible to the public, may be constitutionally protected."

The Fifth Amendment constrains compulsory self-incrimination. The Fifth Amendment asserts in part that, "Nor shall any person ... be compelled in any criminal case to be a witness against himself...." As explained in *Griswold v. Connecticut,* 381 U.S. 479, 484 (1965), the Fifth Amendment's self-incrimination clause "enables the citizen to create a zone of privacy which government may not force him to surrender to his detriment." The Fifth Amendment privilege "respects a private inner sanctum of individual feeling and thought and proscribes state intrusion to extract self-condemnation" (*Couch v. United States,* 409 U.S. 322, 327 (1973)).

The Ninth Amendment reserves to the people unenumerated private rights against the federal government. The amendment provides that the enumeration in the Constitution, of certain rights, shall not be construed to deny or disparage others retained by the people. A rarely relied upon right, in *Griswold v. Connecticut,* 381 U.S. 479 (1965), the case that decriminalized the use of birth control by married couples, the Supreme Court argued that a right of privacy emanated from the penumbra of the Bill of Rights, including the Ninth Amendment.

The Fourteenth Amendment emerged in the 1970s as a major basis for rights of privacy relating to childbearing and health, following the prominent role its guarantee of liberty played in the *Griswold* case and then in *Roe v. Wade,* 410 U.S. 113 (1973), the decision that decriminalized abortion. State and federal courts have cited the Fourteenth Amendment as a source of rights of privacy in cases relating to the right to die, assisted suicide, surrogate motherhood, and gay rights.

2. Statutory Law

Privacy is one of the main values driving a host of federal legislation and state statutes protecting against harmful intrusion, surveillance, disclosures, and unfair information management practices. Although federal regulators entered the arena in the 1990s, state law was the traditional source of most medical privacy, and confidentiality rules have traditionally been almost entirely a matter of state law. Federal law includes comprehensive statutes enacted by Congress governing the privacy and confidentiality of bank records, telephone calls, and government records. Major privacy-related statutes include the following acts, their precursors, and amendments: the Fair Credit and Reporting Act of 1970, the Privacy Act of 1974, the Family Educational Rights and Privacy Act of 1974, the Right to Financial Privacy Act of 1978, the Privacy Protection Act of 1980, the Electronic Communications Privacy Act of 1986, the Video

Privacy Protection Act of 1988, the Employee Polygraph Protection Act of 1988, the Computer Matching and Privacy Protection Act of 1988, and the Children's On-Line Privacy Protection Act of 2000.

3. Common Law

Tort law primarily consists of the common law of personal injury embodied in the individual cases whose aggregate holdings serve as precedent in civil cases in the United States. As previously noted, American tort law includes four rights of privacy. Inspired by a 1890 *Harvard Law Review* article written by Samuel Warren and Louis Brandeis, a privacy tort was first recognized by American judges in the early 20th century. No state's supreme court officially recognized the right to privacy until 1905 when the Georgia high court in *Pavesich v. New England Life Ins. Co.,* 50 S.E. 68 (1905), allowed a man, whose photograph was used without his consent in an insurance advertisement, to assert a right of privacy. Today the common law of privacy recognizes four basic physical, informational, and proprietary privacy rights (but no decisional privacy right as such), first distinguished by William L. Prosser in 1960 in the *California Law Review*. The four are rights against: (1) intrusion upon seclusion, (2) publication of embarrassing private facts, (3) publicity placing a person in a false light, and (4) appropriation of name likeness and identity.

In tort law, telling the truth can result in liability. A distinctive feature of the common law privacy tort is that, subject to exceptions for newsworthy publications and First Amendment freedoms, it permits lawsuits against persons who simply publish or disclose truth. The right to privacy aims to protect persons whose feelings and sensibilities are wounded by having others discover truthful, but embarrassing or intimate, matters of fact as a consequence of highly offensive conduct. So conceived, the privacy torts are especially controversial with members of the media who believe the threat of lawsuits constrains freedom of speech and press. In fact, some members of the press are First Amendment absolutists who advocate that it should never be unlawful to publish a true statement merely because it is wounds feelings and sensibilities. Other journalists recognize a need to strike a balance between the public's right to know and the privacy rights of the public.

IV. THE POLITICS OF THE RIGHT TO KNOW

Political parties and movements come to be defined partly by reference to the stance they take on resolving conflicts between privacy and the public's right to know.

A. Political Parties

In the United States where the major parties are the Democratic and Republican parties, and where Independents and Libertarians also have a modest national presence, there are no party platforms for or against the public right to know in the abstract. We associate libertarianism with a robust regard for freedom of speech and press, and with the ideal of a small, transparent government. We expect libertarians to take up the banner of individual privacy, though, when faced with the prospect of government demands for personal information and aggressive surveillance of private citizens. We associate Democrats with a partisan preference for strong rights of personal decision making when it comes to abortion and sexual orientation. But we know that the administration of the government programs Democrats favor require that citizen beneficiaries yield vast quantities of personal information to a potentially cumbersome and paternalistic bureaucracy. We also know that liberal democrats demand high degrees of public accountability of the corporate sector. We associate Republicans with the ideal of keeping government out of the family to maximize private authority over traditional families. But we expect probusiness Republicans to disapprove of government regulation of the consumer data management and marketing practices of corporations and to approve of aggressive law enforcement practices that subordinate privacy to crime detection.

B. Political Scandals

The public's right to know has been the centerpiece of a number of the United States' most historic scandals and ordeals. In the late 1940s the House Un-American Activities Committee attempted to compel Hollywood film makers and actors to disclose their Communist party affiliations and the names of others who had been or were Communists. During the McCarthyism era, 1950–1954, Senator Joseph McCarthy led a reckless witch-hunt for Soviet and Communist sympathizers in hearings designed to bring personal associations and private political beliefs to light. Many liberals and intellectuals of the period thought the efforts to ferret out un-American sympathies violated privacy norms essential to democratic freedom, ironically in the name of the preservation of democratic freedom. Others disagreed with McCarthy's deceptive and abusive tactics but agreed that the public had a right to right to know about the extent of the Communist threat. During the Vietnam War era of the 1960s and 1970s, liberal, radical, and militant critics demanded openness and accountability of civilian government, the military, and industry sufficient to reveal the underlying motives for continuing the war in southeast Asia. Ralph Nader's pioneering efforts on behalf of the public to reveal corporate wrong-doing in the auto industry in 1965 made him the target of privacy invasions so egregious—surveillance, intrusion, and harassment—that he brought and won successful legal action. "You expose us, and we'll expose you," Nader's foes seemed to say. When President Richard M. Nixon used the doctrine of "executive privilege" in seeking constitutional protection for the infamous Oval Office tapes reflecting his involvement in covering up the 1970s illegal Watergate break-in, partisan Democrats and liberals were among the critics of presidential privacy. The secret arms for hostages deal of the Iran-Contra scandal was an opportunity for Democrats to accuse a Republican White House of violating the public's right to know. The impeachment trial of Democratic President William J. Clinton in 1998 raised the question of presidential privacy in a lurid, sexual context. Although many felt that the details of the adulterous sexual affair between the President and Monica Lewinsky was a private matter and no one's business, others thought the public had a right to know the specific dates, times, and types of sex acts to establish whether the President was guilty of "high crimes and misdemeanors" warranting removal from office. The impeachment of President Clinton raised sharply for the nation whether the personal should be political.

C. Political Movements

That "the personal is political" was a slogan of the women's rights movement of the 1960s and 1970s. Advocates of equal rights for women urged that concerns about the welfare of women and families once relegated to the male-dominated domestic sphere and secreted behind closed doors be made a matter of public knowledge, debate, and action.

The gay rights movement has also called for greater openness about "private matters" related to sexual orientation. An implicit message of the movement has been that the public needs to be informed about the prevalence and nature of homosexuality. Involuntary "outing" of closeted gays and lesbians in the gay press has been a way of making gay men and women in positions of authority and prominence accountable to the public, particularly where they have taken public stances on issues relating to homosexuality that are at odds with their own lifestyles and practices. Roy Cohn, for example, was a gay attorney (ultimately disbarred) who first gained notoriety for his collaboration with Senator Joseph McCarthy. Cohn falsely denied having AIDS, from which he died in 1986, and publically attacked gay rights.

The civil rights movement used the media to expose the atrocities of southern violence and deprivations of blacks' rights. *New York Times v. Sullivan,* 376 U.S. 254 (1964), the Supreme Court case that established the "actual malice standard" for defamation cases brought against the press, originated in the struggles of African-American activists to call public attention to southern injustice. An Alabama public official sued the *New York Times* for publishing a full page advertisement placed by civil rights leaders condemning Alabama for complicity in attacks on the homes of black leaders, and for allegedly locking college students out of their cafeteria and ringing their campus with armed police. Although the fund-raising advertisement contained hyperbole and several factual inaccuracies, the Supreme Court held that the *New York Times* would not be liable unless it published the ad with actual knowledge of its falsehood.

V. PRIVACY IN JOURNALISM ETHICS

The press is a partisan advocate for the public's right to know. Ethical journalistic practices may nevertheless require respect for the public's privacy rights. The *Code of Ethics* of the Society of Professional Journalists places the right to know and the right to privacy on a seesaw and attempts to balance them by requiring a presumption in the favor of personal privacy that can be overcome in the business of journalism by the public's weighty right to know. The Gannett Company (publisher of the middle-brow nationally circulated newspaper, *U.S.A. Today*) issued ethical guidelines for news-gathering in 1999 that take a different approach. There is no seesaw. The guidelines are notable for the fact that the word "privacy" does not appear anywhere in them, nor are any of the obvious conflicts between privacy and news reporting expressly acknowledged.

The Society of Professional Journalists adopted its current *Code of Ethics* in 1996. The Preamble to the *Code* names "public enlightenment" as the "forerunner of justice and the foundation of democracy." The Preamble states that the duty of "conscientious" journalists from "all media and specialities" is to further the ends of justice and democracy by "providing a fair and comprehensive account of events and issues" with "thoroughness and honesty." Members are exhorted to serve the public "by seeking truth and providing a fair and comprehensive account of events and issues." Recognizing individual rights, the *Code* nonetheless demands that they not trump the public's right to know. For example, the *Code* maintains that criminal suspects' fair trial rights should be balanced with the "public's right to be informed."

The *Code* identifies four main requirements of ethical journalism. They are (1) seek truth and report it; (2) minimize harm; (3) act independently; and (4) be accountable. Three of the four imperatives, 1, 3, and 4, conflict with the goal of respecting privacy. The first imperative does because the truth sought and reported may be of personal matters cloaked in privacy. The third imperative conflicts with privacy because acting independently may mean that a journalist reports information that privacy seekers pressured the journalist not to report. The fourth imperative conflicts with privacy because being accountable may require disclosing information to persons to whom one has responsibility, even though the information is about others' private lives.

Although the *Code* asserts the vital importance of the public's right to know, it also demands the protection of privacy. Imperative 2 requires minimizing harm, observing that "ethical journalists treat sources, subjects and colleagues as human being deserving of respect." Respecting privacy is one way to respect people as human beings. The *Code*'s general imperative to minimize harm is accompanied by eight specific harm minimization requirements. These implicitly and explicitly acknowledge privacy intrusion as a harm. Thus the *Code* asks journalists to "recognize that gathering and reporting information may cause harm or discomfort." It asks that journalists "be sensitive when seeking or using interviews of photographs of those affected by tragedy or grief." The *Code* contains one notable provision expressly calling for privacy protection. After an instruction that journalists "recognize that private people have a greater right to control information about themselves than do public officials and others who seek power, influence or attention," the *Code* observes that "only an overriding public need can justify intrusion into anyone's privacy." This statement could be read to say that journalists must give presumptive priority to protecting privacy.

The *Code* goes even further to recognize privacy interests. Provisions of the Code recognize privacy-related interests in anonymity. Journalists are asked to "be cautious about identifying juvenile suspects or victims of sex crimes." Yet in the interest of the public's right to know, the *Code* is predictably skeptical about anonymity when demanded of news sources. The general imperative to "seek truth and report it" is followed by a specific imperative to "always question sources' motives before promising anonymity." The *Code* is also skeptical of government demands for bureaucratic concealment, beseeching journalists to "recognize a special obligation to ensure that the public's business is conducted in the open and that government records are open to inspection." This special obligation is a corollary of the public's right to know. On the other hand, the *Code* recognizes that secrecy and deception may have value to journalists in gathering the news and uncovering truth, but urges avoidance: "Avoid undercover or other surreptitious

methods of gathering information except when traditional open methods will not yield information vital to the public." Thus the press can conceal its tactics only in the interest of the public's right to be informed—the public's right to know.

The Gannett Company's 1999 ethical guidelines for news-gathering and reporting reflect a commitment to "serving the public interest" by "seeking and reporting truth in a truthful way." The public's right to know is at the heart of Gannett's conception of the public interest. Gannett's commitment to serve the public interest includes commitments to "uphold First Amendment principles to serve democratic process"; "be vigilant watchdogs of governments and institutions that affect the public"; "provide the news and information that people need to function as effective citizens"; see solutions as well as expose problems and wrongdoing; "provide a public forum for diverse people and views"; "reflect and encourage understanding of diverse segments of our community"; "provide editorial and community leadership"; and finally "to seek to promote understanding of complex issues."

Gannett's guidelines include ethical standards for managing confidentiality requests from news sources, but no promise that confidentiality will be honored, overall. In a section concerning the ethics of investigative journalism where one might expect to see some mention of privacy, there is none. On the contrary, the core commitment to finding and reporting truth is the sole theme: "Aggressive, hard-hitting reporting is honorable and often courageous in fulfilling the press' First Amendment responsibilities, and it is encouraged." The Gannett code contains no explicit commitment to protecting privacy. Such a commitment might be inferred, however, from the promise to "treat people with dignity, respect and compassion." A commitment to privacy protection might also be inferred from general commitments to "acting ethically and honorably in dealing with news sources"; "to obey the law"; "to observe common standards of decency"; and "to try to do the right thing." The laws that must be obeyed include the privacy laws. Privacy norms may be included among common standards of decency, and respecting privacy can be, on occasion, the right thing. Although these inferences are possible, it is plain enough that Gannett sought to avoid elevating the public's privacy interests to the level of the public's interest in access to information.

The fact that Gannett left privacy protection in the shadows for inference and implication suggests a conscious effort to stand tall for the public right to know and press freedom in the face of the factors that prompted its statement of ethical guidelines. Those factors included, quoting Gannett's press release, "public distrust of the media," and "a need to address the increase in lawsuits focusing on news gathering methods and not on the truth of stories." It is clear that Gannett is troubled by the idea that the press should ever be liable to publishing what is true, even if doing so is highly offensive to a person's privacy and even if the facts were obtained through methods that violate privacy expectations.

VI. CONCLUSION

The public's right to know will surely continue to clash with the public's right to privacy. Where the public interest in information and disclosure is muted or uncertain, privacy may prevail over knowledge. But then again, it may not. The demand for news, information, and perspectives now extends to domains that traditions of official prerogative and conventions of sexual, family, and medical privacy once defined as out of bounds. Yet ways of knowing—the mechanisms of mass communication—are increasingly numerous and efficient. Information is a valuable commodity. Commercial opportunities abound for media who can consistently deliver the kind of information—news or gossip—consumers want. Cautious, caring polities will want to preserve some of the traditional boundaries between the public and the private for the sake of individual dignity and justice. Yet, on global scales, access to news and information is key to development, democracy, and freedom. There is dignity and justice on the side of knowledge as well.

Bibliography

Alderman, E., & Kennedy, C. (1995). *The right to privacy.* New York: Random House.

Bennett, C., & Grant, R., Eds. (1996). *Visions of privacy: Policy choices for the digital age.* Toronto: University of Toronto Press.

Branscomb, A. W. (1994). *Who owns information? From privacy to public access.* New York: Basic Books.

Dienes, C. T., et al. (1997, 1998 (supplement)). *Newsgathering and the law.* Charlottesville, VA: Michie/Lexis Law Publishing.

Etzioni, A. (1999). *The limits of privacy.* New York: Basic Books.

Foerstel, H. N. (1999). *Freedom of information and the right to know: The origins and applications of the Freedom of Information Act.* Westport, CT: Greenwood Press.

Itrona, L. D. (1997). Privacy and the computer: Why we need privacy in the information society. *Metaphilosophy* **28**(3), 259–275.

Markesninis, B. S., Ed. (1999). *Protecting privacy.* New York: Oxford University Press.

Rotenberg, M. (1999). *The privacy law sourcebook 1999: United States law, international law, and recent developments.* Washington, DC: Electronic Privacy Information Center.

Turkington, R., & Allen, A. L. (1999). *Privacy law.* Minneapolis, MN: West Publishing.

Professional Ethics

TIMO AIRAKSINEN
University of Helsinki

I. The Primacy of the Sociological Definition of Professionalism
II. The Types of Professional Ethics
III. Values and Service in Professional Life
IV. Engineering as a Pseudoprofession
V. Truth, Science, and Information as Professional Fields

GLOSSARY

audience That segment of society that is not influenced by given professional practices.

classic profession One of the traditional service-orientated professions such as education, law, and medicine, characterized by its members' theoretical knowledge and training, service ideal, autonomy, authority, and relatively high status.

client A direct recipient of professional services.

code of ethics In this context, an officially accepted document that spells out the values and obligations of a given profession, from the point of view of the profession itself.

exclusivity A status of professional practice in which (i) it is licensed and (ii) professionals treat outsiders as charlatans or impostors.

paternalism The attitude that a professional knows better than a client what is good for him or her.

professional ethics The considerations that determine the good conduct of professionals together with, or independently of, legal and prudential factors.

professional knowledge Abstract and theoretical knowledge, often measured in terms of a Ph.D., that (i) forms the basis of professional work and explains its efficiency, and (ii) whose possession is a necessary condition of entering into the profession.

professional power The ability of a member of a profession to make his working environment promote his own varied goals; professional authority.

pseudo profession A profession that has no classic value-based service ideal.

subprofession A professional group whose work is under the jurisdiction of another.

theoretical profession A profession that serves truth, knowledge, and information.

the public Those who are influenced by professional practices without being clients.

PROFESSIONAL ETHICS govern the work of professionals in addition to more specific legal considerations. In many cases legal constraints must be supplemented with ethical norms so that professional life can be better understood, and controlled. Most professions publish their own codes of ethics for this purpose. Philosophical ethics studies professional life, and tries to understand the foundations of professional values and obligations. Other important philosophical questions concern the analysis of the power of professions in a democratic society, professional authority, paternalistic practices, clients' rights, and the nature of professional knowledge. Professional ethics as a general field can be supplemented by such disciplines as the ethics of work, medical ethics, bioethics, legal ethics, and environmental ethics. Another important aspect of professional ethics is the criticism of professions that it affords. Some radical theorists, such as I. Illich, claim that professional power and privilege are unjustifiable. Professional ethics as an independent field of philosophy is still underdeveloped in the sense that not much theoretical unity can be found among the wealth of practical examples and social problem cases. However, there is no question that professional ethics is an important field of study, especially for the public. The public and the audience of the professions cannot leave the regulation of professional work and service in the hands of professionals alone. Legal controls have limitations as well, mainly because the law steps in only after the harm is done. Ethical practices prevent harm and other problems before they occur.

I. THE PRIMACY OF THE SOCIOLOGICAL DEFINITION OF PROFESSIONALISM

Life in modern society is in many ways dependent on professionals and their work. The terms "professional" and "professionalism" may be understood either as technical terms or everyday ideas. Usually, "profession" is used in the latter way to denote a paid occupation, in contrast to a mere hobby. In this sense a professional ballplayer is different from an amateur one. A car mechanic is a professional in the sense that he earns his living by working on cars instead of only on his own vehicles. Here the term "professional" has a contrastive rather than an independent and well-defined meaning.

"Professionalism" is often taken to mean one's serious and conscientious attitude towards one's own work. A professional works hard to achieve her goals. She is persistent and yet flexible when she confronts problems. A professional attitude towards one's work is clearly a virtue in modern societies, which are permeated by the "Protestant work ethic."

Professional ethics can be understood in two different ways: first, by focusing on paid occupations, and second, by utilizing the sociological definition of a profession. The first approach leads to the ethics of work, which governs the practices, rights, and duties of the members of paid occupations, or workers. We shall not discuss them here because the ethics of work is a field that is only marginally relevant to professional ethics proper. Workers have no autonomy or power in the same sense as professionals. Therefore, it seems advisable to leave the ethics of work out of the field of professional ethics because, by starting from the technical definition, we find a rich field of problems that are only remotely connected to work as such. In other words, we have two different fields here, work and professionalism, each of which leads to very different considerations and theories.

Such a commonsense usage of the term is clearly a problem when discussing professional ethics from a philosophical point of view. Therefore, we may want to use the technical definition borrowed from the sociology of the professions. No exact definition exists, of course, although something like the following can be suggested: a professional is a member of an exclusive group of individuals who possess a value-based service ideal, and an abstract knowledge of their own field. Professionalism is the relevant ideology with its behavioral and policy-orientated counterparts. It must be emphasized that the concept of a profession is an essentially contested one in the sense that no single meaning emerges from the literature. It is difficult to select the single correct one among the countless sociological suggestions of a definition. Such a state of affairs must be simply accepted in philosophy that cannot create for it its own definition.

A simple way to understand what professions are is to consider examples of professionals, such as certified public accountants, physicians, teachers, lawyers, social workers, and psychologists. Their occupations can be called the classic professions. Other occupations, such as nursing, engineering, and various business jobs can also be mentioned. The following classification can be suggested. We call the members of first list "classic professions," or "professions" for short. Nursing has traditionally been a subprofession because it has been under the authority of another profession, namely medicine. The same can be said of psychology. Engineering is a pseudoprofession for reasons that are related to its service ideals: engineers do not seem to have their own values in the sense to be explained below. Business is not a profession and, therefore, business ethics is an independent field for the simple reason that business is not an exclusive occupation. However, the business community must comply with the standards of related professions, such as law, accounting, and medicine. Anyone can start a business or apply for a job in a corporation or enterprise. Moreover, no abstract knowledge is required. Science and research have also been professionalized, and it is interesting to ask what kind of profession they form.

Understood as a theory of professions in general, professional ethics is not a unified field of study. The philosophical study of professional ethics has suffered from such definitional difficulties as those mentioned above. The understanding of the term "profession" has been too wide. This leads to fragmented views without any underlying unity, for instance, when professions, business, and work become confused. On the other hand, if a sociological definition is adopted, it may lead to overtly technical considerations and to a narrow perspective. Moreover, the sociology of the professions is a very complicated field. It seems advisable to narrow down the field of study, but at the same time to keep it simple and intuitive.

II. THE TYPES OF PROFESSIONAL ETHICS

A. Codes of Ethics

Professional ethics can be studied from several points of view. Most professions have their official codes of ethics. It is possible to focus on these codes, in order to criticize and develop them. Professional practices can be understood as embodiments of their codified values and obligations. What such codes are and how they work is indeed an interesting question.

B. Quandary Ethics

Professional practices are often controversial. Therefore, professional ethics includes the criticism of professional malpractice and in general the kinds of dramatic problems and dilemmas associated with a given professional field. Professions are open to criticism; for instance, psychiatrists may have sexual relations with their incompetent, but consenting clients. Medical experiments with animals are often condemned even when they have beneficial consequences for people. Such a focus belongs to an approach that can be called "quandary professional ethics," is a new term is needed.

The quandary approach is diametrically opposed to the view that focuses on codes of ethics, which are highly idealistic documents. The quandary approach is at the same time useful and dangerous. It is useful because professionals often hide behind their official declarations of values even when their practices are dubious. Quandary ethics wants to go beneath the facade to uncover the most dramatic problem areas. This, however, is the weakness of the approach: by focusing on some dramatic examples, a more balanced picture is lost. The teaching of professional ethics becomes difficult, because no professional is enthusiastic about cases in which negative interpretation may stigmatize their own field of work.

This criticism of quandary professional ethics must be taken seriously. Professional ethics cannot be just a theory based on negative rhetoric where the purpose is to degrade professionalism. Many aspects of professionalism deserve criticism, but the quandary approach runs the risk of exaggerating this need. Professional ethics imply positive ethical standards. It cannot be expected that professionals listen to moral experts outside their own field, if their message is exclusively problem-oriented. The professionals' negative response means that promoters of professional ethics have lost their following. For example, this may be true in the accounting profession in United States because companies expect internal accountants and auditors to have as their first priority being loyal to their company and not to their profession. The professionals may study professional ethics independently without the help of ethical experts. But this tends to lead them back to their official moral codes and their self-serving idealism. The media tend to use the quandary approach because it is often entertaining.

C. The Standard Approach

Instead of focusing exclusively on dramatic problems in professional life, it is possible to develop standard professional ethics. By this term we mean an approach that first lays out the features of the field of professional practices, and then applies ethical concepts of duties and rights. In this field it is often claimed that there is no professional ethics as such, but only an ethics applied to everyday social relations in professional life. For instance, a teacher has obligations to pupils and parents, but he or she also has various rights, such as the right to evaluate the pupil's progress in the classroom, or to discipline the pupil within some well-defined limits. Like all professionals, the teacher has the right to make decisions that promote his or her own success both professionally and extraprofessionally. Such an extraprofessional right is strong in the case of the legal professions and in medicine, but less so in teaching or in social work.

It is evident that normal moral considerations apply to professional life. This fact should make one cautious in using the term "professional ethics" because one may think that the term refers to a special type of ethics. This is not plausible, although it must be admitted that some professional practices may look morally extraordinary, even supererogatory. A doctor has a stronger duty to provide help than a member of the public. Professionals may have the right to do things that nonprofessionals cannot be expected to do. For example, a teacher can punish his students, unlike a member of the public. In Great Britian, social workers have had the right to decide where a young delinquent should be placed within the child-care system. No parent, as a member of the public, has such a right. The existence of such rights and duties is one of the reasons why professionalism is such an important social category.

D. Professional Virtues and the Demise of Obligations

The most recent approach to professional ethics is through virtue ethics, which focuses on the good life of a professional who is able to find fulfillments as a professional. The motivation of such an approach is clear. In philosophical ethics, this trend clearly leads away from the deontology of duties and obligations via rights toward virtues and character ethics. The body of literature on ethical rules, understood as universalized prescriptions, has recently been labeled as dubious, especially by postmodernists. While we need not decide whether their relativism and value nihilism is justified, the challenge must be recognized.

Such an applied field as professional ethics has a strong practical influence and therefore its development must be taken seriously. It seems true, however, that the codes of professional ethics must not be left as too dispersed and underdeveloped to follow the trends of ethical theory. As a corrective, one can focus on the practices of the professional and compare them to those of other professionals. One need not pay too much attention to those unattractive quandaries, nor play with unrealistic descriptions of idealized values and obligations. At the same time the theory can locate professional life within the structure of a modern democratic society.

What are the virtues of a good nurse or a good lawyer? It seems that they are different simply because their characteristic practices are so different. The virtue approach should also look attractive to the professionals themselves, including students. Such an approach uses the first person in a way that is not egoistic. A young and aspiring professional sees the importance of becoming a good professional and a happy person, in the Aristotelian sense of the term, according to which happiness is fulfillment, or reaching one's goal. Indeed, the first and most important message of professional ethics to professionals should be that they not only aim at their own success but at competent service. According to virtue ethics, these two goals are not in conflict, as they would be from some other ethical viewpoints. Professional practices are goal-oriented so that the success and happiness of professionals can be measured in terms of their ability to reach the goal, defined in terms of their service ideal. If, on the contrary, success is measured, say, in money, a good professional practice may be detrimental to success.

III. VALUES AND SERVICE IN PROFESSIONAL LIFE

A. Characteristic Professional Values

If professional ethics is going to be more than a collection of particular considerations taken from the law, medicine, and education, among other fields, an account of the values that the professions promote should be

provided. In their philosophical study, some complex issues must be simplified so that their logic becomes visible, while at the same time the real world is kept in sight. A simple method of doing this is to list the values of different professions using the shortest possible name for each key value. The truth of this presentation can be checked from the accepted code of ethics of the profession. It seems that it is possible to do so. Among the benefits of this method is its teachability and its connection to virtue ethics, as we shall see in due course.

In Table I the name of a profession is accompanied with its ideal value and goal, together with its real function in social life. Another consideration that must be taken into account separately is the dysfunction of a given profession; in other words, what the clients and the audience are afraid of, as well as the characteristic factor of the individual success of an individual professional. These two factors may be more or less detached from the real function. All the characterizations in Table I are tentative and should be used with caution, keeping in mind that professional ethics involves the study of the above-mentioned issues.

B. The Gap between Facts and Values in Professional Ethics

Lawyers value the goal of justice, but in real life they may merely utilize the law in the following sense. If a society is unjust, like Hitler's Nazi Germany or Stalin's Soviet Union, its laws are also unjust. In such a situation, lawyers may have no other choice but to do what the law says and thus pretend that they act justly. In most real-life cases, lawyers pay more attention to the law itself than to the justice of the law. In normal democratic conditions, this is justifiable, but it is also dangerous if the social conditions degenerate. A standard counterargument, for instance, is that the Nazi laws are not laws in the full legal sense. It follows that the law professionals of Nazi Germany were not lawyers at all, surprising as this sounds.

In order to see how the emphasis on values and on the service ideal work in professional ethics, let us briefly

TABLE I

Profession	Value	Real function (example)
Law	Justice	Utilization of law
Medicine	Health	Medicalization of life
Education	Human growth	Socialization
Psychology	Autonomy	Social adjustment
Social work	Welfare	Stigmatization
Accounting	Fairness	Measurement of income and assets

review an interesting quandary in legal ethics. A defense attorney defends successfully an accused person whose guilt is evident to everybody, including the attorney: Is this a moral problem? Such a case cannot be understood properly if some abstract deontological principles are applied to the case, because then one must say that both the principle of social utility and the Kantian obligation of justice are violated. If a guilty person should go free, why should the attorney try to free him? The answer must focus on the concept of justice that is the goal of the attorney, namely, on the moral fact that every person has the right to defend himself and the right not to be punished before he is found guilty by the court. These rights cannot be realized without the help of the attorney who, therefore, needs not refuse to defend his client. It may happen that he helps to set the guilty party free, but this is irrelevant to the service ideal understood as justice.

Medicine is one of the strongest of the professions. This is shown, for instance, by the fact that its service ideal and real function prima facie coincide. Of course, values and reality, ideals and facts never really meet, but in the case of medicine one needs to develop a complicated and problematic theoretical account of what the facts of medicine are. It indeed looks as if everything physicians do is supposed to take care of the health of clients. However, it is possible to argue that a hidden real function of medicine is to medicalize the social environment, in the following sense. The definition of health is so broad that more and more human physical and psychological conditions can be classified as illnesses for which cures should be found. Human life becomes open to medical intervention in all of its stages. The advancement of medical science is taken to support such a view, often uncritically.

Teaching as a profession is troubled by the wide gulf between its ideal and its reality. If teachers' moral sensitivity and self-knowledge are sharp enough, they cannot avoid noticing this gulf, and professional ethics requires such awareness. The rift is between the needs of society and the rights of individual pupils. The task of education is the reproduction of culture so that the new generation can find its place in that process of history that leads to an open future from an unalterable past. This means, at the same time, the socialization of youth who, when they learn about the features of their own culture, not only continue it but become socialized by it.

Yet, from the point of view of pupils, they have the right to expect their education to make them flourish as persons. It might seem as if these two faces of education would be compatible, at least in normal cases. However, radical theorists of education have suggested that the task of education is to make pupils accept the social norms of injustice. In social life injustice is unavoidable, so that those who do not accept the relevant norms are troublemakers and self-destructive individuals. As logical as this argument may sound, it is hardly possible to maintain that an ideal ethical teacher should participate in such an educational system. Yet, teachers are expected to do so. According to this radical argument, there is a moral dilemma at the core of the teacher's work: socialization is not enough and yet human growth is an unrealistic ideal. An ethical teacher recognizes the problem and tries to do whatever he or she can to overcome its negative effects.

Psychology aims at the autonomy of the client. What this means is perhaps easiest to understand via the opposite of autonomy. People have unrealistic fears, neuroses, and addictions. One may conceptualize the situation by saying that such factors do not allow one's mind to work autonomously, in the sense that one's decisions are one's own. On the contrary, they are determined regardless of his or her free will, making the person at the same time less responsible as an agent. This condition need not be classified as an illness and, therefore, cannot be located within the jurisdiction of psychiatry.

Regardless of such a service ideal, which can be expressed in terms of moral psychology, the reality may be different. A psychologist helps the client to adjust to society even in cases where the person is troubled because of the imperfections of the norms of social life. For instance, working life in society may make unjustified and unrealistic demands on the worker whose ability to cope becomes more and more difficult. A psychologist helps him to adjust even in such cases where adjustment is personally undesirable in the long run. Perhaps it is too difficult to change the dynamics of the social structure so that such a possibility is never even conceptualized. Another example is marriage and divorce: in modern society a life-long marriage may be simply too demanding a norm and yet the clients may seek help to allow them to continue their married life. A psychologist cannot change the social institution, but she may be able to help the client to adjust to it.

Social work has a value ideal that may be understood in the minimalistic sense of the concept of welfare. Clients receive support, which allows them to avoid the final disaster that would make them unable to return to a normal, self-supporting lifestyle. A system of welfare is a safety net that catches those who would otherwise fall into the void. In other words, social work opposes marginalization and, therefore, its service ideal is not, like that of the majority of professions, a perfectionist one. However, the facts are disturbing. It has been argued, especially by conservative theorists, that welfare systems are highly stigmatizing in the sense that they consolidate the social positions of those caught in the safety net. The system makes the clients dependent on it so that they are not willing or able to live a life without it. The social welfare machinery produces its own clients and their life-style. What should be a brief interlude in their lives becomes their stable social position from which they have no escape. Whether such a description is valid or not is, of course, an open question whose political relevance is obvious.

The discussion above has focused on the key aspect of professional ethics, the virtue of self-understanding, which makes the professional a better person in his or her chosen social role. He or she should be aware both of the values, of the service ideal, and of the social reality of the profession.

C. Professional Practices and Their Virtues

To make the argument for the importance of virtue ethics for professional life more interesting, the following thesis can be presented. Professional values are both objective and internal to professional practices. Such a view is necessarily controversial. The concept of objective values is far from clear as is also the idea of practice-internal values. At the same time it seems important to indicate certain steps that virtue ethics of the professions might take.

Objective values: Such values as health, autonomy, human growth, welfare, and justice are objective in the following limited sense. One cannot sensibly maintain that one does not want to be healthy, which is to say that the denial of such values is false. It follows that these values are unavoidable, and this can be taken to indicate their objectivity. At the same time, it must be admitted that at the individual level, some people maintain that they are not interested in, say, justice or health. Perhaps such values are social values in the sense that in general, and at a policy level, it cannot be supposed that people would reject these values.

Internal values: Professionals work in order to realize social values that are generally perceived as unavoidable and as such objective. These values are internal to the work of professionals in the following sense. A physician who does not recognize health as the goal of his work is no longer a physician, in the intended sense of the term. The Nazi "physicians" were impostors for this very reason when they performed cruel experiments with prisoners of war. Abortions can be criticized from the point of view of professional ethics in the same way, because it requires the killing of a fetus that may be perfectly healthy, in a situation in which the mother has no valid medical reason to want an abortion. If health is the internal value of the medical profession, abortion as well as euthanasia present crucial problems.

Teaching as a profession is anchored to the development of personality so that mere socialization is not the goal of a teacher. The same argument can be repeated in the case of each of the professions. The definition of professional work is offered in terms of the value that defines the relevant service ideal.

D. Professional Power and Responsibility

Such a description of professional ethics in terms of practice-internal values allows us also to understand professional power and responsibility. Professional values, although they are objective, are always open to redefinition. What "health" or "justice" means is neither self-evident nor unchangeable. Historical studies show that both concepts have developed in the course of time. For instance, "health" can mean the absence of disease, a negative and perfect concept, although the current meaning is more like "optimal function of the mind–body unity," a positive and imperfect concept. The former kind of health can be perfected in the sense that a person is free from illness. In the latter sense, no one is ever perfectly healthy. Professions have the ability and power to redefine the relevant value concepts. For instance, "autonomy" is a psychological notion. Such value terms are often naively supposed to be natural and unproblematic so that their meaning is fixed independently of the professional work as if the meaning were independent of professional power.

In an almost paradoxical manner, professions make value-based goals internal to their practices and, consequently, to their work, but the meanings of these values are their own product. This fact emphasizes not only the power of professions but the difficulty of controlling them in modern, democratic societies. In fact, as has been argued, professions wield invisible and uncontrollable social power. At the same time, such a power must be balanced by the responsible behavior of professionals. They should realize that their position is unique in the sense that their profession enjoys an exclusive status; because there is no challenge to their expertise, they should use their own definitional power with caution. They should understand that the value terms that they use are not only based on their scientific theories or abstract learning, but that the meaning of such value terms always reflect some social factors that are difficult to specify. As a recommendation it makes sense to say that professional groups should not isolate themselves from the public discourse. Their members should remain open to external opinions and questions. This is a part of professional virtue.

E. Service and Success: Is There a Conflict?

To put these issues in a sharper focus, we may discuss briefly the application of the social contract theory of ethics to professional life. It seems plausible to suggest that professionals and their clients make an implicit social contract that regulates their relations. Professionals commit themselves to the service ideals that are beneficial to their clients and acceptable to the audience. Their level of cognitive competence is high. Professionals may be required to perform supererogatory acts, or to do more than is normally required, demanded, or expected. In exchange they gain the permission to pursue their own success, which may look less than desirable to clients. Professional fees may be expensive, the availability of services may be relatively scarce, and their status may be artificially high.

A counterargument shows the weak points of this application of the social contract theory. The clients can argue that the contract is invalid because it is based on coercion. Because the clients need the services provided by professionals, these services are necessary for them. Moreover, if they reject the services, they cannot find an alternative source. In other words, if professional values are objective and the profession is an exclusive provider of the relevant services, the clients have no choice but to accept the contract as it is defined by professionals. This is, technically speaking, coercion that invalidates the contract. The alternative sources are named impostors and charlatans who are unable to provide services for clients.

To make the contract work, professional ethics should dictate that an open attitude be adopted toward alternative services offered by other providers. It seems unlikely that any official professional code of ethics would include such norms. The reason is easy to understand on the basis of the idea of professional competence based on abstract knowledge. There is no alternative knowledge, according to professional cognitive objectivism. It follows that the professionals' benefits are high and the opportunities of social success very attractive.

The clients and the audiences of professions must tolerate their success-oriented claims. This is to say that professional ethics cannot be based solely on the service ideal, however important that seems to be. The service is always exchanged for money, status, and privilege. This is evident in law and medicine, but much less so in education and social work. In these latter fields, professionals have not been very successful in their efforts to transform their services into success and benefits. It is not easy to explain why this is so even if the problem certainly deserves studying.

A service ideal entails professional altruism that conflicts with the demands of success. This fact creates the peculiar moral atmosphere that surrounds modern professional life. The standard argument as presented by professionals is that their services are so valuable that they deserve their success. From the clients' and the audience's point of view, this may sound dubious. If the professional ideology is service-oriented and so altruistic, it does not seem to contain any right to claim excessive benefits. The case of those professionals who work for a company or organization is different and must be treated separately.

If the professionals' own argument is utilitarian, the other side represents the deontology that makes it the professionals' duty to provide the relevant services. Such a view is also reflected in official codes of ethics, although the right to success then becomes something of a mystery. A utilitarian may argue that the right to success is based on the maximization of the public good measured in terms of the services provided to clients. The maximization of social good follows from large benefits and good services. However, if professionals have a duty to provide the services, it is difficult to see what is the basis for their claims to success. The performance of one's duty does not entitle one to a reward.

Obviously, the ethical aspects of the relations between professionals and their clients deserve our careful and critical attention. It seems that in philosophical literature, too strong an emphasis has sometimes been placed on the notion of professional obligations. Certainly, professionals have many obligations, but it may be unrealistic to suppose that deontology is the ultimate explanatory theory of professional life. For example, a professional has a moral obligation to be honest when he or she deals with clients. However, he or she has no duty to provide special services. A professional exchanges the services for benefits, a fact that entails freedom-rights. There are exceptions, of course, like emergency medical treatment and an occasional free legal service for the poor.

IV. ENGINEERING AS A PSEUDOPROFESSION

A. The Nature of Engineering Ethics

It has been remarked that engineering is a profession that failed. Such a judgment might be unrealistically harsh considering that engineering is one of the major professions of industrial society. However, it is true that engineers' relationships to a service ideal and its values are problematic, or at least they must be understood differently from the classic professions discussed above. Because the engineering profession faces tremendous challenges in our time, it is sensible to ask whether this profession is able to assume the responsibilities of the leadership role when pollution, war, and the overuse of natural resources become a problem. It is unlikely that engineers want to claim that such issues do not belong to their expertise.

The key issue here is the service ideal. What kind of value-based service is provided by engineers? It is clear that they provide some kind of service. For instance, when people move from one place to another, they use automobiles, trains, and airplanes instead of their own legs, horses, or homemade carriages. When nations go to war, they use highly sophisticated weapons. When soldiers come back from war, they often need medical care, which again is made possible by the achievements of engineers. The engineers first design factories that pollute, and then they design water- and air-cleaning equipment. The blessings of engineering seem to be mixed. It is, however, clear that the modern world is a technological world.

The engineers' code of ethics mentions the safety, health, and welfare of the public as their service ideals, or as is said in the code, those factors should be held "paramount." It is not easy to specify the intended meaning of such a word. Certainly, for instance, a car should be safe. Cars also promote human well-being by allowing us to travel from place to place with the maximum ease. One can, of course, ask whether the notions of health, safety, and welfare are the same as those mentioned by medical professionals, the police, the armed forces, and social workers. The answer must be in the negative. Therefore, it seems plausible to suggest that such values are side-constraints rather than goals in engineering. Their main task is to produce good designs, when the goodness is evaluated according to standards that are internal to the practice of engineering.

The concept of side-constraint can be understood as follows. The physician must promote health. But though an engineer must take care that his design does not risk health, the design need not promote health. Cars may be good, but they are never healthy in the medical sense.

The following can be suggested as a blueprint for engineering ethics. An engineer is responsible for serving an employer by producing good designs that allow the employers to achieve their goals. The designs must be safe and, say, economical. Unlike the second, the first requirement is self-evident. Yet it is obvious that safety alone is not sufficient for a good design. The exact characterization of the sufficient condition must be one of the main tasks of engineering ethics. Certain additional observations can also be offered. Engineers are responsible for providing good designs for an employer, but they should also keep the interests of the public in mind. Here it is important to see how different their relation to employers and clients are, compared to, say, lawyers or teachers. The latter professions have their clients and audience; engineers have their employers and the public. Teachers provide only one type of service, regardless of their employer, unlike engineers who serve many employers with different goals. A teacher's audience is an external one, unlike the public that, say, buys cars. The idea of externality means that the audience is not directly influenced by the work of teachers: they are not taught and they do not learn anything.

B. The Need-Based Service Ideal

Engineers provide a service that is based on needs and desires, not on objective values. The following practical syllogism illustrate this point:

Medical profession:
I believe that the only way to stay healthy is to follow medical advice and do X.
I want to stay healthy.
Therefore, I do X.
Engineering:
I believe that the only way to build a bridge is to use engineering knowledge and to do Y.
I want to build the bridge.
Therefore, I do Y.

We notice that in the first syllogism we cannot reject the first premise, simply because health is an objective value, in the special sense of the word explained above. In the second syllogism, the second premise can be rejected because it is possible simply not to want to build the bridge. The engineer's employer may offer a bridge to his client who, after considering it, refuses to buy it. But if he wants to build the bridge, we can interpret Y as follows:

Y: let a responsible engineer design a bridge so that it is safe, beautiful, practical, ecologically viable, and economical to use and maintain in the long run.

In sum: the engineers provide a service to the public by creating designs that the public wants and that are safe and "good," in the special sense of the word, and that the employer will offer to the public.

Engineers serve also their employers whose goals vary widely, and in some cases are ethically problematic. An example is the weapons industry where, for instance, the infamous neutron bomb was supposed to kill people but leave material objects intact. Such a weapon was considered by the public as morally repulsive because it implied ideologically that people are less important than material objects. Engineers succeeded in reaching their employer's goal but they offended the public. This example shows how difficult it is to pinpoint the exact nature of the ethical side-constraints of engineering designs, which can be offensive almost in the same sense as pornography.

C. From Paternalism to Clients' Rights

A useful way of approaching some recent trends in professional ethics is to start from engineering ethics and then focus on the classical professions. These have tended to be, at least to some degree, paternalistic in the sense that a professional is supposed to know what is good for a client independently of the client's own opinion. Such a position of authority is evident especially in medicine. In recent years the client's rights have become stronger and stronger so that a kind of breakdown point has been reached. In this situation the professional can only advise the client without possessing any authority over his or her decisions. The patient, for instance, can insist on unnecessary treatment that is futile and ineffective. The same phenomena can well occur also in education where parents may want to bypass the teacher's expertise and insist on a certain kind of teaching that the professional sees as ineffective and potentially harmful to a child.

We may then ask what is the difference between "body engineers" and physicians, between "mind engineers" and psychologists, or "socialization engineers" and teachers. It is a useful exercise in professional ethics to try to answer these questions because then one can focus on the nature of the goals and responsibilities that constitute the basis of professional authority. It seems that the basic intuition suggests that medicine cannot be a matter of body engineering, although physicians are highly dependent on engineering designs. In other words, those who design the tools are yet incapable of using them because of some ethical, goal-orientated reasons.

What would happen if physicians were body engineers? One way to accept this is to focus on patients' rights. Suppose a cancer patient wants to try a new treatment that was promising some time ago, but that is now ineffective. The patient has a right to the treatment, if he can afford it financially. It is his physician's duty to inform him that the treatment does not work; but he does not have the right to withhold the treatment from the patient, simply because the patient has the right to determine what happens to his own body. According to such examples, the physician's role approaches that of a body engineer. In engineering the employer may want results so that he insists on working on the technical side of the problem even when engineers deem it futile. An example is the American Star Wars defense program. Interestingly, engineers may have more authority over such a decision than the physicians have. In both cases the clients may make an effort to find more compliant professionals if those whom they originally contacted want to refuse.

Notice that such an example indicates clearly why medicine, unlike engineering, is an ethical profession. Even when physicians are body engineers, their patients have the moral right to the treatment they choose, unlike the employer of an engineer who has no such right over

the engineers' projects. Unlike a physician, an engineer can refuse much more easily.

An even more illuminating example is cosmetic plastic surgery, which seems to present a moral problem from the point of view of the medical code of ethics. In this type of case, a person wants to have a more beautiful face, just as he may want to have a more beautiful car. In such a case, the doctor does not violate a code of ethics. Instead, he bypasses his moral role as a member of the medical profession, because the patient has no moral right to the treatment. Compare this case to that of the cancer patient.

It is possible that the nature of the classical professions is changing along with the recognition of strong patients' rights. This means that professionals provide the services requested by their clients without having any authority over those decisions. They do what they are hired to do on the basis of their technical expertise. Nevertheless, these professions retain their moral basis simply because a client's rights are moral rights, which create a strong obligation to the professionals to provide the service in question. The expertise of the professional becomes more technical in nature.

Another related trend is the emergence of alternatives to the services provided by the classic professions. It seems that their members have difficulties in defending their exclusive epistemic status. The concepts of charlatanism and fakery become more difficult to apply. This is evident in medicine where the ideas of faith healing and of alternative medicine are gaining ground. In the legal professions, the law has been compared to literature. In education, different minority groups have successfully argued against the mainstream educational ideas under the banners of political correctness. In such a process, educators have not much authority and certainly no motive to be paternalistic.

V. TRUTH, SCIENCE, AND INFORMATION AS PROFESSIONAL FIELDS

A. The Concept of Theoretical Profession

An important segment of professionalism can be found among the information professions. These are different both from the classical professions and engineering. Their key concepts are truth, knowledge, and information. We can mention librarians, who are the oldest of them, as well as scientists, journalists, and information-management people.

Let us first suggest why such professionals are not to be classified together with those in the classical professions. The main reason is that truth, knowledge, and information are not ethical terms. In fact, they have no practical value component built into them. The fact that lay people miss this point creates confusion when they discuss professional ethics in this field. It is easy to see why this is so. Truth is either logical or empirical, and empirical truth is simply the property of a sentence such that a true sentence corresponds with facts. Accordingly, "Snow is white" is true if, and only if, snow is white. Knowledge is, according to its classical definition derived from Plato, a justified, true belief. In this definition "justification" means epistemic acceptability, according to some more or less exact but always theoretical criteria. "Information" has many meanings, but the general idea is that information is a variation of a signal.

Some of the related ethical concepts are "truthfulness," "reliability," and "honesty." The idea that the truth must not be concealed or twisted seems to give some credibility to the thesis that truth as such is a value. It is also clear that from the pragmatic perspective, it is easy to accept the proposition that knowledge is useful. The Marxists claim that knowledge is a force of production. However, one should not forget in this context the standard fact-value distinction, or the distinction between theoretical and practical considerations and, indeed, values. There are theoretical values and also theoretical virtues, according to Aristotle.

In what sense are scientists professionals? The answer to this question allows us to understand the ethics of science from a specialized perspective. It is clear that scientists are in most cases professionals, in contrast to the amateurs of the Royal Society of 17th-century England, for instance. It is also interesting to recall that the first famous philosopher who was a professional in the sense of being a university professor is Immanuel Kant at the end of the 18th century.

We can argue that even if truth and knowledge are not values, access to them is. Therefore, the scientific profession has its own service ideal that is based on values. The main question is: What has science to do with truth and knowledge? It is notorious that neither the above-mentioned definition of truth nor the definition of knowledge applies to modern science. The offered definitions must be scientific in nature, so that science seeks for scientific truth and knowledge, which are not unproblematically related to the everyday notions of truth and knowledge. Perhaps the best way to put it is to say simply that scientists serve science in the sense that they try to add to the body of literature concerning certain disciplines and theories. Their aim is the advancement of science, which indirectly seems to entail the betterment of knowledge. It is not easy to characterize the goals of the scientific enterprise, if one takes the ideas of the philosophy of science seriously. Nevertheless, it seems obvious that scientists provide an access to something that is called scientific knowledge, and which is valuable in a modern technological society.

Scientists as professionals have no clients, if their students are not regarded as such. Consequently, they have no obligation to produce useful or entertaining data for the consumers of knowledge. Of course, society at large, or its political segment, often criticizes science for remaining in an ivory tower, which is to say that science is not useful enough and that scientists have too much autonomy in matters of science. Such a challenge should be taken seriously, of course, although it may be difficult to see how modern science could be more consumer-friendly. The scientific enterprise is supremely difficult to understand anyway.

Consequently, the ethics of science must focus mostly on the obligations of scientists toward each other, although the relations to various funding agencies are important as well. At least two levels are relevant here: norms between master and disciple or teacher and student, and between equal colleagues. At the first level, it is important, for instance, that the teacher does not exploit the ideas of the student. At the collegial level, it is important to avoid plagiarism. But what about forging the data that seems to be a growing concern in a present-day competitive scientific environment? Do scientists have a duty to the public not to do that, or do they have a duty toward each other? The answer must depend on the specific view of science one takes, which also determines one's ethics of science. An easy example is a case where forged data are used in an effort to gain a grant from public funds. This case has the moral status of stealing.

Perhaps it is possible to apply the Aristotelian notion of theoretical virtues to the professional ethics of science. The classic practical virtues are wisdom, courage, moderation, justice, and benevolence. Their theoretical counterparts can be listed as follows: theoretical understanding, creativity, logical consistency, criticism of others and oneself, and clarity. A good scientist should possess all of these virtues, and his training must facilitate their acquisition.

B. The Obligations of Journalists

Journalism is an important profession in modern society. Its service ideal is to provide access to information about society to the public. It seems that it has a direct responsibility to the public rather than to its employer. It is often said that the public has the right to know. This is taken to be a moral right, although it is not easy to see how such a right should be understood.

Here, just as in science, the idea of the professional serving truth seems to prevail. In the case of journalism, this may be misleading. It is hardly the responsibility of a journalist to find out whether publishable material is true or not, although he or she must be reasonably certain that what he or she writes is reliable information. It can also be argued that there is no value-free knowledge or information. All knowledge is contaminated by some social interests and background values. This is also to say that the transmission of information and knowledge is tied to social power. How all this happens is not at all easy to understand. It seems clear, however, that journalists cannot pretend that they just serve the truth. On the contrary, it is part of their moral responsibility to understand the aspects of social interest and power that are connected to the information they create and transmit to the public. The professional ethics of scientists and journalists are different, although the work of both focuses on knowledge, truth, and information.

Bibliography

Abbott, A. (1988). *A system of professions.* Chicago: Chicago University Press.

Airaksinen, T. (1994). Service and science in professional life. In R. Chadwick, (Ed.), *Ethics and the professions.* Avebury, U.K.: Aldershot (pp. 1–13).

Bayles, M. D. (1989). *Professional ethics* (2nd ed.). Belmont, CA: Wadsworth.

Cohen, W. (1995). *Ethics in thought and action: Social and professional perspectives.* New York: Ardsley House.

Harris, E. C., Jr., Pritchard, M. S., & Rabins, M. J. (Eds.). (1995). *Engineering ethics.* Belmont, CA: Wadsworth.

Shrader-Frechette, K. (1994). *Ethics of scientific research.* Lanham, U.K.: Roman & Littlefield.

Sprinkle, R. H. (1994). *Profession of conscience.* Princeton, NJ: Princeton University Press.

Windt, P. Y., et al. (Eds.). (1988). *Ethical issues in the professions.* Englewood Cliffs, NJ: Prentice-Hall.

Wueste, D. E. (Ed.). (1994). *Professional ethics and social responsibility.* Lanham, U.K.: Roman & Littlefield.

Sexual Content in Films and Television

JOHN WECKERT

Charles Sturt University

GLOSSARY

conceptual structure The knowledge, beliefs, and attitudes that form the framework within which a person acts and perceives.

eroticism Material intended to stimulate sexual desire.

freedom of expression In John Stuart Mill, the position that people should be able to live their lives and express themselves as they wish, providing that no harm is caused to others.

pornography Sometimes not distinguished from eroticism, but more often considered as sexual material of a violent, degrading, and exploitative nature.

sexual content *Explicit* sexual content comprises material such as human copulation. *Indirect* or *implicit* sexual content is implied or suggested, and is often "in the eye of the beholder."

SEXUAL CONTENT IN FILMS AND TELEVISION is not easy to define. While there are core examples, in many instances whether or not something counts as sexual depends on the context and on the beliefs and attitudes of the viewer. The chief moral issues raised by sexual material concern pornography, particularly in films, the portrayal of women in television commercials, the protection of children and the formation of moral attitudes in educational programs, and privacy and victimization in news bulletins. Finally, there are questions regarding the restriction of sexual material, which raises the issues of freedom of expression.

I. SEXUAL CONTENT: WHAT IS IT?

The title of this article probably evoked images or thoughts of humans engaged in explicit sexual activity, and perhaps of material that would typically be called pornographic or erotic. When considered more carefully, however, it becomes unclear just what constitutes sexual content in film and television, and what is morally interesting. While the pollination of pumpkins and the courtship of peacocks are undoubtedly sexual, and films or television programs about these would undoubtedly have sexual content, it is difficult to see any interesting moral issues here, so the discussion will be restricted primarily to human sexual activity.

The most obvious sexual content is human copulation depicted or discussed explicitly and in detail. It might be pornographic or erotic, or perhaps neither, perhaps factual. Such content could be in a film or an educational program, but probably not in a news bulletin, a sitcom, or a soap opera. Sexual content also comprises references, perhaps oblique, to sexual activity, language involving certain innuendos, as well as scenes that infer sexual activity. For example, the statement, "Last night I went back to Bill's place and we did it" is clearly sexual in the context of a sitcom about very attractive people in their twenties whose lives revolve around relationships with members of the opposite sex. Similarly, a couple walking up the stairs can, in the right context, imply immanent sexual enjoyment, and so counts as sexual content. These examples however raise an interesting question. Where the sexual reference or scene is not explicit, to what extent is sexual content "in the eye of the beholder"? We will return to this shortly.

Sexual content can form part of the artistic or the entertainment content of films (including sitcoms and soap operas), where there would normally be some intent to portray a level of sexuality. But it is not all like this. In educational programs, news bulletins, and documentaries it could be just factual, and there may even be an intention to downplay the sexuality in some scene or discussion. This could and should be the case in news reports of, for example, rape, pedophilia, and litigation for sexual harassment, and in educational programs dealing with sexual, particularly human, reproduction.

Finally, a comment on television commercials, which frequently have, or so it is claimed, sexual content. This is rarely explicit. It is much more likely to be in the form of young and attractive people, perhaps wearing seductive clothes or in seductive poses, or using sexually suggestive language. The impression often given is that the purchaser of the relevant product will be as sexually attractive as the person or people in the advertisement.

The sexual content of commercials is usually implicit rather than explicit, which takes us back to the question raised a moment ago regarding this content being "in the eye of the beholder." What does it mean to say this? It means, generally, that sexual "content" is in the mind of the viewer and not in the material itself. In Wittgenstienian terms we might say that the viewer *sees* the material *as* sexual (Wittgenstein 1968: 193–194). Another viewer might not see it in this way. While care must be taken in claiming that we *see as* rather than just see, we can and do see things differently depending both on the context in which things are couched, and on our own knowledge and beliefs (our conceptual structure) and perhaps on what is uppermost in our minds at the time of viewing.

This issue of seeing material in a sexual way makes it very difficult to specify just what constitutes sexual content. Explicit scenes of human copulation are obviously sexual, but what about fondling, hugging, kissing, and sexually suggestive language? It clearly depends on the context and on the viewers. But once it is conceded that context and viewers are important it is difficult to know where to stop. A meal scene in the well-known *Tom Jones* movie is said to be highly sexual, presumably because it excites the imagination in some way. Young schoolboys might fall down laughing at a shot of a banana, or someone might look lustfully at a preacher extolling the virtues of celibacy. Do these constitute sexual content? Perhaps not, but consider a different case. Suppose that a group of people brought up with public nudity see a film containing scenes of people frolicking nude in a swimming pool. These viewers might see nothing at all sexual in this, although another group probably would. If sexual content is that which evokes images or thoughts of sexual activity, then the scenes of the banana and of the preacher are as sexual as the nude frolickers. If it cannot be extended to this type of material, the latter should not be included either. Clearly, apart from the core examples, sexual content can only be defined in terms of the context of the scene and the conceptual structures of the audience.

II. THE MORAL ISSUES

Given the importance of sexual activity for sexually reproducing organisms, it is something of a wonder that the sexual content in films and television is worth discussing in an ethical context. It is as vital for the survival of many species as is eating, and this is certainly true in the case of humans. While there may be some ethical discussion of gluttony, there is not much of eating in general. In the case of human sexual activity, however, it is not just overindulgence that is thought to raise ethical issues; it is the activity as such. Furthermore, it is not only those activities that engender debate, it is also their portrayal in film, in television, and in the written and spoken word. Why is sexual activity considered so much more important ethically than eating when both are common, and indeed must be if the species is to survive? Perhaps, because everyone must eat to survive while sexual activity is not essential for the survival of an individual. Perhaps, too, it is partly because of the difficulty of always separating this activity from emotional bonds that it can promote and enrich. This leads to what is probably the most important point. Sexual activity normally involves another person, and possibly the creation of more. It is social, usually, and as such is essentially ethical. The rights of both, or all, the participants must be considered.

Although sexual activity itself may necessarily involve ethics, it does not follow that its portrayal necessarily does. The ethical questions in this sphere arise because of the harm or supposed harm caused by some sexual material, and the offense it gives to some people. It could be argued that sexual material is immoral in itself regardless of its consequences. This view would normally be closely associated with particular religious beliefs, and nothing much of significance can be said about this without an examination of those beliefs. In any case, holders of this position would probably be offended by sexual material, so to some extent it will be covered by offense. We will first consider what the moral issues might be in films, and then in television.

A. Films

Most discussion of what is wrong with sexual material in films, whether shown in theaters or on television, concerns pornography. It is not easy, however, to say what pornography is. First, definitions vary widely. The most moderate define it as sexual content of a film, or whatever, that is designed to arouse sexual desires, or perhaps to satisfy sexual desire. Other accounts make it anything but innocuous. It is sexual content that is combined with one or more of violence, abuse, degradation, dominance and conquest. Second, to what content do these definitions refer? Does the first refer to something that was designed to arouse sexual desire but regularly fails to, because it was done so badly? And what about scenes that were not designed for this purpose, but that regularly do? The second definition does not fare much better. While physical violence and abuse are not too difficult to describe, degradation, for example, can take many forms, and what one person sees as degrading another may not.

These criticisms of the definitions do not show that the word "pornography" is too vague to be useful. What they show is that care must be taken when discussing it. There is little point in merely saying that pornographic films should be censored. There may be a lot of point in saying this once a clear statement of what is meant by pornography is given.

Some writers distinguish between the pornographic and the erotic, while others claim that there is no difference. A middle position is that eroticism is a weaker form of pornography. A useful way to differentiate the two is to use "pornography" in the second sense above, where it is linked to violence abuse, dominance, coercion, inequality, and the like, and to use "eroticism" for sexual content that concerns sexual desire but that is free from any violence, dominance, and so on.

Not all sexual content is necessarily pornographic or erotic. Some is simply for artistic purposes (eroticism, of course, could be artistic). The film is better with it than without it. Just what constitutes art, or what distinguishes art from nonart is not easy to say; nevertheless, importance is placed on this distinction. It is

much less common for sexual material to be condemned if it is considered artistic than if it is not.

The most controversial sexual content is the pornographic, in the sense where it is distinguished from the erotic. The main reasons advanced for the wrongness of this material are that it causes harm, both to individuals and to society, that it is degrading, particularly to women, that it is exploitative, and that it is offensive.

1. Harm

It is argued sometimes that there is a causal link between pornographic material in films, and rape and other violence, against women in particular. While there is some anecdotal evidence for this, the hard evidence is more ambiguous. It appears that so far no strong case has been established for a causal link, or for the lack of one. On the other side, there is also some evidence, again inconclusive, that watching pornographic films can have a beneficial effect on some, by reducing aggressive and violent behaviour.

The more general claim that pornographic and erotic material weaken society is even more difficult to substantiate, partly because it is essentially ideological. The claim often is that this material encourages promiscuity, weakens marriage and the family, etc. Even if a causal link were established, more argument would be required to show that that is undesirable.

2. Degradation

It is difficult to make a case that erotica is degrading to anyone, but it is plausible to say that pornography is. There is a sense in which it is degrading to all participants, including the viewers, but it is especially so to the individuals or groups who are the recipients of violence or who are subservient, usually women. It seems equally degrading to the victims in pornography if they suffer violence or other indignities against their will, or if they play the parts willingly.

3. Exploitation

Another common criticism of pornography is that some of the participants, namely, those playing the subservient roles, are exploited. Undoubtedly in many instances this is true. However, where women, and in some cases men, willingly participate, it is difficult to see where the exploitation lies. It might be argued that nobody would willingly play those roles, but this is demeaning to those who do. It implies that any people who willingly and without any coercion decide to play subservient roles, are not really acting freely, and are deluding themselves if they think that they are. Many, of course, who are not coerced, may only "voluntarily" participate because they are so poor that they see no other alternative to escape poverty. Their participation is therefore hardly voluntary. However, there could be cases where there is no such necessity. In any event, this sort of exploitation could be eliminated now with the use of current computer simulation techniques and image manipulation. It may be that some consumers would not find this material as enjoyable if they knew that there were no real people involved in the activities that they were watching, but that is another matter.

4. Offense

Sexual material of any sort, but particularly pornography, is sometimes condemned on the grounds that it is offensive. Because of the perceived importance of this objection in relation to anything sexual, and because the nature of offence is seldom discussed in any detail, we will return to it in Section III.

B. Television

In this section we will concentrate on the nonfilm component of television, in particular on commercials, educational programs, and news bulletins. Here pornography is not particularly important, and neither is erotica, except to a limited extent in commercials. The moral issues raised therefore will be slightly different from those discussed previously, although there is some overlap.

1. Commercials

Advertisers want to sell products, so generally will try to avoid material offensive to their target audience. As already mentioned, the sexual content is likely to be inferred rather than explicit, therefore it could be argued that the content itself is not sexual. But this, as we have also seen, is a dubious claim. What are the moral issues in this context? In commercials, sexual material is almost always unnecessary, and therefore, perhaps, has more potential to portray people, usually women, as sexual objects, even where there is nothing very significant about the content if it were in another context. As is often the case in popular quiz shows, the women involved are little more than decorations—they look attractive and perhaps stimulate the imagination, but they do little that is necessary. The moral issues here revolve around whether this portrayal harms women, and whether it is offensive. One argument is that it helps perpetuate the view that women are not capable of much beyond looking good and giving pleasure to men. This reinforces typical male attitudes and

the male dominance of society. As such, this material is offensive to many. Counterarguments to this might be first, that such material cannot be offensive to too many, because "sex sells"—the commercials work, and second, that the material does not, or cannot, harm women in the way suggested because is must be seen in a certain way to be classed as sexual. It is not sexual in itself. The first response clearly must be rejected. Something is not morally right simply because it works. Ends do not always justify means. Neither does the fact that these commercials work show that nobody is justifiably offended by them. The second response is too glib. Certain material can count as genuine sexual content even though it must be seen in a certain way, and it could still be harmful.

2. Educational Programs

Educational programs can be aimed at people of any age, but the main moral concerns tend to be over whether certain material is appropriate for children of certain ages, and whether the material is dealt with in a proper manner. Should, for example, homosexuality be portrayed as acceptable? Even in moderately tolerant societies, this question generates heat. Some see an affirmative answer as obvious, while others believe that portrayal will help lead to the undermining of traditional family and other religious values. A similar issue is whether sexual activity should be shown as an end in itself, or whether it should always be shown as part of a loving relationship. Another question is to what extent are children upset or psychologically damaged by nonviolent explicit sexual material?

There appear to be two main moral issues here: first, how much should we protect children for their own good, and second, to what extent should we try to stop children acquiring "false," or "morally bad," values? Adults certainly do have an obligation to protect children from harm, and the issues here are what material is harmful, and how long this protection should last. The second main moral issue will always be a problem in any society in which a wide variety of moral values are tolerated. Almost nobody in a civilized society would want children to believe that violence is acceptable in sexual relationships (or in any other), but it is not so obvious what "false" or "morally bad" beliefs are with respect to nonviolent and consensual sexual activity.

3. News Bulletins

The sexual content of television news bulletins raises some moral issues that are different from those discussed so far, because news items are, supposedly, of real events. People usually become the subjects of these news items through misfortune, with no intent of making their private lives public; therefore, the most important moral issues concern privacy and victimization. And it is frequently not only a victim of, for example, rape or sexual harassment who should be taken into account. Anyone close to the victim, say a child or parent, should also have their privacy respected. This respect for privacy should also extend to close associates of accused persons, even if and when they are convicted. There will frequently be conflicts between society's right to know and an individual's right to privacy, but society does not have a right to all details, and journalists do not have the right to victimize people in order to get details.

III. OFFENSE

Because sexual material is undoubtedly offensive to many, it is worth looking more carefully at giving and taking offense. Offense is a sort of unhappiness, mental distress, or some other sort of suffering. An offended person has his or her feelings hurt in some way. An important point is that something will only offend someone if that person *takes* offense. Offense is closely related to beliefs, attitudes, feelings, and so on.

Two questions emerge: (1) What, if anything, is wrong with giving offense? and (2) Why do people take offense? In answer to (1), one may be inclined to say that there is nothing really wrong with giving offense. After all, if people are so silly or sensitive that they become hurt at something said or seen, so much the worse for them. While this contains an element of truth, it is a bit hard, but we will return to this after a brief look at (2).

Obviously, offense is taken for different reasons by different people and over a wide range of areas, but here our only interest is in sexual material in films and on television. Part of the explanation for the offense taken clearly has to do with upbringing and socialization. But this is not a complete explanation. There might be anger where something is not liked because it is thought that it will have harmful consequences. For example, it will lead to rape or to the lowering of moral standards. Offense, however, seems to involve something more than this. If I find something offensive I take it personally in some way. I am *hurt*, not just angered. A reasonable explanation of why I am hurt is that I identify closely with beliefs that this sort of behavior is wrong, and in a way I feel violated. If you expose me to these things that you know I do not like, then you are not showing me the respect that I deserve as a person. Even if it was not directed at me in particular,

I may feel that people like me are not respected enough. In both cases we may feel devalued as persons.

A related point is that material that denigrates a particular group or in some way portrays that group to be inferior can offend because one has no choice in belonging to that group. A relevant example is the portrayal of women in pornography and in some television commercials. There is a real sense here in which our self-image and self-respect can suffer. Offense will more often be bound up with self-respect.

We find that there is a close connection between the taking of offense and self-respect or self-esteem. When someone displays material that we find offensive, we feel that we are not being respected as humans. Our self-respect may be lessened to some extent. Too many of these comments can cause us to see ourselves as people of little worth. If something that is an integral part of me is ridiculed, say my gender or my moral or religious beliefs, this is evidence that others do not value me as a person. They are not showing me the respect that I deserve as a person. Perhaps what is wrong with giving offense in general is that it is showing a lack of respect for others and that it may cause them to lose some of their self-respect.

This account shows that the giving of offense needs to be taken seriously. It can be more than a matter of few oversensitive or old-fashioned people having their sensibilities attacked. The problem, of course, is that almost any sexual material will be offensive to some, so if all offense is taken as a reason for restriction, almost nothing of a sexual nature could be portrayed. Offense must be taken seriously in the sense that it ought not be brushed aside as irrelevant in all cases. A plausible argument might be that material that is generally offensive to a group whose members have no alternative but to belong to that group, say women or any racial group, could be restricted in some way, but that material found offensive in other situations should not. There seems to be a relevant difference between material that is offensive to women because it degrades them as a group, and material that is offensive to some people simply because they find it embarrassing or they do not like it for some other reason.

IV. RESTRICTING SEXUAL CONTENT

Restrictions of various kinds are often placed on material of a sexual nature. It might be banned altogether, or it might just be given a code to indicate its content or the kind of audience for which it is intended. Such codes warn audiences of what they might expect to see or hear. If they do not heed the warnings, they have little cause to complain if they find the material offensive. It is easily avoidable. In the case of television programs, there might also be restrictions placed on when they are allowed to be shown. Programs containing explicit sex scenes might only be allowed to be shown late at night when young children are less likely to see them.

The arguments against restrictions tend to revolve around freedom of expression. Some of the best-known come from J. S. Mill. Mill's conception of a good human life is one in which we think, reflect, and rationally choose for ourselves from different beliefs and life-styles according to what seems most true or meaningful to us. This is shown in his arguments for the freedom of expression. His central tenet here is that people ought to be allowed to express their individuality as they please "so long as it is at their own risk and peril" (Mill 1975: 53). The basic argument is that the diversity created has many benefits. One is that "the human faculties of perception, judgement, discriminative feeling, mental activity, and even moral preference, are exercised only in making a choice" (Mill 1975: 55). And exercising this choice makes it less likely that we will be under the sway of the "despotism of custom" (Mill 1975: 66). If there is this diversity, each human will be more aware of the various options available, and so more competent to make informed choices in life-style and self-expression. We will be able to lead happier and more fulfilled lives.

This and other such arguments for freedom of expression do support the claims for lack of restrictions and control of sexual material in films and on television. However the support is qualified, because one person's right to freedom of expression can impinge on another's rights, and can clash with other goods. There is little sense in the idea of complete freedom of expression for all. So the issue now becomes one of where to draw the lines for this freedom. Common criteria are harm to others and the giving of offense. Mill places particular emphasis on the former. We should be able to express ourselves more or less as we like providing that others are not harmed by our actions.

While many arguments concerning sexual content commonly revolve around pornography and obscenity, others involve the protection of children even from material much more benign. Viewing that might not be detrimental to adults, might be to children. Or perhaps it might instile in them undesirable values. In this context, television is more important. Not only are films on television more accessible to children, but sexual material can also be found in educational programs, news broadcasts, and documentaries. Of concern here are not so much the pornographic and erotic, but more "harmless" sexual material, perhaps nudity in general, and open discussion of sexual issues, and perhaps even the mating behavior of the high mammals. Mill, it should be noted, did not include children in his argument, chiefly because they could not, according to him, be improved by free and rational discussion.

V. CONCLUSION

This article has concentrated on problems of deciding what constitutes sexual content in films and television, on what the main moral issues are, and on questions concerning restriction or control of sexual material. Sexual content is not easy to define, largely because much is not explicit but rather depends on the context and on the viewer. In films the chief concern is pornographic material, although there is disagreement about what pornography is, and why it is objectionable, if it is. The central arguments against it are based on harm, degradation, exploitation, and offense. Offense, while it cannot be an overriding consideration, does deserve serious consideration. In the nonfilm component of television, the important moral issues arise in commercials, educational programs, and news bulletins. In commercials the primary concern is the portrayal of women, and in educational programs, the type of sexual material to which children ought to be exposed, and its effect on them. Because news bulletins deal with real events, privacy and victimization of victims of sex crimes are of paramount importance. Finally, there are strong reasons for allowing freedom of expression, even where the material is of a sexual nature.

Bibliography

Baird, R. M., & Rosenbaum, S. E. (Eds.). (1991). *Pornography: Private right or public menace?* Buffalo, NY: Prometheus Books.

Baker, R., & Elliston, F. (Eds.). (1984). *Philosophy and sex* (New Revised Edition). Buffalo, NY: Prometheus Books.

Belliotti, R. A. (1993). *Good sex: Perspectives on sexual ethics.* Lawrence: The University Press of Kansas.

Christensen, F. M. (1990). *Pornography: The other side.* New York: Praeger.

Davies, S. (1991). *Definitions of art.* Ithaca, NY: Cornell University Press.

Dines, G., & Humez, J. M. (Eds.). (1995). *Gender, race and class in media: A text reader.* Thousand Oaks, CA: Sage Publications.

Feinberg, J. (1985). *The moral limits of the criminal law. Vol. Two: Offense to others.* Oxford: Oxford University Press.

Fink, C. C. (1988). *Media ethics: In the newsroom and beyond.* New York: McGraw-Hill.

MacKinnon, C. A. (1989). *Toward a feminist theory of the state.* Cambridge: Harvard University Press.

Mill, J. S. (1975). *John Stuart Mill On Liberty: Annotated Text, sources and background criticism,* Spitz, D. (Ed.). New York: W. W. Norton & Company.

Oshima, N. (1992). *Cinema, censorship, and the state: The Writings of Nagisa Oshima 1956–1978.* Edited and with an introduction by

Annette Michelson. Translated by Dawn Lawson. Cambridge: MIT Press.

Russell, D. E. H. (Ed.). (1993). *Making violence sexy: Feminist views on pornography*. Buckingham: Open University Press.

Steinem, G. (1978, November). Erotica and pornography: A clear and present difference. *Ms* magazine. Reprinted in Baurd and Rosenbaum (1991), 51–55.

West, M. I. (1988). *Children, culture and controversy*. Hamden, CT: Archon Books.

Williams, B. (1981). *Obscenity and film censorship: An abridgement of the Williams report*. Cambridge: Cambridge University Press.

Wittgenstein, L. (1968). *Philosophical Investigations*. (G. E. M. Anscombe, Trans.) Oxford: Basil Blackwell.

Tabloid Journalism

SEUMAS MILLER

Charles Sturt University

GLOSSARY

autonomous public communicator A person who communicates information and comment to the community via the print and electronic media, and does so wholly on the basis of his or her own judgment. An autonomous communicator is not simply the communicative instrument of someone else. Newsreaders are not autonomous public communicators, while current affairs correspondents are supposed to be.

investigator A newspaper, TV, or radio journalist who unearths, or seeks to unearth, previously unknown—or not widely known—information for the purposes of disseminating it to the public at large.

normative Of, or pertaining to, standards or principles governing what ought to be, as distinct from what in fact is. One category of normative judgments or statements is the moral or ethical.

postmodernism A contemporary intellectual movement associated with the writings of Derrida, Barthes, Lacan, Rorty, and Foucault. Influential in literary and communication studies. Key elements are rejection of the literal–metaphoric distinction, and of rationality and the unitary self, and the tying of knowledge to power.

public forum A meeting place or communicative space in which individuals or representatives can communicate to the community at large.

theoretical Of or pertaining to a theory. A theory is a general account of some type of object or kind of practice, including journalism, which identifies the main features of that object or practice, displays their relationship to one another, and differentiates that object or practice from other sorts of object and practice. A theory enables us to better understand the object or practice in question.

TABLOID JOURNALISM, in the modern sense, refers to the quality of said journalism. "Tabloid" initially referred to the size and layout of a newspaper. Tabloids were distinguished from broadsheets in that they used smaller sheets of paper. Tabloids were more akin to a magazine format than the large, wide broadsheets. However, over time "tabloid" has come to be used to refer to lower quality newspapers and, more recently, certain lower quality TV programs. The *Sun* newspaper published in the United Kingdom is a paradigm of tabloid journalism in this newly established sense.

I. DESCRIPTION OF TABLOID JOURNALISM

A. Content

Taking the *Sun* as our paradigm, let us first look at its overall content. Firstly, there is very little hard news or analysis in the newspaper. Rather it is largely given over to sports, advertising, and so-called human interest stories. Secondly, there is a good deal of space given over to depiction of young female bodies in sexually provocative poses. Most notably there is the page 3 pinup girl. The overall space given to hard news and

The Concise Encyclopedia of Ethics in Politics and the Media

analysis relative to "trivia" is one indicator of the emphasis of tabloid journalism. Another indicator is the relative lack of prominence of hard news and analysis within the structure of the publication.

Typically, the lead story of the *Sun* is "sensational" and oriented to sex scandal. In short, the lead story is often unimportant news—at least from any perspective other than that of sex scandal. This is not to say, of course, that a sex scandal is always and necessarily unimportant. The Christine Keeler episode, for example, was important and newsworthy.

B. Characteristic Features

Some of the characteristic features of tabloid stories—whether in newspapers or on television—follow.

As already indicated, the lead stories in a tabloid publication are often sensationalist in nature. The private lives of prominent public figures, including politicians, Princess Diana, and the British Royal Family, are a particular obsession of the *Sun.* Other favorite issues for tabloid publications throughout the world are gruesome crimes and exotic and/or bizarre events or conditions. The Yorkshire Ripper and the so-called House of Horrors stories provided the UK tabloids with a feast of headlines and lead stories; as did the woman who took fertility drugs and then decided to try to give birth to all of the resultant eight fetuses.

Second, many of the stories are highly moralistic, the morality in question being popular sentiment. Such moralistic stories include those expressing moral outrage at the (allegedly) light sentences handed out to vicious criminals and those giving vent to nationalistic fervor in the context of war. In this latter connection, consider the jingoism and lack of concern for the lives of Argentina naval personnel on the occasion of the sinking of the *Belgrano* during the Falklands war.

Thirdly, the stories rely heavily on cliches, stereotypes, and even abusive slang. Argentinians become Argies, and French men and women, Frogs. To take some recent examples from the Australian press, Ivan Milat, the murderer of backpackers in the Belangalo Forest, became the Belangalo Butcher, and Martin Bryant, the murderer of 36 people in Tasmania, a Blonde Blue-Eyed Beast. There is an overrepresentation of young women in sexually provocative poses. There is the tendency to present adherents to the Moslem faith as members of chanting violent crowds. Young black youths are typically represented as the perpetrators and victims of violent crime. And so on and so forth with the portrayal of various ethnic and sexual stereotypes.

Fourthly, there is a blurring of the distinction between drama and actuality. This is partly a result of a lack of concern for the truth. The truth is often hard to obtain. If one is not resolutely striving for it, then one is not likely to arrive at it. Tabloid journalists have no great concern for the truth. Hence their tendency to exaggerate, and their frequent recourse to the tactic of the news story "beat up." Indeed, on occasion the tabloids quite literally forgo any attempt to represent preexisting truths and simply create the news themselves. For example, recently the Australian tabloid TV program "A Current Affair" arranged for the teenage members of the Paxton family in Melbourne to be offered jobs in Queensland and then flew them there; when they refused the jobs, the program "exposed" and castigated them as "welfare cheats."

A lack of concern for truth was dramatically demonstrated recently by the *Sun.* The *Sun*'s publication of alleged pictures of Princess Diana frolicking with her lover turned out to be a hoax. The pictures were of actors pretending to be Princess Diana and her lover. The *Sun* had evidently not taken sufficient trouble to check the authenticity of the pictures.

But the blurring of the distinction between drama and actuality has a more fundamental cause. Tabloids overuse and misuse dramatic forms. Events are not related sequentially, nor are dramatic forms simply used to heighten the sense of reality of newsworthy events. Rather the drama and emotion—whether real or imagined—surrounding an event in effect become the "event" to be communicated to an audience, and communicated for the purpose of triggering an emotive reaction in the audience. The point of the exercise is not to communicate truth, but to capture and keep audiences.

Thus tabloid style TV current affairs programs often provide "reconstructions" of events which are in fact dramatizations. These dramatizations often focus on and exaggerate sensational, scandalous and morally loaded aspects of the events treated. What for? Not for the purpose of informing the audience or assisting in the process of understanding these events. The purpose is rather to trigger and manipulate an emotive response in the audience—whether it be sexual desire, envy, horror, moral outrage, or merely perverse pleasure in the misfortunes or inadequacies of others—and thereby keep it watching.

C. Macro-institutional Context

This description of tabloid journalism would not be complete without some account being offered of the macro-socioinstitutional context in which tabloid journalism is produced. This context includes the large, sometimes transnational, corporations which produce a great amount of tabloid journalism. One such corporation is Rupert Murdoch's News Ltd.

Governments and political leaders are dependent on

these media corporations for favorable treatment, for governments and political leaders rely heavily on the media for the presentation of themselves and their policies to the public. Yet the media, including tabloid journalism, are, at least in Australia and the USA, largely owned by these corporations.

Moreover, these large media corporations in part own, and in part are owned by, other nonmedia corporations. This raises the issue of the independence of the media as an institution from nonmedia business corporations.

This general issue of the independence of the media from both business and government has been raised recently in Australia. On the one hand there is an alliance between Murdoch's News Corporation—which owns a majority of Australian newspapers as well as one of the major TV networks—and the government-owned telecommunications provider, Telstra, to create the cable TV operation Foxtel. On the other hand in this overall context, the government is seeking partly to privatize Telstra.

A second element comprises the corporate advertisers whose business is so important to the media in general, and to the producers of tabloid journalism in particular. Indeed the point has been reached where the bulk of the revenue of tabloid newspapers comes not from sales of the newspapers but from fees paid by advertisers. (Tabloid TV is wholly dependent on advertising revenue, and all the points to be made below can equally be made in relation to tabloid TV.) This being so, there are at least three aims the producers of tabloid newspapers have, it being no longer clear which of these is the most important.

The first aim of a tabloid newspaper is to inform or entertain its readership. The second aim is to sell as many newspapers as possible. The third aim is to attract advertising revenue. Obviously these aims are interdependent. If readers are informed and entertained they are more likely to buy a newspaper, and if a newspaper has a large readership then advertisers are more likely to want to buy advertising space. However, the existence of this interdependence does not settle the issue as to the means–end relationship between these three different aims. It might be that the overriding de facto aim of a tabloid newspaper is to make a profit. But advertising is the largest source of revenue. So perhaps the aims of selling large numbers of newspapers and informing/entertaining readers are subsidiary to attracting advertising revenue. In short, perhaps in the overall context of making a profit, tabloid newspapers exist principally in order to sell advertising space rather than to inform/entertain or even to attract a large readership. Certainly the huge amount of space devoted to advertising in tabloids provides some evidence for this view.

A third element comprises the mass audiences or consumers of tabloid journalism. Given the points just made about advertising, we need to conceive of these consumers as consumers not only of the information and entertainment presented in the tabloids, but also, and perhaps most importantly, as consumers of the advertisements. Indeed, given the already-mentioned tendencies of the tabloids to exaggerate, sensationalize, titillate, and run together fact and fiction, perhaps the distinction between tabloid news/entertainment and advertisements has been undermined—scrutiny of the advertisements reveals them to have many of the properties of the nonadvertising material.

Consider in this connection the page 3 pinup girl. Is she there as part of the nonadvertising section or part of the advertising? She is presumably not part of the news stories. Presumably she is there to attract readers to buy the newspaper. But if a reader is attracted by the pinup girl and then simply reads the ads, rather than the news stories, surely the pinup girl has served its purpose. Moreover, in what sense is the pinup girl any different from the picture of Princess Diana allegedly frolicking with her lover? Certainly one posed and the other did not, but from the consumer's point of view, wherein lies the difference? Both pictures titillate. Perhaps the purpose of both is to get the reader to buy the newspaper and then go on to read the ads. Further, the ads themselves involve scantily clad young women. (Unlike the page 3 pinup and Princess Diana, these women are associated with specific products.) At any rate the general point to be made here is that there is a real question about the substantive nature of the distinction between advertising and nonadvertising sections within tabloids.

Perhaps the final element of the macroinstitutional or social context is the new communication technologies and their impact on tabloid journalism, including in particular the capacity of satellite and cable operators to project tabloid journalistic products to larger transnational audiences. This projection to larger, including transnational, audiences relies not simply on technology, but on the existence of relatively homogenous consumer societies, or at least of transnational consumer groups, albeit different ones within any given society.

It would not be unfair to say that this macroinstitutional context of tabloid journalism is one which locates tabloid journalism as a highly successful mass consumer product, albeit a differentiated one. Tabloid journalism not only sells well, it advertises well. Moreover, it appears to do so in part not only by blurring the distinction between information and entertainment, but also by blurring the distinction between information/entertainment and advertisements. The most obvious example of this cocktail of information, entertainment, and advertisement is so-called infotainment.

II. NORMATIVE THEORETICAL ACCOUNT OF THE MEDIA

Having provided a descriptive account of tabloid journalism in the opening section, there is a need to offer a normative theoretical account of the role of the media, and its proper relationship both to other institutions, including government and the business sector, and to individual citizens.

A. Media as Both Industry and Institution

The print and electronic media are at one and the same time an industry and a public institution. As an industry in the private sector the media produces saleable commodities (including advertisements), employs workers and managers, and has investors and owners. It is simply another business, or set of businesses, within the market economy. As such its function is economic; it exists to make profits, provide jobs, and satisfy consumer demand. As a public sector industry funded by government, it also has an economic function; it employs workers and managers and is, to an extent, market oriented, e.g., "consumption" levels are of importance.

The media is also an institution. By "institution" it is here meant that it is an organization, or set of organizations, that has a particular sociopolitical function in respect to public communication. Here a number of points need to be made.

Firstly, in distinguishing between the media as an industry and the media as an institution—between its economic and its sociopolitical function—it is not being maintained that the functions do not overlap and are not linked. Indeed it is commonplace in political and social theory that economic functions intermesh with sociopolitical functions, and that political interests are served by particular economic arrangements and economic interests by political arrangements. This goes as much for the media as for any other major social institution. Notwithstanding their interdependence, there is an important distinction between the economic and the sociopolitical functions of the media. Therefore any conception that seeks to collapse the political and/or the social role of institutions, including the media, into their economic role or vice versa should be resisted.

It follows that crude Marxist views should be rejected, for these views in effect occupy an a priori theoretical position according to which institutions such as governments, universities, and the media must be construed principally as agents of the ascendant economic classes.

But equally to be rejected is the view implicit in much of the rational choice theory deployed by "liberal" economists that the social functions of institutions are simply the logical product of the (unexplained) preferences of individual rational agents making choices in a (typically distorted) market economy.

Secondly, we need to distinguish between the de facto function(s) of the media and the function(s) it ought to have. Perhaps the chief function of the mainstream media is to buttress the capitalist system. Whether or not this is so is an empirical question which cannot be addressed here. As far as a normative theory is concerned, we need to ask what the function or functions of the media ought to be. Naturally, a normative conception is not a fanciful conception. A normative conception of an institution is a conception of what realistically could be. Indeed normative issues, far from being the idealist distractions self-styled "real world" advocates proclaim them to be, are in fact central and unavoidable in our common life. When at one level of theorizing neo-Marxists and others dismiss normative claims as ideology, at another level of theorizing the very same theorists appeal—albeit implicitly—to their own unacknowledged set of normative commitments. The point is to argue for and against explicit normative standpoints, whether they be Marxist, Liberal, Postmodernist, or none of these.

Thirdly, as is the case with any organization or institution, the media and the fulfillment of actual and/or legitimate purposes are constrained by the moral rights of individuals. In the case of the media—an institution of public communication—these rights include especially the rights to privacy, to a fair trial, and to not be defamed.

Let us now put forward the following normative theoretical standpoint. In relation to news and comment, the media as an institution—whether it be publicly or privately owned—has the general function of public communication in the public interest. Here the reference to public communication is self-explanatory. The news/comment institution of the media is principally a vehicle for public communication. This is so notwithstanding the emergence of new communications technologies which may well facilitate private interactive communication and do so to some extent at the expense of public and "one way" communication.

The notion of public interest is much more problematic. Suffice it to say here that attempts to explain away the notion of the public interest in terms of sectional or class interests have been unsuccessful. So has the attempted reduction of the notion of the public interest to sets of individual preference or desire. What is in fact in the public interest is not necessarily what the public wants to hear or "consume," and still less what will generate profits for the media industry. Naturally, if the elements of the media in the private sector are to survive they will need to be commercially viable, and this will entail that what is communicated is to an extent what the public will consume. But the point is that if the media is not discharging its obligations as an institution there is no great cause for concern if it does not survive. Normatively speaking, the media—as defined here—is a business, but it is not principally a business; it has other and more important responsibilities than its purely economic ones. It exists to enable public communication in the public interest.

B. Functions of the Media as Institution

Public communication in the public interest involves at least the following subsidiary functions or roles.

Firstly, the media provides a public forum enabling communication by government and other institutions, and by interest groups and individual citizens, to the public at large, and enabling that communication to stand as a public record (media as public forum). Secondly, the media, or at least members of the media, has the task of unearthing and disseminating information of importance to the public (media as investigator). Thirdly, members of the media themselves function as public communicators. In this role members of the media communicate both information and comment (media as autonomous public communicator).

Moreover, these functions, in respect to public communication, are the chief justification for the existence of the (news and comment) media.

1. Media as Public Forum

The media as a public forum enables individual members of the public and representatives of groups and organizations (including the government) to communicate to the public at large. In some of these instances of public communication there is a dispute, and it is in the public interest to be informed about this dispute, for example, the dispute in the United Kingdom in relation to membership of the European Community. These disputes can be about the truth of particular claims, e.g., concerning an alleged "third force" in South Africa, or about the workability or justice of particular policies, e.g., affirmative action policies in relation to Australian Aboriginal education. Here the role of the media is simply to provide a forum for the various disputing parties, and thereby enable them to communicate to the public at large.

Other cases in this category are ones involving basically the communication of information. For example, the government may wish to make known the details of its budget. Here the media provides a mechanism for communication by members of the public (individuals or groups or organizations, including the government) to the public at large.

2. Media as Investigator

The second category of communications involves the media as an investigator. There are cases in which the media investigates matters of public interest and unearths information that is of legitimate interest to the public. For example, consider the role of the journalists Bob Woodward and Carl Bernstein in relation to Watergate, or the sections of the press in South Africa, including, notably, the *Weekly Mail,* who for many years brought to light various covert operations of the South African government and its security agencies.

While this category of cases necessarily involves investigation, it also involves public communication; the journalist investigates in order to communicate his/her discovery to the public. A journalist is not simply a private detective unearthing information for a fee.

In the cases in which the media provides a forum, or finds out and communicates what the public has a right to know, the media is not an autonomous public communicator. Rather in these cases the media exists to ensure that rights to communicate and to know are realized.

3. Media as Autonomous Communicator

The category of cases in which the media acts as an autonomous public communicator comprises such things as editorial comment, and comment and analysis provided by members of the print and electronic media itself, as opposed to comment and analysis in the media provided by academics, community leaders, and others. Political and economic comments are prominent in this category.

In this category the media has an active role as an independent communicator. The media is not simply a mouthpiece or the provider of a forum for other communicators, nor is it simply discharging its obligation to provide information which the public has a right to possess. Rather in these cases the media is a genuinely autonomous communicator.

The general justification for the existence of the media as a public forum is that in a democracy, in respect to certain matters, members of the public and of interest groups—or at least their representatives—have a moral right to address the public at large, and representatives of public institutions have a moral duty to do so. Therefore, there is a need for a forum for public communication, and the media in a modern society is the chief mechanism enabling such public communication. The existence of such a channel or channels of public communication raises important questions of access, particularly given that only limited access is possible.

The general justification for the existence of the media as an investigator/disseminator is the public's right to know in relation to certain matters of public interest and importance.

The general justification for the existence of the media as an autonomous public communicator is more problematic. Suffice it to say here that there are a range of pragmatic reasons why professional journalists and media commentators might be desirable. In the last analysis these reasons come down to the quality of the comment and analysis provided. Note that such reasons do not include the existence of a moral right to exist as an autonomous public communicator.

III. ETHICAL ANALYSIS

In light of the descriptive account of tabloid journalism provided in the first section, and the normative theoretical framework outlined in the second, let me now offer an ethical analysis of tabloid journalism.

Tabloid journalism is ethically problematic on two general counts. Firstly, it is inconsistent with the societal and institutional ethical values which underpin the media as an institution. Secondly, it tends to infringe a number of important individual moral rights, including the rights to privacy, to a fair trial, and to not be defamed.

A. Institutional Ethical Values

As far as the media as an institution is concerned, the following points can be made. In relation to the role of the media as a public forum, we saw in the opening section that tabloid journalism fails to represent important social and economic interest groups; indeed it often misrepresents and stereotypes particular groups, including women and minorities. Moreover, it overemphasizes and focuses attention on individuals and groups who are wealthy and/or glamorous and/or powerful, including not only politicians, but movie actors, sports figures, and members of the Royal Family.

In its role as investigator, the tabloid press pursues the sensationalist and trivial rather than what is important in terms of the public interest. For example, it relentlessly investigates and exposes the sexual lives of politicians and members of the Royal Family, but is not prepared to pursue difficult and expensive investigations of serious public corruption or of internationally significant military conflicts. Moreover, it has scant concern for

the truth, preferring rather to provoke and manipulate emotive reactions.

In its role as autonomous communicator, the tabloid press displays little or no objectivity or analytical depth in its comment. It fails absolutely to critically analyze powerful social and institutional interest groups. Indeed ultimately it is at the service of large business corporations, and therefore tends to reproduce and reinforce the consumer ideology.

In short, tabloid journalism is seriously deficient in each of the three roles of public forum, investigator, and autonomous communicator. As such, tabloid journalism—to the extent that it dominates the public communication of news and comment—is ethically problematic. For if most, or even very large numbers, of people rely on the tabloids as their main source of news and comment, then the citizenry will be ill informed and lack understanding of matters of public importance. In short, the dominance of tabloid journalism entails that the media as an institution of public communication has failed in its institutional purposes.

Moreover, tabloid journalism—if it becomes the dominant voice in public communication—will inevitably over time have a corrosive effect on public morality. The point is not that reading about gruesome crime or viewing the page 3 pinup girl pollutes one's mind. The analogy is rather with pornography. Pornography titillates and sexually arouses, but it does not follow that it is an evil that should be eradicated. However, if a person gets to the point where his or her sexual life is principally lived through pornographic images—to the exclusion of sexual relationships with real people—then that person has a moral problem. Similarly, with tabloid journalism.

If a society gets to the point where its principal mode of public communication in relation to news and comment is tabloid journalism, then that society has a moral problem. What is the problem? The problem is that in eschewing important news and quality comment, and in trivializing fundamental moral attitudes by manipulating them for the purposes of sustaining audience attention, the tabloids not only deprive citizens of information and understanding of important events, they ultimately contribute to an undermining of the capacity of audiences to make discerning moral and political judgments on these matters, and thereby to the impoverishment of public morality and a deterioration of the conditions of democratic life.

B. Individual Moral Rights

Tabloid journalism often infringes, or threatens to infringe, individual moral rights, especially the rights to privacy, to a fair trial, and to not be defamed. On occasion it also threatens other moral rights, including the right to life. Consider in this connection the Cangai siege in NSW Australia. Children were being held hostage by armed killers. The tabloid TV journalist Willessee insisted on phoning up the killers and speaking to the children to get a story, notwithstanding the dangers this course of action posed for the safety of the children.

It is obvious that the right to privacy of members of the Royal Family and of Princess Diana is not respected by the tabloid press. As public figures these people can reasonably expect more media attention and scrutiny than persons who are not public figures. Nevertheless, even public figures have a right not to be the objects of what amounts to ongoing intrusive surveillance. Long-range cameras are used by the paparazzi to provide the tabloids with a diet of photographs of Princess Diana at home, in intimate company on holidays, and so on. Another favorite target of tabloid journalists is the grief-stricken. The families of miners were contacted at 3 A.M. by the tabloids for their reactions to the Moura mine disaster in Australia in 1987.

Nor are these infringements of the right to privacy morally insignificant, for the right to privacy is an important moral right. It is not possible to establish and maintain intimate personal relations without a measure of privacy.

Autonomy depends in part on privacy. A measure of privacy is necessary for a person to pursue his or her projects, whatever those projects might be. For one thing reflection is necessary for planning, and reflection requires privacy. For another, knowledge of someone's plans can enable those plans to be thwarted. And there is this further point. Autonomy consists in part of having the capacity to undertake one's public roles. However, certain facts pertaining to a person's public roles and practices are regarded as private in virtue of the potential, should they be disclosed, of undermining the capacity of the person to function in these public roles or to fairly compete in these practices. Evidently, the tabloid press has undermined the potential of many public figures to adequately undertake their public roles, and has therefore undermined their autonomy. For example, the tabloid press in the United Kingdom has clearly undermined the capacity of members of the Royal Family to function in their public roles.

Tabloid journalism frequently violates the individual's right to a fair trial by presenting an accused person as in effect guilty. One method is to ascribe guilt to an individual in the headline, and then qualify this ascription of guilt in the news report itself by making sure terms such as "suspect" and "alleged" are used. This was the case with Martin Bryant. More generally, the possibility of a fair trial can be reduced by saturating the public mind with stories which link the "suspect"

with the crime, whether as guilty or innocent. The O. J. Simpson trial is an example.

Another related feature of tabloid journalism is defamation. It feeds on scandal and rumor. The preceding methods of headlines without qualifications and saturation coverage have the effect of defaming someone, even if in technical legal terms that person has not been defamed. Consider, for example, the recent case of the Australian senior diplomat John Holloway. He was named by the tabloids as a suspected pedophile, yet subsequently charges against him were dismissed. He has been found innocent, but his reputation has suffered greatly.

C. Arguments in Support of Tabloid Journalism

Let me now consider some attempts to defend tabloid journalism. Firstly, it is argued, while tabloid press might be uninformative, devoid of analysis, and preoccupied with "girlie pics" and the scandalous lives of show business personalities, it is what the people want and therefore is justified on this basis.

However, on the normative conception outlined above, matters which the public may have a *desire* to know about are to be distinguished from those which they have a *right* to know about, or a legitimate interest in knowing about, and the former are of secondary importance in the following senses.

As indicated, such wants or desires do not of themselves justify the existence of the media as a fundamental sociopolitical institution of modern societies. If the function of the media were merely to satisfy desires for information, comment, and/or entertainment then there would be no pressing reason to establish the media as an institution. Rather it should be viewed as an economic organization, or complex of organizations, and we could have or not have the media depending on whether there was a demand for its products and there was sufficient economic benefit to shareholders, advertisers, managers, journalists, and so on.

Again, matters in respect of which the public only has a desire, but not a right or a legitimate interest, for access ought to exist on the channels of public communication only after the latter have been adequately catered for. Public communication in respect of which the public has a right to or a legitimate interest in must take precedence over public communication whose purpose is simply to entertain or otherwise satisfy a desire.

In this connection it is also worth noting that it is by no means clear that there is some sort of logical connection between being a high-profit-making media organization and satisfying consumers' desires. Profits are a function of the difference between revenue from sales and costs. It may well be that most members of the public would prefer certain kinds of high-quality media products to tabloid products. However, such high-quality newspapers and TV programs for general audiences are very expensive to produce, especially compared to many low-quality tabloid products. For this reason media organizations driven only by profit might produce tabloids rather than high-quality general audience newspapers and TV programs. However, if so, this would not necessarily reflect a preference on the part of audiences for tabloid products over high-quality general audience media products.

Secondly, it is often argued that the media cannot provide objective communicative content of high quality since the notion of such content is meaningless or hopelessly naive. It is suggested that the reasons for this are manifold and include the views that communicative content always reflects a standpoint, that mechanisms of media communication necessarily mediate and therefore distort, that quality is simply in the eye of the beholder, and so on.

There is not space to deal with all these kinds of arguments in detail, though it is not difficult to show that they do not demonstrate the strong position they are intended to. Suffice it to say here that the notions that one cannot aim at truth, and on occasion approximate it, and that every piece of analysis and comment is as good as every other are self-defeating and, if accepted, would render communication pointless. It is a presupposition of communication in general, including both linguistic communication and visual representation, that there is something to be represented, and that on occasion this is achieved. If this were not so, communication of news would be rendered pointless and cease to take place. Moreover, it is a presupposition of comment and analysis that not every piece of analysis and comment is as good as every other one since there is always as least one which is regarded by the communicator as inferior, namely, that which is the negation of the one put forward.

Thirdly, there is a tendency to try to ground an (alleged) right of the media to communicate what it sees fit, irrespective of objectivity or quality, on the right to property. Roughly, the idea is that if someone wants to use his own money to set up a newspaper or TV station—to set up, that is, a mechanism of public communication—in order to communicate his own views (or the views of his editors or journalists) or to provide low-grade entertainment, or indeed to provide communicative content of whatever sort he likes, then he has a right to do so. After all, it is argued, he owns it.

There are a number of problems with this line of argument. For one thing, it simply does not follow from the fact that a person has a right to set up a mechanism of public communication that the person has a right to use that mechanism to communicate to the public at large any more than it follows from the fact—if it is a fact—that McDonnell-Douglas has a right to build fighter aircraft that the corporation then has a right to establish a military air force and fly sorties against its corporate enemies.

For another thing, everyone, whether he or she is the owner of newspapers or TV stations, has a right to communicate to the public at large. Moreover, this basic right does not derive from, and is not enlarged or extended by, property rights in general, and the right to set up a mechanism for public communication in particular. The right of a citizen to address the public at large is not somehow increased by virtue of the fact that the citizen has the property right (and the money) to set up a newspaper or TV station. Indeed any such extension of the right of owners in particular (or their employees, including editors and journalists) to public communication would constitute an infringement of the equal right of all citizens to communicate to the public at large. This fundamental equality is not undermined by the fact that on particular issues it is more important that certain members of the public be heard than others.

Bibliography

Cohen, E. D. (Ed.) (1992). *Philosophical issues in journalism.* New York: Oxford Univ. Press.

Christians, C. G., Ferre, J. P., & Fackler, P. M. (1993). *Good news: Social ethics and the press.* New York: Oxford Univ. Press.

Dahlgren, P., & Sparks, C. (Eds.) (1991). *Communication and citizenship.* London: Routledge.

Denton, R. E. (1991). *Ethical dimensions of political communication.* New York: Praeger.

Goodwin, G., & Smith, R. F. (1994). *Groping for ethics in journalism* (3rd ed.). Ames, IA: Iowa State Univ. Press.

Patterson, P., & Wilkins, L. (Eds.) (1994). *Media ethics: Issues and cases* (2nd ed.). Madison, WI: Brown and Benchmark.

Taitte, W. L. (Ed.) (1993). *Morality of the mass media.* Austin, TX: Univ. of Texas Press.

Terrorism

SUE ASHFORD

Murdoch University and The University of Western Australia

GLOSSARY

freedom fighters A relative term used to describe individuals who commit, in the name of freedom or some other political principle, the kinds of acts of violence that others may regard as acts of terrorism.

legitimacy The idea that a government rules by the consent of its peoples.

meliorism The doctrine that over time the world tends to become better, largely through human effort.

political expediency A view that typically advocates some prudent course of action but that may lay claim to notions such as the political good of a society, justice, or the notion of legitimacy to justify that particular course of action. The achievement of these notions—through, for example, the establishing of a new form of government—may not be the true ends of the strategy that has been advocated.

social contract The idea, typically invoked as a metaphor or as a rhetorical device, that at some stage in our history, human beings formally undertook a contract to join together as members of a society.

terrorism A policy that promotes the use of violence to induce fear of death or injury in individuals.

urban guerrilla warfare A term used to describe the kind of violence that others may regard as acts of terrorism; those who use this term believe that the violent acts are actions toward some ultimate good and that those engaged in the warfare (otherwise called terrorists) are involved in a just war.

TERRORISM is the use of violence—as a matter of policy—to cause terror in people, usually so that those individuals will change their beliefs or allegiances. While terrorism is violence that is usually executed against a government or a political system to effect political change, the immediate victims of terrorist acts of violence are typically ordinary citizens, rather than members of government or public property. Terrorism is also a policy used by governments against their citizens, or against the citizens of other states, to intimidate the population or sections of it.

I. ORIGINS OF THE TERM

Terrorism is defined by the *Oxford English Dictionary* as a "system of terror." The *Oxford English Dictionary* is organized on historical basis: hence the dictionary collects chronological illustrations of the uses of a term.

Two instances are given of the early uses of the term terror to describe such systems. The first comes from a particular historical illustration that gave rise to the coining of the term terrorism. The example is the government by intimidation as directed and carried out by the party in power in France during the Revolution of 1789–1794, and, in particular, the system of the "Terror" during 1793–1794. More specifically, the period of the Terror is held to have begun in July 1793, the month when the "Committee of Public Safety" was formed under the aegis of Danton and Robespierre. The Terror is usually considered to have ended in July 1794, after the fall and execution of Robespierre, and hence after the abolition of the Commune of Paris.

The second instance given of the use of the term is of a more general conception: that of a policy intended to strike with terror those against whom it is adopted, the employment of methods of intimidation, the fact of terrorizing or the condition of being terrorized.

A. The Ground of Difference

A difference can be seen between the two uses of the term terrorism. The first instance is a case of violence concerning governments: the original use of the term was used to refer both to violence executed against a presiding government and then, after the Revolution, to violence against the people—the citizens of the new government. The second use of the term concerns the psychological and social effects of the use of violence. This ground of difference is significant when arguments in favor of acts of violence against particular governments are considered, acts that are also termed acts of terrorism by those who support the existing regime but which are considered to be legitimate and necessary acts of warfare by those who oppose the acting government.

II. HISTORICAL BACKGROUND

The concern that the very act of revolution undermined the process and nature of government itself, together with illustrations of the types of uses of violence evidenced during the French Revolution, was the basis for the use of the term *terror* to beget the term *terrorism*. Thus, Edmund Burke, in his *Reflections on the Revolution in France,* used the term terror to illustrate his claim that the mob ruled the National Assembly with the result that true government was made impossible. In his *Reflections* Burke draws a picture of the National Assembly in which the individual members of the Assembly and the king have become actors who are constrained to play a role whose nature is determined by the dictates of those whose power lies in physical force rather than in political legitimacy:

With a compelled appearance of deliberation, they vote under the dominion of a stern necessity. They sit in the heart, as it were, of a foreign republic: they have their residence in a city whose constitution has emanated neither from the charter of their king nor from their legislative power. There they are surrounded by an army not raised either by the authority of their crown or by their command, and which, if they should order to dissolve itself, would instantly dissolve them. There they sit, after a gang of assassins had driven away some hundreds of the members, whilst those who held the same moderate principles, with more patience or better hope, continued every day exposed to outrageous insults and murderous threats. There a majority, sometimes real, sometimes pretended, captive itself, compels a captive king to issue as royal edicts, at third hand, the polluted nonsense of their most licentious and giddy coffeehouses. It is notorious that all their measures are decided before they are debated. It is beyond doubt that, under the terror of the bayonet and the lamppost and torch to their houses, they are obliged to adopt all the crude and desperate measures suggested by clubs composed of a monstrous medley of all conditions, tongues, and nations (pp. 77–78, Edmund Burke *Reflections on the Revolution in France.* ed., with introduction, Thomas H. D. Mahoney (1790; 1955) The Liberal Arts Press Indianapolis, IN: Bobbs-Merrill Co.).

Here, Burke presents two forms of political legitimacy that have been breached by what he calls "the mob": the charter of their king and the legislative power of the National Assembly. The situation that he portrays is thus ironic: those who once held legitimate political power are now puppets whose political actions are dictated by others. As a result, the content of their political actions is really legitimized not by their authority as members of the National Assembly, but by those who are now in a position of what might be thought of as real power—the power that comes from causing an experience of terror, an experience that results from the threat of loss of life and personal property. Burke's irony goes further: in establishing this "foreign republic" in which the members of the National Assembly have become unwilling, even accidental residents, there is a sense in which the puppeteers have forged another kind of constitution—albeit a constitution dictated by and one that prescribes fear.

III. THE COMPLEX NATURE OF TERRORISM

The notion of terrorism is complex and this complexity can be seen in the historical origins of the term, although of course the kinds of behavior that we term terrorism have their origins in human history, not in the French Revolution. On one view the term terrorism was derived from a particular perception of the French Revolution. On this perception the Revolution was to be deplored: the very idea of a revolution against what was hitherto regarded as a legitimate government was regarded as wrong and dangerous. Hence, the action of this Revolution was not an extreme (perhaps justifiable) form of political dissent but rather it was seen as a form of violence that rendered the normal political processes, including legitimate political debate and dissent, impotent. Thus the reason for the perceived danger of the Revolution lay not only in the particular acts of violence that were perpetrated against the institutions of government, against members of the government and ordinary citizens, but also (and what was perhaps more troubling for political theorists) in the concern that the very act of revolution undermined the process and nature of government itself. On this view, revolutions are instruments of social instability and do not simply cause short-term civil strife for a long-term gain of better government; instead, revolutions destroy the very fabric of a society.

There was another form of response to the Revolution. Support for the Revolution (and subsequently for acts of violence regarded by adherents of the first view as acts of terrorism) often came from a reconstruction of the idea that the act of revolution undermined the process and nature of government itself. Reconstruction of the idea that government is undermined by revolution proceeds by affirming both the undesirable nature of the old or existing system of government and the need for change; hence, it is claimed, the current government *must* be undermined. According to this line of thought, the kind or degree of change required can only be achieved by destroying the prevailing form of government. Then, and only in the wake of a revolution, a new and superior form of government or social order can be instituted. Once given the institution of a new form of government, then, according to this line of thought, the acts of violence perpetrated in the name of the Revolution are in one or another sense acceptable. That is, while the effects of particular acts of violence may not be condoned (although they may—for example, the acts of violence may be seen as punishment or justified retribution), these kinds of acts of violence will be considered at least to be the necessary means to the goal of reestablishing a proper social order. Thus, according to the second response to the Revolution, the very content of a concern about the act of revolution—that the bare act of revolution undermined the process and nature of government itself—was often used as a basis for endorsement of the Revolution. This line of thought is still adopted as a way to sanction acts of violence that are termed acts of terrorism by opponents, opponents who typically uphold the incumbent government.

IV. PROPER SOCIAL ORDERS: ONE MOTIVE FOR TERRORISM

Burke was arguing for the legitimacy of a constitutional monarchy. From our perspective, some 200 years later, it is easy to think that while Burke's sentiments against violence may be appropriate, his support for a form of government that has been largely superseded in the modern world is merely an illustration of Burke's conservatism and a reflection of his place in history. The French Revolution is often regarded as one of the precursors of modern and contemporary political movements. A line of thought that is often encouraged by these contemporary movements is that those governments that are considered not to be directly representative of their peoples are held to be wrong, even immoral, kinds of government. If a government is seen to be unrepresentative of its people, then some may argue that that government has no true basis for power over its people. A government of this kind, the argument goes, does not have a proper basis as a government: hence attempts to overthrow the governing power structure—by means that may include violence—are right-minded political actions.

The style of representative government that is characteristically upheld today as the proper kind of government, and hence the political basis for discriminating between acts of terrorism from other kinds of acts of violence against government, is that of democracy. From this vantage point, those acts of violence that Burke deplored, because they were acts of violence against a legitimate government, can be regarded as politically *necessary* steps toward overthrowing an essentially corrupt form of government. But because this vantage point may change, or may not be held by a theorist, the claim that the acts of violence are *necessary* steps toward political progress is undermined.

Why it matters which kind of government is considered the right form of government is that we need some basis to discriminate those acts of violence against particular governments that are to be rightly regarded as acts of terrorism. For not all acts of violence against governments are acts of terrorism. Acts of banditry, for example, are not necessarily acts of terrorism although they may be directed against governments. Thus we need to distinguish acts of terrorism from those acts of violence against particular governments that are either held to be necessary actions in order to try to destabilize that government (there being good reasons to wish to remove that government and for needing to remove it by force, rather than by peaceful means), or that are believed to be legitimate acts of war (either between nations, or when the acts of violence are regarded as acts of, say, modern urban guerrilla warfare).

We want, then, to be able to distinguish acts of terrorism from acts of violence that may be regarded as actions of a just war. The notion of a just war has a long philosophical and theological history. Medieval philosophers distinguished between two notions, the idea of the *jus ad bellum,* which is the right to make war and the idea of the *jus in bello,* which is a matter of how a war should be waged (of what kinds of actions are permissible ways of conducting a war). Both notions are relevant to the issue of discriminating acts of terrorism from other kinds of acts of violence. From certain vantage points, acts that some of us may describe as acts of terrorism may be held to be strategic actions of a just war: that is, these acts may be authorized, as it were, by the concept of the *jus ad bellum.* But even if this is the case and acts of violence against a government are legitimized in some way, as acts of a just war, we may still want to distinguish between those acts that are appropriate kinds of violence for just warfare and those acts that are impermissible. Not everything is permitted in a just war: some kinds of conduct may be acts of terrorism even within the waging of a just war. However, to determine some sense of when the notion of a just war is applicable, more needs to be said about the basis for discriminating between different kinds of violence in terms of the intention to have a desirable and proper social order (see Sections VI and VII).

V. THE ARGUMENT FROM POLITICAL EXPEDIENCY: A SECOND MOTIVE FOR TERRORISM

The idea that violence may be waged against a government as part of a just war (when some part of the citizenry attempts to bring about a better form of government), must be used with caution. Although the rhetoric of many terrorist organizations relies on the idea of waging a just war, the rhetoric of a just war is often a gloss on the real motives of the combatants who are really terrorists attempting to win support for their actions. (Of course, when the notion of waging a just war is employed, those who carry out violence against the government do not describe themselves as terrorists: the term terrorist is employed by those who condemn the violence.)

The line of thought that terms acts of violence against governments and their citizens as instances of a just war can be also described in terms of an argument from the political expediency of violence. Usually, when this line of thought is adopted, the acts of violence in question are not called acts of terrorism by those who execute the acts or by those who support those actions. Instead the relevant events are redescribed as (say) urban guerrilla warfare (for example, Irish Republican Army bombings of English cities) and those who carry out the violence may be known as freedom fighters (for example, the Tamil Tigers in Sri Lanka).

Expediency is the consideration of what is expedient, of what is conducive to a particular purpose. The idea

of political expediency is this: a course of action may be upheld as the right and only political strategy to achieve a certain goal. The strategy is determined as right by means of a notion like justice or representative government or the public good. However, why this strategy is in truth an argument from political expediency and not a full-blooded appeal to political principles such as justice is because it is some other goal that is actually desired by the combatants; and the political principles that are invoked in the name of that goal are relevant in truth only to achieving that end. These political principles are not truly invoked as ends in themselves; the violence is not a means to achieving that which is right (or just, or representative). Because the putative justification for violent political action is spurious (the true goal is, say, the achievement of political power), there is no necessary connection between the espoused political principles and the use of violence to achieve the activists' political ambitions.

When an argument from political expediency is employed, the kinds of justifications brought to the argument often give the impression that a particular kind of government is the goal of the political action: in a sense, the justifications are employed to sanction the use of violence. Given that the kinds of justifications are—in contemporary times—ideas like representative government, justice, equality, and liberty, it is easy to think that again the typical goal of political change is some form of democratic government.

However, the argument from political expediency is not only used to justify violence against a people in order to bring about democracy: this line of thought was, for example, invoked to justify the Russian Revolution (the Bolshevik Revolution of November 1917) and the establishment of a communist state. The justification for the "trials" that marked Stalin's purges was that certain elements of the Soviet population needed to be eliminated for the good of the state. Thus the argument from political expediency regards the loss of human life, or the infliction of pain upon individual citizens of a state, as necessary—perhaps regrettable—stages in a struggle for a better or a just government. The goal of the political good is then used to justify or rationalize the uses of violence.

Thus there is nothing in the argument from the political expediency of violence that enables a theorist, let alone a revolutionary, to claim that the changes in government and society that are sought through violence should be changes toward any one particular kind of government or society. There is nothing in the argument from the political expediency of violence, in itself, to confirm that any one particular style of government is superior to another. While an exponent of the argument from political expediency will typically turn to notions like the political good of a society, to justice or to the notion of legitimacy in order to use these notions to justify a particular employment of the argument, this argument can be used to justify any form of new government that promises to satisfy the desired criterion (whether that is the political good, justice, or legitimacy).

Thus the argument from political expediency gives us two ways to think about terrorism. The first is cautionary: although the invocation of the concept of a just war may be appropriate to argue that particular acts of violence are not, in fact, acts of terrorism, the availability and use of an argument from political expediency warns us that not all appeals to the notion of a just war should be accepted. The second line of thought is that when the idea of a just war is appealed to, there are no clear-cut principles to determine when the concept of a just war is correctly invoked.

VI. HISTORICAL APPRECIATIONS OF REVOLUTIONS

The thrust of Section V was that the idea of a just war could be manipulated for the purposes of political expediency: in such cases the argument for a just war can be reduced to an argument from political expediency. In this section, the theoretical issue is rather that some historical instances of the argument from political expediency may be treated as arguments for a just war.

When theorists evaluate a particular revolution in terms of its political consequences, the argument from the political expediency of violence often gains a foothold insofar as those consequences are determined and evaluated some time after the revolution has occurred. That is, the political consequences need not be immediate and may be, as in the case of the French Revolution, largely symbolic rather than clear and actually realized gains for the citizenry.

There are two problems for the notion of terrorism with this style of retrospective appreciation of political movements such as the French Revolution. The first is a matter of when it is right to call an act of violence an act of political terrorism. The second is the question of when an act of violence aimed at a particular government should be applauded, perhaps to be seen as a step on the path to reforming or overthrowing that government.

A. The Problem of Meliorism

Meliorism is the doctrine that the world tends to become better, or that it may be made better through human effort. According to the meliorist's perspective, the forms of government of the nations of the world are in a continual process of change, and these changes are movements toward an improvement. In a particular version of the meliorist's view, these changes will continue until each nation is represented by, say, a duly elected, democratic government. Thus, in this version of meliorism, the past 300 years of Western civilization can be seen as a model for the transition to proper government, a form of government that will eventually occur across the world. On this account, the dissolution of the Soviet Union, and of other communist states, is a straightforward example of political progress.

B. Meliorism, Styles of Government, and Justifications

One problem is that if we decide that we should approve of the French or some other revolution because that revolution is a step toward transforming the political processes of a country from (say) nondemocratic to democratic (or more democratic) forms of government, then we may commit ourselves to a meliorist view of political history.

However, this view of melioration is self-justifying: there needs to be an argument in order to claim that a democratic political state is the ideal form of human government. Typically an argument to support this claim relies on enunciating the properties of a democratic political state and declaring these properties to be virtues: for example, that it is the form of government that represents the people, that democratic governments are duly elected and legitimized in virtue both of the democratic voting system and a pledge to uphold the rights of the citizens of that state.

But it is not obvious whether the move to expound the properties of a democracy and to declare these properties to be political virtues, is itself an argument for the claim that a democratic government is the best kind of government for human beings. There are two problems here. The first problem—whether the restatement or the proclamation of the properties can be considered an argument for democracies—is that an opponent can claim, with some force, that all the proponent of democracy has done is to describe a democracy and that nothing in that description, per se, demonstrates that democracies are intrinsically superior forms of government. The opponent, then, denies that the acts of violence can be considered events in a just war. As a result, if an opponent of this putative argument for the meliorist view of democratic government wishes to undermine the meliorist's position, the opponent can go on to claim that acts of political violence, perpetrated in the name of furthering democracy, are in fact merely acts of terrorism. The second problem is that the meliorist will also want to be able to recognize some acts of violence—committed in the name of democracy—as acts of terrorism. Here the issues in play rely on the distinction between the concept of *jus ad bellum* (the right to make war) and the idea of the *jus in bello* (how a war should be conducted).

C. From What Style of Government Do We Discriminate Acts of Terrorism?

It is not the case that whether an act of violence against a government is an act of terrorism depends solely on what style of government is in power. There are further aspects of how we discriminate acts of terrorism that will be discussed later. In this section the issues of how to discriminate acts of terrorism, however, are tied to claims about types of government.

Another problem for the meliorist is more practical. The nations of the world are governed by a variety of political processes. From time to time, a democratic government may act to undermine (explicitly or implicitly) the political processes of a country where that government is deemed to be undemocratic and unjust. A instance of this kind of international intervention is the Gulf War (August 1990 to June 1991) when the United States and a number of largely Western allies attempted to rebuff an Iraqi invasion of Kuwait. Although the war was justified among members of the Western Alliance by the Iraqi incursion into Kuwaiti territory, a widespread hope among the allied leaders was that the government of President Saddam Hussein of Iraq would be undermined, perhaps even weakened to the extent that Iraqi political dissidents might be able to overthrow Hussein. However, criticism of this war often amounted to the claim that the attacks on Iraq were simply acts of terrorism (and, viewed from the perspective of supporters of Hussein's government, such claims seem inevitable: members of a governing class are liable to see attacks on their authority as acts of terrorism). A second kind of criticism that was made is that in attacking Iraq, the United States and its allies were unprincipled, in that while agreement could be found that the Iraqi government was corrupt and unjust, much the same kinds of criticism could and should be leveled at a number of neighboring Arab states, especially Kuwait itself (the government which was being supported, in effect, by the Western alliance).

The problem here, then, is that if acts of terrorism are discriminated according to whether or not the acts are perpetrated against democratic governments, and if democratic government is held to be the just form of government, then any act of violence against a nondemocratic government that is executed with the intention to undermine that government, seems to have the right kind of pedigree for acceptance as justified violence, as an act of war. However, if this pedigree is challenged, then the proponents of change toward democracy appear to lack an argument for their actions. Their acts take on the guise of acts of faith or acts of self-interest.

VII. THE IDEA OF LEGITIMACY

One argument that democratic countries can turn to is to claim that their governments are legitimate, whereas the governments of (say) dictators are not. The notion of legitimacy is a complex one, and the boundaries of its application need to be explored. A notion of legitimacy is technical: this conception of legitimacy rests on the idea that a government's power and role is justified by an act of consent by its people or through a covenant with the people. Discussions of this notion of legitimacy were once framed in terms of an idea called "the state of nature," an idea that directed attention to the first assembly of government—from human kind in a state of nature to human kind in a society (see Section 1, below). This technical conception of legitimacy may be termed a constitutional notion of legitimacy. The idea employed below is related but much looser: it is simply the idea that a government must be able to justify its power in terms of its relation to the peoples it governs, and that this justification must not rest on sheer power over its people alone. Thus the notion of legitimacy is at least related to notions of representational government and the idea of a society.

A. Which Governments Are Legitimate?

Suppose that an act of violence is executed against a nondemocratic government with the intention to undermine that government. Consider, then, the claim that in this case, just because the government that is being resisted is nondemocratic, the acts of violence that precede or accompany the change of government can be considered as acts of justified violence or as an act of war rather than as acts of terrorism. Surely this claim needs clarification and supporting argument. For it is not usually the case that democratic governments—such as those of the United States and many NATO countries—count acts of violence against nondemocratic states as thereby acts of war: more usually the acts are counted as instances of terrorism. International politics is a pragmatic business, and the world's nation-states provide instances of a wide range of kinds of democracies and of kinds of nondemocratic governments. Furthermore, the issue of what kind of state is a democratic state is a matter of contention: while democracies are often thought to be capitalist states with representative governments, the term democracy has even been used to describe communist states, and these states have claimed that their system of government is representative of their peoples.

Yet the problem remains that we are rarely willing to claim that any act of violence against any government is an act of terrorism, simply because it is an act of violence against a prevailing government. Attempts to assassinate Adolf Hitler, at one stage a popular leader who had widespread support among the German people, are not necessarily considered acts of terrorism: rather, those reflecting on the political state of the Third Reich may well regret that the assassination attempts were unsuccessful.

It is commonplace, in the course of human history, for there to be widespread agreement that a particular government is wrong, unjust, corrupt, insupportable, and that for the sake of those governed by it (as opposed to the sake of nation-states whose affairs are somehow affected by that government) this government should be overthrown.

Situations of this kind may seem to constitute one powerful argument for democracies: the claim is that governments could be changed through the ballot box. However, to make this claim assumes that the democracy in question is a democracy whose government can be changed by the exercise of the will of the people through the ballot box; that the democratic system ensures actual changes of government; and that democracies are the best system of government. Consider what is at stake here: to agree with these assumptions suggests, for example, that were we to think that the government of Germany's Third Reich was wrong, and were we to make this strong claim in favor of the system of democracy, then we should feel assured that Hitler would not have been voted into office by popular election. In particular, to assume that democracies are the best system of government is, in a sense, question begging: for what properties of a democratic government can we appeal to so that we can claim that democracy is the best system of government? (Or, alternatively, what properties of some other system of government might we point to should we wish to claim that this other system of government is a better or the best system of government?)

B. The Claim for Legitimacy

To distinguish acts of violence against governments as acts of terrorism clearly depends, in some way, on the vantage point and interests of those who make the assessment that these are acts of terrorism (as opposed to other kinds of acts of violence, or rather than acts of warfare). There is a certain circularity in definition here:

unless we are prepared to accept that decisions to describe such acts of violence as terrorism are simply *relative* to the interests, history, and values of the observers, some property of government must be determined for use as a benchmark to evaluate acts of violence as acts of terrorism. What is needed is a property that may be lacking in certain forms of government or absent in particular governments and which we can claim *must* be present for rightful government. Then, although perhaps the kinds of governments that display this property will vary (and not all will be democracies), the presence or absence of this property can be a mark of good (or just) or bad (or unjust) government. Then assessments of which acts constitute acts of terrorism will not be relativistic (that is, relative to the values, interests, and history of those who make the discriminations). We need, therefore, a more basic criterion than whether a government is a democracy or not to decide when acts of violence against particular governments will be considered acts of terrorism.

One property of government that has been held to constitute a more basic criterion is that of legitimacy, or legitimized or legitimate governments. The notion of legitimacy has its origins in the works of English political theorists of the seventeenth and eighteenth centuries whose thinking was influenced by the civil disturbances of the English Civil War and its complex political and social effects. The theorists include Thomas Hobbes in *The Leviathan;* Robert Filmer, *Patriarcha;* James Tyrrell, *Patriarcha non Monarcha;* and John Locke, *Two Treatises on Government.*

1. Social Contract Theory

The notion of legitimacy was often discussed against an idea that acted as a particular mode of exploration of the basis for society and hence for the existence of governments: this idea was the device of a social contract, the idea that at some stage in our history, human beings formally undertook a contract to join together as members of a society.

While the idea of a social contract was often expressed as if the event of a social contract actually occurred, the use of this idea is typically metaphorical or rhetorical: the idea is used to focus attention on the ingredients for the development of society. The ingredients include self-protection, mutual protection, the protection of property, and the use of language for communication (as a matter of utility or for the pleasure that communication can bring). Use of the device of a social contract also ensures attention to the rights and obligations that come with being a member of a society. Hence the device also focuses attention on the constituents or role of society such as the provision of justice, protection, commerce or livelihood, stability, and fellowship.

2. Consent

Central to discussions of social contract theories is the notion of consent: this is the idea that what justifies or legitimizes a society is that its citizens consent, in some form or manner, to being governed and to being subject to particular rules and obligations in return for the particular rights and privileges that are provided by the society. Quite how the notions of consent, a social contract, and the very idea of a society are developed vary from theorist to theorist. These issues have continued to be debated, although not always through the medium of the notion of a social contract (however, two contemporary political theorists who have made use of this device are John Rawls and Robert Nozick).

C. The Place for Legitimacy

The notion of legitimacy, then, is cashed out in terms of an explication of the role of society and the relation between society and its individual members. In particular, the notion of legitimacy is tied to the idea that members of a society consent, in some sense, to their government—to its laws and demands. If, however, citizens of a society find their government burdensome and withdraw their consent, then—according to the terms of this theory—these citizens may argue that the political systems which governs them is illegitimate.

VIII. WHAT COUNTS AS AN ACT OF TERRORISM?

The discussion so far has taken for granted that we can discern, at some level, acts of violence that are candidates for being described as acts of terrorism (even though some may wish to redescribe these acts as acts of warfare, say). But there is a more fundamental issue for the question of what counts as an act of terrorism. The issue has become more problematic of late because there is a tendency to use the term terrorism outside its more traditional place as a form of violence against governments and their citizens. In some feminist discussions, for example, the notion of terrorism is explored to indicate the kind of power relation that holds between men and women in society: in one version, women may be regarded as terrorized by men. In this view, rape and acts of domestic violence may be viewed as terrorist acts, but regarded likewise may be instances of male verbal abuse of females. Another instance of extended

uses of the term terrorism can be found in debates about multiculturalism, racism, and racial vilification: exposure to constant racial insults and threats is sometimes described as a form of violence and as a form of terrorism. Yet another domain in which the term terrorism is used is that of apparently random mass murders. Such events are described as acts of terrorism because an emotion or a cognitive state of terror is engendered in the victims, bystanders, and those who learn of the actions.

There are many kinds of acts of violence that cause feelings of terror in those who witness or who learn of these actions. For example, on March 13, 1996, a lone gunman in Dunblane, Scotland, killed 16 children and one teacher at a primary school. On April 28, 1996, a gunman killed 35 adults and children at Port Arthur, Tasmania, a historic site visited by tourists and picnickers. Both affairs received considerable publicity in the Western world. Typical responses to each massacre, over and beyond sympathy for the victims and their families, were feelings of outrage and fear. In both Britain and Australia, the incidents also provoked debate about gun laws and have led, in both countries, to further restrictions upon gun ownership.

That each incident caused terror, not only among those who were wounded and bystanders but also among members of the wider communities in Britain and Australia, seems clear. A relatively ordinary act—going to school or going on a picnic—took on the possibility of domestic and national tragedy. People's beliefs were changed or galvanized: both incidents caused widespread debate about an aspect of government, namely legislation controlling the ownership of guns, and about the rights of citizens of the state (whether the right to own guns is established by the right to protect one's self and one's family). What is not clear is whether either incident can be regarded as an act of terrorism. Instead, once the immediate emotional effect of the killings has calmed, both events tend to be regarded as horrendous acts of violence committed by an individual who is estranged from his society (which is not to say that the gunmen were necessarily insane).

We do seem to need more than an act of widespread violence in order to term an act of violence an act of terrorism. Certainly we seem to require an intention to cause civil instability or unrest, and these elements appear to be missing in the mass murders at Dunblane and Port Arthur. Yet there are other acts of violence that are often described as acts of terrorism and yet where an express intention to cause civil unrest is absent. Two examples are the explosion of a bomb on Pan Am Flight 103, which destroyed the plane over Lockerbie, Scotland, in December 1988, and the bombing in Centennial Park in Atlanta during the 1996 Olympic Games.

Both of these incidents have been termed acts of terrorism and yet neither was acknowledged by a particular terrorist organization (whereas, typically, bombings on the British mainland are owned by, say, the Irish Republican Army). Neither bombing was accompanied by a demand for a political response (say, the release of political prisoners). That these bombings are deemed acts of terrorism seems to rest on their capacity to produce fear, on the willful destruction of civilian life, and on their potential to undermine confidence in an area of life regulated by governments—that is, international travel and a traditional international celebration of sport. And yet, while there seems to be an intuitive basis for distinguishing these bombings from the cases of Dunblane and Port Arthur, all of the characteristic effects of the bombings can be claimed for Dunblane and Port Arthur (going to school and going to a tourist venue that is a historic site are also areas of life that are regulated at some level by governments).

A further ground for distinguishing acts of terrorism from other kinds of acts of violence is the question of sanity: but it is not clear how this criterion works. If we consider, say, the example of the United State's technology terrorist, the Unabomber, we might well question whether sanity is a relevant criterion: in the case of the Unabomber, there appears to be a clear purpose on the part of the bomber. His manifesto against technological change has been widely publicized (for example, by negotiation in the *Washington Post*). While the views he expresses may find sympathy with many individuals, many of these people would abhor and condemn his methods of publicizing these ideas. The example of the Unabomber is interesting for another reason: his attacks were carried out over a period of time, and his choice of targets was not obvious. There is a sense in which we may question whether his actions caused terror in individuals other than those directly affected by his actions. Yet there also seems good reason to call the Unabomber's attacks acts of terrorism.

Perhaps the intuition, whether it is valuable or not—that the cases are different, that only the plane crashes or the bombing attacks may be acts of terrorism—rests more on the sense that to cause a plane to explode probably requires organization by some number of individuals who are all dedicated to that end. The idea that the planning behind the acts of violence is in some way relevant to determining whether the violence is an instance of terrorism, instead of some other kind of violence, seems applicable just because terrorism is typically carried out by organizations, however small their membership. Even this suggestion does not take us very far. Given the illustration of the Unabomber, and the possibility that the Centennial Park bombing was executed by one person, these examples seem to undercut

the criterion of membership of an organization; however, that these bombings required considerable organization seems plain.

An alternative appeal to the intentions of those who execute the acts of terrorism is to regard terrorists as socially displaced individuals who enjoy violence. But even if this psychological characterization of (at least some) terrorists is correct, this psychological profile is an inadequate basis to distinguish terrorists from (say) freedom fighters. We cannot be assured that organized terrorist groups such as the IRA or the GIA (the Algerian Armed Islamic Group), who are held responsible for a series of bombings in France during 1995, do not include members who enjoy violence for violence's sake—whose primary motive, perhaps, is not political but psychological.

IX. THE APPEAL TO ABSTRACT PRINCIPLES

If it is the case that acts of terrorism are typically carried out by organizations, however small their membership, perhaps what is important to the members of these organizations is not simply that their acts of violence are planned but that these acts are typically executed under the belief that their actions are acts of war. Furthermore, it is usually the case that terrorist groups are organized on one or other kind of military model (hence they are often described as paramilitary groups).

Thus to distinguish acts of terrorism from other kinds of acts of violence such as mass murder, we seem to need to turn to the idea that the terrorist acts under the belief that she or he is an agent for political change. As such, the terrorist perceives himself to be a member of a group that is waging war against an illegitimate or unjust or corrupt government. Thus the acts of violence are legitimized, in the minds of the terrorist and his supporters, by an appeal to abstract principles.

A caveat needs to be entered here. So far the discussion of acts of violence against the citizens of a state—acts that seem strong candidates to merit the description of terrorism—has been in terms of individuals or organizations who wish to develop an alternative form of government or simply to gain power for power's sake (an example here, perhaps, is the role of the Cosa Nostra in Italian politics). But there are other alternatives: these include some varieties of anarchism and of nihilism. The belief that guides individuals to adopt violence as a tactic here is a belief that government itself is wrong or unjust or contrary to human needs. An abstract principle is appealed to here, but the kind of principle that is turned to is radically different from those that have been considered so far. So some extent, this conception of terrorists is the picture familiar in fictional representations of terrorism (for example, in Joseph Conrad's *The Secret Agent* and Doris Lessing's *The Good Terrorist*).

Sometimes an alternative approach is developed to the question of which acts of violence are acts of terrorism, an approach that uses the appeal to abstract principles only in part. On this view what distinguishes acts of terrorism from acts of violence that are executed as part of a "just war" is that the intended targets of acts of terrorism are civilians whereas the intended targets of participants in a just war are combatants whose allegiance is to the enemy—the incumbent government or social order. On this view, then, the loss of civilian life in the plane crash at Lockerbie, the 1995 bombing at Oklahoma City that caused 168 deaths, or the use of the nerve gas Sarin in the Tokyo subway on March 20, 1995, which killed 12 people and injured thousands (allegedly caused by the Aum Shinrikyo cult), are clear cases of terrorism. In contrast, the killings of prominent members of a society—say, the assassination in 1978 of Italian prime minister, Aldo Moro, by the Red Brigade, or the execution of German bankers Alfred Herrhausen and Jürgen Ponto by the Red Army Faction and the Baader-Meinhof group—are held to be instances of carefully targeted violence, the kind of targeted violence that constitutes warfare.

Here, then, are two arguments that appeal to abstract principles in order to discriminate acts of terrorism from other kinds of acts of violence. Both arguments attempt, in particular, to discriminate terrorism from those acts of violence that—by an appeal to their political expediency—can be justified as acts of violence that are believed, by those who execute the violence, to be necessary moves toward a desirable political end.

X. ARGUMENTS AGAINST THE APPEAL TO ABSTRACT PRINCIPLES

But by the very appeal to abstract principles, either kind of argument tends to suggest that acts of violence that may be termed terrorism in an everyday manner should, upon reflection, be redescribed as acts of some kind of warfare, even if it is warfare against the ordinary citizens of a state or nation. However, this method of distinguishing acts of terrorism from other kinds of acts of violence raises a problem. The appeal to abstract principles—for example, that acts of violence against an incumbent government are necessary steps in the engagement of a war for a change of government, a war which is conducted in the name of (say) justice—can be perceived as an instance of the argument from political expediency (see Section V). If the appeal to abstract principles is allowed, then the distinction that has been

sought—a basis for discriminating acts of terrorism from other kinds of acts of violence—breaks down.

The types of acts of violence which remain described as acts of terrorism are acts of violence against civilian life: but these acts of violence now become difficult to distinguish from mass murders such as the killings at Dunblane or Port Arthur. Attempts to distinguish the acts of terrorism (violence against civilians) from these kinds of mass murder rely on the intentions of the terrorists (beliefs that they hold in common with agents of terror who chose noncivilian targets) and their preference for civilian (or "soft") targets. Once this move is made, though, it is no longer clear that a distinction between terrorist and, say, pathological, violence can be drawn.

The argument against these appeals to abstract principles can proceed in three ways. The first line of rebuttal is to question the distinction, made above in Section IX, between the idea that terrorism is distinguished by the loss of general civilian life rather than by the deaths of politicians or other individuals who are prominent members of their society.

The second line of rebuttal is to explore a problem raised by the appeal to abstract argument and the appeal to a distinction between civilian and combatant victims. The problem is this: if one accepts the appeal to abstract argument, or the general direction of the argument from political expediency, then how do we describe acts of violence that are perpetrated by governments rather than by a group of individuals working against a particular government. There are two types of cases to consider. The first is acts of violence that a government executes against other states with which it is at war. History repeatedly provides illustrations of governments whose acts of war exceed military targets. Two controversial examples from World War II are the British bombing of Dresden and the U.S. nuclear bombings of Hiroshima and Nagasaki: in both cases, it is arguable that the targets were the civilian populations rather than military and tactical goals, and that the accomplishments of each event was the spreading of terror among the civilian population. If we turn to the terminology of just-war theory, then these cases may be described as cases of *jus in bello,* a matter of how war should or should not be conducted. Yet many who reflect on incidents of these kinds would wish to go further than the boundaries of just-war theory, and to call these events acts of terrorism not acts of military misconduct.

The second kind of case to consider is that of acts of violence carried out by a government against members of its own civilian population, acts that were designed to cause terror and to subdue the citizens. An example is allegations that leaders of South Africa's former National Party government ordered the 1988 bombing of a

Johannesburg trade union building and numerous other attacks on or assassinations of trade union members and other opponents of apartheid. If we accept the appeal to abstract principles and the idea that only the use of civilian targets to destabilize the government distinguishes acts of terrorism from acts of legitimate warfare, then we face a dilemma in how we may describe cases where a government acts against civilian targets: for on what grounds do we draw our distinctions? Yet surely these kinds of cases are instances where we want to apply the term terrorism.

There is a further and fundamental problem with the appeal to abstract principles. The procedure of appealing to abstract principles in order to redescribe acts of violence as something other than acts of terrorism erases or etiolates the very acts and events that are our grounds of evidence for making a judgment at all. It is the act of violence that causes terror that leads us to consider terming that action an act of terrorism. If we appeal to abstract principles to find guidance for our description and classification of that act, we may lose sight of the terror itself and the effects of that fear. To lose sight of the terror that violence brings just seems wrong, for we then ignore the fact that violence is cruel.

Furthermore, to overlook the terror—the effects of violence—should lead us to question why violence is used if terror is not an effective weapon. But terror is a standard result of violence, and the use of violence to achieve subjugation or suffering is often effective: hence terrorism has its uses for those who wish to bring about certain ends, and its efficiency means that its use is thereby justified by those who wish to promote, at almost any cost, certain ends.

Bibliography

Bar On, B. A. (1991). Why terrorism is morally problematic. In C. Card (Ed.), *Feminist ethics,* pp. 107–125. Lawrence KS: University of Kansas Press.

Berlin, I. (1978). *Russian thinkers.* Harmondsworth: Penguin.

Coady, C. A. J. (1985). On the morality of terrorism. *Philosophy* **60,** 47–69.

Crenshaw, M. (Ed.). (1983). *Terrorism, legitimacy, and power: The consequences of political violence.* Middletown, CT: Wesleyan University Press.

The Economist (1996, March 2). What is terrorism? Website http://www.economist.com/issue/02-03-96.

Ewin, R. E. (1991). *Virtues and rights: The moral philosophy of Thomas Hobbes.* Boulder, CO: Westview Press.

Hare, R. M. (1979). On terrorism. *Journal of Value Inquiry* **13,** 241–249.

Johnson, J. T. (1975). *Ideology, reason, and the limitation of war.* Princeton, NJ: Princeton University Press.

Johnson, J. T. (1981). *Just war tradition and the restraint of war.* Princeton, NJ: Princeton University Press.

Mandelstam, N. (1976). *Hope abandoned.* (M. Hayward, Trans). Harmondsworth: Penguin.

Plamenatz, J. (1963). *Man and society.* (Vol. 1). London: Longman.

Robb, P. (1996). *Midnight in Sicily.* Potts Point, NSW: Duffy & Snellgrove.

U.S. Department of State (1996, April). Patterns of global terrorism, 1995. ⟨http://www.hri.org/docs/USSD-Terror/95/index.html⟩.

Walzer, M. (1978). *Just and unjust wars.* London: Allen Lane.

Wootton, D. (Ed.). (1993). *John Locke: Political writings.* Harmondsworth: Penguin.

Truth Telling as Constitutive of Journalism

JOHN O'NEILL

Lancaster University

GLOSSARY

practice A complex human activity that has internal
ends that are partially constitutive of that activity.
professional virtues Those excellences of character and
technique that enable a person to realize the internal
goods of the practice a profession sustains.

CERTAIN HUMAN PRACTICES, such as medicine, have internal ends that are constitutive of the kind of activity they are. Journalism is among such practices. Truth telling is an internal and constitutive end of journalism. This is not to say that journalism necessarily delivers truth, but where it fails to do so it fails in a special way: it points to an internal failure in the journalistic enterprise. Truth telling as a constitutive end of journalism also defines qualities that are characteristic of a good practitioner of the professions—particular virtues and excellences of a journalist as journalist. These include both technical excellences and broader ethical excellences such as honesty and integrity. Even contested virtues such as "objectivity" are contested in terms of the relation to the internal end of truth telling.

I. THE PRACTICE OF JOURNALISM

Journalism is a practice. I use the term practice in the Aristotelian sense to refer to human activities that have internal ends that are partially constitutive of the kind of activity they are. The concept has been elaborated thus by MacIntyre:

> By a "practice" I am going to mean any coherent and complex form of socially established cooperative human activity through which goods internal to that form of activity are realized in the course of trying to achieve those standards of excellence which are appropriate to, and partially definitive of, that form of activity ... (MacIntyre (1985). *After virtue* (2nd Ed.). London: Duckworth, p. 187).

Medicine is for example a practice in the Aristotelian sense. Medicine is an activity that has a particular point for which it is done, causing individuals to be healthy, which defines the nature of the activity and the excellences of activity and practitioner that are characteristic of the activity. Journalism is a practice in this sense. Just as health is an internal and constitutive end of medicine, so truth telling about significant contemporary public events is an internal and constitutive end of journalism. As an end truth telling distinguishes journalism from other practices akin to it, but distinct from it—for example, those of pure entertainment. The object of the journalistic enterprise—significant, contemporary public events—distinguishes journalism from other truth-oriented practices such as science and history.

Truth telling in the context of journalism involves more than simply the presentation of accurate information. Two points are of particular significance here. First, the journalist works within certain norms of communication. Some of these are particular to the practice, for example, those governing that very particular genre, the newspaper headline. Others are general norms of communication that have particular relevance in the journalistic context. Thus, something like Gricean conversational implicatures set up inferences among readers between what is strictly said in a story and what is meant. Hence, Gricean principles of quantity and relevance assumed in standard conversation—that one supplies all relevant information—can convert partial truths into falsehoods. (Grice, H. (1975). Logic and conversation. In P. Cole & J. L. Morgan (Eds). *Syntax and semantics 3: Speech acts.* New York: Academic Press.). For example, reports of wars are often slotted into a narrative structure in which they are solely a conflict with a particular tyrant. Now, this may in part be true but it sets up implicatures that this is all they are, which is rarely if ever true. One can depart from truth telling through the presentation of true propositions that set up implicatures that are false. For similar reasons, the selection of stories matters in virtue of the implicatures set up by what is not reported.

A second feature of the journalist's art that raises special issues of truth lies in the very fact that journalists standardly write a story. Events are presented within narrative structures. That this is the case does not entail the radical constructivist conclusion that the concepts of truth and falsity no longer apply, that we merely have different constructions of social reality. It does however raise special and difficult issues about what it is for a story to be "a true story." A story can be false in fairly straightforward ways. The particular events it describes never happened as the story says. Its descriptions are inaccurate. However, it can also depart from truthfulness through the choice of narrative structure for connecting the events. Thus, problems of truthfulness are often a question of the genre in which a story is placed, and this turns on normative appraisal of events and their structure that goes beyond "mere" reportage. The choice of narrative genres involves the normative appraisal of the actors, their relationships to each other, and the social order to which they belong: a strike might be presented either as a struggle of the powerless and exploited workers against rich and powerful employers or as unreasonable demands of producers who despite good living standards are willing to "hold the public to ransom." The story will have structure, as Aristotle has it, a "beginning, middle, and end," and the genre to which the story belongs, epic, tragic, or whatever, depends upon its ending, and again the appraisal one makes of it: the story of a strike can be presented as success or failure, and as such, as a sad defeat or as a splendid victory.

These features of the news story raise two distinct problems about truthfulness. First, given that the genre depends upon normative appraisal, if the concept of truth is to apply, it must be possible to have criteria to distinguish true and false normative characterizations of events: for example, it must be possible to assess the truth or falsity of the claim that workers are exploited and powerless. Truthfulness applied to narratives presupposes some form of cognitivism about norms. Second, it must be possible to assert that sequences of events have a narrative structure that we capture in our descriptions more or less adequately and are not merely contingently related to each other. It must not be true that, as Mink has it, "Stories are not lived but told. Life has no beginnings, middles or ends..." (Mink, L. (1970). History and fiction as modes of comprehension. *New literary history* 1, pp. 541–558, 557). If Mink is right, then we merely project stories upon a world; we do not make assertions about the world. Truthfulness assumes some form of narrative realism. I believe that both normative cognitivism and narrative realism should be accepted. The most plausible versions of the denial of cognitivism about norms and the denial of narrative realism share a deep scientism: all that is true of the world is that which can be captured by a true physical theory; because reference to norms and narrative structure make no appearance in physical theory, they are not part of the furniture of the world to be captured by truth claims. This scientism should be rejected. As far as journalism goes we should argue the other way. Because we can make perfect sense of the distinction between true and false narratives about historical and contemporary events, scientism should be rejected. This philosophical worry should, however, be distinguished from a different and more important worry about the actual narratives that appear in newspapers. It is true that much popular journalism appeals to a narrow range of narrative structures and it forces stories into them. The result often is a failure of truth telling.

To assert that truth telling is constitutive of journalism is not to say that journalism always delivers the truth any more than it is true to say that medicine always delivers health because health is the constitutive end of medicine. Rather, it is to say that where these practices do fail to deliver such goods they fail in a special way. To criticize a doctor or medical institution for failing to provide adequate health care for patients is to make an internal criticism. It is to criticize them for failing to realize the very ends that the practice of medicine aims to serve. Likewise, to criticize a journalist, a newspaper, or radio or T.V. news programs for failing to report significant events truthfully is to accuse them of failing to perform that function constitutive of the very practice of journalism. Thus, while it is true that some doctors are bad doctors or that medical institutions may systematically fail to solve health problems—and may perhaps even create them—it remains true that health as an end is constitutive of medicine. Likewise, although some journalists may cease to report truthfully, and some newspaper may systematically distort the truth, it remains true that truth telling is constitutive of journalism.

Indeed, that truth is constitutive of the practice is perhaps most apparent where the journalist is under pressure to depart from it. Consider for example the pressure both from the state and self-censorship on truth telling in time of war. Arguments about the justifiability of the failure to report truthfully presuppose that the journalistic activity itself has that end. Hence, the remark of one war correspondent for World War II: "We were a propaganda arm of our governments. At the start the censors enforced that, but by the end we were our own censors. We were cheerleaders. I suppose there wasn't an alternative at the time. It was total war. But, for God's sake let's not glorify our role. It wasn't good journalism at all" (C. Lynch, cited in Knightley, P. (1982). *The first casualty: The war correspondent as hero, propagandist and myth maker*, p. 317. London: Quartet). It failed as good journalism because truth telling is suspended. The failure is justified because, it is claimed, journalism here has to be subordinate to more pressing ends: as Hopkinson, the wartime editor of the *Picture Post* puts it, "in wartime there is something more important than truth" (cited in Williams, K. (1992). Something More Important Than Truth: Ethical Issues in War Reporting. In A. Belsey & R. Chadwick (Eds.). *Ethical issues in journalism and the media*, p. 154. London: Routledge). This claim that the constitutive ends of journalism should be thus abandoned is clearly open to dispute. The central arguments to that dispute point not just to its implications for the practice of journalism as such but to the relation of the internal goods of journalism and wider public goods.

The internal end of journalism in truth telling about events of public interest has a general social and political significance in modern society: it forms a central component of debate in the public sphere. The internal end is sometimes stated in professional codes as a duty to inform a public correlative to a right of the public to be informed: "The public's right to know of events of public importance and interest is the overriding mission of the mass media" (Society of Professional Journalists *Code of Ethics* adopted 1926, revised 1973). It is in virtue of that informing role that journalism has traditionally been held to have a special role within democracies, where it is understood as a forum. Thus, for example, the third Press Commission defined press freedom in terms of such democratic responsibilities:

> We define the freedom of the press as that freedom from restraint which is essential to enable proprietors, editors and journalists to advance the public interest by publishing facts and opinions without which a democratic electorate cannot make responsible judgements (Royal Commission on the Press Cmnd 6810 (1977), Chapter 2, paragraph 3).

There are two components to the view that free journalism is a necessary condition for democracy. The first is that the media acts as a watchdog in government. Even where the press gains immense independent powers, it acts as a "fourth estate" that provides a check on the other estates of government. The second is that the press is a necessary condition for an informed and critical citizenship. It provides information on major issues without which the public would not be able to make intelligent judgments. Ideally, it functions as a forum for public debate about such issues, serving to ensure that a diversity of opinions is heard. It is clear that there is a necessary relationship between the internal goods of journalism and the functions that journalism is assumed to perform. Because truth telling about significant contemporary public events is constitutive of journalistic practice, where excellence in journalism exists, journalism will serve the creation of an informed and critical political citizenry. The deliberative institutions in democracy rely on a "public sphere" in which debate can be conducted, and the role of the media in representing the issues and different perspectives is critical both to the possibility and to the quality of that sphere. Hence, not just the direction suspension of the practice of journalism as a truth-seeking activity, but also its corrosion by political and commercial institutions (see Section III, below) disrupt a central component of democratic life.

To say that truth telling is a constitutive end of journalism is not to say that all truths come within its domain nor that their are no ethical limits upon its investigative activities. Standardly, the contemporary events that form a legitimate object of journalistic inquiry are taken to be those in which a "public interest" exists. Those facts about the "private lives" of individuals that have no bearing on the interests of the public do not form proper objects of scrutiny. In modern societies there is taken to be a sphere, central to a person's identity and a condition for her autonomy, that is not a permissable object for the public gaze. While this limitation standardly finds itself into journalistic codes, it leaves open considerable room for argument, for example, over what counts as an object of public interest and what criteria demarcate the "private" sphere.

II. THE VIRTUES OF THE JOURNALIST

The constitutive ends of journalism define specific virtues of the profession, those qualities characteristic of a good practitioner—the particular excellences of a journalist as journalist. Among these are those technical skills that are part of the journalist's craft—the ability to construct a story, to tell it well. However, they also include broader ethical virtues that are associated with truth telling—with the recognition and discovery of important truths and a willingness and courage to report them. Thus, typical virtues used by journalists to describe their peers are "honest," "perceptive," "truthful." Closely associated with these virtues of honesty and truthfulness is that of integrity—for example, the subeditor who insists on rewriting a front-page story to eliminate systematic bias in it. Another, more contested, virtue that is often raised here is that of "objectivity." The virtue of "objectivity" is often rejected by some of the best journalists of our day. Thus, James Cameron writes that:

> I do not see how a reporter attempting to define a situation involving some kind of ethical conflict can do it with sufficiently demonstrable neutrality to fulfil some arbitrary concept of "objectivity." It never occurred to me, in such a situation, to be other than subjective, and as obviously so as I could manage to be. I may not always have been satisfactorily balanced; I always tended to argue that objectivity was of less importance than the truth, and that the reporter whose technique was informed by no opinion lacked a very serious dimension. (Cameron, J. (1969). *Point of departure*, p. 74. London: Grafton Books.)

Two comments are in order. First, Cameron's rejection of objectivity stays within the circle of values of journalism. Objectivity is rejected in terms of a contrast with "truth" and, later with the need to present an account that can be "examined and criticized" such that it will: "encourage an attitude of mind that will challenge and criticise automatically, thus to destroy the built in advantages of all propaganda and special pleading—even the journalist's own" (Cameron (1969), pp. 74–75). The criticism of objectivity stays within the particular set of virtues associated with truth telling. Secondly, and relatedly, the rejection of objectivity in journalism appeals to an argument that is accepted by traditional defenders of objectivity in the social sciences—notably by Weber—that if values are to enter in to the reportage of empirical matters of fact, it is better that they do so explicitly rather than implicitly (see Weber, M. (1949). *The methodology of the social sciences* (E. Shils & H. Finch, Trans.). New York: Free Press.). This has particular importance in journalism: given the degree to which the selection and presentation of news is value-laden, the critical faculties of the audience are better served by making those values explicit. "Objectivity" in the sense of reportage that best allows the audience to appreciate the complexities of a situation may be better served by the nonobjective presentation of events. Journalism, then, is a practice constituted by its own goods and a set of virtues among its practitioners that are necessary for the realization of such goods.

III. CORRUPTION, VIRTUES, AND INSTITUTIONS

Practices are open to corruption from the institutional settings in which they occur, for such settings may involve the pursuit of external ends that are distinct from the internal ends of a practice and are potentially in competition with them. Hence, Aristotle's comments on the corrupting effects of markets upon practices: it is not the internal end of medicine to make money, but within a market setting it can be pursued for that end. Similarly, it is not the end of philosophy to make money, but within the market it can be pursued with that end. The pursuit of external ends can corrupt a practice: where a practitioner has been so corrupted, he or she takes the pursuit of the external ends to have priority over the internal ends. Hence, sophism is a corrupt form of philosophy: "the art of the sophist is the semblance of wisdom without the reality, and the art of the sophist is one who makes money from apparent but unreal wisdom" (*De Sophisticis Elenchis,* I (1928). (Trans. W. Pickard-Cambridge). London: Oxford University Press). The virtues required for the pursuit of a practice are then not just those excellences that enable an individual to perform a function well, but also those that enable a practitioner to resist the temptations of putting aside the internal goals of the practice for external goods: the virtues of courage and integrity are of particular significance in this regard.

These general Aristotelian observations about practices have particular relevance to journalism, which exists in the world of commerce or is subsidized by political institutions as a public organ. Both are potentially corrosive of the internal ends of journalism. That political power is potentially corrosive of the internal ends of journalism is widely recognized. Where the press has no independence of political power, then both positive powers of patronage and negative powers of coercion entail that the journalist's pursuit of the end of truth telling may depart radically from the ends of personal advancement or even survival. Hence, the virtues of personal courage and integrity are particularly evident.

The same virtues are also required by the journalist in the commercial press, for the reasons that Aristotle notes: the semblance of truth may sell better than truth itself. A press within a market setting has to satisfy the preferences of its consumers. As De Tocqueville puts it: "A newspaper can survive only on the condition of publishing sentiments or principles common to a large number of men" (De Tocqueville, A. (1945). *Democracy in America* (Vol. II), p. 113. New York: Knopf); or as Balzac more cynically puts it: "Every newspaper is ... a shop which sells to the public whatever shades of opinion it wants" (de Balzac, H. (1971). *Lost illusions,* p. 314 (H. Hunt, Trans.). Harmondsworth: Penguin). This market imperative is potentially corrosive of the internal goods of journalism. Save where there already exists a self-critical audience, the end of giving apparent truth that satisfies the desires of an audience can take precedence over the internal aims of the practice. The marketplace encourages the producer to present news in a way that is congruent with the preexisting values and beliefs of its audience. It does not pay to present news that is outside of the dominant cultural framework of the audiences addressed. Hence, mass journalism will tend to work within the confines of the dominant culture in which it operates. Relatedly, the value of truth telling becomes at best subsidiary in the presentation of news, for it is not always the case that the truth about significant public events is what the consumer prefers to hear or read. What is portrayed in the press, how it is portrayed, and how much it is portrayed is, within a free market, shaped by consumer preference. What ought to be portrayed, how it ought to be portrayed, and how much it ought to be portrayed might be quite odds with such preferences. Hence, while truth telling might be constitutive of journalism as a practice, the institutional setting of the market can be corrosive of that end. The "news value" of a story is rarely a function of its truth value. It is, rather, a function of the perceived market at which the story is aimed. At its worst this leads to the abandonment of the internal ends of journalism so that media become mere vehicles for entertainment produced by entertainers employing traditional journalistic skills. Consider Murdoch's telling comment during the Hitler diary hoax: "we are in the entertainment business" (Evans (1983). *Good times, bad times,* p. 404. London; Weidenfield and Nicolson). Some newspapers are no longer vehicles for the practice of journalism and are not perceived to be so. There is evidence, for example, that readers of many popular newspapers are sceptical of the accuracy of what they read, while in the United Kingdom papers like *The Sunday Sport* are explicitly unconcerned with the truth value of what they "report" such that the entertaining hoax becomes the object of paper. This distancing of newspaper production from the values of truth telling and its recharacterisation as entertainment allows the easy relativism that identifies "quality" with "satisfaction of market preferences." None of this is to deny the value of entertain-

ment: it is rather to contest the claim that the practice of journalism can be treated purely as entertainment and to criticize the increasing tendency for the traditional vehicles of journalism to be thus subverted.

Even where entertainment values are not pursued to the exclusion of journalism's constitutive values, the demands of the market systematically shape what is reported in a news story. The consequence of this is not so much the reporting of falsehoods in the media—although this occurs—but the failure to report what is of significance and to simplify the presentation of events. Hence, the standard complaints about modern mass journalism are that it decontextualizes events, it prefers news that fits standard narrative structures and it presents it in these terms, it personalizes domestic and international politics, it has a systematic bias towards European and American issues, and so on. The consequence is not so much a departure from truth telling as such, but from truthfulness. This is exhibited in the failure to report significant events—and most censorship is a suppression of truth rather than the statement of falsehood—and the presentation of partial truths that, while not false in themselves, depart from what in a court of law might be called the "whole truth." For reasons noted earlier such failures matter in that they virtually create implicatures among readers that are false. These biases are often compounded by economic pressures on the supply of information. Gathering information is costly, and there are pressures on newspapers to accept ready-made news stories from potential suppliers. Those with a particular viewpoint to present will effectively subsidize the media in the costs of gathering news; hence, the growth of press agents and public relations officers. In doing so they are forced to present the press with versions of events that will sell within a particular market niche.

These pressures point to those virtues in the journalist that are required for the pursuit of the internal ends of the practice. The journalist exists in two worlds: he or she enters a practice that is characterized by a commitment to truth telling, and at the same time he or she is an employee who works for a wage and is expected to produce a story of the kind demanded by his or her newspaper, magazine or television station. The nature of such stories is determined by political and commercial pressures that can clearly conflict with the internal ends of journalism. Conflicting demands are placed upon the journalist. Where this occurs, the journalist exhibits vices and virtues that are characteristic of the trade. Of the vices perhaps the most characteristic is that of cynicism concerning the values constitutive of journalism and the divorce between the journalist's written word and his or her own beliefs and temperament. To be a cynical journalist is to believe that truth telling in journalism is a sham and that the practice is universally pursued for narrow, self-interested aims. However, while the cynic does not believe that the goods of journalism are anywhere realized, either in his or her own work or that of others, the attitude presupposes a view of what the constitutive goods of journalism are supposed to be. The cynicism is parasitic on the acceptance of a shared view that the end of journalism is truth telling. The virtues that the journalist exhibits are those familiar in biographies of particular journalists: mention of the virtues of integrity and courage are common. Such virtue is required not only in the performance of a practice, but in resisting those external pressures that undermine its goods. The history of journalism is full of examples of principled resignation by editors and journalists. The tension between the practice of journalism and the market framework in which it operates then produces characteristic virtues and vices. This is not to say that journalists fall into two classes—villains and heroes. Many may find themselves forced to compromise the constitutive values of journalism, while at the same time insisting that some of the standards be enforced. The copy editor may still have reservations about the final form of a story he or she has rewritten, yet be able in the process of rewriting to remove some of the bias, simplification, and falsehood. That the constitutive values of journalism are still realized in the modern world is in part a consequence of the resistance of journalists to the pressures of both marketplace and state power.

Bibliography

Belsey, A., & Chadwick, R. (Eds.). (1992). *Ethical issues in journalism and the media.* London: Routledge.

Bennet, W. L. (1988). *News: The politics of illusion* (2nd ed.). New York: Longman.

Bok, S. (1983). *Secrets.* New York: Random House.

Cohen, S., & Young, J. (Eds.). (1981). *The manufacture of news* (2nd ed.). London: Constable.

Curran, J., & Gurevitch, M. (Eds.). (1991). *Mass media and society.* London: Edward Arnold.

Curran, J., & Seaton, J. (1991). *Power without responsibility* (4th ed.). London: Routledge.

Entman, R. (1989). *Democracy without citizens.* Oxford: Oxford University Press.

Evens, H. (1983). *Good times, bad times.* London: Weidenfield and Nicolson.

Jones, J. C. (1980). *Mass media codes of ethics and councils: A comparative international study on professional standards.* Paris: Unesco.

Keane, J. (1991). *The media and democracy.* Cambridge: Polity Press.

Klaidman, S., & Beauchamp, T. (1987). *The virtuous journalist.* New York: Oxford University Press.

Lichtenberg, J. (Ed.). (1990). *Democracy and the mass media.* Cambridge: Cambridge University Press.

McQuail, D., & Siune, K. (Eds.). (1986). *New media politics.* London: Sage.

Violence in Films and Television

MARIAN I. TULLOCH and JOHN C. TULLOCH
Charles Sturt University

GLOSSARY

arousal A nonspecific physiological response.

catharsis A discharge of hostile feeling in response to watching violence.

correlational research Relation of individuals' measured characteristics and behaviors.

cultivation effects The way television cultivates a distorted view of social reality in the minds of viewers.

desensitization Reduced emotional arousal to aversive stimuli.

disinhibition Reduction in the constraints against behaving in a socially undesirable way.

effects research Research into the direct behavioral consequences of television viewing on individuals.

experimental research Research undertaken in controlled conditions with relevant variables manipulated by the experimenter.

longitudinal panel studies Studies undertaken with the same subjects being measured at intervals over a period of time.

meta-analysis A statistical procedure for combining the results of multiple research studies.

VIOLENCE IN FILMS AND TELEVISION has been a subject of wide public concern since the inception of these media forms. Although a range of issues have been raised by the conjuncture of new media forms and the mass reception of representations of violence (associating violence with subcultural categories of gender, class, and ethnicity), it is the category of age, particularly children, that has attracted most attention. Extensive research has been conducted into the possible negative effects, particularly on children, of exposure to the frequent portrayal of acts of violence, but there has been disagreement as to the conclusiveness of these findings and the appropriate policy implications. Cultural differences in legal and constitutional frameworks, the organization of the communications industry, and the sociopolitical climate have led to countries finding different approaches and solutions to issues of media violence. More recently research has extended both to public perceptions of media violence and its influence on the way audiences view their world and to a study of public attitudes toward portrayals of media violence and appropriate policy interventions. In addition to concern about the extensive portrayal of fictional violence are the particular issues raised by violence in factual television. The media plays a role in shaping public attitudes to violent national and international events as well as impacting directly on those involved in violence, especially victims. This survey will focus primarily on ethical and methodological considerations in the policy, media, and research debate surrounding children and violence in films and television. Having overviewed the historical and institutional context within which research and policy are formed, the article will examine the psychological effects approach to film and television violence, and will then consider a range of research and policy traditions which have in recent years moved away from or critiqued that tradition.

I. CULTURAL CONTEXT

A. Historical Overview

1. Mass Entertainment and the Fear of Violence

Fear of the potential harmful consequences of mass entertainment preceded the moving image. Continuities have been drawn between the avowed dangers of music halls, "penny dreadfuls," or "dime comics" in promoting crime and violence and reducing traditional authority, and subsequent anxieties, sometimes termed "moral panics," at each new technological development: film, television, video, cable and satellite TV, and the Internet. The advent of film led to claims that the moving image bypasses the thinking areas of the brain to impact directly on the subconscious, and therefore unprotected, mind.

> Before these children's greedy eyes with heartless indiscrimination horrors unimaginable are … presented night after night…. Terrific massacres, horrible catastrophes, motor-car smashes, public hangings, lynchings. All who care for the moral well being and education of the child will set their faces like flint against this new form of excitement. (April 12, 1913. Cinematography and the Child, *The Times*, London)

Because moral panics have been so clearly associated with the relationship between media violence and mass audiences, they have sometimes been dismissed as an attack on popular culture by a middle-class elite. Yet the ubiquitous nature of the TV violence debate suggests an ongoing and widespread concern with possible links between a diet of screen violence and problems of social aggression.

2. Early Research into Film Violence

Of all the potential harmful effects of film and television, by far the greatest emphasis has been on the consequences, particularly for the young, of excessive portrayals of violence. The first major study of this issue was established by the National Committee for the Study of Social Values in Motion Pictures and financed by a private philanthropic foundation, the Payne Fund (1928–1933). Despite their negligible effect on public policy, these studies represent an important breakthrough in establishing the role of social scientific research in policy debates, raising issues of public concern, and causing some disquiet in the motion-picture industry. The notion of powerful direct communication effects underlying the research was a simplistic one, later characterized as the "hypodermic model" because it neglected the possible mediating role of viewer characteristics. Although effects models have increased in theoretical and methodological sophistication, they have remained guided by a search for a causal connection

between on-screen and real world violence, with the individual viewer as the unit for analysis.

B. Structural and Industry Contexts

Despite the important role assigned to psychological principles in explaining the effects of media violence, the impact of television and indeed public concern about that impact are extensively mediated by specific cultural contexts. The amount and type of violence in the media vary greatly between cultures. In the multiple-channel deregulated U.S. market, the level of violence is much higher than that in many other cultures where less violence is presented or is contextualized quite differently. Japanese television has a heavy diet of television violence, but heroes themselves are more frequently subjected to violence with a greater focus on their resultant pain and suffering. The role of the United States as the major exporter of film and television, however, means that American shows are a standard part of the viewing offerings in very diverse societies.

C. Changing Communication Technology

Changes in communication technology have also altered the availability of violent material. Cable and satellite technology has vastly increased the range of available products, and in the many countries where television can be accessed from neighboring states there are limited governmental powers of control. For instance, Canadian attempts to reduce violence on television affects Canadian stations but not the cable and satellite programs from the United States available in the majority of Canadian homes. Britain has not imposed the same regulatory regimes on satellite as terrestrial services. The advent of the videocassette recorder means that systems of regulation relying on the exclusion of underage cinema patrons from certain film screenings no longer ensure the restriction of material to adult viewers. Children's access to violent materials through video or pay channels has become an important focus of current public concern.

II. PSYCHOLOGICAL STUDIES OF TV VIOLENCE AND AGGRESSION

A. Psychological Processes

A variety of psychological processes have been posited as mechanisms by which the viewing of violence on film or television can influence behavior. The focus of this research paradigm is on explaining individual differences in aggressive behavior and tolerance for aggression as a function of differential exposure to violent programs.

1. Desensitization

One hypothesized effect of viewing violence is a gradual emotional desensitization, not only to screen violence but to real life violence. For instance, R. S. Drabman and M. H. Thomas asked children to monitor by video the behavior of some younger children. Those who had watched a violent program were found to be less likely to intervene to prevent a fight among younger children in their charge than children who had not seen the film. A subsequent study in which the physiological and emotional responses of the children were monitored found that those who had previously watched violent programming were subsequently less aroused by what was purported to be real life violence (1974. *Developmental Psychology*, 17, 399–407).

Desensitization, at the physiological level, has been demonstrated in the lower arousal to violent scenes among heavy vs light television viewers. Repeated viewing of extremely violent videos has been frequently presented as an explanation for the blunted sensibilities of those who perpetrate acts of extreme violence. A concern with the regular portrayal even of factual violence is that it serves to blunt the public's sensitivities and the power to shock or feel.

2. Imitation

Social learning theorists who emphasize children's ability to learn by observing the behavior of others see television as a prime source of aggressive models. Experimental studies have investigated a range of variables that influence the level of imitative aggression. In A. Bandura's classic studies, children watched a live or filmed model performing aggressive acts against a large plastic Bobo doll. When left alone to play in a room containing the doll, children who had witnessed the aggression produced similar actions to a much greater extent than children who had not. If the model was rewarded rather than punished for their aggression the level of imitation increased, a finding relevant to the tendency of television to portray the final triumph of the forces of good (e.g., in crime series or war movies), by means often as violent as those of their enemies (1973. *Aggression: A Social Learning Analysis*. Prentice-Hall, Englewood Cliffs, NJ).

Several studies have investigated direct imitative effects via fluctuations in suicide rates following television coverage of a suicide—whether actual, as in the case of Marilyn Monroe, or of a major fictional character.

3. Disinhibition

Portrayals of media violence may lower social inhibitions against violent behavior, making aggression appear permitted or even approved. Frequent viewing of violence can make it appear more socially acceptable; violent behaviors are seen to benefit the aggressor or to be judged situationally appropriate. Such lowering of inhibitions can facilitate the enactment of learned behavioral responses.

4. Arousal

One difficulty in research on the consequences of screen violence is in determining whether the effects could be the product not of violence specifically but of emotional arousal in general. The impact of material that is exciting or inspires strong feelings may depend on the viewer's prior mood and the way that arousal is perceived. For instance, arousal in a frustrated viewer witnessing violent action is more likely to be self-perceived as anger. Young children have become more restless and aggressive after watching very fast-paced, fragmented material, whether or not it contains violence. It is possible that what has been interpreted as an effect of violence may sometimes be a more generalized arousal effect.

5. Catharsis

It has been suggested, applying the traditional Aristotelian notion of catharsis, that viewing violence is a harmless way of draining off aggressive energies. While a few studies have found evidence of lowered aggression after violent viewing, support for the catharsis hypothesis from researchers within the effects paradigm has been generally very low.

6. Cognitive Approaches

As psychological theories have shifted from stimulus response to cognitive models, processes of social learning of aggression have been reformulated in cognitive terms. The child is seen to internalize patterns of social action organized into narrative scripts. Scripts contain both images and conceptual representations, providing guides to behavior in specific contexts. Television can play a role in the encoding of violent scripts and the maintenance and rehearsal of scripts by repeated exposure, and may cue the enactment of scripts in everyday contexts, a process that may be fostered by the child's identification with aggressive characters. Such a model can incorporate various psychological processes: social learning, arousal, disinhibition, and the triggering effect of specific cues. One such source of cues can be the "antisocial" toys that are marketed in conjunction with certain violent cartoons, a possibility that has been specifically studied. The way aggressive scripts may be learned and then cued and reenacted has been investigated in a study of preschool children by A. Sanson and C. Di Muccio. They found that children who watched a violent cartoon and then had "spin-off" toys to play with behaved more aggressively than other children who watched a neutral cartoon and/or received neutral toys. (1993. *Australian Psychologist, 28,* 93–99.)

With psychologists conceptualizing the TV violence–aggression relationship increasingly in cognitive terms, the gap between psychological and cultural theorists has diminished. The psychologist Leonard Berkowitz terms his approach "cognitive neoassociationism," and although presenting his theories in terms of memory networks and associative pathways, he considers the audience members' response to a communication as contingent on their prior ideas and the way these shape their interpretation. These ideas and interpretations may determine whether thoughts about violence activated by a program lead to overt aggressive behavior.

G. Comstock, in a review of a large number of experiments, has endeavored to conceptualize the multiplicity of factors that have been found to relate to differences in audience responses to televized acts of violence. Four conceptual dimensions have been identified to make sense of the range of factors affecting program impact: efficacy of violence, normativeness (the morality of violent acts), pertinence (their relevance to the viewer), and viewer susceptibility. Although recognizing that the first three dimensions can depend on viewer perception, effects researchers continue to operate from the position that the properties of the program (for instance, the justifiability of violence) can be determined by the researcher rather than identified by a study of audience readings.

B. Types of Effects Research

1. Laboratory Experiments

Numerous studies on the effects of viewing violence under carefully controlled experimental conditions have been conducted within a psychological paradigm. The significant differences in subsequent aggression found in most of these studies between groups that have viewed violent and nonviolent excerpts have been taken as strong evidence that violence on screen can affect viewers' behavior. The strength of laboratory studies lies in an ability to study the consequence of very specific manipulations under carefully controlled conditions. They have been criticized, however, for the artificial

nature of the viewing context and the measures of aggression that are employed, and for the demand characteristics operating in a laboratory setting, including the lack of social prohibitions or apparent negative consequences for perpetrators or victims of aggression. A study by W. A. Collins and S. K. Getz, with its use of a button to measure aggressive responses, is typical of traditional laboratory studies. Collins and Getz presented children with an episode of "Mod Squad" that had been edited in two ways. The protagonist responded to interpersonal provocation either constructively or aggressively. Children who viewed the aggressive behavior were less likely to demonstrate a desire to cooperate when given an opportunity to assist a peer by pressing a "help" button and more likely instead to press a "hurt" button. (1976. *Journal of Personality, 44,* 488–500). Questions have been raised as to the generalizability of the findings to a natural viewing context and also whether a cumulative impact of violent viewing can be inferred from short-term effects.

2. Field Studies

Field experiments can offer opportunities to study behavior within natural social contexts over longer time periods. However, the real life environment often comes at the expense of the stringent controls operating in the laboratory, possibly leaving findings open to plausible alternative explanations. If preexisting groups are studied they may well differ in initial characteristics. Moreover, while purporting to use the individual as the unit of analysis, ongoing groups are inevitably affected by group processes, reflecting the social reality that aggression is an interactive social behavior, not a unidirectional personal response. It may also be hard to keep those who rate the children's behavior unaware as to which TV programs a given individual is being shown. Even the imposition of particular viewing regimes within a naturalistic environment may be difficult; subjects may be bored by their programming diet or object to the absence of regular favorite programs, suggesting that real life experiments, despite their appeal, can be difficult to implement effectively.

Some of the ethical issues posed by researchers' manipulation of viewing have been overcome in what have been termed naturally occurring experiments. A comparative study of three similar communities in British Colombia in which, for technical reasons, television was introduced at different times found an overall increase in children's playground aggression with the introduction of television, but not a specific relation between quantity of viewing and aggressive behavior. Moreover, the levels of children's aggression in the town that received television during the study became higher than those of children in the towns which already had access to television. The shift appeared in part to reflect overall changes in community social life, suggesting the need for a broad consideration of the impact of television on a community (In T. M. Williams, Ed., 1986. *The Impact of Television: A Natural Experiment in Three Communities.* Academic Press, New York).

The gradual introduction of television on a national level can also be viewed as a natural experiment. A comparison of U.S. cities receiving television before or after the 1949–1952 licensing freeze found television associated with increases in larceny but not with crimes of violence. The introduction of television to a whole country was studied by South African psychologists. Levels of television viewing were found to relate to increased aggressiveness in children in the white community.

3. Correlational Research

Another approach to demonstrating the effects of screen violence on viewer aggression is to relate individual differences in viewing levels to measures of naturally occurring aggressive behavior. Self or parental reports of viewing habits or program preferences, viewing logs, clinical interviews, peer or teacher nominations of behavioral aggression, and records of criminal convictions have all been employed in correlational research and have a variety of potential sources of measurement error. Although these weaknesses can be seen to limit the validity of research conclusions, an alternative view is that it produces an underestimation of the effects of viewing violence. While it has been clearly shown that the frequency of television viewing is associated with higher levels of aggressive behavior, demonstrating a causal linkage is difficult. Studies have attempted to control factors likely to contribute to the association, such as socioeconomic status, educational performance, parenting practices, intelligence, and personality. Studies of preschoolers have found TV viewing and everyday aggressive behavior to be related when a set of other factors are controlled.

One of the most complex attempts to control a range of over 200 variables was made by W. A. Belson in a study of adolescent boys in London. When heavy and light viewers of violence were statistically equated on these possible explanatory variables, heavy viewers were still significantly higher on a set of indices of aggression, particularly seriously harmful acts. This data gave little support to the alternative hypothesis that more aggressive boys sought out more violent entertainment (1978. *Television and the Adolescent Boy.* Teakfield, Farnborough).

4. Longitudinal Research

The problem of inferring causality from association in nonexperimental research can be addressed by studying the same group of children over an extended period of time, although longitudinal studies tend to be plagued by high attrition rates. Cross-lagged correlations that measure the association between two variables at two points in time test specific hypotheses about the direction of relationships. Work by Eron, Huesmann, and colleagues in which the same individuals were studied at ages 9 and 19, and again one and two decades later, did find some support for a bidirectional model: preference for violent TV predicted later aggression even when the level of earlier aggression was controlled, and aggressive children later chose to view more violent programs. For some commentators on these studies, the stability of aggression over time and the importance of child-rearing variables in predicting aggressive behavior are seen as more substantial findings than the relatively small long-term effects of violent viewing. The evidence points to any contribution of violent viewing to aggressiveness being most influential in the elementary school years, with attitudes and patterns of behavior established then having the potential to act cumulatively on aggression in adolescence and adulthood. Eron, L. D. Leftkowitz, M. M. Huesmann, L. R. & Walder, L. O. (1972. *American Psychologist*, 27, 253–263).

Because of the technical statistical complexity of such analyses, there is great scope for varying interpretation. A notable example is Milavsky's study sponsored by the NBC network which claimed negligible evidence of long-term effects. While the reinterpretation of the statistical analysis in this study has led many experts in the United States to present the data as supporting the viewing–violence link, several overseas reviews have cited it as more convincing than other American studies, focusing in particular on Milavsky's concern about the inaccuracies evident in some respondents' viewing reports.

5. Cross-Cultural Studies

Cross-cultural research in which the same techniques and measures are used in different countries is a powerful way to test the generalizability of psychological explanations across cultures. A major cross-cultural project included studies in countries as diverse as Australia, Finland, Israel, the Netherlands, Poland, and the United States. Again interpretations diverge, with some reviewers claiming a consistent pattern of support for the hypothesis that TV violence causes aggression, while others find the data patchy and inconclusive, with demonstrable effects so small as to lack practical import

(L. R. Huesmann and L. D. Eron, Eds., 1986. *Television and the Aggressive Child: A Cross-National Comparison*. Erlbaum, Hillsdale, NJ).

6. Meta-analysis

Meta-analysis is a statistical technique which combines the findings from a large number of studies. A recent analysis by Paik and Comstock combined findings from 217 studies dating from between 1957 and 1990 and demonstrated moderate positive effects of screen violence on aggressive behavior. Their analysis aimed to answer some of the perennial criticisms of effects research by comparing the size of measured differences in aggression according to the ecological and design validity of the studies. They found no evidence that substantial effects were produced only in studies characterized by the artificiality of their setting and of the aggression measures employed. As a summary of a large number of effects studies, the meta-analysis supports the link between greater viewing of film and television violence and increased aggressive behavior.

However, for those who reject this paradigm the aggregation of studies serves only to confuse rather than clarify the complex questions of definition, measurement, and process raised in relation to individual studies. It reflects a broader dispute between those who believe that when looked at separately none of the various types of studies can stand alone and the alternative position that the similarity of conclusions from different types of research together support claims for effects of television violence.

III. ALTERNATIVE PARADIGMS: PERCEPTIONS OF VIOLENCE

A. Content Analysis of TV Violence

Violence on television has the potential to influence not just viewers' behavior but their perceptions—how they understand violence and its place in the world. Content analysis attempts to quantify the extent of this violence. In 1992 the American Psychological Association estimated that the average American child has viewed 8000 dramatized murders and 100,000 acts of televized violence before leaving elementary school. With the advent of unrestricted cable TV, these numbers are likely to increase. Saturday morning television, with its diet of cartoons aimed at children, has violence in over 90% of programs with cartoons having an average of 32 violent acts an hour. The most extensive attempt to quantify television violence has been made by George Gerbner and his colleagues.

Gerbner has attempted to measure and monitor violence on television with a Violence Index. He has defined violence as "the overt expression of physical force (with or without weapon) against self or other, compelling action against one's will on pain of being hurt or killed or actually hurting or killing" (G. A. Comstock et al., 1978. Television and Human Behavior. Columbia University Press, New York, p. 64), a definition that has guided much content analysis but omits notions of intentionality generally central to the meaning of aggression. The Violence Index provides a formula for quantifying fictional violence, taking account of its type, its duration, and the role of the protagonists within the program. The Violence Index is calculated by adding together %P, the percentage of programs in which there is violence; $2(R/P)$, twice the number of violent episodes per program; $2(R/H)$, twice the number of violent episodes per hour; %V, percentage of leading characters involved in violence, either as victim or perpetrator; and %K, percentage of leading characters involved in an actual killing, either as victim or perpetrator. But, as many culturally oriented commentators have pointed out, content analysis suffers from taking little account of narrative encoding, genre, and audience decoding.

B. Cultivation Effects

Instead of concern with the direct behavioral effects of screen violence, Gerbner's cultivation analysis asserts that television has affected the way viewers perceive their world; the diet of television drama is a "message system" with a relatively simple myth structure for modern society. For Gerbner, messages about violence are messages about power and authority, creating a symbolic cultural environment that protects dominant forces within society and legitimizes their social control, while conveying to their audience messages of vulnerability and insecurity. "Risk ratios," which measure the relative likelihood of different demographic groups being represented as aggressors or victims in television drama, define a social pecking order that affects the way in which particular groups in society, women, the elderly, and racial minorities are perceived and view themselves. Their underrepresentation and victimization represent a symbolic annihilation, weakening their sense of identity and esteem while legitimizing the status quo that relegates them to positions of powerlessness.

One aspect of the construction of social reality through television is the claim that heavy viewing makes people more fearful, coming to see the world as a meaner place. Although high viewing levels have been associated with greater fear of crime, the limitations of correlational evidence make the causal role of television questionable, with the association reduced by control for demographic characteristics. Gerbner has accepted that residents of high-crime neighborhoods have a greater fear of crime and violence but has argued for a resonance effect whereby television reinforces and amplifies fear among heavy viewers in these areas. Research outside the United States has produced mixed findings, although differences in the nature of television programming and viewing patterns may alter the relevance of the cultivation model. In assessing violent incidents on television, viewers have proved capable of fine discriminations; British viewers react differently in rating the perceived realism and disturbance felt at police violence in American and British drama. The level of TV viewing in Swedish adolescents was found not to be related to fear of violence, but higher levels of viewer involvement and identification were linked to exaggerated perceptions of societal violence. As stable individual differences in the way people perceive their world have been associated with fear of victimization, perceptions of danger and threat may be better viewed as part of an individual's more global sense of lacking environmental control rather than being contingent on viewing crime and violence on television. It is possible that fearful viewers retreat to the security of their home and television set; reassuring themselves with crime and action drama which, despite its level of violence, frequently portrays the ultimate triumph of law and order.

An underlying assumption of both the cultivation model and the behavioral effect approaches is that the impact of television is gradual and cumulative. An alternative position is that critical images may affect a viewer more dramatically than the continual repetition of predictable violence. One narratively justified moment of aggression by an heroic sheriff or law enforcement officer in a Western may have more ideological "effect" in supporting the status quo than numerous deaths and mutilations in cartoons, news, etc. Under this "drench hypothesis" innovative and challenging portrayals may make a substantial impact on audience perspectives, an approach particularly important to those concerned with the potential of film and television to contest accepted realities.

C. Viewers' Perceptions of Violence

While body counts and violence indices deproblematize the measurement of violence, research into how viewers perceive violence indicates the importance of factors other than the number and severity of injuries. Larry Gelbart, creator of "M*A*S*H," claimed people can tolerate 5000 killings on TV shows, but not one meaningful death of a character they love. The realism of the genre, features of the setting, gender of protagonists, and age, gender, and personality characteristics of

the viewer all affect the extent to which an incident is deemed violent. The distinction is particularly marked in responses to cartoons. Both adults and child viewers themselves judge many cartoons, because of their unreality and humor, as low in violence, and quite young children demonstrate clear understanding of modality cues. Ratings based on content analysis of the frequency of violent incidents, however, place cartoons among the most violent forms of programming. What disturbs viewers relates strongly to a show's relevance to their own personal concerns.

A study by Tulloch and Tulloch of children's responses to depictions of violence indicated that the seriousness with which young people responded to violence was a function of context, not the extent of injury inflicted (J. C. Tulloch and M. I. Tulloch, 1993. In *Nation, Culture and Technology: Australian Media and Cultural Studies* (G. Turner, Ed.). Routledge, London). Thus the slaughter of a group of villagers in a war movie or actual injury on the sporting field was rated less disturbing than a fictional depiction of offscreen violence by a husband against his wife despite an absence of serious injury. Perceptions of violence can interact in a complex way with gender and developmental processes; younger children are more accepting of violence by authority figures, though generally violence is more disturbing to younger and female viewers. Specific social understanding may increase the impact of violence. Although older children are often less disturbed than younger children by portrayals of violence, they have been found to be more disturbed by depictions of nuclear war.

D. Understanding Violence: Qualitative Studies

Additional insights into how viewers perceive violence have been gained from qualitative studies. Researchers exploring the media literacy of children through qualitative techniques reveal how their understanding and responses are mediated by a sophisticated knowledge of generic conventions which are too often ignored in quantitative research. Qualitative research is particularly valuable in exploring the meaning of violent viewing for particular subcultural groupings. For instance, young males may use the viewing of excessively violent material to demonstrate their toughness and masculinity, while first nationals in one country may applaud the violent screen exploits of another first national group (e.g., Native Americans).

One research technique that has uncovered valuable insights into viewers' responses to violence that even qualitative interviews often miss requires participants to identify how they would edit a tape for broadcast. This task elicits strong emotional reactions to very specific details. A key factor in the decision-making processes demanded by the editing task is the extent to which portrayals of violence challenge and threaten an individual's view of the world. When the level of viewer engagement was shallow, violence could be deemed entertaining or merely personally distasteful, but violence that threatened individuals' views of their world provoked more intense though varied responses. Some viewers felt that scenes of disturbingly graphic aggression portrayed important social issues that should be broadcast uncut, while other viewers saw a shocking undermining of established values that was quite unacceptable as television fare (D. Docherty, 1992, *Violence in Television Fiction: Public Opinion and Broadcasting Standards*. Libbey, London).

Such depth of involvement is not confined to nonfictional material. The complexity of viewers' responses to fiction is dramatically demonstrated in an Australian study where female viewers' tense responses to what they were aware of as a fictional portrayal of rape were diffused when they discovered that, within the narrative, the rape was staged, not genuine. In some instances screen violence can provoke intense emotional responses which can mobilize attempts to diminish violence, not to emulate it.

IV. NONFICTIONAL VIOLENCE

A range of quite specific ethical issues emerge if we apply cultural considerations to nonfictional representations of violence.

A. Reporting of Violent Crime

1. Values in News Reporting

A television producer's primary concern in reporting violent crime is with newsworthiness. Accuracy may be sacrificed to the constraints of timing in highly competitive markets that demand an appealing and, most importantly, a current product. Reporting is often accused of sensationalism: pandering to an audience's perceived bloodthirsty enjoyment of violence, with graphic, often gruesome images of blood, injuries, body bags, and distraught victims or relatives. On the other hand, the representation of official violence, as in police attacks on picketers or public marches, can be weakened, effaced, or even suppressed. In either case, the focus in television news on the dramatic moment results in a virtual ignoring of underlying explanations of both violent crime and "official" victimization. Official perspectives on violence remain unchallenged and are frequently further cemented by a close cooperative relationship between

journalists and authorities which promotes the flow of violent images, not analysis. Instead reports of violence tend to promote stereotypes and a scapegoating of minorities and outsiders.

2. Media and Victims Rights

The handling of victims of violence by the media involves a balance of rights between the public right to know and the victim's right to privacy. While recent constitutional interpretation has favored media freedom, ethical concerns about the treatment of victims has led to calls for a media code of ethics on dealing with victims. Because of the immediacy of TV news coverage, victims of violence are particularly vulnerable to intrusive, insensitive treatment, and the search for a voyeuristic or prurient angle can lead to victims feeling further victimized and blamed. Australian research found the practice of interviewing victims of violence or their relatives to be the most objectionable aspect of news coverage of violent incidents, eliciting greater public concern than close-ups, bodies, or blood. On the other hand, some parents argued at the hearing on the Dunblane massacre that, in order to strengthen support for antigun legislation, the public should be fully acquainted with the graphic details of the physical damage that modern weaponry inflicted on their children.

B. War, Terrorism, and Public Disorder

Although public concern with violence on television has often focused on the effects of fictional violence or personalized aggression, an important component of violence on television is the news coverage of public acts of violence, whether perpetrated against the state, as in terrorism or civil unrest, or by the state, as in war. Defining these distinctions is itself part of the role of television; the labeling of terrorists as distinct from resistance fighters implies not only the value attached to their violent actions but to those of the government which they oppose, with the potential to justify repression and terror by security forces. Discourses about riots can range from a stigmatizing of rioters as the "younger generation" out of control or of the structurally unemployed as a "race riot," to a critique of state-imposed economic and social repression. Frequently, the positioning of television cameras behind police lines presents a "natural" view of protesters or picketers as aggressors. A remarkably different view of police and strikers was presented by Ken Loach's film *Which Side Are You On?,* a documentary on the 1984 British Miners' strike where cameras and vox pop interviews presented the police themselves as violent aggressors. For Loach, the film was designed to both critique the "commonsense" status quo and to mobilize support for the miners.

Television images of demonstrators attacked with fire hoses and the brutal treatment of freedom riders have also been important in mobilizing support for the civil rights cause. Powerful images of social disorder can be feared by people positioned differently in the social hierarchy as promoting copycat violence, encouraging support or criticism of forces of law and order, or serving as a stimulus to social change.

Despite frequent claims that television sensationalizes violence, the horrors of real violence are often too graphic to present in viewers' lounge rooms. News reporters have been put at risk attempting to film scenes of carnage in a form sufficiently sanitized to be acceptable for public broadcast. A British survey of viewers' responses to violence in factual television indicated that viewers are more upset when the incident is closer either geographically or through perceived similarity, when they are unaware of the eventual outcome, and when the victim is seen as innocent rather than provoking or deserving the attack. Viewers recognize that although the reality of factual violence makes it more disturbing, it is also the reason why the public needs to be informed. Graphic depictions, however, are often viewed as unnecessary to the provision of adequate information.

Particular violent images, such as the summary execution of a Vietcong collaborator in the streets of Saigon or the beating of Rodney King, can also become iconic, playing an important role in the mobilization of public opinion. Aware that nightly images of violence eroded public support for American intervention in Vietnam, state control of media coverage in wartime has become a very sophisticated process. As a result the Gulf War was largely seen through images of high-tech "smart" weaponry and pyrotechnics. It is no coincidence that a study of young British viewers found the most frequently mentioned distressing image of that war was of struggling sea birds drenched in oil. At the same time, militarily and politically controlled "sanitized" imagery of this kind can be used to support continued massive funding of smart weaponry, whereas later evidence cast considerable doubt on its effectiveness.

V. PUBLIC ATTITUDES TO VIOLENCE ON TELEVISION

A. Extent of Public Concern

Opinion polls have suggested widespread American anxiety about media violence, with the majority favoring more regulation to control it. The extent of public concern depends a great deal on the type of questions asked.

In both the United States and Britain, audiences endorse statements that there is too much violence on television but are less likely to be critical of specific violent television shows. Nearly 80% of British respondents felt people are justified in being concerned about the impact of TV violence on children, and 60% agreed there was too much violence on TV. Yet viewers generally accepted that violence was part of television as it was part of life, favoring warnings, late scheduling, and parental vigilance rather than censorship. An ABC study found that around half of a national sample of television viewers felt there was too much violence on television, yet having rated the "The A-Team" as one of the most violent shows, respondents indicated that the level of violence was acceptable. Much greater concern was expressed about the violence available on cable services. Frequently excessive media presentation of both sex and violence was perceived as the cause of social ills, with 67% of American adults surveyed attributing increases in teenage violence to this cause, and 73% then favoring greater controls on television portrayal of sex and violence.

VI. CENSORSHIP AND PUBLIC POLICY

Responsibility for the regulation and control of film and television in different countries can be examined as a continuum from individual to state control. The model of individual regulation with philosophic roots in the work of Thomas Paine espouses a belief in an informed citizenry capable of protecting themselves and their families from harm. Any intervention by the state is deemed an unwarranted infringement of civil liberties. The United States' deregulated approach to media control most clearly typifies this approach. At the other end of the spectrum are authoritarian systems with tightly controlled, state-run media where public opinion on media products is unsolicited and unwelcome. Somewhere between an investiture of responsibility solely with either the individual viewer or the state lie the mixed systems operating in Australia, Canada, Britain, and other countries in Western Europe. Here an important regulatory and control role is delegated to expert bodies who exercise a degree of responsibility for television content. The rhetoric of threats to democratic freedoms have been far less often voiced in countries of Western Europe. Initiatives such as the British 9:00 P.M. watershed are generally perceived by their audience as a realistic compromise, enhancing parental control without depriving the public of adult programs. A degree of regulation has been accepted as responsible, and the possible threat of license losses encourages greater industry self-regulation. In such mixed systems, the existence of clear, informative labeling of products and accessible viewer complaint procedures are part of the combination of individual and delegated responsibility. In the United States, where the level of violence on TV is greater and concern among researchers much more intense, there is great resistance, even from many of these same researchers, to regulatory powers that smack of censorship or restriction of individual freedoms. The lack of complaint from citizens of European democracies in response to greater controls has itself been presented as evidence of the dangers inherent in such a direction.

A. Regulation and Censorship in the U.S. Context

1. Public Inquiries, Regulation, and Policy Issues

a. Regulatory Role of the Federal Communications Commission (FCC)

The Broadcasting Act of 1934 established the FCC as the governing agency responsible for the granting licenses and the oversight of the radio and television industries. Properties of the broadcast spectrum which limit access have permitted a degree of regulation and extensive investigatory powers. Despite the requirement that broadcasters "serve the public interest," this test has never been used to refuse a license. Historically the FCC has not concerned itself with program content so it has not served the same role as regulatory bodies in many other countries which restrict the level of violence on television.

b. The Surgeon General's Report and Beyond

The emphasis on the effects of media violence on children has led to major government-funded research in this field. The 1972 Surgeon General's Report (by the Surgeon General's Scientific Advisory Committee on Television and Social Behavior) was a major attempt to resolve the issue of television violence effects by the accumulation of scientific evidence, including the commissioning of a series of studies as part of the investigation. Parallels were drawn explicitly with the way scientific research established a link between smoking and lung cancer. Preference was given to researchers within a quantitative social scientific paradigm, particularly from the psychology discipline where support for the demonstrability of violence effects has been greatest. Causal effects of television violence on aggression were accepted, although in a qualified way, in the report, a view reiterated over a decade later by the National Institute of Mental Health (1982), the U.S. Attorney General's Task Force on Family Violence (1984), and the American Psychological Association (1985).

2. First Amendment and Libertarian Concerns

Debate in the United States about regulation and censorship has been fought in the context of the freedom of speech rights granted in the First Amendment. Even a voluntary network agreement not to broadcast violent programs between 7 and 9 P.M. was ruled unconstitutional. The history of U.S. broadcasting has been replete with investigation into the potential psychologically harmful effects of television violence, with a minimum of legislative control. More federal dollars have been spent researching the effects of televized violence than any other social effects of the commercial media. Yet any attempt at government regulation or censorship has been forcefully resisted by civil libertarians and commercial interests.

a. Creativity and the Suppression of Ideas

Any attempt to address the issue of screen violence by censorship can be seen as an attack on individual freedom of speech and creativity. Violence plays a dramatic role in many artistic products. It has been argued that the condemnation of screen violence relates to its mass consumption, thereby demonstrating an elitist distrust of popular art forms. Because of the complex links between political issues and violence, codes to restrict violence can serve also to control critical and subversive challenges to the state. Inasmuch as violence is a reality, not just a representation, any attempt to define unacceptable portrayals of violence potentially restricts the use of graphic depictions of violence in morally or politically challenging ways.

At the heart of legal analysis of the First Amendment is the notion of the free marketplace of ideas, yet within America supporters of diversity in television have identified the commercial pressure of ratings as stifling creativity and diversity. They argue that nowhere is this more evident than in the homogeneity and violence of children's programs. More generally, the sovereignty of the mass audience is seen to limit the forms in which violence is presented. Institutional imperatives work to pull experimentation, at least on network television and mainstream cinema, back toward the safe and acceptable. By contrast the ideology of authorship made possible within the combined public and commercial broadcasting structure of a country like Britain has allowed a wider range of drama and documentaries, promoting within mainstream broadcasting greater variety in the organizing of discourses about violence.

b. The Linking of Sex and Violence

Consideration of screen violence cannot be separated from issues of pornography and sexual violence. Responses in this area involve a complex of political and ideological positions from conservative moralists, to feminists concerned about the impact of demeaning portrayals of women, and to libertarians concerned that threats of sexual violence are being used to countenance tighter control on nonviolent erotica. Research on the impact of sexual violence poses particular dilemmas; experimental study of the effects of portrayals of sexual violence on adolescents has been deemed unethical in a way that studies involving nonerotic physical violence have not. Studies using college students have found that viewing sexual violence has increased male endorsement of rape myths, diminished sympathy for victims of sexual assault, and decreased the length of sentences deemed appropriate for such crimes. While the Attorney General's Commission in 1986 recognized that research findings identified violence, not sex, as the crucial variable in creating antisocial effects, their legislative recommendations were related more to the strengthening of the obscenity laws than to controlling sexually violent material.

3. Lobbying and Citizen Action

The power of citizens to influence what is broadcast can be applied by pressuring for regulations and more directly by commercial pressure on broadcasters. The latter strategy has been particularly prominent in the United States where reluctance to regulate is greater than that in Europe or other English-speaking countries. Such pressure can take the form of direct approaches to networks to modify the content of particular programs, or by organizing boycotts of companies whose advertising is linked to excessively violent shows. Such strategies have been quite effective in encouraging withdrawal of sponsorship and changing programming schedules.

An alternative strategy is lobbying for direct action accompanied by orchestrating public opinion through media campaigns. Such campaigns, viewed by their opponents as "moral panics," may spring out of specific incidents as in the case in England where child murderers were supposed to have viewed a particular violent video. These media campaigns are frequently characterized by sweeping claims, including simplified or distorted presentation of research findings and generalizations from individual cases, often on the basis of misreported information.

B. Children, Violence, and Public Policy

1. Protecting Children: The Vulnerable Child/The Active Child

Underlying much of the TV violence debate have been assumptions about the nature of the child viewer. The idea that children are uniquely vulnerable and in need of protection has been central to demands for a reduction in screen violence. Children, it is argued, are unable to differentiate fact from fantasy and lack an understanding of the constructed nature of fictional portrayals or, at an older age, of the atypicality of the events and solutions portrayed in TV drama. By contrast, a more robust view of children sees them as active viewers. Hodge, working within a cultural studies tradition, has shown how children possess quite sophisticated media decoding abilities and a range of resistant practices through which they actively reframe the programs that they watch. From this perspective, regulatory practices serve to exert control over children and to define children's needs and interests from an adult perspective (R. Hodge, 1989. In *Australian Television: Programs, Pleasures and Politics* (J. Tulloch and G. Turner, Eds.). Allen & Unwin, Sydney).

The active audience perspective has, however, been criticized for ignoring the role of economic and institutional forces in shaping children's television, overemphasizing individual agency, and ignoring any possible role for the media in shaping children's attitudes or behavior. There are signs that a "third generation" audience analysis is developing within cultural studies which will focus equally on structural, textual, and active audience determination of meanings received from the media.

In countries concerned with development of quality children's television, the focus at the professional media level has been as much on the encouragement of diversity and creativity in children's programming as on the removal of violence. For instance, the Australian Children's Television Foundation was funded in order to foster the development of "high-quality" children's programs. Attempts to sanitize children's viewing by censorship of violent programs may simply produce a bland, uncritical, unvaried diet.

2. Educational and Informational Alternatives

An alternative strategy to censorship or regulation of violence lies in informing and educating the viewing public.

a. Ratings

Many countries implement a system of ratings for cinema and television which can have a regulatory or purely informational purpose. The complexity of U.S. rating systems has been criticized, and the need for public education to clarify the meaning of rating codes has been advocated. Ratings can reflect the presence of profanities, explicit sexuality, or violent content and thus lack clear informational value. Moreover, such systems are often driven by notions of what is offensive rather than what is harmful. Introducing programs with warnings that specifically identify levels of coarse language, sex, or violence has the potential to provide the viewer or parent with much clearer guidance as to program content. While ratings serve to inform parents, they can also serve as a guide to young people seeking material that has been defined as "forbidden fruit." A current subject of debate is the technological extension of the ratings system via electronic blocking devices that respond to program classification signals, with the aim of enabling parents to establish controls over the channels or types of content they deem appropriate.

b. Educational Programs

The possibility of lessening the impact of violence by educational programs that promote nonviolent values and emphasize the fictional and unrealistic nature of much violence on television has been supported by specific research showing their effectiveness in reducing the link between viewing and aggressive behavior. The extension of educational interventions to mitigate the effects of exposure to portrayals of sexual violence have been canvassed after some preliminary work conducted on college students. Both in studies with children focusing on general television violence and with adults focusing on sexual violence, the strategy of requiring participants to produce antiviolence messages has been found to impact subsequent beliefs and attitudes. Programs of media education in schools can promote children's awareness of the processes of media construction, and this construction–deconstruction approach to media education has developed in a number of Western countries.

Dutch researchers developed a curriculum to increase the awareness of elementary school students of the consequences of real violence both physically and psychologically for victims and for the police involved in shooting suspects. In addition to gaining novel information from credible sources, students were encouraged to use their newfound knowledge analytically in response to violent incidents in crime series. A demonstrable impact of this program lasted over a period of 2 years, with children more ready to perceive acts as violent, less accepting of violence by good characters, and with lowered perceptions of televized violence as being realistic. This study did not aim to reduce child aggression but to encourage children to assess depictions of violent scenes in crime drama more critically (M. W. Vooijs and T. H. A. van der Voort, 1993. *Journal of Research and Development in Education*, 26, 133–142).

The potential educational role of the media in promoting antiviolence messages has become increasingly recognized. The film *Schindler's List* is an instance of a high-profile film aimed at raising public awareness of the Holocaust. A growing genre of dramatized documentaries have explored a range of issues concerning violence: rape, wife battering, child abuse, police abuse, and terrorism.

C. Investigation and Regulation: Comparative Perspectives

Government initiated investigations into screen violence have been a recurring response to public concerns, although their nature, findings, and policy implications have varied with the temporal and cultural contexts in which they occurred. It is an irony of the particular constitutional and socioeconomic culture of the United States that in the country where violence on television is very high and the scientific community most united in its belief in the harmful effects of television violence, regulation has been so resisted. By contrast the very different relationship of public and commercial broadcasting in Britain, with its greater diversity of programming within a much smaller set of broadcast options, presents a very different climate for policy development in the television violence area. The Broadcasting Standards Council was set up in 1988 to "consider the portrayal of violence, of sex, and matters of taste and decency in broadcast and video works," both monitoring and researching in the area of broadcasting standards. The publications produced by this body have not generally taken an effects approach, the very title of a monograph on mass media effects, *A Measure of Uncertainty*, indicating a more questioning appraisal of effects research. Concern with the portrayal of violence has led to an exploration of viewer responses in order to assess public concerns in both fictional and factual violence.

A similar shift was evident in the approach of the Australian Broadcasting Tribunal (1990) investigation of violence on television which was part of a much broader investigation into violence in Australia prompted by community concern following a spate of multiple killings. Research commissioned as part of this study moved away from the concerns of the effects tradition and used both quantitative and qualitative methods to look at viewers' perceptions of television violence, what disturbed them, and what they believed should be controlled. This represents a paradigm shift from a scientific determination of what is harmful to an examination of community perceptions and concerns.

Epistemological issues are at stake here, since the paradigm shift also involves a move from positivist notions of effects measured objectively by scientific "experts" to hermeneutic, constructivist, and even relativist notions of "the real," as constructed through the language, discourse, and theoretical assumptions of the contextualized observer. This survey of ethical concerns relating to violence in film and television has itself been structured by this epistemological debate, as it has traversed a path from single-nation (U.S.) focused "scientific" assumptions about the effects of media violence to more comparative, relative, and cultural approaches to this field.

Bibliography

Comstock, G. (1991). "Television and the American Child." Academic Press, San Diego.

Gauntlett, D. (1995). "Moving Experiences: Understanding Television's Influences and Effects." Libbey, London.

Gerbner, G. (1994). The politics of media violence: Some reflections. In "Mass Communications Research: On Problems and Policies" (C. J. Hamelink and O. Linné, Eds.). Ablex, Norwood, NJ.

Hargrave, A. M. (1993). "Violence in Factual Television, Vol. 4, Broadcasting Standards Council Public Opinion and Broadcasting Standards." Libbey, London.

Paik, H., and Comstock, G. (1994). The effects of television violence on anti-social behavior: A meta-analysis. *Communication Research* **21,** 516–546.

Warfare, Strategies and Tactics

JOHN D. BECKER
United States Air Force Academy

GLOSSARY

continuum of national security The range of national security issues that includes war, Operations Other Than War (OOTW), and peacetime concerns.

operational art Serves as the connecting link between strategy and tactics. Operational art concerns itself with employment of larger military units, usually echelons above the corps level, and it focuses on campaigns or a series of battles.

Operations Other Than War (OOTW) Those operations that involve the employment of military and nonmilitary resources, but without the intention of using violent force as a primary means to achieve a specific end or set of ends. OOTW include such actions as peacekeeping, counterdrug operations, and disaster relief.

peacetime concerns The important political and economic concerns that nations normally conduct with each other, when not at war or in hostile conflict. These include both defense and deterrence, as well as diplomacy, trade actions, and economic concerns.

spectrum of morality The range of ethical positions that deal with war. These positions include nihilism, just warism, and pacifism.

strategy In general, a plan of action, using available resources, to obtain certain goals over time. Strategy is often considered both an art and a science, in that it requires both intuition and rationality. There are different types of strategy including national strategies, grand strategies, and military strategies.

tactics The employment of military units in combat operations. This employment includes the ordered arrangement and maneuver of those units in relationship to each other to maximize their full potentiality and defeat enemy forces. The units are usually divisions or smaller in size and are concentrated on battles.

war A state of open armed conflict between states (or coalitions of states), or between parties in a state, carried on by force of arms for various reasons. There are various types of wars, ranging from attacks or raids, low-intensity conflicts, limited wars, general wars, and nuclear war.

WAR is the state of open armed conflict between states (or coalitions of states), or between parties in a state, carried on by force of arms for various reasons. There are various types of wars, ranging from attacks or raids, low-intensity conflicts, limited wars, general wars, and nuclear war. War is considered the most serious of a state's national security issues and one that receives the most attention.

I. OVERVIEW

War is only one piece of the continuum of national security. There are also nontraditional operations, Operations Other Than War (OOTW) and peacetime concerns. OOTW are those operations that involve the employment of military and nonmilitary resources, but without the intention of using violent force as a primary means to achieve a specific end or set of ends. OOTW include such actions as peacekeeping, counterdrug operations, and disaster relief. Peacetime concerns are the important political and economic concerns that nations normally conduct with each other, when not at war or in hostile conflict. These include both defense and deterrence, as well as diplomacy, trade actions, and economic concerns.

Warfare is traditionally broken into two parts—strategy and tactics. Strategy is a plan of action, using available resources, to obtain certain goals over time. Strategy is often considered both an art and a science, in that it requires both intuition and rationality. There are different types of strategy, including national strategies, grand strategies, and military strategies. Tactics, on the other hand, is the employment of military units in combat operations. It includes the ordered arrangement and maneuver of those units in relationship to each other to maximize their full potentiality and defeat enemy forces. The units are usually corps level and below, and they concentrate on battles.

There is also a third part, called operational art. It serves as the connection between strategy and tactics. Operational art concerns itself with employment of larger military units, usually echelons above corps, and it focuses on campaigns or a series of battles.

In addition, as part of war, applied ethical issues are raised and considered. These issues include traditional just war concerns which are often broken into two types—*jus ad bellum* (justice of war) and *jus in bello* (justice in war). They also include questions about nontraditional issues, such as OOTW and future war forms, such as information warfare, space warfare, and virtual warfare.

II. STRATEGIES

A strategy is simply a plan of action, using available resources, to obtain certain goals over time. Strategy is often considered both an art and a science, in that it requires both intuition and rationality. There are different types of strategy, including national strategies, grand strategies, and military strategies. At the national level, strategy is a state's plan to attain its interests and objectives, which is done by fusing all of its available resources. A national security strategy will normally include two other strategies—a grand strategy and a military strategy. A grand strategy involves employing national power under all circumstances to exert desired degrees and types of control over a state's enemies or opponents. Threats, force, indirect pressure, diplomacy, subterfuge, and other imaginative means are all employed in grand strategy.

For example, the United States developed and employed a grand strategy for the war in Panama in 1989. This strategy included the administration's use of media in establishing the basis for intervention; the use of various forms of diplomatic and economic sanctions against Panama and its leader Manuel Noriega; the establishment of a political support from neighboring countries in attacking Panama; statements of support by both the Congress and the United Nations; and the integration of special operations forces and psychological warfare forces in the strategy. These parts were woven together into a single, integrated plan—a grand strategy for going to war with Panama.

Military strategy, an element of grand strategy, is predicated on physical violence or the threat of violence. It seeks to support national security interests and objectives through the use of arms and the attainment of military objectives. It involves, as General Karl von Clausewitz noted, the use of engagements to attain the object of war. There is a variety of approaches to military strategy, including sequential and cumulative, direct and indirect, deterrent and combative, and counterforce and countervalue.

In the example of Panama, the U.S. military strategy was to use multiple attacks at varied targets throughout the country. Joint military forces, including ground, sea, and air elements, conducted a synchronized attack on key installations and Panamanian forces.

The difference between grand strategy and military strategy is a simple one: grand strategy is the purview of political leaders while the military strategy is the territory of generals. Moreover, military strategy should be understood as a subset of the larger, grand strategy.

III. TACTICS

As mentioned before, tactics is the employment of military units in combat operations. It stresses the ordered arrangement and maneuver of those units in relationship to each other to maximize their potential and to defeat enemy forces. Tactics include numerous factors, such as maneuver, firepower, protection, sustainment, and leadership. For example, maneuver allows friendly forces to gain the positional advantage over the opposing forces while firepower provides destructive bombardment to exploit that advantage. Simultaneously, friendly force must be protected during the fight and sustained before, during, and after the battle. Leadership is the glue that holds these factors together.

Tactics, like strategy, is both an art and a science, but it employs all available military means to win battles and engagements. Tactics is also thought of as a battlefield problem-solving method—one that is usually rapid and dynamic in its very nature.

There are two types of operations that tactics support—offensive and defensive. Offensive operations are aggressive, forward movements to close with and destroy enemy forces. They are distinguished by rapid momentum, taking advantage of opportunities provided by the enemy, and the destruction of that enemy. Surprise, concentration, tempo, and audacity are important offensive characteristics. Defensive operations are meant to stop and defeat an enemy attack. They are often used to buy time, hold key terrain, or erode enemy resources. Key defensive characteristics include prepared positions, security, disruption, mass and concentration, and flexibility.

In planning and conducting tactical operations, both offensive and defensive, careful consideration is given to the elements of METT-T. This acronym refers to mission, enemy, terrain and weather, troops, and time available. Various plans, including operations orders, make use of these elements.

IV. APPLIED ETHICAL ISSUES

In warfare, there are a number of applied ethical issues raised and discussed. These issues fall into two general categories—*jus ad bellum* and *jus in bello*. The first category, *jus ad bellum* (or justice of war) focuses on whether a state is justified in starting or engaging in a war. Consideration is given to criteria like just cause, right intention, proportionality of ends, last resort, reasonable chance of success, and the aim of peace. If a state can satisfy these criteria, then the war is most likely a just one, rather than an unjust one. *Jus ad bellum* has traditionally been seen as an issue for statesmen and political leaders.

The second category, *jus in bello* (justice in war), focuses on the conduct of the war itself. These issues generally concern soldiers and their leadership and the manner in which they are waging the war. Questions include whether the use of certain weapons and tactics is ethical, what is the proper proportionality of means in the war, and who is a legitimate combatant in the war. These questions are raised on a continuous basis throughout the war.

Similar questions are raised and discussed about both OOTW and peacetime concerns. Their limited use of force requires some modifications of both of those questions and their answers. Nonetheless, the ethical element of warfare often finds itself manifest even in these operations, in things like the names of conflicts, such as Provide Hope and Provide Comfort (recent U.S. OOTW).

In sum, warfare is often thought of as having a dual nature—both practical and ethical. On one side is the strategic and tactical element; the "how to" approach, while on the other side is the ethical element, asking "when should" it be used approach. Both must be addressed in this most serious of a state's endeavors.

Bibliography

Field Manual 100-5, *Operations,* Headquarters, Department of the Army, 1993 Edition, Washington, DC.

Fotion, N. & Elfstrom, G. (1986). *Military ethics.* Boston: Routledge & Kegan Paul, Boston, MA.

Lykke, A. F., Jr. (1989). *Military strategy: Theory and application.* Carlisle Barracks, PA: U.S. Army War College.

Summers, H. G., Jr. (1992). *On strategy II: A critical analysis of the Gulf War.* New York: Dell Books.

Walzer, M. (1992). *Just and unjust wars* (2nd ed.). New York: Basic Books.

Index

ISBN 0-12-166255-1

90038

9 780121 662554